RENAISSANCE DRAMA

New Series VI ❧ *1973*

Renaissance Drama

NEW SERIES VI

Essays on

Dramatic Antecedents

Edited by Alan C. Dessen

Northwestern University Press

EVANSTON 1973

Copyright © 1975 by Northwestern University Press
All rights reserved
Library of Congress Catalog Card Number 67-29872
ISBN 0-8101-0454-7
Printed in the United States of America

Second Printing, 1976

THE ILLUSTRATION on the front cover is an engraving of Rubens' bust of Seneca, from the 1615 edition of Seneca's works, ed. Justus Lipsius. Courtesy of the Newberry Library, Chicago.

THE ILLUSTRATION on the back cover is from John Waley's edition of *The Interlude of Youth* (ca. 1557). Courtesy of the British Museum.

Publication of this volume was made possible by a grant from the College of Arts and Sciences, Northwestern University.

Preface

FOR MANY YEARS the study of Renaissance Drama was largely the study of dramatic sources, influences, and antecedents. Like the Renaissance critics themselves, modern scholars sought and found models in the past, particularly in Roman drama, that had shaped fifteenth-, sixteenth-, and seventeenth-century plays all over Europe. With such debts acknowledged to Seneca, Plautus, and Terence, other scholars turned to liturgical plays, morality plays, cycle plays, saint's plays, and folk plays to explain the evolution and distinctive features of Renaissance drama.

Inevitably the pendulum swung. For example, the evolutionary model assumed by Young, Chambers, and others was attacked as inadequate or misleading; the scholar who found the hand of Seneca everywhere was confronted with equivalent passages in Ovid. But revisionism could not hold the field. As a medium, drama is often closely linked to traditions and conventions evolved over a long period of time. Expectations of both dramatists and audiences are often conditioned if not shaped by vestiges of the past impinging upon the present, even though it may be difficult if not impossible, now, to define or clarify those expectations. Both Roman and medieval drama are of obvious importance for our understanding of the plays that follow, even though interpretations of that importance may produce debate and new problems.

In assembling the essays for this volume, the Editor therefore sought

to encourage reexamination of such questions in the hope that some of
the old chestnuts of historical scholarship (the "influence" of Seneca or
Plautus or Guarini or the Vice) still retained some meat and flavor.
The essays that resulted vary widely in scope, assumptions, and conclusions with the authors going off in their own distinctive directions.
Certainly, none of the essays is revolutionary; few are controversial (in
the sense of a "new interpretation" of *Hamlet*). Rosemary Woolf, for
example, does not quarrel with the traditional approach to sources but
rather argues for some unacknowledged links between the mystery
cycles and the emergent Elizabethan popular drama as represented by
several tragedies from the 1560's. Franco Fido discusses the development
and achievement of Angelo Beolco, a major sixteenth-century dramatist
largely unknown to English readers, stressing the many elements syn-
thesized in his plays. In her own evolutionary terms, Charlotte Stern
treats Spanish drama from 1490 to 1530 as a movement from medieval
ritual (with its emphasis upon music, dance, and communal spirit) to
Renaissance art (associated with aesthetic distance, a written text, and
professional poets).

Several of the essays reconsider familiar problems but argue for new
solutions or relationships. Taking another look at the Vice, Robert C.
Jones raises the question: how could the audience be engaged by such
an entertaining figure and at the same time be taught to reject everything for which he stands? His answer includes some provocative suggestions about the importance of such techniques for later Elizabethan
drama. Gail Kern Paster starts with the standard link between Roman
and Elizabethan comedy but develops that link in her own distinctive
terms, concentrating upon the concept of the city as revealed in the plays
of Plautus and Middleton. Tackling another much-discussed phenomenon, Ervin Beck redefines the Prodigal Son pattern in comedy, setting
up a paradigm by which to evaluate such plays and arguing that such
a paradigm is, in part, a reaction against the values of New Comedy.
G. K. Hunter considers another often-cited "influence" upon the age of
Shakespeare, Italian tragicomedy, offering new evidence for its importance and concluding with some suggestive links to several early
seventeenth-century plays (*The Malcontent, All's Well that Ends Well,*
and *Measure for Measure*).

Of particular importance for the larger questions about dramatic antecedents are the essays by Bruce R. Smith, Catherine Belsey, and David Riggs. Smith shows how the performances of Roman comedies in both England and Italy were interspersed with other elements (*intermedi,* pageantry, masked dancing) that supplied appeals demanded by Renaissance audiences; by themselves, Plautus and Terence were not enough. In her treatment of the origins of the Elizabethan deliberative soliloquy, Belsey challenges the usual sense of "influence," arguing instead for the confluence or creative interaction between elements from Seneca and from the native morality tradition. Riggs demonstrates in detail how sixteenth-century critics concerned with "plot" in comedy dealt with the "middle" or "digression," especially the way such critics consistently misread Aristotle, Horace, and the other authorities in order to "find" the desired concepts of form. All three essays in their own distinctive terms disclose an interaction of various forces that belies any simplistic sense of "influence"; moreover, all three offer suggestive evidence of how the context in which such an "influence" is received can accommodate, transform, or reject it.

The problems posed by this group of essays are complex and not readily resolved. The literature on the subject is immense, as indicated by the two review articles: on studies of Senecan tragedy (by Anna Lydia Motto and John R. Clark) and studies of the English mystery cycles (by Stanley J. Kahrl). But the questions raised here and some of the answers, however tentative, often juxtapose old problems and new evidence in a way that should prove helpful to the reader interested in the history and development of drama. The past is prologue.

ALAN C. DESSEN

Contents

Preface   v

BRUCE R. SMITH Sir Amorous Knight and the Indecorous Romans; or,
Plautus and Terence Play Court in the Renaissance   3

GAIL KERN PASTER The City in Plautus and Middleton   29

ROBERT C. JONES Dangerous Sport: The Audience's Engagement with
Vice in the Moral Interludes   45

CATHERINE BELSEY Senecan Vacillation and Elizabethan Deliberation:
Influence or Confluence?   65

ROSEMARY WOOLF The Influence of the Mystery Plays upon the Popular Tragedies of the 1560's   89

ERVIN BECK Terence Improved: The Paradigm of the Prodigal Son in
English Renaissance Comedy   107

G. K. HUNTER Italian Tragicomedy on the English Stage   123

DAVID RIGGS "Plot" and "Episode" in Early Neoclassical Criticism   149

CHARLOTTE STERN The Early Spanish Drama: From Medieval Ritual
to Renaissance Art   177

FRANCO FIDO An Introduction to the Theater of Angelo Beolco   203

Review Article ANNA LYDIA MOTTO and JOHN R. CLARK Senecan
Tragedy: A Critique of Scholarly Trends   219

Review Article STANLEY J. KAHRL The Civic Religious Drama of
Medieval England: A Review of Recent Scholarship   237

Notes on Contributors   249

ix

RENAISSANCE DRAMA

New Series VI ❧ *1973*

Sir Amorous Knight and the Indecorous Romans; or, Plautus and Terence Play Court in the Renaissance

BRUCE R. SMITH

CARDINAL WOLSEY'S BANQUET was just beginning when into the great hall at Hampton Court burst some uninvited guests—a company of shepherds. No wayfarers from the muddy January fields outside, these merrymakers; they claimed to speak no English and asked for a French interpreter. "Havyng understandyng of thys yo' tryhumphant bankett," their translator explained to Wolsey,

> where was assembled suche a number of excellent fayer dames [they] cowld do no lesse under the supportacion of yo' grace but to repayer hether to vewe as well ther incomperable beawtie as for to accompany them at Mume chaunce And than After to daunce w^t them And so to have of them acquayntaunce. . . .[1]

1. George Cavendish, *The Life and Death of Cardinal Wolsey*, ed. R. S. Sylvester, EETS, no. 243 (London, 1959), pp. 25–28. In this and other quotations in old spelling I have made the consonants *v* and *j* accord with modern orthography. Cavendish does not date the incident he recounts here, but King Henry's flamboyantly dramatic entry in disguise is a prominent event in the Venetian secretary's account of Wolsey's banquet and entertainment at Hampton Court on 3 January 1526/27. With a few changes Shakespeare incorporates this famous incident into *Henry VIII* (I.iv.).

3

At the end of their game of mumchance, Wolsey had to confess to the French interpreter his suspicion that "there shold be among theme some noble man whome I suppose to be myche more worthy of honor to sitt and occupie this rome & place than I to whome I wold most gladly (yf I knewe hyme) surrender my place accordyng to my dewtie. . . ." There was indeed such a man, the shepherds reported through their interpreter, but Wolsey would have to pick him out. The cardinal chose wrong. Delighted, King Henry VIII jerked off his visor "& dasht owt w' suche a pleasaunt Countenaunce & cheare that all noble estates there assembled seying the kyng to be there amoong them rejoysed very myche. . . ." After this grand chivalric gesture the "shepherd"—such an admirer of noble ladies—doffed his disguise, changed to royal attire, and stayed on for the evening's entertainment.

The royal sports Henry enjoyed that January night in 1526 / 27 began not with a show of the exploits of Amadis de Gaul but with a performance of Plautus' *Menaechmi* by some of the gentlemen of the cardinal's household—and in Latin, at that. The whole affair was impressive enough for the Venetian ambassador's secretary, Gasparo Spinelli, to write home about it the next day; most historians of English drama have found the occasion less worthy of comment.[2] Here was an attempt to revive classical drama, not at school (where Terence at least was studied as a text and occasionally acted by students), but at the court, in Latin, for fun. Wolsey's entertainment came less than fifty

---

2. Spinelli's letter is calendared and translated in *Calendar of State Papers Venetian*, IV, 2–3, from which I take my subsequent quotations. I have checked this translation against the Italian original, reprinted in *I Diarii di Marino Sanuto*, ed. F. Stefani, 58 vols. (Venice, 1879–1902), XLIII (1890), cols. 703–704, from which I have occasionally inserted the Italian in parentheses. Productions of Plautus and Terence at Henry VIII's court receive only passing mention in F. P. Wilson, *The English Drama, 1485–1585* (Oxford, 1969), pp. 102–103, and only Sydney Anglo has examined the documentation in detail. In "The Evolution of the Early Tudor Disguising, Pageant, and Mask," *RenD*, N.S. I (1968), 3–44, he shows how the miscellaneous sports of Henry's court—classical comedies included—were given form and order. In *Spectacle, Pageantry, and Early Tudor Policy* (Oxford, 1969), Anglo examines royal shows as political propaganda. There were earlier productions of Latin comedy at Cambridge in 1510–1511 and 1522–1523. See Wilson, p. 102. My attention centers on the court.

years after the earliest-known revival of Terence in Italy—a fact that
should dislodge rigid notions that it took more than a century for the
splendors of Italian Renaissance culture to reach cold, remote England.
Several recent scholars have described a kind of proto-Renaissance at the
court of Henry VIII. English painting in the sixteenth century, Roy
Strong has shown, moves in a decidedly un-Renaissance direction:
painters during Elizabeth's long reign discarded the psychological verisimilitude of Hans Holbein's portraits of Henry VIII's courtiers in favor
of the iconographical "neomedievalism" of Nicholas Hilliard's jewel-like
miniatures and Elizabeth's official portraits.[3] Mark Girouard has described
a similar pattern in sixteenth-century English building. Incipient classicism in such buildings as Longleat House (begun 1559) gives way to
romantic fantasy in Elizabethan dream castles like Wollaton Hall (begun 1580).[4] At Henry's court, as much as at Elizabeth's, lessons in
princely magnificence were learned more immediately from Burgundy
and France than from far-off Urbino.[5] But classical comedies appear
among Henry's courtly revels at an impressively early date.

Just as remarkable is the intimacy with which we in the twentieth
century can *see* these early productions. The rather full documentation
that Sydney Anglo has set out gives us a vivid sense of the dramatic
context in which Henry and his courtiers listened to the colloquial Latin
of Plautus and Terence and followed their plots toward inevitable happy
endings. We not only know when and where certain Roman comedies
were acted; we know also, to some degree at least, how the viewers saw
them. It is this dramatic perspective that I have essayed to explore. How
did Plautus and Terence fit in with men and manners a thousand miles
and seventeen-hundred years away? What did their tricky slaves, braggart soldiers, greedy whores, doting old fathers, and lusty young men

3. Roy Strong, *The English Icon* (London and New York, 1969), pp. 5–21, and
Portraits of Queen Elizabeth I (Oxford, 1963), pp. 33–41.

4. Mark Girouard, *Robert Smythson and the Architecture of the Elizabethan Era*
(London, 1966), *passim*.

5. John Stevens, *Music and Poetry in the Early Tudor Court* (London, 1961),
does a masterful job of placing the pursuits of Henry's court in their European
cultural context. I am particularly indebted to Stevens' discussion of courtly love as
a social game, pp. 154–202.

look like to an audience who just the afternoon before may have been delighting in a tournament, complete with a fictional "plot" drawn afar from medieval romance? How were these new and strange Romans accommodated within the more usual disports of an evening? Did their appearance at the court of Henry VIII have any lasting influence on English court dramatists? Hazarding answers to these questions will take us to three places: first, to Henry's court, where we shall examine what Spinelli and others have to tell us about the three revivals of Roman comedy that were given written record; then to Italy, where we shall see how plays by Plautus, Terence, and their Italian imitators were mounted and performed; and finally to Queen Elizabeth's court, where we shall look briefly at how Roman comedy as staged at Henry's court left its mark on later court plays.

I

Not a courtier but a solid London citizen gives us one of the fullest and earliest descriptions of how splendid and various an evening's pastime could be at the Tudor court. With its menus of Lord Mayors' feasts recorded in rapturous detail, the manuscript *Great Chronicle of London,* kept up by the City corporation and still preserved in the Guildhall library, is not notable for the compilers' reticence and *sprezzatura.* When one of the chroniclers records King Henry VII's knighting of the Lord Mayor at Twelfth Night 1493 / 94, he is impressed with the setting, the company, and the entertainment, and he tells us so in some detail. After the king and his party entered the hall at about an hour before midnight there was first of all "a goodly Interlude" put on by "the kyngys players." [6] Before the players had quite finished their play, however,

Cam In Ridying oon of the kyngys Chapell namyd Cornysh apparaylid afftyr the Fygure of Seynt George, and aftir Folowid a Fayer vyrgyn attyrid lyke unto a kyngys dowgthyr, and ledyng by a sylkyn lace a Terryble & huge Rede dragun, The which In Sundry placys of the halle as he passyd spytt Fyre at hys mowth. . . .

6. *The Great Chronicle of London,* ed. A. H. Thomas and I. D. Thornley (London, 1938), pp. 251–252.

Nothing like this in Cheapside! When he had ridden before the king, Cornish declaimed "a certayn speche made In balad Royall." Then "wyth lusty Corage" he and some of his fellows of the Chapel Royal, who had assembled near by, sang an antiphon addressed to St. George, Cornish first singing out, *"O Georgi deo Care"* ("O George, dear to God"), the others answering, *"Salvatorem Deprecare, ut Gubernet Angliam"* ("Entreat the saviour that he might govern England"). After this spectacular emblem underscored with political sentiment, Cornish and his dragon disappeared, the rescued virgin was led to the queen's box, and from the end of the hall came suddenly the music of "a small Tabret & a subtyle Fedyll." In came twenty-four "Costiously & goodly dysguysid" ladies and gentlemen who danced an artfully choreographed ballet to conclude the evening's sports. After a feast of spectacular dishes brought in with a flourish by the twelve gentlemen-dancers, the mayor and his party embarked for the City. Day was breaking as they rowed down the Thames. It had been a big night, and the newly knighted mayor must have been self-satisfied and mellow: "Then the mayer kyst hys wyffe as a dowble lady." That may be the best-observed detail in the whole account.

What impressed the Guildhall chronicler is what impresses us: the spectacle, the costliness, the variety. This William Cornish astride the dragon was at a later time, we know, the deviser of many entertainments before young Henry VIII. Whether or not he devised the show on this occasion, the pageant of St. George was a clever choice: it made possible, all at once, a display of religious sentiment, a political compliment, and a vivid scene out of medieval romance, complete with bold knight, rescued lady, and fiery dragon. Anglo has called attention to this occasion in 1493 / 94 as the first on which we encounter the three-part paradigm of play-pageant-dance that obtains throughout Cornish's career at court and imposes some expected order upon the variety that Henry and his courtiers so clearly relished.[7] It was just this three-part pattern that Cornish used when he and the children of the Chapel Royal acted one of the earliest court plays we know by name. *Troylous and Pandor,* the bit of popular romance they dramatized before Henry at Epiphany

7. Sydney Anglo, "William Cornish in a Play, Pageants, Prison, and Politics," *RES*, N.S. X (1959), 347–360.

1516, is the first in a long series of plays on romance subjects that remained popular at court down through Elizabeth's reign.[8]

We can return now to Henry at Hampton Court that January night in 1526 / 27 with a clearer sense of just what a noble audience might expect of an evening's pastime. What difference did it make when in among the dragons and love-languishing knights the Menaechmus twins were thrust on? Very little. Spinelli's account describes the familiar three-part paradigm: first the play, then a pageant, finally a masked dance. About the *Menaechmi* itself he has little to say. It was acted by some of "the Cardinal's gentlemen," he notes, on "a very well designed stage" [*"una molto ben intessa scena"*].[9] As with the Guildhall chronicler, it was the afterpieces that especially impressed Spinelli. The end of the play was immediately set off with speeches: one by one the actors bowed before the king and declaimed Latin verses in his praise. After a pause for refreshments, the audience was treated to an amorous mythological afterpiece. Elegant oratory, brilliant trumpet music, beautiful dancing, and a chariot entry reminiscent of Petrarch's *Triumph of Love* were combined in a dramatic event that was essentially a debate. Spinelli was charmed:

> . . . a stage [*uno solaro*] was displayed, on which sat Venus, at whose feet were six damsels, forming so graceful a group for her footstool, that it looked as if she and they had really come down from heaven. And whilst everybody was intently gazing on so agreeable a sight, the trumpets flourished and a car appeared, drawn by three boys stark naked—

8. C. R. Baskervill's long essay, "Some Evidence for Early Romantic Plays in England," *MP*, XIV (1916–1917), 229–251, 467–521, is still the best discussion of the vogue of romantic plays in the sixteenth century and the probable continuity of conventions and audience taste from the fifteenth century. Also relevant: L. M. Ellison, *The Early Romantic Drama at the English Court* (Chicago, 1917); James Paul Brawner, "Early Classical Narrative Plays by Sebastian Westcott and Richard Mulcaster," *MLQ*, IV (1943), 455–464; and Arthur Brown's corrections of Brawner, "A Note on Sebastian Westcott and the Plays Presented by the Children of Pauls," *MLQ*, XII (1951), 134–136.

9. None of these court productions, unfortunately, comes under Richard Southern's sharp scrutiny in *The Staging of Plays Before Shakespeare* (London, 1973). "Stage" may or may not be the best translation of Spinelli's word *scena;* all the evidence Southern adduces, pp. 45–55, would lead us to expect not a raised platform but some properties and perhaps houses on the floor in front of the screen at the lower end of the hall.

How more picturesque and Italian could the spectacle be?—

on which was Cupid, dragging after him, bound by a silver rope, six old men, clad in the pastoral fashion, but the material was cloth of silver and white satin. Cupid presented them to his mother, delivering a most elegant Latin oration in their praise, saying they had been cruelly wounded; whereupon Venus compassionately replied in equally choice language, and caused the six nymphs, the sweethearts of the six old men, to descend, commanding them to afford their lovers all solace, and requite them for past pangs. Each of the nymphs was then taken in hand by her lover, and to the sound of trumpets they performed a very beautiful dance.

The king and his favorites then joined in, and the dancing became general. Always an eager participant in court revels, Henry had favored such grand conclusions to an evening's pastime since the precedent-setting occasion in 1512 when, presumably "after the manner of Italy," the audience and maskers danced together rather than separately.[10]

At first glance the mythological trappings of this pageantry might make us suppose that Venus and Cupid had been summoned to heighten the classical atmosphere set by Plautus' play. A second look at these six languishing shepherds with their fantastically elegant garb tells us, however, that this is the Venus of Chaucer's *Knight's Tale* and not the Venus of Quattrocento painting. These shepherds—like Henry himself, flaunting his disguise at the banquet's beginning—have wandered in not from a Virgilian eclogue but from a medieval *pastourelle*.

What should interest us in Spinelli's account is the proportion of attention he gives to each of the entertainment's three parts. We may regret that he gives us so few details about the play, but he spares no Italian superlatives in conjuring up for us the pageantry and dance. A sober English viewer like Edward Hall could be equally taken with visual splendor. Wolsey's production of the *Menaechmi* is not, in fact, the earliest performance of a classical comedy at Henry's court. Hall describes an occasion on 7 March 1519 / 20 when Henry and his court watched "a goodly commedy of Plautus."[11] Hall does not bother to say just which goodly comedy it was or even who acted it, but he withholds no essential

---

10. On the controversy surrounding "after the manner of Italy," cf. Anglo, "Evolution of Early Tudor Disguising," pp. 4–8.

11. Edward Hall, *The Union of the Two Noble and Illustre Famelies of Lancastre and Yorke,* ed. H. Ellis (London, 1809), p. 597.

details of the pageantry and dancing that followed the play. Henry had an audience of noble French hostages to impress. Even if they did not appreciate such an up-to-the-minute humanistic gesture as mounting a Plautine comedy, they must surely have been impressed with the splendid spectacle that ensued: an entry of sixteen ladies and gentlemen "tired like to the Egipcians very richely." Plautus made his first documented appearance at the English court, not in historically accurate Roman dress, but adorned with exotic Egyptian ornaments.

The *Menaechmi* at Hampton Court came seven years later. On the third occasion for which we have production details, the surface splendor of the earlier two productions was complemented with didactic depth. Just a year after the *Menaechmi* Wolsey sponsored a court performance of Terence's *Phormio*. Spinelli once again was among the guests at festivities that marked a politically important occasion: the Pope's release from captivity by the Holy Roman Emperor Charles V.[12] After dinner the children of St. Paul's School recited Terence's comedy—and with such spirit (*"galantaria"*) and good acting (*"bona attione"*) that Spinelli was frankly astounded. Inscriptions at the front of the hall announced the name of the play, *Terentii Phormio,* and dedicated the performance *"Honori et laudi Pacifici,"* with an unsubtle allusion, as Spinelli realized, to Wolsey's title *Cardinalis Pacificus.* Other inscriptions at the side of the platform and around the hall celebrated this triumph of peace and gave a preview of the pageantry that would follow the play.

No sooner were true identities revealed, Spinelli reports, no sooner were irate fathers calmed and lovers allowed to marry then

three girls richly clad appeared. The first was Religion, the second Peace, the third Justice. They complained of having been expelled well nigh from all Europe, by heresy, war, and ambition; detailing the iniquities perpetrated by the enemy, saying they had no other refuge than in the most generous Father, whom they besought to assume their protection and defence, each of them concluding their harangue with the following lines:—
   "Ast tibi pro meritis meritos tribuemus honores,
      Et laudes cecinit nostra Thalia tuos."
When the girls had finished, a little boy, who had already recit with great applause the prologue of the comedy, delivered a Latin oration, celebrating

12. Spinelli's letter is translated in *Calendar of State Papers Venetian,* IV, 115–116, from which I take my quotations. The Italian words in parentheses are taken from the original letter, rpt. in *Sanuto,* XLVI (1897), col. 595.

the day as one of great thanksgiving on account of the release of the Pope, who had escaped from the hands of the most iniquitous men in the world, worse than the Turks; vituperating greatly their cruelty, and also that of the Emperor, *omisso nomine*, in a paragraph to the effect that these calamities proceeded *"ab unius labidine qui cuncta sibi subjicere cupide admodum conabatur."*

For this sort of artless political allegory there had been several precedents in recent years at court, but none of them had been combined in this way with a conventional play.[13] Even more than the *Triumph of Venus* that followed the 1527 production of the *Menaechmi*, this *Triumph of Peace* for the 1528 production of *Phormio* evinces a real delight in fitting Plautus and Terence into the context of the occasion at hand, a delight in surrounding the verisimilar canvas of satiric comedy with a gilded frame of ideas.

From the details that Spinelli and Hall have obligingly left, we can see three things clearly: first, that Plautus and Terence were certainly shown no pious deference but were asked to fit in with the variety that was traditional in court revelry; second, that the audience saw no incongruity in laughing one minute at the high jinks of Roman comedians, then turning to marvel at a spectacular display of ideas in the game of courtly love or the game of Renaissance politics; and, third, that the audience remembered most vividly the pageantry, not the play. Aristotle would *not* have approved. Henry and his courtiers show a perverse delight in keeping *mythos* and *dianoia* as far apart as possible. Worse still, their written accounts give us no choice but to conclude that thought, spectacle, and music were far more important than plot, characters, and turns of phrase—hardly the order of elements Aristotle had in mind.

II

Just how perverse were Henry and his courtiers? Their Italian compeers have left us even fuller documentation of how *they* produced,

13. During the Emperor Charles V's visit to England in 1522, for instance, a political play, probably by William Cornish, had been performed at Windsor. Five years later Charles had become an enemy, and on November 10, 1527, the boys of St. Paul's school performed a Latin morality play at Greenwich before Henry and some French ambassadors dispatched on the occasion of the capture of Rome. Cf. Hall, *Union of the Famelies of Lancastre and Yorke*, p. 735.

watched, and remembered Roman comedy.[14] As in England, the earliest productions of classical drama in Italy were under scholarly auspices. During Carnival at Florence in 1476 Girgio Antonio Vespucci directed his students in three performances of Terence's *Andria*, once at the school, once in the Medici palace, and once in the Palazzo della Signoria. The cultural climate in late fifteenth-century Florence favored such humanistic endeavors, and in May, 1488, some seminary students staged an immediately famous production of Plautus' *Menaechmi* under Pablo Comparini's direction. For the occasion Angelo Poliziano, Lorenzo's celebrated humanist-in-residence, contributed an elegant Latin prologue that tells us something about the expectations of the audience. Plautus' original Prologue could not be more droll and facetious: he yawns over what a hackneyed play the audience is about to see! Poliziano's Prologue starts out facetiously enough, but soon he takes a scholar's stance and prepares the audience for the heady new pleasures they are about to experience. In *this* play, he warns them, there will be nothing clumsy, ill-chosen, or Greekish, such as certain would-be authors trifle with. The language they will hear is the unadulterated domestic speech of ancient Rome—the very accents the Muses use whenever they speak in Latin. Not authors but actors receive Poliziano's most pointed attack. His description of noisy, lightheaded, hooded, clubfooted entertainers dis-

14. The two fullest accounts of the drama in Italy are in Italian: Alessandro d'Ancona, *Origini del teatro Italiano*, 2d ed. rev. (Turin, 1891), II, 61 ff., and Ireneo Sanesi, *La Commedia*, 2d ed. rev. (Milan, 1944), I, 199 ff. Briefer English accounts are offered by Marvin T. Herrick, *Italian Comedy in the Renaissance* (Urbana, Ill; 1960), pp. 61–65, and Douglas Radcliff-Umstead, *The Birth of Modern Comedy in Renaissance Italy* (Chicago and London, 1969), pp. 59–63. In "Circumstances and Setting in the Earliest Italian Productions of Comedy," *RenD*, N.S. IV (1971), 185–197, Bonner Mitchell provides a vivid picture of occasions and physical settings and makes an apt comparison between courtly audiences then and high society at an opera today: in both cases the occasion is so grand and the production so lavish that no one seems to mind not understanding the foreign language. In Latin or in translation, productions of Plautus and Terence in the sixteenth century were never so numerous elsewhere as in Italy, and England was quite distinguished by the early date of productions at court. Clerics mounted a comedy by Terence in the episcopal palace at Metz in 1502, but it was not until Jodelle's *Eugène* at court in 1552 that Roman comedy began to exert dramatic influence in France. H. W. Lawton discusses the survival of medieval tastes in *Terence en France au XVIᵉ siècle: Éditions et traductions* (Paris, 1926), pp. 48–61.

perses the *commedia dell'arte* figures that may be lurking in the audience's mind. What are they, sneers the Prologue, but "eyebrow-raising, crook-necked cattle"![15]

Rome, too, could boast some lavish productions of ancient Roman drama, beginning with an *Epidicus* (1486), mounted by Pomponio Leto (Julius Pomponius Laetus) under Pope Paul's patronage. A contemporary witness singles out Pomponio Leto's revivals of classical comedy as the first theatrical ventures in modern times to use painted scenes.[16] It was at Ferrara, however, that classical drama found its most enthusiastic audience. The auspices here were not scholarly but noble, and Duke Ercole I (d. 1505) became not only an eager patron but a translator and director as well.[17] The patronage of the d'Este court had an immediate effect on native drama. A staging of an Italian translation of the *Menaechmi* in 1486 was the first in a series of lavish productions of Plautus and Terence that continued into the sixteenth century, but in the very next year the court was treated to an *original* "classical" play as well, Niccola da Coreggio's *Cefalo*. Niccola's model is clearly Poliziano's *Orpheo*, the first secular play of the Italian Renaissance, and like that earlier "fable" (*favola* is Poliziano's own term) his play is more classical in its Ovidian subject than in its rambling form. Both playwrights redact their classical stories into the leisurely episodic structure of the old medieval *sacra rappresentazione*. In *Cefalo* and in *Orpheo* we move from local detail to local detail just as we do in reading a medieval tapestry.[18]

15. "Praefatio in Menechmos," identified at the end as "Recitata Florentiae" (rpt. in *Omnium Angeli Politiani operum* . . . [Paris, 1519], fols. xcvi^v–xcvii). Poliziano's attack on the actors gives the Prologue a very unclassical mouthful to splutter: "Sed qui nos damnant histriones sunt maxumi. / Nam Curios simulant, vivunt bacchanalia. / Hi sunt praecipue quidam clamosi, leves, / Cucullati, lignipedes, cinti funibus, / Superciliosum incurvicervicum pecus" (ll. 38–42).

16. Joannes Sulpitius Verulanus makes a note to this effect in an edition of Vitruvius dedicated to Cardinal Rafaele Riario: "Tu etiam primus picturatae scenae faciem, quum / Pomponiani comoediam agerent, nostro saeculo ostendisti," quoted in W. Parr Greswell, *Memoirs of Angelus Politianus* [*et al.*] . . . 2d ed. rev. (Manchester, 1805), p. 143.

17. One wonders how court audiences managed to respond politely to such ponderous translations. Cf. Sanesi, *La Commedia*, I, 189 ff.

18. There are two editions of Poliziano's play, the original one printed about 1472 and a second one, labeled *Tragedia*, published about 1776. Louis E. Lord

Both Poliziano and Niccola take their fables not from the satire of Roman comedy but from the sensuous mythology of Ovid's *Metamorphoses*. Both plays pleased, and no one, apparently, thought to label them unclassical. Nor did admirers of Ovid think it unclassical when the splendid divine creatures of the *Metamorphoses* mingled onstage with Plautus' and Terence's very earthy Romans. By 1491, at least, when a sumptuously decked out *Amphitrion* was mounted at Ferrara to celebrate Alfonso d'Este's marriage to Anna Sforza, interludes of music, mythological disguise, and showy philosophizing had become crowd-pleasing adornments of productions of Plautus and Terence.[19] These shows, dispersed between the acts, the Italians called *intermedi*. Alternating with the confusions that ensue when a god seduces one's wife, the audience watching the 1491 *Amphitrion* saw a choral dance by ivy-clad youths, Apollo singing an ode in praise of the d'Este house, a rustic farce, an entry of Bacchus and Venus, and a pantomime of the judgment of Paris. Alfonso's second marriage in 1501—this time to a lady of no less renown than Lucrezia Borgia—called for an even more stupendous array of Latin comedy and mythological spectacle. On three successive days there were performances of *Mercator, Captivi,* and *Asinaria,* all of them enlivened by splendid *intermedi.* Two letters from Alfonso's sister Isabella to her husband Francesco Gonzaga describe these festivities in rapturous detail—and in so doing show where the audience's real interest lay. Isabella is mostly enthusiastic about the *intermedi,* particularly about a mock battle that was staged between soldiers in antique costume.[20]

Tastes like Isabella d'Este Gonzaga's could lead only to ever more

---

translates both versions into English prose on facing pages in *A Translation of the Orpheus of Angelo Politian and the Aminta of Torquato Tasso* (Oxford, 1931), pp. 74–103. John Addington Symonds includes an agreeable verse translation of Poliziano's play among his *Sketches and Studies in Italy and Greece,* new ed. (London, 1898), II, 346–361. Unfortunately, Symonds bases his translation on the suspect 1776 version, which alters the play in the direction of "regular" tragedy. A verse rendering of the earlier version, less successful than Symonds', is Henry Morgan Ayres, "A Translation of Poliziano's *Orfeo,*" *RR,* xx (1929), 13–24.

19. Modern readers are more familiar with this production than most from Jacob Burckhardt's full description in *The Civilization of the Renaissance in Italy,* trans. S. G. C. Middlemore (Vienna, n.d.), pp. 163-165.

20. Isabella's letters are reprinted in Sanesi, *La Commedia,* I, 187–188.

extravagant displays. Somewhat later in the century the celebrated play-wright Antonfrancesco Grazzini ("Il Lasca") had had enough. In a satiric madrigal called "The comedy that aches with *intermedi,*" he groans in mock horror at the artistic servitude he finds himself in:

> My grief! Those people who waited on me
> And once for adorning me hung about—
> They're wrecking it all, they're wearing me out!
> Little by little this villainous rout
>> Have taken my breath and vigor
>> And now have so much favor
> That all of them abuse me—they mock and flout.
>> And all this troop demand one thing,
>> With gaping stare, with hankering:
> The wonder—alas!—of *intermedi,*
>> "And you'd better have one ready . . ."
> Or at once of my life they'll bereave me.
> Have pity! Ah Phoebus, help me! help me![21]

Yet on occasion Il Lasca himself could satisfy that "hankering"—and with a measure of artistic integrity, too. In 1565 he collaborated with the composers Alessandro Striggio and Francesco Corteccia in devising a series of *intermedi* on the fable of Cupid and Psyche for a grand production of Francesco d'Ambra's comedy *La Confanaria.* The occasion was grand (the festivities marked the marriage of Francesco de' Medici and Johanna of Austria at Florence), and so was the production (scenic design was in the hands of Giorgio Vasari and Bernardo Timante). In 1593 the *intermedi* were published with a new edition of d'Ambra's play, and Il Lasca wrote a foreword that carefully explains

---

21. Except where noted, this and all other translations from Italian are my own. "La Comedia che si duol degli intermezzi": "Misera, da costor che già trovati / fur per servirmi e per mio ornamento / lacerar tutta e consumarmi sento. / Questi empi e scelerati a poco a poco / preso han lena e vigore / e tanto hanno or favore, / ch'ognun di me si prende scherno e giuoco, / e sol dalla brigata / s'aspetta e brama e guata / la meraviglia, ohimè! degli intermedi; / e se tu non provvedi, / mi fia tosto da lor tolto la vita; / misericordia! Febo, aita! aita!" (Antonfrancesco Grazzini, *Le Rime Burlesche,* ed. C. Verzone [Florence, 1882], p. 229.) Grazzini was not unknown in England in the sixteenth century: his comedy *La Spiritata* was translated into English anonymously as *The Bugbears* (rpt. *Early Plays from the Italian* [Oxford, 1911]).

the plan that he and his collaborators had followed in coupling the Cupid and Psyche fable with the play proper:

All the intermedii . . . were taken from the story of Cupid and Psyche, so pleasingly related by Apuleius in his romance, "The Golden Ass"; and we proceeded by selecting the parts which appeared to be the leading ones, and fitting them to the Comedy with all the skill at our command, with the intention of making it appear as if that which is enacted by the Gods in the fable of the intermedii, is likewise enacted—as it were, under constraint of a higher power—by the mortals in the Comedy.[22]

From Apuleius' fable Il Lasca and his collaborators chose six episodes, not, apparently, because they were important to the narrative (several key events in the story have to be inferred between the six episodes), but because they are visual and musical emblems in a figurative pattern. To begin with, all is cosmic accord (Venus descending in her chariot accompanied by the Graces, the Hours, and Cupid); then discord disrupts the pattern (Cupid's abandonment of Psyche; a wild *moresca* danced by Discord, Anger, Cruelty, Rapine, Vendetta, the two Anthropophagi, and the Furies; a tearfully sung lament by Psyche descending to the Underworld). The *intermedi* end with a triumph of union and renewed concord (a celebration on Mount Helicon and a descent of Hymen, who "personalizes" this dramatic wedding gift with compliments to Francesco and Johanna and relates its cosmic vision to the occasion at hand). Despite the organic connection that Il Lasca claims between *intermedi* and play, however, the *intermedi* had enough intrinsic interest to be published separately within a year after the performance. *Intermedi* for other occasions were often published in just this way.

From Il Lasca's testimony and from examples like the 1565 Florence production of d'Ambra's *La Confanaria*, it is clear that *intermedi* could serve some kind of choric function at the same time that they delighted courtly taste—a fleshly "hankering," Il Lasca would have it—for spectacle,

22. Il Lasca's description, translated by Theodore Baker, is printed by O. G. Sonneck, "A Description of Alessandro Striggio and Francesco Corteccia's Intermedi 'Psyche and Amor,'" in *Miscellaneous Studies in the History of Music* (1921; rpt. New York, 1968), pp. 269–286, from which this quotation is taken. There is a description of the whole affair in Alois M. Nagler, *Theatre Festivals of the Medici: 1539–1637*, trans. G. Hickenlooper (New Haven, Conn., 1964), pp. 15–21.

music, and dance. The connection between play and *intermedi* that Il Lasca suggests is *causal,* but in the case of his Cupid and Psyche sequence such a relationship must remain strictly in the beholder's eye, since the gods of the *intermedi* never actually come into contact with the mortals of d'Ambra's play. The real connection of play and *intermedi* is not causal but *thematic.* And it is just this role of thematic commentary that Angelo Ingegneri used to defend *intermedi* later in the century.

As a treatise on methods of staging, Ingegneri's *Della Poesia Rappresentativa Discorso* (Ferrara, 1598) is more than scholarly speculation. The author was able to put his ideas to practical use in the monumental production of *Oedipus Rex,* complete with proto-operatic *intermedi,* that opened Palladio's Teatro Olimpico at Vicenza in 1585.[23] More than a century and a half later Ingegneri's treatise was evidently still being read: the Folger Library copy of the *Discorso* is bound with other Italian theatrical treatises in a volume once owned by David Garrick. Ingegneri treats *intermedi* as choruses. What the traditional chorus is to tragedy, *intermedi* are to comedy and pastoral drama. An important distinction is to be made, however: in tragedy the connection of the chorus with the main fable is causal; in comedy and pastoral the connection is strictly thematic. In tragedy, Ingegneri explains, the chorus must be organically related to the main fable—as in effect, an actor in the play proper, indispensable to the action. In comedy, on the other hand, the role of a chorus, if there is one, is more dispensable: it moves in a sphere separate from the play itself. In conjoining the matter of *intermedi* with the main fable of a play, an author steers a precarious course. He must choose "an action that doesn't seem to be remote from such a conjunction, yet still does not look like a continuation."[24] Here, if anywhere, is the Renaissance

23. The translated play and the complete text and music for the *intermedi* are edited with a superb introduction by Leo Schrade, *La Representation d'Edipo Tirrano au Teatro Olimpico* (Paris, 1960). A. M. Nagler's *Sources of Theatrical History* (New York, 1952), pp. 81–86, includes an English translation of Filippo Pigafetta's letter describing the whole affair.

24. "Deiquali intermedi, & della loro rappresentatione, così quanto all'attione, come quanto à i personaggi, & particolarmente dintorno all'imitare co'l moto, & co'l gesto regolato, over colla musica, & non con semplici, & ordinarie, parole, & sopra tutto circa'l concertar la materia colla favola principale, in modo però, che

demand for unity-in-variety: play and *intermedi* must combine two discrete, but mutually appropriate, orders of reality.

In considering *intermedi* as choruses, Ingegneri had, if he had needed it, some classical precedent. Along with scattered references in Horace and Cicero, medieval and Renaissance critics alike got most of their information about the history and nature of the Greek and Roman stage from Aelius Donatus, the fourth-century grammarian who was St. Jerome's tutor. Prefaced to Donatus' commentary on the plays of Terence is a treatise *De comoedia* that makes up in magisterial neatness what it lacks in length. Donatus' handy compendium of fact and hearsay found its way into virtually every fifteenth- and sixteenth-century edition of Terence.[25] Greek Old Comedy, says Donatus, had two features that Latin comedy lacks: a chorus and a device for laying out the plot. Where Terence brings on extra characters at the beginning of a comedy to tell us the situation, some Latin writers "after the manner of the Greeks" bring on *dei ex machina* "for making the argument known." By conflating these two forgotten features of Greek and Latin comedy, a deviser of courtly revels could find some justification for using classical deities to punctuate the play and to clarify the argument.

Capable of serving as a thematic chorus, *intermedi* could stand as a kind of frame for helping the audience adjust their perspective. The problem concerned proportion. The chorus of Old Comedy, according to Donatus, kept shrinking in size until impersonators took over the play. Bored with interruptions between the acts, recalcitrant audiences finally succeeded in getting rid of choruses altogether. Just the reverse was likely to happen with *intermedi*: they threatened to take over the play itself. Il Lasca, like other sixteenth-century Italian playwrights, could use the prologue to a comedy for self-conscious critical discussion. In the prologue to *La Strega* two characters, Argumento and Prologo, lament such times as the present, when *intermedi* are more important than the plays they adorn:

non parendo essi à fatto lontani dal concerto di quella, non sembrino tuttavia continoatione, over parte della medesima, non dirò altro, non essendo ciò stato da principio di mia intentione. . . ." (Angelo Ingegneri, *Della Poesia Rappresentativa . . . Discorso* [Ferrara, 1598], p. 25.)

25. *Aeli Donati quod fertur Commentum Terentii,* ed. Paul Wessner (Leipzig, 1902–1908). Donatus' discussion of choruses occurs in section III of *De Comoedia.*

ARGUMENTO

. . . I say that in these comedies that are hardly any good and hardly worth looking at [*intermedi*] come in just like ugly middle-aged women who, the more they try dressing themselves up in silk and gold, with garlands and pearls, the more they try ornamenting themselves, making themselves glitter, and powdering their faces so they'll look pretty and young, the more they show they're really old and dried up.

PROLOGO

No doubt that the richness and beauty of the *intermedi*—which mostly show muses, nymphs, *amori*, gods, heroes, and demi-gods—darken the comedy itself and make it look poor and ugly.

ARGUMENTO

And what a thing this comedy is! All of sudden onstage there's an old man, a parasite, a servant, a widow, and a serving girl—what a group!

PROLOGO

What can you do? That's how the world is nowadays. You just have to get used to the customs.

ARGUMENTO

A *custom*, you say! Once they used to put on *intermedi* to serve the comedies; now they're doing comedies to serve the *intermedi*—What do you say to that?

PROLOGO

I'm with you. But you and I can't change the minds people have today.[26]

26. "*A*. . . . anzi dico che alle commedie poco belle e poco buone, interviene come a certe donne attempate e brutte, che quanto più si sforzano, vestendosi di seta e d'oro, e con ghirlande e vezzi di perle, e ornandosi, lisciandosi e stribbiandosi il volto, di parer giovani e belle, tanto più si dimostrano agli occhi dei risguardanti vecchie e sozze.

"*P*. Non è dubbio che la ricchezza e la bellezza degl'intermedi, i quali rappresentamo per lo più muse, ninfe, amori, dèi, eroi e semidei, offuscano e fanno parer povera e brutta la commedia.

"*A*. E di che sorte! veggendosi poi comparirvi in scena una vecchio, un parassito, un servidore, una vedova e una fantesca; bella convenevolezza!

"*P*. Che vuoi tu fare? il mondo va oggidí cosí: bisogna accomodarsi all'usanza.

"*A*. Un'usanza da dirle voi! Giá si solevon fare gl'intermedi che servissero alle commedie, ma ora si fanno le commedie che servono agl'intermedi: che ne di' tu?

"*P*. Intendola come te in questa parte, ma né tu né io semo atti a riformare i cervelli di oggidí." (From Antonfrancesco Grazzini, *Teatro*, ed. G. Grazzini [Bari, 1953], pp. 185–186.)

It is clear enough where this gaudy "custom" comes from, Argumento volunteers: from pedants. Replete with opportunities for showing off a humanist's recondite learning, the mysteries of pagan mythology could titilate the mind as well as the senses.

Il Lasca's choice of images in this interchange from *La Strega* is telling. Unflatteringly observed flesh contrasts with splendid ornament; the mundane, very unheroic personages of the play ("an old man, a parasite, a servant, a widow, and a serving girl—what a group!") contrast with the sublime, marvelous creatures of the *intermedi* ("muses, nymphs, *amori,* gods, heroes, and demi-gods"). The first set of characters are objects of satiric laughter; the second set are objects of what Il Lasca's madrigal calls "wonder" (*meraviglia*). Play and *intermedi* present an audience with two sharply juxtaposed worlds. It is just this sharp juxtaposition, in fact, that Trissino, that thoroughgoing Aristotelian, finds most objectionable. In division VI of the *Poetica* (1563) he, like Ingegneri, chooses to talk about *intermedi* as a kind of chorus. Instead of the traditional choruses of tragedy, Trissino complains,

in the comedies that are staged today they bring on songs and dances and other things that *intermedi* call for—things that are very different from the action of the comedy; sometimes they introduce a troupe of jesters and jokers who perform another whole comedy (something very out of place) that does not allow us to savor the theme of the comedy itself, the function of which is to move us to laughter not by means of every possible kind of action, but only by those means peculiar to itself [*col suo proprio*]—that is, by biting at ugly, wicked things and reproving and ridiculing them.[27]

The persons of comedy, Aristotle had said, were characters who are "worse" than average; the means by which comedy works, like the means by which tragedy works, are emotional. Tragedy arouses pity and fear; comedy arouses ridicule. Comedy's function (and on this point Horace and Cicero were in agreement with Aristotle) is to "laugh folly

---

27. ". . . ma in vece di questi tali Cori ne le Commedie, che oggidì si rappresentano, vi inducono suoni, e balli, et altre cose, le quali dimandano Intermedi, che sono cose diversissime da la azione de la Commedia, e talora v'inducono tanti buffoni, e giocolari, che fanno un'altra Commedia, cosa inconvenientissima, a che non lascia gustare la dottrina de la Commedia, l'officio de la quale non è di muovere riso per ogni modo che si può, ma solamente col suo proprio, cioè col mordere, e riprendere, e deleggiare le cose brutte, e viziose." (Giangiorgio Trissino, *Poetica,* in *Tutte le Opere* [Verona, 1729], I, 122).

out of countenance." With their splendid personages who play on the emotion of "wonder," *intermedi* failed to satisfy both terms in Aristotle's definition of comedy. From Trissino's critical perspective, *intermedi* distract attention from those objects that *are* appropriate to comedy; quite simply, *intermedi* confuse the emotional means by which comedy works.

Trissino may have raged; Italian audiences raved. When we look over a century of productions of the comedies of Plautus and Terence and of the *commedie erudite* they inspired, we can see in Italian courts exactly that "hankering" for dramatic variety that we have found at the court of Henry VIII. In the eyes of a Renaissance courtier Roman comedies were bound to be found wanting. Bernardo Bibbiena, himself a writer of *commedie erudite,* explains the situation well on the second night of the conversations Baldassare Castiglione records in *Il Libro del Cortegiano.* Man is the only creature that can laugh, Monsignor Bibbiena reminds his noble interlocutors, and laughter

alwaies is a token of a certaine jocondnesse and merry moode that he feeleth inwardly in his minde, which by nature is drawne to pleasantnesse, and coveteth quietnesse and refreshing.

"For which cause," he concludes, "we see men have invented manie matters, as sportes, games and pastimes, and so many sundrie sortes of open shewes." [28] Monsignor Bibbiena's emphasis is on many and sundry.

By themselves, Plautus and Terence were unable to supply three elements in particular that a noble audience had come to expect: spectacle, didactic message, and love interest. The last element is the most crucial. The wide-ranging mythological allusions and the pretentious allegory of some of the *intermedi* may prompt us to applaud their highbrow classicism, until we realize that almost always the allegory points to a statement in the idiom of courtly love. It was an idiom in which Ovid was well versed and versed well—or so it seemed to his medieval and Renaissance admirers. Italian courtiers, no less than Henry's English courtiers, were doing more than watching plays: they were playing an elaborate and very old social game. Jousts and tournaments with all their medieval romantic trappings remained as popular at Italian courts down through the century as they did at the court of

28. Trans. Sir T. Hoby as *The Book of the Courtyer,* Everyman's Library (London and New York, 1937), pp. 35–37.

Queen Elizabeth.[29] With great displays of ingenuity the devisers of courtly revels in both countries managed to persuade the unlikely characters of Plautus and Terence to conform with the social code of courteous love. The Italians were simply better at carrying the business off with artistic integrity. What we observe in both countries is an attempt to accommodate the distant world of teeming urban Rome to a small and closed society that liked to see itself, as Ariosto, Tasso, and Spenser all remind us, in the image of the legendary courts of medieval romance. Like their d'Este compeers, Henry VIII and his courtiers looked at Plautus and Terence with their own eyes, not with the eyes of literary historians conscious of cultural contexts.

III

When playwrights made the displaced Romans of Plautus and Terence speak Italian in native imitations like d'Ambra's *La Confanaria* and Bibbiena's *La Calandria,* they kept a scholar's eye on their models, depending on *intermedi* to give that wider frame of reference that brought the play home to the audience. English adapters of Plautus and Terence were, on the whole, less respectful. There were fitful attempts in England at *commedia erudita,* but when we survey these experiments in classical comedy erudite is hardly the adjective that comes to mind. English imitators of Plautus and Terence could not help letting more immediate objects divert their eyes from distant classical models. The earliest English translation of Terence starts off the tradition conservatively enough: the English *Andria* of about 1520—grandly set forth as *Terens in englysh*—is as scrupulous as the Italian versions by Ercole d'Este. As a master of ceremonies for Terence's comedy the anonymous translators introduce a figure they style "the Poet." In a critically self-conscious prologue the Poet calls attention to the medium (the translation is an attempt to enrich the still uncultivated English language) before going on to lay out the matter. In the appended epilogue the Poet turns finally to the play's *sentence* and assures us of the translation's integrity:

29. Elena Povoledo, "Le Théâtre de tournoi en Italie pendant la Renaissance," in *Le Lieu théâtral à la Renaissance,* ed. Jean Jacquot (Paris, 1964), pp. 95-104, with excellent plates.

> Syth we have playd now this lytill comedy
> Before your wisdoms as we pretendyd
> To tak it in gre we besech you humbly
> And to forgyne us where we hane offendid
> The translatours know well it may be Amendyd
> By theym that be wyse & wold take the payne
> It forrede & to corect agayn
>
> Wherfore the translatours now Req[ui]re you this
> yf ought be amys ye wold consyder
> The englysh almost as short as the latten is
> And still to kepe ryme a dyffycult matter
> To make the sentence opynly to appere
> Which if it had a long expocyson
> Then were it a comment & no translation[30]

This rough but vigorous translation, obviously intended for acting, deserves to be better known than it is.

Later writers of "erudite comedy" in English show little of the Poet's tact and reserve. Mid-century plays like *Ralph Roister Doister* and *Jack Juggler* are as bumptious and locally colorful as any groundling could wish. There is more than knockabout farce, however, in the best-known English adaptation of Roman comedy. In *The Comedy of Errors*—surely England's best exercise in *commedia erudita*—young William Shakespeare alters Plautus' *Menaechmi* in a characteristically Renaissance direction. Like the Italian producers of Roman comedy, like the devisers of Henry's revels, he heightens the love interest. The already married twin is reconciled with his wife; the unmarried twin falls in love with his brother's wife's sister. The twins' father is reunited with their mother, and so all the family with each other. The denouement could not be more symmetrical, or more cozily domestic, or more chastely un-Italian. Ben Jonson, on the other hand, might have found Plautus' sardonic irony more to his own way of looking at things. After one of his conversations with Jonson in 1618, William Drummond made this note: "he had ane intention to have made a play like Plaut[us'] Amphitrio but left it of, for that he could never find two so like others that he could persuade the spectators they were one." [31]

---

30. *Terens in englysh*, STC 23894, p. 137.
31. Ben Jonson, *Works*, ed. C. H. Herford and P. and E. Simpson, 11 vols. (Oxford, 1925–52), I, 144.

In English imitations, however, Plautus and Terence could not hope for favor at Queen Elizabeth's court. *Commedia erudita* has suffered almost as much as Ben Jonson himself in the comparisons literary critics like to draw with Shakespeare. Who would prefer the musty academy to the sweet-smelling English greenwood? Sir Philip Sidney, for one. Like Trissino, Sidney has read his Aristotle. We may well wonder what Sidney would have said had he seen Shakespeare's plays, but surveying English drama in the early 1580's he can see nothing but naïveté in the confused incidents that converge willy-nilly in a typical English play:

> Now you shall have three Ladies walke to gather flowers, and then we must beleeve the stage to be a garden. By and by we heare newes of shipwrack in the same place, then we are too blame if we accept it not for a Rock. Upon the back of that, comes out a hidious monster with fire and smoke, and then the miserable beholders are bound to take it for a Cave: while in the meane time two Armies flie in, represented with foure swords & bucklers, and then what hart wil not receive it for a pitched field.

If dramatists take such freedoms with place, what do they do to time?

> Now of time, they are much more liberall. For ordinarie it is, that two yoong Princes fall in love, after many traverses she is got with childe, delivered of a faire boy: he is lost, groweth a man, falleth in love, and is readie to get an other childe, and all this in two houres space: which howe absurd it is in sence, even sence may imagine: and Arte hath taught, and all auncient examples justified, and at this day the ordinarie players in *Italie* will not erre in.[32]

Sidney had been to Italy and should know firsthand.

The high adventures Sidney describes delighted not only farmers in provincial innyards but Elizabeth and her court in the great halls of Greenwich, Nonsuch, and Whitehall. *Aulularia* was acted for Elizabeth at Cambridge in 1564, the boys of Westminster School played *Miles Gloriosus* for her in 1565, and a *History of Error* is mentioned in the Revels Office accounts for 1577, but there are conspicuously few Roman comedies among the court performances that have left behind some written record. Other dramatic forms, we must conclude, better suited court taste. Throughout Elizabeth's reign belated morality plays instructed her; when her hosts had academic pretensions, imitations after

32. *The Prose Works of Sir Philip Sidney*, ed. A. Feuillerat (Cambridge, 1912), III, 38.

classical tragedy admonished her; but another dramatic kind entertained her. Though the plays themselves are almost all lost, most titles mentioned in the Revels Office accounts during the 1570's and early 1580's point to a rich and well-worked mine of narrative. During these years Italian princes may have been yawning through *commedie erudite;* but Elizabeth and her knights and ladies were sitting rapt before the adventures of *Herpetulus the Blue Knight and Perobia* and *The Knight of the Burning Rock.* The titles and property lists that survive in the Revels accounts are teasingly obscure and should keep us wary about making easy generalizations. Where only a Latin or Italian proper name survives, the lost play could *perhaps* have been an English variation on the model of Plautus or Terence. But, in a wide-ranging survey of possible sources of these lost court plays, Carter Anderson Daniel has found that most titles suggest links with four great treasuries of narrative: classical history and legend, Greek romance, medieval romance, and Italian *novelle.*[33] In the last three, certainly, love motives and high adventure dominate the action. *Sir Clyomon and Sir Clamydes,* perhaps revived near the end of the century and then put into print, is virtually the only survivor of a genre that enjoyed royal favor for at least fifteen years.

What hopes had the comedians of Plautus and Terence in a world of dragons, battles, and fortune-crossed lovers? What of the pagan gods who shared attention with them at the court of Henry VIII? Their fortunes are linked. When Richard Edwards, master of Queen Elizabeth's Chapel Royal, turned Chaucer's *Knight's Tale* into a celebrated court play in 1566, he took the romantic intrigue of his source and both lowered it and heightened it.[34] Under-plot clowning by one Tercatio caused Elizabeth to exclaim, "God's pity, what a knave it is!" Over-plot philosophizing turned Palamon and Arcite's combat into a contest of ideas. In Chaucer's tale each knight prays for success to his own patron

33. Carter Anderson Daniel, "Patterns and Traditions of the Elizabethan Court Play to 1590" (diss., University of Virginia, 1965).

34. The fullest of several eyewitness accounts is by John Bereblock, Dean of Exeter College, and is translated (sometimes very loosely) from the Latin original by W. Y. Durand in *PMLA*, XX (1905), 502–528. Details from the comic subplot are recounted by Anthony à Wood in his biographical notice of Edwards in *Athenae Oxoniensis*, I, 152, in the 2d ed. (London, 1721).

deity; in Edwards' play Diana, Venus, Mars, and Saturn apparently held counsel on stage to make the thematic argument vivid and immediate—just as gods would have done in an Italian *intermedio*.

What Edwards' noble audience saw that night in Christ Church Hall, Oxford, was a play on three levels: disputatious gods clarified issues at the top; amorous knights played out their intrigue in the middle; Tercatio romped at the bottom. Edwards managed to combine not only a hierarchy of three plots but a hierarchy of three traditions of court entertainment. Behind Diana, Venus, Mars, and Saturn stand the pageant gods whose splendid oratory and even more splendid appearance dazzled the court of Henry VIII. Provoking Elizabeth's laughter at the bottom of the play, Tercatio may well proclaim his ancestry with his Italian name. Certainly the wily servants who carry on the comic business in Edwards' earlier court play *Damon and Pythias* leave no doubt that they have migrated to England from Terence's Rome. The main focus in Edwards' play, however, was apparently not on gods or the quipping comedian but just where Isabella d'Este Gonzaga, Gasparo Spinelli, Edward Hall, and Sir Philip Sidney would lead us to expect it: on the amorous knights and their adventures. Edwards scored a triumph. Though the text itself has been lost, *Palamon and Arcite* was memorable enough for several eyewitnesses to record it in detail and for Anthony à Wood to give the occasion singular attention when he set down Edwards' biography more than a century later. We know more about the performance and audience reaction on this occasion than we do for many court plays that survive intact.

Down through the sixteenth century, Italian poets catered to their patrons' delight in amorous poses and grand chivalric gestures not by writing new plays on subjects from romance (as did writers of Renaissance epic) but by framing productions of Plautine and Terentian comedy with the marvelous wonders of amorous mythology—or, better, mythologized *amours*. English court dramatists were different: in England the play was the thing. Classical mythology and classical comedy were merely fashionable adornments. Edwards' plan for *Palamon and Arcite* had variety, unity, and imitators. His hierarchy of sententious gods, languishing lovers, and satiric observers confronts us in such master-moves in the game of courtly love as John Lyly's *Sapho and Phao, Gallathea,* and *Love's Metamorphosis.* The showy classical trappings of Lyly's court comedies are used to very unclassical ends: they serve motives that the Roman audiences of Plautus and Terence would not have understood. Court drama, after all, is not art for art's sake but art for the prince's sake.

Strangers to the world of medieval romance, unread in Ovid, unpracticed in speaking the language of courtly love, Plautus' and Terence's indecorous Romans could not confront Renaissance courtiers without a proper introduction. In England as in Italy, when we chart the fortunes of Roman comedy among the revels of Renaissance courts, we discover a series of attempts to accommodate new dramatic materials to old thematic interests. Audiences may have had a fresh appreciation for the classics; they had at the same time more than a passing fancy for spectacle, didactic message, and amorous intrigue. Alone, Plautus and Terence could not satisfy their expectations. To establish their perspective, to see Roman comedy from the most gratifying angle, Italian and English courtiers demanded a made-to-order Renaissance frame.

The City in Plautus and Middleton

GAIL KERN PASTER

IT HAS BEEN SAID that while Terence had a greater influence than Plautus on the themes of Jacobean comedy, Plautus had more impact on specific character types and situations.[1] Since Plautus' comedies outnumber Terence's by a score of twenty to six, the greater incidence of Plautine sources in Jacobean comedy is not surprising. What is surprising is that, as a writer widely studied in English schools and universities from the early sixteenth century, Plautus' authority was considerable, despite the fact that he is not usually thought to have had a large spiritual following on the Jacobean stage. We tend to think of *The Comedy of Errors,* for instance—the most Plautine of any Elizabethan play—as an early experiment that Shakespeare fortunately outgrew. The element of romantic love permeating the atmosphere of so much of Elizabethan and Jacobean comedy is totally missing from the

---

1. This is, at least, Richard Hosley's contention in "The Formal Influence of Plautus and Terence," in *Elizabethan Theatre,* ed. John Russell Brown and Bernard Harris, Stratford-upon-Avon Studies (London, 1966), IX, 131. Hosley's notes, p. 130, provide a good summary of relevant criticism of Plautus and Terence.

Plautine scheme of things. The young men of Plautine comedy may mouth romantic sentiments, but most of them are really prompted by what we would identify rather as sexual appetite.[2] In Terence's comedies, however (and in that Plautine anomaly, the *Captivi*), characters are stirred by nobler motives and moved to higher ends. Walter Beare comments that Terence's plays "invest the themes of daily life with a certain nobility."[3] Even Erich Segal, who goes farther than anyone else in asserting the ulterior significance of the Plautine canon, would hardly make such a claim.[4] The adjective *Plautine* describes comedy that is broad, bawdy, and filled with farcical incident at the expense, seemingly, of more serious thematic concerns. Shakespeare's addition of a second pair of twins in *The Comedy of Errors* brings to the surface deeply riddling questions of identity that lie submerged in Plautus' original. Yet Plautus does have a legitimate heir on the Jacobean stage, an heir whose detached and rather cynical perspective on the spectacle of human absurdity matches his own. As M. C. Bradbrook almost alone has noticed,[5] Plautus' comedies find their most accurate reflection not in those plays specifically indebted to him for a character or situation, but in the city comedies of Thomas Middleton, especially (I would add) the best of them—*Michaelmas Term; A Mad World, My Masters; A Trick to Catch the Old One;* and *A Chaste Maid in Cheapside.* Her observation that Middleton takes over the cruel atmosphere of the Plautine world is worth exploring in some further detail for the light it may shed on the grounds for comparison between a realistic comedy of seventeenth-century London and classical comedy from the late third and early second centuries B.C.

The differences between the two playwrights may seem more apparent at first glance. Although several city comedies—*Epicoene,* for

2. H. B. Charlton, *Shakespearian Comedy,* 4th ed. (1938; rpt. London, 1949), p. 56.

3. In *The Roman Stage: A Short History of Latin Drama in the Time of the Republic,* 3d ed. rev. (1950; rpt. London, 1964), p. 112.

4. *Roman Laughter: The Comedy of Plautus,* Harvard Studies in Comparative Literature (Cambridge, Mass., 1968), Vol. XXIX.

5. In *The Growth and Structure of Elizabethan Comedy* (London, 1955), p. 158.

example—have Plautine antecedents, the important sources of Middleton's best comedies are to be found not in Roman comedy at all, but in the cony-catching pamphlets of the 1590's, cases in the law courts, and the rough texture of daily life on the city's streets.[6] Furthermore, even though the common stock of comic conventions that Middleton draws on stems from ancient comic traditions, the differences between theatrical conditions in Renaissance London and republican Rome outweigh the similarities. In terms of cultural differences, for example, the slave of Roman comedy becomes perforce the wily servant of Renaissance comedy, and the young gentlewoman so prominent in Renaissance comedy could never appear on the Roman stage except in the person of a newly translated courtesan.[7] The ancient playwright was limited not only by the visual and acoustical difficulties of outdoor performances in the amphitheaters, but also by the conventions which prohibited interior scenes or the mention of any Roman, living or dead. Of course there were restrictions in the Jacobean theater, too, despite the greater flexibility of the unlocalized stage. The "realism" of any Jacobean comedy is always limited by the convention of boys taking women's parts, for example, and in the case of most of Middleton's comedies is even further complicated by the manipulations of the dramatic illusion so frequent in the productions of the children's companies.[8] Yet on the Roman stage there was even greater stylization: the large masks the actors wore identified them with one of the stock roles—*servus, senex, adulescens, meretrix,* and so forth. Plautus, moreover, had to adhere to the stultifying fiction that his were Greek plays, mere translations of the Greek

6. For literary sources, see David George, "Thomas Middleton's Sources: A Survey," *N&Q*, CXVI (1971), 16–22; but also see Richard Levin's introduction to his edition of *Michaelmas Term*, Regents Renaissance Drama (Lincoln, Neb., 1966), pp. xi–xii and notes; and Samuel Schoenbaum, "*A Chaste Maid in Cheapside* and Middleton's City Comedy," in *Studies in the English Renaissance Drama: In Memory of Karl Julius Holzknecht*, ed. Josephine W. Bennett, et al. (New York, 1959), p. 291.

7. For the transmutations of other roles, see Hosley, "The Formal Influence," pp. 137–42.

8. Michael Shapiro discusses the children's effects on city comedy in "Children's Troupes: Dramatic Illusion and Acting Style," *CompD*, III (1969), 49–51; and in "Toward a Reappraisal of the Children's Troupes," *ThS*, XIII, no. 2 (1972), 13–16.

originals of Menander, Philemon, and Diphilus.[9] Thus he had to set his scene in Athens or Ephesus, even though his real concern, like Middleton's, was the conditions of life in his own city.

Despite all the differences between them in time and place, it is the shared interest in the city which draws Middleton and Plautus together for comparison, because (with the exceptions of Plautus' *Rudens,* the *Captivi,* and *Amphitruo*) all of the plays in question take the city for their subject as well as their setting. Analogous preoccupations with money, power, sexual politics, battles of wit and cony-catching, and often intricate questions of law define the atmosphere and punctuate the comic action. These preoccupations are, in fact, indigenous in some degree to plays that make significant use of a realistic urban background, and some of the comparisons that can be drawn between Plautus' comedies and Middleton's could also be extended to other city comedies such as *The Devil Is An Ass* or *The Dutch Courtesan.* Yet Middleton's comedies are Plautine not simply because of the common urban setting, but because of a common mood and point of view which override even important differences among them. The rather cynical detachment variously evident in these plays creates a cold and competitive urban world in which a predatory dynamic of conflicting appetites threatens a whole network of social and familial relationships. Only the most astute of their critics have understood that this detachment masks ethical concern, and that both playwrights use the oblique techniques of irony and satire to comment critically on the societies in which they live.[10]

Both Plautus and Middleton use the different resources of their respective theaters to reach beyond the limits of dramatic form to bring the entire city metaphorically on-stage. Plautus turns what would otherwise be a handicap into an advantage by using the fixed location of his

9. The best general account of Roman comedy is George E. Duckworth, *The Nature of Roman Comedy: A Study in Popular Entertainment* (Princeton, N.J., 1952).

10. For instance, Erich Segal in *Roman Laughter;* Schoenbaum, *"A Chaste Maid in Cheapside";* and R. B. Parker in the introduction to his edition of *A Chaste Maid in Cheapside,* The Revels Plays (London, 1969). The reader interested in Middleton and/or city comedy should consult Brian Gibbons, *Jacobean City Comedy: A Study of Satiric Plays by Jonson, Marston, and Middleton* (Cambridge, Mass., 1968); and Alexander Leggatt, *Citizen Comedy in the Age of Shakespeare* (Toronto, 1973).

stage as a crossroads connecting the forum, the harbor or the country, and the household. Unable actually to present the busy life of the forum or the intimacies of life behind the threshold, Plautus makes the neutrality of an unidentified city street significant as the point of intersection for the public and private spheres. Set between the truly public and the thoroughly private, then, the plays share something of the nature of both. Furthermore, because off-stage action is more important to Roman comedy than to a comic tradition with more flexible stage conventions, expository narrative becomes an essential part of the verbal texture and comic action of the plays. Off-stage places take on a reality that they rarely do in plays where expository narrative is a tiresome chore, perfunctorily dispensed with. The forum, particularly, provides important verbal images in many of the plays, and the sense of the movement and activity of city life which these images generate helps to disguise the limitations of action and characterization that are inevitable in such formulaic comedy. Vivid descriptions of urban detail sometimes stand out from the action as virtuoso set pieces with their own unity and inner life. In the *Aulularia,* for instance, the wealthy Megadorus moves from the question at hand—the wisdom of marrying poor women—to an elaborate portrait of rich women in the city:

Wherever you go nowadays you see more wagons in front of a city mansion than you can find around a farmyard. That's a perfectly glorious sight, though, compared with the time when the tradesmen come for their money. The cleanser, the ladies' tailor, the jeweller, the woollen worker—they're all hanging round. And there are the dealers in flounces and underclothes and bridal veils, in violet dyes and yellow dyes, or muffs, or balsam scented footgear; and then the lingerie people drop in on you, along with shoemakers and squatting cobblers and slipper and sandal merchants and dealers in mallow dyes . . .

(*Aulularia,* ll. 505–514)[11]

Megadorus goes on at such length, and with such precision of catalogue, that the accumulation becomes comic. Meantime, however, he has conjured up the vision of a host of tradesmen who will never come on-stage but who, by being given such specific acknowledgment, connect the long, narrow stage to the great urban world. Such examples abound:

11. All quotations from Plautus are from the Loeb Classical Library edition, trans. Paul Nixon, 5 vols. (London and Cambridge, Mass., 1937–1938). For the sake of space I have quoted only Nixon's English translation and line citations.

there is the vibrant picture of returning soldiers tramping through streets crowded with baggage animals, captives, excited relatives, and eager harlots, in *Epidicus* (ll. 208 ff.); the street scene of cloaked, book-laden Greek tutors and ball-playing slaves in *Curculio* (ll. 280 ff.); the picture in the *Poenulus,* which the courtesan Adelphasium creates with contemptuous detail, of prostitutes from all over the city worshipping at the temple of Venus (ll. 265–270); or the long monologue of Ballio, the pimp in the *Pseudolus,* which calls into being the various city tradesmen from whom Ballio is demanding birthday tribute (ll. 133 ff.). The most famous example of this kind of word painting occurs in *Curculio,* when an actor representing the company's property manager comes forward to "show you where you can readily find men of every variety" (ll. 467–468):

> In case you wish to meet a perjurer, go to the Comitium; for a liar and braggart, try the temple of Venus Cloacina; for wealthy married wasters, the Basilica. There too will be harlots, well-ripened ones, and men ready for a bargain, while at the Fish-market are the members of eating clubs. In the lower forum citizens of repute and wealth stroll about; in the middle forum, near the Canal, there you find the merely showy set . . .
>
> (*Curculio,* ll. 470–476)

By interrupting whatever dramatic illusion the play had thus far created in order to present his travelogue of downtown Rome, the stage manager draws attention away from the world of the play toward the actual city surrounding both play and audience. Also, by underscoring the relationship between the city's geography and its moral topography, his words turn Rome into a quasi-allegorical landscape and suggest possible connections between the actual world and the moral categories implicit in the play world of prostitutes and parasites, married wasters, and citizens of repute and wealth.

This city scene in *Curculio* is the most obvious example of the wealth of irrelevant detail which Plautus strews throughout his plays—"irrelevant" because such detail rarely contributes to the stage action to which it ostensibly is connected. It does, however, add greatly to a sense of life and movement existing apart from the action. Because such detail is so often gratuitous—an example perhaps of the playwright's exuberant and generous creativity—it becomes better evidence for the actuality of the characters and intrigue on-stage. It is obvious, of course, that Plautus does not make realistic use of the Greek settings of his plays. On the contrary, he uses the recognizable features of daily life in Rome to provide whatever "local color" his comedies possess. The point is not, as some critics have complained, that Plautus fails to create a consistent play world;[12] it is rather that he borrows from the manifest "reality" of Rome to breathe vitality into otherwise conventional comic plots and to provide rather trivial comic intrigue with a credible social context. The familiarity of the dramatic background is especially important, moreover, in view of Erich Segal's thesis that the action and characters of Plautine comedy present an inverted picture of the moral and social order of republican Rome and that this inversion, obvious to Plautus' audience, constitutes the essence of his art.[13]

Middleton, too, uses the city to expand a play's range of implication and to deepen the sense of actuality of both action and character. He does not bring the city into the plays as Plautus does through large visual images that stand apart from the action, and he tends not to exploit the flexibility of his stage by sharply localizing individual scenes in London's more familiar places. Miss Bradbrook has even suggested that his plays create a sense of London through a familiar, easy style rather than through the thick application of local color that Dekker, for instance, relies on to give his plays topical interest.[14] Primarily, however, Middleton creates a recognizable urban milieu by presenting characters who are aware of themselves as city-dwellers having specifically urban kinds of experience. They see themselves in an urban tradition and different from, if not superior to, the nonurban population. This urban self-consciousness is particularly intense in *Michaelmas Term*, through its emphasis on the class warfare of merchant and gallant. Indeed, the characters of that play think of themselves less as individuals than as representatives of a class and a position in the urban struggle. There is, among the characters, a common understanding of the nature of the urban experience—what the gallants Rearage and Cockstone call the "city powd'ring" (I.i.56),[15] and which they are ruefully proud to

---

12. Duckworth, for example, *Nature of Roman Comedy*, p. 136.

13. *Roman Laughter, passim.*

14. *Growth and Structure of Elizabethan Comedy*, p. 159.

15. I have chosen to quote Middleton in the modern editions of the plays where possible, rather than in the outdated, though standard edition of Bullen (1885–

have acquired. Characters often voice their assessments of the rapacious-
ness of urban living in the accents of familiar truths—platitude or
proverb—set off from surrounding dialogue by rhymed couplets. Thus
Quomodo reminds Shortyard of the deadly enmity of merchant and
gallant, "which thus stands: / They're busy 'bout our wives, we 'bout
their lands" (I.i.106–107); and later in the same scene sends him off with
the command, "Oh, my most cheerful spirit, go, dispatch! / Gentry is the
chief fish we tradesmen catch" (131–132). The pandar Hellgill tells
the Country Wench he has enticed into the city, "Virginity is no city
trade, / You're out o' th' freedom, when you're a maid" (I.ii.43–44).
Middleton suggests that the city has its own body of folk wisdom. Shortyard's boy laments:

Alas, poor birds that cannot keep the sweet country, where they fly at
pleasure, but must needs come to London to have their wings clip'd, and
are fain to go hopping home again.

                                                              (III.ii.19–22)

Such civic consciousness is more casual in *A Trick to Catch the Old
One* and *A Mad World, My Masters*. Phrases like "here i'the city" not
only serve to remind the audience of location, but also suggest that the
location is itself essential to an understanding of the action. Furthermore,
in both plays, as in *Michaelmas Term,* characters not only harbor base
expectations about human nature, but are rather self-consciously aware
of the ease with which they accept the many forms of human viciousness. *A Mad World, My Masters* opens with Dick Follywit's proud account of his decline from virtue. Later in the same scene, the Courtesan's
mother reminds her daughter in the matter-of-fact accents of Middle-
tonian platitude that "every part of the world shoots up daily into more
subtlety" (I.i.140):

              The shallow plowman can distinguish now
              'Twixt simple truth and a dissembling brow,
              Your base mechanic fellow can spy out

1886). I will quote from the following without further citation: *Michaelmas Term,*
ed. Richard Levin, as above; *A Mad World, My Masters,* ed. Standish Henning,
Regents Renaissance Drama (Lincoln, Neb., 1965); *A Trick to Catch the Old
One,* ed. G. J. Watson, New Mermaids (London, 1968); and *A Chaste Maid in
Cheapside,* ed. R. B. Parker, as above.

> A weakness in a lord, and learns to flout.
> How does't behoove us then that live by sleight
> To have our wits wound up to their stretch'd height!
> (I.i.143–148)

Her words are belied by the play itself, of course, which demonstrates among other things the permanence of gullibility. More to the point, characters seem to understand the complacent acceptance of vice as an urban attitude because they accept as manifest truth the conventional contrasts between city-dwellers and country folk. Thus Lucre, the miser in *A Trick to Catch the Old One,* remarks, "There's more true honesty in such a country servingman than in a hundred of our cloak companions" (II.i.145–146). The plays themselves, of course, undercut whatever grain of truth lies in such easy assumptions. The point is, however, that Middleton's urban characters think and act on a set of assumptions which they characterize as belonging to the city. They see themselves in an urban context, as merchant or gallant or city wife or just sly urban fox. In these plays, at least, Middleton's use of local reference is simply a final guarantee, as it were, of the familiar credibility of the comic milieu.

The most significant use of local reference in Middleton's city comedies occurs in *A Chaste Maid in Cheapside.* As R. B. Parker has pointed out in his edition of the play, place names become evaluative metaphors that serve to establish moral connections between a character and his physical setting. Thus, the idiotic Tim Yellowhammer searches for his sister by way of Trig Stairs, *trig* being Elizabethan slang for coxcomb. His mother goes to Puddle Wharf, an appropriate place for a woman of equivocal moral standards in a play that associates women with incontinence. Cheapside's commercial importance gives to the title of the play the second meaning, "chastity for sale," the truth of which is obvious to even the most casual reader.[16]

Middleton's dramatic use of the city, however, goes beyond the imaginative local reference of *A Chaste Maid.* With a potential cast of characters substantially larger than Plautus', he uses minor or anonymous characters to help evoke the larger urban world which stretches out beyond the play and for which Cheapside is the symbol. There is a sense

---

16. See the introduction by Parker, pp. xlvi–xlvii.

that Middleton's characters have relationships and connections extending beyond the play world. On hearing of Witgood's reacquired fortune in *A Trick to Catch the Old One*, three creditors whose existence has till then been unknown appear and try to collect. One of the play's editors points out the number of nameless people we hear about but never see in the course of the play: the widow-hunters Witgood mentions in III.i.253–258; the widows hunting Witgood whom Lucre imagines in II.i.310–319; or the matches that Lucre boasts of having made in II.i.333–335.[17] The most significant examples of this use of the anonymous community occur in *A Chaste Maid*, which includes in its list of dramatis personae designations for thirty-one anonymous characters from the Puritan gossips at the Allwit christening to Tim Yellowhammer's Cambridge tutor. Unimportant as characters in their own right and barely noticeable (one suspects) in a production, these anonymous figures are nevertheless part of the play's physical background. They give depth to the reality of the city's presence on-stage and reinforce the social context in much the same way that dramatically irrelevant detail authenticates Plautus' fictive locales. The incident of the Country Wench and the two Lenten promoters in II.i and II.ii, for instance, has no effect on the action: the promoters' hostile encounter with Allwit vividly establishes the rankness of the season, and after the Country Wench has slyly deposited her bastard with them, she and they disappear from the stage. Precisely because it is connected so loosely to the action, the incident serves to widen the implications of that action beyond the actual borders of the stage to the surrounding urban community into which the girl and the promoters have merged. Major characters seem aware of subtle pressures from this community in their references to neighbors and the neighborhood. "All the whole street will hate us, and the world / Point me out cruel," says Yellowhammer (V.ii.92–93), on learning of his daughter's death. Sir Oliver Kix makes the same point: "I would not have my cruelty so talk'd on / To any child of mine for a monopoly" (V.iii.27–28). Such references, like Plautus' mention of the forum, place the characters' lives in a much broader social context and make stage action part of a larger, busier urban continuum.

17. Watson, introd. to *A Trick to Catch the Old One*, p. xix.

Plautus and Middleton, then, make the entire city an important symbolic presence in the comic action in order to provide a significant background and resonant context for what is always their more limited focus—the interaction within and between several family groups. The emphasis in New Comedy is, in general, domestic rather than social or political. In part, too, Plautus' interest in the family as the important dramatic unit is a function of his stage, which had as a permanent backdrop two or three houses on a long Roman street. The main characters belong logically to one or the other of the houses—and thus, in a sense, to each other. Furthermore, as Erich Segal has suggested, Roman society was so strongly patriarchal that it was family-obsessed, and Plautus is merely picking up on this obsession in the father-son relationships in his plays.[18] Middleton, however, is more interested than his contemporaries in how the urban struggle affects family relationships.[19] To be sure, there are families in other city comedies—the Touchstones of *Eastward Ho,* for example. But family relationships tend to dominate the action in Middleton's city comedies because the playwright is preoccupied with the often disastrous effect of city life on family harmony and stability. Beyond the predatory relationships of gull and rogue in *Michaelmas Term,* there are three distinctly unfortunate parent-child relationships—Quomodo and son Sim; Andrew Lethe and Mother Gruel; and the Country Wench and her father—which constitute the focus of thematic interest. In *A Mad World, My Masters* and *A Trick to Catch the Old One,* the predatory relationship and the family relationship coincide in the schemes of a grandson against his grandfather in the one, and a nephew against his uncle in the other. The cast of characters of *A Chaste Maid* is almost wholly bound together by a complicated network of family ties. The action of the play creates more relationships than it dissolves, most of them ironic, and by the end it is possible to connect almost all the characters in legitimate and recognized, or illegitimate and unrecognized ties of blood and marriage.

One of the striking similarities between Plautus' and Middleton's comedies is that in plays where there are so many families there is so little love. The sons in a Plautine comedy are at a distant remove from

18. *Roman Laughter,* pp. 16 ff.
19. Schoenbaum, "*A Chaste Maid in Cheapside,*" p. 292.

the dutiful Roman ideal of *pietas*. Plautine sons dread the day father comes home from a trip to find the family finances in disarray. Far from assuming the obligation of every Roman son to increase the family wealth, they even look forward to their fathers' deaths and encourage their wily slaves to ever more outrageous deceptions of the credulous old men. Philolaches in the *Mostellaria* wishes "for news now of my father's demise" (l. 233), and his thoughts are seconded by many other Plautine sons.[20] But they are also seconded by several of the young men in Middleton's comedies, who fit Dryden's famous description of the *adulescens* of Roman comedy as a "Debauch'd Son, kind in his Nature to his Mistress, but miserably in want of Money."[21] Fitsgrave asks the young gallants of *Your Five Gallants,* "Are your fathers dead, gentlemen, you're so merry?" To which one of them replies, "By my troth, a good jest!" (IV.viii.288–289).[22] Quomodo counterfeits his own death in order to have the pleasure of seeing himself mourned, only to find that both his wife and his son rejoice instead. Sim declares: "I am glad he's gone, though 'twere long first; Shortyard and I will revel it, i'faith" (*Michaelmas Term*, IV.iv.43–44). Follywit, the madcap hero of *A Mad World, My Masters,* complains about the stinginess of elders to their heirs, and that of his grandfather in particular:

I think one mind runs through a million of 'em; they love to keep us sober all the while they're alive, that when they're dead we may drink to their healths; they cannot abide to see us merry all the while they're above ground, and that makes so many laugh at their fathers' funerals.

(I.i.42–47)

While there may not have been as strict an emphasis on family obligation in Middleton's London as there was in the repressive age of Cato the Elder, the family relationships in Middleton's comedies still represent inversions and distortions of any reasonable standard of love and duty. Like Plautus' *adulescentes,* Follywit is eager to trick his

20. See Segal, *Roman Laughter*, pp. 16–17. He also quotes this line, in his own translation.

21. "An Essay of Dramatick Poesie," *The Works of John Dryden*, Vol. XVII: *Prose 1668–1691*, ed. Samuel Holt Monk, et al. (Berkeley, Los Angeles, and London, 1971), p. 25.

22. Here the quotation is from A. H. Bullen's edition of *The Works of Middleton* (London, 1885), Vol. III.

grandfather out of enough funds to escape sobriety a while longer, though, unlike the less colorful young men in Plautus, Follywit does not entrust the mechanics of the deception to a clever servant. Witgood, the bankrupt hero of *A Trick to Catch the Old One,* is equally eager to catch "that old fox, mine uncle" (I.i.78–79). Lethe in *Michaelmas Term* not only hides his identity from his mother, but employs her as his servant as well. The father figures are far harsher in Middleton's comedy than they are in Plautus, at times denying the existence of family duty and seemingly unable to accept as natural the manifestations of youthful folly. Sir Bounteous Progress, for example, considers his grandson's shameful marriage to his own whore as fit retribution for Follywit's deceptions. Lucre, Witgood's uncle, denies any bond with the nephew from whom he has profited:

What acquaintance have I with his follies? If he riot, 'tis he must want it; if he surfeit, 'tis he must feel it; if he drab it, 'tis he must lie by't; what's this to me?

(I.iii.30–32)

All the inhabitants of Cheapside seem to regard their children as investments with expected dividends: "The child is coming and the land comes after," exclaims Sir Oliver Kix (V.iii.14), on learning of his wife's pregnancy.

There is only one outcome in Middleton's comedy of the conflicts between self-interest and family ties, between material concerns and human claims, between money and love. The contest is rarely more explicit than in *Michaelmas Term,* where Quomodo responds contemptuously to Shortyard's insinuation that he might desire a woman:

> Puh, a woman! Yet beneath her,
> That which she often treads on, yet commands her:
> Land, fair neat land.

(I.i.99–101)

In the same scene Andrew Lethe weighs the claims of his mother against those of his new position, symbolized by new clothes:

My mother! Curse of poverty! Does she come up to shame me, to betray my birth, and cast soil upon my new suit? Let her pass me, I'll take no notice of her. Scurvy murrey kersey!

(I.i.236–239)

In *A Trick to Catch the Old One,* Theodorus Witgood brands his cast-off courtesan as "the secret consumption of my purse" (I.i.28–29), and readers have observed the constant degrading of human worth through insult and innuendo in *A Chaste Maid.*

The cruel atmosphere of Middleton's London, then, results in large part from the characters' cold assessments of one another and the consequent amorality of a body of citizens governed by self-interest. The chilly climate is all the more striking, of course, because the characters are so often related to one another. But characters outside the family structure tend to receive even worse treatment. Courtesans in particular—treated and described contemptuously with a heavy emphasis on venereal disease—are generally so much excess baggage to be fobbed off on someone else as quickly and as profitably as possible. They contract marriages which Middleton and his other characters treat either as good jokes or as deserved punishment. Never is there any sympathy intended or merited for the courtesan or for her victim. Even a character like Dick Follywit, who is certainly the most attractive character in *A Mad World, My Masters,* finds that his marriage to the most outrageous courtesan in all of Middleton's comedies earns only his grandfather's derisive laughter. In such an indifferent world even the victims lack the self-awareness to pity themselves, and Dick Follywit manages to say only, "Is't come about? Tricks are repaid, I see" (V.ii.261). There could hardly be a more casual pointing of the moral.

In Plautus, it is the slave rather than the courtesan who bears the brunt of human indifference. By far the most clever character in his particular comic world, the slave manages the intrigue amid a barrage of threats of whippings and beatings. Erich Segal has argued that all the talk of whippings and beatings rarely leads to actual punishment and that, in the inverted order of the Plautine world, the slave wins his freedom and ends triumphant over a submissive and humbled master.[23] The verbal violence of these threats is often quite specific, however, in its catalogue of proposed tortures of "hot irons and crosses and gyves, and thongs, chains, cells, shackles, fetters, collars, and painters—painters keen as can be and intimate with our backs" (*Asinaria,* ll. 549–551). Actual violence may not be a part of the Plautine world, but in a world

23. *Roman Laughter,* p. 141.

created by words it is not possible to discount verbal violence—a violence directed at the slave and a permanent feature of life in the Plautine city. Indeed, since this verbal violence hardly ever results in action, it is in a sense all the more gratuitous—casually accepted as an idiom of social intercourse the way obscenity is in Middleton's London. And, even if Plautus usually prevents anyone—character or spectator—from taking threats of beatings seriously, it is still a rather cruel kind of fun, appropriate to a world in which the young men for whom intrigues are undertaken seem wholly absorbed in providing for their own physical requirements. The exchange between the slave Epidicus and his young master Stratippocles is typical. Epidicus has succeeded in buying a slave girl at Stratippocles' urgent request, only to find out that Stratippocles has a new object for his affections. To Epidicus' objections that he is being victimized and will surely be punished, Stratippocles airily replies:

Come, come! this is mere chatter. I am a man that needs a hundred and sixty pounds piping hot, in a hurry, to pay off a money-lender, and no time to lose.

(Epidicus, ll. 141–142)

The point is not that Plautus asks us to care a great deal about whether Epidicus or his fellow slaves ever get the beatings they are threatened with, but that on the contrary there is very little emotional involvement with any of the characters or their situations. If Plautus seldom allows anyone to take threats of whippings seriously, he can hardly expect the audience to take seriously the moral sententiousness which is also a part of a Plautine character's vocabulary. Moral behavior in these plays is as rare as violence, and sententiousness is often given an ironic context. Thus Charinus, the *adulescens* in the *Mercator,* condemns Athens— "where vice grows more rampant day by day, where the friendly and the faithless are indistinguishable" (ll. 838–839)—because his father has appropriated his mistress. In these comedies, as in Middleton's, characters tend to think of each other in terms of usefulness—parents being useful for the money they control, slaves for the wit and energy they bring to bear on the problem at hand, and pimps for the women whose fates they direct.

The lack of emotional involvement or interest in a particular comic world is part of what distinguishes farce from comedy, and the important

elements of farce in both Plautus and Middleton can hardly be ignored. It is important to recognize, therefore, that the two playwrights
make farce the level of human interaction as a way of suggesting an
ethical position—albeit an oblique one. The success and prominence of
the undutiful sons and triumphant slaves of Plautine comedy in a comic
world that, like all comic worlds, affirms the values of wit, energy,
youthfulness, and fun constitutes the essence of Plautus' implicit criticism
of contemporary society. Like other kinds of dramatic art, farce, too,
has to stand in some sort of critical relation to the actual world. It is
precisely because Plautus makes the urban background of his plays
familiar to his spectators that his satiric technique of comic inversion can
be successful. Though Middleton chooses the different methods of
caricature and exaggeration, he too relies on the sense of actuality of a
specifically urban background. The city is more than a silent witness to
the contests of merchant and gallant, of uncle and nephew, or of rogue
and gull. In fact the city is deeply implicated in the struggle. The ethical
position of Plautus and Middleton, then, is finally negative, even
though, as Schoenbaum has remarked, "we laugh at what, under other
circumstances, might well horrify us."[24] For both Plautus and Middleton, the cruel mechanization of personal relationships is intimately tied
to the greater urban world that stretches beyond the smaller worlds of
the individual plays and gives them much of their social coherence.

24. Schoenbaum, "*A Chaste Maid in Cheapside*," p. 307.

Dangerous Sport: The Audience's Engagement with Vice in the Moral Interludes

ROBERT C. JONES

W E NO LONGER SNIFF at morality plays and moral interludes as mere "specimens of the pre-Shaksperean drama." But our growing receptiveness to the dramatic vitality of the moralities actually accentuates an apparent problem noted by a generation of unamused scholars—namely, that the bawdy, scurrilous vices tend to steal the show from the wholesome but tiresome virtues. Recent critical studies of these plays—borne out by the increasing availability of performances—have made us aware of their engaging theatricality and especially of their lively use of interactions with the audience. The characters who carry on most of that lively interaction are, of course, the comic vices. Hence the apparent conflict between theatrical attraction and moral purpose that was implicit in the advertisements of the plays themselves when they lured their audiences with promises of the mirth and game to be provided by the vices: what engages the spectators is the representation of the very vices that it is the play's business to make them reject. My concern here, then, is with the ways in which the morality dramatists worked to resolve that conflict, and to reinforce rather than subvert the doctrine of their plays through the theatrically engaging antics of their sportive vices.[1]

Perhaps I can best illustrate the nature of the dramatists' problem by citing C. L. Barber's description of the mood created by what he terms festive comedy: "Behind the laughter at the butts there is always a sense of solidarity about pleasure, a communion embracing the merrymakers in the play and the audience, who have gone on holiday in going to a comedy."[2] It is not hard to imagine something like this happening at the performance of moral interludes that include large measures of the sort of merrymaking that almost always turns at some point on laughter at the butt of a joke or trick—laughter in which the audience is openly invited to join by the merry prankster himself. But if this communal spirit actually united the merrymakers on-stage and in the audience with no counterforce to break the union, it would be absolutely subversive to the moral purpose of the plays, since the tricksters on-stage who ignite our mirth are always the chief representatives of vice (or "the Vice"), and the poor dupe at whom we are asked to laugh is often the figure of mankind. In other words, insofar as the vices' mirth is theatrically successful in Barber's terms, the audience is put in the position of laughing at the representation of its own ruin.

1. Though Bernard Spivack's *Shakespeare and the Allegory of Evil* (New York, 1958) and David M. Bevington's *From "Mankind" to Marlowe* (Cambridge, Mass., 1962) are in many ways the most substantial recent studies of the later moralities and moral interludes, the apology for the plays' theatrical effectiveness may best be represented by T. W. Craik, *The Tudor Interlude* (Leicester, 1958); the Introduction to *English Morality Plays and Moral Interludes*, ed. Edgar T. Schell and J. D. Shuchter (New York, 1969); and Robert C. Johnson, "Audience Involvement in the Tudor Interlude," *TN*, XXIV (1970), 101–111. These three works touch on the problem I am dealing with here (as does Spivack), but they are more concerned with illustrating the theatricality of the plays than reconciling that theatricality with moral instruction. I should add that my own attempt to do so here ignores another vexed question regarding the comic vices—their historical derivation and development. I am only trying to show how dramatists made use of the combination of clowning and vice in these characters, not how that combination came about. For some suggestions about derivation, see (in addition to Spivack) Francis H. Mares, "The Origin of the Figure called 'the Vice' in Tudor Drama," *HLQ*, XXII (1958), 11–29; and Peter Happé, "The Vice and the Folk-Drama," *Folklore*, LXXV (1964), 161–193.

2. *Shakespeare's Festive Comedy* (Princeton, N.J., 1959), pp. 8–9.

Of course, though the vices may have the last laugh, they never have the last word. Virtue always triumphs, and in the end Virtue (along with the repentant victims of the vices) always expounds. In the typical structure of the moral drama, the vices' engaging sport is framed by solemn instructive buffers at the beginning and conclusion of the play.[3] Even when the introductory lesson is confined to a prologue, so that the play itself is opened by a festive Vice, Virtue remains firmly in place at the conclusion to pass its weighty judgment. But if entertainment and instruction were simply the separate provinces of the vices and virtues respectively, the conflict between theatrical attraction and moral doctrine would not really be resolved at all; and the fact that the instructive buffers tended to shrink, while the Vice emerged more and more as the dominant character, indicates that if the entire burden of doctrine were left to the virtues, doctrine would be losing the battle to entertainment. The doctrine had to be sustained in some way by the entertainment itself, and by the vices who provided it, in order to stand up theatrically.

I

Since the problem of the audience's engagement in the vices' sport would seem especially acute in those later moralities in which the Vice both directs and presents most of the action, let me begin with such a play—Ulpian Fulwell's *Like Will to Like* (1568)—to show how the sort of communion of merrymakers that Barber speaks of is purposefully averted. As in some other later moralities, the Vice's dupes at whom we laugh in Fulwell's play are not representatives of mankind in general but types of folly and knavery from which we are meant to dissociate ourselves. The butts of the Vice's jokes are therefore the proper objects of our derision. But the basic problem remains the same. We may be, quite soundly, laughing at Tom Tosspot or Cuthbert Cutpurse; but if we are laughing altogether *with* the Vice, Nichol Newfangle, as he snares his victims into the Devil's party, we are sharing a point of view

3. For a detailed account of the evolving structure of the moral interludes, see Bevington, *From "Mankind" to Marlowe*.

that is perilous for us according to the play's morality. Fulwell turns this danger to our advantage by making the spirit we might share with Newfangle, or our possible kinship with him, an object of satire, with Newfangle himself acting as the satirist in his interactions with us. That is, much of the fun he has with us is precisely on the subject of our likeness to him, playing on the proverb that gives this interlude its title. He rubs our noses in our presumed alliance with him in a way that may make us laugh—but we must laugh self-consciously, rejecting his innuendoes for our own sakes, and thereby rejecting him. Here is how it works.

After a Prologue has explained the play's title, Nichol bounds in, laughing jauntily, and starts things off by tossing down a playing card in front of one of us (it is, apparently visibly, the knave of clubs). His first lines explicate the business:

> Ha, ha, ha, ha! now like unto like: it will be none other,
> Stoop, gentle knave, and take up your brother.
> Why, is it so? and is it even so indeed?
> Why then may I say God send us good speed!
> And is every one here so greatly unkind,
> That I am no sooner out of sight, but quite out of mind?
> Marry, this will make a man even weep for woe,
> That on such a sudden no man will let me know,
> Sith men be so dangerous now at this day:
> Yet are women kind worms, I dare well say.
> How say you, woman? you that stand in the angle,
> Were you never acquainted with Nichol Newfangle?
> Then I see Nichol Newfangle is quite forgot,
> Yet you will know me anon, I dare jeopard a groat.
> Nichol Newfangle is my name, do you not me know?
> My whole education to you I shall show.[4]

Notice here that Nichol's fun comes in the form of taunts that play satirically on our imputed friendship with him; and that, as Nichol's lines make clear, our response to his gibes, however amused we may be, must involve embarrassed rejection of his familiar advances and insinuations of our likeness to him. So the dramatist, in this fairly simple and direct way, turns his Vice's sport, which is the play's main theatrical

4. *The Dramatic Writings of Ulpian Fulwell*, ed. John S. Farmer (London, 1906), pp. 4–5.

attraction, into a means for detaching the audience from the Vice. The rest of the play is devoted to reinforcing that rejection through the illustrative examples of the characters on-stage who welcome or rebuff Newfangle's proffered friendship.

This sort of confrontation, in which our theatrical response defines our relationship to the Vice (or vices), is constant throughout the morality plays. From *The Castle of Perseverance* on, we are invited to join company with the vices, and thereby are put in the position of acting out our refusal to do so:

> Cum speke wyth Lust and Lykynge belyue
> And hys felaw, yonge Foly.
> > Late se whoso wyl vs knowe.
> Whoso wyl drawe to Lykynge and Luste
> And as a fole in Foly ruste,
> > On vs to he may truste
> And leuyn louely, I trowe.[5]

Or, turned the other way, the extent of our complicity with the scheming Vice can be pointed up by making us share in a conspiratorial silence with him:

> Peace, peace! she commeth hereby.
> I spoke no word of her, no, not I! [6]

I will return to the uses of this sort of "complicity" in more detail when we look at *Mankind*. What I want to stress here is that in these plays the very theatricality through which the vices engage the audience gives the satire its special effect. It is not just that the plays satirize vices and follies which they attribute to their audiences—though they do plenty of that as well. They go beyond the direct gibes which, though aimed our way, allow us to respond or not as we will. They interact with us, and the point of the confrontation is made to depend on our response. We are repeatedly made aware of our theatrical responses and their implications. Thus, when the Vice Inclination in *The Trial of Treasure* becomes the mocker mocked (an occupational hazard for his kind), we laugh at him—but, beyond that, we are made conscious of

5. *The Castle of Perseverance*, ll. 519–525, in *The Macro Plays,* ed. Mark Eccles, EETS, no. 262 (London, 1969).

6. *Nice Wanton*, ll. 457–458, in *Specimens of the Pre-Shaksperean Drama,* ed. John M. Manly (1897; rpt. New York, 1967), I, 476.

our laughter and of the fact that it dissociates us from him: "Ye have no pity on me, you, I see, by your laughing."[7]

When this happens, of course, as with all such self-conscious theatricalism, we are made aware of our situation as an audience at a play.[8] In most instances, however, the characters act as though we are responding to them as "real" embodiments of the vices they represent—as though we belong to the same world they do, in which Envy, or Iniquity, or Idleness holds sway. That is how the satiric association they claim with us gets its point. Occasionally, however, the vices add to this theatricalism the further twist of openly acknowledging their status as actors in a play whose business it is to entertain us:

> What, I ween all this company are come to see a play!
> What lackest thee, good fellow? didst thee ne'er see man before?
> Here is a gazing! I am the best man in the company when there
>   is no more.[9]

This emergence of the actor out of his role, this coupling of his role as a particular vice with his skill as a performer, can add a further dimension to the conflict between the virtues and vices and to the significance of our responses to them. The competition between the merry vices and the moral virtues *as* theatrical attractions is exposed and, together with their competition over the mankind figure, becomes part of the play's concern.

A clear instance of this concern can be seen in *The Nature of the Four Elements*. Apparently written by John Rastell around 1518, this play is about education rather than salvation, and therefore its mankind figure, Humanity, is prompted by such specialized virtues as Studious

---

7. *The Trial of Treasure*, in Robert Dodsley's *Select Collection of Old English Plays*, ed. W. C. Hazlitt (1874–76; rpt. New York, 1964), III, 279.

8. See Johnson, "Audience Involvement in the Tudor Interlude."

9. *The Marriage of Wit and Wisdom*, in *Five Anonymous Plays*, 4th ser., ed. John S. Farmer (London, 1908), p. 264. The application of the lesson of the play as such to the audience by the virtues, repentant sinners, and even the vices is common enough at the end of a play or a sequence in a play, and may be distinguished from the sort of emergence of actors as entertainers that I am discussing here. Ann Wierum deals with the vices' deceptive "acting" within the plays, but not with this sort of open allusion to the play as performance, in "'Actors' and 'Play Acting' in the Morality Tradition," *RenD*, N.S. III (1970), 189–214.

Desire and beset by such vices as Ignorance. The lectures on the composition of the world in this play are meant to instruct us as well as Humanity, of course; so we are placed, perhaps even more directly than in most moralities, in the same situation as spectators of the play that Humanity fills within the play. As he learns, so do we.

The one surviving copy of this play is imperfect, but its general pattern and primary techniques are clear enough. After a hiatus in the middle of the play, we discover Humanity (who has been vacillating between Studious Desire and Sensual Appetite) cowering on the ground. Apparently there has been a fracas, and for the moment the vices have the upper hand, for holding the field where Humanity has fallen we find not only Sensual Appetite, whom we have seen misleading him before, but a new character, Ignorance, who is introducing himself to us:

> I would ye knew it, I am Ignorance!
> A lord I am of greater puissance
> Than the king of England or France,
> Yea, the greatest lord living!
> I have servants at my retinue,
> That long to me, I assure you,
> Herewith in England,
> That with me, Ignorance, dwell still,
> And term of life continue will,
> Above five hundred thousand.[10]

Here, then, is a simple, direct satiric association of the vice with the English audience. But a little later, when Ignorance lists "the most part" of the audience among his servants, he points out a more specific aspect of our relationship to him. He is congratulating Humanity on his decision to follow Sensual Appetite back to the delights of the tavern and to forsake the tedium of his virtuous instructors:

> Then thou takest good and wise ways,
> And so shalt thou best please
> All this whole company [the audience];
> For the foolish arguing that thou hast had
> With that knave Experience, that hath made
> All these folk thereof weary;

10. Dodsley, *Old English Plays,* I, 41.

For all that they be now in this hall,
They be the most part my servants all,
And love principally
Disports, as dancing, singing,
Toys, trifles, laughing, jesting;
For cunning they set not by.

(pp. 45–46)

Here Ignorance extends the Like-Will-to-Like principle, applying it
not only to our imputed service under him in general but also to our
enjoyment of that part of the *play* in which he and his cronies take
the lead. In other words, if we prefer the merrymaking in the play to
the serious matter, we are in the camp of Ignorance. We may be prodded
by Ignorance's gibes into a heightened awareness that when (for
example) Sensual Appetite had popped in earlier in the play to interrupt Studious Desire's good progress in enlightening Humanity, it
was our enlightenment that was cut short as well; and that if our hearts
leaped up at the merry note that Sensual Appetite had injected into the
action at that point ("Make room, sirs, and let us be merry, / With
huffa gallant, sing tirl on the berry, / And let the wide world wind!"
[p. 20]), we were experiencing precisely the temptation that leads
Humanity astray in the play, not simply watching him be tempted.

Thus we are made to see that our very responses to the play are
actual manifestations in ourselves of the better and worse impulses in
man that are being represented on-stage; and we can accordingly place
our delight in the vices as something in us to be guarded against. This
technique is perhaps the fullest theatrical realization of the possibilities
of instruction through entertainment in the moral plays. That it serves
the instructive purposes of the plays does not make the entertainment
itself any less lively. The techniques I have been describing here depend
on the satirical bite that stings us into an awareness of what our
laughter means and, in the case of *The Four Elements,* a spirit of mirth
that is engaging enough to have caught us up, with Humanity, in the
mood of the tavern so that we can then be made conscious, with
Humanity, of the perils of getting lost in that mood. This more complex
process of making us actually undergo the experience of the mankind
figure in the play is especially direct in *The Four Elements* since this
play is for us, just as it is for Humanity, a series of instructive lectures

interrupted by frivolity. But to the extent that we do move from engagement in the entertainment of the vices to judgment that places that sort of entertainment in perspective for us—a movement that is built into the typical structure of these plays—virtually all of the moralities involve us in this process.

II

I want to turn now to a more thorough analysis of the uses of comic theatricalism in a single morality play. I choose *Mankind* (ca. 1471) because it is an outstanding example: representative in the sense that it uses the techniques I have been describing, but unusual in the boldness with which it uses them—especially in the degree to which it invites our engagement with the comic vices as entertainers. No doubt this is the reason that it has also served as the outstanding example of decadence in the scholarly view of moralities that used to prevail. Here, according to literary histories that are still very much in use, moral instruction has abdicated in favor of bawdy entertainment. It is, we are told, "a play in which the comic scenes are vulgar but not funny and almost swamp the moral scenes." [11] Or again, "most of the play is given over to horse-play and coarse humor. Some of the lines are unprintable. As a morality play it is so debased as to be rather a contradiction of the type." [12] Though I clearly disagree with these assessments, I have enough respect for the scholars who made them not to presume to use them simply as straw men. And if these attacks on the "coarse humor" of *Mankind* are misplaced, they are by no means implausible reactions to comic business in the moralities. For one thing, their apparent assumption that comedy and morality are separable elements in these plays and that the bent of the comedy was purely diversionary could be supported by the

11. F. P. Wilson, *The English Drama: 1485–1585* (Oxford, 1969), p. 5.
12. Tucker Brooke, in *A Literary History of England,* ed. Albert C. Baugh, 2d ed. (New York, 1967), p. 286. Even Bernard Spivack, whose analysis of the comic vices more closely approximates mine, feels that "the author of *Mankind* . . . is responsible for so lavish a seasoning of buffoonery that it comes perilously close to obscuring, for modern eyes at least, his serious primary meaning," (*Shakespeare and the Allegory of Evil,* p. 193).

apologies offered by the morality dramatists themselves for the admixture of mirth. In their prologues, they customarily spoke of the plays' "sport" as though it were absolutely detachable from the moral matter, or attached to it only as bait to lure the audience into swallowing both together. Rastell's Messenger, who introduces *The Four Elements,* is typical in this respect:

> But because some folk be little disposed
> To sadness, but more to mirth and sport,
> This philosophical work is mixed
> With merry conceits, to give men comfort,
> And occasion to cause them to resort
> To hear this matter, whereto if they take heed,
> Some learning to them thereof may proceed.

(p. 10)

And the title-page advertisement of the surviving copy of this play foresees what we might imagine to be an inevitable tendency for performers with an eye to their audience's pleasure and their own profit to alter the proportions of the mixture: "which interlude, if the whole matter be played, will contain the space of an hour and a half; but, if ye list, ye may leave out much of the sad matter, as the Messenger's part, and some of Nature's part, and some of Experience's part, and yet the matter will depend conveniently, and then it will not be past three-quarters of an hour of length." If this tendency prevailed, we might expect that the comic scenes would, in Wilson's terms, "swamp the moral scenes." And if the comic and serious matter were in fact no more integrally related than the prologues suggest, the comedy might well become an obstacle to the plays' instructive purpose. It would be overzealous to claim that this was never the case, though the satiric confrontation with the audience through the comedy is at work to prevent it from happening in virtually every surviving play.[13] It is not the case in *The Four Elements* (at least as we have it) because of the way in which the play makes its

---

13. For example, some of the Vice's antics at the most serious points of the trial scene in Thomas Garter's *Virtuous and Godly Susanna* (published 1578) seem to me to be purely disruptive—though this Vice, Ill Report, taunts the audience through the play (especially the women for their lechery) in the familiar manner of Nichol Newfangle. In this case, of course, it particularly suits the Vice's character to slander us.

audience aware of the diversionary and potentially obstructive nature of its "sport." And *Mankind* forces this same sort of awareness upon us by having its sportive vices and instructive virtue openly vie for audience approval in a manner that directly parallels their competition for Mankind's allegiance in the play.

This parallel is established through the first two sequences of the play in which we see the same pattern repeated. Mercy opens the play with a cautionary sermon to the audience, warning us against the sort of "neclygence" that would corrupt our souls: "Dyverte not yowrsylffe in tyme of temtacyon, / That ye may be acceptable to Gode at yowr goyng hence." [14] This good instruction is then rudely cut short (though not too short) by the entrance of Mischief, a ringleader to the vices, who mocks Mercy's sermonizing with a raucous parody. Mischief is soon joined by his henchmen Newguise, Nowadays, and Nought, who dance and disport themselves at Mercy's expense until he manages to drive them out. The same sequence is then virtually replayed after Mankind's entrance. This time Mercy's lesson (in a rather more homely version) is delivered to Mankind; but it is again interrupted and mocked by the sportive vices, against whom Mercy gives Mankind a "specyall" warning before leaving him on his own: "Gyff them non audyence" (ll. 293–300).

Through this repeated pattern our relationship to Mankind in the play is dramatically established. Not only does he "represent" us in the play; but also, as Mercy's pupils and potential victims of the vices, we are being put through the same experience as he is. Yet at the same time the *distinction* between our situation as audience at the play and his position as character in the play is emphasized by the way that all of the characters (including Mankind) address us as performers addressing an audience. [15] At this level, as performers, both the sober virtue and the festive vices assume our allegiance and our disapproval of their antagonists in the play. And at this level, I should think, there can be little question that the vices have the best of it through the first half of the performance. Mercy assumes he is speaking for us when he reacts to

14. *The Macro Plays,* ed. Eccles, p. 154.
15. Anne Righter considers this conscious attention to the audience an unhealthy aspect of "the tyranny of the audience" in the period of the later moralities and interludes (*Shakespeare and the Idea of the Play* [London, 1964], pp. 29–42). What I am arguing here is that the audience was played upon deliberately.

Mischief's first interruption: "Why com ye hethyr, brother? Ye were not dysyryde. / . . . Ye ben culpable / To interrupte thus my talkyng delectable" (ll. 53–65). But surely few of us would wish Mercy's sermon longer. As an audience we welcome Mischief's diversion, and when the merry vices leave we can hardly be expected to share Mercy's relief, as he supposes we do: "Thankyde be Gode, we have a fayer dylyuerance / Of thes thre onthryfty gestys" (ll. 162–163). Again, when the interruption of Mercy's lesson to Mankind comes in the form of the vices' off-stage taunts, Nowadays' derisive response to Mercy's warning that the vices will appear as soon as he leaves must catch our mood as an audience accurately enough:

> The sonner the leuer, and yt be ewyn anon!
> I trow yowr name ys Do Lytyll, ye be so long fro hom.
> Yf ye wolde go hens, we xall cum euerychon,
>   Mo then a goode sorte.
> Ye haue leve, I dare well say.
> When ye wyll, go forth yowr wey.
> Men haue lytyll deynte of yowr pley
>   Because ye make no sporte.
>
>   (ll. 261–268)

When the vices do come on after Mercy's exit, they pay no attention at first to Mankind (who is piously delving the earth), but instead, assuming their place as eagerly anticipated crowd-pleasers, greet us warmly and ask us (or the yeoman among us) to join them in a bawdy song:

> NOWADAYS
>
> Make rom, sers, for we haue be longe!
> We wyll cum gyf yow a Crystemes songe.
>
> NOUGHT
>
> Now I prey all the yemandry that ys here
> To synge wyth ws wyth a mery chere.
>
>   (ll. 331–334)

To the extent, then, that we are caught up in this festive spirit, we are distinguished from Mankind in the play, who sternly rebukes the vices for their "derysyon and . . . japyng" (l. 349); and in this mood we can scarcely be heartened by Mankind's promise to us, once he has chased the vices off again by buffeting them with his spade, that "thes felouse wyll no more cum here" (l. 401).

The point about this disparity between our responses as an audience being entertained and the attitude of the virtue (and the still virtuous Mankind) in the play is that, as the whole context makes clear, there is no *real* distinction between the vices as performers and at least some of the vices that they represent; no *real* distinction between us as an audience being entertained and us as "mankind" whose attitudes may be good or bad according to the play's Christian ethic. Insofar as we indulge in the vices' mood, we are falling into precisely the "neclygence" and "derysyon" that Mercy had warned us against (ll. 23, 168). At the mid-point of the play it becomes clear how far the audience is expected to get caught up in that mood and what its ultimate implications are. For at that point the vices rebound from their initial failure with Mankind by enlisting that "Fend of helle" Titivillus in their campaign against him; and so sure are they that this superfiend will be, for us, the main attraction of the play that they stop the show altogether and make us pay before we get to see him:

> Ye, go thi wey! We xall gather mony onto,
> Ellys ther xall no man hym se.
> Now gostly to owr purpos, worschypfull souerence,
> We intende to gather mony, yf yt plesse yowr neclygence.[16]
>
> (ll. 457–460)

Newguise's last phrase (whether it be a slip of the tongue, a malapropism, or a direct taunt) points out exactly how our situation can be judged in the play's terms. We are paying to suit the pleasure of the "neclygence" against which Mercy's opening sermon had warned us.

Once Titivillus comes on, our engagement with the vices is intensified, for we are put in the position of acting as his confidants and accomplices in his successful deception of Mankind.[17] From the moment of his entrance he treats us as admiring potential henchmen whom he is

16. Happé, in "The Vice and the Folk-Drama," cites this collection in *Mankind* as one of the factors linking the morality Vice to the folk play.

17. Spivack reviews this sequence and comments on Titivillus' "concern . . . with his audience" in *Shakespeare and the Allegory of Evil*, pp. 123–125.

taking under his wing and teaching the tricks of his trade: "Titivillus kan lerne yow many praty thyngys" (l. 572). First he warns us, as insiders, to watch out for *our* belongings as he sends Newguise, Nowadays, and Nought out to plunder our neighbors in the local countryside (ll. 476–524). Then he proudly reveals his scheme against Mankind to us, promising us "goode sport" in his execution of it, and beseeching our conspiratorial silence as he carries it out:

> Ande euer ye dyde, for me kepe now yowr sylence.
> Not a worde, I charge yow, peyn of forty pens.
> A praty game xall be scheude yow or ye go hens.
> Ye may here hym snore; he ys sade aslepe.
> Qwyst! pesse! the Deull ys dede! I xall goo ronde in hys ere.
>
> (ll. 589–593)

The audience is not likely to take this stage fiend's "abhomynabull presens" or his bag of tricks very seriously, of course, but that is just the point. We are being caught up in the "sport" of the thing without thinking much about its implications. It is only when the trap is successfully sprung and Mankind has succumbed to Titivillus' deceptive spells that we are brought up suddenly and rudely against the full consequences of this "praty game." The turn comes when Titivillus, having done his business, leaves us abruptly (and no doubt with an abusive gesture). The tone of camaraderie is gone as he points out exactly what he has accomplished:

> Farwell, euerychon! for I haue don my game,
> For I haue brought Mankynde to myscheff and to schame.
>
> (ll. 605–606)

After Titivillus has departed, the play takes on a new tone. As Mankind awakens with his faith in Mercy entirely broken, our old friends the vices return to welcome him into their company. But they return with a difference. Bawdy songs and raucous pranks have been replaced by bloody murders and the hangman's noose. Newguise staggers on with half a halter around his neck, soon followed by Mischief with the remnants of fetters on his arms. What he has been up to is more than mischief:

> Of murder and manslawter I haue my bely-fyll.
> . . . .

I was chenyde by the armys: lo, I haue them here.
The chenys I brast asundyr and kyllyde the jaylere,
Ye, ande hys fayer wyff halsyde in a cornere;
A, how swetly I kyssyde the swete mowth of hers!

(ll. 639–645)

Moreover, their demeanor toward us has changed as well. Whereas they had earlier wooed us into sharing their festive spirit, they now shoulder us aside rudely as they come on:

Make space, for cokkys body sakyrde, make space!

(l. 612)

Avante, knawys, lett me go by!

(l. 636)

Out of my wey, sers, for drede of fyghtynge!

(l. 696)

Thus we are being dissociated from them theatrically as well as through our responses to their starkly exposed sordidness and viciousness. There is more "horseplay," to be sure, in the vices' formal investiture of Mankind as one of their own; but the sport now revolves around such utter degradation of Mankind as he commits himself to a life of crime that it cannot be taken in the same humor as the earlier high jinks:

NEWGUISE

Ye xall goo robbe, stell, and kyll, as fast as ye may gon.
"I wyll," sey ye.

MANKIND

I wyll, ser.

NOWADAYS

On Sundays on the morow erly betyme
Ye xall wyth ws to the all-house erly to go dyn
And forbere masse and matens, owres and prime.
"I wyll," sey ye.

MANKIND

I wyll, ser.

MISCHIEF

Ye must haue be yowr syde a longe da pacem,
As trew men ryde be the wey for to onbrace them,

Take ther monay, kytt ther throtys, thus ouerface them.
"I wyll," sey ye.

MANKIND

I wyll, ser.

(ll. 708–717)

We must agree with Mercy, who reenters at this point, that "this maner of lyuynge ys a detestabull plesure" (l. 766). Whereas the vices have become openly rude to us, Mercy's courteous manner as he apologizes for any annoyance his anguished discomposure over Mankind's fall may cause us must now win the sympathy he had assumed he had from us in his first set-to with Mischief: "My inwarde afflixcyon yeldyth me tedyouse wnto yowr presens. / I kan not bere yt ewynly that Mankynde ys so flexybull" (ll. 740–741). If in that earlier interchange we had welcomed the diversion provided by the vices' mocking interruption of Mercy's solemn lesson, we surely cannot share the spirit of their gloating mockery at Mercy's distress as he seeks to aid Mankind in spite of the latter's betrayal: "Yf ye wyll haue hym [Mankind], goo and syke, syke, syke! / Syke not ouerlong, for losynge of yowr mynde!" (ll. 777–778). In fact, the vices no longer seem to be playing *to* us as they had in those first sequences. They make no gesture toward sharing with us their last-ditch scheme to drive Mankind to suicide; and there are no farewells to us when, this having failed, they scramble frantically off-stage for the last time:

MISCHIEF

Helpe thisylff, Nought! Lo, Mercy ys here!

He skaryth ws wyth a bales; we may no lengere tary.

NEWGUISE

Qweke, qweke, qweke! Alass, my thrott! I beschrew yow, mary!
A, Mercy, Crystys coppyde curse go wyth yow, and Sent Dauy!
Alasse, my wesant! Ye were sumwhat to nere.

(ll. 806–810)

Even for them the fun has gone out of it.

It is left for Mercy, having lectured Mankind once more in the aftermath of his experience, to turn and exhort us in the aftermath of ours: "Now for hys lowe that for vs receywyd hys humanite, / Serge your condicyons wyth dew examinacion" (ll. 907–908). We have been made more fully aware of our "condicyons" not only through the dramatized *exemplum* of Mankind, but through our realization of the impulse toward "derysyon" that the vices had evoked in us and the dangerous and destructive potential of our participation in their mocking mood. We have been "proved," just as Mankind has (l. 283). In this light, it is possible to see a double sense in Mercy's warnings to the audience in the introductory sermon:

> Dyverte not yowrsylffe in tyme of temtacyon.
> . . . .
> For yowr gostly enmy wyll make hys avaunte,
> Yowr goode condycyons yf he may interrupte.
> (ll. 19–28)

and again, after the vices' first appearance:

> Ye may conseyue by there dysporte and behauour,
> Ther joy ande delyte ys in derysyon
> Of her owyn Cryste to hys dyshonur.
>
> Thys condycyon of leuing, yt ys prejudycyall;
> Be ware therof, yt ys wers than ony felony or treson.
> (ll. 167–171)

This serves, of course, as a lesson for our lives in general as we encounter (like Mankind) the dangers that these vices represent. But it also applies to our experience of the stage representation itself, where our "gostly enmy" *does* "make hys avaunte" in order to "dyverte" us, and where we are surely lured into "joy ande delyte" in the "dysporte" of the very vices against whom Mercy warns us. Here again, then, and in a far more thoroughgoing way than in *The Four Elements,* we are engaged by the festive mood of the vices only to be made fully aware of the implications of that engagement.

Few moralities make the audience's experience of the play so fully analogous to the mankind figure's seduction by the vices as *Mankind* does. Even when (and perhaps because) the Vice took over a larger proportion of the action in the later interludes, most dramatists were careful to prod the audience into dissociating itself from the Vice early in the play, in the very process of being entertained by him. Nichol Newfangle's opening confrontation is the more common technique. In

The Tide Tarrieth No Man (1576), for example, where the Vice
Courage, along with his allies and victims, has the first three-fourths of
the play to himself before we get a glimpse of a virtue, we are made to
act out our initial rejection of Courage at once by not taking up his
opening invitation to join him on the Barge of Sin:

> To the Barge to!
> Come they that will go.
> Why sirs, I say "When?"
> It is high tide,
> We may not abide,
> Tide tarrieth no man.
> If ye will not go,
> Why then tell me so,
> Or else come away straight.
> If you come not soon
> You shall have no room,
> For we have almost our freight.[18]

But I would stress, finally, the likenesses, not the differences, among
these plays. All of them work on our awareness of the way we respond
to the vices who so directly confront us; all turn our experience of the
play, at some point, into an expressed rejection of these vices. So the apparent conflict between entertainment and morality that I proposed at
the beginning of this essay is resolved. The very theatricality through
which the vices engage us is used to make us act out the lessons that
the plays expound.

III

The heirs of the Vices—those mischievously intriguing knaves, villains,
and revengers who initiate and direct so much of the action in the
drama of Shakespeare's time—continued to engage their audiences, of
course. In what must be a cursory concluding glance ahead at these
later schemers, however, I want to insist on an obvious but crucial dif-

---

18. *The Tide Tarrieth No Man,* in *English Morality Plays and Moral Interludes,*
pp. 312–313.

ference between them and their morality forebears. The thrust of recent scholarship has been to document continuity between the popular drama of the earlier and later English Renaissance, and the family likeness of Vice, Knave, and Villain has helped to establish that unbroken line. Along with other characteristic traits, the Elizabethan and Jacobean intriguer may also inherit the Vice's capacity for involving his audience in the "dangerous sport" of experiencing much of the action through his sardonic point of view. But there is a fundamental distinction to be made here. Though the Shakespearean villain and Jonsonian knave appeal to us theatrically, they do not openly interact with us, or even (except by way of inviting our applause at the end of a comedy) overtly acknowledge our responses as an audience. For all the versatile theatricalism that allows them their explanatory soliloquies and mocking asides, they no longer jostle us, taunt us about our behavior toward them, or invite us to join in their activities as their earlier counterparts in the interludes had done. In the move from hall to theater, from "place" to stage, the Vice's heir has detached himself from us to this extent. He may still play *to* us, but he does not make us participating actors *in* his play; he does not make us self-consciously act out our conspiratorial engagement with him ("Ande euer ye dide, for me kepe now yowr sylence"), or our dissociation from him ("Ye have no pity on me, you, I see, by your laughing").

This may mean that the audience's engagement with a vicious schemer at the Globe or Blackfriars was even *more* "dangerous" than it had been with the interlude Vice, for the very reason that it was not forced into the open through such direct confrontations. It means, in any case, that the job of tracing the audience's awareness of its engagement with viciousness would be a good deal more complex in the later plays than in the interludes. Plausible assertions have been made about the later plays that sound very much like my thesis about *Mankind,* nonetheless:

So Shakespeare in *Richard III,* a play which owes a great deal to the moralities, induces the audience to assent to Richard's activities through the first half of the play by making him an audaciously comic character, and then forces them to awake with a shock to the evil at which they laughed.[19]

19. *English Morality Plays and Moral Interludes,* p. ix.

But it is indicative that such assertions tend to rely much more heavily on assumptions about the "secret" feelings of the audience than I have had any occasion to do with the interludes:

Although we may feel uneasy about it, our virtuous superego is lulled, and the naked id awakes to vicarious enjoyment of Richard's virtuosity in villainy.[20]

If we reserve most of our scorn for the three birds of prey, if we laugh *at* them and *with* Volpone and Mosca during most of the action, it is not only because Corvino, Voltore, and Corbaccio are so repellent, but because Volpone and Mosca act out with such marvellous aplomb our own secret craving to dominate and manipulate others. We really want to see them get away with it, but Jonson will not indulge us that far.[21]

These assumptions about the audience's psychology may be fair enough; but if we do "feel uneasy" about our enjoyment of these audacious virtuosos in crime, neither Richard nor either of Jonson's rogues embarrasses us by exposing our attraction to him publicly. And by the same token, none of them embarrasses us into publicly rejecting him, as Nichol Newfangle had done.

Though this distinction between the earlier and later plays is an essential one, a convincing argument could be made to show the ways in which Shakespeare and Jonson actually direct our positive and negative reactions to their engaging knaves and villains. Such an argument, however, would demand careful analysis of verbal and dramatic gestures subtler than those of the moral interludes, where the audience's responses are written so largely into the action of the plays themselves.

20. Waldo F. McNeir, "The Masks of Richard the Third," *SEL*, XI (1971), 173.
21. *Volpone, or the Fox*, ed. Jonas A. Barish (New York, 1958), p. x.

Senecan Vacillation and Elizabethan Deliberation: Influence or Confluence?

CATHERINE BELSEY

THE PROBLEM of Seneca's role in the formation of English tragedy remains unresolved. A generation of critics made out a case for his influence, a case which has subsequently been severely questioned, but meanwhile scholars have continued to argue for his formative significance in certain areas.[1] Such continuing critical disagreement may be attributed to a difficulty inherent in the concept of influence itself. The temptation, particularly in the earlier studies, has been either to focus on Seneca to the apparent exclusion of all other possible influences, or to clutch at all other possible influences in order to argue that Seneca's can be ignored. The difficulty is located by G. K. Hunter, who points out "that the etymology of *influence* suggests no single link, but rather a stream of tendency raining down upon its object. . . . We should not' discuss 'the influence of Seneca on Elizabethan tragedy' except in the

---

1. For a review of the entire controversy see the review article by Anna Lydia Motto and John R. Clark at the end of this volume. Recent studies include Wolfgang Clemen, *English Tragedy before Shakespeare,* trans. T. S. Dorsch (London, 1961), and Reuben A. Brower, *Hero and Saint: Shakespeare and the Graeco-Roman Tradition* (Oxford, 1971), pp. 141-172.

context of the other competing influences that were raining down at the same time."[2]

This truth is disheartening. To isolate the single influence of Seneca in the "stream of tendency" is tacitly to ignore any non-Senecan elements and so to risk giving the impression that the Renaissance dramatists were little more than passive imitators; but to analyze the relationship between all the "competing influences" in order to assess the extent of one would be a daunting task.

It is perhaps possible, however, to make a beginning by isolating a specific area in the drama and examining it as the conjunction of two distinct contributory traditions. This means (I fully admit) continuing to do less than justice to the complexity of the whole "stream of tendency." But such an approach has the advantage of treating "influence" as "interaction," or perhaps "creative interaction," thus suggesting that the final product is more than parasitic, that it is, in fact, a transformation of its adopted parts.

J. W. Cunliffe found one of the sources of Seneca's influence in the tendency of his heroes to soliloquy and self-examination, drawing an analogy between Senecan self-doubt and "the scruples of Macbeth and the self-analysis of Hamlet"; F. L. Lucas also mentions the influence of Senecan "introspection." Wolfgang Clemen, who, with some caution, finds in Seneca the ultimate source of set speeches revealing states of mind and feeling, draws attention to his special preoccupation with uncertainty and vacillation, while Reuben Brower argues that "however far short Seneca may have come from creating true speech for the inner life, he gave a cue and a direction that was not lost on his Elizabethan translators and imitators."[3]

Curiously enough, the arguments for the influence of Seneca in this particular sphere largely overlook the English morality tradition which, at the time of the Senecan translations in the 1550's and 1560's, had been

2. "Seneca and the Elizabethans: A Case-Study in 'Influence,'" *ShS*, XX (1967), 18.

3. John W. Cunliffe, *The Influence of Seneca on Elizabethan Tragedy* (London, 1893), pp. 16–17; F. L. Lucas, *Seneca and Elizabethan Tragedy* (Cambridge, 1922), p. 104; Clemen, *English Tragedy before Shakespeare*, p. 47; Brower, *Hero and Saint*, p. 168.

dramatizing states of mind and feeling for over a century and a half. The morality plays of the fifteenth and sixteenth centuries consistently analyzed in allegorical terms the doubts, uncertainties and inner struggles of their heroes. The physical battle between vices and virtues disappeared during the fifteenth century, but the *psychomachia* remained in the form of a conflict between good and evil for possession of the hero's soul. Broadly, the stage represented the consciousness of the central figure, and on it personifications of his inner impulses engaged in disputes designed to persuade him toward virtue or sin, salvation or damnation. According to Brower, "It is hard to believe that the Elizabethans would have found a medium appropriate for dramatizing the private life of the soul merely by continuing the narrative tradition of *The Mirror for Magistrates*" (pp. 167–168). In view of their morality heritage, the Elizabethans had no need to look to the narrative tradition for such a medium, but Brower is presumably taking up the arguments of Howard Baker, whose claim that the "Senecan" elements in Elizabethan drama can all be found in the native tradition also largely ignores the morality plays.[4]

Soliloquies expressing hesitation are characteristic both of Seneca and of Elizabethan tragedy. Here, then, is a specific area in which Seneca may have had an influence on the sixteenth century. But *pace* Cunliffe, Senecan hesitation seems to me substantially different from "the scruples of Macbeth and the self-analysis of Hamlet." Seneca's soliloquies characteristically show his protagonists as the helpless victims of wildly fluctuating passion: Renaissance dramatists tend to use deliberative soliloquies as a means of exploring, however passionately, the relationship between conflicting arguments in the processes of ethical choice. In this they are surely the heirs of the morality tradition. But the morality plays attribute the arguments to externalized abstractions, and the moralities before the period of the Senecan translations do not contain fully developed deliberative soliloquies. It is my hypothesis that Seneca provided Elizabethan drama with the concept of the soliloquy which passionately expresses uncertainty, but that the substance of Renaissance deliberation owes much more to the morality analysis of

4. Howard Baker, *Induction to Tragedy* (1939; rpt. New York, 1965).

inner conflict; that the scruples and uncertainties of Elizabethan soliloquies are the result of a confluence of the native and the classical traditions. If so, then in this respect at least, Seneca contributed to the formation of English tragedy, but not in the dominant way suggested by Cunliffe and his successors. Instead of waiting passively for a classical master to transform it, the native tradition would appear to have employed and adapted a Senecan mode which was useful in the process of its own development.

I

Vacillation in the plays ascribed to Seneca is concerned only indirectly with ethics. In accordance with Stoic values, passion is seen as a destructive force which causes nothing but suffering for the hero and his victims. The Senecan figures themselves, however, do not choose in soliloquy between passion and reason, but only between conflicting passions.[5] They are presented as overwhelmed by the force of their own emotions. The audience may condemn their subjection to passion, but the characters themselves are beyond the realm of moral responsibility. Their hesitation is not ethical but a product of the fluctuation of unwilled and violent feeling, and it is expressed not by means of argument and counterargument but in terms of waves of conflicting emotion succeeding and displacing one another.

In the *Troades,* for instance, Ulysses, seeking Astyanax, threatens to raze Hector's tomb where Andromache has hidden her son. Andromache is torn between saving her son's life and sacrificing it to protect her husband's ashes (ll. 642–662).[6] The conflict is between the contending passions of a wife and a mother. The play does not evaluate these passions in moral terms. Andromache's predicament is emotional, not

5. The rejection of reason is characteristically shown not in soliloquy but in dialogue between the protagonist and a *nutrix* or *satelles*. The latter puts forward rational arguments that are overruled by the driving passion of the central figure. Reason is thus the property of another contrasted character, not an inner source of restraint.

6. References to Seneca are to the Loeb edition of *Seneca's Tragedies,* trans. F. J. Miller, 2 vols. (London, 1917).

ethical. Similarly, Clytemnestra[7] (*Agamemnon,* ll. 108–124) makes reference to the ethics of her situation, but only in order to dismiss all
thought of virtue: "clausa iam melior via est" (the better way is already
closed—l. 109). Morality has no serious part in her vacillation: "periere
mores ius decus pietas fides" (good customs, law, honor, duty, faith are
gone—l. 112). As Brower points out in his excellent analysis of this
speech, "She tosses off her losses with ease—periere" (they're gone—
p. 161). These references to virtue serve primarily to emphasize
Clytemnestra's total rejection of all ethical considerations. Self-accusation
alternates violently with self-assertion, but the only real choice is between
weak-minded flight and commitment to unbridled crime. She is no
more capable of controlling her own hysteria than the shifting floods in
a tempest to which she compares it (ll. 138–140). And so "omisi regimen
e manibus meis— / quocumque me ira, quo dolor, quo spes feret, / huc
ire pergam; fluctibus dedimus ratem. / ubi animus errat, optimum est
casum sequi" (ll. 141–144). She has abandoned all thought of control
and is driven wherever anger, grief, or hope carry her, blindly following chance.

   Like Clytemnestra's hesitation, Medea's serves predominantly to stress
the frenzy of her state of mind. Committed to vengeance from the beginning of the play (*Medea,* ll. 25–55), she is subject to a tumult of
feelings (ll. 116 ff.). Can Jason be so cruel? Does he think her powers
of evil are exhausted? These are rhetorical questions. "Incerta vaecors
mente vaesana feror / partes in omnes; unde me ulcisci queam?" (ll.
123–124). She is perplexed, tormented, insane, but her only serious
doubt is how to be avenged. In a long soliloquy (ll. 895 ff.) she steels
herself to kill her sons. She begins, "quid, anime, cessas" (why, soul,
do you hesitate?) but again the question is apparently rhetorical, and
almost at once she continues, "fas omne cedat" (let all right give way—
l. 900). Her rage and her determination mount. The crimes she has
committed already are as nothing: "Medea nunc sum" (now I am Medea
—l. 910). But before she can destroy her children there is a moment of

---

7. Neither Clytemnestra nor Andromache is alone, but they are both addressing
only themselves in the equivalent of pure soliloquy. The fact that the plays were
recited, not acted, would presumably tend to blur the distinction between real
soliloquy and monologue in the presence of another character.

real hesitation (ll. 926 ff.) when she is torn between love for her sons and anger against Jason. But the furies, sent by the brother she has killed, impel her onward and she is resolved on destruction. The whole passage is a portrait of madness showing Medea helpless before a driving passion. Only another passion, love for her children, can restrain her, and the restraint is momentary. There is no reasoned dispute between the passions, no attempt to order her own experience. One passion simply gives way to another, and she submits to the rage which is dominant over all other impulses.

This Senecan combat of the passions differs fundamentally from the deliberative soliloquies of Elizabethan tragedy, where choice is repeatedly presented as ethical choice, an attempt to resolve the conflicting claims of vice and virtue. However passionately they confront their dilemmas, these Renaissance figures are neither mad nor helpless.[8] Renaissance deliberation reflects the workings of a mind attempting, however inadequately, to order its own experience in terms of arguments. The choice of evil often represents a submission to passion, but it is a willed submission made in defiance of reason or on the basis of self-deception which is the result of false reasoning. Elizabethan tragedy inherited from the morality plays the concept of ethical deliberation as a process of reasoned choice between conflicting arguments.

Arden of Faversham offers a brief but striking example of the characteristic Elizabethan pattern of deliberation. Arden's servant, Michael, has promised to leave the door unlocked for Arden's murderers. In return, he is to marry Susan, Alice's servant and Mosbie's sister. When the moment comes, however, Michael is assailed by doubts: "Ah harmles Arden how, how hast thou misdone, / That thus thy gentle lyfe is leveld at?" (ll. 991–992).[9] Arden's many kindnesses to him must be repaid by betrayal. But he has given oaths to Mosbie, to Alice, and to the hired murderers, Black Will and Shakebag, and he fears the effects of their "lawles rage" (l. 1002). In consequence,

8. Elizabethan drama does contain figures that in some ways resemble Seneca's— Lady Macbeth, for instance, or Vindice. But these characters do not deliberate. If they pause, it is only to invent new stratagems or to draw attention to their achievements.

9. *Arden of Faversham,* ed. H. Macdonald and D. N. Smith, Malone Society Reprints (Oxford, 1967).

> Tush I will spurne at mercy for this once.
> Let pittie lodge where feeble women lye,
> I am resolved, and Arden needs must die.
>
> (ll. 1003–1005)

The abstractions (mercy, pity) may recall the morality tradition. In the following scene Michael's resolution falters again, and the imagery of the *psychomachia* evokes more strongly the dilemma of the morality heroes:

> Conflicting thoughts incamped in my brest
> Awake me with the Echo of their strokes:
> And I a iudge to censure either side,
> Can give to neither wished victory.
>
> (ll. 1070–1073)

Again he recalls his master's kindness, his own oaths, his love for Susan. With horror he visualizes Arden's murder, and then his own:

> Me thinks I heare them aske where Michaell is
> And pittiles black Will, cryes stab the slave.
> The Pesant will detect the Tragedy.
>
> (ll. 1090–1092)

Resolution is overthrown and he calls to Franklin for help against the murderers. The language conveys the emotional tension of Michael's predicament but the soliloquies follow the morality pattern of dispute between good and evil impulses. Finally pity and prudence prevail over his commitment to evil.

Michael's hesitation forms a single episode in *Arden of Faversham.* In *Doctor Faustus* the waverings of the hero dominate the action. In the mind of Faustus, grace struggles against pride, heaven against hell until the great final soliloquy in which the desire to repent contends violently with despair. In *Hamlet,* too, a series of soliloquies analyze the conflict between "resolution" and "thought" which is at the center of the play.

But deliberative soliloquies do not always explore both sides of the case in this way. Wendoll's long monologue in *A Woman Killed with Kindness* (vi.1–52)[10] represents an attempt to overcome his passion for

10. Thomas Heywood, *A Woman Killed with Kindness,* ed. R. W. van Fossen (London, 1961).

Anne Frankford. The arguments he puts forward concern Frankford's kindness, his own ingratitude, his damnation. The soliloquy embodies the warnings of conscience, the efforts of virtuous reason to prevail over the impulse to evil. Finally, Wendoll cannot resist his passion, but the soliloquy indicates that he gives way to vice in defiance of reason, not in its absence.[11] Similarly, Macbeth's great soliloquy in Act I, scene vii, consists almost entirely of arguments against Duncan's murder. The jerky and elusive syntax, the kaleidoscopic imagery reflecting the turbulence of his state of mind, cannot disguise the fact that Macbeth is assembling ethical arguments against the ambition which spurs him on: "We still have judgment here . . ."; "He's here in double trust . . ."; Duncan's virtues; "The deep damnation of his taking-off"; "pity . . ." In each case it is as if the Good Angel of the morality tradition held the hero's attention for a moment before his final plunge into evil.

Deliberative soliloquies may equally recall the arguments of the vices. Conventionally the vices worked through a process of deception. Disguise, false names, and false arguments combined to persuade the hero to choose the values of this world by blinding him to those of the next. In *The Castle of Perseverance* Covetousness lures Humanum Genus from the stronghold of virtue with the plausible argument that his purse will be his best friend in old age (ll. 2492–2530).[12] In the Elizabethan *Enough Is as Good as a Feast* the vices in disguise persuade the protagonist that he ought to make money in order to be charitable (ll. 822–828).[13] Rationalization resembles right reason, and the hero chooses evil as a result of self-delusion. This is the pattern of Leantio's soliloquy in *Women Beware Women* (III. ii. 322–350).[14] His transition from the contented innocence of married poverty to avarice and adultery is accomplished by Bianca's infidelity and Livia's blandishments, but

11. It is perhaps worth noting in relation to the morality tradition that, although Heywood analyzes Wendoll's temptation and Anne's repentance, in both cases the processes are represented in the most general terms, so that it is as if Wendoll-Anne replaces Mankind and inherits his characteristic inner conflicts.

12. *The Macro Plays,* ed. Mark Eccles, EETS, no. 262 (London, 1969).

13. W. Wager, *The Longer Thou Livest* and *Enough Is as Good as a Feast,* ed. R. Mark Benbow (London, 1967).

14. Thomas Middleton, *Women Beware Women,* ed. Roma Gill (London, 1968).

not before Leantio, alone on the stage, has argued himself into hatred and corruption. He begins:

> Is she my wife till death, yet no more mine?
> That's a hard measure. Then what's marriage good for?

Bianca is "gone for ever—utterly" (l. 330). Why, then,

> should my love last longer than her truth?
> What is there good in woman to be loved
> When only that which makes her so has left her?
>
> (ll. 333–335)

To remain committed to his own sin and her shame "were monstrous."

> Then my safest course,
> For health of mind and body, is to turn
> My heart and hate her, most extremely hate her!
> I have no other way.
>
> (ll. 339–342)

The reasoning is plausible, to some extent sympathetic, but false. It follows the promptings of natural impulse, not virtue. Marriage, as Leantio himself recognizes, is a commitment "till death." In insisting that he has "no other way" than hatred, he is blinding himself to the way of patience and forgiveness. Reason, which should dominate the will, has become subject to it, and thus distorted. The play demonstrates that Leantio's choice achieves neither "safety" nor "health" of mind or body.

Women Beware Women shows the influence of a corrupt society on a series of individuals.[15] Leantio is not strong enough to resist the evil which dominates the world he lives in. Chapman's *Byron* plays are differently constructed; the hero is a more autonomous figure whose tragedy is more the result of his own free choice of evil. Byron is proud and ambitious, but loyal, until Savoy and La Fin tempt him with flattery and the promise of power to believe that obedience to the king is thankless and degrading. Here, too, it is in soliloquy that Byron

---

15. In this it recalls the "estates" moralities. Livia brings about the corruption of a series of innocents of different social classes, primarily through deception, the characteristic method of the vices. For a detailed analysis of the survival of the "estates" play structure in *The Alchemist,* see Alan C. Dessen, "*The Alchemist:* Jonson's 'Estates' Play," *RenD,* VII (1964), 35–54.

commits himself to evil (*Byron's Conspiracy*, II.i.145–173),[16] and here
again the process is one of false reasoning. The prospect of a struggle
against the king challenges his courage:

> How fit a sort were this to handsel Fortune!
> And I will win it though I lose myself.
>
> (ll. 145–146)

Ironically, Byron wins nothing, and does indeed lose himself, to regain
his true nature only in the face of execution.

> If to be highest still, be to be best,
> All works to that end are the worthiest.
>
> (ll. 154–155)

The argument is persuasive but false: "highest" in power is patently
not highest in virtue, and therefore "best" here is not synonymous with
"worthiest."

> Truth is a golden ball, cast in our way,
> To make us stript by falsehood.
>
> (ll. 156–157)

Byron's treachery fails to outstrip justice, and his rejection of truth
achieves only his own moral degradation and physical death.

In a similar way Brutus, "with himself at war" (*Julius Caesar*, I.ii.46),
rationalizes his assassination of Caesar ("Fashion it thus . . . ," II.i.30),
and Othello his murder of Desdemona ("It is the cause, it is the cause,
my soul," V.ii.1). The arrogance of Faustus entraps him in a false
syllogism (I.i.39–46),[17] and in rejecting divinity he also rejects salvation.
These tragic figures choose evil on the basis of apparently rational principle, in accordance with spurious arguments which seem to be the
product of right reason.

Senecan vacillation displays the overwhelming power of passion;
Elizabethan deliberation, when it issues in the choice of evil, characteristically displays the power of the corrupted will to defy or distort the
reason. The distinction, of course, reflects the difference between

---

16. *The Plays and Poems of George Chapman*, ed. T. M. Parrott, 2 vols. (London,
1910).

17. Christopher Marlowe, *The Tragical History of the Life and Death of Doctor
Faustus: A Conjectural Reconstruction*, ed. W. W. Greg (Oxford, 1950).

Stoicism and the main current of Christian orthodoxy, which stresses the freedom of the will and man's consequent responsibility for sin. The morality plays, with rare exceptions,[18] consistently show their heroes as responsible for their choices, using allegory to analyze in detail the ethical conflicts which occur in the processes of temptation and repentance. Elizabethan tragedy discards the allegory but absorbs into the deliberative soliloquy the processes it represents.

II

So far it would seem that there is little need to adduce the influence of Seneca to explain the emergence of this particular form. But there remains the problem of the transition from allegory to the literal drama, and I suggest that here Seneca's influence worked in conjunction with the morality heritage to transform the dispute between vices and virtues into the deliberation of a single mind. Brower urges that "the example of an ancient playwright must have been enormously useful to dramatists writing in a vigorous native tradition . . ." (p. 168), but he is not concerned with tracing the process of interaction between the external example and the native tradition. It seems, however, that it is necessary to examine this process in order to judge with any accuracy just how useful the ancient example may have been. Cunliffe's "classical" tragedies at the Inns of Court do not provide an obvious bridge to the later drama, but the period of the Senecan translations (1559–66) also witnessed a development in the popular drama. *Cambises, King of Persia* (ca. 1558–69), *Patient Grissell* (1558–61, pr. 1566?), *Apius and Virginia* (1559–67, pr. 1575) and *Horestes* (pr. 1567) are the real antecedents of Elizabethan tragedy,[19] and these plays have certain patterns in common

18. See, for instance, Lewis Wager's Calvinist *Mary Magdalene*. Moros, the hero of W. Wager's *The Longer Thou Livest* is too foolish to be capable of rational choice.

19. In terms of their energetic action and vigorous dialogue, for instance. They include the low comedy (often parodying the central action) characteristic of the Elizabethan stage. For the continuity of the popular drama see especially Bernard Spivack, *Shakespeare and the Allegory of Evil* (New York, 1958); and David M. Bevington, *From "Mankind" to Marlowe* (Cambridge, Mass., 1962).

which may suggest an interaction between Senecan influence and the native morality tradition.

Their roots are clearly in the morality tradition. Like the moralities, they contain personifications of abstractions, including in each case a vice, who fulfils the traditional role of tempter and simultaneously provides a source of low comedy. At the same time it has been widely assumed that these early "tragedies" show some traces of Senecan influence.[20] It is difficult to estimate with any certainty the precise extent of their debt to Seneca: some of their characteristics which are new in the popular drama could be derived either from Seneca or from native nondramatic works. The truth is probably that in general the plays absorbed those features of Senecan tragedy that other sources had already made congenial to English taste. The "tragedies" are filled with violent action and passionate rhetoric. Emotional set speeches introduce a strong element of pathos. Three of the plays have "classical" settings, though their immediate sources are, of course, more recent.[21] Fourteeners, the staple meter of most of the Senecan translations, are used in these plays for the first time on the popular stage. Unlike the moralities, each of the "tragedies" dramatizes a specific narrative. The moralities, of course, tell a story, but it is the story of mankind's inner life. Even when they deal with a particular type of hero, like *Magnificence,* or with a specific period of his life, like *Lusty Juventus,* their narrative is conceived in the most general terms, with little or no reference to time and place. The early popular "tragedies," however, set out to tell a specific story, and often one which is well known, like that of Orestes or Griselda, just as Senecan tragedy dramatizes familiar narratives. The central figure in each play is a particular individual, and there is a specific situation located in the phenomenal world of time and place.

Further, all these plays deal to some extent with the intense emotions involved in intimate personal and family relationships. This is not

20. H. B. Charlton, *The Senecan Tradition in Renaissance Tragedy* (Manchester, 1946), p. clxviii; Spivack, *Shakespeare and the Allegory of Evil,* p. 115; Clemen, *English Tragedy before Shakespeare,* pp. 193–194.

21. The story of Cambises is from Richard Taverner, *The Second Booke of the Garden of Wysedome* (London, 1539); *Apius and Virginia* is derived from Chaucer's *Physician's Tale;* and *Horestes* from Caxton, *Recuyell of the Histories of Troye* (1469).

characteristic of the moralities, where social relationships tend to be of the most generalized kind, showing how landlords oppress tenants, or masters servants (*The Longer Thou Livest, The More Fool Thou Art; Enough Is as Good as a Feast; The Tide Tarrieth No Man*). When the native tradition dramatizes marriage, it does so in order to provide a model of domestic happiness (*Virtuous and Godly Susanna*), or to show the folly of marrying young (*The Disobedient Child, The Tide Tarrieth No Man*). On the other hand, passionate and tragic relationships between husbands and wives, parents and children, are the stuff of Senecan drama.

Above all, as far as I know, the four early "tragedies" are the first secular plays to include the analysis of inner conflict. Deliberation is a feature of *Cambises* and *Patient Grissell,* and is central in the action of *Apius and Virginia* and *Horestes.* In each case the vices participate in the processes of deliberation, but they no longer dominate the heroes as the morality vices do. The role of the vice is diminished and the heroes achieve a corresponding measure of autonomy. Further, their deliberations are conducted with varying degrees of emotional intensity, and while they are never blind slaves of passion in the Senecan manner, the rhetoric of the deliberative processes of Gautier, Apius, and Horestes is not derived from the morality tradition. These heroes anticipate Othello, Macbeth, and Hamlet, who also express their ethical dilemmas in the (infinitely more powerful) language of passion. Passionate rhetoric alone, of course, is not evidence of Senecan influence, but the emergence of passionate deliberative soliloquies in the very period of the Senecan translations does seem to me to suggest that the native drama took something from Seneca in the course of its development. If so, the early popular "tragedies" provide a bridge between the moralities and Elizabethan drama in that they absorb the form, though not the substance, of Senecan vacillation.

Deliberative soliloquies do not, I think, occur before this period in the fully allegorical morality plays, where it is the abstractions who articulate the nature of the hero's choice. *The Castle of Perseverance* offers an instance of the traditional division of roles. At the beginning of the play the Good and Bad Angels compete for the soul of Humanum Genus. After they have put forward the respective claims of the World and God, Humanum Genus describes his dilemma:

Whom to folwe wetyn I ne may.
I stonde and stodye and gynne to raue.
I wolde be ryche in gret aray
And fayn I wolde my sowle saue.
As wynde in watyr I wave.
þou woldyst to þe Werld I me toke,
And he wolde þat I it forsoke.
Now so God me helpe and þe holy boke,
I not wyche I may haue.

(ll. 375–383)

The protagonist describes the experience of wavering, but the arguments are confined to the abstractions. Similarly, the hero of *Mankind* laments that he is composed "Of a body and of a soull, of condycyon contrarye" (l. 195), and that the soul which should dominate the body is in a state of subjection. Mankind is not attempting to make an ethical choice but simply recording his divided condition. His speech describes a state of conflict but it does not record the struggle itself. In Medwall's *Nature* the hero also gives a long account of his dual composition (sig. A3).[22] Like *The Castle of Perseverance*, *Nature* is a leisurely play which consistently comments on its own action, and after a long debate between Reason and Sensuality, Man exclaims,

O blessyd lord / what maner stryf is thys
Atwyxt my reason / and sensualyte
That one meneth well / and that all other amysse.

(sig. Br˅–2)

He goes on to complain that he is "wonderously / entryked in this case / And almost brought / into perplexyte" (sig. B2). Here, too, the argument itself is conducted by the personifications. The hero merely draws attention to his own confusion. Later and briefer moralities tend to take for granted the wavering and perplexity of their heroes. Debate is confined to the abstractions; the protagonist resists or capitulates without giving an account of his feelings.

I suggest, then, that it is possible here to identify a specifically Senecan influence on the early popular "tragedies." Senecan vacillation showed that it was possible to express hesitation in soliloquy without the intro-

22. Henry Medwall, *Nature*, ed. John S. Farmer, Tudor Facsimile Texts (Oxford, 1908).

duction of personifications. The early "tragedies" absorb this lesson to a certain extent, allowing their characters a measure of formal autonomy, and in some cases the language of passionate feeling, while retaining the traditional vices to reinforce the arguments for evil. The substance of this hesitation, however, is in no real sense Senecan, since it preserves the morality tradition of ethical choice between conflicting arguments.

Though he may have something in common with the Nero of *Octavia,* Thomas Preston's Cambises owes more to the medieval Herod than to any of Seneca's heroes, and the episode in which the king shoots the young son of his virtuous counsellor, Praxaspes, may recall the Massacre of the Innocents. But the king himself, who has no inner doubts, needs no vice to encourage him in cruelty, and the real victim of Ambidexter, who seems to stand for double-dealing, is Sisamnes, appointed governor in the king's absence. Sisamnes begins by exulting in his new power:

> Now may I abrogate the law as I shall thinke it good;
> If any-one me now offend, I may demaund his blood.
>
> > (ll. 117–118)[23]

But then he hesitates:

> But oftentimes the birds be gone while one for nest doth grope.
> Doo well or il, I dare avouch some evil on me wil speake.
> No, truly—yet I do not meane the kings precepts to breake;
> To place I meane for to returne my duty to fulfil.
>
> > (ll. 122–125)

Despite this resolution, he begins to accept bribes, but later hesitates again:

> Now and then some vantage I atchive; much more yet may I take,
> But that I fear unto the king that some complaint will make.
>
> > (ll. 309–310)

On this occasion Ambidexter appears and hastens to reassure him and urge him on to greater excesses:

> Ye are unwise if ye take not time while ye may;
> If ye wil not now, when ye would ye shall have nay.
> What is he that of you dare make exclamation,

23. *Chief Pre-Shakespearean Dramas,* ed. J. Q. Adams (New York, 1924).

Of your wrong-dealing to make explication?
Can you not play with both hands?

(ll. 317–321)

I have quoted at such length in order to show that it is Sisamnes himself who takes the initiative in expressing his state of hesitation, while the vice merely takes advantage of the opportunity that is offered him. Ambidexter is a subordinate figure in the temptation. The debate between good and evil is conducted at least partly by Sisamnes himself ("Now may I abrogate the law . . . But oftentimes . . . No, truly . . ."), and though some of the forms of dialogue remain to suggest the morality ancestry of the technique, Sisamnes is arguing with himself in soliloquy.

It is clear that Sisamnes owes little to Seneca unless it is simply the concept that hesitation can be internalized. The inner debate is anything but passionate, and while it is true that the ethics of Sisamnes are crudely prudential, nonetheless, like the morality heroes, he is concerned with the arguments for and against an evil course of action. The hesitation of Gautier in John Phillip's *Patient Grissell,* however, is emotional as well as ethical. Here the vice, Politic Persuasion, seems to be introduced in an attempt to provide a psychological explanation of Gautier's inhumanity. Gautier, an otherwise exemplary ruler, is persuaded that it would be "politic" to test Grissell's fidelity, meekness and devotion. Though the introduction of the vice is not a particularly satisfactory solution to the psychological problems that the story has always presented, it is evidence of the dramatist's interest in the state of mind of a man who behaves with great cruelty. Here, at the very point at which the play is closest to the morality tradition, it is also closest to the kind of tragedy that explores the inner experience of a tyrant. In this respect, perhaps, Seneca and the morality tradition meet in *Patient Grissell,* which in turn points forward to Elizabethan tragedy.

When Gautier, in obedience to Politic Persuasion, is on the point of sending Grissell home to her father, he unexpectedly hesitates:

Oh hart now reaue and rend, now breake thou cleane in sonder
The heauens aboue and lumiuing stars, at this attempt may wonder [*sic*]
All liuinge wights that heare thys fact will me reward with shame
No condinge praise, but ill report, shall thunder forth my Fame,
Shall I forgoe my wedded wife, whose wiflye troth is such,

That aye to do hir husband good, hir life thinketh not much,
What though from simple stocke, hir nature be deryude,
Hir vertues yeld such equall dome, that honors she atchiude,
And shall I then reieckt, as abieckt from my syght,
My Lady deare, whose vertues all, my sences much delight,
No no not so, plucke backe thy feete, such acts exile thy thought,
Let no such sinne against thy loue in any wyse be wrought.

(ll. 1568–1579)[24]

Like Sisamnes, Gautier has begun on a course of action but suddenly experiences doubt, and he, too, takes the initiative in expressing it.

The themes of Gautier's deliberations belong to the Renaissance— fame, the duties of a wife, the nature of true nobility, the obligations of a husband—and the debate is the familiar conflict between virtue and vice. But the emotion, however clumsily expressed, is not characteristic of the morality tradition. The "sinne" which Gautier hesitates to commit is one against his "loue," and the rejection of Grissell threatens to break his heart. Gautier's situation is not precisely Senecan since his cruelty is a result of false reasoning, not of passion, but his conflict of feeling is new to the native tradition. Seneca's Clytemnestra hesitates on a similar account: "Amor iugalis vincit ac flectit retro" (love for my husband conquers and turns me back—l. 239). But Aegisthus persuades her that retreat would be imprudent. Politic Persuasion, too, rallies at once: "What bodie a me, my Lord plucke up your hart . . ." (l. 1580) and convinces Gautier that he must be stern. He determines that he will go on with his plan after all, "Followinge the mosyons of Polliticke Perswasion" (l. 1588).

R. B.'s *Apius and Virginia* has received more critical attention than *Patient Grissell,* and Spivack has noted that Apius soliloquizes in the manner of Angelo, Macbeth, or Richard III.[25] Here more than 200 lines of a total of 1032 are devoted to the exploration of his tortured state of mind. At his first appearance he debates the folly of his irresistible love for Virginia and the inevitable dishonor of giving way to it (ll. 411–449).[26] The vice of the play, Haphazard, personifies a spirit of recklessness.

24. John Phillip, *The Play of Patient Grissell,* ed. R. B. McKerrow, Malone Society Reprints (Oxford, 1909).
25. *Shakespeare and the Allegory of Evil,* p. 271.
26. R. B., *Apius and Virginia,* ed. Ronald B. McKerrow, Malone Society Reprints (London, 1911).

He stands for the conviction that, since consequences are unpredictable and strange things happen by chance, man might as well hazard everything in pursuit of his desires. The moment Apius has given expression to his state of doubt, the vice urges him on with a scheme for making Virginia a ward of court. Almost at once, however, Apius falters again, and here the play provides a remarkable instance of the conjunction between the allegorical tradition and the emergent form of the deliberative soliloquy. It is worth quoting in full:

Here let him make as rhogh he went out and let Consince and Iustice come out of him, and let Consience hold in his hande a Lamp burning and let Iustice haue a sworde and hold it before Apius brest

> But out I am wounded, how am I deuided?
> Two states of my life, from me are now glided,
> For Consience he pricketh me contempned,
> And Iustice saith, Iudgement wold haue me condemned:
> Consience saith crueltye sure will detest me:
> And Iustice saith, death in thende will molest me,
> And both in one sodden me thinkes they do crie,
> That fier eternall, my soule shall destroy.
>
> (ll. 499–508)

Apius is "deuided." Conscience and Justice are visibly personified, but at this point they are silent. In order to express his state of conflict, Apius attributes dialogue to them ("Consience saith . . . Iustice saith"). What they have to tell him finally is the traditional message of the morality plays, sustained in the imagery of so much Elizabethan drama: that the price of his sinful course is damnation. But the personifications have dwindled to little more than shadows, and their arguments are expressed by Apius himself. At once the vice exclaims contemptuously, "Why these are but thoughts man? Why fie for shame fie" (l. 510). Thus restored, Apius renews his determination, while Conscience and Justice remain behind and complain that they are overruled by will and lust (ll. 538–539, 549–550).

The situation of Apius is in no real sense Senecan. He is guilty of the sin of lechery and he knowingly incurs damnation. The analysis of his inner conflict bears a clear formal resemblance to the inner warfare of the morality tradition. At the same time, however, his soliloquies stress the passionate nature of his sinful impulse. It is true that R. B.'s rhetoric asserts rather than conveys the nature of the hero's emotions ("Oh perelesse dame, Oh passing peece, Oh face of such a feature . . ."— l. 417), and it is clear to Apius as well as to the audience that he ought to resist his passion. Nonetheless, it is possible to see a parallel here between Apius and the heroes of Senecan tragedy, helpless before a passion which they cannot control.

Pickering's *Horestes* concerns the question of whether or not it is right for the hero to avenge Agamemnon by killing his mother. The conflict is by no means confined to the mind of Horestes, and at various stages Idumeus (Idomeneus) and his Counsel, as well as Menelaus and Nestor, participate in the debate. Nature and Revenge personify the hero's conflicting impulses, but here, too, the problem is raised initially by Horestes himself, whose first speech is a deliberative soliloquy that shows him perhaps more fully aware of the complexity of his situation, and more in command of the arguments, than Sisamnes, Gautier or Apius. Again, despite its length, the speech is worth quoting in full, since it has received relatively little critical attention and because it displays the combination of ethical argument and emotional intensity that characterizes so many later soliloquies. Cumbrous fourteeners and awkward inversions combine with the rhetoric rather than with the language of feeling, but the speech has moments of naturalness, and its structure does seem to reflect the workings of a divided mind. This is no longer the stilted antithesis of morality debate but fully-fledged soliloquy. In the morality manner it records an attempt to order a confused ethical situation, but the dilemma of Horestes has its roots in conflicting emotions prompted by family relationships. His mother's murder and adultery, as well as her threat to his own life, side with filial piety toward his father against the natural impulse of pity for his mother:

> To caull to minde the crabyd rage of mothers yll attempt
> Prouokes me now all pyttie quight, from me to be exempt:
> Yet lo dame nature teles me that, I must with willing mind
> Forgiue the faute and to pytie, some what to be inclynd.
> But lo be hould thad ulltres dame, on hourdome morder vill
> Hath heaped up not contented, her sponsaule bed to fyll:
> With forrayne loue but sought also, my fatal thred to share
> As erst before my fathers fyll, in sonder she dyd pare.
> O paterne loue why douste thou so, of pytey me request,

Syth thou to me wast quight denyed, my mother being prest:
When tender yeres this corps of mine, did hould alas for wo
When frend my mother shuld haue bin then was she chefe my fo
Oh godes therfore sith you be iust, unto whose poure & wyll,
All thing in heauen, and earth also; obaye and sarue untyll.
Declare to me your gracious mind, shall I reuenged be,
Of good Kynge *Agamemnones* death, ye godes declare to me
Or shall I let the, adulltres dame, styll wallow in her sin . . .
                                                        (ll. 200–216)[27]

As usual, the vice, Revenge, comes in at once. He says that he is
called Courage, and, claiming to be a messenger of the gods, he urges
Horestes to go to war against Clytemnestra. Horestes is quick to respond
to his persuasions: "My thinkes I fele corrage prouokes, my wil for ward
againe" (l. 249). As in the other early "tragedies," soliloquy and personified abstraction work together in the analysis of inner conflict.

But Pickering's departures from the morality tradition are striking.
In the morality plays the hero's ethical position is clear. *Horestes,* however, does not resolve the moral ambiguities of revenge, since Revenge
is both a vice and a source of justice. When he has accomplished
Clytemnestra's death, Horestes reappears as king, accompanied by his
Nobles, Commons, Truth, and Duty, clearly a worthy ruler of a purged
and reunited realm. The disputing abstractions no longer represent
simple good and evil: Nature and Revenge also represent opposed
emotional impulses. This is the first English play to take the conflicting
feelings of the revenger as its central concern, and while I accept
Howard Baker's argument that revenge is not a wholly new theme in
English literature,[28] his point seems to me to have a bearing on my own
more general one: if Senecan tragedy had an influence in England, this
was precisely because the Senecan stream flowed into a native river
which was already predisposed to absorb it. The confluence transformed
both constituents: Pickering's treatment of the revenge theme differs
as greatly from Seneca's as Elizabethan deliberation differs from Senecan
vacillation.

I suggest that this process of transformation is the origin of the diffi-

27. John Pickering, *Horestes,* ed. D. Seltzer and Arthur Brown, Malone Society
Reprints (Oxford, 1962).
28. *Induction to Tragedy,* pp. 148–149.

culty inherent in the concept of influence. If external influences tend to take effect not simply because they become available but because they in some way echo concerns that already exist independently (revenge, hesitation), they are themselves transformed in the process of transforming the native treatment of those concerns. It is for this reason that arguments that attempt to isolate the influence of Seneca have proved inconclusive.

III

It seems possible that the bridge between inner conflict in the moralities and deliberation in the predominantly literal early "tragedies" is provided not by Seneca himself but by the translations of Seneca. The rhetoric of Apius and Horestes is closer to the language of the translators, who frequently amplify the extravagances of the original, than it is to Seneca's own.[29] Further, the English versions succeed to some extent in moralizing Senecan vacillation. Their fidelity to the text prevents them from changing the soliloquies into ethical debates, but they do contrive, by a series of minor modifications, to intensify the moral responsibility of Seneca's protagonists for their crimes. Thus in Studley's version Medea's momentary maternal impulse becomes a virtue. "Materque . . . redit" (l. 928) appears as "pitious mothers mercy milde restoreth natures face" (p. 138).[30] The emotion to which Seneca attaches no moral evaluation is transformed to the point where it evokes the medieval concept of the Virgin Mary. Seneca's Medea asks what crime her dying children will expiate, and answers: "Scelus est Iason genitor et maius scelus / Medea mater" (ll. 933–934). Their only crime is that they are the children of their parents. In Studley's version, "Upon their Father Iason right all blot of blame should lye. / Medea yet their Mother I am worser farre then hee" (p. 138). The translation replaces

---

29. The Prologue to *Cambises* includes a reference to Seneca (ll. 11–14), which Cunliffe traces to *Thyestes*, ll. 213–217 (*Influence of Seneca*, p. 56), but this is a very free rendering of the original, and it is no closer to Jasper Heywood's version than it is to Seneca's.

30. *Seneca His Tenne Tragedies* (1581), in *The English Experience: Its Record in Early Printed Books, Published in Facsimile* (Amsterdam and New York, 1969).

the dismissive irony of the original with Medea's ponderous recognition of her own moral culpability, which is greater even than Jason's. In Seneca's version, "ira pietatem fugat / iramque pietas" ll. 943–944 (rage drives out maternal love, love rage). Studley translates *pietas* as "vertue," an understandable rendering, but one which thoroughly moralizes the conflicting passions of the original. But perhaps the most telling alterations occur in Studley's version of Clytemnestra, who turns momentarily from a woman lashed on by her own frenzy to a calculating Eve. The "femineos dolos" (l. 116) she will employ become "The wylie traynes, and craftie guyles of wicked womankind" (p. 143ᵛ), and the extremes of any faithless wife beside herself with blind passion ("impos sui / amore caeco," ll. 117–118) are transformed into "What any diuelish trayterous dame durst do in working woe" (p. 143ᵛ). Fevered irresponsibility becomes craft, and blindness becomes the cunning treachery of the devil. Seneca invites us to condemn his heroine's hysteria: Studley's heroine judges and condemns herself. Seneca's Clytemnestra is beyond the reach of ethical considerations: Studley's at this moment is as morally culpable as the archetypal sinner of Christian theology.

The translations are thus in some instances marginally nearer than the original to the ethical argument of the English tradition, and their portraits of vacillation might well seem to offer the authors of the early popular "tragedies" a mold into which they might pour the analysis of their own rather different kinds of inner conflict. Once this had occurred, deliberative soliloquies could become part of the mainstream of the native tradition, and there was no need for subsequent dramatists to look directly to Seneca for the mode. This would perhaps explain why the later soliloquies I have discussed are so markedly different from Seneca's. One final example may substantiate the point.

Marlowe's *Doctor Faustus* is in essence a single protracted deliberative soliloquy, ironically punctuated by a series of comic episodes. At the beginning of the play Faustus, alone in his study, chooses a way of life and with it his own damnation; in the final scene he confronts death, racked with alternating remorse and despair; in between we see his recurrent impulse to repent repeatedly quelled by fear or by devilish distractions. There is no need to argue for the continuity between *Doctor Faustus* and the morality tradition, and indeed, as far as I know, it has not been suggested that the play is directly indebted to Seneca. But the hero owes his tragic stature not only to Marlowe's magnificent language but also to the existence of the soliloquy as a means of expressing doubt.

The morality plays, even those that end unhappily, lack the grandeur of tragedy. This is at least partly a product of the allegorical form. The inner conflicts of Humanum Genus are argued out on his behalf by his Good and Bad Angels. The dazzling figure of the World towers above him on his scaffold, with power, riches, and delights at his command. Humanum Genus is a ready victim of the arguments put forward by dominating external figures. Of course, if the allegory is "translated," the entire action takes place within the mind of the central figure. But the form determines the experience of the audience, and the form diminishes the hero. In later moralities, as the vice figures become more central, the pattern is similar. We are drawn to the vices as to a Barabas or a Volpone because they are so much cleverer than their victims, the nominal heroes of the plays. The central figures in the morality tradition cannot be heroic. When their separate characteristics are isolated in personifications, any qualities that lend them stature, whether for good or evil, are separately personified, and the heroes are formally passive.

But in *Doctor Faustus* the relationship between the abstractions and the central figure is reversed.[31] The Good and Bad Angels do not debate with Faustus or with each other. They appear in response to the hero's hesitation and do not attempt to initiate it. The Seven Deadly Sins conduct no *psychomachia* and are confined to one ironic pageant. The pliant Mephostophilis appears in obedience to the hero, who needs no tempter. Instead of adopting a disguise to deceive Faustus, this melancholy vice does so on the hero's instructions. The shadowy personifications and the obedient vice are diminished in proportion to the dominance of a hero who, because his conflict is largely internalized, has achieved the dramatic and formal autonomy of tragedy.

It is in this context that it seems to me most arguable that Seneca's influence contributed to the formation of Elizabethan tragedy. Brower has drawn attention to the "immense sense of self," the grand scale of Seneca's protagonists.[32] They have that passionate autonomy which the morality heroes lack and which determines our response to the tragic

31. Douglas Cole, *Suffering and Evil in the Plays of Christopher Marlowe* (Princeton, N.J., 1962), pp. 235–242.

32. *Hero and Saint,* p. 169.

heroes of Elizabethan drama. The emergence of the soliloquy was a necessary condition of this autonomy if the analysis of inner conflict developed in the morality tradition was to be incorporated into Elizabethan tragedy.

The grandeur of Seneca's heroic figures is directly proportional to the scale on which they experience passion: the Renaissance heroes I have discussed, figures like Faustus, Macbeth, and Byron, owe much of their greatness to the scale on which they confront temptation. They sin, and sin greatly, but their stature is derived not only from their deeds but also from their inner experience. I suggest that while the morality tradition was the main source of the substance of this experience, Seneca provided the concept of the soliloquies in which it is expressed, that the classical and the native streams of influence converged in the development of this specific feature of Elizabethan tragedy.

The Influence of the Mystery Plays upon the Popular Tragedies of the 1560's

ROSEMARY WOOLF

THREE TRAGEDIES of the 1560's, *Apius and Virginia, Cambises,* and *Horestes* are usually called popular by modern scholars in order to distinguish them from the three Inns of Court tragedies, *Gorboduc, Gismond of Salerne,* and *Jocasta,* which were written during the same decade. The term *popular,* however, does not necessarily indicate that the authors (unknown or only conjecturally identified) were unlearned or that the place of performance was exclusively envisaged as the inn-yard: *Horestes,* for instance, was almost certainly performed at court. The popularity lies rather in the fact that the dramatists deliberately mingled themes and conventions from the Senecan tradition with those of native dramatic origin, the result being plays more vigorous but also more crude than the formal imitations of Seneca. The most important of the native traditions here imitated and adapted are generally agreed to be the use of personifications, including the figure of the vice, intended to display the moral state of hero or villain, and the use of a comic subplot, a structural element without precedent in classical tragedy (though occasionally used in Roman comedy), which most probably developed from the sixteenth-century moralities in which scenes of super-

fluous horseplay and verbal jesting among the vices were interspersed
with the main and serious matters of the heroes' moral trials.[1] To these
important borrowings from the living tradition of allegorical drama
should be added the almost equally substantial borrowings from the
mystery plays, which were still frequently performed, though they had
ceased to represent a living tradition of drama. The authors of the three
popular tragedies seem to have been influenced by the cycles in the
choice and treatment of some of their tragic themes and may also have
borrowed matter from the cycles in order to fill out their subplots.

The influence of the mystery plays is most interestingly seen in *Apius
and Virginia*. This story, told in Livy to illustrate the wicked and
tyrannous conduct of the second Decemvirate, had undergone successive
adaptations in the Middle Ages, through which it became transformed
into a striking parallel to the Sacrifice of Isaac.[2] The first modification
of it was made by Jean de Meung who, stripping it of political, legal,
and narrative complications, turned it into a neat exemplum about an
unjust judge. But the changes that Jean de Meung made to this end,
such as the omission of the young man to whom Virginia was betrothed
and the alteration in the method of killing from stabbing to beheading,
prepared the way for Chaucer to retell the story with an entirely different patterning:[3] for in the *Physician's Tale* the interest lies in the
relationship between father and daughter, with a touching depiction of
Virginia's willingness to die and of Virginius' agony at the ineluctable
obligation of slaying his own daughter. The movement of the dialogue

1. Cf. Richard Levin, *The Multiple Plot in English Renaissance Drama* (Chicago
and London, 1971), and David M. Bevington, *From "Mankind" to Marlowe* (Cambridge, Mass., 1962), pp. 170–198.

2. On the story before Livy, see R. M. Ogilvie, *A Commentary on Livy Books
1–5* (Oxford, 1965), pp. 476–479, and, for later versions, O. Rumbaur, *Die
Geschichte von Appius und Virginia in der englischen Litteratur* (Breslau, 1890).

3. *Le Roman de la Rose par Guillaume de Lorris et Jean de Meun*, ed. Ernest
Langlois, SATF (Paris, 1920), pp. 263–266. Why Jean de Meung altered the method
of killing is unclear: Langlois (*Origines et sources du Roman de la Rose* [Paris,
1890], p. 118) suggests the poet was writing from a faulty recollection of Livy, who
had said: "Pectus deinde puellae transfigit respectansque ad tribunal: 'Te,' inquit,
'Appi, tuumque caput sanguine hoc consecro.'" It had long been a commonplace
of the literary and iconographic tradition that Abraham's method of sacrificing
Isaac would have been to cut off his head.

in lines 213–250 is so similar to that in the plays of Abraham and Isaac that it is tempting to believe that Chaucer was directly influenced by a play on this subject. There are obvious chronological difficulties in the way of this hypothesis since, although Chaucer undoubtedly knew the lost London cycle, all extant plays are later than the *Physician's Tale*.[4] It might also be urged that Chaucer as an acknowledged master of the art of pathos needed no model at this point. Nevertheless, the source of pathos in the *Physician's Tale* is different from the typical pathetic situation of cruel villain and helpless victim of which Chaucer presents so many variations. Admittedly, Chaucer has explicitly accommodated the Roman story to a Christian Biblical pattern by making Virginia compare herself to Jephthah's daughter. But, though there were many medieval versions of this story,[5] none would provide so adequate a model for Chaucer's treatment of the scene between Virginius and Virginia, and it would not be uncharacteristic of Chaucer to call attention to one analogue while in fact drawing substantially upon another.

From the point of view of *Apius and Virginia*[6] it of course makes no difference whether the resemblance between the *Physician's Tale* and the plays of Abraham and Isaac was coincidental or the result of direct borrowing. In either case the dramatist observed, and indeed was probably attracted by, the resemblance which he then deliberately sought to heighten. The direct indebtedness to the mystery plays may be seen in Virginia's first reaction when she finds her father weeping, "Why do you waile in such a sorte? why do you weepe and mone?" This innocent unawareness of possible danger to herself recalls the initial compassionate response of Isaac to Abraham's tears found in several of the plays. In the Chester cycle as in the Brome play, Isaac asks as they arrive on the scene of the sacrifice, "But why make you so heavie

---

4. On Chaucer's allusions to the mystery plays elsewhere in *The Canterbury Tales,* see Kelsie B. Harder, "Chaucer's Use of the Mystery Plays in the *Miller's Tale,*" *MLQ,* XVII (1956), 193–198, and Woolf, *The English Mystery Plays* (London, 1972), p. 208.

5. Cf. W. O. Sypherd, *Jepthah and His Daughter: A Study in Comparative Literature* (Newark, Del., 1948).

6. The edition used is the Malone Society Reprint, ed. Ronald B. McKerrow (London, 1911).

cheare? / are you any thing adred?," and in the *Ludus Coventriae* he
more movingly attempts to comfort his father:

> Lat be good fadyr your wepynge,
> your hevy cher agrevyth me sore;
> tell me fadyr your grett mornyng,
> and I shal seke sum help ther-fore.[7]

In itself this resemblance could be coincidental. That it is not is proved
by Virginia's later plea to her father:

> Yet stay a whyle, O father deare, for flesh to death is fraile,
> Let first my wimple bind my eyes, and then thy blow assaile.

Like Isaac, Virginia feels a natural fear, though freely offering herself
to death at her father's hands. In the cycles this was a realistic touch
encouraged and permitted by Christ's own expression of fear of death
during the Agony in the Garden. The way in which Virginia formulates
fear in her plea that her eyes may be covered ultimately goes back to an
iconographic detail already found in the twelfth-century *Winchester
Psalter,* where Isaac is shown blindfolded.[8] The manipulation of this
iconographic tradition for the effects of pathos is, however, confined to
the related Brome and Chester plays, in both of which Isaac in a last
moment resurgence of fear begs Abraham to bind his handkerchief
round his eyes, "Father, if you be to me kinde, about my heade a
kercher bynde . . ."[9] The author of *Apius and Virginia* has of course
plausibly substituted Virginia's own wimple for Abraham's handkerchief (though the stage direction oddly specifies a *handkercher*), but
it is a striking resemblance, all the more telling for the fact that Chaucer
had conceived of the moment of death more softly and evasively, Virginius performing the deed while his daughter lies unconscious in a
swoon.

Though quotations from some of the most simple and moving of the
mystery plays may unhappily draw attention to the stilted style of

---

7. EETS, E.S. no. 120, p. 47. In this quotation, as in all quotations that follow
from whatever source, I have substituted *th* for thorn, *y* for yogh, and, when appropriate, *sh* for x. For quotations from the *Ludus Coventriae,* I have also provided
modern punctuation.

8. Francis Wormald, *The Winchester Psalter,* (London, 1973), pl. 6.

9. EETS, E.S. no. 62, p. 80; cf. EETS, S.S. no. 1, p. 51.

Apius and Virginia, it would be fair to conclude that in terms of the larger working out of a theme the anonymous dramatist used the works that influenced him imaginatively. He did not imitate the *Physician's Tale* uncritically. On the one hand, with the help of moral-allegorical drama he learned to disregard the hagiographical pattern of the *Physician's Tale* according to which Apius' wickedness is something given from the outset and instead shows an upright man lapsing into vicious desires: Apius has thus become a faint but unmistakable anticipation of Angelo. On the other hand, with the help of the mystery plays the dramatist observed the pathos and dramatic force of the theme of a father compelled by some higher law to kill his child, and exerted his skill to make this scene the emotional center of the play. It would be a mistake to suppose that the latter was the inevitable tenor of the story. Webster's *Appius and Virginia* written about 1620 under the influence, it would seem, of Shakespeare's Roman plays, shows that the story could be recast in a quite different way with the clash between Appius and Virginius in the court scene providing the dramatic climax.[10] It is a taste formed by the mystery plays that would be likely to prefer tenderness and pathos to passion and conflict.

The influence of the plays of Abraham and Isaac upon one of the four major episodes in *Cambises* is even clearer,[11] for here the dramatist did not begin with a source that already had affinities with this subject, nor does he show an independent imaginative power that might have led him to fashion a similar scene through pure coincidence. The story of Cambises, first related coherently and effectively by Herodotus, had considerable currency in Western Europe during the Middle Ages: as in Herodotus, there were two separate stories about Cambises, one of his three great crimes and his death, the other of his so-called one good deed when he inflicted a severe punishment upon the unjust judge Sisamnes. In the sixteenth century these two stories were united and related in chronological order by Richard Taverner in his little volume of moral histories, *The Garden of Wisdom.* It is almost certainly from this source that Preston took his plot, retaining in full its crude outlines

10. *The Complete Works of John Webster,* ed. F. L. Lucas (London, 1927), III, 155–224.

11. The edition used is *Specimens of the Pre-Shakespearean Drama,* ed. J. M. Manly (1897; rpt. New York, 1967), II, 159–210.

and the weakness of its moral patterning.[12] To make a successful play the story urgently needed recasting and reinterpreting: as told by Taverner and dramatized by Preston it has two major weaknesses. The first is that when the story is set out in chronological order, the brutal savagery of Cambises in his three crimes seems to be anticipated in the punishment that he imposes on Sisamnes (after he has been executed the skin is flayed from the corpse in front of Sisamnes' son): Preston does nothing either to bring out this implication or to contrive that it should not arise. The second is that the medieval view that Cambises' crimes arose from drunkenness is inadequate (Herodotus had seen him as the victim of a terrible madness): but Preston seems to accept this traditional motivation readily and unthoughtfully.

This timid treatment of the outlines of the plot suggests that one should not expect any large and felicitous inventiveness in the management of the individual episodes. It is therefore not surprising to find that the episode in which Cambises kills the young son of his councilor Praxaspes, which is the most sensitively and consistently developed of the four, indeed has a source, namely, a play on the subject of the Sacrifice of Isaac.

Taverner's account is brief and in narrative terms imprecise:

. . . he [Cambises] commaunded Prexaspes to be called afore him, and bad him bryng unto hym hys yonger son. For he wold declare, how wel he coulde seme sobre even when he had most of al dronken for he sayd he wold even when he were dronken with hys bowe shote at Prexaspes sonne, and yf he myght wyth hys arowe stryke through his herte, than it myght be iudged, that in the myddes of hys cuppes he wanteth not the practse of counsaylle, and iudgement of reason. Yf not, that he were worthye to be called a dronkard. To be short, when Cambyses had thoroughly washed hys braynes wyth wyne, he shotte at the chyld as at an appointed marke . . .[13]

Such a scheme would seem to be the fruit of devilish or maniacal arrogance, but, as we have said, Preston was not concerned to develop the

---

12. Cf. W. A. Armstrong, "The Background and Sources of Preston's *Cambises*," *ES*, XXXI (1950), 129–135; Don Cameron Allen, "A Source for *Cambises*," *MLN*, XLIX (1934), 384–387.

13. Richard Taverner, *The Garden of Wysdome* (London, 1539), II, 17–21 (abbreviations have been expanded silently). Johan Carion's version is identical in outline though briefer.

figure of Cambises in this way. Instead he turned to the plays of the Sacrifice of Isaac and by the invention of one apt detail, namely, that the cruelty of Cambises extended to an insistence that Praxaspes himself should place his son on the right spot to form his target, he contrived an immediate parallelism. This invention permitted the presentation of a touching relationship between Praxaspes and his son (the player must have been a small boy, since the part is doubled with that of Cupid) and the introduction of a new character, the wife of Praxaspes, reproachful and inconsolable at her child's death.

When Praxaspes, distressed and weeping, brings his son to Cambises, the child is at first uncomprehending of his own danger, and in innocent bewilderment he is concerned only at his father's grief:

> O, father, father, wipe your face,
> I see the teares run from your eye:
> My mother is at home sowing of a band;
> Alas! deere father, why doo you cry?

Here the child's compassionate response is, like Virginia's, reminiscent of Isaac's; but, unlike the author of *Apius and Virginia,* Preston has deliberately and successfully caught the tone and style of the mystery plays. Asked to identify this quotation, one might reasonably guess that it was Isaac speaking in one of the cycles. The child's pathetically random thought of his mother is resumed in the last two lines that he speaks:

> Alas, alas! father wil you me kill?
> Good Master king, doo not shoot at me, my mother loves me
>   best of all.
>   (ll. 552–553)

The child's assumption at this late stage that his father is responsible for his death (though no doubt justified at this moment by Praxaspes, obeying the king's command to place the boy in front of his drawn bow) is certainly suggestive of the origins of this scene, as are also the small boy's childish thoughts of his mother. For the latter there are analogues in all the plays that present Isaac as a child, with the exception of the *Ludus Coventriae.* Chester and Brome both show Isaac wishing that his mother was at hand so that she might save him, and Brome also has Isaac urging that the truth may be concealed from

Sarah for "sche lovyt me full wyll." In Towneley Isaac pleads for his
life "ffor my moder luf," and in the Northampton plays Isaac's thoughts
of his mother are emphasized, as when he says, "For of my modre, I
wot wel, I shal be myst. / Many a tyme hath she me clipt and kyst." [14]
    It is conceivable that Preston also borrowed from the mystery plays
the idea of introducing the child's mother; but this is no more than a
tentative possibility, partly because among extant texts Sarah appears
only in the Northampton play, partly because this invention could
alternatively derive from classical models, such as Clytemnestra and
Hecuba or imitations of these, such as the unbiblical wife of Jephthah
named Storge, who speaks a brief lament at the end of Buchanan's
Jephthes.[15] Nevertheless, the treatment of the wife of Praxaspes strongly
recalls the English tradition. Though the intention of the style is consistently that of dignity, the manner in which she reproaches herself and
blames her husband, "What ment I, that from hands of him this childe
I did not keepe?" (earlier at line 538 Praxaspes had confessed that his
wife did not know for what purpose he had taken the child from her),
is reminiscent of the Northampton play in which Isaac argues that had
his mother known what was happening "I had not riden out from her
this day," and Abraham with unexpected tartness replies, "Thi modre
may not have hir wille all way." This interchange in itself reveals that
behind Sarah stands the figure of Noah's wife in the mystery plays and
behind her the shrewish wife of fabliau tradition (in tone it is far
removed from the movingly controlled and carefully argued speech in
which Storge claims the same right to save her child's life as Jephthah
has to sacrifice her). Similarly, the same kind of immediacy and directness can be seen in the formal lament spoken by the wife of Praxaspes.
Again, of course, the Senecan tradition could have furnished examples
as it did for the laments in so many Renaissance tragedies.[16] But the
speech itself is remarkably free from conventional and generalized
rhetorical themes (represented here by a half-line such as, "O hevy day
and dolefull time" and neologisms, such as *perpend,* so notoriously char-

14. EETS, E.S. no. 71, p. 47; EETS, S.S. no. 1, p. 38.
15. *Jephthes sive votum tragoedia* (Paris, 1557), p. 31.
16. Cf. Wolfgang Clemen, *English Tragedy before Shakespeare,* trans. T. S. Dorsch
(London, 1961), pp. 211–286.

acteristic of this play).[17] A more likely source for this lament of a bereaved mother is a *planctus* of the Blessed Virgin, whether the influence came directly from a play of the Burial of Christ or from the store of religious lyrics upon which the authors of the mystery plays often drew.[18] Particularly reminiscent of some of the lyrics is the way in which the mother's former happiness as she nursed and fondled her child is contrasted with the agony of the present. It is even likely that, as in some of the lyrics, this theme was pointed by the mother holding the dead body of her son in her lap (cf. ll. 582–583), thus making the exquisite distress caused by the contrast of past joy and present grief visually as well as verbally plain. While the use here of the now ill-famed Poulter's measure does not permit the stylistic simplicity and economy of the child's address to his father, there is throughout the speech a recollection of touching homely detail, as in ". . . and danced thee upon my knee to bring thee unto rest," which very strongly brings to mind the native as opposed to the Senecan tradition of lamentation.

Preston turned to the mystery plays not only for the effects of serious pathos but also in part for the two low comic scenes which interrupt the plot near the beginning and end of the play. These scenes are only loosely related to the main narrative: the characters in the first are soldiers of Cambises who have taken part in his recent wars against Persia; in the second they are peasants who talk of the evil deeds of Cambises. Thematically, the scenes are related by the presence in them of the vice, Ambidexter, who, according to his opening monologue will bring destruction "To all kinde of estates" (l. 157). In terms of both story and theme the connections are thus tenuous. Insofar as these comic episodes have a dramatic point it is that of a quarrel: in the first the boasting soldiers and Ambidexter, who has solidified into the stock figure of the *miles gloriosus,* fall to quarreling over which one of them shall successfully buy the company of "Mistress Meretrix" for the night; in the second the peasants Hob and Lob are provoked into fighting each

17. Cf. M. P. Tilley, "Shakespeare and his Ridicule of 'Cambyses,'" *MLN,* XXIV (1909), 244–247.

18. Cf. Woolf, *The English Religious Lyric in the Middle Ages* (Oxford, 1968), pp. 255–265; and for further comment on the Digby Play of the Burial of Christ, *English Mystery Plays,* pp. 332–333.

other by the instigation of Ambidexter, who threatens to betray them
for their treasonous talk about Cambises. Oddly enough, however, the
quarreling and fighting in both scenes are resolved in the same way: in
the first Meretrix suddenly intervenes and lays about her with the staff
that she has been carrying; as a result the Vice runs away, as does Snuf,
who throws away his weapons as he runs. Ruf remains to be thoroughly
beaten and to have his weapons taken away by Meretrix, who returns
them to him only when he pledges to be her servant. In the second episode the Vice is similarly treated: Marian, Hob's wife, firmly parts the
fighting peasants and then turns upon the Vice, knocking him down
and beating him with her broom. The comic pattern here is that of
many versions of the Massacre of the Innocents, in which Herod's
foolishly boastful soldiers are terrified of the mothers who often beat
them vigorously, using for weapons any household tool at hand—such
as a cooking ladle or distaff.

A probable explanation for the denouement of the comic scenes in
Cambises is that it deliberately repeats a well-liked motif in the mystery
plays. Traditional allegorical intention is out of the question: one has
only to try to formulate an interpretation along the lines of a *psychomachia* to realize how inappropriate such an approach would be; while
a recent and freer suggestion that the two women represent "a healthy
life force (of a comic Earth Goddess, perhaps, divided into her sexual
and maternal aspects)" illustrates the kind of wildly improbable and
anachronistic solution that is inevitably found by the critic who tries
to reconcile the mood of the comic scenes with a rational moral pattern
that embraces the whole play.[19] If, then, the double beating and putting
to flight of the Vice does not represent the banishment of anger and
dissension, then its only point seems to be to provoke laughter. An appeal to the comic pattern of the mystery plays also explains the otherwise inexplicable presentation of the Vice in the traditional role of the
miles gloriosus. An immediate influence here may have been the earlier
comedy *Thersites*, in which the braggart warrior, like the vice in
Cambises, undertakes "to fight against a snaile,"[20] and whose armor is
also a source of comedy: on the one hand Ambidexter has appareled

19. Levin, *Multiple Plot*, p. 145.
20. *Select Collection of Old English Plays*, ed. W. C. Hazlitt (1874–76; rpt. New
York, 1964), I, 394–431.

himself in kitchenware for his battles[21] while for Thersites nothing less will do than armor forged by the weaponsmith of the gods. For the portrayal of this type of figure, Roman comedy and the mystery plays are twin influences difficult to disentwine, the one no doubt reinforcing the other in the drama of the sixteenth century. Nevertheless, the native tradition seems the aptest source for the unsophisticated treatment of this stock jest in *Cambises*. Its influence may even be seen in the much more polished version of the theme in *Roister Doister,* where Dame Custance and the *knightesses* of her household drive Ralph Roister Doister and his companions into trembling and cowardly retreat:[22] though in narrative terms this episode may have been suggested by the farcical scene in Terence's *Eunuch,*[23] in which the braggart Thraso and his slaves lay siege to the house of Thais, in tone Custance and her formidable servants seem to be the direct descendants of the mothers in the Massacre of the Innocents.

A comic scene, very similar to those in *Cambises,* occurs also in *Horestes.* The main comic subplot in this play is quite well related to the story, the peasants, Rusticus and Hodge, satisfactorily representing and expressing the fears of the common people who will suffer from the passage of the armies engaged in the prosecution of the high quarrels of their rulers. Their vulnerability at a comic level to the Vice's encouragement to vengeance (with Rusticus setting upon Hodge because his dog has killed his pig) is also well done. There is, however, one isolated comic scene that does not have this simple aptness. It occurs immediately before the climax of the play in which Horestes, to avenge the murder of his father Agamemnon, takes his mother Clytemnestra prisoner and has her put to death. The dramatic point of the placing of the scene is plain: Pickering relaxes the tension with a short piece of knockabout comedy in order to tighten it the more in the successfully taut and horrific scene that is to follow. But the subject of the scene,

---

21. For detailed commentary on the armor of Ambidexter, see Richard Southern, *The Staging of Plays before Shakespeare* (London, 1973), pp. 512–513. The derivation of this armor is further discussed below on p. 105.

22. Nicholas Udall, *Roister Doister,* IV, vii–viii; Manly, *Specimens of the Pre-Shakesperean Drama,* II, 75–84.

23. Cf. D. L. Maulsby, "The Relation between Udall's *Roister Doister* and the Comedies of Plautus and Terence," *Englische Studien,* XXXVIII (1907), 263–265.

namely, how a Mycenaean woman turns upon one of the soldiers in Horestes' army and gives him a good beating on the ground before confiscating his weapons and taking him prisoner, is irrelevant to the main theme. To see it, for instance, as a comic inversion of Horestes' capture of his mother, would be to impose a pattern upon the play that is not felt to arise naturally from the text. Again, therefore, as in *Cambises,* the introduction of this subject is best explained as the borrowing of a popular element in the mystery plays that was available to a dramatist who sought a successful moment of comic diversion.

At this point in *Horestes* a recognition of a source in the mystery plays casts light on the inclusion of an episode puzzlingly irrelevant to the main plot. There is, however, another passage in the play where the recognition of an antecedent in the mystery plays may have a bearing upon the interpretation of the whole work. There has been a tendency among critics, particularly among recent critics who interpret *Horestes* as a play mirroring the political situation, to assume that the vice may give good counsel.[24] This interpretation is inherently unlikely and certainly impoverishes the play. Crude though *Horestes* is, Pickering shows in it that he has understood the two important elements in its Greek ancestors: first, that, whatever the duties of filial revenge, it is a very terrible and unnatural thing for a son to kill his mother; second, that the play may nevertheless have a happy ending because in a new era of conciliation, the unending chain of cause and effect, crime and vengeance which has bound the house of Pelops will be snapped. To express these two ideas, Pickering resorts quite effectively to the morality-play tradition, contriving the antithetic roles of the Revenge (the Vice), and of Nature, and also the banishment of the Vice at the end of the play after he has tried to attach himself to Menelaus in order to provoke a further round of revenge. How Pickering gained these insights is not known: it was certainly not from either of his postulated sources,

---

24. Cf. James E. Phillips, "A Revaluation of *Horestes* (1567)," *HLQ*, XVIII (1954-1955), 227-244, and E. B. de Chickera, "Horestes' Revenge: Another Interpretation," *N&Q*, CCIV (1959), 190. A similarly unquestioning attitude to the Vice in *Cambises* is shown in W. A. Armstrong, "The Authorship and Political Meaning of *Cambises*," *ES*, XXXVI (1955), 289-299. The best analysis of the Vice in *Horestes* as a giver of evil advice is that of Willard Farnham, *The Medieval Heritage of Elizabethan Tragedy* (Oxford, 1956), pp. 258-262.

Caxton's *Recuyell of the Historyes of Troye* or Lydgate's *Troy Book*, for neither shows any awareness of the patterning of the tragic dilemma and its solution.[25] The *Recuyell* does not question the fittingness of Horestes' revenge, even though it is the more horrifyingly unnatural in that Horestes himself rips off his mother's breasts and has her body thrown to the dogs and birds while Lydgate positively commends the virtue of Horestes in taking vengeance upon Clytemnestra, "rote of al falshede."[26] Gower's *Tale of Horestes,* with its perceptive moral insights, might, however, have drawn Pickering's attention to the pattern of reciprocity, the unnatural crime of wife murdering husband being punished by the unnatural vengeance of son murdering mother,[27] while Pickering's understanding of the aesthetic value of bringing the successive acts of a vengeance to a close might have come from Greek sources, even if Pickering only knew of the plays of Aeschylus and Euripides at secondhand.

This interpretation of *Horestes* depends upon the recognition of the Vice, whose proper name is Revenge though he masquerades under the alias of Courage, as a character not to be trusted: he is in part a personification of revenge, which is at best a particolored quality that needs to be controlled by certain virtues, while in part as Vice he is an unscrupulous and malicious tempter who seeks to promote the quality that he represents without restraint. This understanding of the nature and role of the Vice is confirmed if his first approach to Horestes is seen as an echo of the devil's approach to Eve in a play of the Fall of Man. Horestes in a soliloquy has been considering the conflicting obligations of avenging his father and showing filial compassion toward his mother. As he speaks his mind becomes set upon revenge, and he appeals to the gods for guidance, formulating his dilemma in a highly tendentious way: shall he, he asks, avenge his father or shall he let "the adulltres

25. Cf. F. Brie, *"Horestes* von John Pickeryng," *Englische Studien,* XLVI (1912–1913), 66–72; Karen Maxwell Merritt, "The Source of Pikeryng's *Horestes,*" *RES,* NS, XXIII (1972), 255–266.

26. William Caxton, *The Recuyell of the Historyes of Troye,* ed. H. Oskar Sommer (London, 1894), II, 684–686; Lydgate's *Troy Book,* III, EETS, E.S. no. 106, pp. 814–823. The savage detail of the revenge derives ultimately from the *Roman de Troie* of Benoit de Sainte-Maure, SATF (Paris, 1908), p. 283.

27. *Confessio amantis.* EETS, E.S. no. 81, pp. 281–283.

dame, styll wallow in her sin"? He then ends with an appeal which shows that he has unconsciously answered his own question, "Oh godes of war, gide me a right, when I shall war begyn" (ll. 216–217). Pat upon this prayer the Vice enters and speaks as follows (the first line with its punning resumption of the word "war" being a snappy and sinister aside addressed to himself):

> Warre quoth he, I war in dede, and trye it by the sworde,
> God saue you syr, the godes to ye: haue sent this kind of word
> That in the hast you armour take, your fathers fose to slaye
> And I as gyde with you shall go, to gyde you on the way.
> By me thy mind ther wrathful dome, shalbe performd in dede
> Therfore Horestes marke me well, & forward do procede.
> For to reueng thy fathers death, for this they all haue ment
> Which thing for to demonstrat lo, to the they haue sent me.
>
> (ll. 219–226)[28]

Questioned by Horestes, the Vice further adds that he was in the heavens when the gods resolved that Horestes should avenge his father and that he comes with the express permission of Mars. There are two notable points in the Vice's claims. First, the minor one, that he refers specifically to Mars: in other medieval versions the gods are referred to vaguely, whereas in the Greek tradition Horestes received his command from the oracle of Apollo. Second, and more importantly, Pickering has already presented the Vice on stage (untypically he opens with a comic scene), and therefore from the audience's point of view the Vice has manifestly come not from a council of the gods but from provoking a silly, ill-tempered quarrel between a pair of peasants.

The moral ambivalence of the oracle of Apollo is an element in the Greek story entirely ignored in the Middle Ages. Most versions seem tacitly to assume that an order of the gods was right and had to be obeyed; the exception is Lydgate, who boldly but unfelicitously explains that the command of the gods was the command of God. Pickering seems ingeniously to have done the reverse, and the Vice's proclamation that he comes bearing a message of the gods is surely to be understood as the deceptive lie of a cunning tempter, equivalent to the lie in the 1533 Norwich play of the Fall in which the serpent, after urging Eve to

28. *The Interlude of Vice* (Horestes) 1567, ed. Daniel Seltzer, Malone Society Reprints (Oxford, 1962).

eat the apple, adds the assurance, "Almyghty God dyd me send."[29] It would not have been necessary for Pickering's audience to recognize this point of resemblance, since all that is required for a true understanding of the play is that the Vice should be taken for a liar. In a period, however, when this understanding is neglected, it is worth noting that Pickering may well have modeled the Vice's first approach to Horestes upon that of the father of lies.

A detection of echoes of the mystery plays in the works of mid-sixteenth-century dramatists is not in itself startling. Though it is not possible to show a historical connection between the authors of the popular tragedies and the cycles (uncertain identification of the three writers and the loss of important texts makes such external evidence irrecoverable), the general probability that they would have seen a cycle of plays is high: for the great northern cycles and the famous (though now almost entirely lost) cycles of London and Coventry had either been acted regularly up to 1570 or had been revived during the reign of Mary (1553–1558).[30] Furthermore, the influence of the mystery plays on the Biblical drama of the sixteenth century (both English and Latin) is well established, and allusions to the cycles in the works of secular dramatists, writing before and after the 1560's, are well known: there is, for instance, a reference to the lost Coventry Harrowing of Hell in *The Four PP* of John Heywood, while two stock themes of the Massacre of the Innocents are referred to by Shakespeare—the ranting style of Herod in *Hamlet* and the screaming of the mothers in *Henry V*.[31]

The importance, therefore, of these echoes does not lie primarily in their existence but in their nature. This is self-evidently different from that of the allusions to the mystery plays in *The Four PP* or *Henry V*,

29. EETS, S.S. no. 1, p. 10. This detail was omitted from the revision of 1565, that is, approximately at the time that *Horestes* was written (it was printed in 1567 and was probably performed at court in 1567–1568).

30. Cf. Harold C. Gardiner, *Mysteries' End, YSE*, CIII (1946), and E. K. Chambers, *The Mediaeval Stage* (Oxford, 1903), II, 329–406. It may be worth noting that all the most important borrowings, both tragic and comic, could have come from the Chester plays, of which there were apparently five performances (and conceivably more) in the ten years from 1551 to 1561.

31. Cf. Hardin Craig, *English Religious Drama of the Middle Ages* (Oxford, 1955), 364–377.

which serve only to enlarge the field of reference of these plays for comic or declamatory purposes. And it is also different from the use that Marlowe probably made of the figure of Herod in *Tamburlaine*.[32] There is an obvious general resemblance between Herod and Tamburlaine, but at one point it is also specific. When in one of his earliest magniloquent speeches Tamburlaine declares, "I hold the Fates fast bound in yron chains, / and with my hand turne Fortunes wheel about," these godlike claims are a classical equivalent to such typical boasts as the following, "I dynge with my dowtynes the devyl down to helle / for bothe of hevyn and of herthe I am kyng sertain," or "For I am evyn he thatt made bothe hevin and hell, / And of my myghte powar holdith up this world rownd."[33] In the mystery plays, however, there is a grotesque and morally pregnant discrepancy between Herod and his hyperbolic claims: through the magnitude of such boasting he shrinks in size; whereas Tamburlaine through the vastness and splendor of his image of himself grows to superhuman size, and when at last and inevitably he is shown to be the subject and not the ruler of fortune, his earlier claims retain an imaginative truth. If, then, Marlowe drew upon the traditional figure of Herod in his creation of Tamburlaine, he did so in order to achieve a new and different effect. By contrast, when R. B. in his treatment of Virginius and Virginia turned to the traditional and analogous figures of Abraham and Isaac and in particular borrowed Isaac's touching plea to have his eyes bound, he did so in order to achieve precisely the same effect of pathos that he found in his source.

The same intention may be seen in *Cambises*, where paradoxically Preston may sometimes adopt a detail from another source in order to imitate more feelingly the effects of pathos or comedy that had pleased him in the mystery plays. When Preston modeled the episode of Praxaspes and his son upon the plays of Abraham and Isaac, he obviously needed to make some change in order to accommodate the differences between the endings, one happy, one tragic. While the possibility that the introduction of the mother was influenced by the Northampton play

32. The resemblance between Herod and Tamburlaine has of course been noted before, for instance by Harry Levin, *The Overreacher* (Cambridge, Mass., 1952), p. 31, who considers it "probably more than a coincidence."

33. *Ludus Coventriae*, EETS, E.S. no. 120, p. 151; *Two Coventry Corpus Christi Plays*, EETS, E.S. no. 87, p. 17.

has been mentioned, on present (though limited) knowledge it is more likely that Preston arrived at this happy extension of the story himself, either by pondering the implications of the plays themselves about what Sarah's reactions would have been both realistically and typologically if Isaac had been killed, or, as we also suggested, by recalling the analogous figure of Storge, or perhaps by a blending of the two. That Preston had understood the devotional pattern of the plays is suggested by the precise echoes of the *planctus* of the Virgin in the mother's lament. If the Biblical Isaac had died, it is surely thus that the authors of the mystery plays would have made Sarah mourn.

The comic episodes in *Cambises* indicate a similar method of working. As we have seen, the treatment of the Vice in these scenes could not fail to recall the treatment of Herod's soldiers in the Massacre of the Innocents. Nevertheless, the unexplained kitchen armor of the Vice is more immediately reminiscent of the harnessing of Roister Doister, where, though the joke appears to be an elaboration of the theme of the kitchen weapons of the mothers of the Innocents, it is in itself naturalistically motivated, since it is only to the kitchen that Roister Doister can quickly turn in his pressing need for armor. Though Udall seems here to have found a further twist for a traditional comic theme, it is an invention not out of keeping with some of the mystery plays—one could well, for instance, imagine the Digby Watkin dressed in makeshift armor—and stripped of narrative function, it serves to enhance the likeness to the mystery plays, which is felt in the colloquial interchanges and abuse and the extraordinary placing of farce in the general context of brutal and tragic action.

In the popular tragedies of the 1560's, therefore, we find the transplantation of certain popular and striking effects of the mystery plays to the new context of secular drama. In course of time some kinds of comedy lose their power to amuse, and nowadays there seems little to value in the imitations of the rout of the soldiers from the Massacre of the Innocents. But the medieval treatment of the story of Abraham and Isaac retains its power to move, and the scene in *Cambises* modeled upon it is one of the most successful in the plays of the 1560's, including the regular tragedies.

Terence Improved: The Paradigm of the Prodigal Son in English Renaissance Comedy

ERVIN BECK

A Comedie, I meane for to present,
No Terence phrase: his tyme and myne are twaine:
The verse that pleasde a *Romaine* rashe intent,
Myght well offend the godly Preachers vayne.
George Gascoigne, *The Glass of Government*

T HE STORY of the prodigal son is the most ubiquitous one in comedy of the English Renaissance (1500–1642). Appearing as the main or subplot in almost forty plays, it germinates in *The Interlude of Youth* (Anon., ca. 1513) and is last found in the Frederick subplot of Shirley's *The Lady of Pleasure* (1635).[1] Many of these plays, and certainly the best ones, were written during the greatest years of English drama, with at least fifteen coming from between 1593 and 1610. Except for Lyly and Peele, every important known comic playwright had a hand in at least one prodigal-son comedy. Shakespeare, in fact, used the archetypal story in six plays: *The Two Gentlemen of Verona* (Proteus), *The Taming of*

---

1. The Appendix gives a chronological list of prodigal-son comedies in England. Some of the early ones, such as *Nice Wanton* and *The Glass of Government,* are prodigal-son *plays,* rather than prodigal-son *comedies* proper.

the Shrew (Lucentio), *Henry IV, Parts 1* and *2* (Prince Hal), *All's Well that Ends Well* (Bertram), and *The Tempest* (Caliban).

Ever since Charles H. Herford's *Studies in the Literary Relations of England and Germany in the Sixteenth Century*,[2] literary historians have studied the prodigal-son tradition in English drama and have acknowledged its indebtedness to the "Christian Terence" movement in Continental drama. But they have usually limited their concerns to early sixteenth-century drama, particularly the tradition as it emerged following John Palsgrave's translation of Gnapheus' *Acolastus* into English in 1540. R. Wever's *Lusty Juventus* (ca. 1550), *Nice Wanton* (Anon., ca. 1550), Thomas Ingelend's *The Disobedient Child* (ca. 1560), *Misogonus* (Anon., ca. 1570), and George Gascoigne's *The Glass of Government* (1575) are the early British plays incorporating the prodigal son that seem to merge the native morality tradition with the Christian Terence tradition of Continental drama. F. S. Boas is typical in claiming that with Gascoigne's stultifying tragedy "the day of the Prodigal Son dramatic cycle was passing."[3]

In actuality, it had only just begun. More than thirty identifiable prodigal-son plays were written after 1575, the most obvious ones being *Henry IV* (ca. 1597), *The London Prodigal* (ca. 1604), and *Eastward Ho* (1605). Some critics—notably Hardin Craig, Madeleine Doran, J. Dover Wilson, Robert Y. Turner, Muriel C. Bradbrook, and Alan R. Young— have been aware of the continuing tradition and have tried, in part, to account for it. But the exact nature of the tradition and, in particular, its relevance to seventeenth-century comedy have remained murky topics. In this confusion, a useful tool for describing and analyzing Renaissance comedy has remained unrefined.

Hardin Craig, who says that "the pattern of the Prodigal Son may be said to permeate Elizabethan drama," apparently regards most plays concerned with erring youth as examples of prodigal-son comedy. Consequently, his delineation of the tradition is too broad to be very useful. Robert Turner uses the term in referring to a play whose hero abandons wife or sweetheart for a harlot, undergoes a traumatic experience, is converted, and returns to his first love. Turner apparently follows

2. (1886; rpt. New York, 1966), pp. 70–164.
3. *An Introduction to Tudor Drama* (Oxford, 1933), p. 41.

Muriel C. Bradbrook, whose list of prodigal-son plays implies a similar definition. But as Robert Hapgood rightly points out, such a description skews the meaning of "prodigal son" since it emphasizes the hero's marital, rather than his filial, waywardness. The most recent study of the tradition, a dissertation by Alan R. Young, comments on many of the plays, but offers no conceptual framework for meaningful use of the term.[4] His *ad hoc* approach to individual plays leads him to ignore such important plays in the tradition as *The Two Gentlemen of Verona, All's Well that Ends Well, The Wise Woman of Hogsdon,* and *The Wild-Goose Chase.*

The concept of "prodigal-son comedy" is a fruitful critical tool only if it is regarded as an archetype or paradigm; that is, as a universalized story-structure that contains certain deep motifs and meanings which persist despite surface variations in character, event, and tone. In its absolutely perfect form, of course, this archetypal plot would be faithful to the sequence of events found in Christ's parable in Luke 15:11–32, thereby consisting of ten "segments" of action: the request (vv. 11–12a), the granting of the request (v. 12b), the trip to the far country (v. 13a), the riotous living (vv. 13b–14), the recourse to work (v. 15a), the bondage-humiliation-despair (vv. 15b–16), the recognition-repentance-return (vv. 17–20a), the generous reception (vv. 20b–21), the celebration (vv. 22–24), and the elder brother's response (vv. 25–32). One would hardly expect a group of plays, however, to adhere faithfully to the details of the Biblical story. Such literal plotting would be trite indeed.

In my judgment, the essential prodigal-son archetype concerns a young man who has newly come of age and has therefore arrived at a state of moral, social, and economic accountability. He rebels against or rejects a father-figure or, more generally speaking, his inheritance from a preceding generation. In going his own way, he brings himself to some kind of humiliating defeat. He undergoes a conversion and tries to

---

4. Craig, *English Religious Drama of the Middle Ages* (Oxford, 1955), p. 384, and "Morality Plays and Elizabethan Drama," *SQ*, I (1950), 64–72; Turner, "Dramatic Conventions in *All's Well That Ends Well*," *PMLA*, LXXV (1960), 497–502; Bradbrook, *The Growth and Structure of Elizabethan Comedy* (London, 1955), pp. 127–133; Hapgood, "Dramatic Conventions in *All's Well That Ends Well*," *PMLA*, LXXIX (1964), 177–182; Young, "The English Prodigal Son Plays to 1625" (Diss., University of Alberta, 1970).

return to the people and to the values against which he had originally rebelled. In most cases, he succeeds so well that a happy ending is possible. Even if he does not return to what he originally rejected, the assumption of the play is that he ought to do so. The most important fact about the hero, therefore, is not that he is a *prodigal*, but that he is a *son* who denies or misvalues his heritage and has to learn through experience to appreciate it.

Such a definition does not assume that the author necessarily had the Biblical parable in mind when he wrote his play. The full sequence of events in the paradigm need not be dramatized. A prodigal-son comedy may begin with the young man's request (*All's Well that Ends Well, The Two Gentlemen of Verona, Eastward Ho*); it may begin with his riot (*The London Prodigal*); or it may begin with his attempted return (*A Trick to Catch the Old One*). The prodigal may be the elder brother rather than the younger; there may even be no brother; the father himself may be "prodigal" in some fashion; the restoration of the son to former values may be effected by an act of mercy or by the son's own design. The quintessential element in the paradigm is that a young man has departed from the values of his forebears—values which the play assumes he ought to reembrace.

This understanding of prodigal-son comedy is grounded less in the details of the parable itself than in the recognition that the prodigal-son paradigm contrasts strikingly with the paradigm of youth that dominates the Roman comedy of Plautus and Terence—as in Terence's *Phormio*, for example. The typical plot of New Comedy is concerned with a young man whose desire for a girl is thwarted by some external opposition, usually parental; the young hero is usually vindicated and the older generation is discredited. Henry Ten Eyck Perry says that "Plautus and Terence . . . contented themselves with the feeling that hope for a better society in the future rests with the younger generation, which must always be considered right in its conflict with miserly old age and selfish parental authority."[5] Hence the basic assumptions of prodigal-son comedy are fundamentally opposed to those of Roman New

5. *Masters of Dramatic Comedy and Their Social Themes* (Cambridge, Mass., 1939), p. xx.

Comedy: New Comedy is *adulescens triumphans;* prodigal-son comedy is *senex triumphans.*

To delineate prodigal-son comedy according to its relationship to Roman New Comedy is not a mere academic exercise but is justified by important historical and critical considerations. The historical justification derives from the fact that the first prodigal-son comedies were written, beginning about 1510, by Continental humanist schoolmasters who sought substitutes for the supposedly immoral plays of Plautus and Terence as pedagogical materials for teaching language and rhetoric. Accordingly, they dramatized the story of the prodigal son in the mode of Roman comedy. But the drama that resulted constituted more than the ideological patchwork implied by Herford, who says that the humanists reproduced "as far as was consistent with a Biblical subject and a pious intention the art, the colouring, the society, the atmosphere of Plautus and Terence" (p. 85). In actuality, *Térence moralisé* resulted in a precise inversion of the paradigm of youth in New Comedy.[6]

The critical justification derives from the influential criticism of Northrop Frye, who claims that the New Comedy paradigm of youth has been the normative one for Western comedy since Plautus and Terence. Because prodigal-son comedy represents a diametrically opposed archetype, Frye's observations on New Comedy offer a valuable point of reference for generalizations regarding the nature and implications of prodigal-son comedy—its precise foil.[7]

Frye says that, in its social significance, New Comedy portrays a single movement from an old, effete society to a new one that forms around a young hero. Since the young hero usually plays a subordinate role in his own play, his character—hence the nature of the emergent society—remains undefined. The new society ushered in by the happy ending, however, recalls a golden age prior to the opening of the play when the natural order had not yet been usurped by the senex society

---

6. Noted in passing by Young, "English Prodigal Son Plays," p. 380, and W. E. D. Atkinson in his translated edition of Gulielmus Gnapheus, *Acolastus,* Studies in the Humanities, no. 3 (London, Ont., 1964), p. 26.

7. Unless otherwise indicated, the observations on New Comedy that follow are adapted from Frye's *Anatomy of Criticism: Four Essays* (1957; rpt. New York, 1968), pp. 163–186 *et passim.*

and its unnatural, irrational laws (which included the idea that money is more important than love).

Prodigal-son comedy, on the other hand, portrays a twofold change in society. It begins with the desirable, aged society in control; experiments with a new, disorderly society initiated by the young hero; but finally returns and re-forms around the original, stable society. Prodigal-son comedy is conservative, not revolutionary, in its social implications. But it is not merely reactionary; its return to the original society also involves a renewal of that society, since the former society now incorporates the vitality of youth into the old order, thus insuring its lively perpetuation. Because the old, desirable society was present in the play from the beginning, the norms of the society re-formed at the end are well understood, and, throughout, the deviation from them by the young man is clearly perceived for what it is: a violation of natural law. The society formed at the end of prodigal-son comedy is no "golden age" or "Edenic" existence; rather, it is a social order formed within the fallen world, aware of the cruel realities of life but somehow transcending them.

Since the chief conflict of New Comedy is between generations, its plot moves toward rendering harmless those members of the old society who oppose the will of the young. Frye calls such people "blocking" characters; usually they are parents, members of the senex generation. Normally they are not converted or changed; instead, they are somehow rendered harmless so their presence may be tolerated by the new order. They are usually put in their place by some kind of trick or arbitrary discovery. The vices or humors of the blocking characters often make them the most interesting characters in the play.

The essential concern of prodigal-son comedy, however, is the re-forming of the internal desires of the young hero. New Comedy is concerned with subduing the senex that threatens from without, but prodigal-son comedy is concerned with getting rid of a different kind of senex—the internalized "old man" of the New Testament: "put off . . . the old man, which is corrupt according to the deceitful lusts; and be renewed in the spirit of your mind; and . . . put on the new man, which after God is created in righteousness and true holiness" (Ephesians 4:22–24). This conflict between the "old" and the "new" men within the prodigal son makes him the most fully developed, and therefore the most interesting, character in his play. His reformation is effected not by arbitrary device, or merely factual discovery, but rather by a causative process that leads to his self-recognition and a purgation of his vicious humor. The final stage in his self-recovery—his generous reception by a long-suffering father—affirms the dominance of *agape* in prodigal-son comedy, as opposed to the dominance of *eros* in New Comedy.

In his early essay, "The Argument of Comedy," Frye claims that New Comedy is Aristotelian, in contrast to Aristophanic comedy, for instance, which is Platonic; Dantean *commedia,* which is Thomist; and Shakespearean green-world comedy, which derives from folk feelings.[8] In calling Roman comedy Aristotelian, Frye may have in mind Aristotle's preference for plots that observe probable cause and effect, as well as his observation that comedy is "an imitation of characters of a lower type" than tragedy, which represents people superior to us.[9]

But the late classical, medieval, and Renaissance commentators on Terence noticed a more profound way in which New Comedy is Aristotelian. In Aristotle's *Rhetoric* and *Ethics* they found human beings from various stations in life described according to their most typical traits of personality. Thus, an old man is typically pessimistic, petty, selfish, expedient, dishonorable, avaricious, calculating, and malicious. Conversely, a young man is normally idealistic, honorable, prone to excess, inexperienced, innocent, overconfident, and hopeful. The tradition of such character description reached its peak in the ethical characters of Theophrastus (371–287 B.C.), Aristotle's pupil at the Academy, and was apparently transmitted to Menander (343?–?291 B.C.), who is traditionally regarded as the originator of New Comedy.[10] In literary criticism, this kind of understanding of character shows its greatest influence in the neoclassical doctrine of decorum, whereby a character is required to do and say only those things appropriate to his age and station in life.

Since New Comedy respects this kind of decorum, its characters offer few surprises. Because they are Theophrastan types, they act as one

8. *English Institute Essays 1948* (New York, 1949), pp. 65–67.

9. *Poetics,* trans. S. H. Butcher (New York, 1961), p. 52.

10. Edwin W. Robbins, *Dramatic Characterization in Printed Commentaries on Terence,* Studies in Language and Literature, XXXV, no. 4 (Urbana, Ill., 1951), pp. 68, 73 *et passim.*

would normally expect people of their station in life to act. Consequently, they do not change significantly through the course of a play. The typical senex, for instance, remains avaricious; his will changes only because he knows that the seemingly base young lady actually has money and social status.

Prodigal-son comedy, grounded in Christian theology and morality, assumes that character can and should change—and significantly so, since change from one moral state to another has everlasting consequences. It is true that prodigal-son comedy introduces its own character type, the young man who changes from good to bad to good again; but this character type implies a radical departure from the assumptions underlying the classical understanding of decorum of character. One important consequence for drama is that, in its protagonist, prodigal-son comedy offers a character that is subject to multiple variations in development, as opposed to that of the adolescent of New Comedy, whose role is more or less fixed.

As an anthropological critic, Northrop Frye has a great interest in the social meanings of comedy, which are well reinforced by this Theophrastan concept of frozen social types. In New Comedy, the social process is redeemed because there is always a group of maturing young men and women, fertile and strong, who eventually work their will over the effete senex class. In anthropological terms of seasonal ritual, youth defeats age just as—or because—spring inevitably replaces winter and renews the earth.

Romantic as this idea may seem to be, it is actually based on a primitive, naturalistic understanding of the human condition that is much more cynical than Aristotle's understanding, which sees reason as a saving grace. The characters of New Comedy are locked in, so to speak, to the roles that their physical bodies and their social station require. Just as saplings become large trees, so young men inevitably become old men, and there is nothing they can do to thwart the process.

Prodigal-son comedy, however, offers a Christian alternative. Man need not be a victim of his physical or social existence. Age and social position merely determine certain of his modes of being, through which his true self may nevertheless emerge, thus transcending the limitations of the physical and social realms. For instance, the prodigal son's conversion does not change his age or his social role, but it does allow his true self—that part of him that transcends seasonal change—to be born. In Roman comedy adolescent and senex will never merge; they are eternally separated by age and social conditions. But in prodigal-son comedy the son attains the wisdom customarily associated with age, and the father remains "young at heart" in the best sense of that cliché. Thus the characters of prodigal-son comedy realize fully the old *topoi* of classical and medieval rhetoric—the *puer senex* (the young old man) and the *senex puer* (the old young man)[11]—in a dramatic context that recognizes these paradoxical states to be manifestations of true self-recognition and self-fulfilment.

To view New Comedy and prodigal-son comedy side by side is, in effect, to recapitulate the famous scene in *As You Like It* in which Jacques, Theophrastus-like, describes the seven inevitable ages of man. They culminate in "second childishness . . . sans teeth, sans eyes, sans taste, sans everything." But Jacques's wry generalization is immediately undermined by the appearance of Orlando, who bears on his back the exhausted Adam—an old man who has saved Orlando from Oliver's wrath and therefore means "everything" to Orlando.[12] Jacques's speech is in the spirit of New Comedy—*puer* and *senex;* but Orlando's action affirms the spirit of prodigal-son comedy—*puer senex* and *senex puer.*

Prodigal-son comedy finds no welcome place within Frye's six phases of the "Mythos of Spring: Comedy." With considerable distortion, it might fit into Phase I, the most "ironic" phase of comedy, which shows the defeat of the young, emergent society by the usurping, established social order. Frye's explanation of this kind of comedy assumes that the emergent society is good, and that the established society is undesirable; hence the quality of "irony" in the phase. However, prodigal-son comedy usually endorses the old society and always condemns the revolutionary, chaotic society.

Prodigal-son comedy is probably best seen as a Renaissance version of Dantean-Thomist *commedia.* It is redemptive comedy, which means that it is concerned with resolution of internal contradictions and progress toward right integration of personality. In religious terms, it

11. Ernst R. Curtius, *European Literature and the Latin Middle Ages,* trans. Willard R. Trask (New York, 1953), pp. 98–101.

12. The implications of the appearance of Orlando and Adam were first pointed out by O. J. Campbell in "Jacques," *Huntington Library Bulletin,* VIII (1935), p. 100.

portrays the salvation of the individual's soul and the social reconcili-
ation and renewal that naturally result from the emergence of the hero's
true self. Northrop Frye will hardly admit *commedia* to the ranks of
real comedy. It is what he would call "moral comedy," which, Frye
implies, is inferior comedy: "It is of course quite possible to have a
moral comedy, but the result is often the kind of melodrama that we
have described as comedy without humor, and which achieves its happy
ending with a self-righteous tone that most comedy avoids." [13] Many
prodigal-son comedies—especially the early ones—do illustrate this objection. However, the problem of asserting moral norms by laughter
rather than by heavy didacticism and melodramatic devices is one that
prodigal-son comedy eventually overcomes. It merges morality and
laughter most successfully when, as in Middleton's *A Trick to Catch
the Old One,* it takes seriously the techniques and structural qualities
of Roman comedy—although such flirtation with Roman conventions
frequently modifies some of the implications of the paradigm.

Prodigal-son comedy, then, constitutes what seems to be a noncon-
formist comic tradition. Best described in contrast to Roman comedy, it
presents a certain narrative sequence and contains a certain insight into
human experience. The insight into human experience derives from
Christian theology; the narrative sequence imitates—often imperfectly—
the parable in Luke.

With both the parable and the Roman paradigm of youth in mind, it
is possible to isolate more precisely the discrete elements in prodigal-son
comedy that, together, constitute a *sine qua non* for the tradition.

1. The hero rebels against or disappoints a father or father-figure—
whether a foster-father, an uncle-guardian, a teacher, or a man who previously had advised his father. This element distinguishes prodigal-son
comedy from the "faithful wife" play, in which a young man deserts a
faithful sweetheart or wife, as in *The Fair Maid of Bristow.* That tradition can merge with the prodigal-son tradition, however, if the deserted
girl is strongly associated with the will of a living or deceased father.
Such is the case with *All's Well that Ends Well* and *The Wise Woman
of Hogsdon.*

2. The hero's departure from established values is a perverse, radical

13. *Anatomy of Criticism,* p. 167.

action; it is a "fall" from some kind of "grace," and not merely a well-intentioned mistake that is easily amended by advice and education. This feature rules out the "Wit and Science" plays, which teach a prudential lesson in education. Normally the hero, Wit, has the right goal in mind, but he tries to take a short cut to Dame Science's abode and is waylaid by Tediousness and Idleness.

3. The prodigal son's "fall" is implicitly an initial departure from innocence, a first step toward self-realization. This element rules out plays about middle-aged people, and, again, distinguishes prodigal-son comedy from plays about deserted wives. A hero's marriage to a good wife implies an initially healthy volition directed toward self-realization and maturity as symbolized by marriage. But a prodigal son's first movement toward self-realization is a perverse one. His return to grace is often rewarded with marriage to a good girl, which becomes a token of his permanent regeneration.

4. The paradigm assumes that its hero *ought* to return to the good state from which he has fallen. This assumption rules out a play such as Dekker's *Northward Ho,* which concludes with the older generation's endorsement of the young hero's prodigal bent.

5. The paradigm is not obscured by a more prominent, even if similar, archetypal story. Hence *The Sun's Darling* and *Old Fortunatus* are not prodigal-son comedies, even though they vindicate the father and discredit the son. *The Sun's Darling* is dominated by the Phaëthon-Helios myth; *Old Fortunatus,* by the Fortunatus legend.

Although thirty-odd plays share the prodigal-son paradigm in overt or latent content, the tradition is not as homogeneous as the preceding discussion of archetype implies. The vast time span covered by the plays, as well as the sheer quantity of titles and authors, guarantees lively variation from play to play. Nevertheless, upon examination, the comedies often share special characteristics that enable the mass of plays to be sorted into subgroupings other than those based on author or chronological proximity.

Among such interesting classifications is one based on the role played by the young prodigal in addition to the primary one of "son." He may be a student (*Nice Wanton, The Taming of the Shrew, The Lady of Pleasure*); a prince (*James IV, Henry IV, If This Be Not a Good Play*); an apprentice (*If You Know Not Me, Eastward Ho, Greene's Tu*

Quoque); or a lover (The Two Gentlemen of Verona, The Wise Woman of Hogsdon, The Wild-Goose Chase). Such plays encourage the study of the themes of education, politics, economics, and romance that inevitably arise from the prodigal's truancy from responsibility in these spheres.

Another kind of grouping is based on the relative abridgment of the prodigal-son narrative. Some plays begin with the request (*Acolastus, All's Well that Ends Well, Eastward Ho*); many begin with the riot (*Henry IV, The London Prodigal, The English Traveller*); others with the return (*A Trick to Catch the Old One, The Wild-Goose Chase, The Ordinary*); and one even begins with the generous reception (*The City Madam*). As a general rule, the more the paradigm is abbreviated the more the resultant play imitates Roman comedy, both in idea and in form.

The most helpful classification centers on the distinctions observable among "moral," "romantic," and "satiric" plays within the tradition. In this case, genre is only superficially a matter of observable tone (e.g., sober, wondrous, or critical). Of greater importance is the nature of the play's intrigue, which seems to determine the resultant tone.

The "moral" comedies are obvious descendants of the English morality play tradition. In a moral comedy, the primary intrigue is carried on by vice figures, and is at least temporarily successful. If the prodigal himself is also an intriguer, his intrigue is usually very ineffective. The important quality of the intrigue in the moral comedies is that it is directed toward a recognizably evil end, the ruination of the prodigal son.

Since all prodigal-son comedy is interested in the conflict between virtue and vice in the prodigal's experience, all of the plays are, in a general sense, moral comedies. But certain of them are so in a special sense. What might be called the "pure" moral comedies are essentially *commedias,* in which the purification of the hero's character is the sole reason for rejoicing. That is, the play excludes the *gamus* that usually concludes other kinds of comedy. In fact, moral *commedia* is quite misogynistic. Romantic love is confined to the prodigal's riot, where his attraction to a girl is evidence of his sensual abandon. The comic celebration honors his return to the father, not his romantic union with a sweetheart. The earliest English prodigal-son comedy, *The Interlude of Youth,* is a prime example of the type. Other prominent *commedias* include *The Famous Victories of Henry V, Henry IV, Eastward Ho, If You Know Not Me You Know Nobody, The Tempest,* and *The English Traveller.*

A species of moral comedy that complements moral *commedia* can be called "moral satire." Plays in this tradition also feature evil intrigue, but since they do not show the prodigal restored to the position from which he has fallen, they are not true *commedias.* Instead, the prodigal is comically censured either for failing to reform or for getting himself into a situation from which he cannot extricate himself even though he has repented. Massinger's *The City Madam* is the purest example of the type. Other moral satires include *Pater, Filius and Uxor, The Disobedient Child, The Taming of the Shrew, The Drinking Academy,* and *The Lady of Pleasure.*

Unlike the moral *commedias* and the moral satires, the "romantic" comedies of the prodigal son celebrate the prodigal's romantic affection for a virtuous girl. The hero may perversely court other girls in his riot, but his return to a former love and his subsequent marriage to her betoken his spiritual regeneration and offer a traditional excuse for the celebration that ends the play. In these romantic comedies, the primary intrigue is managed by virtuous figures for the good end of reforming the prodigal. Usually the sweetheart (who becomes a kind of Patient Griselda in the abuse that she endures) is the primary intriguer. Often she is aided by the prodigal's father; always she is endorsed by him. The most interesting of such romantic comedies are *The London Prodigal* and *All's Well that Ends Well.* Other similar plays are *The Two Gentlemen of Verona, The Wise Woman of Hogsdon, The Wild-Goose Chase,* and *The Staple of News.*

Prodigal-son comedies in the "satiric" mode begin with a wastrel hero, newly repentant, whose primary task in the rest of the play is to recover his lost inheritance and social status. Since he carries out the primary intrigue in the play for his own benefit, and since his efforts usually culminate in the removal of a senex blocking-figure, the satiric plays almost duplicate the dramaturgy and the ideas about the nature of man found in Roman New Comedy. Nevertheless, since the plays take for granted the fallen nature of the young hero and the necessity of his reformation, they remain true to the Christian assumptions inherent in the prodigal-son paradigm. Such plays include *A Mad World, My*

Masters, A New Trick to Cheat the Devil, A Trick to Catch the Old One, A New Way to Pay Old Debts, The Ordinary, and perhaps *Ram Alley* (but not Chapman's *All Fools* or Dekker's *Northward Ho,* which endorse the prodigal's riotous conduct). Although these satiric plays usually culminate in the marriage of the hero, the romantic interest is minimal.

Many of the plays, of course, do not fit exclusively into a single mode. *Wit without Money* mixes almost equally the satiric and the romantic modes. *James IV* is a *commedia* that concludes with the hero's reunion with his faithful wife. *Michaelmas Term* is, in a sense, the prototypical satiric comedy, but it also includes much intrigue by vice figures, and its hero is eventually saved by the affection and cleverness of a woman. *Greene's Tu Quoque* exploits all four of the modes: moral *commedia* in Spendall's fall and repentance; moral satire in the career of Bubble; romantic comedy in his surprising rescue from prison by a widow; and satiric comedy in the career of Staines.

An explication of one of these prodigal-son comedies would relate the play to commentary on the Biblical parable by the church fathers, medieval theologians, Renaissance humanists, and Protestant reformers. It would also examine carefully the tension between elements of dramaturgy adapted from the traditions of Roman comedy and the medieval morality play. But at the center of the study would be a testing of the play in terms of the paradigm: How does the play rearrange or abridge the segments of the full archetypal story? What elements are omitted or added? What is the effect and import of such variations?[14]

For, although the full paradigm is relevant to all prodigal-son comedies, it may seem to "fit" some better than others. But that is no indictment of the paradigm as a critical tool. In fact, disparity between paradigm and play is to be expected. The paradigm is a kind of Platonic ideal. When it is brought to bear on a play that contains its shadow, the resulting tension serves to define the unique achievement of the individual play as well as relate it to a larger tradition. Many otherwise

14. For studies of *Youth, The London Prodigal, All's Well that Ends Well, A Trick to Catch the Old One, Wit without Money,* and *The City Madam,* see my dissertation, "Prodigal Son Comedy: The Continuity of a Paradigm in English Drama, 1500–1642" (Diss., Indiana University, 1972).

neglected plays are thereby placed within a critical context that enhances their proper appreciation, and the entire tradition of prodigal-son comedy is properly emphasized as one of the earliest, most persistent, and most important strains in drama of the English Renaissance.

Appendix
Chronological List of English Prodigal-Son Plays

A single date indicates the known date or the best approximation; a double date (e.g., 1513–1529) gives the earliest and latest possible dates for a play whose dating is unknown. The dating of *The Interlude of Youth* is based on Edgar T. Schell, "*Youth* and *Hyckescorner*: Which Came First?," *PQ*, XLV (1966), 468–474. All other dating follows the Harbage-Schoenbaum *Annals of English Drama, 975–1700* (London, 1964).

1513—Anonymous, *The Interlude of Youth* (1513–1529)

1530—Anonymous, *Pater, Filius and Uxor, or The Prodigal Son* (ca. 1530–ca. 1534 [?])

1540—Gulielmus Gnapheus, *Acolastus,* trans. John Palsgrave

1550—R. Wever, *Lusty Juventus* (1547–1553)

—Anonymous, *Nice Wanton* (1547–1553)

1560—Thomas Ingelend, *The Disobedient Child* (ca. 1559–1570)

1570—Laurence Johnson (?), *Misogonus* (ca. 1560–1577)

1575—George Gascoigne, *The Glass of Government*

1586—Anonymous, *The Famous Victories of Henry V* (1583–1588)

1590—Robert Greene, *The Scottish History of James IV* (ca. 1590–1591)

(?)—Anonymous, *The Comedy of the Prodigal Son* (printed in Germany, 1620)

1593—William Shakespeare, *The Two Gentlemen of Verona* (ca. 1590–1598)

1594—William Shakespeare, *The Taming of the Shrew* (ca. 1594–ca. 1598)

1597—William Shakespeare, *Henry IV, Part 1* (ca. 1596–1598)

—William Shakespeare, *Henry IV, Part 2* (ca. 1597–ca. 1598)

1599—John Marston (reviser), *Histriomastix, or The Player Whipped* (1589–1599)

1602—William Shakespeare, *All's Well that Ends Well* (ca. 1601–ca. 1604)

1604—Anonymous, *The London Prodigal* (1603–1605)

—Thomas Heywood, *The Wise Woman of Hogsdon* (ca. 1604?)

1605—Thomas Heywood, *If You Know Not Me You Know Nobody, Part 2*

—George Chapman, Ben Jonson, John Marston, *Eastward Ho*

—Thomas Middleton, *A Trick to Catch the Old One* (1604–1607)

1606—Thomas Middleton, *A Mad World, My Masters* (1604–1607)

—Thomas Middleton, *Michaelmas Term* (1604–1606)

1607—Francis Beaumont, *The Knight of the Burning Pestle* (1607–ca. 1610)

1608—Lording Barry, *Ram Alley, or Merry Tricks* (1607–1608)

1611—John Cooke, *Greene's Tu Quoque, or The City Gallant*

—Thomas Dekker, *If This Be Not a Good Play, the Devil Is in It* (1611–1612)

—William Shakespeare, *The Tempest* (ca. 1609–1611)

1614—John Fletcher, *Wit without Money* (probably revised in 1620)

1621—John Fletcher, *The Wild-Goose Chase* (1621?)

—Philip Massinger, *A New Way to Pay Old Debts* (1621–1625)

1625—Robert Davenport, *A New Trick to Cheat the Devil* (ca. 1624–1639)

—Thomas Heywood, *The English Traveller* (1621–1633)

1626—Ben Jonson, *The Staple of News*

1629—Thomas Randolph, *The Drinking Academy, or The Cheaters' Holiday* (1626–1631)

1632—Philip Massinger, *The City Madam*

1635—William Cartwright, *The Ordinary, or The City Cozener* (1634–1635)

—James Shirley, *The Lady of Pleasure*

Italian Tragicomedy
on the English Stage

G. K. HUNTER

T HAT SHAKESPEARE was unlike Jonson is well known and widely believed. That Shakespeare was *like* anyone else (Heywood and
Dekker are the names Webster suggests[1]) is found less plausible.
We tend to suppose that he worked by the light of his own genius—
usually called the light of nature ("Shakespeare and Nature were, he
found, the same"). Yet this dramatist, like the others, spent his creative
life in the literary-theatrical milieu of a town the size of a modern
provincial center. Are we to suppose that the fashions, the enthusiasms,
the feuds, inevitable in such an environment, left him totally unmoved?
Were the forms of his works never affected by rivalry, a new literary
model suddenly discovered, a new generic possibility opening up? Our
prejudgments lead us to believe not. When we notice that his vision

---

1. John Webster, Preface to *The White Devil* (1612), speaks of ". . . the right
happy and copious industry of Master Shakespeare, Master Dekker and Master
Heywood."

expresses itself inside traditional genres, our first effort is to seek explanation in his personal psychology, or, if that is too obviously crude, in the
subject requirements of the particular play. We do not normally attribute
to Shakespeare any desire to fulfill external expectations based on genre.
Rather, we describe (for example) the set of tragedies he wrote after
1600 as reflections of a "tragic vision" particular and personal to Shakespeare; and though the final "romances" are sometimes explained by the
new Blackfriars theater or by the influence of the court masque or
some other external aspect of the age, our deepest sense of these plays
still arises from our response to Shakespeare the individual.

The group of "problem plays" or "dark comedies" written 1601–1604
faces us with the same situation in a slightly different form. Can
this group of plays be defined as belonging to an aesthetically distinct
genre or broadly shared fashion? The fact that the genre was defined as
separate only as late as F. S. Boas's *Shakspere and His Predecessors* of
1896 must make us pause. The obvious alternative explanation would
attribute any repetitiveness of form or content among the "problem
plays" to the pressure of Shakespeare's individual vision. One time-
honored explanation sees these plays as the fairly helpless personal
response of an artist caught in the grip of a tragic view of the world,
but committed to the comic forms in which he had generally expressed
himself, and which his audience expected from him.

The suggestion I wish to offer here is that much in *All's Well that
Ends Well* and *Measure for Measure* can be seen as response to the
stimulus of a new genre absorbed by a number of dramatists at approximately the same time. I believe it can be shown that Shakespeare
is drawing in these plays on a sense of genre which he, along with his
fellow playwrights, perceived through "the spectacles of books." If I am
right, he shows himself an artist very much aware of the European
avant-garde and quick to respond to the latest seductions of cinquecento
taste.

It confirms our standard expectations about the Renaissance to hear
that it was Italy that provided Shakespeare and his fellows with critical
stimulation. That there was an "Italian influence" on Elizabethan drama
has been asserted for so long that we tend to assume it must exist, for
this reason if for no other. And of course it is true that many plays
of the Elizabethan popular theater are set in a so-called "Italy," or refer

to things or habits as "Italian."[2] But if we define influence with any degree of literary severity, restricting it to the area implied by the question, "What Elizabethan plays are direct imitations of Italian plays?," then we are given an interestingly muted answer.[3] The one section of Elizabethan drama which shows a direct and significant debt to Italian drama is occupied by that sterile and unrepresentative group of plays written by gentlemen amateurs for their privileged peers. This situation is not altogether surprising; for these plays are the only English ones that reproduce, even approximately, the social conditions of the serious Italian drama. The fact that influence can be detected here gives us good reason why we do not find it elsewhere. The Elizabethan professional theater, the context of all the worthwhile drama of the period, had, if it were to succeed commercially, to satisfy audience requirements far outside the scope of amateur or Italian drama.

The situation is certainly curious. The professional drama was the peculiar glory of the English Renaissance. But in one respect it seems to be quite distinct from other aspects of the English literary Renaissance. Italian works such as Ariosto's or Tasso's epics were not only talked about, translated, and reprinted in England; they provided the necessary precondition for England's attempts to achieve its own monuments. In music, in art, in love lyric, civil treatise, and short story, the Italian example fired the English imagination. But the Italian play seems not at all necessary to explain the nature or the growth of the English play.

There is, however, one exception to this general truth. When we consider the reception and translation of Italian plays in England, we notice first of all the poverty of the connections. But two or possibly three Italian plays must be allowed to be exceptional; and all these plays belong, significantly enough, to the same new genre, and are in fact its first mature expressions[4] as well as its most celebrated exemplars.

2. For the distinction between the true Italy and the dramatized Italy, see G. K. Hunter, "English Folly and Italian Vice," in *Jacobean Theatre,* ed. J. R. Brown and B. Harris (London, 1960), pp. 85–111.

3. See David Orr, *Italian Renaissance Drama in England before 1625* (Chapel Hill, N.C., 1970) for a refreshingly objective look at the actual evidence.

4. In saying this I am treating previous pastoral plays, such as Giraldi's *Egle* (1545), Beccari's *Il Sacrificio* (1554), and Argenti's *Lo sfortunato* (1567) as experimental rather than mature examples.

The two plays I refer to are Tasso's *Aminta* and Guarini's *Il Pastor Fido*, and the third is Bonarelli's *Filli di Sciro;* the new genre is, of course, pastoral tragicomedy. The *Aminta* stimulated at least five separate English translators in the first hundred years or so of its existence.[5] *Il Pastor Fido* was translated by five seventeenth-century Englishmen, and nine editions of English versions were published in the same century.[6] *Filli di Sciro* enjoyed two English and one Latin translation in the first half of the century.[7] And all this is, we should remember, in the context of a situation where no other Italian play had more than a single translation and where the vast majority had none.

The response to the new genre was continuous throughout the seventeenth century. But this might be taken to reflect Caroline rather than Elizabethan or Jacobean taste. More important for our purposes is to note how early the English response appears. *Aminta* was first published in 1580; *Il Pastor Fido,* first published in 1590, did not reach its final revision till 1602, in the twentieth edition. But as early as 1591 Italian texts of both plays were published in London, from the press of John Wolfe. Wolfe had published a number of Italian texts in the eighties, but these can be explained by impeccably commercial motives; no question of taste arises.[8] The edition of the two pastoral plays seems,

5. The *Aminta* was first translated by Abraham Fraunce in 1591, and later by Henry Reynolds in 1628, (in part at least) by Kenelm Digby in 1635, by John Dancer in 1660, and by John Oldmixon in 1698.

6. *Il Pastor Fido* was translated by "Dymock" (first published in 1602; rpt. 1633), translated into Latin for a Cambridge performance by ?W. Quarles about 1604, retranslated by Jonathan Sidnam (1630), by Sir Richard Fanshawe (1647; rpt. 1664, 1676, etc.), and adapted from Fanshawe by Settle (1676; rpt. 1689, 1694).

7. *Filli di Sciro* was first published in 1607. It was translated into Latin by Samuel Brooke in 1613, into English by Jonathan Sidnam in 1630 (published in 1655), and translated again by Gilbert Talbot in 1657 (while the author was in exile in Paris and hoping for a providential intervention to turn the Stuart tragedy into a tragicomedy). *Filli di Sciro* is not only the third most translated play; it is also the third play in the sequence of Italian pastoral tragicomedies, derivative from *Il Pastor Fido* as *Il Pastor Fido* is from *Aminta.*

8. The works that might seem most directly comparable with the 1591 volume are Wolfe's editions of two Machiavelli comedies (1588) and of four Aretino comedies (1588). The commercial justification for these volumes is, however, very clear. They belong to a large-scale plan to publish the complete works of the two

however, not to have been a commercial venture. It was printed, the title page tells us, *a spese di Giacopo Castelvetri*. Giacopo (or Giacomo) Castelvetro[9] seems to have had considerable acquaintance among the educated nobility of Britain, to many of whom he acted as tutor in Italian; his pupils included King James of Scotland, the ninth Earl of Northumberland, Lord North, and Sir Charles Blount. As Miss Rosenberg has remarked, it was part of his role as cultural middleman to "offer himself as a purveyor of fashionable masterpieces *e transmarinis partibus*" (p. 126). What is interesting, from the point of view of this article, is that *Il Pastor Fido* should have occupied this category as early as 1591. Castelvetro's dedication of the volume to Sir Charles Blount (the successful lover of Sidney's Stella, we may remember) dilates in a very interesting way on the reasons which prompted him to procure the publication.[10] It appears from what he says that literary relations

---

most scandalous Italian authors, Machiavelli and Aretino, which Wolfe worked on between 1584 and 1589. The Machiavelli is slightly more complete. In 1584 Wolfe published the *Principe* and the *Discorsi*. In 1587 appeared the *Historie fiorentino* and the *Arte della guerra*. *L'Asino doro* and the comedies were published in 1588. The set of volumes is bound together by the prefaces to the early ones, which promise the later publications. The order of publication shows the nature of the market at which they were aimed: the most scandalous works appear first and secure public interest, and the more insipid works follow in their wake. The same pattern appears with the Aretino. The first and second parts of the *Ragionamenti* appear in 1584. The preface to the first part promises later publication of the letters, the religious works, the comedies. The comedies appeared in 1588; the letters were licensed to Wolfe in 1588, but never published. In 1589 Wolfe published the third part of the *Ragionamenti,* and that (so far as we know) was the end of his adventure to exploit English fascination with Italian wickedness and the desire to read, even if in a half-understood language, works never likely to be available in English.

9. For comment on the life of Castelvetro and his literary work, see Sheila A. Dimsey, "Giacopo Castelvetro," *MLR,* XXIII (1928), 424–431, and Eleanor Rosenberg, "Giacomo Castelvetro, Italian Publisher in Elizabethan London and His Patrons," *HLQ,* VI (1943), 119–148.

10. He tells us that the fame of *Il Pastor Fido* had quickly traveled from Italy to England and that thus there was caused, among the English *singulari spiriti,* a great desire to see it. Castelvetro had tried to use his connections in Italy to raise a copy, but found this very difficult; eventually, however, he received one exemplar. On reading it he realized what a treasure it was, and how difficult it would be for others to share the pleasure. So he resolved to have the work reprinted. Other

between London and Italy were closer than is usually supposed. In mid-1591 he seems to regard it as remarkable that a book published in Ferrara in 1590 is difficult to find in London. He seems also to be saying that the *Aminta* is now getting harder to find (presumably again in London); and this I take to imply that it was once quite easy. We have not normally thought that the latest Italian literature was looked for in London. Castelvetro's words imply that there is an audience in London, small perhaps but important, of persons who have an immediate response to the Italian graces of *Il Pastor Fido* and (he assumes without question) to "l'Aminta del gran TASSO." But English taste for these early portents of *seicentismo* is less surprising if we remember how well known in the nineties were the swooning madrigal verses of the Italians.[11] The long Italian dialogue between Antonio and Mellida, in Marston's play of that name (1599), is very much in the manner of the lyric verses of Tasso and Guarini. As early as 1605 Ben Jonson is rounding on the imitators of Guarini, who are thought to have already weakened the moral fiber of English poetry. In *Volpone* Jonson puts into the mouth (or rather parrot beak) of the literary Lady Would-Be an ironic praise of Italian authors, including Guarini:

> Here's PASTOR FIDO . . . . All our *English* writers,
> I mean such, as are happy in th'*Italian*,
> Will deigne to steale out of this author . . .
> He has so moderne, and facile a veine,
> Fitting the time, and catching the court-eare.
>
>   (III.iv.86–92)[12]

---

gentlemen *fornite di maggior letteratura & di maggiore agutezza d'ingegno* agreed as soon as they read the work that it must not be lost sight of. Castelvetro resolved to reprint *Il Pastor Fido* in a double volume, together with *Aminta*, since *chi legge il Pastor Fido divenghi volonteroso di veder l'Aminta, & poi anchora perche di lei si ritrovano hoggi pochissimi essempi da vendere.*

11. The relationship between *Il Pastor Fido* and current madrigal verse was much noted by Italian critics of the play. G. P. Malacreta calls it *una dissipata raccolta di madrigali*; Udeno Nisiely speaks of *filza di madrigali amorosi;* N. Villani says that Guarini *potrai coglier da questa favola una sessantina di madrigaletti.* (All quoted in N. J. Perella, *The Critical Fortune of Battista Guarini's "Il Pastor Fido,"* [Florence, 1973], pp. 21, 35; cf. p. 50).

12. Ben Jonson, *Works,* ed. C. H. Herford and P. and E. Simpson, 11 vols. (Oxford, 1925–1952), V, 73–74 (hereafter cited as "Herford and Simpson").

Jonson clearly regards Guarini as the kind of effeminate and relaxing author whose chief appeal will be to women.[13]

In accepting the predictive value of the 1591 volume, one should not lose sight of the differences between the two plays it contains and the different kinds of success they were to enjoy in England. The *Aminta* is a short and simple work; its charms are those of a gentle and polished eroticism, of psychology, of style, and of sentiment. It has little direct to offer to the sophisticated technical demands of the theaters of the English metropolis. The response to it is, in consequence, primarily a literary response, deriving from an established taste for pastoral poetry. Thomas Watson's *Amyntas* of 1585 has been hailed as the first English acknowledgment of its existence, and if any connection between the two works could be established, Watson's poem would mark an extraordinarily early assimilation into England. Alas, the point cannot be made in these terms. Watson's volume (a set of eleven, hundred-line, Latin lamentations, in which Amyntas mourns for the death of Phyllis, at the rate of a hundred lines a day) exhibits no connection whatsoever with Tasso's play.

Abraham Fraunce, who translated Watson's eclogues into English in 1587, seems in fact to be the first who conceived of them as *parerga* to Tasso. In 1591 he added to his Watson translation a translation of Tasso's *Aminta* (newly available in Wolfe's edition) in the same meter, English hexameters. Further, he doctored Watson's text so that the eclogues would seem to follow naturally from the play. He sees good generic reasons for linking them:

> But Tassoes is Comicall, therefore this verse [hexameter] unusual: yet it is also pastoral, and in effect nothing els but a continuation of aeglogues, therefore no verse fitter than this.
>
> (sig. A2)

In its rather pedantic terms this is an interesting early expression of the idea of a mixed genre, which was later to be a central concern of tragicomedy. The *Aminta* is a comedy (it ends happily), it deals with the private emotions of humble persons, but it is seriously poetic as

---

13. The condemnation of *Il Pastor Fido* as a dangerously relaxing, sentimental, and effeminate work is also found among the Continental critics. See Perella, *The Critical Fortune of "Il Pastor Fido,"* pp. 50 ff.

well, and so justifies hexameters. The theatrical problems of tragicomedy do not arise here, of course; the play being "nothing els but a continuation of aeglogues," the context is poetic rather than dramatic. There is no evidence indeed of any of the translations of the *Aminta*, before Oldmixon's of 1698, being designed for the stage.

Il Pastor Fido shares with *Aminta* (and derives from it) many of the basic features of pastoral tragicomedy; but it pushes these in a direction which, while it may be destructive of the poetic charm of pure pastoral, nonetheless makes possible a tenuous but effective relationship with the practical English theater. The elaboration and complexity of Guarini's play, its careful imitations of the *Andria* and the *Oedipus Rex*, ensured that it should be of technical interest to English playwrights in a way that the poetically charming but dramatically slight *Aminta* could hardly be. Moreover, though the *Compendio della poesia tragicomica* attached to the 1602 edition of *Il Pastor Fido* does not seem to have been translated into English in the seventeenth century, it does seem to have been known. There can be little doubt that Fletcher's preface to *The Faithful Shepherdess* (1610) indicates some knowledge of it (or of the *Verrati* which preceded it, in 1588 and 1591). It seems likely that Fletcher knew the *Compendio* before he wrote the play—about 1608. Any knowledge of the *Compendio* must, of course, have sharpened the focus of dramatists' technical interest in the new genre.

Il Pastor Fido can be seen as pushing toward the test of actual performance the claim of pastoral tragicomedy to represent a significant imitation of reality. This is a test that Italian tragedy had signally failed to pass; and the possible reasons why are not irrelevant to thoughts about the cultural transmission of the tragicomic form. The lack of contact between Italian tragedy and English public performance must be due, in large part, to the different views of reality found in the two theatrical traditions. Italian tragedy is, by and large, centered on the figure of the tyrant, seen together with his (often female) victims. A tyrant is by definition one who has subjugated social responsibility to personal passion. The royal power of Dolce's Herod or Giraldi's Sulmone is shown mainly in the freedom with which he can indulge in himself and promote in others the personal violences of jealousy, suspicion, anger, and revenge. But the Elizabethan tragic sense seems to have demanded more explicitly political conflicts. The tyrant, when we meet him in Elizabethan public tragedy, is part of a fully represented political scene. So it is (for example) with Macbeth, with Piero (in Marston's *Antonio's Revenge*), or with the Duke in *The Revenger's Tragedy*. In such plays the passions of the individual tyrant are always judged in terms of social and political responsibility.

It is hard to resist the assumption that these opposed forms of tragedy reflect the day-to-day political experience that author and audience brought to the composition and reception of tragedies, rather than any simply aesthetic tastes. If this is a fair assumption, we find in it a clue to the theatrical as well as poetical claims of pastoral tragicomedy in England. The material of Italian tragedies encroached on the English tragic vision, but the terms of its development prevented it from expressing a full political meaning, and therefore it seemed to the English to be stunted and incomplete. Pastoral tragicomedy was, on the other hand, quite without political pretension. The social structure of Guarini's Arcadia is more defined than that of the *Aminta,* but its utmost definition is only vaguely theocratic. Montano, the chief priest, exercises the only visible authority, but his function does not fully emerge till the end of the play, when he conducts the sacrifice to Diana. No hierarchy or system of government is declared. One can say that society here is represented (and even more obviously in the *Aminta*) by loving (or about-to-be-loving) couples, acknowledging only the authority of their parents and the gods. The great affairs of oracles, plagues, sacrifices, etc., impinge directly on private individuals and their families, without the intervention of any state apparatus.

The generic "openness" of tragicomedy—the quality so often cited against it in the critical controversy around *Il Pastor Fido*—can be paralleled by a blankness in its political dimension. Having nothing at all to say about political life, it could pass into the English theater through the barrier of different audience assumptions about power and its distribution; in this area it offered nothing for rejection. But the political blankness or blandness of the genre may be seen not as an advantage but rather as a deprivation. This seems to have been a natural early response in England. Ben Jonson's comment on Guarini's "moderne and facile . . . veine" (cited above) makes this point with characteristic directness. Guarini's ability to give meltingly smooth expression to tremulous love-emotions and feminine reticences seems to

Jonson to be both trivial ("moderne") and facile. *Il Pastor Fido* reads to Jonson like a confession of poetic irresponsibility, an abandonment of the traditional Humanist position: that poets gave advice to princes, so that even the public stage had a moral role.

The English public-theater audience might be thought to have made the same point in their rejection of Fletcher's attempt to infuse Guarini neat onto the London stage in *The Faithful Shepherdess* of ca. 1608. Fletcher, in his supercilious epistle "To the Reader," represents this as only an ignorantly conservative reaction to the new mode, a reaction in which the public took tragicomedy to be Sidney's "mongrel" genre, combining mirth and killing as well as clowns and kings, and also supposed (sympathetically) that pastoral meant "lower class." They were, therefore, on both counts, unadjusted to the blending of gods and economically independent shepherds that Fletcher intended. In this case Jonson's difficulty, caught between Humanist political serious-ness and upper-class loyalty, is nicely exposed. In his sonnet to Fletcher, Jonson condemned the audience who

> had, before
> They saw it halfe, damd thy whole play, and more.

The moral Jonson makes of the occasion is interestingly different from Fletcher's:

> Their motiues were, since it had not to do
> With vices, which they look'd for, and came to.
> . . . thy Innocence was thy guilt.
>   (Herford and Simpson, VIII, 370)

The moral blankness or evasiveness of the Guarinian play, its lack of interest in the social dimension of crime and violence, is now alleged to be a sign of innocence rather than triviality. Here friendship with Fletcher and hatred for the mob seem to have betrayed Jonson into a position very close to that of his much-despised colleague, Samuel Daniel. It is often supposed that Jonson had Daniel in mind when he made Lady Would-Be tell Volpone that English authors steal out of Guarini. The two men, however, seem to be at one in describing the relationship of Guarini to the English stage, though Jonson's valuation differs sharply, outside the poem to Fletcher. *Il Pastor Fido* provides the obvious model for Daniel's *The Queen's Arcadia* (1605), described on the title page as "a pastoral tragicomedy presented to her majesty and her ladies by the University of Oxford." In the prologue Daniel speaks of his properly humble and apolitical mode of writing as entirely appropriate for students, who share with shepherds the innocency of a secluded existence:

> And though it be in th'humblest ranke of words,
> And in the lowest region of our speach,
> Yet is it in that kinde, as best accords
> With rurall passions; which vse not to reach
> Beyond the groues and woods, where they were bred:
> And best becomes a claustrall exercise,
> Where men shut out retyr'd, and sequestred
> From publike fashion, seeme to sympathize
> With innocent, and plaine simplicity:
> And liuing here under the awfull hand
> Of discipline, and strict obseruancy
> Learne but our weakenesses to understand.
>
> (ll. 9–20)[14]

For Daniel, this scholarly quasi-pastoral seclusion allows the student actors to avoid the vices of the public stage, for such actors

> dare not enterprize to show
> In lowder stile the hidden mysteries,
> And arts of Thrones; which none that are below
> The Sphere of action, and the exercise
> Of power can truely shew: though men may straine . . .
> Whereby the populasse (in whom such skill
> Is needlesse) may be brought to apprehend
> Notions, that may turne all to a tast of ill . . .
>
> . . . .
> Yet the eye of practise, looking downe from hie
> Vpon such ouer-reaching vanity,
> Sees how from error t'error it doth flote,
> As from an unknowne Ocean into a Gulfe:
> And how though th'Woolfe, would counterfeit the Goate
> Yet euery chinke bewrayes him for a Woolfe.
> And therefore in the view of state t'haue show'd
> A counterfeit of state, had beene to light
> A candle to the Sunne.
>
> (ll. 21–45)

14. *The Complete Works in Verse and Prose of Samuel Daniel,* ed. Alexander E. Grosart (1885; rpt. New York, 1963), III, 213–214.

In Daniel's view the sovereign would be most improperly served by the political and social commentary that was the staple of the public stage. And the public stage itself is censured for meddling in mysteries above the capacities of the "populace." It is clear that Guarini provides a model of how the stage can avoid these strong and dangerous excitements. It is equally clear that the English populace had no intention of doing without them.

The Malcontent of John Marston is the play that shows most brilliantly how pastoral tragicomedy and the English stage could be brought into a relationship more fruitful than that envisaged by Daniel, or achieved by Fletcher. As I have pointed out before,[15] The Malcontent has many quotations from Il Pastor Fido, which are taken literatim from the 1602 "Dymock" translation. Borrowing from Il Pastor Fido proves, of course, that Marston had been reading Il Pastor Fido but does not prove that the shape and nature of Marston's play is affected by Guarini's. There is some evidence, however, of this further and larger connection. Marston's play was entered in the Stationers' Register as "An Enterlude called the Malecontent Tragicomedia." Such entries often reflect something written on the manuscript; internal as well as external evidence suggests that Marston was deliberately experimenting with a new genre for which Guarini's play provided the most celebrated and most embattled example. The Malcontent is not, need I say, a simple reproduction of the mode of Il Pastor Fido; the surface appearances of the two plays could hardly be more distinct. The one is as much a critique of the other as an imitation. Perhaps it should be seen as a critical return to the roots of the genre. The pastoral tragicomedy form had grown out of attempts to reinvent the Greek satyr play.[16] The satyr and the shepherd are presented by the theorists as its alternate protagonists. The English awareness of this notion is nicely illustrated by the engraved title page to Ben Jonson's Workes (1616 and 1640). In this design Tragicomoedia appears aloft, supported on one side by Pastor and on the other by Satyr. In the Compendio della Poesia Tragicomica Guarini traced back the origins of the new form to

15. See Hunter, "English Folly and Italian Vice."
16. See, for example, Giraldi's Egle, and the theoretical gloss supplied in his Discorso sulle satire atti alle scene,

the *tertium quid* (between Tragedy and Comedy) that the satyr play provided:

> Ma niuno meglio d'Orazio nella sua poetica *Pistola a' Pisoni*
> ci ha descritta la tragicommedia con questi versi:
>   mox etiam agrestes satyros nudavit et asper
>   incolumi gravitate iocum tentavit eo quod
>   illecibris erat et grata novitate morandus
>   spectator, functusque sacris et potus et exlex.
>   Verum ita risores, ita commendare dicaces
>   conveniet Satyros, ita vertere seria ludo . . .[17]

In such a passage the satyr ceases to be simply the wild man of the pastoral scene and becomes the urban expression of irreverence and license, the presiding genius of sophisticated satire. Marston has re-worked Guarini's idyllic pastoral in terms of the tragicomic urban satyr rather than the shepherd, so that the surface appearances are bound to be wholly different. The nonpolitical world of Arcadia becomes the charged political confine of an Italian palace (as imagined by Englishmen); the intervention of the gods to fulfill the promise of the oracle becomes a political revolution to overthrow the usurpers and reestablish the legitimate duke.

But these political happenings in *The Malcontent* are tragicomic rather than tragic because Marston has taken from Guarini a primary

---

17. P. 247 in the Laterza edition (1914) in the "Scrittori d'Italia" series. The quotation is from Horace's *Ars Poetica*, ll. 221–226. The passage reads in English: But no one has done better than Horace, who in his poem *Epistle to the Pisos* has described tragicomedy in these verses:

> Hee . . . soone after, forth did send
> The rough rude Satyres naked; and would try,
> Though sower with safetie of his gravitie,
> How he could jest; because he mark'd and saw,
> The free spectators, subject to no Law,
> Having well eat, and drunke (the rites being done)
> Were to be staid with softnesses, and wonne
> With something that was acceptably new.
> Yet so the scoffing Satyres to mens view,
> And so their prating to present was best,
> And so to turne all earnest into jest.

The translation of the Horace is Ben Jonson's (Herford and Simpson, VIII, 319–321).

concern with love, faithful and unfaithful, reworking it in urban terms
and in the context of court intrigue. The danger of death is omnipresent
but no one dies; revenge is limited to satiric ends—the public exposure
of the wicked, assisted self-discovery for those who have lost their moral
bearings, and expulsion for the incorrigible. And this limitation is possible because erotic corruption provides the primary terms for the social
viciousness that issues also in usurpation, atheism, Machiavellian plot-
tings, and intended murder. Mendoza's claim to the throne of Genoa
derives from his exploits in the Medici Duchess's bedchamber; and it
was she who engineered the earlier coup when her husband Piero replaced Altofront, the virtuous and legitimate ruler. The pattern of
loves that Guarini establishes in his play, with the separated ideal pair,
Mirtillo and Amarilli, flanked on one side by the less perfect Silvio and
Dorinda, and on the other by the largely corrupt and opportunist Satyr
and Corisca, is repeated in *The Malcontent,* Altofront and Maria representing the ideal, Pietro and Aurelia the imperfect, Mendoza and
Maquerelle the corrupt. The pattern repeats, but of course the tone
and range of reference is entirely different. The love attitudes of *The
Malcontent* may provide the basic analysis of the material, but every
love attitude turns out to have a train of political consequences. The
ideal love of Altofront and Maria establishes not only an emotional
relationship between individuals but also a model of the political fidelity
of self-consciously righteous sovereigns. The infidelity of Aurelia has
its most poignant treatment as personal loss but its most elaborate
development in terms of political betrayal. And it is in the public sphere
that these relationships are finally fixed—as versions of the political
responsibility that arises from personal integrity.

Marston's satyric bias also leads him to give greater emphasis to the
bottom end of this scale of love than Guarini does. The passages of
Il Pastor Fido that attract Marston's direct imitation (or rather tran-
scription) belong predominantly to the satyr and to Corisca the libertine
nymph. Corisca's *carpe diem* advice is transferred to Maquerelle, the
court bawd, while the satyr provides rhetoric for the cuckold-maker
and usurper, Mendoza. These attitudes toward love thus become political forces. Both Tasso and Guarini give emphasis to nostalgia for a
bella età de l'oro, when tyrant honor did not frustrate natural love-
making. In *The Malcontent* the nostalgia is rather for the old simplicities

of patriarchal rule and family fidelities, before sophisticated female rulers turned political action into sexual intrigue.

The Malcontent is not a freak play standing alone in the dramatic world of its time. It is one of a series of plays that reflect, in the period 1602–1604, a movement away from the grand confrontation with corruption that *Hamlet* had implied and toward the compromises by which justice and forgiveness could be embodied in the action. *Hamlet* had dealt with the overthrow of order when the sovereign mind was dispossessed of command both of the state and of itself. The hero's "disguise" in madness, designed to give him room to maneuver for the cure of corruption, operates in the manner of *The Malcontent* only in that small part of the action dealing with Gertrude. Elsewhere, Hamlet's estrangement from the corrupt court lies under the pressure of the Ghost's command. The answer to corruption implied by Hamlet's verbal control and his conceptual transformation of its images is not allowed to be an adequate response. In the world of Fortinbras and the elder Hamlet only active physical opposition is "real"; the stains of corruption can only be washed out by decimation and a tide of blood. But in the group of later plays with which I am concerned—Shakespeare's *All's Well* and *Measure for Measure,* Marston's *The Malcontent* and *The Fawn,* Middleton's *The Phoenix*—the sovereign mind, though eclipsed and dispossessed of its effortless superiority, is able, in the midst of corruption, to retain an adequate control through disguise and cunning and verbal superiority.

The reason why these plays appear at this time has been discussed at what might seem inordinate length, given the inconclusiveness of the results, especially, of course, Shakespeare's so-called "dark comedies" or "problem plays," which have been seen as resulting from "mythical sorrows" (dark ladies, etc.) or from the new political tone of James's reign. If Guarini's *Il Pastor Fido* is a factor in this change of direction in the Elizabethan public repertory, then the whole movement begins to look more technical, more deliberate than has been supposed. This does not mean, of course, that the vogue of these plays has no connection with the intellectual temper of England in the years 1602–1604. The fact that *Il Pastor Fido* exercised an influence I am prepared to call decisive is in itself a measure of the responsiveness of the time to this exotic model.

The early and seminal influence of *Il Pastor Fido* is focussed for critics of Shakespeare by a number of parallels between that play and Shakespeare's *All's Well that Ends Well*.[18] My sense of the relationship was first stimulated by reading the speech in Act III, scene v, in which the lecherous nymph Corisca advises Amarilli that love is more natural than chastity:

> Qual è tra noi più antica,
> la legge di Diana o pur d'Amore?
> Questa ne' nostri petti
> nasce, Amarilli, e con l'etá s' avanza;
> né s'apprende o s'insegna,
> ma negli umani cuori,
> senza maestro, la natura stessa
> di propria man l'imprime.[19]

18. A connection between the two plays was long ago noticed in passing by J. L. Klein, *Geschichte des Dramas* (Leipzig, 1867), p. 198. Klein, in the course of an extended treatment of *Kusswissenschaft,* mentions the similarity between Dorinda's reluctance to ask openly for the kiss she desires:

Vorrei senza parlar esser intesa (II.ii.61),

and Helena's similar reluctance:

I would not tell you what I would, my lord (II.v.83).

The absence of verbal connection weakens the case here if taken as basic; but given the other examples cited in this article it may be thought to lend confirmatory strength.

19. Pp. 98–99 in the Laterza edition. The 1602 translation is here, as elsewhere, rather curt, and appears to be, if anything, more remote from Shakespeare than the original:

> . . . which is more auncient among us
> *Dianaes* lawes or loues? this in our breasts
> Is bred and growes with vs, *Nature* her selfe
> With her owne hands imprints in our hearts breasts.

(sig. H4)

I am not anxious to use anything in this article as a basis for an assertion that Shakespeare must have known Italian. The evidence suggests that Shakespeare read the original rather than the 1602 translation of *Il Pastor Fido* but is not substantial. It is commonly supposed, of course, that Shakespeare in the years about 1603 read the *Othello* story in Italian (it was not translated into English). A detailed response to the stylistic qualities of *Il Pastor Fido* implies a better reading ability than any made necessary by a capacity to get the gist of Cinthio's story of the moor of Venice, but this is where the existence of the 1602 translation may be important. It is certainly an interesting coincidence that Shakespeare was

We should compare with this the Countess's speech in Act I, scene iii, of *All's Well,* where she comments on the discovery that Helena loves her son:

> If ever we are nature's, these are ours; this thorn
> Doth to our rose of youth rightly belong;
> Our blood to us, this to our blood is born:
> It is the show and seal of nature's truth
> Where love's strong passion is impress'd on youth.
>
> (ll. 120–124)

The general argument that love is natural is, of course, too commonplace to justify any claims of relationship. But it is remarkable that in both authors the theme is particularized by the image of Nature stamping itself (*imprime / impress'd*), as in a seal or a signature, directly on to the physical constitution of the person (*umani cuori / our blood*) and justifying its authenticity by the legal evidence of *propria man* or *show and seal*.[20] Secondary evidence of Shakespeare's knowledge of this passage may be found slightly later in the same scene of *All's Well*. Helena tells the Countess that she will know how to pity her predicament if she herself did ever

> Wish chastely and love dearly that your Dian
> Was both herself and love.
>
> (ll. 203–204)

The antithesis of *Dian* and *love* here is perfectly intelligible. The editors usually tell us that we should substitute *Venus* for *love*. But the English idiom is somewhat strained, since *love* cannot normally mean "the goddess of love." The same idiom is, however, much more acceptable

---

writing *All's Well* in the year of the translation or the year after. The existence of the crib may have made it possible for him to work fruitfully with the Italian as well as the English, deploying the two in a manner familiar to most students of the foreign classics.

20. My colleague, Miss Jennifer Lorch, whose help I sought to uncover the range of meaning in *propria man* writes to me as follows:
"Professor Domenico De Robertis of the Accademia della Crusca confirmed that 'di propria man l'imprime' can be understood in a regal/legal sense with implicit reference to *sigillo*. But he stresssed that this was only one of a number of possible meanings and that there was nothing in the text to support that interpretation rather than another."

in Italian. If Shakespeare had in his mind here Guarini's *la legge di Diana o pur d'Amore,* we would have an explanation of the appearance of the un-English idiom at this point. Exactly the same English wording (*Diana . . . love*) appears, we may note, in the 1602 translation.

A more important connection between the two plays appears to be established in the denouements. Act V, scene iii, of *All's Well* is the first example in Shakespeare and (so far as I know) in Elizabethan drama of a resolution of a dramatic tangle by bittersweet, self-consciously legal and sophistic juggling, where the anagnorisis is achieved by the unwilling testimony of morally dubious characters, dragged out of them in paradoxes by a half-comic, half-punitive method. In *All's Well* this process is presented twice, first with the evidence of Parolles and then with that of Diana. The whole passage is therefore rather long, but I hope it may be represented fairly by the following:

KING

Tell me, sirrah—but tell me true I charge you,
. . . .
By him and by this woman here what know you?

PAROLLES

So please your Majesty, my master hath been an honourable gentleman; tricks he hath had in him which gentlemen have.

KING

Come, come, to th' purpose. Did he love this woman?

PAROLLES

Faith, sir, he did love her; but how?

KING

How, I pray you?

PAROLLES

He did love her, sir, as a gentleman loves a woman.

KING

How is that?

PAROLLES

He lov'd her, sir, and lov'd her not.

KING

As thou art a knave and no knave.

. . . .

KING [to Diana]

This ring, you say was yours?

DIANA

Ay, my good lord.

KING

Where did you buy it? Or who gave it you?

DIANA

It was not given me, nor I did not buy it.

KING

Who lent it you?

DIANA

It was not lent me neither.

KING

Where did you find it then?

DIANA

I found it not.

KING

If it were yours by none of all these ways,
How could you give it to him?

DIANA

I never gave it him.

(V.iii.232 ff.)

In Act V, scene v, of *Il Pastor Fido,* Carino, the supposed father of Mirtillo, uncovers to Montano (the true father—about to sacrifice his son on the altar of Diana) the complex circumstances of Mirtillo's early life, a process that will lead in the end to the discovery of true paternity. The machinery of this anagnorisis is derived from the *Oedipus Rex,* but the tone and detail of the discovery is quite un-Sophoclean:

CARINO
Perché nol generai, straniero il chiamo.

MONTANO
Dunque è tuo figlio, e tu nol generasti?

CARINO
E, se nol generai, non è mio figlio.

MONTANO
Non mi dicesti tu ch'è di te nato?

CARINO
Dissi ch'è figlio mio, non di me nato.
. . . .

MONTANO
Chi è dunque suo padre,
se non è figlio tuo?

CARINO
                        Non tel so dire;
so ben che non son io.

MONTANO
Vedi come vacilli?
E egli del tuo sangue?

CARINO
Né questo ancora.

MONTANO
                        E perché figlio il chiami?
. . . .

MONTANO
Il comprasti? il rapisti? onde l'avesti?

CARINO
In Elide l'ebb'io, cortese dono
d'uomo straniero.

MONTANO
                        E quell' uomo straniero
donde l'ebb'egli?

CARINO

A lui l'avea dat'io.

MONTANO

Sdegno tu movi in un sol punto e riso.[21]

---

21. Pp. 186–187 in the Laterza edition. The 1602 translation reads:

CARINO

I call him Stranger, for I got him not.

MONTANO

Is he thy sonne, and thou begots him not?

CARINO

He is my sonne, though I begot him not.

MONTANO

Didst thou not say that he was borne of thee?

CARINO

I sayd he was my sonne, not borne of mee.

. . . .

MONTANO

How can it be sonne, and not sonne at once?

. . . .

MONTANO

Who is his father since hee's not your sonne?

CARINO

I cannot tell you, I am sure not I.

MONTANO

See how he wauers, is he not of your bloud?

CARINO

Oh no.

MONTANO

Why do you call him sonne?

. . . .

MONTANO

Bought you him? stole you him? where had you him?

CARINO

A courteous straunger in *Elidis* gaue me him.

The obvious verbal connections here are between the "He lov'd her and lov'd her not . . . knave and no knave" and the Italian "figlio e non figlio,"[22] together with the contradictions about possession: "Where did you buy it . . . who gave it you . . . lent it . . . find it . . . give it?" and "It was not given . . . I did not buy it . . . was not lent . . . I found it not . . . I never gave it," set against the Italian "Il comprasti? Il rapisti? onde l'avesti? . . . donde l'ebb'egli?" (with the implied contradiction of the first two and the absurd answer to the last: "[l'ebb'egli] a lui l'avea dat'io"). Shakespeare turns this final paradox into its negative form: Carino claims he does not own the child because he received him from a stranger to whom he had already given him; while Diana denies having given her ring to Bertram, because she never possessed it in such a way as to be able to give it; but the common play on possession and giving links the two, in my mind, in undeniable fashion.

It is worthwhile trying to establish verbal correspondence, for without this it is difficult to argue for a necessary relationship. But much more interesting, from a critical point of view, are the more vague and general points that may be made about the tone of these passages taken as wholes. The final line of the quotation from Guarini makes an important point about this tone:

Sdegno tu movi in un sol punto e riso

The questioner is seen, in terms of the play, as moving, though slowly and circuitously, nearer to the truth, but to himself he seems only to be sinking deeper into paradox and absurdity. The clash of tragic urgency on one side with cumbrous levity on the other establishes a tone important to the tragicomic effect. The tragic potential of the situation is

---

MONTANO

And that same straunger, where had he the childe?

CARINO

I gaue him.

MONTANO

Thou mou'st at once disdain and laughter.

(sig.O4v–P1)

22. Compare the later "guilty and not guilty" paradox (l. 283) and the having a husband but not married situation in *Measure for Measure* (V.i.170–178).

not simply contradicted by the happy ending. Eventually, the collision of two opposed attitudes, *sdegno* and *riso* on one side, and the passionate gravity of the situation on the other, resolves into a sense of the divine dispensation by which the flaunted impossibilities surrounding Carino's son or Diana's ring are shown to belong to a higher simplicity. But before the sudden and unexpected unknotting of the paradoxes an atmosphere of social insolence and moral rejection is powerfully established. From the point of view of Providence, *sdegno* and *riso* may be seen as inevitable parts of human response to its processes, but we are not allowed to forget that in the human terms that provide the substance of the play there is a painful and unbridged gap. The route to the genuine comedy of a providential reestablishment of social cohesion involves a seeming dissolution of order, more alarming than comic. Montano's loss of authority and understanding can only provide, in the asocial world of *Il Pastor Fido,* a muted paradigm. But one can see why the politically self-conscious world of Jacobean drama should seize upon it to express a radical unease. We can think of the uncharacteristic effrontery of Diana to the King at the end of *All's Well:*

> Great King, I am no strumpet, by my life;
> I am either maid, or else this old man's wife.
>
> (V.iii.286–287)

The same uneasy atmosphere pervades what may well have been Shakespeare's next play—*Measure for Measure*—which appears to be, whatever the chronological detail, a second attempt to achieve Guarinian tragicomic effects within an English theatrical context. There are this time, so far as I know, no verbal parallels with *Il Pastor Fido.* Perhaps one should not expect them. The English tragicomic convention of the duke who observes his subjects' license while moving among them in disguise has here almost completely absorbed the Guarinian basis of oracular confusion and discovery. *Measure for Measure* resembles *The Malcontent* (it seems impossible to say which way the debt—if there is any—is owed) not only in its use of this convention, but in its whole approach to political corruption through sexual license. In an even more skeletal form than in Marston's play, it offers the structure of a range of couples who show kinds of loving relationships, extending from perfect through imperfect to corrupt. Clearly, Duke-Isabella achieve the ideal politico-moral position. Claudio-Juliet and Angelo-Mariana may be seen as alternative versions of morally damaged but recoverable relationships (comparable to Marston's Pietro and Aurelia), while Lucio and Kate Keepdown (the eventual representative of the brothel world of Mistress Overdone) mark the nadir of presumably irrecoverable corruption. Shakespeare's characteristic concern for the individual psychology of his characters weakens, however, the exemplary force of the relationships, so that the structural point is hardly evident.

But the most interesting element in relationship to Guarini remains, in *Measure for Measure* as in *All's Well that Ends Well*, the final unknotting. Here again we face the painful process of sifting through absurdities and social solecisms to reach a truth which seems to claim validity almost because of the bizarre processes and paradoxes that its discovery has involved. The role of Lucio in the final scene of *Measure for Measure* has puzzled many critics. His comments seem designed to bring into ridicule the processes of a justice that elsewhere claims a quasi-divine sanction.

Take, for example, Mariana's paradox-laden entry in Act V:

[*Enter Mariana veiled*]

DUKE

Is this the witness friar?
First let her show her face, and after speak.

MARIANA

Pardon, my lord; I will not show my face
Until my husband bid me.

DUKE

What, are you married?

MARIANA

No, my lord.

DUKE

Are you a maid?

MARIANA

No, my lord.

DUKE

A widow, then?

MARIANA

Neither, my lord.

DUKE

Why, you are nothing then; neither maid, widow, nor wife.

LUCIO

My lord, she may be a punk; for many of them are neither maid, widow, nor wife.

DUKE

Silence that fellow. I would he had some cause
To prattle for himself.

LUCIO

Well, my lord.

MARIANA

My lord, I do confess I ne'er was married,
And I confess, besides, I am no maid.
I have known my husband; yet my husband
Knows not that ever he knew me.

LUCIO

He was drunk then, my lord; it can be no better.

DUKE

For the benefit of silence, would thou wert so too!

LUCIO

Well, my lord.

(V.i.167–190)

What is the dramatic point of Lucio's interruptions here? How are they related to the context into which they obtrude? Are we meant to laugh at him or to sigh with the Duke at his ineptitude, feel *riso* or *sdegno*? Given the connection suggested above, we may guess that Shakespeare is here compacting with even greater boldness than in *All's Well* the *sdegno e riso* of Guarini's denouement, together with the providential movement toward understanding and forgiveness. Mariana's paradoxes here resemble those of Carino and of Diana Capilet. But here they are subject not only to the contemptuous disbelief of her questioner but also to the further debasement of Lucio's interpretations. To the world as it really exists, Shakespeare seems to be saying, such high-strained paradoxes of salvation are only dirty jokes. With Donnean brilliance he impacts against the providential figure of the Duke the *contempt* which is shown here as a fully realized figure. What in Guarini is only a fleeting impression of *sdegno,* in *All's Well* only a psychological response, becomes in *Measure for Measure* a man of flesh and blood with a whole social milieu to support him and give him depth of reality. When Lucio pulls the hood from the supposed friar and reveals the duke beneath the cowl, two totally disparate views of what the scene is about are pushed together. For Lucio, slander, evasion, and disguise are the natural processes of society. He knows himself and assumes that the rest of the world shares with him the desire to wriggle out of every responsibility as it arises, without a thought beyond the immediate advantages that are opened up. And, in truth, the un-covering of the situation in *Measure for Measure* cannot be wholly divorced from some such sense of shuffling subterfuge. If we are to see in perspective the quasi-providential and self-denying responses of the Duke and Isabella, we cannot afford to forget the world of Vienna, where the very flesh, through which they too operate, is subject to *sdegno e riso.*

It is a long time since *Il Pastor Fido* read like a crucial text; it is hard for us even to imagine what shock of novelty it could ever have imposed upon its readers. We therefore find ourselves unwilling to allow that it could ever have had a crucial effect on a mind as original and actively creative as Shakespeare's. On the other hand it becomes increasingly clear that Shakespeare's originality operated inside formal and generic assumptions which he shared with his fellow dramatists and which can eventually be fitted into the larger European context. In particular, it begins to appear that his "discovery" of tragicomedy was, in part at least, like that of his fellow dramatists, a discovery of Guarini. Only in his case, however, was the discovery so handled that it gave every appearance of spontaneous personal creation.

"Plot" and "Episode" in Early Neoclassical Criticism

DAVID RIGGS

THE BATTLE of the ancients and the moderns persists in our literary histories. Ever since Sidney's *Apology for Poetry*, critics have been tempted to argue that everything in the various terrain of Elizabethan drama can be assigned to either of two categories: neoclassical or native, elite or popular, academic or professional. During the past fifty years the effort to segregate the two strains has become a vast scholarly project. The earlier part of this century saw full-scale studies of *Early English Classical Tragedies* (1912), *University Drama in the Tudor Age* (1914), *Seneca and Elizabethan Tragedy* (1922), *The School Drama in England* (1929), and *William Shakspere's Small Latine and Lesse Greeke* (1944).[1] Partly in reaction to this emphasis on neoclassical

A version of this essay was delivered at the Shakespeare Institute, Birmingham University, in December, 1973. I wish to thank the Director of the Institute, Professor T. J. B. Spencer, and the members of his faculty-graduate seminar for their suggestions, criticisms, and encouragement.

1. John W. Cunliffe, *Early English Classical Tragedies* (Oxford, 1912); F. S. Boas, *University Drama in the Tudor Age* (Oxford, 1914); F. L. Lucas, *Seneca and Elizabethan Tragedy* (Cambridge, 1922); T. H. V. Motter, *The School Drama in*

sources, more recent works, such as *The Medieval Heritage of Eliza-bethan Tragedy* (1936), *Shakespeare and the Popular Dramatic Tradi-tion* (1944), *Shakespeare and the Rival Traditions* (1952), and *From "Mankind" to Marlowe* (1962), have all stressed the formative influence of "native" traditions.[2] Valuable as these books are, they have all re-inforced the idea that the two categories—neoclassical and native—are mutually exclusive. Stressing the importance of one tradition invariably involves minimizing or rejecting the other. An earlier generation's preoccupation with Udall, and Sackville and Norton, led it to conclude that the morality "can hardly be said to lie in the direct line of evolu-tion between the Miracle and the legitimate Drama," but rather was "an abortive side-effort, which was destined to bear barren fruit."[3] Alfred Harbage, who stresses the importance of playwrights like Preston and Pickering, finds that "the 'landmarks' of the early drama rise not from the mainland but from academic archipelagoes; and the various 'firsts' often prove to be also practically the 'lasts' of their particular kind."[4] In the current, and perhaps definitive, phase of this scholarly debate about what is central to the development of Elizabethan drama, the native tradition is very much in the ascendant. The old *psychomachia*, the "Estates" morality, "moral histories," holiday enter-tainments, and naïve romantic comedies are taken to stand behind the things one values most in Elizabethan drama—Marlowe, Shake-speare, and even Ben Jonson.[5] Interest in Senecan tragedy, in neo-

---

England (New York, 1929); T. W. Baldwin, *William Shakspere's Small Latine and Lesse Greeke* (Urbana, Ill., 1944).

2. Willard Farnham, *The Medieval Heritage of Elizabethan Tragedy* (Berkeley, Calif., 1936); S. L. Bethell, *Shakespeare and the Popular Dramatic Tradition* (Lon-don, 1944); Alfred Harbage, *Shakespeare and the Rival Traditions* (1952; rpt. Bloomington, Ind., 1970); David Bevington, *From "Mankind" to Marlowe* (Cam-bridge, Mass., 1962).

3. John A. Symonds, *Shakespeare's Predecessors in the English Drama* (London, 1884), p. 149. Quoted in Bevington, *From "Mankind" to Marlowe*, p. 1.

4. *Shakespeare and the Rival Traditions*, p. 58.

5. Along with the books by Farnham, Bethell, Harbage, and Bevington men-tioned above, one could cite any number of further instances: John Dover Wilson, *The Fortunes of Falstaff* (London, 1943); *Woodstock: A Moral History*, ed. A. P. Rossiter (London, 1946), Introduction; Bernard Spivack, *Shakespeare and the Allegory of Evil* (New York, 1958); C. L. Barber, *Shakespeare's Festive Comedy*

Terentian comedy and comic theory, and in neoclassical precept is at a low ebb.

In this essay I want to reexamine one aspect of neoclassical tradition, the theory of plot, and to offer some fresh conjectures about its relevance to the Elizabethan popular drama. My purpose is not to strike a blow for the ancients as against the moderns, but rather to suggest that the whole practice of setting the one side against the other has obscured an underlying consistency in the world of sixteenth-century letters.

I

Anyone attempting to locate Seneca and Terence, or Aristotle, Horace, and Donatus, within sixteenth-century dramatic traditions must try to deal with these writers not as we read them today, but as they were read during the Renaissance. At first glance this proviso only seems to heighten the isolation of the neoclassical man of letters. It has often been argued that the Renaissance Aristotle is even more remote from Shakespeare than the Greek original; for the whole neoclassical idea of verisimilitude, which leans heavily on the pseudo-Aristotelian "unities" of time and place, runs quite contrary to the accepted practices of the popular stage. Moreover, the repeated attempts to revive the external conventions of the classical stage—the *nuntius,* the Greek and Senecan choruses, the unities of time and place—never really took hold in the vernacular drama. But there was more to neoclassical theory of plot. The rigid conservatism of the early critics, Madeleine Doran has convincingly argued, is largely a surface impression: "everywhere seeming to agree with him [i.e., Aristotle], they are actually always implying quite different ways of seeing. And in spite of themselves those ways of seeing were formed by the narrative and dramatic traditions of the Middle Ages." The critics repeatedly cite Aristotle's precepts about "unity of action," but they also make provision for "plenty" of action

---

(Princeton, N.J., 1959); Northrop Frye, *A Natural Perspective: The Development of Shakespearean Comedy and Romance* (New York, 1965); and Alan C. Dessen, *Jonson's Moral Comedy* (Evanston, Ill., 1971).

(*copia*), and in this regard "they were at one with the least scholarly-minded of the popular dramatists." [6] So there are grounds for arguing that the Renaissance Aristotle was not conceived in bookish disregard for the native dramaturgy of its day. In many instances commentators took the opposite tack and rewrote Aristotle to suit the popular taste.

The pressure to adapt classical theory was at its most intense when the Renaissance critic dealt with the classical idea of fictional unity. As everyone knows, Aristotle's own remarks on the subject in chapters 7 and 8 of the *Poetics* are fairly uncompromising. The unity of a fictional action arises from the fact that its events succeed one another in logical fashion (*propter hoc* rather than *post hoc,* as Aristotle says in chapter 23), so that every event is implicated in the ongoing chain of causes and effects. In the large-scale periodic structure that comprises the fictional "whole," the *beginning* is an uncaused situation from which something else follows, the *middle* is that which follows logically from the beginning and entails in its turn the *end* from which nothing necessarily follows. Set this paradigm alongside the sixteenth-century popular drama, with its multiple plots, plays-within-plays, and allegorical tableaux, its accessory clowns, dumb shows, and incidental entertainment, and it is clear that some adjustment between theory and practice was inevitable. In Aristotle's ideal plot every incident helps to bring about the single change of fortune on which everything turns. He simply does not make allowance for autonomous events lying on the periphery of the action which present analogous instances of what is happening in the "main" plot.

Aristotle would, of course, allow for the symbolic resonance of an incident such as the "carpet scene" in the *Agamemnon:* crushing the rich tapestries underfoot as he crosses the portal, Agamemnon becomes, for a moment, an emblem of his own destruction. But (and this is the point) Aeschylus allows no disjunction between this symbolic moment and the steady unfolding of the one "action." The destruction of the

---

6. *Endeavors of Art* (Madison, Wis., 1954), pp. 265–266. Miss Doran's suggestion that sixteenth-century critics modified Aristotle's unity of action to suit contemporary taste by their "interpretation of episodes" (p. 273) is the point of origin for this essay. Pages 273–277 of her study anticipate much of what I have to say about the distortion of the *Poetics* in particular.

House of Agamemnon, the man and the possessions that define his status, goes on apace. An Elizabethan playwright would be just as likely to make the point about "waste" by interpolating a scene depicting two drunken soldiers. And however we choose to differentiate between the two kinds of dramaturgy, it seems clear that the "modern" playwright had a sense of allegory, an interest in illuminating the *idea* through whatever sort of episode would best get it across, that is wholly alien to Aristotle.[7] Here the early neoclassical critics faced a crucial choice: either to reject their native literary traditions, which still were conditioned by the digressive and allegorical conventions of the later Middle Ages, or to reformulate the classical, and especially the Aristotelian, theory of plot to the point where it could accommodate those conventions without undue strain. I shall argue that critics took the latter alternative and developed a set of ideas about plot structure that turned ancient terms to modern uses.

The natural starting point for an essay of this kind is the great series of commentaries on Terence, on Horace's *Ars poetica,* and on Aristotle's *Poetics* that were published during the sixteenth century. These provide remarkably thorough discussions of the seminal commonplaces, but they need to be used with care where Elizabethan drama is concerned, because they were all done by Continental scholars. The discussions of comedy affixed to editions of Terence undoubtedly enjoyed the widest circulation, since these were set texts in Tudor grammar schools.[8] The editions of Horace appealed to a more learned circle but the *Ars poetica* was studied at grammar schools (it was universally known in any case), and the commentaries provide our best evidence as to what the sixteenth-century reader made of it.[9] Aristotle's *Poetics* was still an esoteric text in Elizabethan England; we cannot be sure that it ever circulated outside university circles. But Aristotle was an important presence in sixteenth-century letters even where his treatise was unread. Terms, propositions, and fragments of theory from the *Poetics* figure prominently in editions of Horace and Terence that appear from the

7. For the point about the "carpet scene," see John Jones, *On Aristotle and Greek Tragedy* (London, 1962), pp. 85–88.
8. See T. W. Baldwin, *Shakspere's Five-Act Structure* (Urbana, Ill., 1947), pp. 312–346.
9. See Baldwin, *Shakspere's Small Latine and Lesse Greeke,* II, 497–525.

mid-sixteenth century onward. To know those authors (and everyone did) was to know something of Aristotle.[10] Indeed, it is difficult to get at the really seminal propositions in Renaissance criticism by studying any of the ancient critics in isolation; for the specific texts that mattered were those that could be readily translated from one system of critical thought to another.

In developing their ideas about plot, the early neoclassical scholars emphasized four texts that are mostly ignored today, even by critics who are interested in neoclassical theory. These were (1) lines 146–152 of the *Ars poetica,* in which Horace advises the poet to begin *in medias res;* (2) chapter 17 of the *Poetics,* in which Aristotle divides the process of composition into two stages: first the "argument" is worked out, then the "episodes" are added; (3) Aristotle's superficially similar analysis of tragic performances into three nonchoral parts, Prologue, Episode, and Exode (*Poetics,* chapter 12); and (4) Donatus' analysis of Terentian comedy into its three constituent parts, *protasis, epitasis,* and *catastrophe.* The centrality of these passages is amply borne out by the extended sections of interpretation that accompany them both in the commentaries and in the earliest "arts" of poetry. This is in itself a striking fact, since only one of these texts, to our way of thinking, really addresses itself to the theory of plot construction. Donatus does aim to distinguish between the beginning, the middle, and the end in a systematic way. But Aristotle probably has no such intention in either of the two passages just cited, while Horace simply offers a beautifully concise suggestion about where to begin.

We may ask at the outset, then, why commentators and critics were so intent on developing a theory of plot based on these passages. The answer, I believe, is that all of these texts appear to make some division between a "main" plot and a body of accessory material that is "added"

---

10. See Bernard Weinberg, *A History of Literary Criticism in the Italian Renaissance* (Chicago, 1961), I, 111–155 (chap. 4, "The Tradition of Horace's *Ars poetica:* II. The Confusion with Aristotle"); and Marvin T. Herrick, *The Fusion of Horatian and Aristotelian Literary Criticism, 1531–1555* (Urbana, Ill., 1946). Herrick's monograph, *The Poetics of Aristotle in England* (New Haven, Conn., 1930) provides an inventory of direct references to Aristotle in the writings of sixteenth-century English humanists. For the conflation of Aristotle and Donatus, see Baldwin, *Five-Act Structure,* pp. 264–311.

on to it. Of course, Aristotle would not have meant this two-tiered arrangement to apply to the *structure* of the plot, for that is an order in which every successive incident is as "probable or necessary" as the last. But the Renaissance critic did not want to talk about structure in precisely this way. So he took the distinction between main plot and accessory episodes where he could find it and turned it to his own purposes. By virtue of the several interpretations and distortions that we have now to consider, the commentators managed to read each of these four passages as if it were saying roughly the same thing as the other three. In other words, beneath the surface distortions there is an underlying consistency, a privileged theory of fictional form, that does not find an exact parallel in any of these passages, but draws on each of them for its terms and propositions and classical authority.

To summarize the theory briefly: Horace, Donatus, and Aristotle all were supposed to have analyzed fiction in roughly the following way: there is a linear, time-bound "argument" (or main plot) localized at the beginning and the end, and there is a congeries of additional material (retrospective, ornamental, or merely diverting) localized in the middle. The ancient texts provided a selection of descriptive phrases that carried varying inflections within the universe of neoclassical criticism, but the kind of plot being described was, so far as the commentators were concerned, essentially the same regardless of the critic's particular choice of words. In the pages that follow, I will trace the formation of this paradigm in European criticism by looking at a number of passages from commentaries and treatises.

Much of what ensues will deal with minor distortions, misleading cross-references, and overly-ingenious interpretations. Taken as a whole, these small-scale interpretive choices involve an act of literary judgment that is far greater than the sum of its parts. In effect, the sixteenth-century critics were decisively rejecting Aristotle's theory of plot and substituting one of their own contriving. Their theory tried to allow for both the "single action" recommended by Aristotle and Horace *and* the plenitude of diverse exempla that goes into the native allegory and romance. The emergent sense of classical unity defines itself in the containing sequence represented by the beginning and the end, both of which are fixed in a limited expanse of time and space. The residual sense of "multiple unity," to borrow Heinrich Wöllflin's descriptive phrase for late medieval art, persists in the plotless yet illuminating variety of episodes sequestered in the middle.

II

Let us begin with the passage from Horace:

nec reditum Diomedis ab interitu Meleagri,
nec gemino bellum Troianum orditur ab ovo;
semper ad eventum festinat et in medias res
non secus ac notas auditorem rapit, et quae
desperat tractata nitescere posse, relinquit,
atque ita mentitur, sic veris falsa remiscet,
primo ne medium, medio ne discrepet imum.

Nor does he begin Diomede's return from the death of Meleager, or the war of Troy from the twin eggs. Ever he hastens to the issue, and hurries his hearer into the story's midst, as if already known, and what he fears he cannot make attractive with his touch he abandons; and so skillfully does he invent, so closely does he blend facts and fiction, that the middle is not discordant with the beginning, nor the end with the middle.[11]

Horace's advice has to do with the problem of knowing where to begin a story. The skillful poet contrives to notify his readers at the outset about the limits of his fable—about the kind of end they can look forward to—by beginning *in medias res* and filling in the background as he goes along. By beginning with the warning of the oracle, Sophocles sets a finite boundary to what his play is going to accomplish: the discovery and punishment of Laius' murderer. In the concise phrasing of the commentators, "he takes his listener forward as if to things already known." [12]

As scholars undertook to elaborate on Horace's advice and to reconcile it with other parts of literary theory, they incorporated suggestions about plot structure into their annotations. Most of these respond to one peculiar crux in the Horatian formula: those events that constitute

11. *Satires, Epistles, and Ars Poetica,* ed. and trans. H. Rushton Fairclough (London, 1926), pp. 462–463.

12. Giovanni Fabrini, *L'Opere d'Oratio poeta lirico, Comentate da Giovanni Fabrini* (Venice, 1566), p. 374: " . . . e conduce il suo uditore come a cose note."

the bulk of the poem must all be represented within that brief space of time which elapses before the end; yet they must also possess sufficient "magnitude" to sustain a fully developed periodic structure through its beginning, middle, and end. Considered as part of a linear time span, the middle should be brief—so brief that the poem is always at the crisis point or near the end; considered as part of a fictional structure, it should be "big"—big enough to carry its own weight in the over-all design. Horatian scholars resolved this problem by claiming that in the economy of fiction *previous* events (the origins of the story, *ab ovo*) should be brought forward and inserted between the beginning and the end of the poem. The middle should contain plenty of action, but—somewhat paradoxically—this action will not take up any more story time than is required for the retelling of it. *Oedipus Rex,* for example, begins *in medias res* on the morning of the final day, proceeds to recount the beginning of things in the retrospective accounts of Oedipus' life, then concludes with his exposure and downfall. Sophocles' order of events, from middle to beginning to end, "disturbs" the natural order, but corresponds exactly to the beginning, middle, and end of a finished plot. Neoclassical critics refer to this kind of structure as the "artificial" or "poetic" order and, as we know, they thought of it both as a prototype and definition of the fictional plot.[13]

13. For a brief, informative discussion of the artificial order and its importance in neoclassical letters, see Doran, *Endeavors of Art,* pp. 259–265; also see Herrick, *Fusion of Horatian and Aristotelian Literary Criticism,* pp. 16–20. Horace's remarks about order in lines 42–45 of the *Ars poetica* also were used as a basic text from which to expound the artificial order. Following the practice of the commentators, I have treated the two passages as virtually interchangeable; when I refer to commentary on the artificial order, the citation may be to glosses either on ll. 146–152 or on ll. 42–45. The artificial order also figures in the commentaries on Terence. See especially, *Aeli Donati quod fertur commentum Terenti accedunt Eugraphi commentum et Scholia Bembina,* ed. Paulus Wessner (Leipzig, 1902), I, 38: "Perspecto argumento scire debemus hanc esse virtutem poeticam, ut a novissimis argumenti rebus incipiens initium fabulae et originem narrative reddat spectatoribus auctoremque praesentem scilicet ibi exhibeat, ubi finis est fabulae. Hunc enim orbem et circulum poeticae virtutis non modo secuti sunt tragici comicique auctores, sed Homeres etiam et Vergilius tenuerunt." Melancthon makes the same point in his seminal commentary: see Terence, *Poetae lepidissimi comoediae* (Paris, 1552), p. 3. Adrianus Barlandus offers a still more thorough explanation of the artificial order as it applies to Terence in his commentary on the *Andria,*

In order to assess the impact of "artificial order" on Renaissance theory of plot, we shall have to look beyond the rather superficial analyses that the Horatian scholars provided and attempt to excavate some of the assumptions on which they were based. First of all, the responsibility for creating a sense of continuity or "plot" is not evenly distributed throughout the various parts of the whole, as it would be in Aristotle's paradigm. It falls primarily on the beginning, which is supposed to intercept the latent "historical" sequence at the moment of critical change. The poet "hastens to the end because he narrates the beginnings in an 'open' way, so that by them the earlier events may be understood: and he takes his auditor forward as if to things already known."[14] The pressure inevitably relaxes during the middle period; for the middle is not given any functions of this kind, and its contents are distinguishable only insofar as they fall outside the chronological perimeters that form the beginning and the end. In a strictly Aristotelian appraisal, the middle of the artificial order looks quite amorphous, for it is essentially devoid of "paralogical" functions. But this problem does not occur to the Horatian commentators, despite their increasing familiarity with the *Poetics* itself. Instead, they emphasize the pleasure that stems from unforeseeable and eccentric additions in the middle of the story line. "Even if [the poets] return later to earlier events and draw out the tale longer than at first seemed likely," Giason DeNores explains, "nevertheless they give delight."[15] The "middle" of the artificial order, as the commentators see it, is like an amalgam of "episodes."

This reading was ill-informed, but it was important, since it altered the original meaning both of the passage from the *Ars poetica* and of its companion texts in the *Poetics*. The first of these comes from chap-

---

V.iv: again, see the variorum edition published in Paris, 1552, p. 193. These passages are quoted in James E. Robinson, "The Dramatic Unities in the Renaissance" (diss., University of Illinois, 1959), pp. 98–99, 108–110.

14. Fabrini, *L'Opere d'Oratio*, p. 374.

15. *Opera Q. Horatii Flacci . . . commentariis illustrata* (Basel, 1555), p. 1203: "nam etsi ad priora revertuntur, et longius protrahunt narrationem, quam primo videbantur, ita tamen delectant, dum hoc nos quasi errore fallunt, ut ad exitum usque sine fastidio, et satietate, ejus modi etiam cum voluptate perducant, ut id quidem vix sensu percipiatur" (my translation). Hereafter, this work is cited as "Horace, *Opera, 1555.*"

ter 17 in a passage where Aristotle offers some advice about composition: first the poet should frame his "argument" or plot-in-brief and then proceed to flesh it out with "episodes" or accessory incidents. "The argument of the *Odyssey*," he notes, "is not a long one"—Odysseus has been in exile for many years; he eventually returns home and overcomes the suitors who have wasted his substance and plotted his son's death—"everything else in it is episode" (*Poetics* 17. 1455^{b}17-23).[16] To see where the commentators went wrong, it is crucial to bear in mind that Aristotle refers here to two stages in the process of composition but *not* to two (or three) stages of the completed poem as it unfolds in time. He does not, in other words, suggest that a successful work of narrative or drama should itself begin with a brief exposition of the plot, then proceed to a section of episodic materials, and then conclude by bringing the original "plot" to an end. But the parallel between what Aristotle says in chapter 17 and what Horace says about beginning when things are almost over and then digressing in the middle made sense to the commentators precisely because they did read the passage from Aristotle in this highly misleading way.

Why did they fail to get this right? First of all, because they wanted to draw a parallel between Horace-on-Homer and Aristotle-on-Homer. The passage where Aristotle commends Homer for achieving a proper balance between the argument and the episodes affords at least a superficial basis for doing so.[17] Horace praises Homer for beginning near the end and digressing in the middle; Aristotle praises him for keeping the argument brief and interposing a copious variety of episodes. Aristotle's "argument" corresponds to Horace's beginning and end, Aristotle's "episodes" to Horace's displaced middle. This reading originates with the early Italian commentator Vircenzo Maggi, who maintained that Horace was referring to "episodes, which are brought in when the

16. Quoted from *Aristotle's Art of Poetry*, trans. Ingram Bywater (Oxford, 1920). All citations in my text from the *Poetics* are to this translation, hereafter cited as *P*.

17. Commentators also stressed the parallel between the "artificial order" passage and *P* 1459^{a}30-39, where Aristotle praises Homer in similar terms: "As it is, he has singled out one section of the whole; many of the other incidents, however, he brings in as episodes, using the Catalogue of the Ships, for instance, and other episodes to relieve the uniformity of his narrative."

whole story is drawn out."[18] It is well established by the middle of the century.[19]

Quite apart from the sheer exigencies of parallel-hunting, though, the alliance with Aristotle actually puts the artificial order on a far more flexible footing than it had hitherto enjoyed. In the strictly neo-Horatian version, the "middle" of the artificial order consists entirely of retrospective narration. But once critics begin to think of the middle as an amalgam of "episodes," in Aristotle's sense of the term, this section of the poem becomes the natural place to insert a wide variety of digressive materials. As Aristotle's oft-cited discussion of *Iphigenia in Tauris* reveals, a series of "episodes" would include particular incidents, explanations, and "background" material that clarify the story yet remain "outside" the main plot. It would also include, as one learns from chapter 23, ornamental set-pieces, such as the Catalogue of the Ships in the *Odyssey*. In other words, almost any particulars or details not accounted for by a summary outline of the main plot could be absorbed into this part of the play. By this very loose (and quite incorrect) interpretation, Horace and Aristotle would simply be saying that the middle should be full of richly varied entertainment—as it is in medieval romance.

The critics' readiness to modernize classical precepts under the guise of a purified classicism is even more apparent when one considers what the supposed parallelism does to the passage from Aristotle. Taking his language out of context, the commentators foisted upon him a new

18. So Francesco Lovisini:

Madius tamen, huius, et superioris memoriae philosophorum facile princeps, non de ordine hic arbitratur Horatius praecipere, id est, de dispositione poetica, sed de episodiis, quae inducuntur, cum non tota explicatur fabula: ejus autem verba haec sunt. Ut jam nunc dicat, hoc est, ut poeta aliquid narret, quod ad fabulam spectet, jam nunc debentia dici pleraque; differat, id est, quae gratia fabulae sequi deberent, differat atque; aliquid in eorum locum, quod congruat substituat: per hoc enim, quod dicit, pleraque; differat, episodia multa innuit epico carmine inserenda.

Horace, *Opera*, 1555, pp. 1049–1050.

19. See Grifoli's gloss in Horace, *Opera*, 1555, p. 1161: "Brevissima est historia Odysseae, ut ostendit Aristotle. Verum longissima intercedunt Episodia, ut idem testatos, et re ipsa comprobatur." Fabrini's comparable comments may be found in his *L'Opere d'Oratio*, p. 359. See also G. B. Giraldi, *Discorsi . . . intorno al comporre de i Romanzi, delle Comedie, e delle Tragedie* (Venice, 1554), pp. 18–20.

kind of periodic sequence that naturally emerges as a rival to the canonical pair of chapters 7 and 8. The new order proceeds from a preliminary exposition of the argument (the beginning), to a loose congeries of episodes (the middle), to the completion of the original argument (the end). As in the Horatian paradigm, the beginning and the end, as bearers of the "argument," carry the primary responsibility for establishing a sense of probability. The middle has the rather different function of "lengthening out the poem" (*P,* 17. 1455^{b}16–17).

The violence that is done to Aristotle's ideas by this interpretation is writ large in Renaissance editions of the *Poetics.* The thin edge of the wedge, as I have already indicated, is Aristotle's division of the fable into argument and episode (*P* 17. 1455^{a}37^b–24). The crucial fallacy that crops up in most of the glosses on this passage lies in supposing that Aristotle thought of the "episodes" as one distinct part of a periodic structure, rather than a stage in the process of composition. The earliest published commentator, Francisco Robortello, sets the pattern by insisting on the parallel between this passage and the Horatian idea of fictional order. He is followed by Maggi and Lombardi, who see the episodes as essentially parallel to the digressions in a formal oration. They also note that Aristotle uses the same term (*episode*) to describe the middle part of tragedy in his discussion of the so-called quantitative parts in chapter 12: first the Prologue, *then* the Episode, then the Exode. Here again, Aristotle's point about compositional order gets confused with the commentator's assumptions about structural order. (For a full and lucid account of this false parallelism based on Castelvetro, the reader should consult Madeleine Doran's *Endeavors of Art,* pp. 273–277.) The cross-reference to chapter 12 and the "quantitative parts" also appears in the influential commentaries of Castelvetro, Buonamici, and Beni.[20] It was here that Aristotle proved to be totally vulnerable.

---

20. See *Francisci Robortelli . . . in librum Aristotelis de Arte poetica explicationes* (Florence, 1548), p. 201; *Vincentii Madii . . . et Bartholomaei Lombardi . . . in Aristotelis librum de poetica communes explicationes* (Venice, 1550), pp. 190–191; Francesco Buonamici, *Discorsi poetici Nella Accademia Fiorentina in difesa d'Aristotile* (Florence, 1597), p. 61; *Pauli Benii . . . in Aristotelis poeticam commentarii* (Padua, 1613), p. 434. These texts are hereafter cited by the name of the editor, or editors, and the year of the edition—"Robortello, 1548," etc.

About half-way through his discussion of the tragic plot, Aristotle writes:

The parts of Tragedy to be treated as formative elements in the whole were mentioned in a previous chapter [i.e., chapter 6]. From the point of view, however, of its quantity, i.e., the separate sections into which it is divided, a tragedy has the following parts: Prologue, Episode, Exode, and a choral portion. . . . The Prologue is all that precedes the Parode of the chorus; an Episode all that comes in between two whole choral songs; the Exode all that follows after the last choral song (P 12. 1452^{b}14–23).

Disregarded today, this text was universally cited during the Renaissance. The modern commentator will rightly point out that this particular section of the *Poetics* does not, in fact, deal with the structure of tragedy in any literary sense at all; it merely sets forth certain facts and terms pertinent to the staging of tragedies in the Greek theater.[21] The Renaissance critic thought otherwise. For him, this passage was important not because of what it said in its own right, but because it served as a crossroads for a cluster of texts dealing with plot structure. Indeed, its conceptual poverty may paradoxically help account for its rich development in the commentaries. For once, Aristotle provides merely a list of terms, terms that found imprecise and suggestive echoes in rhetorical treatises, in Donatus, and in other parts of the *Poetics*. As a result, critics were free to synthesize under the ubiquitous headings of Prologue, Episode, and Exode most of the essential precepts that dealt with the structure of drama as they understood it.

Thus, the "argument" and "episode" that Aristotle describes in chapter 17 became virtually interchangeable with the Prologue and Episode of chapter 12. The confusion between "argument" and "Prologue" arises because the commentators took the latter term in its rhetorical sense. Like the proem of an oration, the Prologue or first part of the play gives a brief preliminary exposition of the issues that are to be treated in the work as a whole. And by this definition it naturally seemed to resemble the brief plot-summary ("argument") that Aristotle takes as the poet's starting point in chapter 17. The further confusion of "episodes" and the Episode, as Professor Doran has painstakingly shown,

---

21. Gerald F. Else argues that it is suspect on textual grounds as well. See *Aristotle's Poetics: The Argument* (Cambridge, Mass., 1957), pp. 359–363.

follows from Aristotle's own failure to distinguish explicitly among his manifold uses of this slippery term. The sixteenth-century editor naturally reasoned that Aristotle would want to put the episodes in the Episode or middle part of the poem. And here again he reconfirmed the misreading by remembering that the argument comes before the episodes, while neglecting to notice that the point about priority refers only to the order of composition. So each passage turned into a mirror image of the other, and once again the new whole was greater than the sum of its misconstrued parts. Read in the light of chapter 12, the argument-episodes formula turns into a clear periodic structure with the episodes firmly entrenched in the middle. Read in the light of chapter 17, the undifferentiated technical terms of chapter 12 take on definition and point. The Prologue gives a brief introductory outline of the plot; the Episode consists of digressive and ornamental passages. The basic transference of terms begins with Robortello, who assigns the brief version of the plot (argument) to the Prologue, while the "part added to the argument which has been proposed" becomes the Episode. It reappears in the influential commentaries of Maggi and Lombardi, Castelvetro, Buonamici, and Beni, and, as we shall see, leaves its mark on the basic vocabulary of sixteenth-century criticism.[22]

Looming behind this whole misinterpretation of Aristotle was yet another paradigm, the neo-Terentian division of comic plots into protasis, epitasis, and catastrophe, which corroborates all of the local distortions we have been following. The frequency with which scholars were taken in by the superficial similarity between Donatus'

---

22. Robortello, 1548, pp. 119–120; Maggi and Lombardi, 1550, p. 149:

Sciendum est, Tragoediam (pro faciliori verborum Aristotelis intelligentia) in tres partes commode secari posse, in Proemium, Exodum, et in id, quod ab his duobus extremis clauditur. In prooemio fabulae scopus, atque propositum, et si non exacte, modo tamen quodam aperitur; adeo ut qua de re agendum fit intelligi possit. ut in Oedipode tyranno, quod Oedipus vult Laii interfectorem investigare, ut eum debito supplicio afficat. hoc in prooemio ponitur. In exodo vero ea, quae secuta sunt, ex tali investigatione mortis Laii, verbi causa Jocastae suspensionem, et Oedipus caecitatem. et hoc in exodo. In parte vero intermedia ponitur tota illa negociatio, atque investigatio. quae cum habeat cantus choricos ad relaxandos animos audientium permixtos.

And see Buonamici, 1597, p. 61; Beni, 1613, p. 319. For Castelvetro, see Professor Doran's account, cited in my text.

nomenclature and Aristotle's does not require any comment here.[26] Behind the facade of imprecise cross-references, though, the critics forged
some important links between neo-Terentian precept and the ideas about
dramatic form that were germinating in commentaries on Horace and
Aristotle. The functions assigned to each "part" of the plot in all three
traditions were highly comparable; and the synthesizing of Donatus
and Aristotle served mainly to consolidate the points of likeness while
suppressing the differences.

The stress fell upon the seminal phrases from the *De comoedia* and
from the *Evanthius de fabula*.[24]

Protasis is the first act of the play, in which part of the argument is un-
folded, part concealed so as to hold the expectation of the audience; epitasis
the involution of the argument, by the elegance of which it is knotted together; catastrophe the solution of the play, through which its outcome is
made good.

(De comoedia)

The protasis is the first act, and beginning of the drama. The epitasis is the
increase and progression of the turbations and the whole, as I might say,
knot of the error. The catastrophe is the conversion of affairs into a happy
ending.

(Evanthius de fabula)

Commentators may well have begun by assuming that these phrases
must correspond to Aristotle's quantitative parts simply because the two
sets of terms looked alike. But even as the hypothesis was formed, they
must also have found that everything in their emergent interpretation
of the quantitative parts fell into place within the Terentian framework.
The key phrases from Donatus and Evanthius were like so many route-
markers, pointing in the direction of Aristotle's remarks about "argument" and "episode," and—more distantly—to the beginning-digressing-
and-ending syndrome of neo-Horatian theory. When, for example, the
critic took Evanthius' definition of the protasis—a preliminary exposition of the argument, anticipating its eventual outcome—and compared

23. See Baldwin, *Five-Act Structure*, pp. 264–311. Besides the commentaries on
Aristotle cited by Baldwin, see Buonamici, 1597, p. 65; Beni, 1613, p. 324; and
Antonio Riccoboni, *Poetica Aristotelis, ab Antonio Riccobono Latine conversa*
(Padua, 1587), pp. 61–63.

24. The translated passages are quoted from Baldwin, *Five-Act Structure*, p. 33.

it to Aristotle's Prologue, he must have noticed that this made a close parallel to the definition of the "argument" that Aristotle provides in chapter 17 of the *Poetics*.[25] Similarly, the familiar definition of the epitasis as "an intension [literally, a 'stretching out'] and exaggeration of matters" would inevitably call to mind Aristotle's discussion of "episodes" and his observation that they serve to "lengthen out" the plot to its proper magnitude (*P* 17. 1455^{b}2–3). The epitasis was also supposed to take in a marked diversity of styles ("many kinds of style, and those intermixed in short sections, and then suddenly broken off," as Willichius explains it),[26] and this requirement links up with Aristotle's observation that episodes "relieve the uniformity" of the main plot (*P* 23. 1459^{a}37–39). Finally, Donatus' famous description of the epitasis as a "knot of error" (*nodum erroris*) evokes a further set of parallels between the complication and the unravelling (*P* 18), the epitasis and the catastrophe, the Episode and the Exode.

Reduced to simple diagram, the whole network of parallels and cross-references looks like this (the "parts" in each of the vertical columns can be thought of as roughly analogous to one another):

Horace, *Ars*	Beginning	Middle	End = historical order
poetica,	Middle	(Beginning)	End = artificial order
ll. 146–152			
Poetics,	Argument	Episodes	(order of
chap. 17			composition)
Poetics,	Prologue	Episode	Exode (stage
chap. 12			movements)
Donatus, *De*	Protasis	Epitasis	Catastrophe
comoedia			

This schematic arrangement inevitably oversimplifies matters. No one supposed that the "plot" simply disappears during the middle of a play.

25. The parallel was unavoidable, since the Terentians, like the Aristotelians, saw the first "part" of drama as analogous to the rhetorical proem or *narratio*. For the confusion between Aristotle's use of 'Prologue' in chapter 12 and the rhetorical sense of the term, see, for example, the passage from Maggi and Lombardi given at note 24 above. Compare Robortello, 1548, p. 118; Riccoboni, 1587, pp. 60–63; and Beni, 1613, p. 319. The conflation of Donatus' *protasis* and the rhetorical *propositio* is pointed out in Baldwin, *Five-Act Structure*, p. 177.

26. Quoted and translated in Baldwin, *Five-Act Structure*, p. 241.

And critics would not have regarded all of these elements as being strictly interchangeable. They knew perfectly well, for example, that Aristotle's "episode" carried different nuances in different chapters of the *Poetics*. They made rather little of the parallel between Horace's "artificial order" and Donatus' threefold division (which is not surprising, since Horace's recommendation of the five-act structure made the more obvious parallel to Donatus in any case). Taken in its entirety, though, this network of texts and glosses represents the most ample and highly integrated theory of plot to emerge during the sixteenth century. Of course it is difficult to be absolutely certain about the opinions of a writer like Robortello, Maggi, or Buonamici. When they juxtapose lines from Horace to a text from the *Poetics,* the actual point that is being made may correspond to neither passage but lie somewhere in the interstices between them. However, one premise usually holds good: this middle ground is a suitable place to argue that the ideal fictional order is one of beginning, digressing, and ending. I think we must allow that the sixteenth-century critic did not find his way to this position by merely accidental judgments. The reinterpretation of Aristotle, in particular, is so ingenious and methodical that the scholars who devised it must have had a fairly clear idea of what they wanted him to say.

The complement to the learned commentaries are the "arts" of poetry and treatises on drama written by such men as Giraldi, Minturno, and Rossi. All of these derive from the editions of Horace, Aristotle, and Terence, and from the rhetoricians, but they enjoy one advantage over the parent volumes. Since these treatises dispense with the format of serial commentary, the authors have to make some effort to see their subject as a whole. What they have to say about plot does not differ a great deal from comparable passages in the commentaries. But they do bring into focus the main problems for critical theory. What exactly is the common ground shared by the argument and the episodes? What kind of relatedness binds together the main plot and its accessory materials? It is easy to see why the sixteenth-century critic would have missed Aristotle's point that every incident should follow from its antecedent in "probable or necessary order," for this criterion is alien to late medieval narrative and drama. It is not so easy to decide what criterion he might have put in its place. "Unity of action" is a perennial problem for literary theory; the sixteenth-century critic finally had to resolve it on his own terms. By looking at some representative passages from the criticism of Minturno and Giraldi, we can get a clearer picture of the kind of solution that the early neoclassical writers had in mind.

Minturno's *L'Arte poetica* (1563) makes a good starting point because he keeps his discussion on a practical plane. His object is to differentiate clearly between two sorts of material, *favola* and *episodii*, and to describe their functioning within particular plays. The fable is a very simple thing. In Terentian comedy, for example, it comprises "una sola faccende," the victory of the son and parasite over the father, which results in the marriage of the principals. Everything else is episode. The use of minor characters to elicit background information or to "enrich the poem" and "increase the pleasure" falls into this category. Narrative set-pieces about previous events form yet another species of episode (as in the artificial order): they "adorn and enlarge the poem, and they are extraordinarily pleasing."[27] When Minturno goes on to analyze Terence's *Andria,* he treats the previous life of the principals, the entire subplot involving the second pair of lovers, and the "Tormento" of the intriguer as further varieties of episode. Like any critic of the Renaissance, he knows far more about Terence than any other classical dramatist, but, he also recognizes that the kind of structure he is describing resembles the Old Comedy of Aristophanes.

And, as in any comedy they [episodes] are more frequent than in tragedy: so in the old [comedy] they occur most frequently of all. Therefore, while all comic writers bring in many things that fall outside the plot, so as to give pleasure to the onlookers, nevertheless the old ones, as they have the freedom to scold and to "bite" [satirize] their neighbor, cover a more large and spacious ground, and jest with more liberty.[28]

Minturno proceeds to analyze Aristophanes' *Plutus* into its argument and episodes. The analysis comprises little more than a plot summary

27. Antonio Minturno, *L'Arte poetica* (Venice, 1563), pp. 122–126.

28. "E, come che in ogni Comedia sieno piu spessi, che nella Tragedia: pur nella vecchia spessissimi si trovano. Perchioche, quantunque tutti i Comici per dar piacere a riguardanti molte cose fuori della favola introducano: nondimeno gli antichi, come havevano licenza di riprendere, e di mordere altrui: cosi discorreano per piu largo, e spatioso campo; e con maggior liberta mottegiavano." My translation from Minturno, *L'Arte poetica,* p. 123.

of the play, but there is enough to indicate that Minturno's judgment is sound. Aristophanes takes a very simple plot line—an honest countryman comes upon Plutus, god of riches, and cures him of his blindness—and enlarges it by adding numerous characters who pertain to the satire on wealth. So long as one thinks of comedy as an amalgam of episodes contained within a single "action," Aristophanes makes a better model than Terence. Minturno's reference to Old Comedy is especially revealing. Since Minturno's interpretation of Aristotle leads him to put the diverse episodes, rather than the single action, at the center of things, he cannot grasp "unity of action" in the classical sense at all. The logic of his position inevitably leads him toward the "multiple unity" of late medieval allegory and romance—a unity of diverse exempla, grouped around a single unifying theme. The *vetus comoedia,* which mingles allegorical figures, mythological personages, and shrewdly realistic character portrayals is the one form of ancient drama that actually does develop this kind of unity; hence Aristophanic comedy offers a genuine parallel to the "hybrid" forms of sixteenth-century drama, such as the morality, the allegorical romance, and the mythological pastoral, where Sophocles and Terence do not. (Ben Jonson may have been mindful of this peculiar affinity between the neoclassical and the native when, in the Induction to *Every Man Out of His Humour,* he announces his intention to imitate the *vetus comoedia.*) When Minturno praises the Old Comedy because it gives the playwright more freedom to invent episodes than do the regular forms of classical comedy and tragedy, he is using Aristotle's language to confute Aristotelian precept, while sketching in a classical precedent for the truly native forms of Renaissance drama.

Giraldi also assigns the episode a central place in his discussions of plot, but, unlike Minturno, he keeps the overarching structure of "quantitative parts" firmly in view. He sees the episodes not as a form of pure entertainment brought in to enliven the argument at random moments, but rather as one distinct element in a three-part structure.

I do not want you to think that the Episode, or the digression, as we call it, is the kind of digression that does not contain in itself part of the plot. Rather, that entire stretch of the plot which we have spoken of is called "Episode" because the part that is contained between the two ends (the ends are the Prologue and Exode as has been noted) is most apt and suitable to receive digressions. These very digressions, however, contain, mixed in themselves, that part of the plot [i.e., the Episode] on which they are based: so that, however much the poet ranges over commonplaces, such as praising, blaming, consoling, reproving, counseling, in his episodes, they ought to conclude with the subjects of the plot [*cose della favola*]; as the choruses of Seneca do also, which I judge (as Erasmus already has, and wisely) to be more praiseworthy than all those of the Greeks . . .[29]

Like Minturno, Giraldi retains a deep attachment to the digressive and allegorical modes of late medieval romance. In the earlier part of his *Discorsi*, which deals with the romanzi of Ariosto and Sannazaro, he grants the poet "a liberal space for making episodes, i.e., pleasing digressions" (p. 25), even though this means discarding the single action recommended by Aristotle. In this passage he manages to resolve the apparent contradiction by proposing that when the individual digressions are taken as a group and sequestered in the middle (the section "most apt to receive them") they become a functioning part of the plot from which they digress. Like the Senecan chorus, they must distinguish themselves from the main action in order to achieve a distinct perspective on it. (The Greek choruses, on the other hand, speak more as participants within the main action.) In other words, it seems fairly clear that Giraldi, like Minturno, conceived of the episodes as incidents which enlarge upon the *themes* of the play even as they digress from its *plot;* and this interpretation confirms our suspicion that the pseudo-Aristotelian "episode" is the Trojan horse that imports the allegorical unity of late medieval literature into the middle of the classical plot. At the same time, the distinctive frame of reference secured by the two *termine,* Prologue and Exode (the one "a summary of the plot," p. 249,

---

29. My translation from Giraldi, *Discorsi,* p. 252:

Ne voglio che voi crediate che l'Episodio, o la digressione, che la chiamiamo, sia cosi digressione, che non habbia in se parte della favola. Ma si chiama Episodio tutto quel tratto della favola, c'habbiam detto, perche la parte che tra que due termini si contiene (i quali termini sono il Prologo, e l'Essodo, come s'e detto) e attissimo et convenevolissimo a ricevere le digressioni. Lequali pero hanno in se mescolata quella parte di favola, che e lor fondamento: che quantunque il Poeta ne gli Episodii scorra in cose comuni; come lodare, biasimare, confortare, riprendere, consigliare; debbono nondimeno terminare nelle cose della favola, come anco fanno i Chori di Seneca, i quali giudico io (come gia se Erasmo, e giudiciosamente) molto piu degni di loda, che quelli di tutti i Greci.

the other "a way of settling the plot," p. 253) puts a clear limit on the cultivation of *cose commune* for their own sake. The digressive sections should conclude with *cose della favola*. Episodes provide bulk and ornament; the argument provides those predefined limits which give shape and consistency to the whole.[30]

III

I think that this attempt to treat "plot" and "episode" as distinct varieties of fictional experience, joined together in a single poem, carries over into the construction of Elizabethan plays. Now, the reader may agree that these theories appertain to badly constructed plays, but he will probably entertain some doubts about their relevance to the more highly integrated drama of Shakespeare and Jonson. Madeleine Doran takes this position, and her reasoning is very cogent.

The effect of these modifications and extensions of the sense of "episode" is to narrow the interpretation of "the action" to the main outline of the story and to enlarge the sense of "episode" to include all the detail, whether extraneous or not. And the logical consequence of this interpretation is that far from constricting anyone's impulse to variety, it enlarges it. . . . if these episodes need be there only to give delight, not to clarify the fable, then you may have as many episodes as the physical length of your play will allow you.[31]

These remarks bring out the intrinsic weakness of beginning, digressing, and ending. The paradigm allows such a wide variety of accessory materials, and pays so little attention to the relationship that obtains between these materials and the main plot, that it looks suspiciously like a mere pretext for avoiding the problem of form altogether.

The crux of the matter lies in the precise form of the attachment between the "probable or necessary" sequence that comprises the main plot and the episode which is "added on" to it. A number of descriptive terms and phrases are at hand in Renaissance criticism. Episodes "fill in" and "enlarge" the plot; they "enrich" and "adorn" it; they "clarify" and "illuminate" it; they are linked to it "according to verisimilitude."

30. Niccolo Rossi's *Discorsi . . . intorno alla Comedia* (Vicenza, 1589) and *Discorsi . . . intorno alla Tragedia* (Vicenza, 1590) include chapters on the quantitative parts that are comparable to these sections in Minturno and Giraldi.

31. *Endeavors of Art*, pp. 276–277.

Before trying to determine what these words mean in this context, I think we must agree with Miss Doran that they do *not* entail the sort of verisimilitude that Aristotle has in mind in his discussion of *Iphigenia in Tauris*. That is, the Renaissance critic did not think of the episodes as an interlocking chain of incentives, motivations, and explanations which assist the serial development of the main plot.

Miss Doran concludes that Renaissance criticism does not provide *any* satisfactory answer to the question we are raising. The real use of episodes, she finds, was to give "delight" through "copie" (p. 276). Her conclusion doubtless holds good in certain cases. There are second-rate critics, like Pino da Cagli, who seem to feel that a mindless proliferation of colorful incidents makes for good drama.[32] There are dull plays, like Peele's *Edward I,* that follow this recipe. But the terms that I have put between quotation marks have extremely misleading connotations for modern readers. They derive from a rhetorical theory of ornament that is largely unfamiliar to us, despite the pioneering work of Rosemond Tuve. As she has shown, the pursuit of copie and delightfulness is always subordinate to a "criterion of significancy" in Renaissance poetic. "Exuberance without point is not called delightful," as Miss Tuve remarks, nor do sixteenth-century theorists ever depart "from a conception of 'texture' as unquestionably *logically* relevant."[33] When Renaissance critics say that a copious variety of episodes "adorns," "enriches," or "illuminates" the argument, I think that some form of similitude between the fable and the episode is usually implied. The relationship is a logical one, but it is to be explained by a logic of resemblance rather than a logic of cause and effect. The aptness of the analogies, rather than the intrinsic vividness of the material, is what "delights" the discerning spectator. The same criterion would apply when the critics compare episodes to rhetorical digressions. The skillful orator digresses not to amuse his audience but to embellish his cause.[34]

The Renaissance commentators did not understand what Aristotle

---

32. See his *Discorso . . . intorno al componimento della Comedia,* appended to S. di'Oddi, *L'Erofilomachia* (Venice, 1578).

33. *Elizabethan and Metaphysical Imagery* (Chicago, 1947), pp. 138, 113.

34. See Quintilian, *Institutio oratoria,* ed. and trans. H. E. Butler (New York, 1921), Book IV, chap. 3. Giraldi probably draws on this chapter in the passage cited above, n. 29.

meant by "unity of action," but neither did they fall into a heretical doctrine of variety for variety's sake. Giraldi's description of episodes as "commonplaces" that "conclude with the subjects of the plot," like Minturno's reference to the topical organization of Old Comedy, suggests a different function altogether. Even though the episodes do not assist the serial development of the plot, they are meant to tell us *something* about it. They enlarge the argument at the level of its themes by giving us additional perspectives on its subject matter. In the current critical jargon, they "comment on" the main plot. If this interpretation is correct, the early neoclassical critic had a fairly sophisticated grasp of Renaissance dramatic convention. The subplot of a play such as *The Changeling* is a hopeless irrelevancy by Aristotelian standards, but it succeeds brilliantly as a variation on the theme of love and madness. Conversely, *Edward I* fails because this kind of logical relationship between plot and episode is totally lacking. There is no reason to suppose that Giraldi would not have seen that Middleton's play is more artful than Peele's. There *were* restrictions on the Elizabethan playwright's "impulse to variety," and Renaissance criticism seems to have been aware of them.

During the middle of the sixteenth century, Aristotle's reign had not yet begun in earnest. As a result, criticism was probably better equipped to deal with such devices as "mirror scenes," "umbrella speeches," the multiple plot, the play-within-a-play, and comic burlesques of serious themes than it has been at any time until the twentieth century. It was understood that these devices served to "amplify" (we would say, to "symbolize") issues latent in the dramatic fable—that drama would be "thin" if this dimension were lacking. I think these critics of four centuries ago would have enjoyed the subplots of *Volpone* or *A Midsummer Night's Dream* just as we do, and for many of the same reasons.

Nevertheless, sixteenth-century critics show no interest whatever in the kind of formal unity that fascinates modern exegetes of the "double plot." They could scarcely have done so and still held that the "main" plot's sole function is to create a sense of "probable or necessary order." William Empson's brilliant analyses presuppose that *both* plots "embody" or illustrate general meanings. While this kind of interpretation can reveal an extraordinary degree of integration among the various episodes of a single play, it does require us to jettison the traditional idea of "plot" altogether. Renaissance scholars would surely have objected that literary theory stood to lose more than it gained by this procedure. And one presumes that they would raise similar objections to modern theories of "spatial form" and the play as poem.

The sixteenth-century critics' commitment to *unity* of structure was genuine, but it had its limits. They thought that there should always be some "connection"—some thread of meaning or motivation—linking one incident to another. But they would not have known how to unify an entire play under one formal concept. Since Aristotle's proviso that the episodes should have no autonomy with respect to the plot went unheeded, unity of action was never really understood. On the other hand, Aristotle's insistence that the self-contained "main" plot should obey its own autonomous logic of act and consequence did make a strong impression. Consequently, it never occurred to these critics to look for a *figural* unity among the various parts of the play, even though the native tradition of medieval allegory might have encouraged them to do so. It is only modern scholars who have discovered that plays might be about such matters as "revenge" or "forgiveness" or "justice."

It is difficult to theorize about the "unity" of a dramatic poem without first accounting for the expressive device that does the synthesizing. There has to be some *modus operandi* whereby "plot" and "episode" become one. Early neoclassical scholars did not ignore this problem, but they did not pursue it with much zeal either. When Minturno and Giraldi are called upon to define the two terms, they simply treat them as two categories of experience. They assume that their readers will want a list of the items that fall under each heading. Their internal relation to one another is finally less important than their external relation to different aspects of reality. In other words, "plot" and "episode" are primarily a means to secure completeness of representation. Terence is a good model because he always contrives to include both a single action *and* plenty of episodes. The two parts should be integrated, but not so highly integrated that either loses its distinct character. The single "necessity" of the plot, the associative "richness" of the episodes, are finally qualities that reveal themselves through juxtaposition and contrast.

If these principles are really applicable to Renaissance drama, then modern criticism, like the Aristotelianism that it supplanted, may be

looking for an aesthetic unity that is belied by the plays themselves.
To argue that dramatists consistently wrote within the framework that
I have described would take me well beyond the scope of this essay.
I simply want to propose that these definitions of "plot" and "episode"
correspond to some familiar conventions in late sixteenth-century drama.

Elizabethan plays often begin by involving a few central characters
in some situation that must come to an end within a limited period of
time. Faustus promises to give the Devil his soul after twenty-four years
have elapsed. Antonio agrees to pay Shylock three thousand ducats or a
pound of his flesh within three months' time. Caesar is told to beware
the Ides of March: on that day the senators will either crown him or
assassinate him. Theseus tells the four Athenian lovers that they must
resolve their quandary by the next change of the moon. By establishing
a *terminus ad quem,* these arrangements delineate a "probable or necessary" order of events to be completed in the course of the play. The
completed sequence will comprise the "argument." Those characters
who participate in the argument must abide by certain rules. They have
to be in certain places, and perform specific tasks, within the allotted
limit of time. And these rules are binding on the playwright as well.
In order for the argument to be verisimilar, his solution has to fall
within the limiting conditions set forth at the outset.

These plays also embody a wealth of material that lies "outside the
plot." We have already seen that it is possible to list and classify such
materials. I will not weary the reader's patience with yet more in-
ventories. A few representative instances will have to suffice. Faustus'
servant Wagner raises two devils, Banio and Belcher, in order to bind
the clown Robin to him for seven years. Shylock's daughter Jessica
elopes, steals Shylock's casket, and pawns his wedding ring. Calphurnia
dreams of Caesar's statue spouting blood. As the four Athenian lovers
seek each other in the woods, the mechanicals rehearse a play about two
lovers who met by the city walls and were devoured in the "jaws of
darkness." Anyone who knows how to read Elizabethan drama will see
that these episodes "amplify" the main plot by restating its central
motifs. A logic of resemblance applies in every case. But a consistent
principle of differentiation is also at work here. The episodes are essentially unlike the main plot in that they are exempt from the rules
that apply there. They do not have beginnings and ends, and they do

not appear in any probable sequence or have any likely consequences. Wagner's experiments in demonology do not imply anything about anyone's ultimate salvation, nor, for that matter, do Faustus' banal displays of magic during the middle acts. Lorenzo and Jessica are the spendthrift aesthetes who do not enter into any bonds: they simply drift from place to place. Calphurnia's dream is completely enigmatic and Caesar will go to the senate despite her warning. Pyramus and Thisbe die, but only in sport. The episodes are "outside the plot" in that they do not affect the main action one way or the other, but, more importantly, they are outside the whole *concept* of plot.

If one tries to explain the excellence of these plays by appealing to a concept of formal unity—whether it be a unity of action or an "organic" unity—the results are likely to be disappointing. There is a realm of act and consequence; there is a realm of reflection and restatement. Criticism can trace the linkages between them, but it must also acknowledge that they are formally distinct. The outcome of the plot is "probable or necessary"—but only on its own terms. The episodes remind us that other versions of this story are conceivable, that other outcomes might have been possible.

Shakespearean criticism is happily beyond its period of monistic Aristotelianism. No one supposes any longer that the Porter is "extraneous" to *Macbeth*. But our own "symbolic" interpretation of Shakespeare falls into its own kind of monism by treating "plot" as a kind of metaphor. The sixteenth-century critic's attempts to apportion "plot" and "episode" among the various acts of a play may well strike us as clumsy or naïve. But the distinction that he tried to draw was an authentic one, and it carries over into the drama written by his contemporaries. If we simply choose to neglect it, our criticism runs the risk of unifying perspectives that were originally meant to be sharply diverse.

The Early Spanish Drama: From Medieval Ritual to Renaissance Art

CHARLOTTE STERN

. . . we shall renounce the theatrical superstition of the text and the dictatorship of the writer. . . . And thus we rejoin the ancient popular drama, sensed and experienced by the mind without the deformations of language and the barrier of speech.

Antonin Artaud

A playwright who writes only the lines uttered in a play marks a long series of culminating moments in the flow of the action. . . . The lines of the play are the only guide a good director or actor needs. What makes the play the author's work is that the lines are really the highlights of a perpetual, progressive action, and determine what can be done with the piece on stage.

Susanne K. Langer

H ISTORIANS OF THE EARLY SPANISH THEATER all make the same startling observation: there are no dramatic texts in Castilian between

This paper is an expanded version of a talk presented at the Spanish 3 session of the Modern Language Association convention in Chicago, December 28, 1973. I wish to express my appreciation to Professor John Lihani of the University of Kentucky for inviting me to participate in the program and for reading several versions of this study.

the twelfth-century *Auto de los Reyes Magos* (Play of the Magi)[1] and four short dialogue pieces by the fifteenth-century poet Gómez Manrique.[2] This baffling and frustrating state of affairs has sent scholars scurrying to Spain to comb libraries, churches, and monasteries for manuscripts—concrete evidence that would confirm the existence of a medieval theater. Richard Donovan has made the most exhaustive search, but he has returned almost empty-handed. Reluctantly, he concludes that in the Middle Ages Spanish churches and cathedrals knew only minimal dramatic activity.[3] Fernando Lázaro Carreter and Humberto López Morales also suggest a kind of theatrical stagnation which, they contend, explains the rudimentary quality of Gómez Manrique's pieces. John Lihani, however, undaunted by the absence of texts, postulates the existence of Spanish performances, including popular farces and mummers' plays, that predate the inclusion of dramatic tropes in the Christian liturgy.[4] An entirely plausible explanation for these seemingly incompatible views lies in the recognition of two distinct types of drama: drama as ritual or social pastime, in which recorded dialogue is incidental or nonexistent, and drama as art or literature, in which the written text is paramount.

1. Actually, the Magi piece may not be an authentic Spanish creation but a translation or *refundición* (reworking) of a French or Provençal original. In this regard see Winifred Sturdevant, *The Misterio de los Reyes Magos: Its Position in the Development of the Medieval Legend of the Three Kings* (Baltimore, Md., 1927), and Rafael Lapesa, "Sobre el *Auto de los Reyes Magos:* Sus rimas anómalas y el posible origen de su autor," *Homenaje a Fritz Krüger* (Mendoza, 1954), II, 591–599.

2. They include a Nativity scene, *Representación del Nacimiento de Nuestro Señor* (Play of the Birth of Our Lord), a Passion Play, *Llanto por Nuestro Señor* (Lament for Our Lord), and two brief secular pieces. All four texts are contained in Fernando Lázaro Carreter, *Teatro medieval* (Valencia, 1958), pp. 83–109. Their embryonic structure may be somewhat deceptive, as Harry Sieber has shown in his provocative study "Dramatic Symmetry in Gómez Manrique's *La representación del Nacimiento de Nuestro Señor*," *HR,* XXXIII (1965), 118–135.

3. *The Liturgical Drama in Medieval Spain* (Toronto, 1958), hereafter cited as "Donovan."

4. Lázaro Carreter, *Teatro medieval;* Humberto López Morales, *Tradición y creación en los orígenes del teatro castellano* (Madrid, 1968); John Lihani, *Lucas Fernández* (New York, 1973), pp. 50–54.

In Spain, as elsewhere in Europe, the early Christian era witnessed the disappearance, or at least the misunderstanding, of dramatic poetry as defined by Aristotle. The Renaissance hastened rediscovery of the concept in all its complexity. It is logical, then, to suppose that the medieval Spanish theater reflects a pre-Aristotelian base with a structure and content more in harmony with dramatic ritual than with dramatic art. This essay attempts first to establish the ritual essence of medieval drama and then to trace in some detail the crucial transition from ritual to art that occurred in the late Middle Ages and the early Renaissance. Special attention is given to vigorous Spanish, and to a lesser extent Portuguese, experimentation with the dramatic mode from 1490 to 1530. We hope that the analysis of several important plays by Juan del Encina, Gil Vicente, and Bartolomé de Torres Naharro will support the theoretical position set forth in this study.

Before proceeding, it is necessary to define the essential differences between ritual and art, between delusion and illusion.[5] Theoretically, a clear distinction can be drawn that eliminates all ambiguities, but it is obvious that in actual dramatic practice no single play can be categorized as pure ritual or pure art. Rather, in the plays themselves, it is the predominant tendency, the author's express purpose, that will determine their classification.

In *Feeling and Form,* Susanne K. Langer observes that art, whether painting, sculpture, music, or drama, is concerned with images, charged with reality, but distanced as symbolic forms. "The mind," Mrs. Langer tells us, "dwell[s] on the sheer appearance of things. . . . The knowledge that what is before us has no practical significance in the world is what enables us to give attention to its appearance as such."[6] Dramatic art, then, has this basic attribute: it is an illusion, the unfolding of a

5. Several years ago I examined some aspects of this problem in "Fray Iñigo de Mendoza and Medieval Dramatic Ritual," *HR,* XXXIII (1965), 197–245; see esp. pp. 211–215 on "Drama and Ritual."

6. *Feeling and Form* (New York, 1953), p. 49. Compare also Jane Ellen Harrison, *Ancient Art and Ritual* (1913; rpt. Oxford, 1951), pp. 119–169. Miss Harrison distinguishes between *dromenon*—"the thing actually done by yourself"—and *drama*—"a thing also done, but abstracted from your doing"—(p. 127). Art is *"cut loose from immediate action"* (p. 128; author's italics). We then have "the needful physical and moral distance, and we are free for contemplation" (p. 133).

"virtual future" (p. 307). *Virtual* is used by Mrs. Langer in the same way that physicists speak of virtual space, which is the space behind the surface of a mirror, hence a semblance of reality. In the drama the plot, dialogue, *mise en scène,* dramatis personae, and any spectacular aspects such as music, song, and dance all contribute to an organic whole.[7] Even seemingly insignificant events acquire special importance because the "action is so constructed that a whole piece of virtual history is implicit in it." There exists, then, a "strategic pattern" not a "welter of irrelevant doings." [8]

Because dramatic art is concerned with illusions, it has its own temporal and spatial laws determined by the special requirements of the virtual world. The sixteenth-century dramatic theorist Castelvetro found this difficult to accept. His insistence on highly restrictive concepts of time and place—in fact, on an almost exact correspondence between real time and virtual time, real space and virtual space—came from the fallacious assumption that the theater aimed at delusion, rather than illusion.[9]

But it is precisely this illusory nature of drama that permits the viewer to maintain what the British psychologist Edward Bullough terms *psychical distance,* the aesthetic detachment necessary for the appreciation of a work of art. Bullough emphasizes the highly complex nature of psychical distance: "It has a *negative,* inhibitory aspect—the cutting-out of the practical sides of things and of our practical attitude toward them—and a *positive* side—the elaboration of the experience on the new basis created by the inhibitory action of Distance." [10] Obviously, this is

7. Compare, for example, Robert Edmond Jones's observation on stage setting, which he believes has no independent status but provides the atmosphere for the unfolding of the play (*The Dramatic Imagination* [New York, 1941], pp. 69–71).

8. Langer, *Feeling and Form,* pp. 310–311.

9. Jackson I. Cope, *The Theater and the Dream: From Metaphor to Form in Renaissance Drama* (Baltimore, Md., 1973), pp. 78–80. Cope concludes: "Castelvetro's ideal of drama is coercive, creating an alternative objective world into which the viewer is drawn out of his own" (p. 93).

10. " 'Psychical Distance' as a Factor in Art and as an Aesthetic Principle," *British Journal of Psychology,* V, pt. 2 (June, 1912), 89. A comparable view is expressed by José Ortega y Gasset: "Seeing requires distance. Each art operates a magic lantern that removes and transfigures its objects. On its screen they stand aloof, inmates of an inaccessible world, in an absolute distance. When this de-realization is lacking, an awkward perplexity arises: we do not know whether to

a question not of complete objectivity, of total emotional detachment, since overdistancing can be as destructive as underdistancing,[11] but rather of the adoption of the proper perspective for producing aesthetic pleasure. The playwright contributes to that perspective when he determines the thematic and structural elements in his play together with its manner of presentation. Thus it is within his power to control the level of participation by his audience.

Dramatic ritual, on the other hand, strives for the *maximum* emotional involvement by the audience in the dramatized event. It attempts to delude the spectators into believing that what they are witnessing is real. Moreover, it has a practical, frequently magical function as the performers attempt to transcend the boundaries of their normal existence and exert total or partial control over the mysterious forces of nature. In dramatic ritual the actor fuses his personality with that of the character he is impersonating, and the spectators, if they do not participate actively, at least participate vicariously. The efficacy of the rite depends, it would seem, on the participation by all the people—hence its communal character. Moreover, dramatic ritual is either anticipatory or commemorative. The participants prelive a future event or relive one already past. Consequently, the rite actualizes both the past and the future. The intense emotional involvement and the collective nature of the celebration explain the predominance of the dance in mimetic ritual, to which is added instrumental and vocal music that further heightens its emotional impact. Spoken dialogue is frequently nonexistent.[12] The commemorative aspect is a universal feature: "a rite regularly performed is

---

'live' the things or to observe them" (*The Dehumanization of Art and Other Writings on Art and Culture* [New York, 1956], p. 26). For a more recent and complex analysis of aesthetic distance, see the perceptive essay by P. A. Michelis, "Aesthetic Distance and the Charm of Contemporary Art," *JAAC*, XVIII (1959), 1–45. What Michelis terms "pre-aesthetic distance" appears to be the perspective achieved in medieval dramatic ritual.

11. Compare Oscar Büdel, "Contemporary Theater and Aesthetic Distance," *PMLA*, LXXVI (1961), 278.

12. For a comprehensive examination of the nature and function of mimetic ritual, see Harrison, *Ancient Art and Ritual;* Benjamin Hunningher, *The Origin of the Theater* (New York, 1966), chaps. I, II; C. M. Bowra, *Primitive Song* (New York, 1963); Susanne K. Langer, *Philosophy in a New Key* (Cambridge, Mass., 1942), pp. 144–170.

the constant reiteration of sentiments . . . not a free expression of emotions, but a disciplined rehearsal of 'right attitudes.' " [13] Every detail is important, which explains the lack of variation in established rites. Rather, it is their careful reenactment that assures their continued effectiveness.

Dramatic ritual, then, displays many of the same features as dramatic art: a story is enacted, frequently of death and resurrection; there is impersonation; time and space are redefined; music, song, and dance play a significant role. But because the ultimate purpose of ritual is practical and not aesthetic, the nature and function of these elements have a different import.

Although many unresolved controversies concerning the origin and development of medieval liturgical drama still remain, its ritual character seems to me irrefutable. The effort by medieval composers to achieve total immediacy and thus assure maximum emotional involvement by the audience is strikingly apparent in *La Sibila de la Noche de Navidad* (The Sibyl of Christmas Eve).[14] It was performed as part of the midnight Christmas mass in the cathedral of Toledo, perhaps as early as the thirteenth century.[15] A casual reading of the meager twenty-

13. Langer, *Philosophy in a New Key*, p. 153.

14. The Sibyl celebration has been chosen over the better-known Magi play because the Sibyl tradition is particularly vigorous on the Iberian Peninsula. While it may have been introduced into Spain by the French Benedictines, it underwent new and interesting modifications. Rather than the Erythraean Sibyl sharing the limelight with other prophets, as she does in the Latin *Ordo prophetarum* (Procession of the Prophets), in our little masterpiece she appears alone to intone her grim prophecy. In Vicente's *Auto da sebila Casandra* (Play of the Sibyl Cassandra), however, Cassandra is the protagonist, but Erythraea, Persica, and Cymeria also appear. For a bibliography of critical studies on the Sibyl in Spain and Portugal, see Jack H. Parker, *Gil Vicente* (New York, 1967), pp. 154–155. For the Sibyl in thirteenth-century iconography, see Emile Mâle, *The Gothic Image* (New York, 1958), pp. 336–338.

15. The text was first copied in 1785 by Felipe Fernández Vallejo, canon of the Cathedral of Toledo and later Archbishop of Santiago. Vallejo apparently utilized an early sixteenth-century version of the play. His description of the ceremony was based on firsthand experience and on documents available to him. Joseph E. Gillet reproduces the text in "The 'Memorias' of Felipe Fernández Vallejo and the History of the Early Spanish Drama," *Essays and Studies in Honor of Carleton Brown* (New York, 1940), pp. 264–280. It is also reprinted by Donovan, pp. 39–40.

nine lines hardly conveys the intense emotional impact that the ceremony must have had on the parishioners. According to the stage directions and accompanying sketch provided by Vallejo (fol. 637), the priest
or an acolyte, clad in the oriental attire of the Sibyl, approaches a special
platform erected near the pulpit. She is accompanied by four choristers,
two disguised as angels with swords unsheathed, and two bearing torches
that provide illumination in an otherwise dimly lit cathedral. In a shrill,
doleful voice, the Sibyl prophesies the day of Final Judgment, when

> un Rey vendra perdurable
> con poder muy espantable
> á juzgar las Criaturas.

> A King shall come everlasting
> with terrifying power
> to judge all creatures.

The choir reiterates the dire prophecy:

> Juicio fuerte sera dado
> cruel y de muerte.

> Harsh judgment shall be given,
> cruel and mortal.

Their music is eerie, indeed unearthly: "tan patetica, y poco grata á los
oientes, que no hay uno que no desée se concluia quanto antes" ("so
pathetic and unpleasant to the listeners that there is no one who doesn't
want it to cease as quickly as possible").[16] The Sibyl then proclaims,

> Trompetas, y sones tristes
> diran de lo alto del Cielo
> levantaos muertos del suelo
> recivireis segun hizist[e]is

> Trumpets and sad sounds
> shall proclaim from the heights of Heaven,

Donovan examines in detail various performances of the Sibyl ceremony not only
in Toledo but in Gerona, Vich, Valencia, León, Mallorca, Lluchmaior, Tarragona,
and Lérida, and also provides "A Brief History of the Monologue of the Sibyl"
(pp. 165–167). The translation is mine.

16. Vallejo, fol. 637; Gillet, *Essays in Honor of Carleton Brown*, p. 275. Apparently Vallejo planned to transcribe the music, since there are some blank bars in
the manuscript.

arise ye dead from the earth,
as ye have sown, so shall ye reap.

We can readily imagine the consternation that is generated among the parishioners, for they have just heard those lugubrious sounds.[17] In the final moments the Sibyl recalls Christ's birth when she exhorts the spectators:

A la Virgen supliquemos
que antes de aqueste litijo
interceda con su hijo
porque todos nos salvemos.

Let us pray to the Virgin
prior to that fateful day
to intercede with her Son
that we may all be saved.

Mesmerized by the sheer immediacy of the performance, the audience would certainly take her admonition to heart. The Sibyl's final entreaty has special relevance. Since the midnight Christmas mass lasted several hours, it is not unlikely that the Adoration of the Shepherds was also performed, in which case the traditional Nativity scene was visible in the cathedral. Thus the spectators were permitted to prelive the second coming of Christ, the Judge, while at the same time reliving his first coming as the Infant Jesus. The synchronization of the two advents is no surprise, because the first is in effect a prefiguration of the second, and because, in the spiritual world as in dramatic ritual, past and future melt into an eternal present.

Furthermore, every effort is made to assure the emotional participation of the audience in the performance. The Sibyl addresses *not* the angels who accompany her but the parishioners, thereby involving them directly in the drama. One would be hard-pressed, therefore, to speak of psychical distance between actors and spectators. Even the stage represented by the platform is utterly stark; no backdrop or other props set it off from the surrounding area. Furthermore, although the choir is spatially re-

17. While the performance attended by Vallejo did not include the playing of trumpets, they were at one time part of the liturgical ceremonies in Palma de Mallorca, but there is no evidence that they were blown during the actual performance of the Sibyl play (Donovan, pp. 124–125).

moved from the five actors, it actively participates in the drama, sending down its message of doom and destruction on actors and audience alike. At the beginning, then, the stage is perceived to be the area represented by the platform itself, but when the eerie chant of the chorus resounds through the cavernous cathedral, the stage must expand to incorporate the whole interior, including the area occupied by the stunned parishioners. Thus, by recognizing the existence of only one world that embraces both actors and audience, the spectators are physically engulfed and psychologically involved in the ceremony. This *integralista* view was appropriate in the Middle Ages, when the physical and spiritual worlds were regarded as two manifestations of the same reality. Other features, such as the eerie darkness of the sanctuary, the frightening content of the prophecy, the raised swords that suggest a militant Christ[18] are all carefully orchestrated to inspire fear and trembling before the spectators are permitted to feel the more traditional Christmas emotions of joy and thanksgiving.[19]

The Sibyl play is strikingly different from the conventional Adoration scenes, which are alive with color, raucous with the music of rustic flutes and flageolets, and sprightly with animated country dances. They are also warmly human as humble shepherds make their simple offerings to the Christ Child and regale him with their lusty carols. But the Sibyl ceremony shares with the Visitation of the Shepherds the essential attributes of participatory ritual. Today, from a spatial distance of

18. The significance of the swords is explained in a sixth-century sermon erroneously attributed to St. Augustine: "Quid Sibilla vaticinando etiam de Christo clamaverit in medium proferamus, ut ex uno lapide utrorumque frontes percuciantur, Iudeorum scilicet atque paganorum, *atque suo gladio,* sicut Golias, Christi omnes percuciantur inimici . . . " ("Let us set forth what the Sibyl proclaimed in her prophecy even about Christ: that the foreheads of both the Jews and the pagans be struck by a single stone and that all the enemies of Christ be smitten *by His sword,* just like Goliath" (Donovan, p. 42; author's italics).

19. Vallejo, who was generally opposed to performances in the Church that demeaned the religious service, obviously recognized the moving power of the Sibyl play: "que es preciso mueva el animo de los oientes una voz delgada, y lamentable, que con pausa, y gravedad predice el dia tremendo del Juicio" ("it is inevitable that the spirit of the audience be stirred by a thin, doleful voice that slowly and gravely predicts the awesome day of Judgment" (fol. 633; Gillet, *Essays in Honor of Carleton Brown,* p. 274).

thousands of miles and a temporal span of many centuries, critics tend to view the Sibyl play aesthetically as a remarkably successful specimen of medieval dramatic art. But provoking aesthetic pleasure was certainly not the chief motivation of the unknown composer. His purpose, which he undoubtedly achieved, was instead immediate and practical: a reawakening of religious fervor through the disquieting preview of one Christian event and the happy commemoration of another.

In the fifteenth and sixteenth centuries the Sibylline prophecy and other devout forms of mimetic ritual continued to be enacted in Spanish cathedrals as an integral part of the Christmas liturgy. But the more raucous demonstrations had long since been expelled from the churches and forced to take up residence in the village squares, where they inevitably encountered other deeply entrenched pre-Christian rites. A detailed examination of mimetic ritual in medieval Spain lies beyond the scope of this study, but we should note that the Iberian people shared with their fellow Europeans a variety of activities that could be classified as dramatic ritual.[20] There were festivals to herald the arrival of spring, usually in the form of a combat between Winter and Summer with the predetermined triumph of the latter.[21] Or a pagan rite might yield to a Christianized version such as we encounter in the battle between Carnival and Lent.[22] Still other performances were designed to encourage the

20. Cf. medieval dramatic performances in other European countries: Joseph Bédier, "Les Fêtes de Mai et les commencements de la poésie lyrique au Moyen Age," *RDM*, LXVI° année, quatrième période, CXXXV (1896), 147–172; *idem*, "Les Plus Anciennes Danses françaises," *RDM*, LXXXI année, cinquième période (1906), 398–424; E. K. Chambers, *The Mediaeval Stage* (Oxford, 1903), Vol. I, bk. II, "Folk Drama"; Charles Read Baskervill, "Dramatic Aspects of Medieval Folk Festivals in England," *SP*, XVII (1920), 19–87; *idem*, "Mummers' Wooing Plays in England," *MP*, XXI (1924), 225–272; *idem*, *The Elizabethan Jig and Related Song Drama* (Chicago, 1929); Alice Bertha Gomme, *The Traditional Games of England, Scotland, and Ireland* (1894–1898; rpt., New York, 1964).

21. See Sir James Frazer, *The Golden Bough*, 3d ed. (London, 1911–1915), pt. III, chap. VIII, pp. 254–261; *The New Golden Bough*, ed. Theodor H. Gaster (New York, 1959), pp. 265–268; Chambers, *Mediaeval Stage*, pp. 187–188; Frederick Monroe Tisdel, "The Influence of Popular Customs on the Mystery Plays," *JEGP*, V (1903–1905), 324–325; Hunningher, *Origin of the Theater*, pp. 99–102; Richard Bernheimer, *Wild Men in the Middle Ages* (Cambridge, Mass., 1952), pp. 55–56.

22. For Carnival celebrations in Europe, see Julio Caro Baroja, *El carnaval (Análisis histórico-cultural)* (Madrid, 1965); C. Cabal, *Contribución al diccionario*

vital, regenerative forces of nature and included rustic dances characterized by vigorous leaping and jumping steps.[23] There were also mock wedding celebrations in which the head shepherd recited an erotic monologue, replete with salacious comments, designed solely to stimulate the fertility of bride and groom. Or else the shepherd would reel off an endless list of wedding gifts, hoping to arouse the assembled well-wishers to comparable munificence. The plays usually ended with a burlesque marriage ceremony.[24] While the latter activities imply verbal improvisation if not an actual text, the battle scenes could have been performed in pantomime without accompanying dialogue. These celebrations clearly belong to a pre-aesthetic period, when pantomime, music, song, and dance, together with a host of visual effects, were paramount, and spoken dialogue was relegated to a decidedly inferior position. Therefore the absence of texts should come as no surprise, since the primacy of the text in Spanish drama is a Renaissance phenomenon.

By the fifteenth century, ritual drama was flourishing not only in the cathedrals and outside in the courtyards, but also in the palaces, where it was taken up first by the minstrels and later by professional Renaissance poets.[25] Sometimes the new product was relatively close in spirit

folklórico de Asturias (Oviedo, 1958), "Antroxu"; Gregoire Lozinski, *La Bataille de Caresme et de Charnage* (Paris, 1933); Maximilian J. Rudwin, *The Origin of German Carnival Comedy* (New York, 1920).

23. See Joseph E. Gillet, *Propalladia and the Other Works of Bartolomé de Torres Naharro.* Vol. IV: *Torres Naharro and the Drama of the Renaissance* (Philadelphia, 1961), p. 23 (hereafter cited as *Propalladia*).

24. *Ibid.*, pp. 38–40. See also J. P. W. Crawford, "Early Spanish Wedding Plays," *RR,* XII (1921), 370–384. Crawford deals almost exclusively with sixteenth-century literary texts. He briefly acknowledges the existence of medieval celebrations at the weddings of Spanish royalty and nobility, but there is no discussion of medieval folk ritual. Of particular relevance are the studies by Baskervill in which he stresses popular folk motifs like the shepherd's inventory of his rustic possessions (see n. 20). I have found no trace in Spain of the "Dirty Bride" (*vuile bruid*) tradition, a farcical performance at Flemish carnivals, recorded for us so vividly by Peter Bruegel. See H. Arthur Klein's description in *Graphic Worlds of Peter Bruegel the Elder* (New York, 1963), p. 123, pl. 26. While social satire and parody are not lacking in Encina, Vicente, and Torres Naharro, this particular tradition seems to be unknown in Spain.

25. Compare Baskervill's successive stages in the evolution of medieval English drama: (1) pagan ritual; (2) festival celebrations derived from ritual but viewed

and content to its popular sources. Torres Naharro's prologue speaker, for example, exhibits all the essential talents of a seasoned rustic performer and, like him, never loses contact with his audience for a moment. An erotic epithalamium composed by Francisco de Aldana was clearly part of a wedding celebration, although the bride and groom, parents and friends, were not country bumpkins but a distinguished gathering of Spanish nobility.[26] In such a setting did the erotic monologue still retain its ritual function as anticipatory magic? Frequent references by the monologuist to those present would seem to encourage a participatory attitude on the part of the spectators. The enumeration of gifts comprising the rustic dowry likewise permitted the playwrights to demonstrate their poetic virtuosity, and in plays like Lucas Fernández' *Comedia de Bras Gil y Beringuella* (Comedy of Bras Gil and Berînguella) this event constitutes a significant and delightful scene.[27] At times the list becomes an extraordinary poetic feat. In one of his dialogue songs, Encina catalogues almost a hundred items, everything from *çueco* (wooden clog) and *çapata* (half boot) to *artera* (kneeding trough) and *cedaço* (colander).[28] In the Renaissance, Spanish nobility, greatly attracted to the pastoral life and cognizant of Spain's economic dependence on her shepherds, must have delighted in such enumerations.

Generally, however, by the late fifteenth century, ritual drama submitted to fundamental alterations. Since its purpose was to provide gala entertainment for Renaissance nobility and since the composers were

---

as social pastime; (3) folk festivals taken up by minstrels who convert them into professional entertainment ("Dramatic Aspects," p. 20). Compare Cope, *Theater and the Dream*, p. 98. In fourteenth-century Spain many of Juan Ruiz's minstrel activities derive from medieval folk tradition. Also, festive performances held a century later in the palace of Miguel Lucas de Iranzo belong to Baskervill's third stage and were conceivably more widespread than the scanty records suggest. It is entirely possible that all three stages—pagan ritual, social festivals, and professional entertainment—coexisted in the period under consideration.

26. Otis H. Green, "A Wedding *Introito* by Francisco de Aldana (1537–1578)," *HR*, XXXI (1963), 8–21.

27. John Lihani, *Lucas Fernández Farsas y églogas* (New York, 1969), pp. 71–72; see also Lihani's study *Lucas Fernández*, pp. 90–94.

28. See *La música en la Corte de los Reyes Católicos* IV–2 *Cancionero Musical de Palacio (siglos XV–XVI)*, ed. José Romeu Figueras (Barcelona, 1965), song 309, pp. 408–411.

professional poets, spoken dialogue moved to the forefront, although music, song, and dance continued to play a peripheral role. The drama became the creative expression of the individual poet rather than the religious manifestation of the entire community. Consequently, it is not surprising to discover that what was in many cases the traditional rite was either completely suppressed or accommodated to a narrative presentation. This is particularly apparent in the Nativity plays, but we also find that the ritual battle between Carnival and Lent is narrated in Encina's sixth eclogue, while in Vicente's *Triunfo do inverno* (Triumph of Winter) a boisterous, long-winded Winter yields without a struggle to a benign and gallant Spring.

The dramatists quickly filled the vacuum created by elimination of folk material. The rich lyric tradition, particularly the courtly love motif of the fifteenth-century *cancionero* poets, found a propitious environment in plays by Encina and his followers, while the rather narrow confines of the Spanish pastoral world were expanded to embrace the highly stylized bucolic setting recorded by Vergil and Italian Renaissance writers. In plays on religious themes the inclusion of dissertations on complex theological questions were designed not to arouse the spectators emotionally but to challenge and inspire them intellectually. It is not surprising, then, that in the process the drama lost some of the zest and vitality that had characterized medieval performances.

In spite of the change in content and the greater emphasis on spoken dialogue, Encina and his followers retained many structural features and a theatrical perspective that suggest a transitional or intermediate stage between ritual and art. Encina's earliest dramatic pieces, written in pairs, are all in dialogue form, but in the prefatory ecologues the actors are barely disguised and the topical allusions betray concern for immediate problems; the Duke of Alba and his court are regarded at least as silent participants. These features have led Duncan Moir recently to characterize the plays as a game of charades.[29] The first eclogue provides the distinct impression that the poet Encina and a friend, disguised as Spanish shepherds, have strong ties both with the audience and the virtual world of the second eclogue, where they

29. Edward M. Wilson and Duncan Moir, *A Literary History of Spain, The Golden Age: Drama 1492–1700* (London, 1971), p. 2.

subsequently reappear metamorphosed into Biblical shepherds who are simultaneously the Evangelists John and Matthew.[30] One of their functions, then, is to lead the spectators across the boundary between reality and illusion, between fifteenth-century Spain and Bethlehem in the time of Christ, and in so doing efface, or at least blur, the line of demarcation separating spectators and actors. Here, then, is a kind of play-within-a-play, whose express purpose is to deceive the spectators regarding the virtual world. Paradoxically, however, this technique calls attention to the illusory nature of the theater.

Encina's Carnival eclogues may also be classified as dramatic ritual. In them stage time coincides precisely with the time of the performance: the plays were indeed performed on Shrove Tuesday in 1494. Moreover, the animated, even farcical tone of the plays reflects the spirit of overindulgence and conviviality generated by the Duke and his court. Having just finished glutting themselves, they watch the "stage" shepherds partake of their rustic fare in what could well be a parody of their own Saturnalian orgy. The ties that bind actors to audience are multiple, but the performance of the eclogues on Shrove Tuesday is particularly significant because it is this commemorative spirit that links the plays to dramatic ritual.[31]

In the *Auto del repelón,* according to the stage directions, Johán Paramás, a terrified hillbilly fleeing from some malicious students "se fue a casa de un cavallero, y entrando en la sala [hallándose] fuera del peligro començó a contar lo que le [acaeció]" ("hastened to the house of a nobleman, and entering the drawing room and finding himself out of danger, began to relate what happened to him"). The shepherd does, in fact, appear in a palace room (the Duke of Alba's if the play is really

30. Compare Bruce W. Wardropper, "Metamorphosis in the Theatre of Juan del Encina," *SP,* LIX (1962), 41–51.

31. See *ibid.,* pp. 45–46; Charlotte Stern, "Juan del Encina's Carnival Eclogues and the Spanish Drama of the Renaissance," *RenD,* VIII (1965), 181–195. J. Richard Andrews suggests a strong element of social satire through the juxtaposition of the Duke of Alba and Lady Lent and concludes: "Encina could be symbolically complaining that life under Ducal protection was a continual Lent in secular form" (*Juan del Encina: Prometheus in Search of Prestige* [Berkeley, Calif., 1959], pp. 123–125).

by Encina),[32] where, after recovering his composure, he addresses his startled audience and regales them with a blow-by-blow account of the abuse he has suffered. Here the stage setting and the room in which the audience is assembled coincide. The spectators are deceived into thinking that they are eye-witnesses to a "happening," not spectators at a dramatic performance. Thus both the Carnival eclogues and the *Auto del repelón* reflect an aura of actuality that impedes or at least discourages aesthetic detachment.

The sixteenth-century festival plays also imply in their structure and content a pre-aesthetic or pre-Aristotelian perspective. Torres Naharro's *Comedia Trophea,* performed in Rome in 1514, exemplifies that tradition. Of particular interest is the second act, in which the Spanish rustics Cacoluzio and Juan Tomillo, one of whom we may have already met in the prologue, prepare the room for the *real* performance: the dazzling procession of African monarchs who, in the best *Ordo prophetarum* tradition, pay homage to King Manuel of Portugal and express their desire to be baptized. In the rustic scene we have, in my opinion, a sixteenth-century forerunner of Pirandello's technique in which the inner workings of the theater are revealed. This device drastically reduces the psychical distance between actors and audience. Both yokels subsequently reappear in Act IV and, together with two other shepherds, present gifts to King Manuel's son, Prince John. Gillet observes that Torres Naharro has secularized two liturgical traditions, the Procession of the Prophets and the Adoration of the Shepherds, but in the secularization process both ceremonies retain their ritual function.[33] Gillet further avers, that "[the *Trophea*] is literally re-creation. . . . Indeed, profane time is abolished, and the repeated act coincides with the original one. This may be called *confirmatory magic.* The 'kings' who declare their fealty to Portugal and their desire for baptism were evidently represented by impersonators; their submissiveness was probably a matter of some doubt. Their show of meekness in the play was *anticipatory magic,* intended to produce the attitude desired by the conquerors" (p. 496;

---

32. Oliver T. Myers, "Juan del Encina and the *Auto del Repelón,*" HR, XXXII (1964), 189–201.

33. See Gillet, *Propalladia,* pp. 489–503.

italics mine). Consequently, "the *Trophea* is not, properly speaking, an imitation of a human action but an action pure and simple—a magic action, with a double purpose, to confirm an acquired situation and to produce one yet unrealized."

The festival plays were not uncommon in the sixteenth century, and they enjoyed an even greater vogue in the seventeenth.[34] They were successfully cultivated in the 1520's by Gil Vicente, whose *Auto da fama* (Play of Fame), *Cortes de Júpiter* (Court of Jupiter), *Triunfo do inverno* (Triumph of Winter), and *Farsa das ciganas* (Farce of the Gypsies) display a dramatic structure and content that recalls medieval tradition. The *Auto da fama,* performed in Lisbon in 1520, is, like the *Trophea,* a panegyric extolling recent Portuguese military achievements in Africa, India, and America. *Fama* enumerates them ecstatically, taking special delight in pronouncing the exotic foreign names. The tone of the play is not only laudatory but anticipatory as the actors imply even greater Portuguese achievements in the future.[35] The *Cortes de Júpiter* (1521) celebrates the impending departure of Princess Beatriz, who is about to become Duchess of Savoy. Jupiter summons the moon to calm the seas and assure a safe voyage. Like the *Auto da fama,* it is clearly a piece of anticipatory magic.[36] The *Farsa das ciganas* (1521), the earliest literary work to depict the Iberian gypsies, is hardly a farce. Rather it provides the opportunity for the stage gypsies to circulate among the distinguished

34. The earliest festival play in Castilian is an *égloga* by Francisco de Madrid, performed in 1495 before the Catholic Monarchs. It is a piece of "political propaganda" in which Spain appears as the peacemaker and France the warmonger. See Joseph E. Gillet, "Eglogo hecha por Francisco de Madrid (1495?)," *HR,* XI (1943), 275–303. For additional festival plays in Castilian, see Gillet, *Propalladia,* pp. 498–500.

35. *Obras completas de Gil Vicente,* reimpressão "fac-similada" da edição de 1562 (Lisbon, 1928), fols. CXCVIII^r–CCI^v. Although the 1562 edition gives the date of the play as 1510, I. S. Révah changes it to 1520, basing his revision on internal evidence and the fact that Luis Vicente, who was responsible for publishing the dramatist's works, frequently erred by ten years in dating the plays ("La 'Comédia' dans l'oeuvre de Gil Vicente," *Bulletin d'histoire du théâtre Portugais,* II [1951], 15–16).

36. See Thomas R. Hart's illuminating discussion of the play in *Gil Vicente: Farces and Festival Plays* (Eugene, Ore., 1972), pp. 44–47. Hart appropriately compares Vicente's festival pieces to the English masque.

ladies of the court and tell their fortunes. Here we have the actual physical commingling of actors and spectators.[37]

Vicente's most complex and elaborate pageant is the *Triunfo do inverno,* a veritable extravaganza performed on April 28, 1529, to celebrate the birth of Princess Isabel.[38] The narrator, who addresses the monarchs, bemoans the absence of music, song, and dance in Portugal and sings a traditional ditty to remind everyone of the wonderful by-gone days. He then introduces Winter, who appears dressed as a wild man, a medieval folk character with equally deep roots in classical mythology. Winter behaves, however, like a boastful Spanish shepherd and in an outburst of pride enumerates his many accomplishments, i.e., the miseries he has provoked. In his function as "master of ceremonies" he summarizes the action that unfolds in a series of farcical interludes and further facilitates the viewers' acceptance of those scenes by appearing in them himself. The second part of the play features Spring, a handsome Renaissance courtier enamored of an equally comely Renaissance lady, the *Serra da Sintra* (Sintra mountain range). Like Winter, Spring actively involves the audience in the performance. Then, as a grand finale, a prince arrives on a pageant wagon representing the Garden of Virtues which is presented to the Portuguese monarchs.

In Vicente's festival plays the inclusion of numerous musical interludes and the use of spectacular visual effects seem, according to Hart, "always to be threatening the primacy of the text."[39] But it is precisely the ritual function of these plays as gala commemorations or anticipations of important events that prevents the text from acquiring the supremacy it achieves when theater is viewed as a branch of literature.

All the plays discussed thus far are endowed with such actuality as to invite, indeed encourage, the audience to believe there is no real separation, no sharp division between the world of the spectators and that of the actors. Gillet likewise stresses what he calls the "pre-Aristotelian basis" of the sixteenth-century drama: "It is not an imitation, an interpretation and explanation of reality, but an attempt at simply

37. *Obras completas,* fols. CCXXVI^r–CCXXVIII^r. The play is designated an *auto,* but it appears among the farces. Compare Wilson and Moir, *Literary History of Spain,* pp. 12–13.
38. Hart provides a perceptive analysis of the *Triunfo* in *Gil Vicente,* pp. 47–61.
39. *Ibid.,* p. 42.

presenting it. The dramatist desires to show life-in-the-act, not to make the public vicariously and consciously understand it. This kind of drama is not primarily art, but rather an *act of worship,* an affirmation of the holiness of life, and thus a homage to God." [40]

It is conceivable that in the shift from a pre-aesthetic to an aesthetic perspective the theater had to pass through these transitional phases before the crucial attributes of dramatic art as defined by Mrs. Langer were fully recognized. This recognition was achieved, in my opinion, by 1516 with the performance in Italy of Torres Naharro's *Comedia Himenea.* The play was made available in Spain one year later when copies of the Naples edition of the *Propalladia* reached the Peninsula.

In the *Himenea* Torres Naharro offers us a *fiction* that is a semblance of reality. The impression of dynamic movement toward the future is the most striking feature: each scene proceeds logically, consistently, inevitably toward the "finalmente alegre[s] acontecimiento[s]" ("happy dénouement") in accordance with Torres Naharro's dramatic formula. Even those scenes involving the servants contribute to the forward motion of the main action. The all-important plot (*artificio*) reveals similarities with classical Roman comedy and more immediately with the *Celestina,* but with keen dramatic intuition the poet has replaced Melibea's lyrical but passive father Pleberio with Phebea's aggressive brother the Marqués, the vigilant and determined protector of his sister's and consequently his family's honor.[41]

The *introito* speaker, who prepares the audience for the semblance of reality they are about to witness, does not appear in the *comedia* itself. After presenting his erotic monologue and summary of the action, this intermediary between the actors and spectators withdraws and does not further disrupt the dramatic illusion created in the *comedia.* Rather, the "stage" becomes a closed and self-contained world, charged with reality, but distinct and isolated from the world of the spectators.

The *Himenea* is wholly consistent with Torres Naharro's dramatic theory: the plot predominates over both characters and setting, but the characters, conceived as fictional personalities, and the setting, with its *own* laws of time and space, reinforce the dramatic illusion here created.

40. Gillet, *Propalladia,* p. 567.
41. Cf. *ibid.,* p. 519.

The dark and foreboding night scenes provide the atmosphere of secrecy necessary for the dramatic action, but unlike the medieval Sibyl play, these scenes are designed to instill not fear in the audience but consternation in the hearts of Himeneo's timorous servants, Boreas and Eliso. Hence the darkness belongs exclusively to the virtual world of the actors, not to the real world of the spectators. Likewise, time is fictional time—neither the eternal present of ritual drama nor the empirical time of the audience (which Castelvetro attempts to foist upon us), but time as lived by the characters. Consequently, there are accelerating and decelerating effects that reflect events unfolding in the virtual world, for it is the *comedia* itself that determines the temporal rhythm of the play. Moreover, the actors are fully cognizant of their dramatic roles as distinct and separate from their real selves, and the audience shares that awareness. Hence there is no attempt to draw the spectators into the virtual world nor to delude them concerning the nature of dramatic illusion. Rather, Torres Naharro clearly defines it as a "cosa fantástiga o fingida" ("something invented or imagined").

The *Himenea,* then, is distinct from the *Trophea,* where psychical distance is minimal and audience participation actively sought. In the *Himenea* the necessary aesthetic distance is carefully maintained between actors and audience. The resulting emotional detachment permits the spectators to view the play as art and to derive aesthetic pleasure from it.

The *Himenea* was probably performed as part of a wedding celebration, as suggested by the title. In this regard, then, the art form Torres Naharro calls *comedia* is not yet completely separated from its ritual origins. However, the traditional wedding performance, which is the ribald monologue, is here confined to the prologue, while in the *comedia* itself a piece of a virtual future unfolds before our eyes. Moreover, the secret marriage has an artistic function in relation to the plot rather than a practical purpose with regard to the audience. As an integral part of the dramatic illusion, it makes the happy denouement possible.[42]

42. The secret marriage based on mutual consent of the interested parties, and without intervention of appropriate church or civil authorities, was practiced in medieval and Renaissance Spain until it was prohibited by the Council of Trent. It provided a religious and moral "escape hatch" in a period when concern for the lady's honor was serious. Naturally, it became a common literary theme, par-

The *Himenea* displays sophisticated dramatic techniques not found in Torres Naharro's Spanish contemporaries. Encina's *Cristino y Febea,* written in 1509, and his *Plácida y Vitoriano,* composed in 1513, just three years before the *Himenea,* create a static effect that is diametrically opposite to the dynamic thrust of Torres Naharro's piece. This is the unfortunate consequence of prolonged monologues of a rhetorical nature —Vitoriano's *Vigilia de la enamorada muerta* ("Vigil for the Dead Lover") runs 639 lines!—that bring the dramatic action to a virtual halt.

Torres Naharro's greater comprehension of the nature of dramatic illusion may be attributed to various factors. First, although he had no direct knowledge of Aristotle's *Poetics,* his prolonged stay in Italy permitted him to attend performances of Plautus' comedies in Latin and Italian.[43] These were enacted not in pantomime with a narrator reading the dialogue but as true drama. But Encina also visited Italy and was apparently susceptible to literary pressures, since his later plays clearly display Italian pastoral influence. It would seem, then, that Torres Naharro, although a poet of merit, was truly a man of the theater with an intuitive sense of the dramatic. Encina, on the contrary, was an accomplished poet and musician, and while he achieved some delightfully funny moments in his rustic pieces, he did not fully accept the rich possibilities inherent in the creation of a virtual future. Finally, the *Himenea* was performed not in Spain but in Italy, before Italians and Spaniards residing in Rome who had already been exposed to the fundamental principles of dramatic illusion. The prologue speaker who summarizes the plot was Torres Naharro's only concession to his audience.

---

ticularly in the romances of chivalry. See Justina Ruiz de Conde, *El amor y el matrimonio secreto en los libros de caballerías* (Madrid, 1948). The secret marriage, not yet consummated, between Himeneo and Phebea (V. 124–126) diverts the course of action from what otherwise would have been a tragic outcome.

43. Gillet discusses at length Torres Naharro's knowledge of classical dramatic theory, which ultimately derives from Aelius Donatus, fourth-century grammarian and commentator on Terence (*Propalladia,* pp. 427 ff.). For performances of Plautus in Italy, consult Raymond Leonard Grismer, *The Influence of Plautus in Spain before Lope de Vega* (New York, 1944), pp. 57–80. The *Aulularia* was presented in Rome in 1484, "the first stage performance of a Latin comedy during the Renaissance" (p. 62). Several performances are recorded thereafter, and from 1500 presentations of Italian translations "become too numerous to mention" (p. 64).

In fact, the spectators' recognition of the special character of the virtual world allowed them to accept without shock or dismay such theatrical liberties as the careful manipulation of time and space for artistic purposes.

The *Propalladia* provided, then, a real challenge to Torres Naharro's successors, many of whom failed to measure up to their master's excellence. For example, Gil Vicente's *Comédia de Rubena,* written in 1521, clearly belongs to the New Comedy tradition with its complex plot, forward movement, coincidences, and final recognition scene, but these elements are at times awkwardly manipulated.[44] There is a commentator who summarizes the action, but unfortunately his presence is not confined to the prologue. Rather, he makes repeated and inopportune intrusions into the play itself, thus shattering the virtual world the poet hoped to create. These narrative incursions were, according to Castelvetro, an unpardonable sin.[45] Apparently the complicated plot, the change of scenes, and the passage of time could not be managed effectively without the presence of a narrator. This situation constitutes a definite step backward toward the medieval drama, where a narrator recited the dialogue while the actors performed in pantomime, and it may be the reason for the insistence of some critics that the play was written to be read, not performed on the stage.[46] However, the tragicomedies of *Don Duardos* and *Amadís,* written between 1522 and 1523, display more skillful handling of the plot.

Vicente also perceived significant theatrical possibilities inherent in the complex relationship between the actor and his dramatic role. In several of his *comédias,* beginning with the *Rubena,* there is a disguised

44. Compare Parker, *Gil Vicente,* pp. 83–85, who emphasizes the lyrical quality of the play while playing down its dramatic structure. For relations between Gil Vicente and Torres Naharro, see Joseph E. Gillet, "Torres Naharro and the Spanish Drama of the Sixteenth Century," *Estudios Eruditos in Memoriam de Adolfo Bonilla y San Martín,* II (1930), 437–468; also I. S. Révah, "La 'Comedia,'" pp. 25–33, and Leif Sletsjöe, *O elemento cénico em Gil Vicente* (Lisbon, 1965), pp. 39–40.

45. See Cope, *Theater and the Dream,* p. 80.

46. It has been suggested that the *Don Duardos* was also destined to be read, since it was composed during a period of mourning when a ban on dramatic activities was in effect.

prince, suggested by Torres Naharro's *Aquilana,* who reveals his true identity only in the final scene. Thus a play-within-a-play is created in which the actor is acutely conscious first, that his dramatic role is distinct from his real self, and second, that within his dramatic role he may further "theatricalize" himself to create what Lionel Abel calls "metatheatre" and Orozco Díaz "teatralización." The prince's full awareness of his theatrical pose and his blatant deception of the other characters is conspicuously different from the metamorphosis in Encina's seventh and eighth eclogues where we all watch the squire become the shepherd Gil and Pascuala become a refined lady of the court. While Encina's metamorphosis actually reduces the barriers between the two illusory worlds, Vicente's theatricalization, on the contrary, reflects a heightened awareness of the distinctions between the real world and the two virtual worlds created in the drama.

In this cursory survey, I have attempted to trace the rediscovery of aesthetic distance in Spain and with it the rebirth of dramatic art during the transitional period between the Middle Ages and the Renaissance. The reawakening process extends over several decades. First, there is the gradual widening of distance, physical and psychical, between audience and actors in plays preceding the *Himenea,* but it is Torres Naharro who takes the tremendous leap forward and treats us to a full-fledged example of dramatic illusion. That the change in dramatic perception should occur at that particular moment in history is not surprising. By 1490 drama had ceased to be the exclusive concern of the Church, which used it for edification of the faithful (the Sibyl play), and of the folk, for whom it was a communal activity that sprang from the practical necessities of their uncertain lives (the battle between Summer and Winter). It was also being cultivated by professional poets for whom it became a vehicle for artistic expression. Furthermore, the spectators were not the Iberian peasantry but Spanish and Portuguese royalty and nobility who sought not reassurance in a mysterious universe but intellectual stimulation and sparkling entertainment. Under such conditions, emotional detachment and critical perception developed simultaneously and led eventually to Spanish efforts to imitate classical drama. But the unpopularity of such imitations was the consequence of over-distancing or too great a psychical barrier between the spectators and the performance.

The national theater, on the other hand, achieved a felicitous compromise between medieval involvement and Renaissance detachment. In the decades immediately following publication of the *Propalladia,* López de Yanguas, Diego Sánchez de Badajoz, Jaime de Güete, and other dramatists produced plays that preserve many medieval techniques closely associated with dramatic ritual. These include the dramatic monologue directed to the audience, allusions to contemporary events, the appearance of stock characters such as the boastful shepherd, the medieval fool, the wild man, and a host of allegorical figures, the synchronization of temporally separate events, and the creation of dazzling spectacle through the effective use of colorful pageantry and musical interludes. But these aspects commingle with important Renaissance characteristics essential to dramatic art. The new features stress the preeminence of the written text as the expression of the poet's art, the creation of a virtual future, a dramatic illusion that is self-contained and self-sufficient, the redefining of the laws of time and space in accordance with the special requirements of the virtual world, and finally the audience's acceptance of the play on an aesthetic level.

But this convergence of the old and the new extends beyond Torres Naharro's immediate successors to the Golden Age *comedia* and *auto sacramental.* Lope and Calderón, authors fully cognizant of the nature of dramatic illusion and the principle of aesthetic distance, offer us plays which frequently overflow the confines of the stage to engulf the viewers in a process described by Orozco Diaz as "desbordamiento teatral" ("stage expansion in all directions").[47] Moreover, in an era of heightened sensitivity to reality and illusion, particularly to the illusory nature of reality, it is not surprising that baroque dramatists discover ever new possibilities in the adroit manipulation of the aesthetic-distance prin-

47. See Emilio Orozco Díaz, *El teatro y la teatralidad del Barroco* (Barcelona, 1969), where he discusses the "visión de continuidad espacial" ("vision of spatial continuity"—p. 39) and the "incorporación del espectador a la obra de arte" ("incorporation of the spectator into the work of art"—p. 40). Of special interest are chapters II and IV. "Metatheatre in Calderón's *La vida es sueño*" is analyzed by Lionel Abel, *Metatheatre: A New View of Dramatic Form* (New York, 1963), pp. 59–72. Also of interest is Bruce W. Wardropper, "La imaginación en el metateatro calderoniano," *Actas del Tercer Congreso Internacional de Hispanistas* (Mexico, 1970), pp. 923–930.

ciple.[48] Finally, the religious content and the pre-aesthetic perspective of
the *autos sacramentales* and many *comedias* further support the contention that even in the seventeenth century Spain had not forsaken her
medieval dramatic heritage.[49]   .

Perhaps as a postscript, it should be noted that while the Renaissance
witnessed the rediscovery of dramatic illusion, our contemporary theater
is actively engaged in rejecting that vital concept. Büdel calls attention
to the current trend toward delusion or the elimination of aesthetic
distance. He further avers: "On our modern stage, in comparison, the
audience is to be made part and parcel of the whole performance; it is
to be dragged, as it were, into the play. *With this we move toward the
concept of the theater as a rite, as the liturgical celebration of a community.*" [50] Büdel believes that the new trend is more than theatrical
gadgetry: the artist is himself questioning "whether the work of art as
such, closed in itself, self-sufficient and harmonious, has any legitimate
relation to the complete uncertainty, the problematical nature and the
chaos of our social situation; and, finally, whether all appearance, even
the most beautiful one, and exactly the most beautiful one, has not become a lie in our day" (p. 291). The noted director Peter Brook also
appeals for a new "Holy theater," a restoration of ritual drama on a
truly contemporary level.[51] Finally, the French poet and dramatist
Antonin Artaud condemns as unauthentic the realistic, psychological,

48. The manipulation of reality and illusion is studied by Alan S. Trueblood,
"Rôle-playing and the Sense of Illusion in Lope de Vega," *HR*, XXXII (1964),
305–318. Of special interest are "the shifting planes of actuality and dramatic
fiction" in *Lo fingido verdadero o el mejor representante*. In "Comic Illusion:
Lope in Vega's *El perro del hortelano*," *KRQ*, XIV (1967), 101–111, Bruce W.
Wardropper notes that the Baroque *comedias de capa y espada* (cloak-and-dagger
plays) convince us that life is illusory, while the serious plays ponder the ethical
and theological implications of that problem. These philosophical concerns,
epitomized in the phrases "Life is a dream" and "The world is a stage" are
brilliantly analyzed by Cope, *Theater and the Dream*, who also considers their
implications for European Renaissance drama.

49. The essentially medieval nature of Calderón's *Autos sacramentales* has already been pointed out by Margaret Wilson: "The performance of the *auto* is a
ritual, involving the total response of the spectator at all levels" (*Spanish Drama
of the Golden Age* [New York, 1969], p. 182).

50. "Contemporary Theater and Aesthetic Distance," p. 284 (italics mine).

51. *The Empty Space* (New York, 1968), pp. 38–58.

bourgeois theater, foisted upon us by the Renaissance, in which the written text is supreme, and the actors are on one side and the spectators on the other. He urges a return to the genuine theater as practiced by primitive societies and preserved in the Orient, with its mythic content and its ritual form.[52] Artaud describes at length the elimination of all barriers between the audience and the performance: "The spectacle will be extended, by elimination of the stage, to the entire hall of the theater and will scale the walls from the ground up on light catwalks, will physically envelop the spectator and immerse him in a constant bath of light, images, movements, and noises. . . . Between life and the theater there will be no distinct division, but instead a continuity" (pp. 125–126).[53] We have come full circle.

52. Antonin Artaud, *The Theater and Its Double* (New York, 1958).

53. In Spain, on the contrary, García Lorca, who first embraced Pirandellism, later rejected it. In *El Público* he defends aesthetic distance as indispensable for the survival of dramatic art. See Wilma Newberry, "Aesthetic Distance in García Lorca's *El Público:* Pirandello and Ortega," *HR,* XXXVII (1969), 276–296.

An Introduction to the Theater of
Angelo Beolco

FRANCO FIDO

EW MAJOR PLAYWRIGHTS of the Renaissance are still as little known to English readers as Angelo Beolco, more familiar under the name of Ruzante, who lived, mostly in Padua, from about 1500 to 1542.[1] So far, to my knowledge, only two of his shorter "dialogues," *Bilora* and *Parlamento de Ruzante che iera vegnù de campo,* have been translated into English,[2] and only recently have two critics, Marvin T. Herrick

1. The most reliable information on Beolco's life is found in Emilio Menegazzo and Paolo Sambin, "Nuove Esplorazioni archivistiche per Angelo Beolco e Alvise Cornaro," *IMU,* VII (1964), 133–247. But see also Grabher's and Lovarini's books quoted in notes 4 and 5 below, and the two articles on Beolco—respectively by Carlo Grabher and Nino Borsellino—in the *Dizionario biografico degli Italiani* (Rome, 1966), and in the *Enciclopedia dello Spettacolo* (Rome, 1961). The most important historical sources for Beolco's Paduan and Venetian activity respectively are Bernardini Scardeonii, *Historiae de urbis Patavii antiquitate et claris civibus patavinis libri tres* (Leiden, n.d. [but 1722]), and Marino Sanuto, *I Diarii,* ed. R. Fulin et al., 58 vols. (Venice, 1879–1903).

2. *Bilora,* in *World Drama,* ed. Barrett H. Clark (New York, n.d.), Vol. II, and also in *Masterworks of World Drama, III: The Renaissance,* ed. Anthony Caputi (New York, 1968); *Parlamento,* trans. Angela Ingold and Theodore Hoff-

and Nancy Dersofi, given him the attention and the place that he
deserves in the history of sixteenth-century comedy.[3] Even in Europe
the rediscovery of the Paduan author (famous during his lifetime and
for the rest of the Cinquecento, yet almost forgotten in the two following centuries) is a relatively recent development, due exclusively, in the
nineteenth and early twentieth centuries, to the intelligence and the
labors of two French writers, Maurice Sand and Alfred Mortier, and
an Italian philologist, Emilio Lovarini.[4]

Today, after the studies of Carlo Grabher, Mario Baratto, Ludovico
Zorzi, and Giorgio Padoan,[5] and especially after the splendid edition of

---

man as *Ruzzante Returns from the Wars*, in *The Classic Theatre, I: Six Italian
Plays*, ed. Eric Bentley (Garden City, N.Y., 1958).

3. Marvin T. Herrick, *Italian Comedy in the Renaissance* (Urbana, Ill. and
London, 1960), pp. 43–52; Nancy Dorothy Dersofi, "Ruzzante: The Paradox of
Snaturalité in a *Mondo roesso*," *Yearbook of Italian Studies*, I (1971), 142–155. For
some useful remarks on the Venetian stage in the early sixteenth century, see also
Bodo L. O. Richter, "*La Venexiana* in the Light of Recent Criticism," in *The
Drama of the Renaissance: Essays for Leicester Bradner*, ed. Elmer M. Blistein
(Providence, R.I., 1970), pp. 134–152. Short, but excellent, is the section on Beolco
(by John A. Scott) in *The Continental Renaissance*, ed. A. J. Krailsheimer (Har-
mondsworth, Eng., 1971), pp. 261–262. For an earlier and still authoritative analysis
of Beolco's plays by an English scholar, see Kathleen M. Lea, *Italian Popular
Comedy: A Study in the Commedia dell'Arte, 1560–1620* (Oxford, 1934), I, 233–
238. Since Lea could read only the French translation of Mortier, her intuitions
about Ruzzante's artistry and originality are all the more remarkable.

4. Maurice Sand, *Masques et bouffons (Comédie italienne)* (Paris, 1862), II,
77–118; Alfred Mortier, *Un Dramaturge populaire de la Renaissance italienne:
Ruzzante (1502–1542)*, 2 vols. (Paris, 1925/26); all the essays and papers on
Beolco published by Emilio Lovarini in more than sixty years of scholarly activity
(from 1889 to 1951) are now collected in *Studi sul Ruzzante e la letteratura pavana*,
ed. Gianfranco Folena (Padua, 1965).

5. Carlo Grabher, *Ruzzante* (Milan and Messina, 1953); Mario Baratto, *Tre
Studi sul teatro (Ruzante—Aretino—Goldoni)* (Venice, 1964), and "Da Ruzante
al Beolco: Per la storia di un autore," *Atti del convegno sul tema: "La poesia
rusticana nel Rinascimento"* (Rome, 1969), pp. 85–109; Ludovico Zorzi, "Rassegna
di studi teatrali (In margine a due recenti antologie venete)," *LI*, XIII (1961),
335–363; Giorgio Padoan, "Angelo Beolco da Ruzante a Perduocimo," *LI*, XX
(1968), 121–200. These are only a few—but in my opinion the most important—of
the numerous essays on Beolco published in recent years.

Ruzante's *Teatro* by Zorzi,[6] the phase of rediscovery may be considered concluded; nevertheless, we still have an impressive score to settle with Beolco. After rereading "all Ruzante" in Zorzi's edition, there can be little doubt left that he is the greatest Italian playwright of the sixteenth century, or at least that his plays are masterpieces comparable only to a few others in the Cinquecento: Machiavelli's *La Mandragola*, the anonymous *La Venexiana*, perhaps *La Cortigiana* of Pietro Aretino.

Spanning a period of a little over fifteen years in the first half of the century, from 1520 to 1536 more or less, the chronology for a good half of Beolco's works remains uncertain. However, internal and external evidence permits us to group them in three phases, with the exception of *L'Anconitana*, the date of which is still highly controversial.

The first phase, from ca. 1520 to 1525, is represented by the eclogue *La Pastoral*, that mixes standard Italian with the dialects of Padua and Bergamo, the vernacular *First Oration*, addressed in 1521 to Cardinal Marco Cornaro in Asolo, and *La Betìa*, a *mariazo* or marriage play in verse, also in Paduan dialect. A second phase, between 1528 and 1530/31, includes the *Second Oration*, addressed again in Asolo to Cardinal Francesco Cornaro, Marco's brother and successor, three "dialogues" or one-act plays, two of them being *Bilora* and the *Parlamento*, the best known of Ruzante's works, and two regular comedies, *La Moscheta* and *La Fiorina*. In the final period were written two other comedies imitated from Plautus, *La Piovana* and *La Vaccària* (certainly composed in 1532/33), and the letter to Alvarotto, Beolco's last known work and a sort of spiritual testament, as we shall see.

Our chronological outline shows that Beolco's early activity can be situated between the truce that Venice had signed with the emperor in 1518 and the League of Cognac in 1526: that is, in a period of relative peace and reconstruction for the Venetian republic and her territory, including Padua, after the catastrophes of the League of Cambrai and

6. Ruzante, *Teatro: Prima edizione completa. Testo, traduzione e note,* ed. L. Zorzi (Turin, 1967). Zorzi's notes (more than 300 pages at the end of the volume) constitute an invaluable tool for Ruzante scholars, both for the vastness and precision of his information and the acuteness of his critical interpretation. My citations are all from this edition, with the page number given only in the case of the longer passages. The English translation is mine, unless otherwise specified.

the bloody defeat of Agnadello in 1509; a typical, if ephemeral postwar situation, when culture strives for an equilibrium between the recent horrors and the vitality that nature seems to infuse into the survivors as though to make up for the lives and time lost.[7]

In this context, the young actor Beolco, who was a self-taught man of considerable learning, began his writing career by exploiting—and trans-forming—the two different traditions that he found ready-made within his reach: the tradition of the pastoral eclogue, literary but also po-tentially dramatic, after Poliziano's *Orfeo,* and the popular tradition of the *mariazo,* the bawdy farce or *contrasto* in verse performed during rustic weddings—a ritual form of theater which had its roots in the most remote folklore of the Western world.[8] From this second tradition Beolco inherited the role he used to perform as an actor in his own plays, the *vilàn* or rustic Ruzante, a character that he reshaped in the light of the direct experience of the peasants and peasants' life he had acquired while managing the farms of his brothers and the country estate of his rich protector and admirer Alvise Cornaro.

Confronted by the fashionable Arcadias of his time and the exquisite-ness of their self-styled shepherds, Ruzante asserts from the outset his massive and famished presence on the stage and his unfailing belief in *snaturalité,* naturalness, or rather nature *tout court.* So, for instance, when *La Betìa* is happily concluded by the promise of an erotic com-munal life for the two peasant couples, such an ending mirrors not only the well-known Boccaccian pattern of the "happy foursome," but more directly the sexual collectivism then widespread in the country. And it is not by chance that the whole first act of the same play turns out to be a parody of the lofty, platonic love expounded in the *Asolani* by Bembo: "un gran sletràn, maòr che sea sul Pavàn," as a character says ("a great scholar, the biggest in the territory of Padua"—the adjectives clearly referring to the size of Bembo's body rather than to the quality of his writings).

While in *La Pastoral* the tenuous Arcadian plot—lamentation, suicide, and burial of the shepherd *mal aimé*—is dreamed by Ruzante before the action begins, the rustic recounts his dream to the audience as soon as

7. Cf. Zorzi's Introduction, *Teatro,* p. xxix.
8, See Paolo Toschi, *Le Origini del teatro italiano* (Turin, 1955), pp. 413 ff,

he wakes (*Proemio a la villana:* rustic prologue) and ends by finding himself enmeshed in that same pastoral story as the action proceeds— much to his displeasure. In Ruzante's account, by a process of obvious demystification, the elegant *pastori* (shepherds) become *pegorari,* a word that means the same thing but belongs to a much more down-to-earth register; the gesticulating candidate for suicide, "un vecieto . . . el parea Barba Scati" ("a little old man who looked like Uncle Jerks"); and his melodious playing and singing before dying of love, a ballroom tune:

> Cum l'ave ben zarlò,
> el scomenzé a sonare:
> el fasea vuogia de balare.
>
> (p. 11)

> As his chatter was over,
> he started playing:
> and made me feel like dancing.

Furthermore, when the two worlds come into direct contact, each with its own language, respectively literary Tuscan and the dialect of Padua, it is not the rustic that disturbs the shepherds, as tradition had it, but just the opposite; while Ruzante is about to shoot a bird with his blowpipe, the shepherd Arpino rushes onto the stage calling for somebody to help him bury his dead friend and scares the bird away, rousing the anger of the peasant:

> (A') digo ch'a' vuò guagnarme da magnare;
> ch'a' he tre boche a le spale e mia serore,
> che 'l gh'ha mazò so marìo i Toìschi.
>
> (p. 59)

> I say, I have got to earn my bread,
> for I have three mouths to feed, and my sister,
> since the German soldiers have killed her man.

But when Arpino invokes Pan ("O sacro Pan, pietà d'i servi toi!"), Ruzante suddenly becomes very friendly: "Tu me vuò dar del pan? Mo su, anagùn" ("You want to give me some bread? Let's go"). Obviously, the farcical pun between Pan the god and *pan* as bread implies a more serious confrontation between the *snatural,* natural, parlance extolled by Beolco in all his prologues *a la villana* and the grammatical, Tuscan language spoken by the shepherds. And behind such an opposition there is another one yet, between city and country, *citaìni e contaìni.* As

Beolco will say to Cardinal Cornaro the elder in the *First Oration,*
"These literary pricks, that want to talk grammatically and *a la Fioren-
tinesca,* are after better bread than you can make with wheat."[9]

The *First Oration,* composed in 1521 to welcome Cardinal Cornaro in
Asolo, is the best formulation of Beolco's poetics in these years. On the
one hand, the adoption of the rustic vernacular even on an occasion
such as this corresponds to the intention of entertaining a refined and
aristocratic audience. If the solidarity that the actor feels for the peasants
he impersonates is evident, no less clear is the author's fellowship—not
to say complicity—with his spectators. On the other hand the choice of
the Paduan dialect is a profession of faith in the *snaturalité* as opposed to
everything that is *moscheto,* artificial and sophisticated, and climaxes
with the glorification of the *taratuorio pavan,* the territory or land
around Padua, with its pure air, prodigious fertility and abundance,
and its girls well equipped for hard labor, love-making, and child-
bearing:

In colusion, a' cherzo verasiamen che 'l supia el Paraìso terestro, e tanto pì
belo e megiore, com che là su no se magna, e chialò sì.

(p. 1193)

In conclusion, I truly believe this to be the earthly paradise, all the better
and preferable, because up there they do not eat, and down here we do.

As for the *leze e stratuti* (laws and statutes) that Ruzante suggests to
the cardinal, speaking on behalf of the whole rustic community, they
show, to be sure, more than one trace of evangelical and Erasmian influence—a subject that it is not my purpose to discuss here. I shall only
recall among them the peasants' exemption from fasting; the permission to harvest during religious holidays to save the crop in case of bad
weather; and mandatory marriage for priests, so that, busy in their own
houses, they would stop chasing the rustics' wives and daughters, or at
least could be paid in the same coin.

But these same laws reflect also a youthful season in Beolco's career
when the *snaturalité* seems to be optimistically bound to overcome the
fastubi (worries) and *torbolaziòn* (tribulations) brought upon the peasants by poverty and the abuses of city dwellers. It is one of the

9. See the fine analyses of *La Pastoral* by Baratto, *Tre studi,* pp. 17–25, and
Dersofi, "Ruzante," pp. 145–147. To both I am greatly indebted.

functions of Ruzante's theater to make us believe in the possible triumph of nature over all the bad things that the rustic often summarizes with the image of the *cancaro,* the cancer gnawing at the *roesso mondo,* the "whole world" if *roesso* stands for *universo,* but at the same time and more significantly the "world turned upside down," if *roesso* means *roverso,* overturned, as it also undoubtedly does.

The rural Eden of Ruzante's early plays may well win an easy victory over the literary Arcadia of Sannazaro and Bembo, but it soon shows itself to be a precarious shelter against the violence of reality and history. The works of the central period, written about or shortly after 1528, the year of the great famine, offer a glimpse of the peasants' condition that is no longer merely comic.

In the *Second Oration,* addressed in 1528 to Francesco Cornaro, the desolation of the fields and the hunger of the people lead Ruzante to the bitter discovery that his old *Paradìso terestro* has become the hell of a *tera vegra,* a wasteland:

El disse Messier Ieson Dio al nostro pare Adamo, e an a nu tuti che a' ghe seòn vegnù drio: "In suore vultu tui te magnerè pane tui." Mo el me pare mo che la vaghe a un altro muò, cha nu, che a' se suòm, a' no n'aòn mé, e gi altri, cha no se sua, el magne.

(p. 1217)

Sir God Jesus said to our father Adam and also to us who followed: "In the sweat of your face you will eat bread." Now it seems to me this is not the way things are today, that we, who sweat, do not eat at all, and those eat plenty who do not sweat.

Accordingly, the laws that once again Ruzante proposes to his cardinal have now a defensive slant, half resigned, half polemic—like the one legalizing usury so that in wintertime the peasants may borrow money at an interest lower than that now requested by clandestine lenders, or the project to unify all extant laws into a single codex, which would at last take into account the point of view of Menego, Nale, and all the other farmers:

A' no aòn leza dal nostro lò, né [che] dighe per nu, né che ghe supia stò negun d'i nuostri. A' sento lomé dire la leza de Dato, la leza de Bartole, la leza de Gesto dire cossì; a' no sento mé dire: la leza de Menego, la leza de Nale, la leza de Duozo.

(p. 1217)

We have no laws on our side, none speaking for us, none passed after asking our advice. I keep hearing people invoking the law of Datum, the law of Bartolus, the law of Digest; never do I hear anything about the law of Menego, the law of Nale, the law of Duozo.

Laws are always made in the cities, by and for city dwellers. The plays of this period have in common the theme of the rustic who comes to town and in one way or another finds there his doom. Bilora, the peasant who gives his name to one of the *dialoghi,* is in Venice to look for his wife, Gnua, who came to live here, half mistress half nurse, in the house of the rich old patrician Andronico. Driven away by the woman, Bilora gets drunk with the money she paid to get rid of him. Later he comes back to the old man's house and kills him, almost without knowing, in his drunkenness, what he is doing, thereby making himself an outlaw.

The bilingualism of *La Pastoral* returns here in the contrast between the coarse parlance of Bilora and Gnua and the courtly Venetian of Andronico. But rather than providing an opportunity for antiliterary satire and the celebration of the *snatural,* now this opposition is the sign of an irremediable chasm between two conditions: on one side the hunger and ignorance of the country, on the other the money and culture of the city—this latter remaining an incomprehensible and dangerous world for the peasants, which they call *moscheto,* literally musk-smelling.

In the comedy *La Moscheta* the destruction of the war has forced Ruzante and his wife Betìa to come to live in Padua, where for a while, unfortunately for him, the rustic is convinced that he has become a clever man. Instigated by his comrade Menato, who actually plans to seduce Betìa, Ruzante decides to test her fidelity and calls on her in disguise and talking *moscheto,* that is, pretending to speak Italian. The woman, who at first does not recognize him, and is ready to earn with her favors the money the stranger is offering, later grows so incensed at being deceived that she will betray her husband not only with Menato but also with a neighbor, a soldier whom Ruzante had tried to swindle.

The *snaturalité,* we have seen, can no longer provide the rustic with a rationale and a shelter against military invasions and city tricks. But to betray the *snatural* is to make things even worse; there is, really, no way out. If you, a peasant, pretend to be a *pulitàn de la Talia* (a Neapolitan from Italy) in order to tempt foolishly your wife—as Ruzante does in *La Moscheta*—or impersonate a rough and tough veteran to win her back—as the same character will do in the *Parlamento*—the consequences of this sin will fall back, literally, on your own shoulders.

In the *Parlamento,* again in Venice, where his woman, Gnua, has come to earn a living as a whore, Ruzante is a soldier back from the war, cowardly and plagued with lice, but nonetheless a braggart. When he tries to convince the girl to return to him in spite of his poverty, she refuses with a reflection worthy of Machiavelli: "If I could keep alive on one meal a year, you'd do fine for me. But I have to eat every day . . ." [10] And since Ruzante insists, he is badly beaten up by one of her lovers.

How come, asks his fellow countryman Menato, who witnessed the whole scene, that a man as tough and brave as Ruzante had boasted he had become would take such a beating without even attempting to react? Gnua's sorcery is the reason, answers Ruzante from the ground where he is still lying: she has bewitched him into believing there were a hundred assailants. If he had only known there was just one of them, he would have taken the knave and the bitch and tied them together, and what fun that would have been!

At the end Menato, more and more aghast at seeing how cheerfully his friend is taking the terrible punishment he received, is the one who needs Ruzante's comforting:

10. The English translation of this and the next passage is from Bentley, *Classic Theatre,* pp. 72, 77. Cf. Machiavelli, *Principe,* chap. xviii: "If men were all good, this precept would not be a good one; but, since they are bad . . . ," and a similar passage also in chap. xv. As I hope to show in another paper, numerous passages in Beolco's works (in particular the *dialoghi, La Moscheta,* and *La Fiorina*) seem to be reminiscent of Machiavelli's characteristic way of reasoning and writing, especially in *La Mandragola.* If one remembers that *La Mandragola* was successfully staged in Venice in 1522, a few weeks before the performance of a "comedia a la vilanescha" by "Ruzante e Menato" (Sanuto, *Diarii,* XXXIII, 9), and again in 1526 (after a Venetian edition of the play and a visit of the author to that city), it is safe to guess that not only did Beolco know Machiavelli's masterpiece, but probably the stern exposure of human foibles in *La Mandragola* helped him find the way toward his most original and "cruellest" works; for the exact chronology, see G. Padoan, "La *Mandragola* del Machiavelli nella Venezia cinquecentesca," *LI,* XXII (1970), 161–186.

Poh, compare! Che me fa a mi? O cancaro, la sarae stà da riso, s'a' i ligava!
E sì aessè po dito ch'a' no ve faze pì de le comierie.

(p. 543)

What the hell, Menato? What does it matter? What do I care? It really
would have been a riot, though, if I'd tied the two of them together! But
then, I suppose you'd have told me not to put on any more comedies.

To the violence of history, which by now denies him any possibility
of normal existence, Ruzante can only oppose, at the price of a calculated
self-deception, his own "counter-history," which ends up by reversing the
roesso mondo, by overturning the world turned upside down—not even
a comedy, but the dream of a comedy, whereby the protagonist could
promote himself from the pitiful victim that he really is to the privileged, twofold role of hero and spectator.

In order to bring his peasants onto the stage without betraying them,
but always—we must never forget—for the pleasure of his refined
audiences of Padua, Venice, and Ferrara, Beolco arrives long before
Genet at a theater of mirrors and hallucination in which the characters
try to be *comédiens* to escape their historical destiny of *martyrs.*

As Ruzante's last words to Menato seem to suggest ("You'd have
told me not to put on any more comedies"), it was impossible to go any
further in this direction; and this may explain the return to literature,
the prevalence of the author over the actor and the character that we find
in the comedies written after 1530, no longer for the Venetian stage but
for the Estense court in Ferrara.

In *L'Anconitana (The Girl from Ancona),* if it belongs to this third
group as I believe, Ruzante is no longer the peasant that he used to be
but a servant and a procurer, that is, a Zanni *avant la lettre;* along with
his old and lecherous master Tomao and the three couples of *amorosi*
and *amorose* that the plot punctually leads to the altar, he prefigures
indeed the typology of the Commedia dell'Arte.

La Piovana and *La Vaccària,* of 1532 / 33, blend respectively Plautus'
Rudens and *Asinaria* with inventions of Terence, Ariosto, and Beolco's
own. In the urban setting of these elegant plays, at the same time more
"classical" and more "middle-class" than anything he had written before, there is no room any longer for the character of Ruzante and his
snaturalité. In both, as an actor, Beolco played the same role of a cunning domestic, Garbinelo in *La Piovana,* Truffo in *La Vaccària.*

The practical wisdom of this character, integrated at last into the "civilized" world and akin to the malicious servants of Bibbiena's *La Calandria* and Aretino's *La Cortigiana* and *L'Ipocrito,* is well summarized by Truffo in a reflection that seems curiously to announce Hegel's dialectic of master and servant and the *Volkstück* of Brecht's *Herr Puntila und sein Knecht Matti:*

Faze pur, sti richi, co' i vuole, ch'i no pò fare senza nu; perché, se nu a' no foessàm famigi, igi no serae paruni.

(p. 1071)

They may do what they want, these rich people, but they cannot do without us; because, if we were not servants, they would not be masters.

But Ruzante the rustic, speaking to a certain extent for the author, comes back one last time in the "letter" Beolco wrote in 1536 to his fellow actor Marco Alvarotto, for him to read—or recite—to their common friends who used to gather each winter, during a hunting party, in one of the country houses of Alvise Cornaro (that year, presumably, in the absence of Beolco himself).

To Alvarotto, Ruzante writes that, one day after a hunt, after looking for a long time and in vain into his *compagni libretti,* his friends the books, for the secret of prolonging life indefinitely, he fell asleep on a knoll and began to dream. It is worth noting that Beolco's whole work lies between two dreams, that related by young Ruzante to the audience in the vernacular prologue of *La Pastoral,* and this one, told by the same, older, Ruzante to his friend.[11]

Furthermore, both dreams occur during a hunting expedition, and both are related to the fear of death and the longing for a better life,[12]

---

11. In his provocative and far-reaching book *The Theater and the Dream: From Metaphor to Form in Renaissance Drama* (Baltimore, Md., 1973), Jackson I. Cope mentions Ruzante (pp. 217, 284), but does not focus on this aspect of his theater, though providing the best possible introduction to it.

12. See the *Proemio a la villana* of *La Pastoral:* "A crezo, a la mia fé, / Ch'a sun morto . . . Vergine Maria, / Quando morigi?" (Upon my word, I believe I am dead . . . Virgin Mary, when did I die?—pp. 7–9); and later on: "El m'iera viso / Ch'a' fusse in un Paraìso, / E tante bele pute / Che s'a' la risea tute" (It seemed to me that I was in a Paradise, with a lot of pretty girls, all giggling—p. 9). The recollection of the blessed place dreamed by the character merges with what the actor sees in front of him, the smiling ladies in the audience, so that a

as though in his empathy for the peasants' condition and their fight for
survival, Beolco were able to "dig up," so to speak, the basic elements of
their ancestral mind: a little like the Florentine painter Piero di Cosimo
(1462–1521), who—according to Panofsky's fascinating interpretation—
was enabled by his archaeological, or rather atavistic, memory to reconstruct with startling precision the early history of mankind.[13]

But the allusion to *i compagni libretti* has already told us that in the
letter Ruzante, if he is Beolco more than ever, is a much wiser and
more complex character than in the early plays. In his sleep, he dreams
of Barba Polo, an old friend and fellow showman who had been dead
for some time. And Polo explains that what he had asked of his books,
only Madona Legraçiòn, Dame Joyfulness, can perform. She is able
indeed to prolong life, not *metando una vita da cao de l'altra*, by putting one life on top of another, but by teaching men to be aware and
happy that they are alive: "one hour of life of one who knows he is
alive, is more life, and longer, than the whole life of one who does not
know he is alive."

From the summit of the hill old Polo shows Ruzante the estate of
Lady Joyfulness, populated by Pleasures and Virtues, and defended by
Mea Savianza, Aunt Sagacity, against her mistress' enemies, Sullenness,

---

significant analogy seems suggested between Theater and Paradise (cf. Dersofi,
"Ruzante," p. 147). Finally, in the third one-act play, the *Dialogo facetissimo*, the
soul of a dead friend, Zaccarotto, will explain to the rustics Menato and Duozo
that there are two Paradises: one meant for ascetic and deeply religious people,
whose sole happiness is in contemplating God, and another reserved for men of
action and gallant fellows (*omeni da bene*) who, having led an honest and full
life, are granted up there the same pleasures they used to enjoy here in moderation:
eating, drinking, singing and playing, hunting (pp. 713–719).

13. Erwin Panofsky, "Early History of Man," in *Studies in Iconology* (1939;
rpt. New York and Evanston, 1972). One could easily recognize in Ruzante many
of the psychological and cultural features that Panofsky points out in Piero: "To
him civilisation meant a realm of beauty and happiness as long as man kept in
close contact with Nature, but a nightmare of oppression, ugliness and distress
as soon as man became estranged from her"; or: "In his pictures [plays], primitive
[rustic] life is not transfigured in a spirit of Utopian sentimentality, as is the
case with the poetic and pictorial evocations of 'Arcadia'; it is reenacted with the
utmost realism and concreteness" (pp. 65, 67).

Sadness, Jealousy, etc. On the one hand these and other figures in the villa of Madona Legraçiòn belong to a wide-ranging and illustrious allegorical tradition, which includes—to give only a few examples—the Twelve Months frescoes of Palazzo Schifanoja in Ferrara (second half of the fifteenth century), the train of Folly in the *Moriae encomium* (1509), and, perhaps also known to Beolco, the disquieting passengers of Sebastian Brant's *Narrenschiff* (1494).[14]

On the other hand, one could be tempted to view Ruzante's description of happy life as yet another variation on the theme, so common in the sixteenth century, of the Golden Age and the Earthly Paradise,[15] if it were only to notice how little he dwells on the usual niceties and delights of pastoral life—probably because, unlike many of his fellow writers, he happened to know firsthand how real people lived in the country.[16]

14. The *Ship of Fools* was translated into Latin very soon after its publication, and Beolco could have it in mind also when he was writing *La Betìa*. In the fifth act Nale (a clever rustic who makes his wife believe he is dead and a ghost back from the other world) gives a "Rabelaisian account of his sufferings in hell," and among other things relates "how he was all but buried in an ocean of dung, how he saw on this ocean a boatload of Venetian whores quarreling and fighting among themselves" (Herrick, *Italian Comedy*, p. 45).

15. In addition to the references to Paradise already seen, a passage in the Prologue of *La Piovana* shows that Beolco was familiar with the philosophical assumption on which the myth rested:

A priest told me, that a great philosopher swore to him, that we, who are alive now, have been in this same world thousands and thousands of years ago: I was I and you were you, these ones were these ones, those others were those others; and in as many thousands of years, when I don't know what wheel completes a whole turn, we shall be around again, I standing up here, you sitting down there, I talking you listening . . . and these words, which will have been words, will again be words, and it will seem to you that you heard them before, exactly as it seems to you now" (pp. 887–889).

Beolco is jokingly defending himself from the accusation of having plagiarized Plautus: but he is also aware of the chiliastic belief to which the topos of the Golden Age was related.

16. For its anomalies, Ruzante's "garden of happy life" was of no avail to the scholars who in recent years have thoroughly and brilliantly studied the myths of the Golden Age and the Earthly Paradise. But the reciprocal is not true, and the student of Ruzante can greatly benefit by essays and books such as E. H. Gom-

No less tempting is the analogy with Prospero's airy realm in *The Tempest,* a play that is also a kind of spiritual testament. Ariel's island and Joyfulness' valley, though off the routes usually taken by the people of the brave new world, are within reach of the wise mind. Peace and harmony may be enjoyed there by restraining one's passions; at the end we do not know whether the thin veil of sadness which surrounds both places is due to the disenchantment they require of their inhabitants or to the fact that real people are just visiting there. At the end of Ruzante's dream, of Prospero's exile, the valley and the island will be left once again to the emblems and spirits that are their true denizens.

Finally, even more intriguing is the comparison with another fantasy of the same type (and almost exactly of the same time: 1534), the sumptuous abbey of Thélème, with whose planning and foundation *Gargantua* ends. In this case the similarities are closer and more numerous, starting with Beolco's *buoni compagni* matching verbatim Rabelais's *gentilz compaignons,* and the horrid personifications of anguish barred from the gate of Madona Legraçiòn's garden as well as from Frère Jean's manor; but it is a basic difference that strikes us more. The lordly ways of the Thelemites make a golden tapestry against which the daily life of Dame Joyfulness and her guests stands out in all its plainness: walks, hunts, healthy suppers seasoned by Appetite, evenings spent in company by the fireside; soon after the falling of night everybody goes to bed, as Rest, *un veciaruolo con gi uoci pesuochi,* a little old man with heavy eyes, takes a tour of the house and sends all to sleep: a world much closer to Bruegel the elder than to the masters of Schifanoja. There,

tuto serà metù in riequia, tuto arpasò, tuto acordò, tuto artasentò; perché te no averè in la panza altro che vite. E agno cossa sarà vita: el pan vita, el

---

brich, "Renaissance and Golden Age," in *Norm and Form: Studies in the Art of the Renaissance* (London and New York, 1966; 2d ed. 1971); A. Bartlett Giamatti, *The Earthly Paradise and the Renaissance Epic* (Princeton, N.J., 1966); Harry Levin, *The Myth of The Golden Age in the Renaissance* (Bloomington, Ind. and London, 1969); Terry Comito, "Renaissance Gardens and the Discovery of Paradise," *JHI,* XXXII (1971), 483–506; Gustavo Costa, *La Leggenda dei secoli d'oro nella letteratura italiana* (Bari, 1972); Frank E. and Fritzie P. Manuel, "Sketch for a Natural History of Paradise," *Dædalus* (Winter, 1972), pp. 83–128.

vin vita, e tuto el magnare vita. E col pigiar fiò per el naso, te tirerè su agno bota una vita, e in colusion te no te sentirè atorno se no çielo e vite.

(p. 1243)

all will be rested, all pacified, all reconciled, all silent; because you'll have in your stomach nothing but lives. And everything will be life: bread life, wine life, and all food you eat life. And by breathing through your nose, you will draw in with each breath one life: to make it short, you'll feel nothing around you but sky and lives.

This last hyperbole seems to mark in its recurrence and with its variations the different phases of Beolco's career. In 1521, praising to Cardinal Cornaro the demographic effects of polygamy (which he favored in obedience to God's precept in Genesis, *cressì e smultiplichè*), Ruzante had predicted, with an enthusiasm that today makes us shiver: "Se veerà se lomé cielo e femene gravie e puti e tosati" (One will see nothing but sky and pregnant women and babies and children). Seven years later, describing to Menato the battlefield after the Venetian defeat of Agnadello, Ruzante will say in the *Parlamento:* "Compare, a' no vîvi se no cielo e uossi de morti" (Pal, I saw nothing there, but sky and bones of dead people).[17]

On the one hand, then, we have a mutable element that we might call the dynamic history of Ruzante. The actor carves out of the *mariazi* tradition, and of his own experience, a character socially plausible, the rustic; the author takes charge of him and makes Ruzante the herald of his poetics of *snaturalité*. But at a certain point (in *La Moscheta* and the *Parlamento*) the character forces, as it were, Beolco's hand and superimposes his conscience, his existential logic, on that of the author, a little as Don Quixote's wisdom, in the course of the novel, will increasingly transcend the cultural implications of his folly. When the theatrical autonomy (or solitude) of the rustic seems to threaten the very existence of Comedy, to rescue her Beolco goes back to literature and philosophy until he meets Dame Joyfulness; then Ruzante may return, if not as the protagonist of a play or *parlamento,* at least as an author himself of a letter in which he tells a friend of his dreams.

17. For an exhaustive study of Beolco's language, see Marisa Milani, *"Snaturalité e deformazione nella lingua teatrale del Ruzzante,"* in L. Vanossi et al., *Lingua e strutture del teatro italiano del Rinascimento* (Padua, 1970), pp. 107–202.

On the other hand, we have a permanent element, the extraordinary density and vitality of Beolco's language, which makes possible a representation of the peasants that, though addressed to a social and intellectual élite, is never patronizing: a language thanks to which Ruzante ends always by coinciding with Beolco and goes on offering on his behalf some of the *legraçiòn* needed by the *citaìni* and the *sletràn* of the *roesso mondo*.

Senecan Tragedy: A Critique of Scholarly Trends

Review Article

ANNA LYDIA MOTTO

JOHN R. CLARK

T HE REPUBLICATION in 1927 of Newton's collected edition (1581) of *Seneca His Tenne Tragedies* together with T. S. Eliot's introductory essay[1] may be considered a major event, comparable to the original appearance of this translation in the sixteenth century. Eliot perceived that the 1581 edition was a landmark, not because the Elizabethans needed an English translation (many had read Seneca in Latin in the schools), but because it typified the Roman philosopher's increasing and sweeping influence in that era. It was, as Eliot noted, an "event of capital importance."

Such an Elizabethan "homage" to Seneca may be taken as a type of affirmative criticism, and no more significant "affirmative" criticism has been proposed since that time than Eliot's own 1927 essay.[2] Eliot sensibly argued away many of the standard objections against Seneca the dramatist, and forcibly urged "Seneca's influence upon dramatic

---

1. *Seneca His Tenne Tragedies,* ed. Thomas Newton [1581], intro. T. S. Eliot (New York, 1927).

2. This point is tellingly urged by C. J. Herington, "Senecan Tragedy," *Arion,* V (1966), 422–423.

form, upon versification and language, upon sensibility, and upon thought. . . ." [3] Nonetheless, Eliot fully recognized the climate of disapprobation under which Seneca lay: "In the Renaissance, no Latin author was more highly esteemed than Seneca; in modern times, few Latin authors have been more consistently damned." [4]

But, for all of his essay's importance, Eliot has hardly been able to stem the general critical tide which deplores Senecan drama; most criticism since 1927 has continued to assault the philosopher's talent and his influence. Recently, two scholars of some repute—H. D. F. Kitto and H. J. Muller—have both labeled Senecan work "abominable" and "dreadful." [5] And, if anything, scholarship in the last four decades has continued to vilify or, more mildly, at least to denigrate Senecan tragedy, suggesting that Seneca is in no way akin to Sophocles or to Shakespeare, and perhaps worthless himself. Perhaps an analogy might help to trace the cause. When, in the nineteenth century, it fully came home to academic Englishmen that the great Shakespeare far surpassed "University wits" in the drama without himself ever having gone to school, they immediately postulated that the plays had been written by somebody else. Similarly, the thought that Seneca could have been influential upon our forebears when he was in fact less brilliant and powerful than Aeschylus, Sophocles, or Euripides has driven many a scholar to insist that Seneca had virtually no influence at all. But whatever the reason, Seneca and his tragedies have fallen upon hard times, and the present essay will attempt to sketch the major trends in recent criticism,

3. T. S. Eliot, "Seneca in Elizabethan Translation," *Selected Essays* (New York, 1950), p. 79. Eliot's introduction to the Newton volume is here included in a selection of his essays, a volume which obviously made his opinions about Senecan drama far more widely available.

4. *Ibid.*, p. 52. One of the more severe critics has been Désiré Nisard, *Etudes de moeurs et de critique sur les poetes Latins de la decadence . . . ,* 2d ed. (Paris, 1849), pp. 57–144. For a review of such negative criticism, consult Howard V. Canter, "Rhetorical Elements in the Tragedies of Seneca," *University of Illinois Studies in Language and Literature,* X (Urbana, 1925), 15–18.

5. Herbert J. Muller, *The Spirit of Tragedy* (New York, 1956), p. 132, designates Senecan work "abominable," while H. D. F. Kitto, in "Le Déclin de la tragédie à Athènes et en Angleterre," *Le Théâtre Tragique,* ed. Jean Jacquot (Paris, 1962), p. 68, speaks of "l'effroyable Sénèque," who nevertheless appealed to barbarous Elizabethans, "mes compatriotes assoiffés de sang."

to assess these currents, and, finally, to propose areas in Senecan dramatic studies that deserve encouragement and require further exploration in the future.

I

First, it must be said that there are a number of highly adequate bibliographical tools available to those who wish to explore Senecan drama. In addition to standard sources, the yearly *L'Année philologique* and the brief quarterly bibliographies in the journal *Gnomon,* together with the up-dated treatment of Seneca in Platnauer,[6] a number of specific works certainly prove useful. Most thorough and helpful (because of detailed paragraphs discussing individual works) is M. Coffey's bibliography, covering the years 1922–1955.[7] Two essay-like bibliographies by D'Agostino are similarly helpful, reviewing work for the years 1930–1952 and 1953–1965.[8] A recent essay by Cupaiuolo, furthermore, explores the specific years 1969–1971.[9] Such surveys make it relatively easy to review the general trends in this century in Senecan studies.

When one actually does examine this body of work, one is able, we believe, to discern three rather broad and distinctive "trends." Ultimately, none of these trends is, alas, likely to place Seneca or his work in a very favorable light.

6. Consult W. A. Laidlaw's essay, "Roman Drama," in *Fifty Years of Classical Scholarship,* ed. M. Platnauer (Oxford, 1954), pp. 257–271.

7. "Senecan Tragedies, including pseudo-Senecan *Octavia* and Epigrams attributed to Seneca. Report for the Years 1922–1955," *Lustrum,* II (1957), 113–186. See also H. J. Mette, "Die Römische Tragödie und die Neufunde zur Griechischen Tragödie (insbesondere für die Jahre 1945–1964)," *Lustrum,* IX (1964), esp. pp. 18–23 and 160–194.

8. V. D'Agostino, "Orientamento bibliografico su Seneca filosofo e tragico (1930–1952)," *RSCl,* I (1952), 47–65; and "Seneca filosofo e tragico negli anni 1953–1965. Saggio bibliografico," *RSCl,* XIV (1966), 61–81.

9. G. Cupaiuolo, "Gli studi su Seneca nel triennio 1969–1971," *Bollettino di Studi Latini,* II (1972), 290–295. In addition, much recent criticism—especially adverse criticism—is incorporated in the notes of Isidoro Muñoz Valle's "Valoracion del elemento retorico en las Tragedias de Seneca," *Actas del Congreso Internacional de Filosofia en commemoracion de Seneca en el XIX Centenario de su muerte* (Madrid, 1967), pp. 141–153.

The Greek Influence

A number of critics become too much concerned with the "influence" of Aeschylus, Sophocles, and Euripides upon Senecan drama. Commencing with a "search" in Seneca for "elements" and "particles" that are "Sophoclean" or "Euripidesque," they conclude by perceiving nothing else. All too often, as a consequence, they end by describing and decrying Seneca's single-minded monolithic Grecian debt.[10] Such a patent, predetermined conclusion has been, over the centuries, recurrent. Surely a playwright who employs the machinery of Greek tragedy—its mythic families, its themes and scenes, its choruses, etc.—owes an evident debt to his Hellenic forebears. So much is obvious. Any author writing "plays" is clearly indebted (and who would deny it?) to playwrights. However, all too frequently, such critics, who begin with a simple comparison of Seneca and the great Greek trio of playwrights,[11] conclude by finding Seneca *wholly* derivative or, when he deviates from Greek practice, defective, pathetic, inept.[12] Brecht clearly owes some obligations to Gay's *Beggar's Opera,* Shakespeare in his *Hamlet* is surely obliged to the earlier drama by Kyd. So much is self-evident. Still, it is another

10. B. Seidensticker, *Die Gesprächsverdichtung in den Tragödien Senecas* (Heidelberg, 1970), heavily stresses Greek "models." Pierre Grimal, for instance, in "L'Originalité de Sénèque dans la tragédie de *Phèdre,*" *RELat,* XLI (1963), 297–314, discovers that Senecan "originality" extends to large borrowings from Euripides, while William M. Calder III, "Originality in Seneca's *Troades,*" *Classical Philology,* LXV (1970), 75–82, discerns in Seneca no "originality" whatsoever. Needless to say, one supposes, is the fact that "originality" has become the especial badge of significance since the onset of the romantic movement in the nineteenth century.

11. The disturbing habit of meticulously paralleling Senecan plays with Greek plays was infelicitously fostered by the Loeb Classical Library edition of Seneca, which in an Appendix, on facing pages, proffers detailed résumés of Senecan and Greek dramatic plots on the same themes in so-called "Comparative Analyses": Seneca, *Tragedies,* trans. Frank Justus Miller (Cambridge, Mass., and London, 1917), I, 525–569; II, 491–509.

12. Clarence W. Mendell, *Our Seneca* (New Haven, Conn., 1941), does precisely this in Chapter I. After minutely comparing the Senecan and the Sophoclean *Oedipus,* he concludes that Senecan differences are certifiably defects. It should be evident, of course, that Seneca lacks the greatness of the three consummate playwrights with whom he is compared; to make *that* point over and over again is indeed to whallop a dead horse.

matter for the critic to expect the plays to be entirely alike, and Seneca to be without an iota of merit or "originality." [13]

Seneca's plays are what they are for a great many reasons; and surely no author of the least concern to our literary tradition merely composed by slavish or lackluster imitation. Seneca's plays are often striking and individualized in their own right, and not at all similar to Greek practice. They are, indeed, very often utterly different in intent and in kind from Greek theatrical usage. Moreover, Greek dramatists differed among themselves; there is no reason why the critic should expect Seneca to be the captive, mindless beggar or borrower, nor his plays subject—*in vacuo*—to the assumed "mandates" of Aristotelian poetics. Candidly, there is no reason to expect Seneca to be a Greek in Roman clothing, but "source studies" very often come to expect just that.

The point needs to be stressed, and stressed urgently, that a writer who utilizes a tradition should never be considered to be nothing but the replica of that tradition. No one is in the habit of maintaining that classicists like Dante, Milton, Goethe, or Pound are *nothing other* than the traditions they employ, and Seneca would be better served if he were not entertained as an amalgamator, imitator, and parasite. Or, possibly, as what is worse: as *imitateur manqué*.

The Roman Stamp

At the opposite extreme, a number of critics would "rescue" Seneca from the Greek camp, only to Romanize him with a vengeance. [14] Such a school minimizes the *einfluss* of the Greeks and frequently immerses itself in commonplace and trivial argument. Numerous scholars of this ilk debate endlessly whether Senecan drama was intended for recitation

13. The important study by Wolf-Hartmut Friedrich, *Untersuchungen zu Senecas dramatischer Technik* (Borna-Leipzig, 1933), illustrates such reasoning. After a detailed comparison of six Senecan plays with Greek "originals," he resolves that whenever Seneca deviates from his sources, he loses dramatic coherence and unity.

14. See particularly Moses Hadas, "The Roman Stamp of Seneca's Tragedies," *American Journal of Philology,* LX (1939), 220–231; R. B. Steele, "Some Roman Elements in the Tragedies of Seneca," *American Journal of Philology,* XLIII (1922), 1–31; and Berthe M. Marti, "The Prototypes of Seneca's Tragedies," *Classical Philology,* XLII (1947), 1–16.

or for the stage.[15] Others, knowingly observing that Seneca was a philosopher, and his father a rhetor, attempt to calculate in the plays the prevalence of his *suasoriae* and the forensics of his rhetoric.[16] Most importantly, however, critics of this color wish to persuade us of Seneca's Roman philosophy, and generate for us a Stoical Seneca, one who palpably "invokes" the "lessons" of Stoicism. Or such critics even discern in the plays a progressive system of a deeper and deeper infiltration of Stoic teachings.[17] They salvage Seneca the philosopher, it seems, but they do not much enhance our understanding of Seneca the dramatist.

Indeed, attention to single, isolated "questions" and "problems" in Senecan drama has tended to fracture and fragment the criticism, seemingly reducing the plays to illustrative bits and parts. Such a tendency in the criticism is only aggravated by the determination of modern scholarship that Senecan drama is rhetorical and without coherent dramatic composition.

A Senecan prologue is not only a separable prefix; it may be a summary of the whole plot, as [is] the prologue of Latin comedy. Separable the Senecan chorus is always in providing lyric interludes. It would thereby interrupt the

15. Most critics believe Senecan drama was meant for private reading or public declamation; very few, like Leon Herrmann, *Le Théâtre de Sénèque* (Paris, 1924), argue substantially that the plays were acted. The point, however, is that almost every book-length study devotes a chapter to the question of the dating of the plays and a chapter to the acting recitation debate. There is a certain degree of wastefulness in such conjecturings, for neither of these matters can ever be satisfactorily resolved.

16. See Canter, "Rhetorical Elements in the Tragedies of Seneca," pp. 9–185; and F. Martinazzoli, *Seneca, Studio sulla morale ellenica nell' esperienza romana* (Florence, 1945).

17. To be sure, critics have long urged that Seneca is a "moralizing" tragedian, and authors like T. Birt, "Was hat Seneca mit seinen Tragödien gewolt?," *Neue Jahrbücher für das klassische Altertum*, XXVII (1911), 336–364, and A. Sipple, *Der Staatsmann und Dichter Seneca als politischer Erzieher* (Würzburg, 1938), stress that Seneca was "instructing" Nero in the plays. But a recent school more and more wants to perceive a pervasive and waxing Stoicism abounding in the plays. See F. Egermann, "Seneca als Dichterphilosoph," *Neue Jahrbücher für das klassische Altertum*, III (1940), 18–36, Berthe Marti, "Seneca's Tragedies. A New Interpretation," *Transactions of the American Philological Association*, LXXVI (1945), 216–245, and Norman T. Pratt, Jr., "The Stoic Base of Senecan Drama," *Transactions of the American Philological Association* LXXIX (1948), 1–11.

action if the tragedy had the Greek onward course; but instead Seneca's violent scenes are themselves separable, and his dialogue is sometimes a collection of speeches.[18]

Such a reading of Senecan plays, giving over any possibility of total artistic relevance and integration, has induced a number of scholars simply to write on extracted "parts" of Senecan plays.[19] Such dissecting and dismemberment has not contributed signally to an examination or a comprehension of whole, individual plays. And, we take it, the examination of plays as total units, as works of art, lies precisely at the crux of what critical activity ought to be.

Seneca and the Elizabethans

Although for several centuries Seneca has been assaulted as a dramatist or explored piecemeal as a fragmented author, one of his last great strongholds has nevertheless been the virtually unanimous belief that, whatever his weaknesses, he at least can be viewed as an amazing catalyst and influence upon the great Elizabethan playwrights. The concept of Senecan influence has been general and was, for instance, put forward by Symonds in 1884.[20] Such a view was urged more rigorously than ever before by John W. Cunliffe, who reached into every possible pocket of Elizabethan drama to make his claim in his authoritative dissertation, *The Influence of Seneca on Elizabethan Tragedy* (1893). With him, a view of a pervasive influence was firmly established. It was made further secure by H. B. Charlton's lengthy Introduction in his edition of

18. C. S. Baldwin, *Renaissance Literary Theory and Practice* [1939] (Gloucester, Mass., 1959), pp. 186–187.

19. F. Freznel, *Die Prologe der Senecatragödien* (Leipzig, 1914) and Norman T. Pratt, Jr., *Dramatic Suspense in Seneca and in His Greek Precursors* (Princeton, N.J., 1939) study the prologues; W. Marx, *Funktion und Form der Chorlieder in den Seneca Tragödien* (Cologne, 1932) and J. D. Bishop, "The Choral Odes of Seneca: Theme and Development" (Diss., University of Pennsylvania, 1964) study the choruses; Mary V. Braginton, *The Supernatural in Seneca's Tragedies* (Menasha, Wis., 1933) explores ghosts and visions and the unnatural; and O. Regenbogen, *Schmerz und Tod in den Tragödien Senecas* [1927] (Darmstadt, 1963), surveys scenes of pain and suffering.

20. John Addington Symonds, *Shakspere's Predecessors in the English Drama* (London, 1884), chap. VI.

Sir William Alexander's *Poetical Works* in 1921,[21] and by F. L. Lucas' *Seneca and Elizabethan Tragedy* (1922). And, although Lucas believed the influence of Seneca after 1590 "more diffused and elusive" than did Cunliffe, and although Lucas was reluctant to make sweeping claims for Seneca's "direct" influence upon Shakespeare ("the number and importance of such echoes seem to have been very much exaggerated"),[22] the course was firmly set. After the appearance of Eliot's essay on Seneca in 1927, it is clear that the tide of Senecanism was at its apex.

Now this last great Senecan shibboleth has been challenged and disputed; it has been brought tumbling to the ground. Willard Farnham's *The Medieval Heritage of Elizabethan Tragedy* (1936) began to weaken the "classical origins" hypothesis in favor of a "native tradition." The deathblow was struck by Howard Baker's polemic volume *Induction to Tragedy* in 1939. Baker debunked the obvious exaggerations of Cunliffe's arguments and concluded that Senecan influence was virtually nil.

Thereafter, T. W. Baldwin demonstrated that the five-act structure of plays came to Elizabethan England through Terence, and he observed that Senecan influence upon critics and in the schools was relatively slight:

Seneca's plays are evidently not much impressed on the critics. The small number of editions speaks eloquently of this. Horace and Terence were grammar-school authors, and hence required hundreds of editions. But Seneca was not sufficiently esteemed to attain grammar-school standing, in England at least, till very occsionally toward the end of the sixteenth century; consequently, of him a very few editions managed to suffice.[23]

Since then, two studies have followed, largely confirming Baker, or at least more seriously questioning Seneca's importance.[24]

21. H. B. Charlton, *The Senecan Tradition in Renaissance Tragedy* [1921] (Manchester, 1946).

22. *Seneca and Elizabethan Tragedy* (Cambridge, 1922), pp. 110, 123.

23. T. W. Baldwin, *Shakspere's Five-Act Structure* (Urbana, Ill., 1947), pp. 150–151.

24. Peter Ure, "On Some Differences between Senecan and Elizabethan Tragedy," *DUJ*, XLI (1948), 17–23; and G. K. Hunter, "Seneca and the Elizabethans: A Case-Study in 'Influence,'" *ShS*, XX (1966), 17–26. Hunter expands his argument, minimizing a "pervasive influence" of Seneca upon Elizabethan drama, in his

Where do all of these late developments leave Senecan scholars, with reference to the Elizabethans? With some sense of humility, we hope. We all can recollect how fads have risen up and become the rage for a time, before expiring in a puff or being put down. For a number of decades, for instance, every critic of the period talked solemnly and long about "Elizabethan psychology," before that balloon, postulating a coherent medical thesis and every writer as a knowledgeable doctor, was piercingly burst.[25] Similarly, following the broad circulation of E. M. W. Tillyard's *The Elizabethan World Picture* (1943), it became a critical commonplace for scholars to speak of the "Elizabethan view." Then, in 1964, C. S. Lewis brought out *The Discarded Image*. Without ever once mentioning Tillyard's name, Lewis simply demonstrated conclusively that the "Elizabethan view" was a pervasive one emanating from the classical and the medieval worlds.

Cunliffe's theses in *The Influence of Seneca on Elizabethan Tragedy* were simply too sweeping, too grandiose, too inclusive. He often ransacked and distorted texts to establish his "case." His was another bubble to be exploded. "Influence studies" and *Quellenforschungen* are almost always on ticklish ground.[26] *B* might well do something very like *A*, but it is almost a hopeless affair to determine that *B learned* his strategy from *A*. He might have reinvented the tactic, obtained it from *C*, or even discovered it in *other* traditions or lying in the "public domain." Thus, it is virtually impossible to demonstrate that Seneca specifically influenced a stable of major Elizabethan authors or to show that they had been waiting about for an opportunity to feed from his trough. No one needed to turn specifically to Seneca to discover the "grand style," omens, or ghosts.

Yet, it is nevertheless true that Seneca's works *were* virtually in the

"Seneca and English Tragedy," in *Seneca* (Studies in Latin Literature) (London, 1974), pp. 166–204.

25. Louise C. Turner Forest, "A Caveat for Critics Against Invoking Elizabethan Psychology," *PMLA*, LXI (1946), 651–672.

26. See R. E. Neil Dodge, "A Sermon on Source-Hunting," *MP*, IX (1911–1912), 211–223; Ihab Hassan, "The Problem of Influence in Literary History," *JAAC*, XIV (1955), 66–76; and René Wellek and Austin Warren, *Theory of Literature*, 3d ed. (New York, 1956), esp. pp. 257–258.

public domain. No authority in the field would deny that a certain continuity does exist between Elizabethan and medieval drama,[27] but to overstress *that* thesis would be to topple, as one writer phrases it, from one set of "prefabricated frames and boxes"[28] onto another. Seneca certainly did exert a general and an important influence upon the Italian Renaissance theater, upon Garnier and the French, and upon the Elizabethans. One recent collection of essays continues to survey exactly this general ground;[29] it is clear that scholars simply must proceed more cautiously.

A perfect example of the effects of the deflating of Cunliffe and of a greater caution may be observed in attitudes toward Shakespeare's *Titus Andronicus*. Baker tellingly debunks the tradition that appeared to pronounce Seneca's *Thyestes* as an influential source by convincingly demonstrating that the true source was certainly the Philomel story in Ovid.[30] This point is carefully taken up by Eugene M. Waith, who maintains that "how much [Shakespeare] may have been affected by Seneca is debatable . . . and it seems fair to conclude that however important the Senecan model may have been, Ovid exerted a more direct influence." Later, in speaking of Renaissance interest in arousing "admiration" or astonishment in an audience, Waith concludes: "Seneca was obviously a rich mine, but often it was the Latin writers of verse narrative who furnished models; astonishing passages were freely borrowed or imitated from Virgil, Lucan, Statius."[31]

The truth is, of course, that Renaissance authors were influenced by

27. In addition to Farnham's study, the following explorations of medieval influences are important: Frederick J. Boas, *Shakespere and His Predecessors* (New York, 1906); Bernard Spivack, *Shakespeare and the Allegory of Evil* (New York, 1958); and David M. Bevington, *From "Mankind" to Marlowe* (Cambridge, Mass., 1962).

28. Charles Garton, "Characterisation in Greek Tragedy," *Journal of Hellenic Studies*, LXXVII (1957), 250. Garton is discussing the vexing problem of attempting to discern "real characters" in tragedy; most scholars bring to a play one or another of a series of expectations or pet preconceptions.

29. *Les Tragédies de Sénèque et le théâtre de la Renaissance*, ed. Jean Jacquot (Paris, 1964).

30. *Induction to Tragedy* (New York, 1965), pp. 120 ff.

31. Eugene M. Waith, "The Metamorphosis of Violence in *Titus Andronicus*," *ShS*, X (1957), 40, 48.

many, many medieval *and* classical forebears. In fact, their encyclopedic tastes were a distinct carry-over from the past. In discussing Sackville's long poem, the "Induction," Douglas Bush discovers a rich variety of specific influences—Chaucer's *Pardoner's Tale,* Virgil's *Aeneid,* and Seneca's plays.

Chaucer, Virgil, Seneca—it is a characteristic Tudor combination. And Sackville is not a mere stumbling translator or imitator. . . . His borrowings are wrought into an original poem, at once medieval and classical, which is the most ample poetic expression before Spenser of the moral seriousness of Tudor humanism.[32]

Something similar may be said for a great many of the Elizabethan playwrights. Seneca is far from being utterly abandoned; but he has simply been placed in a saner, more realistic light. If he is to be understood at all, that is precisely where scholars should wish to have him.

II

What, then, are we to make—seriously—of Senecan drama? Why should not his work be scrupulously, meticulously compared to the

32. Douglas Bush, *Mythology and the Renaissance Tradition in English Poetry* (New York, 1963), p. 64. A related point is made by Una Ellis-Fermor: a sense of doom led Jacobean dramatists to discover a sense of fellow-feeling for Seneca and they were attracted to his *sententiae.* "That the Stoic generalizations they reproduced were not necessarily his, were at least equally those of Cicero, Epictetus, Marcus Aurelius and later European borrowers, was beside the point. Except for a scholar like Ben Jonson the source of the thought was immaterial; it was its aptness to their present need that mattered" (*The Jacobean Drama* [New York, 1964], p. 21). Similarly, Reuben A. Brower, in *Hero and Saint: Shakespeare and the Graeco-Roman Heroic Tradition* (New York, 1971), p. 149, observes:

If we should yield to the agreeable temptation to pass over Seneca and his example, we should find a considerable loss in our ability to define the nature of Shakespearian heroic tragedy. There are simply too many instructive analogies and contrasts to leave Seneca out of the story. What matters—to emphasize a point made earlier—for the interpretation of Shakespeare's heroic tragedies is not Seneca alone, or Homer or Virgil or Ovid, but the composite heroic image, language, and style that emerges from their works.

Unfortunately, in dealing with Seneca, Brower is concerned with tracing "the degradation of the Homeric hero" (p. 153), and, exploring but a single Senecan play (the *Agamemnon*), mistakenly, it seems to us, assumes that Seneca *intended* his Agamemnon and Clytemnestra to be fully "heroic."

productions of the Greek dramatists? The answer is quite plain: because his plays are something distinctive, something separate, something else. "Why judge Seneca, in this or other matters, by the standards of fifth-century Greek tragedy, as if nothing had happened since to the world or to the theater?"[33] It is high time that the Senecan plays be looked at for what they are—*in themselves*. Yet, until recently, there have been too many vague or glib attempts merely to describe his plays, or to "sort" them into several "kinds." The studies of Allan Gilbert or of Hardin Craig, for instance, raise more difficulties than they allay, and both suffer ultimately from loose abstractions and broadest generalities.[34] Such writers simply fail to describe accurately Seneca's practice or Senecan plays.

Far more interesting has been Gerhard Müller's suggestion that Senecan plays may be separated into two distinctive types: "tragedies of passion" and "tragedies of fate."[35] This is an attractive distinction, and, of the seven extant plays assuredly by Seneca,[36] it could be argued that *Oedipus, Troades,* and *Hercules Furens* all reveal heroes or heroines defeated and beset by fate, whereas in the *Medea, Phaedra, Thyestes,* and *Agamemnon,* we witness characters giving themselves over to a deliberate and excessive passion. Nonetheless, such a distinction might well prove misleading, since Hercules' madness and Oedipus' weakness and wavering, for example, are similarly displays of a kind of emotion or "passion." To a considerable degree in the Senecan corpus, passions, once

33. Herington, "Senecan Tragedy," p. 445.

34. Allan H. Gilbert, "Seneca and the Criticism of Elizabethan Tragedy," *PQ,* XIII (1934), 370–381, without adducing evidence, assumes that there are "two kinds" of tragedy—Senecan tragedies of state and an alien kind of domestic tragedy. Hardin Craig "The Shackling of Accidents: A Study of Elizabethan Tragedy," *PQ,* XIX (1940), 1–19, conjectures that there are *three* kinds of tragedy: Aeschylean (Aristotelian and fatalistic), Senecan (grossly fatalistic and displaying "titanism"), and Christian. In the course of his discussion, one finds it difficult to distinguish the Aeschylean from the Senecan, and many assertions about these "kinds" simply take a fanciful flight far from particular plays by particular authors.

35. "Senecas *Oedipus* als Drama," *Hermes,* LXXXI (1953), 460.

36. In addition to the seven, a fragment, the *Phoenissae,* is doubtless by Seneca. The *Octavia* is universally understood to be by another author, certainly an imitator of Seneca. As for the *Hercules Oetaeus,* authorship is in doubt.

unleashed, are transmuted into an irrevocable fatality, and characters, as soon as they are caught in the web of violent emotion, are subsequently "driven" throughout their plays.

However that may be, there can be no doubt that the *Oedipus* and the *Hercules Furens* are different in quality and emphasis from Seneca's greater tragedies displaying towering passions—the *Phaedra,* the *Medea,* or the *Thyestes.* Oedipus is merely weak, fearful, and beset from within and from without; and Hercules, as Stoic hero and pattern, is the victim of a madness that has been inflicted upon him and makes it necessary for him to marshall all of his powers and strength of will in order to "accept" his fate or even to endure.

Assuredly, the violent, passionate, and venegeful figures of Medea, Atreus, and Phaedra have exerted an influence upon later drama.[37] And, recently, studies have shown that a separate tradition of the Hercules figure exerted a different but similar influence.[38] It might be argued, as well, that the general conception of "the Stoic hero" constituted another, or a third, vein that captured the attention of innumerable authors in the Renaissance.[39] But as we have said earlier, considerable

37. See, for instance, Clarence V. Boyer, *The Villain as Hero in Elizabethan Tragedy* (New York, 1914); Fredson T. Bowers, *Elizabethan Revenge Tragedy 1587-1642* (Princeton, N.J., 1940); Irving Ribner, *Patterns in Shakespearian Tragedy* (London, 1960); Roy W. Battenhouse, *Marlowe's Tamburlaine: A Study in Renaissance Moral Philosophy* (Nashville, Tenn., 1941), pp. 193 ff. Obviously, Elizabethan ideas about Machiavelli, Italianate melodrama, and the Vice from the morality plays were similarly important.

38. Consult the important studies by Rolf Soellner, "The Madness of Hercules and the Elizabethans," *CL,* X (1958), 309-324, and Eugene M. Waith, *The Herculean Hero* (New York, 1962).

39. See, for instance, Michael Higgins, "The Convention of the Stoic Hero as Handled by Marston," *MLR,* XXXIX (1944), 338-346, and Elias Schwartz, "Seneca, Homer, and Chapman's *Bussy D'Ambois,*" *JEGP,* LVI (1957), 163-176. We believe that the "Stoical hero" is more prevalent in Seneca's prose writings, wherein he repeatedly held up such figures as Socrates, Cato, Mucius, and Rutilius as ideal Stoic heroes, especially when faced with adversity. The efforts of Justus Lipsius and Guillaume du Vair had made Seneca an important exemplar of Stoicism in the Renaissance. Consult Léontine Zanta, *La Renaissance du Stoicisme au XVI° siècle* (Paris, 1914); Robert Hoopes, *Right Reason in the English Renaissance* (Cambridge, Mass., 1962); and Philip A. Smith, "Bishop Hall, 'Our English Seneca,'" *PMLA,* LXIII (1948), 1191-1204.

care must be exercised in sorting out "traditions" that Seneca generated and in distinguishing the "kinds" of plays that he wrote.

Most importantly, criticism must redirect its attention to the particular plays themselves, and critics must read them with a new sensitivity and a more fixed attention. It should not be possible for a critic to make such generalizations as the following: "[Seneca] gave [in the tragedies] a stoic view of the world, showing heroic persons unyielding in their conflict with one another and with Fate." [40] There is nothing whatever "stoical" or "unyielding" about major figures from many of these plays, and one must use a judicious temperance in detecting conventional Stoical moralities parading in Seneca's pages.

Nevertheless, important works *have* been emerging which study particular facets of Seneca's art, and these deserve encouragement and consideration. Studies have appeared which take a thoughtful look at Senecan characters,[41] at the atmosphere and symbolism of his settings,[42] at the psychological intensity of his exploration of painful scenes,[43] at the structure of his imagery,[44] and at the ironies of his plotting.[45] Further studies will be needed: that examine the virtues of

40. B. L. Joseph, " 'The Spanish Tragedy' and 'Hamlet': Two Exercises in English Seneca," *Classical Drama and Its Influence,* ed. M. J. Anderson (New York, 1965), p. 121.

41. Charles Garton, "The Background of Character Portrayal in Seneca," *Classical Philology,* LIV (1959), 1–9; Ronald W. Tobin, "Tragedy and Catastrophe in Seneca's Theater," *CJ,* LXII (1966), 64–70.

42. Norman T. Pratt, Jr., *Dramatic Suspense in Seneca and in His Greek Precursors* (Princeton, N.J., 1939).

43. Particularly in Otto Regenbogen's *Schmerz und Tod in den Tragödien Senecas.* And consult Wolfgang Clemen, *English Tragedy before Shakespeare,* trans. T. S. Dorsch (London, 1961), especially with reference to Seneca, the "dramatic lament," and self-apostrophe," pp. 211–252. The theme of psychological presentations of self is accentuated in Pierre Thevanaz, "L'Intériorité chez Sénéque," *Melanges offerts à M. Max Niedermann* . . . (Neuchatel, 1944), pp. 189–194.

44. See Norman T. Pratt, Jr., "Major Systems of Figurative Language in Senecan Melodrama," *Transactions of the American Philological Association,* XCIV (1963), 199–234; and William H. Owen, "Commonplace and Dramatic Symbol in Seneca's Tragedies," *Transactions of the American Philological Association,* XCIX (1968), 291–313.

45. Anna Lydia Motto and John R. Clark, "Senecan Tragedy: Patterns of Irony and Art," *Classical Bulletin,* XLVIII (1972), 69–77.

his poetry, his artistic creation of "atmosphere," and, most important of all, the over-all "kind" of drama Seneca produces—its qualities, its types, its virtues and achievement.

To date, the best recent general study of Senecan drama has been provided by C. J. Herington.[46] In addition to offering a sweeping defense of Senecan practice and touching upon a variety of themes and strategies in his work, Herington's study particularly traces the "form" of Senecan drama: a temptation to passion or crime, the defeat of reason by passion, and the explosion of evil. Like a musical composition, characters caught in this tangle of almost insane excitation proceed to an accompaniment of choral premonitions, staccato accentuations, and ominous signs and portents, until the unleashing of such savage passions is virtually complete. Such an exacting and precise development of mood and motif in Seneca's plays is altogether different from many of the broader themes and styles of Greek dramatic usage.

Seneca must not be judged by the Greek gauge, because his aims were different. He is concerned, not to justify the ways of gods to men or of men to gods, but to display the capacity for emotional intensity exhibited by characters endowed with extraordinary passions. It may have been part of a Stoic teacher's purpose to show that excessive emotions—"perturbations" the Stoics called them, and insisted that they must be suppressed—have horrible consequences; but for the ordinary reader the principal effect of the display is to demonstrate enormously expanded limits of human potentiality, and this constitutes release and enlargement like that afforded by heroic poetry. These plays, then, are even further than the Greek from any concessions to realism or naturalism, and their language is therefore even more artificial. No ordinary people have ever used such lavish rhetoric, but neither do ordinary people communicate through musical arias, and Seneca's true affinities are not with drama as Europe has come to conceive it, but rather with opera.[47]

The comparison with opera is very nearly right. For Seneca's dramas at their best, as we have indicated, unfold with musical splendor and unnatural tautness. And the explosion of passion, when it comes, is heightened most fearfully, like the bursting of a dam, with all of the attendant suggestions of fury and madness. As Seneca explains

46. "Senecan Tragedy," pp. 422–471.
47. Moses Hadas, Introduction, *Seneca's Oedipus* (New York, 1955), pp. 6–7.

elsewhere, passion and madness are very near allied.[48] In his best (and most tightly organized) plays—the *Medea, Phaedra, Thyestes*—the central character is swept aloft in an agony of devastating frenzy.

He provided the most tragic characters, superhuman villains dominated with one abnormal consuming passion. He provided the most tragic sentiment, morbid introspective self-pity and self-reliance. He provided the superlative tragic style, whether for the utterance of passion, picture, or sentence. Above all, he warranted the use of all these elements extravagantly and without restraint.[49]

Here is the heart of a Senecan drama that requires understanding—and much more extensive exploration.

Such a drama, to be sure, hardly fulfills the ideals that Aristotle proposed for a formal Sophoclean tragedy, and never provides the kind of "catharsis" that the earlier drama could forcibly elicit. Yet Seneca's is a significant dramatic kind, for all of that. His drama, delivered in the high style with the "mighty line," fraught with mythic allusions, generating violent gesture, grandiose events, and the hyperbolic—almost allegorical—contest of Good and Evil, has been conventionally and even matter-of-factly denigrated by critics as "melodrama." However, we see no reason why such *melodrama* (accounting for Hadas' comparison of Senecan performance with opera) should be applied in a pejorative sense. For, at its best, melodrama obtains powerful dramatic effects. Indeed, a recent critic, discussing passages from Balzac and Henry James, attempts to characterize such excessive features as constituting a specific and meaningful "melodramatic mode." It is "a superdrama involving life and death," an essential, urgent drama that strains "to go beyond the surface of the real to the truer, hidden reality. . . ." This critic urges that tragedy slips toward melodrama in an era of cultural decline, when the common belief in traditions and religions has disappeared, when man finds himself more solipsistic, alone, secularized, forced to turn inward upon himself.

The melodramatic imagination is . . . a way of perceiving and imaging the spiritual in a world where there is no longer any clear idea of the sacred,

---

48. Particularly in his moral essays—the *De Ira* and the *De Tranquillitate Animi*.
49. H. B. Charlton, *The Senecan Tradition in Renaissance Tragedy* (Manchester, 1946), p. clxix.

no generally accepted societal moral imperatives, where the body of the ethical has become a sort of *deus absconditus* which must be sought for, posited, brought into man's existence through exercise of the spiritualist imagination.[50]

And he further postulates that this climate of loss has been a Western moral condition for several centuries and that this melodramatic mode has been developing in the novel, from Samuel Richardson all the way to Norman Mailer and other writers of the present day.

We might add that a similar period of metaphysical perplexity and moral void was sorely felt and sharply portrayed by Jacobean dramatists. And, finally, we must remark that in first-century, Neronian Rome, a similar force was very painfully at work and is fully embodied in the masterworks of Seneca's theater. His was, it should become clear, a serious and significant contribution to dramatic art. And what is more, as further studies accumulate, his art will be once again perceived to speak acutely—and relevantly—to our present age.

50. Peter Brooks, "The Melodramatic Imagination," *Partisan Review,* XXXIX (1972), 196, 209.

The Civic Religious Drama of Medieval England: A Review of Recent Scholarship

Review Article

STANLEY J. KAHRL

T HE FIRST THING to make clear in any discussion of recent work on medieval English drama is that the term *pre-Shakespearean drama* is best buried once and for all. As Rosemary Woolf remarks, at the conclusion of her fine study of *The English Mystery Plays*, "The long shadow of Renaissance contempt has lain across the mystery plays almost until the present day."[1] It is to the credit of scholars such as Miss Woolf that we are acquiring the tools with which to assess the strengths and weaknesses of early English drama as a subject worth studying in its own right, rather than as a crude predecessor to the great age of English playwrighting.

Before proceeding to outline the process by which this reassessment has come about, however, I should make it clear that the studies to be discussed will deal primarily with the civic religious drama of the later Middle Ages, those plays called variously "mystery plays" or "Corpus Christi plays," after the festival during which they were most often produced. Because the line of development from the early pro-

1. (Berkeley and Los Angeles, 1972), p. 323.

vincial touring companies to the London companies of which Shakespeare was a part has long been known, the plays put on by the early touring companies have understandably held more interest for students of later drama than have other forms of medieval English drama. The earlier comparative neglect of the cycle plays by medievalists may stem in part from the fact that the poetry of these plays is not their major strength; I am inclined to think, moreover, that because Chaucer wrote no plays and because many medievalists begin their studies through a love of Chaucer, a study of the mystery plays is not of immediate interest to them. Until recently, the best work on medieval drama was done by scholars attracted in the first instance to Shakespeare, thence to his origins. What I am about to outline is a process of revaluation of a relatively negelected corpus of medieval literature undertaken at long last by medievalists who valued that corpus in itself, rather than as a prelude to something else.

It is now generally recognized that the move to revaluate the strengths of early English cycle drama began with the study by Harold C. Gardiner, S. J., entitled *Mysteries' End: An Investigation of the Last Days of the Medieval Religious Stage*.[2] Father Gardiner proposed that the civic drama of medieval England was not moribund at the time of Elizabeth's accession, but was in fact so lively a manifestation of older forms of belief that it represented a threat of some consequence to the new state religion. Gardiner was one of the first modern critics to call attention to the series of edicts (which in fact began during the reign of Henry VIII) forbidding stage plays that treated matters of state or religion. At the same time the city guilds, despite increasing difficulties in raising the capital for producing the plays in a time of changing economic conditions, appear to have been quite eager to continue civic religious plays. Final suppression of the mystery plays appears to have taken place near the period of the establishment of a permanent dramatic company in the Theater in London.

Recognition that the plays still had life in them, though they might have appeared old-fashioned to the new university graduates who preceded Shakespeare as writers for the new stages in London, has led to a series of important studies, all of which have added to our understanding

2. (New Haven, Conn., 1946).

of early English drama. However, these studies did not follow Father Gardiner's work immediately. Not until almost ten years later did F. M. Salter's Alexander lectures on *Mediaeval Drama in Chester* appear.[3] Salter demonstrated, through a return to the dramatic records of Chester, that the production of medieval civic drama in that city was an extremely serious undertaking. Using largely unpublished records, he created a far richer picture of what was really involved in mounting the annual Corpus Christi plays. At the same time, he attacked the accuracy of the sole surviving contemporary description of a pageant wagon, that given by David Rogers in the seventeenth century, thus opening up to future speculation the whole topic of what the pageant wagons looked like. Undoubtedly for subsequent scholars the most important consequence of his lectures was the indication that there was work to be done through a reexamination of the surviving archives, encouraging those who followed to move beyond the dramatic records published by Chambers in *The Mediaeval Stage*.

Given the momentum that was in fact gathering in the wake of these two studies, it was unfortunate that Hardin Craig's *English Religious Drama of the Middle Ages*[4] should have appeared at the same time as Salter's lectures. Craig's work in medieval drama extended back at least to his publication of the *Two Coventry Corpus Christi Plays*.[5] His approach to the plays was very much like that of Chambers, who studied them with the distaste of the Renaissance. Craig could not conceive of the plays as possessing theatrical vitality and used the position he had gained to attack in reviews those subsequent works that sought to draw attention to the dramatic and theatrical strengths of the early drama. For Craig, the plays were strictly museum pieces with no continuing life of their own. From the vantage point of twenty years' hindsight, it is now apparent that Craig's study was an anachronism almost as soon as it appeared.

Yet it did not by any means seem so at the time. Glynne Wickham, in his recent *Shakespeare's Dramatic Heritage*[6] recalls how Craig

3. (Toronto, 1955).
4. (Oxford, 1955).
5. EETS, E.S. no. 87 (London, 1902).
6. (London, 1969).

attacked Volume I of *Early English Stages: 1300–1660*,[7] covering the period 1300–1576, for the tentative suggestion that the liturgical Latin drama of the Middle Ages had an entirely separate life from the vernacular cycle drama. Wickham correctly saw that there was a difference in dramatic quality between the two types of drama, a difference sufficiently great for him to question the traditional account of the development of the early drama. That account, whose main formulators were E. K. Chambers, Karl Young, and Hardin Craig, is still to be found in most popular histories of early English drama. It proposes that the plays, having begun under the auspices of the Church as part of the service of divine worship, got out of hand and had to be moved, first to the precincts surrounding the church and then to the town squares of medieval Europe. With each step the drama was supposedly more secularized, less devout in tone, less under the control of the Church. Such was not the case, as we shall see shortly.

Wickham's three-volume study of the medieval and Renaissance stage, a study like Salter's marked by its use of unpublished or hitherto ignored evidence, is remarkable not so much for its early perception of what we may now call the two traditions of medieval English drama, however, as for the wealth of detail that demonstrates the complexity and rich variety within English theatrical life before, during, and after Elizabeth's reign. Volume I called attention to the structures built for royal processions, indicating how similar these splendid edifices must have been to the structures used in other medieval entertainments. Once having read the accounts Wickham amassed, one can no longer regard medieval stagecrafts as naïve or unsophisticated. His attempt to assimilate the structures of the tournament to theatrical practices does not seem to have been as persuasive as the connections between the pageant structures of the streets and the sets, both movable and fixed, that were used to stage the secular civic plays of the period. His accounts of subsequent theatrical developments in parts 1 and 2 of Volume II[8] need not be touched on here. They are undoubtedly familiar by now to students of Renaissance drama. Suffice it only to say that in

7. Glynne Wickham, *Early English Stages: 1300–1660* (London, 1959), Vol. I, 1300–1576.

8. *Ibid.*, (London, 1963), Vol. II, pt. 1, 1576–1660; (London, 1972), Vol. II, pt. 2, 1576–1660.

Volume II Wickham most carefully reviews the edicts first alluded to by Father Gardiner, and, in a long chapter on "State Control of British Drama, 1530–1642," drawn in many cases from the appendixes to Chambers' *Elizabethan Stage,* he shows how the closing of the theaters was the end of a process which began with the control and then the banning of medieval cycle plays.[9]

The studies mentioned thus far have largely been contextual, concerned more with the conditions under which the plays were produced than with explications of the plays themselves. But with the appearance of Richard Southern's *Medieval Theatre in the Round,*[10] the picture began to change. Southern's book appears at first glance to be an attempt to reconstruct another theater, in this case, the theater in which *The Castle of Perseverance* was performed. Were that all that he had set out to do, the book by now would already be dated, since the theater he proposed—high earthen banks inside a palisade and ditch, with theatrical structures set on small scaffolds on the banks between the rows of seats—is not now generally accepted as an accurate representation of the diagram preceding the text. Southern's major contribution was to demonstrate the dramatic success achieved by the dramatist who constructed *The Castle of Perseverance,* to suggest how well the play, which had before seemed so talky and dull, must come across when properly staged and directed. Those interested in understanding the dynamics of the theater-in-the-round should still begin with Southern's discussion.

Not long after Southern's study, there appeared the first revised history of the early drama to take into account the work of Salter or Wickham. Arnold Williams' *The Drama of Medieval England,*[11] written for the beginning student as Craig's account was not, is marked by sturdy common sense in its presentation of the probable theatrical and social context for the plays, coupled with a good feel for what makes a play successful in the theater. For example, in noting the existence of stock characters in the cycle plays, Williams points out that "dramatists of all ages, Shakespeare among them, have found stock characters and

9. *Ibid.,* Vol. II, pt. 1, pp. 54–97.
10. (London, 1957).
11. (East Lansing, Mich., 1961).

situations useful. . . . The important critical question is whether a stock character comes alive" (p. 121). Commenting on the usual literary sources drawn on for the individual scenes in the cycle plays, he states that "the one source of the cycles that penetrates and controls all others is [a] feeling for life. . . . it keeps the cycles from being over-powered by the miraculous and it provides constant social commentary" (p. 124). It was Williams who inaugurated the Medieval Drama Seminar, which still meets during the annual Modern Language Association meeting, as a forum for those interested in early English drama to exchange information on what plays they had seen in production and how effective those plays were when so viewed. The emphasis on production permeates his book and gives it a quality that readers still find attractive.

In the same year that Williams' history appeared, Stanford University Press published the first of two important books of criticism. Eleanor Prosser's *Drama and Religion in the English Mystery Plays: A Re-Evaluation*[12] attempted to provide a fresh way of looking at the plays, a point of view which took them seriously as works of art, asking that we "grant the possibility that the plays may be the result of conscious artistry" (p. 57). The criteria for which Miss Prosser sought to gain acceptance were four: (1) ". . . All good drama is unified by some core of meaning, some significant insight about man that creates a coherent point of view." (2) "All good drama is unified by some central dramatic question, a question posed in human terms that capture [*sic*] the audience's interest." (3) All drama "is good only when the plot incidents are so closely knit together that nothing in the structure could be either removed or transposed without marring the total effect." (4) "In evaluating characterization . . . the critic does not ask if a character is a fully developed, realistic human being. Rather, he tests traits and actions in terms of a character's function within a play" (pp. 58–60). Such criteria may not seem startling to those accustomed to critical reading of plays they take seriously; it is nevertheless a mark of the state of dramatic criticism in the field of medieval English drama that, when this book appeared, it was regarded by many as marking a radical departure from the past. Miss Prosser then applied her criteria to a group of subjects handled in a number of different cycles, specifically the plays of Cain,

12. (Palo Alto, Calif., 1961).

Joseph, the Woman Taken in Adultery, Mary Magdalene, and Doubting Thomas. I cannot say that I agree entirely with the conclusions that she draws as to which of the plays are the best, for, in evaluating the effectiveness of the plays, Miss Prosser consistently approved of those whose "central dramatic question" was presented with moral earnestness. Comedy was likely to be a negative quantity, no matter how it was employed. In practice her standards too often were not dramatic but doctrinal. It is a reflection on the state of medieval dramatic criticism ten years ago that this book was still the best to be had.

Miss Prosser herself remarked in her opening chapter how much she owed to those predecessors I have already noted with approval. The most radical attack on the assumptions that had governed the study of medieval English drama prior to World War II was the by-now famous attack on the Darwinian school of criticism mounted by O. B. Hardison, Jr., in the opening chapter of *Christian Rite and Christian Drama in the Middle Ages*.[13] Hardison's book, which received the Medieval Academy's Haskins Medal, is principally a reexamination of the whole nature of what constitutes liturgical drama and the actual conditions under which it came into being within the medieval church. His study did much to buttress the growing opinion that the Latin liturgical drama and the vernacular drama were separate and distinct. Having first shown that Chambers, Young, and Craig had used the evidence offered by the early plays selectively and that complex plays do not necessarily come later than simple forms, he then showed, first, that the early Latin plays were tied to the liturgy in far different ways than Chambers or Young had supposed, and, secondly, that a fully developed set of vernacular plays, embodying most of the theatrical and dramatic qualities later to be found in the vernacular Corpus Christi plays of the late fourteenth, fifteenth, and sixteenth centuries, were already in existence in the Anglo-Norman plays of the twelfth century. While Hardison's study has been faulted by William Smolden for its failure to take into account the evidence provided by the musical settings of the early tropes from which the liturgical plays seem to have developed, the major points that he made are still very much worth making.

Two major studies remain to be considered. But before turning to

13. (Baltimore, Md., 1965).

them a word of explanation is needed as to why I have omitted mention of work on the moral interludes. Excellent studies have appeared in this field, such as both books by David Bevington—*From "Mankind" to Marlowe* and *Tudor Drama and Politics*—or T. W. Craik's *The Tudor Interlude*. The fact is that for years it has been accepted doctrine that the interludes and the school and university plays of the mid-sixteenth century exerted the dominant influence on the Elizabethan drama, if for no other reason than that the religious civic drama had collapsed well before the early sixteenth century. Thus, at least from the appearance of W. Roy Mackenzie's *The English Moralities from the Point of View of Allegory* in 1914, if not before, students of the Elizabethan theater have taken the moral interludes seriously. In more recent times, Bernard Spivack's study of Iago's forerunners is a signal example. What I have sought to suggest throughout this review is that there was another body of drama which existed at exactly the same time that the moral interludes were on the stage, a drama which we must take just as seriously and which may have had an equal effect on those plays that came later, a point that simply does not need to be made about the moral interludes.

Certainly the work that has exerted the greatest influence on the recent study of the civic religious plays is the second work published by Stanford University Press, namely, V. A. Kolve's *The Play Called Corpus Christi*.[14] Kolve proposes that there is in fact a form that we can call a Corpus Christi play, a form determined by medieval attitudes toward history. Because medieval writers saw history as cyclic, and those cycles as part of God's plan, they set out, in the plays created to accompany the celebration of the feast of Corpus Christi, to represent the acts of God in the Old Testament and the New that have led to the possibility of salvation. Old Testament scenes were chosen not because they made good plays but because they prefigured scenes that were to recur, transformed, in the life of Christ—and in the life of the ordinary Christian viewing the play as well. The interest of the medieval dramatists in the past "consists not in what it can teach us of the past but in how it can remedy the present. . . . The interest in history re-

14. (Palo Alto, Calif., 1966).

sides in its reflection of the eternal, unchanging plan of God for the salvation of man, and in the moral constants of good and evil which reveal themselves in human behavior" (p. 108). This attitude toward history as providing moral guideposts for the present carries over into the English Renaissance, of course. And it is the continuity of this very attitude of mind which enabled the Elizabethan dramatists to learn from the cycle drama how to present historical material with a moral meaning.

Kolve's study is important, aside from the fact that it contains some excellent critical readings of individual plays, in that he also addressed himself to the difficult question of how the medieval actor could handle such parts as those of God or Christ without feeling either awkward or blasphemous. The answer that Kolve gives is that the actors and audience equally understood that a play is just that— a play, a game, an activity which is known to mimic reality but not to be reality: "The aim of the Corpus Christi drama was to celebrate and elucidate, never, not even temporarily, to deceive" (p. 32). Actors were presenting, not representing, a scene, and the audience was not expected to forget that fact. The theatrical world of the Corpus Christi plays functioned with much the same attitude toward portrayal of character as that espoused in more recent times by such playwrights as Bertolt Brecht.

With the increase of interest in the early English drama, it has become progressively more difficult to write a single book encompassing the entire field. Rosemary Woolf's recent full-length study of *The English Mystery Plays* provides the historical background in great detail and in the discussion of the plays themselves demonstrates a particularly good feel for the uses made by individual playwrights of their sources. But it is clear that to discuss both the origins of the Corpus Christi plays and the plays themselves permits neither an analysis of noncyclic plays nor a full discussion of the early moral interludes. Miss Woolf's own book demonstrates by indirection the truth of one of the points already made earlier in this review, that is, the separate life of the Latin liturgical plays and the later vernacular plays. For, having provided quite a dependable account of the early plays, she finds herself driven to account for the cycle plays as really comprising a new beginning, though this is not stated quite so clearly. She does seem to treat the vernacular plays as a development from *tableaux vivants* in the annual Corpus Christi day procession and, by so doing, provides for the separate life that many of us now feel them to have had.

In discussing the plays themselves Miss Woolf adopts a method of analysis that has been followed by many others in the past when dealing with the Corpus Christi plays as a whole. One wonders, however, if her approach is exactly the best one. Each topic in the cycles is dealt with sequentially, with the analysis focusing on the strengths or weaknesses of the different treatments of specific themes—for example, the Annunciation. In this case her analysis concludes as follows: "All the other cycles treat the Annunciation simply and unremarkably. The author of the *Ludus Coventriae* alone by a brilliant combination of different sources has succeeded in transposing it into a cosmic setting and preserving some of the mysterious grandeur that great devotional writers had seen in the event" (pp. 168–169). Again and again her fine insights seem to come from her intimate knowledge of the sources drawn on by the dramatists rather than from a developed sense of the theatrical situation with which she has to deal. Such sources are important and can be sensed nowhere so well as in this book. The other difficulty with her method of analysis is that one loses a sense of the characteristics of the individual cycles—what makes the work of the Wakefield Master undoubtedly the best of the surviving plays, for example—when each cycle is treated only in relation to the treatments of the same part in other cycles.

It should be apparent from the works mentioned here that the study of medieval drama by and for itself is a rewarding activity. The language of the plays is not difficult, as they were all composed during the fifteenth century. Students can find the plays easily accessible through such a text as A. C. Cawley's edition of *The Wakefield Pageants in the Towneley Cycle*.[15] Some sense of the diverse and growing body of critical articles can be gained from the anthology edited by Jerome Taylor and Alan Nelson, *Medieval English Drama: Essays Critical and Contextual*.[16] For anyone interested in drama as a genre, individual plays

15. (Manchester, 1958).
16. (Chicago, 1972).

will be found that are as good as in nearly any other period of English literature.

But the specialist in the drama of the Renaissance has an additional reason for taking this drama seriously. The civic religious drama of England in the fifteenth and sixteenth centuries provided most of the dramatic fare available to an average Englishman during his lifetime. One has only to read the dramatic records of Kent, published by Giles Dawson in the Malone Society's *Collections* series as *Collections VII, Plays and Players in Kent, 1450–1642*,[17] or my edition of the medieval dramatic records for Lincolnshire, *Collections VIII; Records of Plays and Players in Lincolnshire, 1300–1585*[18] (not to mention the kinds of records cited by Wickham or Salter) to realize how vital the civic drama still was in England in the 1560's.[19] Glynne Wickham, in *Shakespeare's Dramatic Heritage,* mentions some of the specific ways in which familiarity with this dramatic tradition informs one's understanding of specific scenes in Shakespeare. As one reads Marlowe at the close of a course of study devoted to English medieval drama, one becomes increasingly aware of his debt to a variety of medieval dramatic genres. I myself have come to feel, and have so indicated in the concluding chapter of my forthcoming book on *Traditions of Medieval English Drama,*[20] that the medieval habit of treating history in cyclic terms is a far more pervasive influence on the structure of the history plays of the English Renaissance than any of the sources suggested by Tillyard, Campbell, or Ribner. But the specific connections one can make between, say, the Porter in *Macbeth* and the devils' Hellmouth in the cycle plays are less important than the habits of mind, the entire theatrical tradition which was a part of the world of both the early Elizabethan dramatists and their audiences.

17. (Oxford, 1965). See particularly Appendix B for the extensive preparations made at New Romney in 1555 and 1560 for their civic religious play produced on Whitsun.

18. (Oxford, 1969 [1974]).

19. John Murphy, at the University of Colorado at Boulder, in a personal correspondence has informed me that more civic religious drama was put on in Essex in the 1560's than at any other time in that county's history.

20. (London, 1974).

Having said all this, I should also add that there is still a long way to go before the criticism of medieval drama reaches the level of sophistication taken for granted in the study of Renaissance drama. Dramatic structure is being studied in individual plays in occasional articles, but the effects of Kolve's suggestion as to the controlling form for the understanding of cycle drama have hardly been felt. A fascination with what the medieval stages looked like or what sources a dramatist used still too often grips those criticizing the plays. Only when the plays are thoroughly understood as drama can the real connections between medieval and Renaissance drama be made.

For the present, what I would ask is that the student of Renaissance drama approach medieval English drama as he would the drama of the Restoration. Both are interesting in themselves and also as the parts of the history of English drama most closely allied to the plays of the Renaissance. Understanding the continuities enriches one's appreciation of all three periods.

Notes on Contributors

ERVIN BECK, Associate Professor of English at Goshen College, has published an essay on *Tamburlaine* and is working on several prodigal-son comedies.

CATHERINE BELSEY is a Fellow of New Hall, Cambridge, and has published articles on medieval and Renaissance drama.

JOHN R. CLARK is a Professor and Chairman of the Department of English at the University of South Florida. He has written widely on satire, including a book on Swift, and has frequently collaborated with his wife, Anna Lydia Motto, on studies of Seneca and other classical authors.

FRANCO FIDO, Professor of Italian Studies at Brown University, is the author of many essays on Italian literature and of *Machiavelli* (1965), a history of criticism.

G. K. HUNTER, Professor of English and Comparative Literary Studies at the University of Warwick, is well known for his many articles, books, and editions, including the New Arden edition of *All's Well that Ends Well* (1959) and *John Lyly: The Humanist as Courtier* (1962). He has recently completed his edition of Marston's *The Malcontent* for the Revels Plays.

ROBERT C. JONES is an Associate Professor of English at the Ohio State University and the author of articles on various aspects of English Renaissance drama.

STANLEY J. KAHRL, Professor of English and Director of the Center for Medieval and Renaissance Studies at the Ohio State University, has recently completed a book on the traditions of medieval English drama.

ANNA LYDIA MOTTO, Professor of Classics at the University of South Florida, has published two book-length studies and more than twenty scholarly articles on Seneca.

GAIL KERN PASTER teaches English at George Washington University. A National Endowment for the Humanities Younger Humanist Fellow in 1973–1974, she is working on ideas of the city in Elizabethan and Jacobean plays, pageants, and masques.

DAVID RIGGS, Assistant Professor of English at Stanford University, is the author of *Shakespeare's Heroical Histories: "Henry VI" and Its Literary Tradition* (1971). His current project is a book on Ben Jonson and neoclassical realism.

BRUCE R. SMITH is an Assistant Professor of English at Georgetown University. He has published an essay on Jonson's *Epigrams* and is working on a monograph on sixteenth-century court drama.

CHARLOTTE STERN, Associate Professor of Romance Languages at Randolph-Macon Woman's College, has published numerous articles and reviews on Spanish literature of the Middle Ages and the Renaissance and has previously contributed to *Renaissance Drama*. She is currently working on the Sayaqués in the early Spanish drama.

ROSEMARY WOOLF is a Fellow and Tutor in English Language and Medieval Literature at Somerville College, Oxford, and the author of *The English Religious Lyric in the Middle Ages* (1968) and *The English Mystery Plays* (1972).

LA PENSÉE

DE

JEAN-JACQUES ROUSSEAU

ESSAI D'INTERPRÉTATION NOUVELLE

PAR

ALBERT SCHINZ

Docteur en Philosophie
Professeur de Littérature française à l'Université de Pensylvanie
à Philadelphie

> J'ai toujours pensé qu'il faut prendre dans l'écritoire de chaque auteur l'encre dont on veut le peindre.
>
> SAINTE-BEUVE (*Mes Poisons*, p. 126)

PARIS
LIBRAIRIE FÉLIX ALCAN
108, BOULEVARD SAINT-GERMAIN, 108
—
1929

DU MÊME AUTEUR

A LA MÊME LIBRAIRIE

Anti-Pragmatisme. *Examen des droits respectifs de l'aristocratie intellectuelle et de la démocratie sociale*. 1909.

La Pensée religieuse de Rousseau et ses récents interprètes. 1927.

Jean-Jacques Rousseau, a Forerunner of Pragmatism. Chicago, Open Court Publ. Co, London, Truebner, 1909.

La Question du Contrat social. *Nouvelle contribution sur les rapports de J.-J. Rousseau avec les Encyclopédistes* (Tirage à part de la *Revue d'Histoire Littéraire de la France*, oct.-nov. 1912 ; pas mis dans le commerce).

Jean-Jacques Rousseau et le libraire-imprimeur Rey. *Les relations personnelles.* Genève, Jullien, 1916.

French Literature of the Great War. New-York and London, Appleton, 1919.

LA PENSÉE

DE

JEAN-JACQUES ROUSSEAU

A MES COLLÈGUES DE LA SECTION D'ÉTUDES FRANÇAISES

ET A MES ANCIENNES ÉTUDIANTES

DE SMITH COLLEGE

EN SOUVENIR DE QUINZE ANNÉES DE COLLABORATION CHARMANTE

AU COURS DESQUELLES IL EST NÉ

CE LIVRE EST DÉDIÉ

A. S.

LA PENSÉE DE JEAN-JACQUES ROUSSEAU

INTRODUCTION

> La plus puissante des influences qui se
> sont exercées sur l'esprit humain depuis
> Descartes, de quelque manière qu'on la
> juge, est incontestablement celle de
> J.-J. Rousseau.
>
> H. BERGSON (*La Philosophie*, p. 11).

LA MODERNITÉ DE ROUSSEAU

I. — La modernité prouvée : 1. Par les attaques, jamais discontinuées, contre lui. 2. Par une formidable littérature rousseauiste. 3. Le vrai Rousseau et le Rousseau de la tradition.

II. — Les causes le plus souvent invoquées pour expliquer l'action de Rousseau sur ses contemporains et sur la postérité, et l'insusffisance de ces explications : 1. L'art de Rousseau. 2. La personnalité de Rousseau. 3. Rousseau novateur.

III. — Deux observations qui serviront de point de départ à une nouvelle interprétation. 1. Un facteur négligé : l'état des esprits en Europe au moment où parut Rousseau. 2. Les commentateurs amenés à souligner de plus en plus un manque fondamental de cohésion philosophique chez Rousseau.

I

§ 1. Les travaux des érudits des dernières décades ont révisé ou confirmé, en tout cas renouvelé entièrement, peut-on dire, nos vues sur la plupart des grands écrivains : Rabelais, Ronsard, Montaigne, Pascal, Racine, Voltaire, Chateaubriand, Vigny, Hugo... En ce qui concerne Rousseau, on a à peu près piétiné sur place.

Est-ce que Rousseau serait mort ? — nous voulons dire, est-ce que l'œuvre de Rousseau n'aurait rien qui pût encore solliciter notre attention ? C'est juste le contraire. De tous les grands écrivains de France, il est le plus vivant. Bergson le proclamait il n'y a pas longtemps : « La plus puissante des influences qui se sont exercées sur l'esprit humain depuis Descartes, de quelque manière qu'on la juge, est incontestablement celle de J.-J. Rousseau » (*La Philosophie*, p. 11).

Ils sont légion, il est vrai, ceux qui ont voulu le proclamer mort (1) ; depuis cet abbé Cajot, digne précurseur de nos fureteurs modernes, lequel ne voyait en Rousseau qu'un plagiaire, à la fois formidable et minutieux, et qui se faisait fort de « réduire à rien la collection de ses œuvres », et alors « tout était fini, on ne parlait plus de J.-J. Rousseau » ; — en passant par Nisard, écrivant à la veille de la Révolution de 1848 : « Plus célèbre un moment que Montesquieu et non moins populaire que Voltaire, J.-J. Rousseau a le plus perdu avec le temps », et « il a le plus perdu parce que c'est à lui que la mode a le plus prêté » ; — et jusqu'à ce fanatique, L. Moreau, qui voulait persuader, aux autres et à lui-même, que Rousseau « diminue chaque jour, comme penseur et comme écrivain ; ses erreurs vivent sans doute, mais la mort gagne ses écrits »... Moreau vaticinait à la veille justement d'une nouvelle mêlée dont le fracas n'a pas cessé et dont Rousseau est sorti sinon grandi, au moins augmenté. C'est que ces oraisons funèbres passionnées ne furent jamais, il est à peine besoin de le dire, que des certificats de vitalité. On constate la mort, on ne la prouve pas. Qui songerait à écrire de gros volumes pour enterrer le fétichisme ? En effet, l'abbé Cajot déjà était obligé de substituer subrepticement à cette thèse que Rousseau n'exis-

---

(1) Sans compter même ses ennemis personnels, comme Grimm et Diderot, qui avaient un intérêt trop évident à assurer à ceux qui se fiaient à leur parole, que Rousseau était mort-né. Ou, encore, comme Voltaire : « Jean-Jacques n'est bon qu'à être oublié ; il sera comme Ramponneau qui a eu un moment de vogue à la Courtille ; à cela près que Ramponneau a eu cent fois moins de vanité et d'orgueil que le petit polisson de Genève » (Cité FAGUET, *Vie de Rousseau*, 1911, p. 346).

tait pas, ou était mort, cette autre que Rousseau *devrait* être mort : c'était « un détracteur des lois, l'ennemi du bon ordre », n'ayant produit « rien de véritablement utile à la patrie ». De même Moreau : Rousseau ne *devrait* plus être considéré comme vivant puisqu'il était l'auteur « d'idées malfaisantes » et « d'inspirations honteuses », parce qu'il était coupable d'avoir commis « le forfait de la plume », d'avoir professé « le mépris de la vérité », répandu « le goût dépravé du sophisme » ; qu'il n'était « qu'un raisonneur perpétuellement déraisonnable » tout en faisant des « simagrées d'indépendance altières », avec une « attitude de charlatan », du reste homme « abject », « faux », « ivre de cette corruption » contre laquelle il « hurle ».

Et depuis Moreau ces anathèmes, gages de vitalité, n'ont fait que se multiplier :

« C'est en vain qu'on se dit que cet homme est fou d'une folie croissante et caractérisée... On sent que l'âme de l'auteur a toujours été vile et l'on éprouve une sorte de satisfaction à reconnaître qu'avec tout son talent, l'écrivain n'est pas parvenu à déguiser entièrement sa vulgarité native » — écrit Ed. Schérer (1887).

« Rhéteur » ; impossible « à prendre au sérieux » ; n'ayant « qu'un souci, le succès, c'est-à-dire la réputation et l'argent », — écrit A. Espinas (1895).

« C'est la part d'absurdité qui est dans son œuvre qui a permis à Rousseau d'exercer sa prodigieuse influence » — écrit J. Lemaître (1906).

« Ne s'exhale-t-il pas de toutes ces fantaisies, une odeur de cadavre ? » — demande Lasserre (1907).

« Particulariste, borné, intolérant, d'un égoïsme féroce » ; « l'auteur d'une comédie perpétuelle » ; le « salarié de l'apostasie » ; « fourbe », « sycophante », aux « procédés de charlatan et de théologien » — s'indigne A. Dide (1911).

Rien de plus révélateur que le déchaînement de fureur à l'occasion du bi-centenaire de 1912. Le « criminel Rousseau » (*der Frevler Rousseau*) écrit simplement l'Allemand Fryman. « Enchanteur », « extravagant musicien de grandes symphonies », ironise M. Barrès. « Infirme moral » reprend avec une

pitié indignée Bourget, et qu'on ne devrait penser à célébrer
« que dans les préaux de la Salpêtrière, de Bicêtre ou de Sainte-
Anne ». « L'ennemi de la France » (Charles Maurras), « le
chien savant (Dollfus) ; « Le fou et le singe » ; « Le Chienlit »
(L. Daudet). Et le numéro du 25 juin 1912 de la *Revue Critique des Idées et des Livres* est consacré tout entier à maudire
Rousseau.

Après 1912 il y eut comme une trève ; mais elle ne fut pas
longue. Et jamais l'esprit Rousseauphobe ne fut plus violent
qu'en ces dernières années :

« Plat personnage », « plébeien mal né et mal élevé », « auto-
didacte », « un irrégulier et un malade », « un protestant et
un métèque », « cuistre genevois » (E. Ponthot, *Revue soc. et
catholique*, févr.-mars 1920).

« Esprit nébuleux et faible » ; « Forces ténébreuses », par
opposition à Dante « puissance de lumière » ; « Cœur lâche » ;
« Le plus pernicieux et le plus influent des mauvais maîtres »
(Jean Carrère, *les Mauvais Maîtres*, 1922).

« Pervertisseur prodigieux » ; « Laquais de Génie », à qui
nous devons « ce cadavre d'idées chrétiennes dont l'immense
putréfaction empoisonne aujourd'hui l'univers » (Jacques
Maritain, *Trois Réformateurs*, 1925).

Producteur de « sophismes monstrueux », « corrupteur de
conscience », et « déshumanisant l'homme » ; — « L'homme
que les Allemands glorifiaient comme principal inspirateur
de la Kultur » ; — Celui qui « abandonne ses cinq enfants et
qui a une affection inouïe (*unspeakable*) pour son chien » ; —
« Glorificateur de l'instinct » ; — animé de cette sorte de
sincérité « dont les meilleurs exemples se trouvent dans les
asiles de fous » (Babbit, *Democracy and Leadership*, 1924).

Inutile donc d'insister.

> *Je saute vingt bouquins pour en trouver la fin*
> *Et je me sauve à peine au milieu du jardin.*

Terminons par ces mots cueillis récemment dans une revue
pourtant large d'esprit, *Le Mercure de France*, 15 mars 1923,
et signés Émile Magne : « Le grand brigand, le mauvais génie

à qui nous devons tous nos maux, continue à verser son poison dans nos âmes et nos veines. Des gens d'esprit orné sont encore assez fous pour s'intéresser à ses doctrines et pour chanter ses louanges ».

Nous n'avons pas parlé des médecins, qui, eux du reste, en général n'ont pas manqué de sympathique compréhension (nous aurons a en dire quelque chose plus loin), mais dont l'influence s'est manifestée néfaste malgré eux ; le seul fait que des médecins s'occupaient si souvent de Rousseau faisait penser à bien des gens qu'il s'agissait d'un cas suspect et grave ; — sans compter que les termes parfois formidables dont ils se servent trahissent souvent leur pensée aux yeux de ceux qui sont peu au courant du langage de la profession. Et les rousseauphobes ne se sont pas privés d'exploiter ces dispositions du public.

D'autre part, nous ne voulons mentionner que pour montrer que nous n'ignorons pas leur existence ceux qui passent trop nettement les bornes de l'équité. Mais nous refusons de les prendre tout à fait au sérieux. Nous serions tenté de faire rentrer dans cette classe, M. Ernest Seillière lui-même, membre de l'Institut, et qui depuis 1908 n'a jamais cessé ses imprécations contre le « charlatan » Rousseau, le « crâne embaumé », et « l'apôtre de l'Impérialisme irrationnel ». Un de ses derniers livres, *Jean-Jacques Rousseau*, (Garnier, 1921) résume toutes ses précédentes attaques et y ajoute. C'est effroyable. On doit souhaiter, pour la mémoire de Rousseau, que ce livre soit beaucoup lu ; car, le parti pris — sans parler de l'absence parfait d'esprit chevaleresque vis-à-vis de celui qu'on définit comme un malade — est si évident que la victime ne pourra qu'en profiter dans l'esprit du lecteur. Les méthodes employées sont fort simples : On fait un diagnostique du malade, par analogie, et on prouve que Rousseau était un dégénéré par le même genre d'arguments que celui auquel avait recours le Dr Binet-Sanglé pour prouver que Jésus-Christ était fou. On puise ses munitions de préférence dans les *Confessions* et dans les *Dialogues* — les premières devant être interprétées avec les plus grandes précautions (dont M. Seillière ne se soucie pas trop), les seconds que très peu de gens lisent et dont l'action sur la postérité est donc très relative. On avise aussi le moyen le plus commode qui soit, en acceptant le témoignage de Rousseau toutes les fois que ce témoignage le condamne et en refusant le témoignage de Rousseau (comme hypocrite) toute les fois que ce témoignage parlerait en sa faveur ; de même M. Seillière prend pour accordé en quelque sorte que toutes les fois que Rousseau parle de vertu, il ne dit pas sa pensée, et qu'ainsi la « partie rationnelle » de *La Nouvelle Héloïse* — les deux tiers au bas mot — contient des lettres « aux *prétentions* moralisatrices » seulement (p. 106 ; voir aussi p. 25 de ses *Etapes du Mysticisme passionnel*, 1919), et où le Rousseau condamnant Saint-Preux « ne parle que du bout des lèvres », et sans désirer qu'on le « prenne au sérieux ». Peut-on « prendre au sérieux » de tels procédés ?

Veut-on de l'Inquisition ? Voici l'abbé Théodore Delmont, dans son *J.-J. Rousseau d'après les derniers travaux de la critique et de l'histoire* (Lille, 1892) ; très bien renseigné d'ailleurs, il conclut dans le sens de la tradition catholique la plus exaltée. « La vie de Jean-Jacques est faite depuis son enfance jusqu'à 38 ans d'une odyssée aventureuse et des *polissonneries d'un vaurien* ; de 38 jusqu'à 50 ans des passions les plus viles et de l'incommensurable orgueil d'un parvenu *plébéien d'origine, resté peuple au sens fâcheux du mot* ; depuis 50 jusqu'à 66 ans des accès délirants d'une lypémanie douloureuse, d'une folie raisonnante, provoquée hélas ! par des vices et des passions qui ne peuvent avoir droit qu'à la pitié... » L'homme Rousseau est « un vilain sire », à peine supérieur à Voltaire ; l'œuvre de Rousseau est « essentiellement paradoxale et malsaine ».

Et voici l'ouvrage de C. Lecigne, docteur ès Lettres, professeur des lettres françaises aux Facultés libres de Lille, *Le Fléau romantique* (Paris, Lethellieux, 1909). L'*Imprimatur* est donné par H. Odelin, Vic. gén. à Paris. L'auteur part de la définition de Gœthe : « J'appelle le classique ce qui est sain, et le romantique ce qui est malade ». Or, « il faut remonter jusqu'à J.-J. Rousseau. Le mal romantique, on va le voir dans la hideur originelle. Tares physiologiques, tares intellectuelles, tares morales, toutes les tares y sont... Fou... Monstre jusque vers l'âge de trente ans... » qui va tout pourrir. « Otez à Jean-Jacques Rousseau son éloquence, son souffle, ses images, tout ce décor fastueux des couleurs et des attitudes, il ne reste qu'un résidu *affreux*, — amas de corruptions d'où s'exhalent des odeurs de mort... il y a le délire... il y a le cauchemar d'orgueil et la synthèse de tous les vices du romantisme ». M. Seillière et M. Babbitt seraient jaloux des épithètes savoureuses que ce fils de l'Église prêchant la religion de la charité a su collectionner contre Rousseau. Sa violence n'a d'égale que sa candeur, car il répète à chaque pas : Je ne comprends pas : — Alors que vaut le jugement ?

Un autre exemple de fanatisme — aussi poussé qu'inoffensif — est celui de C.-A. Fusil. Dans *Rousseau, juge de Jean-Jacques ou la Comédie de l'Orgueil et du Cœur* (Plon, 1923, VII, 335 p.). Faut-il avoir assez peur du spectre de Rousseau pour se laisser aller à écrire des livres pareils ? et pour avoir la naïveté d'aller dire encore au public intelligent : Pendant un siècle et demi le monde s'est trompé ; mais moi, professeur dans quelque lycée, j'ai lu pour la première fois Rousseau avec intelligence et je vais vous le révéler : « Aujourd'hui après avoir relu Rousseau la plume à la main, nous avons vu clair dans cette confusion. Sans autre préoccupation, ni tentance extérieure, nous avons étudié l'homme, et nous l'avons jugé mauvais. Voilà tout ! » — Hé, oui ! Voilà tout ! M. Fusil a trouvé Rousseau mauvais : Et après ? Toutefois M. Fusil a rendu un service : Quand on voudra démontrer jusqu'où peut aller, non la passion — car la passion peut rester intelligente même en déformant les réalités — mais jusqu'où peut aller la candeur, on lira M. Fusil. Il pratique le plus souvent la même méthode que M. Seillière : Quand Rousseau écrit des phrases qui correspondent à l'idée que M. Fusil s'est faite de sa victime, il estime que le texte vaut très bien ; mais quand Rousseau dit des choses que M. Fusil lui-même trouve fort bonnes, alors c'est que Rousseau est « un faux bonhomme ». On conçoit où l'on aboutit de cette façon : Comme on ne peut nier que Rousseau exprime tout de même certaines choses excellentes, il en résulte que plus Rousseau a raison, plus il est détestable aux yeux de M. Fusil, — car plus il est faux bonhomme.

Veut-on un exemple encore où l'impertinence prend sa source dans ce qu'on ne peut appeler cette fois que de l'incompréhension. Voici un article de M. Francis Waterhouse qui a paru dans *Publications* of *the Modern language Association of America* (mars 1922, pp. 113-127) : « An Interview with J.-J. Rousseau ». L'auteur, professeur à l'Université du Texas cite une « *Selbstbiographie* » d'un Allemand, Christian Felix Weisse, « minor poet » et « Hofmeister » chez le comte von Geyerberg. Le volume cité est à la Bibliothèque de l'Université Harvard. Ce Weisse a rendu visite à Rousseau à Montmorency, en 1760. L'article se compose de deux pages et demie d'entrevue et de *onze pages* de commentaires. C'est bien malheureux. L'interview sans être en rien révélateur, n'est pas sans quelque intérêt. Mais les commentaires sont faits dans un esprit de dénigrement tellement extraordinaire que l'on comprend difficilement comment un périodique sérieux a pu les accueillir. L'auteur descend à des profondeurs insondables pour prouver que les remarques — du reste toujours banales — que l'on prête à Rousseau, trahissent bien son « génie singulier », c'est-à-dire une âme imbécile et tortueuse. M. Waterhouse est un disciple de M. Babbit. Nous serions surpris tout de même que celui-ci se louât de sa progéniture spirituelle.

Il est juste d'ajouter que ces extravagances ont suscité une réaction dans le camp même qu'on voulait servir et dont elles compromettaient la cause. Rappelons ici un maître —, et des moins suspect sur la matière, qui a pris le parti de se moquer de cette manie de nos contemporains à traiter Rousseau de Turc à More. Nous voulons dire le délicat lettré, et penseur — et ironiste — Henri Bremond, de l'Académie Française.

« Si jamais philosophe a tenté — dit-il — de nous persuader que tout est dans tout, ce fut bien j'imagine l'auteur de ces volumes, heureusement innombrables [M. de Seillière], où se coudoient presque sans surprise, La Calprenède et Nietzsche, Fénelon et Gobineau, Mme Guyon et George Sand, beaucoup d'autres encore, tous prototypes ou sosies, ou successeurs de Rousseau, tous associés avec lui, paraît-il, à la naissance du monstre à trois têtes — Impérialisme, Mysticisme, Romantisme — de qui sont venus tous nos maux et la fin de l'âge d'or. J'avoue du reste, à ma honte, que cette hydre m'a tout l'air du Loup-Garou. Ou bien, si elle naquit jamais, ce dut être dans un jardin plus antique de quatre mille ans que les Charmettes. Libre à chacun d'appeler Romantisme ce que nous appelions jadis péché originel, mais à ce jeu qu'on laisse donc tranquille le pauvre Jean-Jacques pour ne plus harceler que le vieil Adam » (1).

Ou qu'on lise, dans le même volume, les pages inspirées par les deux volumes de M. Maréchal, *la Jeunesse de Lamennais*, et *La famille de Lamennais* (Perin 1913). L'article commence ainsi :

« Le Romantisme Catholique c'est Lamennais ; Lamennais c'est Rousseau ; Rousseau enfin c'est le Mal ; telles sont les trois propositions où se réduit, en dernière analyse, le gros volume de M. Chr. Maréchal…. Lamennais, selon cet auteur, est un pauvre damné, et c'est la faute à Rousseau « dont le moi sans cesse en révolte ne sera jamais écrasé ». Comme si, continue l'abbé Brémond, Rousseau était le premier et le seul dont le moi n'a jamais été écrasé, comme si le premier romantique n'était pas Adam ? Voyons : « Rousseau par-ci, Rousseau par là ; ce mot revient à toutes les pages du livre… mais de bonne foi, qu'est-ce que le romantisme et Jean-Jacques ont à faire ici ? Ne lui faisons pas cet honneur, Rousseau n'a pas inventé la sensibilité» (p. 50-51) (2).

---

(1) Plus bas il écrit : « Il me plaît infiniment que M. Seillière rapproche jusqu'à les confondre, Romantisme et Mysticisme. Au lieu seulement de maudire en celui-ci et en celui-là des venins de la même famille, je bénirais plutôt la commune excellence qui les rend très bienfaisants l'un et l'autre ; Romantisme et Mysticisme prenant également leur origine aux sources profondes de notre être dans cette région mystérieuse où s'allume la « docte et sainte ivresse du poète » et où la nature s'offre à la grâce qui l'a prévenue, et qui la prépare à la rencontre de Dieu » (*Pour le Romantisme*, Bloud et Gay, 1923, pp. IX-X).

(2) On voit bien du reste que Bremond n'est pas un fervent de Rousseau en lisant l'essai sur « Sainte-Beuve ou le romantisme impénitent » où il rapproche Saint-Preux de l'Amaury de *Volupté* ; et certes Rousseau n'est pas épargné là !

Un autre cas où l'exagération par trop forte a invité à l'ironie est celui de Maugras ; l'auteur de *Voltaire et Rousseau* (1886) a été arrangé de main de maître par Faguet qui refuse de prendre au sérieux ce « livre ineffable », dans lequel non seulement Rousseau est traité de monstre mais Voltaire de petit saint (*Vie de Rousseau*, 1911 ; p. 271, 345-6 et al.)

Nous le répétons, rien ne prouve mieux l'actualité de la pensée de Rousseau que justement ces anathèmes. Et nous n'avons d'ailleurs qu'un commentaire à offrir sur toutes ces vitupérations : Nous sommes convaincus que le procédé de maudire — ou de bénir — n'est pas le bon. Quand il s'agit du passé particulièrement, les faits se comprennent et ne se jugent point ; et nous allons jusqu'à dire : les idées de Rousseau — dans leur ensemble ou isolées, et aussi bien les idées que souvent *on prête* à Rousseau — pourraient d'ailleurs être mille fois fausses et absurdes, cela n'a qu'une importance secondaire pour l'étudiant d'histoire littéraire dès l'instant où elles ont servi de drapeaux à l'opinion. La seule attitude qui convienne au penser est celle-ci : *Rousseau a été, donc il devait être*. En outre, pour Rousseau, les circonstances sont aujourd'hui les mêmes que dans le passé — elle continuent à l'être ou elles le sont *de nouveau*, et il faut dire encore : Rousseau est, donc il *doit* être ; et il n'est pas digne d'hommes comme Bourget, Barrès, Maurras, Magne, etc. de lancer des injures, de se comporter vis-à-vis d'un écrivain dont on condamne les idées comme l'enfant qui frappe la table à laquelle il s'est cogné. La sagesse, selon nous, consisterait à pénétrer le secret de la bataille royale engagée autour de ce nom, et qui ne veut cesser.

§ 2. La vitalité de Rousseau n'est pas attestée seulement par ces discussions violentes, elle l'est aussi par ce fait que la littérature rousseauiste (1) — même sans compter tous ces écrits

---

(1) Nous suivrons l'usage, malgré la justesse de cette note de l'abbé Bremond à la p. 48 de son volume *Pour le Romantisme* (Bloud 1925) : « Roussien, rous-

de polémique que nous venons de rappeler — s'est enrichie en
ces dernières années au point d'être écrasante (1) ; mais cela
encore n'empêche pas notre remarque d'être vraie, que l'interprétation de Rousseau en somme a piétiné sur place.

1º En effet une proportion considérable de ces publications
ne sont guère que des travaux d'érudition et de minutie :
Rousseau est-il mort naturellement, par suicide, ou assassiné ?
Rousseau a-t-il eu des enfants ? Rousseau a-t-il raison contre
Hume, ou Hume contre Rousseau ? Les *Confessions* contre
les *Mémoires d'Epinay* ou les *Mémoires d'Epinay* contre les
Confessions ; les femmes qui ont fourni des éléments pour
la création de Julie ; — ou de Lord Bomston; Rousseau
« Dromomane » ; Rousseau aviateur ; Rousseau « Thanato-
phobe » ; Rousseau et la prohibition des boissons fermentées ;
Rousseau et la paix perpétuelle ; Rousseau anglicisant ;
Rousseau et le Roman ; Rousseau plagiaire ; Rousseau De-
bussyste, Rousseau et le Bolchévisme, etc., etc. Et d'ailleurs
nous ne voudrions pas dire non plus que telles de ces recherches ne sont pas utiles, voire indispensables. Il est en
certainement de remarquables. Ainsi, concernant la *vie* de
Rousseau, celles de Berthoud, sur *Rousseau au Val-de-Travers* ;
Rey, sur *Rousseau dans la Vallée de Montmorency* ; E. Rod,
sur *L'Affaire Jean-Jacques Rousseau*, Courtois sur *Rousseau
en Angleterre*, Foster sur *Rousseau à Paris de 1770-1778* ; les
deux volumes de Buffenoir sur Mᵐᵉ d'Houdetot (1901, 1905)
et celui sur la maréchale de Luxembourg (1924) etc. Ou,
concernant les *écrits* de Rousseau celles de Morel, sur le *Second
Discours*, Brunel, sur la *Lettre à d'Alembert*, Dreyfus-Brisac,

seauisme nous ne devrions plus employer ces mots monstrueux... M. Pierre de
Nolhac propose rousselien, rousselisme conforme du moins au génie de la
langue ».

(1) Impossible d'aller dans les détails. Nous renvoyons, pour un coup d'œil
général, à notre article de *Modern Philology* (Chicago, nov. 1922). « Le Mouvement Rousseauiste du dernier quart de siècle, Essai de Bibliographie Critique
(p. 149-170), et à celui de *Modern Language Notes* (Baltimore, nov. 1926) :
« Bibliographie critique de Rousseau dans les cinq dernières années » (p. 423-
438).

et Vaughan, et Beaulavon sur le *Contrat Social* ; Mornet, sur
la *Nouvelle Héloïse* ; Masson sur la *Profession de foi* ; Tiersot
sur la musique ; G. Havens, etc. Il n'en reste pas moins vrai
que trop souvent dans ces articles et livres d'érudition on ne
fait que battre les buissons tout autour du sujet lui-même
lequel demeure la *pensée* de Rousseau ; ou bien ce ne sont
encore, comme ceux que nous venons de nommer, que des
travaux d'approche.

2º Quant aux ouvrages qui abordent l'œuvre de Rousseau
du point de vue de la pensée — et nous parlons ici surtout
de ceux qui la prennent dans son ensemble — ils demeurent
fondamentalement traditionnalistes, ceux des sympathiques
ou objectifs, Valette, Bouvier, Ducros, comme ceux des
détracteurs, comme Nourisson, Lasserre, Lemaître, Seillière,
More, Babbitt, Carrère, Maritain, et comme même ceux de
qui l'attitude philosophique et impersonnelle est le moins
contestable, par exemple Faguet ou Hoeffding. Ce sont, en
somme, les mêmes points de vue qui ont prévalu pendant un
siècle et demi, les mêmes appréciations, les mêmes problèmes
d'exégèse, exposés avec les mêmes solutions, les mêmes développements d'arguments pour et contre, — et qui, notons-
le bien, n'ayant pas satisfait hier ceux qui cherchaient à pénétrer au cœur du mystère, ne sauraient satisfaire aujourd'hui.

§ 3. Et c'est ici que se place une observation très importante. Pas une petite part des polémiques sans fin engagées
autour du nom de Rousseau, est due au vague des concepts
philosophiques qu'on fait valoir de part et d'autre dans ces
discussions. Il paraît étonnant qu'à une époque où on ne peut
lire dix lignes sans rencontrer le nom de Rousseau, on se serve
presque toujours, sans effort pour en préciser la valeur, de
tant de termes indéfinis et usés, de clichés démodés, comme
« nature », « raison », « liberté », « vertu », « devoir », « conscience
morale », sentiment religieux », etc. L'explication de cet ana-
chronisme — car c'en est un — est d'ailleurs facile à indiquer.
Elle se ramènerait en grande partie à une simple tradition de
vocabulaire : Rousseau lui-même d'abord s'est servi des

termes philosophiques en cours ; il y a assujetti — de concert du reste avec ses contemporains — sa pensée. Or, lui le premier, il eût dû être prudent ; à leur tour, les successeurs de Rousseau n'évitèrent pas ces termes ; et, en fait, ils les eussent évités difficilement dès l'instant où ils voulaient citer Rousseau pour mieux exposer sa pensée ; mais c'était donc leur donner, à ces termes, droit de cité une seconde fois ; et depuis, ils sont demeurés avec nous, consacrant en quelque sorte la continuité de tant de notions lourdes de malentendus (1).

Si l'on s'étonne d'ailleurs, de ce que cette mise au point des définitions ait justement été négligée pour un auteur comme Rousseau, à propos de qui elle aurait été si particulièrement nécessaire, nous remarquerons que l'anomalie s'explique par le fait même de cette importance. En soi déjà, ce travail réclame un effort de pensée fort sérieux et qu'on ne peut faire au pied levé ; en outre il devenait plus complexe et plus difficile à mesure qu'on en remettait l'exécution ; — car les commentaires s'ajoutaient aux commentaires, c'est-à-dire les explications nébuleuses aux explications nébuleuses. D'ailleurs, le monde qui toujours discutait Rousseau exigeait toujours plus impérieusement des clartés de la part des commentateurs, lesquels de plus en plus pressés trouvaient de moins en moins le repos d'esprit nécessaire pour s'atteler au vrai pro-

(1) Rousseau a senti cette difficulté déjà lui-même et ne l'a pas cachée. Prenez par exemple cette phrase où toute l'imprécision du mot *nature* est franchement reconnue, voire signalée. Le baron d'Étange réclame ses droits *naturels* de père pour marier Julie comme il l'entend, et Saint-Preux ne peut lui répondre qu'en invoquant à son tour les droits *naturels* : « Et quand vous osez réclamer la nature, c'est vous seul qui bravez ses lois » (III, lettre 11). (Et notons tout de suite, pour chercher à pousser d'emblée le lecteur dans l'esprit de cet ouvrage, que c'est le droit — ou plutôt le devoir — naturel tel que l'entend le père, auquel Rousseau donne le pas sur l'autre, après avoir pesé la valeur des deux). Rousseau s'est rendu compte de plus en plus de l'insuffisance de la terminologie de son temps. Dans une *note* au 3ᵉ *Dialogue* parlant *du Système de la Nature* d'Holbach, on lit : « Nos philosophes ne manquent pas d'étaler pompeusement ce mot de *nature* à la tête de tous leurs écrits. Mais ouvrez le livre et vous verrez quel jargon métaphysique ils ont décoré de ce beau nom ».

blème. Bref, à mesure que le travail s'imposait davantage, il décourageait davantage les meilleures volontés. C'est un cercle vicieux.

L'exemple le plus frappant de ce désarroi se trouve chez E. Faguet ; à l'occasion du bicentenaire de Rousseau en 1912, il publiait sur Rousseau cinq volumes remplis d'observations et de critiques qui sont souvent de premier ordre, mais sporadiques et sans aucune valeur finale, et qui aboutissaient à ce bilan : « Chaos d'idées claires ». Il est très certain que Faguet n'eût pas consacré presque en une seule année ces cinq volumes et de nombreux articles au philosophe de Genève si celui-ci n'avait eu à offrir qu'un « chaos » (1).

Mais cette imprécision des termes chez Rousseau et ses commentateurs, a eu des conséquences bien plus importantes que le simple désarroi auquel il a conduit un penseur indépendant et vigoureux comme Faguet. Elle a conduit — et cela de fort bonne heure — à une déviation sérieuse dans l'interprétation de la pensée de Rousseau, laquelle s'aggravant de jour en jour a fini par constituer à côté du *Rousseau original* un Rousseau postiche — le *Rousseau de la tradition*. Et ce n'est pas trop de dire que celui-ci a presque entièrement déplacé celui-là. M. Baldensperger, dans son livre *La Littérature* (1913) n'a pas craint d'affirmer que « les écrivains de marque sont admis *presque en dehors de leurs œuvres et avec celles-ci pour surrogat ou peu s'en faut* à se maintenir dans le souvenir de la postérité » (p. 273). Nous ne sachions d'écrivain dont cela soit plus absolument exact que de Rousseau. Avec le lait de nos mères nous suçons, non pas tant toutes sortes d'idées de Rousseau, mais justement toutes sortes *d'interprétations* de ces idées. Seulement la plus scrupuleuse circonspection peut garantir contre cette hantise des préjugés — contradictoires étonnemment, erronés souvent, imprécis tou-

---

(1) Il avait publié lui-même, bien des années avant, deux études sur Rousseau, — l'une dans son *XVIIIᵉ siècle* (1887), l'autre son ouvrage *Politiques Comparées de Montesquieu, Voltaire et Rousseau* (1902) — beaucoup plus pensées, encore qu'appartenant à la période d'impressionisme littéraire.

jours — harcelant l'esprit à la moindre velléité d'inattention. Edme Champion, *J.-J. Rousseau et la Révolution Française* (1909) examinant par exemple l'influence des divers écrits de Rousseau sur la Révolution Française, était arrivé à montrer en somme que dès la fin du XVIIIe siècle il n'y en eut guère, *mais* que de très bonne heure on en avait affirmé beaucoup. Et aujourd'hui encore, là — comme du reste ailleurs — le Rousseau qui vit, celui autour duquel on se bat, est un Rousseau qui n'exista pas. Nous irons jusqu'à affirmer que jamais les deux pensées, du Rousseau original et du Rousseau postiche, n'ont été aussi loin l'une de l'autre que chez les modernes ; et si on voulait étudier ce que les doctrines de Rousseau *ne sont pas*, on ne trouverait mieux que des livres signés Dide, Seillière, Babbitt. Au fond le grand effort — et le plus illusoire — de ces écrivains se ramène surtout à tâcher d'identifier le Rousseau original et vrai avec le pseudo Rousseau d'une tradition qu'ils continuent (ou parfois qu'ils essaient de créer). Et d'ailleurs, sans doute, il reste toujours quelques rapports du « Rousseauisme » avec Rousseau ; le premier sort toujours du second ; mais vouloir ignorer la nature de ce rapport, c'est d'une étourderie ou d'une mauvaise foi extraordinaire ; et c'est raisonner exactement comme le pédant de Montaigne : « Le jambon donne la soif, la soif désaltère, donc le jambon désaltère », et souvent c'est comme de rendre Jésus-Christ responsable des horreurs de l'inquisition (1).

Pour nous, une conclusion à tout ceci, s'impose : Abstraction faite même des cas d'étourderies ou de mauvaise foi, et

---

(1) Dans son livre *J.-J. Rousseau* (Garnier, 1921) M. de Seillière va juqu'à écrire des phrases comme celles-ci : « Nous savons déjà que Julie va bientôt contredire point par point ces diverses assertions [des droits de l'amour passionné] dans la partie rationnelle du roman. *Laquelle des deux suggestions toutefois a fait le plus de chemin après 150 ans de rousseauisme continu ?* » (p. 350). C'est nous qui soulignons : mais que dire d'un historien des idées qui indique si bien la différence entre le texte de l'auteur et l'interprétation du lecteur, et qui ensuite l'ignore pour mieux s'acharner sur cet auteur que son propre texte absout parfaitement ?

puisque l'entente entre commentateurs de Rousseau paraît aussi éloignée que jamais, — ce sont nous l'avons dit les *mêmes* discussions qui sans cesse renaissent — puisque l'accord n'existe même pas toujours au sujet des idées qu'il faut attribuer à Rousseau, c'est qu'on frappe dans la nuit ou que les armes sont faussées.

Manifestement la chose à faire est de reprendre intégralement l'examen de la pensée de Rousseau. C'est l'objet des pages suivantes. Le lecteur jugera si, profitant des errements de nos prédécesseurs, nous avons mieux réussi.

II

§ 1. Nous serions trop présomptueux cependant, si nous procédions d'emblée à notre exposé, c'est-à-dire sans récapituler rapidement les solutions qu'on a proposées au problème de la fascination toujours encore exercée par Rousseau, et sans expliquer pourquoi, selon nous, elles ne peuvent satisfaire.

On peut les placer sous trois chefs.

D'abord, il y a l'explication de ceux qui ramènent tout à L'ART DE ROUSSEAU : Rousseau aurait été un homme et un penseur médiocre ou détestable ; mais il avait un style qui a suffi à ensorceler le monde. Ce sont du reste surtout des poètes choqués du réalisme de ses sentiments, ou des adversaires de certaines de ses idées philosophiques et en mal d'explications précises qui parlent ainsi, Nisard, Schérer, Lemaître, — et le dernier venu, Ducros : « Ce style est, croyons-nous, la principale cause de sa grande influence » (*J.-J. Rousseau*, p. 218) (1).

---

(1) Nous avons mentionné des auteurs Français ; il en est de même à l'étranger. Rappelons les appréciations du poète anglais Thomas Moore : « C'est une iniquité, c'est une honte. Quel exemple révèle mieux les impostures du génie ? Comme il disperse les ressources de son talent merveilleux d'histrion, qui est

alcan édite :

René **MAUNIER**

Professeur à l'Université de Paris.

INTRODUCTION
à la
SOCIOLOGIE

1 vol. in-16, 124 pages, cartonné......... **10 fr.**

C'est, non pas un traité ou un manuel, mais un précis ou une initiation à l'usage des étudiants et aussi du public curieux et studieux. L'auteur y a donné la quintessence des cours de sociologie qu'il a professés à Alger et à Paris. Par son texte, concentré et condensé, par ses notes bibliographiques donnant l'indication de sources soigneusement choisies, par sa présentation et par sa division méthodique et pratique, il est le livret que tous ceux qui sont occupés des sciences sociales trouveront avec profit sous leur main. Un ample index des matières permet en s'y référant de trouver, sur chaque question, l'essentiel de ce qu'on sait.

Paris, 108 b.ᵈ St Germain·6ᵉ

C'est supposer le monde par trop peu intelligent. Le style seul, c'est-à-dire s'il ne sert pas à souligner une pensée, n'existe pas. Or, ramener tout Rousseau à son style, c'est admettre : *ou bien* que sa pensée est toute banale, — et alors on ne conçoit pas que les meilleurs représentants souvent de l'espèce humaine se soient arrêtés devant un homme qui soulignait sans avoir rien à souligner ; *ou bien* que ce style souligne des erreurs certaines et des folies, — et alors on se refuse à voir la postérité persistant à prendre au sérieux un « malade », et un « fou » (Lemaître) ; *ou bien* que le style sert à dissimuler des pensées d'un auteur consciemment méchant et voulant abuser son prochain, — et alors, encore moins qu'avant, on ne peut admettre que tant de générations aient été dupes d'une imposture. Le mot de Lincoln est ici à sa place : « On peut tromper quelque monde tout le temps, et on peut tromper tout le monde quelque temps ; mais on ne peut tromper tout le monde tout le temps.

§ 2. Ensuite il y a — et davantage récemment — la tentative d'expliquer l'action de Rousseau par sa PERSONNALITÉ : Rousseau est un *étranger* dans la pensée française ; il est *Genevois* ; il est *protestant* ; et on a appuyé sur l'un des trois termes (Nisard, de Voguë, Brunetière, Texte, Seillière, Lasserre, Lemaitre, Vallette, Dide etc.). Ces termes en eux-mêmes, n'ont pas un sens suffisamment arrêté ; et il faut nécessairement commencer par les définir si on veut s'entendre — ce qui finira toujours par ramener le subjectivisme. Le terme *étranger* en particulier, est désespérément vague ; à supposer même qu'on sache précisément ce qu'il faut entendre par « Français », il est évident qu'étranger signifiant

le principe et le ressort de sa vie, à contrefaire toutes les nuances de la pensée, toutes les délicatesses du sentiment à déchaîner tant d'émotions auxquelles il est insensible » (Cité, Houssaye, *Charmettes*, p. 324). Moore était un poète : Burke le grand historien n'est pas plus mesuré que le poète son compatriote quand il reproche aux Français « d'élever des statuts à ce barbare, féroce, vil, dur, père de beaux sentiments généreux » (*Lettre à un Membre de l'Assemblée Nationale*, 1791).

non-Français, nous apprend peu de chose. Le terme *Genevois* est moins imprécis déjà, mais que de causes de confusion encore ! Si on se contente de la notion générale qu'éveille ce mot chez un lecteur, toute démonstration reposant là-dessus sera sans consistance aussi ; si on le définit, ce sera forcément une définition de quelque individu, et toute démonstration se fondant là-dessus restera subjective elle-même. Ce n'est pas tout ; les Genevois sont des êtres humains, et certains de leurs traits les plus accusés se retrouvent ailleurs, — alors pourquoi appeler ces traits chez Rousseau, *genevois* plutôt qu'autre chose ? En fait, Joseph Texte déclare *anglais* chez Rousseau maints traits que Vallette déclare *genevois*. Ainsi, au lieu de dire : Rousseau est genevois, et genevois signifie telle chose, ne serait-il pas plus court de dire directement : Rousseau est telle chose ? Enfin, qu'il soit en somme, genevois ne changera rien au problème (d'expliquer l'influence de Rousseau) qui ne sera que reculé.

En ce sens, le terme *protestant* paraît encore le moins mauvais des trois ; le protestantisme est pour beaucoup une doctrine théologico-philosophique de la vie, qui est saisissable et discutable, comme le catholicisme ou le bouddhisme. Malheureusement, le principe pratique fondamental du protestantisme est l'interprétation individuelle, partant subjective des choses de la religion ; dès lors l'appellation « protestant » cesse de donner prise au penseur ; Bossuet déjà l'avait bien montré. Et les *Lettres de la Montagne* prouvent assez que le Protestantisme de Rousseau n'est pas, par exemple, celui de la majorité des Genevois. Alors, à quoi nous avance la définition du « Rousseau protestant » ?

Il n'y a pas si longtemps, la démonstration de l'illusion de cette explication par le facteur de la personnalité a été faite d'une façon frappante. Deux auteurs — Dide (1910), Vallette (1911) — ont cherché à expliquer Rousseau par sa qualité de Genevois et de protestant ; leurs deux ouvrages, parus presque en même temps, sont cependant aussi différents qu'il est possible : — où l'un dit blanc, l'autre dit noir, — essentiellement parce que tous deux partaient de leur conception per-

sonnelle du Genevois et du protestant, et voyaient Rousseau
au travers de cette conception.

Il faudrait ajouter ici la tentative d'explication — bien
anglo-saxonne — que c'est la *personnalité tout court* de Rousseau qui a hypnotisé le monde ; comme, disons, celle de Napo-
léon ou de Byron ; un peu l'idée du « Hero-worship » de Carlyle.
mais agissant à rebours. C'est particulièrement l'idée des deux
écrivains américains, MM. Irving Babbitt et Paul E. More

« En partie — dit ce dernier — l'influence de Rousseau fut due
à son talent littéraire... mais au fond de tout, il y a la personnalité
démoniaque de l'écrivain, la force inexplicable qui a imposé au
monde l'expérience de cet homme, Rousseau... le rayonnement
magique que les émotions personnelles de cet homme imposait
au monde. Comme le *credo* chrétien a pénétré le moyen âge, coloré
par l'intense figure des *Confessions* de saint Augustin, ainsi la foi
des temps modernes s'est enflammée des *Confessions* de Rousseau »
(*Shelburns Essays* III, « Rousseau », p. 236).

§ **3.** L'explication la plus persistante, cependant, est celle qui
montre en Rousseau un grand NOVATEUR ; pas un simple
iconoclaste comme beaucoup de ses émules du XVIIIᵉ siècle,
il aurait semé quantité d'idées originales dont le monde se
serait emparé. C'est aussi l'explication la plus facilement
vérifiable. Tandis qu'on peut toujours épiloguer à propos des
théories du *génie*, ou des diverses formes de la *personnalité*,
ou de ce qui constitue le fond d'une *nationalité* ou d'une *religion*, il est aisé de s'assurer concrètement si telle ou telle idée
défendue par Rousseau a été vraiment formulée par lui
d'abord. Or, cet examen a été fait ; et, de cet argument, le
plus rebattu et le plus solide semblait-il, l'érudition n'a rien
laissé debout.

Prenons par ordre chronologique quelques-unes des plus
fameuses de ces idées soi-disant nouvelles chez Rousseau.

Voici d'abord le « paradoxe » du *Discours sur les Sciences
et les Arts*. Sans remonter à la Genèse qui nous montre nos
premiers parents mis en garde contre l'arbre de la connais-

sance du bien et du mal, ni même à l'Ecclésiaste (« avec beaucoup de savoir on a beaucoup de chagrin, et celui qui augmente sa science augmente sa douleur » I, 18) ce qui serait suffisant pour rendre un peu ridicule les prétentions d'originalité que des disciples réclament ici pour Rousseau, il serait assez pertinent de se souvenir que ce dernier invoquera lui-même ses ancêtres spirituels, Lycurgue par exemple, Platon et Plutarque ; et il aurait pu encore rappeler Horace opposant les fortes vertus des Scythes aux mœurs dissolues des courtisans d'Auguste ; ou Tacite célébrant les mœurs des Germains pour frapper celles des Romains de l'Empire ; ou Salluste rappelant la simplicité des premiers temps de la République en contraste avec la corruption sortie du luxe de la Rome conquérante ; ou Juvénal surtout, regrettant comme le fera Rousseau les jours où les peuples redoutaient les Fabricius et les Catons. Il faudra se souvenir que la nouvelle morale (chrétienne) proclamée sur les ruines de la Rome impériale fut celle de la vanité des choses du monde, des Arts et des Sciences. Et que, contre le mouvement de la Renaissance menaçante, Agrippa de Nettesheim dressait d'avance un acte d'accusation dans son *De Vanitate Scientiarum* (1530), suivi bientôt par Lylio Gyraldi dans son *Progymnason adversus litteras et litteratos* (1538), et en 1565 par Nicolas de Cusa dans son *De Docta Ignoratione*. Que signifiait ensuite le geste du réformateur Carlostatt, persuadant aux étudiants de Wittemberg de brûler leurs livres et d'apprendre quelques métiers manuels, lui même abandonnant le professorat pour la charrue ? Puis le siècle de Louis XIV avait à peine commencé que Racan lançait son *Discours contre les Sciences* (1635)... et combien lui firent écho : Fénelon, La Bruyère, Fontenelle même ; et davantage encore les grands prédicateurs du XVIIe siècle (1). Pas un instant, cette note n'avait

---

(1) A titre d'exemple, citons une seulement des nombreuses Prosopopées de Fabricius avant la lettre ; elle émane de la plume autorisée de Bossuet alors à Metz : « Paris dont on ne peut apaiser l'orgueil, dont la vanité se soutient « toujours malgré tant de choses qui te devraient déprimer, quand te verrai-je

cessé de se faire entendre depuis l'aube de la civilisation occidentale, et le XVIIIe siècle — celui de Rousseau — était en quelque sorte ouvert par les *Lettres Persannes* (1721) où on lisait ces mots : « Tu m'as beaucoup parlé des sciences et des arts cultivés en occident. Tu me vas regarder comme un Barbare, mais je ne sais si l'utilité que l'on en retire dédommage les hommes des mauvais usages que l'on en fait tous les jours » (*Lettre* 105). Et Rousseau connaissait Montesquieu ; et Rousseau avait été jusqu'à 16 ans à Genève où se faisait entendre tous les jours la voix de Turretini, l'auteur des *Orationes Academicæ* (1735), dont l'une avait pour titre : « De Scientiarum Vanitate et Præstantia ».

On arrivera à la même conclusion si l'on prend la question du luxe. Le XVIIe siècle avait lu l'essai impitoyable de Nicole sur ce sujet, et avait entendu le « Sermon sur les Divertissements » de Bourdaloue, et le « Sermon sur l'Aumône » de Massillon, il avait médité le chapitre de *Télémaque* sur « La Bétique » ; et Montesquieu écrivait son chapitre : « Fatale conséquence du luxe à la Chine » (*Esprit des Lois*, VII, chap. VII), presque à l'heure même où Rousseau composait son *Premier Discours*. Enfin ici encore nous devrions rappeler Genève, car Turretini présidait une députation du vénérable consistoire au magnifique Conseil de Genève, mettant en garde contre les empiètements du luxe sur la moralité de la vie, quand Rousseau avait 12 ans — si celui-ci était trop jeune encore lorsque en 1720 le pasteur Gallatin avait prononcé et imprimé un Sermon sur la Nature du Luxe et ses dangereux effets [Voir l'Opuscule de A. Morize, *l'Apologie du Luxe au XVIIIe siècle et le Mondain de Voltaire* (Paris 1909) ; Masson, *Religion de Rousseau* (1915), vol. I, page 11,

---

« renversé ? Quand est-ce que j'entendrai cette bienheureuse nouvelle : le « règne du péché est renversé de fond en comble dans cette capitale ; ses « femmes ne s'arment plus contre la pudeur, ses enfants ne soupirent plus après « les plaisirs mortels et ne livrent plus leurs âmes en proie à leurs jeux »! Rousseau n'avait donc pas trop mal répondu d'avance à ses maladroits commentateurs quand il écrivait (dans ce Premier Discours même) qu'il prétendait attaquer, lui, un « paradoxe digne d'être né de nos jours ».

27, 82 ; voir encore le grand travail de M. Kaye sur la *Fable des Abeilles* (1925)] (1).

C'est dans le *Second Discours* que Rousseau a discuté surtout la théorie que la postérité a en quelque sorte identifiée avec son nom, celle de l'exaltation de l'homme à l'état de nature. Il se trouve aujourd'hui qu'elle est probablement la moins originale de toutes celles qu'on attribue à Rousseau. Était-ce l'éloge de la vie des hommes de la nature qui serait nouvelle ? D'abord, c'était un lieu commun chez les Anciens ; qu'on relise seulement l'*Epître XC* de Sénèque, à Lucilius, qui résume toute la littérature classique sur ce sujet. Ensuite, plus nous étudions les Encyclopédistes mêmes au milieu de qui Rousseau fait ses premières armes dans le domaine des lettres, plus nous voyons que Rousseau avait baigné en quelque sorte dans une atmosphère saturée déjà de cette idée d'excellence de la nature. Diderot, d'Holbach, Marmontel, Morelly n'en finissent pas d'invoquer la nature. Dès 1895, Lichtenberger publiait son *Socialisme au XVIIIe siècle*, bourré de renseignements montrant combien les idées sur la non-corruption des peuples primitifs étaient répandues bien avant Rousseau. Il y avait toute une « Littérature sauvage » ou « Littérature taïtienne », dont le plus brillant spécimen, le *Supplément au Voyage de Bougainville* (1772) ne devait paraître qu'assez tard, mais qui avait été précédé de toute une série d'ouvrages analogues. *L'Histoire et Description de la Nouvelle France*, du Père Charlevoix, était de 1744. Beaucoup, il est vrai, décrivaient des voyages purement imaginaires, et dans des pays imaginaires, et cela dès le XVIIe siècle — *L'Histoire des Sévarambes* (1677), *Les Aventures de Jacques Sadeur* (1676),

(1) Tout reci rend bien frêle la valeur d'études comme celle de Samuel C. Chew, « An English Precursor of Rousseau (*Mod. Lang. Notes.* June 1917, p. 321-336). On y voit l'auteur chercher une source possible du Rousseau du *Premier Discours*, dans ce qui paraît être une banale imitation de Montesquieu : *Letters from a Persian in England to his friend at Ispaham*, by George, first Baron of Littleton. Mais il y avait des quantités de telles attaques contre la civilisation avant Rousseau et que celui-ci pouvait avoir lues !

l'Histoire de l'Ile de Calagava ou de l'île des hommes raison-
nables (1700) de Claude Gilbert — mais ils partent des théories
de Rousseau (ou attribuées à Rousseau) d'un âge d'or perdu
avec l'innocence de l'humanité. Tout ce groupe de théories
dites « Rousseauistes » se trouve avec une précision frappante
entre autres dans le *Télémaque*, si goûté du reste par
Rousseau ; et c'est le *Télémaque* qui mit à la mode ce genre de
fiction qu'on retrouve entre autre dans le *Roman de Sethos,*
Histoire ou vie tirée des monuments anecdotiques de l'ancienne
Egypte, citée parmi les lectures de jeunesse de Rousseau
(*Verger des Charmettes*). Et Montaigne, deux siècles avant,
avait écrit son essai célèbre *Des Cannibales*.

Depuis le livre de Lichtenberger, les travaux ont continué
dans ce domaine ; tels, ceux de Chinard (un des chapitres de
l'Amérique et le rêve exotique dans la Littérature Française des
XVIIe et XVIIIe siècles est intitulé : « Un continuateur des
missionnaires jésuites, Jean-Jacques Rousseau ») ; ceux de
Geoffroy Atkinson (voir en particulier dans le petit volume,
Les relations de voyage au XVIIe siècle et l'évolution des idées,
1924, tout le chap. IV « le bon Sauvage », où on lit : « Grâce
aux travaux récents, on sait maintenant que cette idée existait
déjà au XVIe siècle et que plusieurs auteurs de livres exotiques
ont employé le terme *le bon Sauvage* bien avant 1600 » ; et
« la bonté naturelle des sauvages paraît être le plus commun
des traits rapportés par les voyageurs du XVIIe siècle »). Men-
tionnons aussi le volume d'Albert Chérel, *Fénelon au*
XVIIIe siècle en France, 1715-1820 (surtout p. 13-17 de l'Introduction). Et dans le domaine de la littérature propre,
nous savons bien qu'avant Rousseau, Prevost dans son
M. Cleveland (1732) brisait une fameuse lance en faveur de la
sensibilité des sauvages : « J'étais persuadé, dit Cleveland,
que les mouvements simples de la nature quand elle n'a point
été corrompue par l'habitude du vice, n'ont jamais rien de
contraire à l'innocence ; ils ne demandent point d'être répri-
més mais seulement d'être réglés par la raison ». Avant lui,
Montesquieu avait fait une place de choix aux Troglodytes
dans les *Lettres Persannes* (12-14 ; Cf. *Esprit des Lois* V, 1).

Avant lui, dès 1704, Gueudeville, dans un ouvrage qui lui valut quelque célébrité, *Dialogues ou Entretiens entre un sauvage et le Baron de La Hontan*, s'efforçait de mettre en lumière les vertus de l'homme primitif ; il fondait sa démonstration sur les affirmations du voyageur qui avait visité des sauvages « n'ayant ni tien ni mien, ni supériorité, ni subordination, et vivant dans une espèce d'égalité conforme au sentiment de la nature ». Rousseau cite à la fin du *Second Discours*, le mot de Buffon : « La vertu appartient à l'homme sauvage plus qu'à l'homme civilisé, et... le vice n'a pris naissance que dans la société ».

L'abbé Morelly, dans sa *Basiliade* (1753) parue l'an même où Rousseau méditait son *second Discours*, attaque la grande erreur des philosophes traditionnels que « l'homme naît vicieux et méchant », et soutient que, tout à l'origine, était calculé en vue du bien général ; le « partage monstrueux » des biens de la terre est le point de départ de toutes les misères, et Morelly propose, lui, le retour à l'état de nature dont Rousseau n'a jamais voulu. Les mêmes idées sont reprises dans le *Code des Mœurs* (1755) du même auteur, sous une forme plus systématique. Turgot, dix ans plus tôt même, exprimait fort souvent des idées qui rappelleront singulièrement celles de son ami Rousseau : « Dans tous les genres nous avons étouffé l'instinct, et le sauvage le suit sans le connaître ; il n'a pas assez d'esprit pour s'en écarter » (Lettre à Mme de Graffigny) ; tout Rousseau, apôtre de la nature, n'est-il pas dans cette phrase du même Turgot : « La nature a mis au cœur de l'homme la semence de toutes les vertus ; il n'y a qu'à les laisser éclore ».

Le théâtre même s'était emparé dès l'aube du XVIIIe siècle de la thèse du bonheur des innocents, et de la littérature sauvage : ainsi, dans *la Coquette du Village* de Dufresny (1715), dans l'*Arlequin sauvage* (1721) et *Timon le Misanthrope* (1722) de Delisle (1) ; dans *l'île des Esclaves* (1725) de Marivaux, —

(1) C'est là qu'on trouve les vers :

Tout le cœur des mortels lorsque rien ne l'altère
Porte de la beauté le divin caractère.

que Lenient caractérise : « un chapitre sur l'inégalité des conditions avant Rousseau ».

Voltaire, en somme, paraît un isolé quand, dans sa lettre à Rousseau sur le *Second Discours* (30 août 1756) il écrit : « On n'a jamais employé tant d'esprit à nous rendre bêtes ; il prend envie de marcher à quatre pattes quand on lit votre ouvrage... » ; et dans son *Mondain*. Nous disons *paraît*, car il faut tenir compte aussi de *L'Ingénu*, et de sa tragédie *Les Américains*.

Le cas de la *Lettre sur les Spectacles* est parallèle à celui du *Premier Discours*. Rousseau, loin de lancer une campagne, continue simplement une discussion séculaire, et, qui plus est, il se range du côté de la réaction (pour des raisons que nous aurons du reste à apprécier). Le travail de M. L. Bourquin *La Controverse sur la Comédie au XVIIIe siècle et la Lettre à d'Alembert*, ayant commencé à paraître dans la *Revue d'Histoire littéraire*, en 1919, est là pour le prouver ; et M. L. Brunel l'avait indiqué déjà dans sa petite édition pour les écoles (Hachette). Comme dans l'antiquité Platon avait défendu le théâtre (*République*) car il distrait de la spéculation ; comme Sénèque (*Lettre à Lucilius*, XC) craint la façon dont, au théâtre, le vice se coule dans les âmes sous forme aimable ; comme au premier siècle de l'ère chrétienne (comme on peut bien s'y attendre), les anathèmes se multiplient (chez Cyprien, Tertulien, Chrysostome, Saint-Augustin), nous voyons qu'en France, dès l'instant où les pièces profanes menacent de remplacer sur la scène les vieux Mystères c'est-à-dire dès le XVIe siècle, l'Église prend des mesures ; Bourdaloue, puis les Jansénistes, Pascal à leur tête (1), s'élèvent contre le théâtre corrupteur des mœurs ; Nicole fait un écrit spécial, *De la Comédie* ; et lorsque le Père Caffaro (1694) essaye de justifier l'existence de la Comédie, c'est Bossuet qui répond par ses *Maximes et Réflexions contre la Comédie*, — et celles-ci

---

(1) Voir les pages 383-84 des *Pensées* (Ed. Louandre) qui contient en essence toute l'argumentation de la *Lettre à d'Alembert*.

expriment si fortement l'esprit de la *Lettre à d'Alembert* qu'on
en demeure confondu : enfin en 1713, Fénelon — si possible
plus directement encore que Bossuet — anticipe Rousseau
dans ses attaques contre le « Grand Molière » dans la *Lettre
sur les Occupations de l'Académie*. Et, chose curieuse, en 1756
paraît la *Lettre sur les Spectacles* [sic !] de Desprey de Boissy
— lequel dans une nouvelle *Lettre* en 1759 invoque le témoignage que Rousseau a apporté à sa plaidoirie contre les
dangers d'exciter les passions de l'amour par la scène.

Tout ceci ne suffit-il pas, on pourrait rappeler le passage
d'une lettre de Rousseau à Jean Sarrasin de Genève (29 novembre 1758) : « Quand j'ose élever ma faible voix sur les
dangers du théâtre, je ne fais que répéter les maximes de nos
pasteurs dont nous devrions mieux profiter ».

En Angleterre, un même mouvement existait contre les
spectacles, avec d'ailleurs des résultats pratiques plus accusés
qu'en France ; c'était le groupe des écrivains du *Spectateur* —
que Rousseau lisait chez Mme de Warens — qui menait la
campagne. Dès 1698, Jeremy Taylor avait publié un célèbre
pamphlet, *Aperçu de l'Impiété et de l'Immoralité du Théâtre
Anglais*, lequel amena à la fondation d'une « Association
pour la Réforme des Mœurs » en 1699 ; en 1700, on défendait
l'accès des théâtres aux femmes portant des masques ; en
1711, la « Convocation » ou « Assemblée de l'Église Anglicane »
rappelait l'attention des pouvoirs publics sur les mêmes dangers ; en 1735, l'Association ci-dessus mentionnée, aurait
compté près de cent mille adhérents.

Passons à la *Nouvelle-Héloïse*. Ce n'était certes pas l'idée du
« roman personnel » comme l'a appelé Merlant, qui était nouvelle chez Rousseau. Et que ce fût, du reste, sous forme de
lettres, de mémoires, ou de romans, Merlant nous montre aux
premières pages de son volume (*Roman personnel depuis Jean-
Jacques Rousseau*, 1905), le « genre » tel qu'il existait avant la
Julie, chez Mme Riccoboni (*Lettres de Mylady Catesby*, et
Histoire du Marquis de Crécy, 1756), et chez Mme de Beaumont
(*Lettre du Marquis de Roselle*), et chez l'abbé Prevost qui,

déviant la passion en la décrivant, se délivre indirectement des tourments de son *moi* (*Cleveland, homme de qualité, Doyen de Killerine*) et chez Lesage... A travers les Mémoires il remonte jusqu'à Courtils de Sandras. En somme, il est inutile de revenir sur ce chapitre aujourd'hui tant étudié de l'histoire littéraire (1).

Quel ravage dans la théorie du Rousseau novateur n'avait pas fait déjà, à lui seul, le volume de Joseph Texte, *J.-J. Rousseau et le Cosmopolitisme Littéraire* (1895) ! Les œuvres de sentimentalisme du Suisse Gessner pénétraient en France à l'heure même où Rousseau se révélait ; celui-ci s'en inspirait dans le *Lévite d'Ephraïm*, et déclarait Gessner « un homme selon son cœur ». Mais surtout, cette voix du sentimentalisme avait retenti depuis longtemps en Angleterre. La mélancolie de Saint-Preux, on l'avait entendue chez Milton, l'auteur du *Penseroso*, (1632), chez Thomson (*Saisons*, 1730), chez Young (*Nuits*, 1742), dans les *Odes* de Collins (1747), et dans *l'Elégie sur un cimetière de campagne*, de Gray (1751) ; les premiers fragments d'Ossian sont d'un an antérieurs à *la Nouvelle Héloïse* et de plusieurs années aux *Rêveries*.

Une autre forme de ce que Texte et autres ont nommé « l'Anglomanie » de Rousseau (et qui assez bizarrement va la main dans la main avec le sentimentalisme) c'est l'esprit pragmatique. Or, comme Texte l'a bien montré — et beaucoup y ont insisté depuis — les interminables lettres de *la Nouvelle Héloïse* sur l'esprit sensé et pratique, ont suivi et non précédé les *Lettres sur les Anglais et les Français*, de Muralt (1725-28), les *Lettres Anglaises* de Voltaire (1734), et, dès 1685, après la Révocation de l'Édit de Nantes, toute la littérature de vulgarisation des Huguenots réfugiés à Londres et en Hollande. En 1742, presque dix ans avant que Rousseau n'entrât en scène comme écrivain, son homonyme Jean-

---

(1) Toutes ces études sont aujourd'hui résumées et complétées par Daniel MORNET, au vol. I. de son Éd. de *la Nouvelle Héloïse* (Collect. des Grands Écr. de la France, Hachette 1926), Ire partie ; chap. I et II : « Le Roman Français de 1741 à 1760 ».

Baptiste Rousseau constatait avec regret les progrès de « ce malheureux esprit anglais qui s'est glissé parmi nous depuis vingt ans ».

S'il est une théorie chère encore à des masses de gens, c'est celle qui veut que Rousseau ait appris aux hommes à aimer la nature. Il n'en peut plus être question (1).

Théocrite et Virgile, dès le xvie siècle avaient leurs disciples. Et les Italiens de la Renaissance, comment peut-on les oublier ? Et Ronsard et la Pléiade, l'*Astrée* et les *Bergeries*, Viaud, Saint-Amant, La Fontaine, Mme de Sévigné ? Tout au plus pourrait-on dire qu'il y a eu dans l'Europe moderne une partiale éclipse du sentiment de la nature à la fin du règne de Louis XIV ; mais Rousseau n'est pas celui qui eut l'honneur de reprendre la tradition interrompue, puisque vers 1750 de nouveau, comme le démontre Mornet « le flot coule abondamment » (p. 19). Avant la *Nouvelle Héloïse*, les *Géorgiques* de Delille étaient commencées, Lambert avait entrepris ses *Saisons*, Rosset son *Agriculture*, et Le Brun son poème sur *les avantages de la Campagne*.

Bien plus, ce fameux sentiment de la nature qu'on veut faire remonter à Rousseau, Rousseau le possède-t-il même ? Mornet n'en est pas sûr : « Rousseau a vécu — dit-il, III ch. IV, — au milieu de tout ce qui pourrait ravir un cœur, et malgré tout il n'a été qu'un peintre médiocre ». Son pittoresque est « presque toujours banal et terne » ; du reste Rousseau ayant fort mauvaise vue il n'en pouvait guère être autrement. Et à ce propos, Mornet indique une distinction qu'on aurait dû faire depuis longtemps et qu'il faudrait pousser vigoureusement, entre le sentiment de la *nature pittoresque* et le senti-

---

(1) Il n'aurait jamais dû en être question après l'ouvrage d'Alfred Biese, *Die Entwickelung des Naturgefuehls*, I. *Bei den Griechen* (1882), II. *Im Mittelalter und in der Neuzeit* (1892). Pour ce qui se rapporte à la période immédiatement antérieure à Rousseau, voir l'article de Pierre Viguié : « *Le sentiment de la Nature au XVIIIe siècle* » (*Mercure de France*, août 1920). Voir aussi aux les premiers chapitres de D. Mornet, *Le sentiment de la Nature en France de J.-J. Rousseau à Bernardin de Saint-Pierre*, déjà cité.

ment de la *nature morale*. Nous ne disons pas qu'il n'y ait
point de rapport entre les deux, mais certes qu'on peut avoir
l'un sans l'autre, ou du moins développer l'un sans développer
l'autre. Rousseau a connu et développé le second très fort ;
il n'a exprimé le premier que rarement. Les auteurs anglais,
Milton, Thomson, Gray, Collins, Young, Chatterton etc., ont
cent fois surpassé Rousseau pittoresque avant que Rousseau
eût même parlé (1).

Parlant toujours de *la Nouvelle Héloïse*, nous ne nous expo-
serons pas au ridicule de réfuter l'idée que Rousseau fut un
novateur en protestant contre le mariage de convention,
contre la tyrannie de la naissance et de l'argent. Mais depuis
les vieilles chansons, des mal-mariées, en passant par les fa-
bliaux, les lais de Marie de France, La Fontaine, Molière
ce n'est qu'un cri ininterrompu des droits du sentiment de
l'amour dans la formation des liens de la famille. Et tout
récemment l'Abbé Bremond dans son *Histoire du Sentiment
Religieux* (1923, vol. I, p. 472) prenait plaisir à relever que le
père Yves dans son *Gentilhomme Chrétien*, insistait avant
Rousseau pour que l'amour ait le pas sur classe et fortune
dans le mariage.

Essaiera-t-on de se rabattre sur des thèmes secondaires
dans *La Nouvelle Héloïse* ? Le résultat sera le même. La discussion (IV, 11) de la supériorité des jardins anglais sur les jardins où la nature est asservie à l'homme — les jardins de
l'intelligence, comme les appelle si pertinemment M. L. Cor-
pechot — remontait à Virgile, lequel, à vrai dire, voulait bien
chanter les bois, mais qui soient des bois « dignes d'un consul ».
En France, Ronsard pressentait le danger du jardin trop artificiel quand il disait :

> *J'aime fort les jardins qui sentent le sauvage.*

Et les phases du débat avant aussi bien qu'après Rousseau,

----

(1) C'est ce que démontre avec une ingénieuse documentation Richard
Ashley Rice dans *Rousseau and the Poetry of Nature in XVIII Century France*
(Smith College Studies in Mod. Languages, VI, 3 et 4 ; April-July 1925).

où le prestige du jardin anglais de Kent et Brown se doublait
du prestige du jardin chinois pour miner le prestige du jardin
français ne donnant que « la tristesse et l'ennui », sont bien
exposées chez Mornet (1907), et chez Charlier (1912) dans des
ouvrages aux titres presque semblables sur le sentiment de
la nature au xviiie siècle.

Dans les deux « Lettres sur le Suicide » on peut presque dire
que Rousseau arrive bon dernier ; les Jansénistes surtout,
et Montesquieu avaient discuté le suicide, et le *Spectateur
Français* de Marivaux avait repris le débat ; et tandis que
Voltaire s'employait à détourner Frédéric II de son projet de
suicide, Gresset fait du problème le sujet de sa pièce *Sidné*, et
La Chaussée et maints autres lui font écho. En Angleterre, le
suicide semblait depuis longtemps une vertu de gentilhomme,
et ce fut Muralt qui signala l'attitude anglaise à Rousseau (1).

De même, lorsque Rousseau discuta dans son roman la
question du duel, il ne pouvait que donner une opinion personnelle sur le débat qui faisait rage en France même, depuis
Richelieu. Mornet donne une vingtaine de références dans ses
Notes à la lettre 57 (Ire partie de *La Nouvelle Héloïse*).

Nous arrivons aux idées politiques. La situation est la même
qu'ailleurs, sinon pire. Depuis longtemps Morley, Ritchie,
Landmann, Lipmann, Faguet, Champion, et autres ont réduit
à néant l'idée d'un Rousseau original en politique. A grand
peine Rodet (*Le Contrat Social et les Idées Politiques de J.-J.
Rousseau*, 1909) sauve-t-il du désastre la théorie de la guerre ;
avant Rousseau la guerre avait été conçue comme un rapport
d'État à particuliers, et depuis celui-ci seulement comme un
rapport d'État à État ; — encore, ces vues « nouvelles » sur la
guerre étaient-elles contenues implicitement dans les théories
générales du droit qui se répandaient au xviiie siècle.

Quant à l'idée d'un contrat social, Rousseau lui-même mentionne les principaux juristes aux vues desquels il se rapporte.

---

(1) Qu'on lise enfin l'imposant volume de A. Bayet, *Le Suicide et la Morale*,
Alcan, 1922.

Chacun connaissait déjà la *République* de Jean Bodin (1570),
la *Politica methodice digesta* d'Althusius (1603), le *De Jure
Belli et Pacis* de Grotius (1625), le *De Cive* (1642) et le *Leviathan*
de Hobbes (1651 à 1668), le *Tractatus Politicus* de Spinoza
(1670), le *De Jure Naturæ et Gentium* de Puffendorf (1672),
les *Discourses concerning Government* de Locke (1689).
Du reste, sous une autre forme, on discutait déjà le « Contrat »
au moyen âge en commentant la distinction d'Aristote entre
le *dikaion phuseï* et le *dikaion nomô* ; déjà on se demandait
si le « Omnis potestas a Deo » devait être interprété au bénéfice des rois. « Quod principi placuit, legis habet vigorem »
disait le *Digeste*, et le *Légiste* du *XVIᵉ siècle* traduisait : « Si
veut le roi, si veut la Loi ». Mais en fait la « *Potestas* » a-t-elle
été donnée au roi souverain directement, ou indirectement
par le peuple en qui Dieu l'avait d'abord déposée ? Dans ce
dernier cas, il devait exister entre le roi et son peuple un
« contrat » et il importait d'en définir la nature. Or, cette idée
que la puissance des rois dépend au moins temporellement du
bon vouloir des nations, les théologiens s'en étaient servi
depuis longtemps. Thomas d'Aquin au XIIIᵉ siècle déclare
déjà (*Summa*, XC-CVIII) que le pouvoir politique *qu'on crée*
vient du peuple. Rousseau dira-t-il autre chose ? Et au
XVIᵉ siècle, lorsque les Jésuites reprennent avec décision ce
principe et lorsque Suarèz répète que « le pouvoir vient
médiatement de Dieu, mais immédiatement du peuple »,
ce sera précisément la doctrine de Rousseau et la doctrine de
la Révolution Française et celle qui servit à justifier Clément
et Ravaillac, assassins de Henri III et Henri IV. Les protestants du reste (en particulier Bèze et Knox). invoquaient la
même doctrine du peuple souverain pour justifier la résistance aux rois catholiques. Et comme au XVIᵉ siècle les
monarques catholiques étaient la règle, c'est chez les protestants que ce dogme politique s'établit le plus fortement ; il
devint le principe politique carastéristique du protestantisme. Rappelons que c'est une des idées chères à Faguet
que « le Contrat Social n'est que le dernier et le plus brillant
de ces ouvrages théologico-politiques des calvinistes qui

vont de Jurieu à Burlamaqui, et qui tous renferment le dogme de l'absolutisme de la souveraineté du peuple » (*XVIII*ᵉ *siècle*, J.-J. Rousseau).

En Angleterre, le passage de la doctrine religieuse à la doctrine politique s'était fait plus rapidement. Ritchie (*Natural Rights*, 1895) montre très joliment comment le fanatisme protestant aboutit au protestantisme social : Rousseau et Locke, tous deux, dans leur politique « résultent directement de la révolte protestante contre l'autorité de la tradition et de la réclamation de jugement personnel, c'est-à-dire de l'appel à la raison et conscience de l'individu ». Du reste, le peuple avait été logique avant eux. Wicliff, prêchait à celui-ci « que quiconque est en état de grâce a véritablement seigneurie sur l'univers entier » ; le peuple remplaça « le juste par l'homme », et cela en s'appuyant sur la Bible comme le fougueux réformateur ; il chantait :

> *When Adam dalf and Eva span*
> *Who was then the gentleman ?*

(Quand Adam béchait et qu'Ève filait, qui faisait alors le gentleman).

Il y aurait beaucoup à dire encore.

On trouvera plus de détails dans notre article de *Modern Philology* (X, nº 2, oct. 1912, « Rousseau devant l'érudition moderne », p. 11-15) ; dans les ouvrages cités de Beaulavon, de Mornet et de E. Champion, et surtout dans les savants volumes de C.-E. Vaughan, *Political Writings of Rousseau* (2 volumes, Cambridge 1915).

Tout impose la conclusion exprimée dans ces mots de Champion : « il n'y a (dans le *Contrat Social*) rien de neuf ; Rousseau ne dit que ce que l'on avait dit et répété avant lui. Il dit même beaucoup moins » (p. 59-60).

Dira-t-on peut-être que c'étaient là des discussions entre savants seulement ? Qu'on lise le petit ouvrage de L. Fontaine : *Le Théâtre et la Philosophie au XVIII*ᵉ *siècle* (Paris, s. d.) ; on y verra le peuple applaudir aux théories des plus révolutionnaires. Avant même que Louis XIV eût fermé les yeux, on avait insulté les rois ; et : « Depuis l'*Œdipe* de Voltaire (1718) la tragédie, dit Fontaine, ne cessa de s'attaquer aux rois, de discuter l'étendue et l'origine de leur pouvoir » (p. 22).

> *Un roi pour ses sujets est un Dieu qu'on révère ;*
> *Pour Hercule et pour moi c'est un homme ordinaire,*

écrivait Voltaire dans *Œdipe* ; et c'était en 1734 que le Franc de Pompignan dans sa *Didon* lançait son vers :

> *Et le premier des rois fut un usurpateur.*

La Chaussé, en 1744, dans *L'Ecoles des Mères*, disait :

> *L'égalité, Madame est la loi de nature.*

Deux ans après, Marivaux donnait son *Préjugé vaincu* — préjugé de classe ; et Voltaire allait faire écho avec *Nanine*.

Devons-nous rappeler que, dès 1291, les vallées suisses *appliquaient* le principe de souveraineté populaire, qu'en 1581 était rédigée la « Déclaration d'indépendance de la Hollande » ; et que le cardinal de Retz entendait en 1649 dans les rues de Paris le cri de « *République* » (1).

Ici comme pour *La Nouvelle Héloïse*, nous nous en sommes tenus aux grandes questions ; et comme pour *La Nouvelle*

---

(1) On a voulu voir un précurseur de Rousseau chez Adhémar Fabri, prince-évêque de Genève, lequel en 1387, promulgua à Genève des « Franchises nationales » (J. VUY, *Origine des idées politiques de Rousseau*, Genève, 1889). C'est une de ces illusions dont l'érudition moderne est fréquemment la victime. Il s'agit évidemment là d'un fait fort banal ; de ces « franchises », étaient accordées tous les jours par les princes laïques ou ecclésiastiques du temps — à leur corps défendant du reste — pour conserver ou assurer l'obéissance de leurs sujets. Si Calvin a aboli ces franchises, ce ne fut pas par haine de la liberté, mais des conséquences funestes pour la moralité et dès lors la sécurité politique de Genève. La question est de savoir quand on a cessé de considérer ces « franchises » comme une grâce du souverain pour y voir un droit du peuple. M. Goyau, dans son ouvrage, *Une ville église*, Genève, (Paris, 1919), reprend la thèse de M. Vuy.

Héloïse, le même manque d'originalité est vrai quant aux doctrines particulières du *Contrat social*. Ainsi Rodet écrit : « A considérer dans son ensemble la thèse de Rousseau touchant la propriété et ses rapports avec l'État, on est bien forcé de convenir qu'elle n'était pas une nouveauté au xviiiᵉ siècle. Sous des traits plus accusés et plus violents c'est au fond la théorie même de Montesquieu : *La propriété est une concession des lois civiles et elle est utile et respectable dans l'état de société* » (p. 202).

De même la théorie, si chère à Rousseau, des avantages politiques et moraux des petits états avait été formulée presque dans les mêmes termes que les siens par Aristote (*Politique*, VII, chap iv) ; puis ç'avait été, par exemple, le rêve de Dante, — un Empire Romain des peuples Européens, avec quantité de petits États, comme ceux d'Italie, qui vivraient une vie indépendante (Dante songeait à l'individualité artistique en même temps que politique). Montesquieu y revient surtout (*Esprit des Lois*, XIII, chap. xvi, IX, i, etc.).

Et quant à ses projets de « paix perpétuelle », Rousseau n'est que le continuateur de l'Abbé de Saint-Pierre.

Le dernier chapitre du Contrat social nous amène aux idées religieuses de Rousseau ; il faut naturellement nous y arrêter.

Sa conception d'une « religion civile », il est à peine besoin de le rappeler, non seulement fut défendue par des philosophes depuis Platon et Aristote, à Spinoza et Hobbes, mais elle fut à proprement parler celle de la cité antique où l'outrage aux dieux de l'État (témoins les martyrs chrétiens), ou la simple incrédulité (témoin Socrate) étaient des crimes publics ; elle fut adoptée par Constantin ; elle guida les Arabes dans leurs conquêtes ; elle inspira les Croisades ; elle fut encore une des idées directrices de la politique de Louis XIV, conseillé par Bossuet, après qu'elle eut présidé à la fondation de la Rome protestante. Elle est indiquée aussi nettement que possible dans *L'Histoire de Sévarambes* (1679) déjà plusieurs fois citée, — et donc quand on a reproché à Rousseau le despotisme de cette doctrine, on aurait dû s'apercevoir que s'il était en désaccord avec ses contemporains, ce n'était pas parce qu'il *devançait* son temps.

On a souvent cru voir un abîme entre la « religion civile » de Rousseau et sa religion telle que conçue dans ses autres écrits, surtout dans la *Profession de foi du Vicaire Savoyard*. Nous croyons que c'est une grave erreur (nous le verrons plus bas). Et en tout cas on ne peut nier une étroite relation entre la religion naturelle de Rousseau et celle du rationalisme théologique. Or celui-ci avait existé dès le XVIe siècle en France sous le nom de « libertinisme », avait été continué et accentué avec Gassendi et avec Bayle en France, et s'affirmait de même dès le XVIIe siècle chez les « Déistes » anglais, Toland, Collins, Tindal, Locke. Rousseau lui-même n'invoque-t-il pas l'autorité du « vertueux Shaftesbury » dans les *Lettres sur la Vertu et le Bonheur*, et de « l'illustre Clark » dans la *Profession de foi du Vicaire Savoyard* ? Et des échos de ce Déisme anglais avaient été entendus en France bien avant la *Profession de foi du Vicaire Savoyard* chez Voltaire (*Lettres Anglaises*, 1734), chez Lamettrie (*Histoire naturelle de l'âme*, 1745), chez Toussaint (*Les mœurs*, 1748), chez Diderot (*Lettres sur les Aveugles*, 1749) ; l'abbé de Prades (successeur de Lamettrie comme lecteur chez Frédéric II) fut cause du déchaînement de l'orage contre les Encyclopédistes en 1751, dix ans avant l'*Emile* (1). Enfin qu'on consulte surtout la gerbe si touffue de titres d'ouvrages (imprimés ou manuscrits) du XVIIIe siècle, cités dans les articles de M. Lanson. « Questions diverses sur l'histoire de l'esprit philosophique en France avant 1750 » (*Rev. Hist. Litt.*, janvier-avril 1912) ; cette poussée anti-orthodoxe est extraordinaire : « Plusieurs des ouvrages les plus hardis ou les plus violents qui furent imprimés après 1750 — dit M. Lanson — de ceux qui nous servent à étudier la grande bataille de 1760-1770, datent en réalité du

---

(1) Il présenta à la Sorbonne une thèse qui parut d'abord insignifiante. Ce fut le public qui en découvrit les hérésies et s'alarma. L'ouvrage fut condamné au feu, et l'auteur à se rétracter. Les miracles de Jésus-Christ étaient comparés aux guérisons d'Esculape.

commencement ou du moins de la première partie du
xviiie siècle. L'*Emile* ne parut qu'en 1761 (1).

Brunetière retrouvait dans l'*Histoire de M. Cleveland* (1732)
comme une édition avancée de la *Profession de foi du Vicaire
Savoyard*. Voltaire dès l'*Epître à Uranie* (1722-31) opposait
nettement la religion naturelle à la religion révélée (2). D'autre
part, dans la patrie de Rousseau le théologien Turretini publiait de 1729-37 une série de dissertations latines sur la
Théologie Naturelle ; et en 1736, un élève de Turretini, Jacob
Vernet traduisait son *Traité sur la Vérité de la Religion Chrétienne*, et des *Pensées sur la Religion*, où l'on trouve ébauchées
quelques-unes des idées les plus importantes du Rousseau de
l'*Emile*. M. Ritter, M. Sayons (dans son *XVIIIe siècle à
l'étranger*), et d'autres ont attiré l'attention sur l'ouvrage en
six volumes, bien connu en Suisse Française, de Marie Hubert,
*Lettres sur la Religion essentielle à l'homme, distinguée de ce
qui n'en est que l'accessoire* (1738 ; 2e éd. 1756). Que reste-il
d'ailleurs à dire à ce sujet après les trois volumes de P.-M.
Masson sur *la Religion de Jean-Jacques Rousseau* (1916), et
son édition de la *Profession de foi du Vicaire Savoyard* (en
1914) ? On lit dans l'Introduction à cette dernière ce passage : « On s'apercevra, en achevant la lecture du Commentaire, qu'il n'y a guère une idée formulée par le Vicaire qui

---

(1) On consultera aussi avec fruit le volume de D. MORNET, *Sciences de la
Nature au XVIIIe siècle* (1911), Première Partie, Chap. II. « La lutte contre le
Merveilleux », Chap. III. « La lutte contre la Théologie ». Et les volumes déjà
cités de J. Atkinson. Empruntons lui cette esquisse de la Profession de Foi du
Vicaire Savoyard que crayonna Pierre Bergeron dans la *Relation de Voyage
en Tartarie* (1634), Vol. III, p. 323 : « Pour ce qui est de leur Religion, ils
croyaient en Dieu, Créateur de toutes choses, tant visibles qu'invisibles, et qui
donne les récompenses et les peines aux hommes selon leurs mérites. Et toutefois ils ne l'honorent pas par prières et louanges, ni par aucun service et cérémonie ». Et après avoir résumé les croyances des Sévarambes du « Troisième
continent, ordinairement appelé Terre Australe » (1677-79), l'auteur écrit :
« De là vient que si leur religion n'est pas la plus véritable de toutes, elle est
du moins la plus conforme à la raison humaine ».

(2) *Songe que de très haut la Sagesse éternelle
A gravé de sa main, dans le fond de ton cœur,
La religion naturelle.*

n'eut été formulée avant lui ; que depuis la théorie du jugement jusqu'au parallèle de Socrate et de Jésus, depuis l'exaltation de la conscience jusqu'au réquisitoire contre les « phi-
losophistes » tout avait été dit et redit par les moralistes et
les apologistes antérieurs » (p. 100).

Resterait encore le Rousseau novateur en éducation. Il
n'est pas plus « neuf » dans ce domaine qu'ailleurs ; et le secret
de l'influence qu'il exerça avec son *Emile* ne saurait être cherché là. Il est peut-être pédant de remonter jusqu'au monde
antique pour y trouver des précurseurs ; cependant, devant
la persistance de l'argument que nous combattons, il ne sera
pas déplacé de rappeler au moins Platon défendant avec zèle
des thèses volontiers attribuées à Rousseau ; telles l'instruction
par le jeu, et dans les méthodes d'enseignement le bannissement
de tout ce qui pourrait sentir la contrainte ; de pratiquer avec
zèle les exercices du corps ; et de ne point offrir de nourriture
trop forte à des esprits trop faibles ; et si Rousseau attend
qu'Émile ait vingt ans pour lui parler de religion, Platon
renvoie après la trentième année l'étude de la Dialectique.
Après Platon, les Stoïciens insistèrent sur l'éducation selon
la nature. Les Plutarque, les Cicéron, et les Sénèque défendirent sous une autre forme, ou seulement moins systématiquement, les mêmes idées. Laissant l'antiquité, nous trouvons un cas assez curieux chez ce père Mapphée-Vegge, que
l'abbé Cajot dans son zèle à trouver Rousseau coupable de
« plagiat » déterra dans la *Bib. SS. PP.*, tome XV (1622).
Entre autres points discutés dans le traité *De Liberorum
Educatione* nous trouvons : livre I, Prescription aux femmes
grosses d'un régime nutritif convenable ; demande qu'elles
allaitent leurs enfants ; endurcir les petits au grand air ; les
pleurs ont leur raison d'être ; tenir compte de l'âge des enfants,
et éviter autant les bontés mal entendues que les excès de
sévérité. Livre II. Ne rien hâter en éducation ; ne pas commencer la lecture avant sept ans ; moyen d'alléger les dégoûts de
l'étude en rendant le travail intéressant ; bien étudier le caractère de chaque enfant et se diriger d'après cela pour le con-

duire et choisir sa profession. Livre III. Les exercices manuels
sont excellents ; maintenir une atmosphère gaie au travail ;
préparer peu à peu aux études philosophiques ; rendre la
vertu attrayante ; cultiver la frugalité.

Amiel (*J.-J. Rousseau jugé par les Genevois d'aujourd'hui*,
p. 454) a fait une découverte analogue à celle de Cajot : « Si,
dit-il, *Emile* est un ouvrage hardi et neuf, il est moins radical
cependant que son prototype du xiiie siècle, demeuré inconnu
à Rousseau ; je veux parler du roman philosophique intitulé
L'Homme de la Nature qui a pour auteur Tophail, un des
philosophes arabes de l'Espagne ». Mais il n'est pas besoin
de se rabattre sur des cas isolés, accidents en quelque sorte ;
à la Renaissance, on discute avec passion l'éducation, et les
plus grands, Érasme, Rabelais, Montaigne, le font dans
l'esprit de Rousseau. « Je trouve, remarque Montaigne, que
nos plus grands vices traînent leurs plis dès notre plus tendre
enfance, et que notre principal gouvernement est entre les
mains de nos nourrices ». Au xviie siècle, les Jésuites et les
Jansénistes continuent à remuer la question d'éducation dans
un sens éminemment progressif ; les premiers par exemple
favorisant les exercices corporels ; et quant aux seconds,
Rousseau avait « dévoré, » dit Compayré, les livres de Port
Royal ; chez Pascal même, il pouvait trouver son grand principe d'Émile : « Il faut donc qu'on ne puisse dire ni il est ma-
thématicien, ni prédicateur, ni éloquent. Cette qualité universelle ; être né homme, me plaît ». Dans la *Logique*, les Soli-
taires s'étaient donné pour but aussi de former « non le gram-
mairien, le savant en aucune science... mais l'homme ».
Ailleurs ce qu'il voulait avant tout apprendre à leurs élèves,
c'était « la science de bien vivre » (Sainte-Beuve, *Port Royal*,
III, p. 544). Rousseau lui-même cite parmi ces prédécesseurs,
et pour en approuver les principes, Locke (son livre de l'*Education des Enfants*, 1693, avait été traduit en Français par
Coste, et publié à Amsterdam, 6e éd. 1743), Buffon, Crousaz,
Duclos, l'abbé de Saint-Pierre, Fleury, Rollin, Turgot.

Si nous entrions dans le détail des théories diverses de
Rousseau, l'énumération des précurseurs deviendrait extrêmement fastidieuse.

La campagne de l'allaitement maternel par exemple était
en train bien avant que parût l'*Emile* ; Tronchin, Buffon en
avaient parlé avec autorité, et combien de moins connus !
Atkinson, dans le chapitre cité, sur le « Bon sauvage » (*Relations de Voyages au XVII*e *siècle*) écrit : « Il est intéressant
de constater qu'elle (l'idée de l'allaitement) fait partie du
contenu moral du bon sauvage » (p. 78). Et Erasme s'en était
occupé dans son Colloque « Puerpera », dès 1516. Les mêmes
auteurs, presque tous, protestaient avant Rousseau contre
l'emmaillotement des bébés. Les conseils pour le développement du corps, jamais abandonnés depuis Rabelais et Montaigne, avaient été — sans compter des auteurs secondaires
— nettement préconisée par Locke en Angleterre, et Turgot
en France. De même, depuis Rabelais et Montaigne, on
n'avait cessé de répéter qu'il fallait donner le pas au développement de l'intelligence sur la culture de la mémoire ; et la
prudence dans la discussion des choses religieuses et philosophiques qui souleva tant d'opposition quand elle fut proposée par Rousseau avait été fortement recommandée ; Bacon
voulait attendre à 15 ans, Crousaz, un Vaudois publiant en
Hollande, parlait dans le même sens, et Bonnet, l'adversaire
de Rousseau en maintes occasions, avait cependant prêché
la même doctrine sur ce point dès 1754 (*Essai de Psychologie*).
Une autre idée dont on a volontiers fait honneur à Rousseau,
celle de l'excellence du travail manuel était déjà chère à
Locke avant Rousseau ; à l'abbé Fleury de même ; et Bossuet
lui-même dans ses *Elévations sur les Mystères* avait exalté le
travail manuel par l'exemple du charpentier de Nazareth...
Et ainsi de suite *ad infinitum* (voir notre article cité de *Modern Philology*, X, 2 oct. 1912, p. 17-19) (1).

---

(1) Notons en passant que M. F. Picavet, dans sa révélatrice *Littérature
Française en langue latine* (1921) ne peut s'empêcher à tout moment, de penser
à Rousseau : c'est, dès le premier siècle de notre ère, Phavorinos qui engageait

Citerons-nous encore — dans un domaine du reste secondaire — ce passage de Louis Dimier, *Buffon* (1919) : « La vogue de ces études (de botanique) dont nos manuels de classe ont inventé de mettre la cause dans Rousseau, était de trente ans plus ancienne. Répandue premièrement sous le nom et avec les méthodes de Tournefort, elle avait pris un essor soudain quand les ouvrages de Linné parurent : depuis les *Fundamenta botanica* qui sont de 1736, jusqu'à la *Philosophia botanica*, qui est de 1751 » (p. 113) ? Ou citerons-nous Culcasi qui fait voir clairement que dans le grand débat au sujet de la supériorité de la musique française ou italienne, Rousseau n'a pris la parole que lorsque tous les éléments du débat avaient déjà été formulés ? (*Gli Influssi italiani nell'Opere di J. J. Rousseau*, 1907).

Tant de témoignages dans tant de domaines ont fait boule de neige,... ont amené à des affirmations plus générales comme celle de Brunetière, lequel, dans ses *Etudes sur le XVIIIe siècle* (1911) parlait de Vauvenargues : « en qui déjà se trouve tout ce qu'il y a de meilleur dans Rousseau » (p. 294) ; à celle même de M. G. de Reynold, qui réduisait à des proportions microscopiques en quelque sorte le Rousseau novateur quand il écrivait dans les *Annales Rousseau* de 1912 « J.-J. Rousseau et la Suisse » (VIII, p. 161-204), qu'il n'y a pas une des œuvres du philosophe dont on ne trouve l'idée exprimée dans des œuvres suisses de l'époque antérieure à 1749, date du *Premier Discours*.

De telles déclarations, il n'y avait vraiment qu'un pas au mot d'apparence si paradoxale de M. René Gillouin, dans son livre sur Seillière (*Un philosophe de l'Histoire moderne et*

---

les femmes romaines à nourrir leurs enfants, et « apporte des arguments que J.-J. Rousseau a reproduits dans l'*Emile* (p. 38) ; c'est « Voltaire et Rousseau (qui) maintiennent une religion naturelle qui rappelle en plus d'un point ce qu'avait enseigné saint Thomas, Raymond Lulle et Raymond de Sebonde ; c'est la politique de J.-J. Rousseau qui descend en ligne droite des pamphlétaires latins du temps de la Ligue » (p. 154), etc.

française) : « On voit que... le prodigieux succès de J.-J. Rousseau a tenu, non point à l'originalité de ses vues, mais tout au contraire à leur vaste diffusion préalable » (p. 68).

Nous n'en doutons pas, du reste ; Rousseau continuera longtemps encore à être proclamé l'écrivain le plus original du XVIIIᵉ siècle, le grand lanceur d'idées : « le Roi est mort ; vive le Roi ! » Ce qui précède n'en démontre pas moins que, parler aujourd'hui d'un Rousseau novateur, est réellement impossible. Ce qu'il faut dire, c'est que l'érudition moderne, en montrant comment on ne peut *pas* résoudre sur ce terrain le problème de la prodigieuse influence de Rousseau, l'a posé une fois de plus et confirmé une fois de plus notre idée de la nécessité d'une nouvelle enquête.

III

Maintenant deux remarques pour préparer à l'examen que nous proposons.

§ 1. D'abord, ne cherchons pas un refuge dans le mot fameux par lequel Mᵐᵉ de Staël a, la première, exposé son embarras, mot qu'on a souvent répété, et qu'on trouve même sous la plume d'érudits aussi remarquables que P.-M. Masson : « Rousseau n'a rien inventé, mais il a tout enflammé ». Le mot n'est pas faux, mais il ne constitue en aucune manière une réponse ; il amène plutôt un nouveau problème. Car enfin, si parmi tous ceux qui, avant Rousseau, avaient discuté les mêmes idées — et il est bien sûr que nous aurions pu allonger indéfiniment notre liste de précurseurs, *numquam nil novum sub sole* — aucun n'a remué le monde comme lui, certains d'entr eux ne manquaient pas d'éloquence ni de style : Platon, Dante, Rabelais, Montaigne, Fénelon, et tant d'autres ! Non, pour que Rousseau pût « tout enflammer », ENCORE FALLAIT-IL QU'IL Y EUT QUELQUE CHOSE D'INFLAMMABLE. Puisque, à égale observation, égale dialectique, égale éloquence, et sou-

vent égale passion, la semence n'avait pas germé, c'est qu'il
devait exister au moment où Rousseau parut, des circonstances qui n'avaient pas prévalu en d'autres temps. Baldensperger (dans son livre *La Littérature*, II, p. 203) dit fort bien :
« Un succès prouve toujours quelque chose : qu'il s'est ren-
contré à de certains moments des coïncidences entre une
œuvre et un groupe ». En d'autres termes, il se pourrait qu'en
cherchant l'explication de l'action surprenante de Rousseau
chez Rousseau, on ait fait fausse route ; et qu'on ait négligé
ce qui justement constitue le facteur décisif dans le problème
à savoir les circonstances et l'état d'esprit public au moment
où Rousseau écrivit et où il reprenait à son tour des idées
préconisées avant lui. Si tel était le cas en effet, le mérite —
ou le démérite — de Rousseau pourrait en être considérablement réduit, ou du moins devrait être apprécié différemment.
Serait-ce une raison pour rejeter l'explication ? Certes non.

Il faut donc commencer — et ce sera le sujet de notre première partie — par faire la part de ce contingent qui explique
probablement tant de choses, souvent toutes choses (1).

§ 2. Et voici notre seconde remarque, bien plus importante
encore. En sondant l'œuvre de Rousseau dans toutes les directions pour aboutir au résultat qu'elle n'était pas celle d'un
novateur, l'érudition en même temps a imposé à notre attention cette vérité qu'il existe entre plusieurs des théories fondamentales du philosophe, des contradictions en apparence
irréductibles. Entre le scepticisme métaphysique de Voltaire,
par exemple, sa tolérance religieuse, son rationalisme moral,
son enthousiasme pour les sciences, son aspiration à la liberté
politique, il y a une unité philosophique ; et certaines incon-

---

(1) Dira-t-on que, si Rousseau n'a inauguré sur aucun point, il a du moins
coordonné en un faisceau unique toutes ces doctrines dont il fut considéré
comme le représentant ? Cela pourrait se soutenir ; mais ce serait réduire
l'affaire à une simple addition, et il est évident que l'addition se serait faite
sans Rousseau. Le problème ne serait-il pas simplement déplacé, ou transformé
en celui-ci : comment Rousseau a-t-il *usurpé* son prestige ?

séquences (comme on en trouve chez chaque auteur) sont des accidents qui n'infirment pas l'inspiration unique. De même Montesquieu est toujours l'adversaire de l'absolutisme politique et social, et l'avocat du contingent. Buffon malgré sa classification hiérarchique des êtres vivants calquée sur la classification aristocratique de la société — et qu'il avait adoptée dans un esprit de tradition — n'en reste pas moins pour son temps un naturaliste imbu d'un esprit méthodique d'observation et un maître dans l'art de la synthèse ; Bossuet est toujours au fond l'apôtre de l'autorité ; Pascal toujours le détracteur de la raison humaine... Mais chez Rousseau, rien de tel ; en vain les critiques divers ont longtemps essayé de tout ramener — selon leur humeur ou leur préférence — à quelqu'une des théories accusées chez Rousseau, le rationalisme philosophique ou la liberté politique, le retour à la nature ou le sentimentalisme moral, ou le sentimentalisme religieux... : un examen attentif des textes, écartant impitoyablement tout impressionisme ou tout subjectivisme, n'autorise plus pareille tentative.

Prenez même — prenez surtout — les pourfendeurs de Rousseau ; ils brandissent l'anathème pour des motifs si contradictoires, que ce serait un jeu de faire une collection de ces accusations disparates. Voici, par exemple, Rousseau malmené pour avoir tué toute énergie en nous par un sentimentalisme stupide et efféminé (ruine psychique de l'individu... eudaimonisme lâche... maladie de la solitude... empire des éléments féminins de l'esprit sur les éléments viriles — *Lasserre*) ; et le voici, pris à partie pour avoir exaspéré l'énergie et créé une atmosphère de passions violentes et de folies furieuses (exaltation du crime à la façon de Nietzsche lorsque celui-ci écrivait : « Quand il tue, vous affirmez qu'il tue pour dérober ; mais je vous dirai quoi : son âme désirait du sang, pas du butin ; il avait soif du bonheur du contenu » — *Seillière*). Étudiez Rousseau à un point de vue plus concret, son influence sur la Révolution : le voici, chez l'un, responsable d'avoir inspiré la Révolution (« le jargon révolutionnaire, c'est la langue de Rousseau mal parlée : Rousseau enchante le peuple par son affirmation de la bonté des pauvres et de la méchanceté des riches... sans lui, il est possible qu'on n'eût pas songé en 1792 à faire la République » — *Lemaitre*) ; mais d'après un autre, les « prodigieux événements » de la Révolution ne lui doivent rien, à ce Jean-Jacques, ce prédicant ordinaire du respect des lois et de la soumission aux pouvoirs établis ». (« Les grands faits révolutionnaires, la convention des États Généraux, l'abolition de la royauté, la mise en vente des biens nationaux, la séparation dans l'État du temporel et du spirituel sont étrangers à Rousseau, ou même se sont produits malgré et contre cette influence » — *Dide*).

On voit bien que c'est la passion qui a conduit à ces formules simplistes, mais il n'en reste pas moins que l'on a pu trouver des arguments pour défendre les plus disparates avec une égale conviction.

Il faut reconnaître aussi ici qu'une partie du mal vient de ce qu'on n'a guère cessé encore d'aborder les théories de Rousseau comme devant former d'emblée un système arrêté ; la contingence d'étapes successives de la pensée chez lui n'a jamais été sérieusement prise en considération ; or la pensée de Rousseau a évolué sur bien des points ; il y a eu des retours, et même des re-retours ; et pas toujours simultanément dans les divers chapitres de sa pensée philosophique, ce qui crée des malentendus sans fin. Qu'on se rappelle seulement combien ont été transformées et illuminées nos appréciations de Rabelais, Ronsard, Montaigne, V. Hugo (pour ne citer que les tout grands) depuis qu'on s'est avisé de substituer une étude de l'évolution et des variations de leur pensée à la notion d'une création intégrale et d'emblée homogène, ou d'emblée hétérogène. De même, on avait oublié trop souvent que Rousseau avait laissé des éléments de sa pensée non développés (il le dit lui-même pour le *Contrat social* qui n'est qu'un chapitre de sa pensée politique). De cette façon, il est trop facile, comme on le fait souvent, d'opposer partie à partie, ou trop difficile de concilier partie à partie.

D'autre part, ni les considérations d'évolutions ou de variations, ni celles de pensées fragmentaires ou suspendues, ne suffisent à expliquer certaines fondamentales incompatibilités. On trouve sous la plume de Rousseau, constamment et même simultanément, des théories qui sont essentielles et qui sont cependant ennemies : bref, c'est dans le tissu même de la pensée qu'il y a des déchirures.

Certains travaux des dernières années nous ont déjà fait pressentir que l'on marche graduellement et irrésistiblement vers cette conclusion. Citons-en quelques-uns.

En 1891, M. Alexis Bertrand, dans un travail lu à l'Académie des Sciences Morales et Politiques sur « Le texte primitif du *Contrat social* » (*Comptes rendus de la société* T. CXXXV, p. 850-884, et chez Picard, 1891) veut établir surtout — en se fondant sur ce texte primitif du *Contrat social* — que le contenu du *Second Discours* est incompatible avec l'œuvre de Rousseau dans son ensemble, que ses paroles sur l'excellence de l'état de nature et l'infériorité de l'état social sont de « simples boutades » ; et que seulement Rousseau n'a pas eu le courage de se dédire. Or, ce n'est en réalité qu'une répétition d'une observation souvent formulée par les érudits les plus compétents. Tels Morley : Les théories du *Contrat* reviennent « à un abandon complet à peu près des principes du *Seconp Discours* » (*J.-J. Rousseau*, II, III, 21) ; Chuquet : « Le *Contrat social* est en désaccord avec l'œuvre entière de R. » (*Rousseau*, p. 147) ; Faguet : « Les idées politiques de Rousseau me paraissent, je le dis franchement, ne pas tenir à l'ensemble de ses idées » (*Dix-Huitième siècle*, p. 383) ; Voir aussi Ducros, *J.-J. R. de Genève à l'Ermitage*, p. 203, note) ; Beaudoin, *J.-J. R., vie et œuvres*, I, 326-7) ; E. Champion, dans ses diverses publications ; etc. Il y a cette différence seulement que le plus souvent quand on attire l'attention sur cette difficulté particulière de réconcilier les idées de Rousseau sur la société civile et celles sur l'état de nature, c'est au contraire le Roussean de l'état de nature qu'on considère comme le vrai, et celui du Contrat social qu'on considère comme étranger.

En 1865, M. Espinas, dans la *Revue Internationale de l'En-*

seignement (Vol. 30, pp. 325-56 ; 425-62), publie des articles conçus dans un esprit de violence tout à fait curieux, traitant Rousseau de « rhéteur », « incohérent jusqu'à l'impertinence » (234), impossible à « prendre au sérieux », car on ne peut voir dans son œuvre qu'une « mystification prolongée » (442). Nous ne revenons pas sur ce qu'il peut y avoir de présomptueux de la part d'un individu — de beaucoup de talent du reste mais sans grand nom quand il écrivait cela — d'accuser de folie le monde entier qui avait honoré Rousseau comme un de ses grands penseurs ; surtout nous persistons à ignorer des arguments sans dignité, tels que « Rousseau n'avait qu'un souci, le succès, c'est-à-dire la réputation et l'argent » (457). Constatons seulement que dans les pages pensées de son étude, et dans un esprit qui rappelle celui de M. Bertrand, M. Espinas oppose surtout le Rousseau défendant l'état de nature et le Rousseau déclarant l'état social supérieur ; — le second serait le vrai Rousseau, et c'est celui des premières années de Paris ; mais Jean-Jacques, par vanité, aurait voulu jouer le rôle du premier ; il y a bien une troisième phase, où Rousseau a voulu faire un compromis entre le penseur et le comédien, mais là « tout s'effondre dans un abîme de contradiction. » Ajoutons, qu'énergiquement pris à partie par M. Dreyfus-Brisac (*Rev. de l'Enseignement*, Vol. 31, pp. 537-48), M. Espinas réplique (Vol. 31, pp. 138-53), en faisant des concessions importantes ; c'est-à-dire disant qu'il n'a proposé son système des trois phases que « comme une hypothèse plausible, avec l'espoir — nous l'avouons encore — que la critique sérieuse nous apprendrait si le problème des perpétuelles contradictions de J.-J. est ou n'est pas soluble de cette façon » (140). Sur ce point des « contradictions perpétuelles » M. Espinas, on le voit, ne peut consentir à céder ; — et en cela il sera de moins en moins un isolé.

Bien plus important, car il ne nous accule pas à la théorie que le monde entier est fou en lisant un Rousseau insincère, est le cas de M. Faguet ; nous y avons fait allusion déjà ; il définit la pensée de Rousseau : un « chaos d'idées claires ». Par exemple, dans son *Rousseau penseur*, il compare les données des *Discours, Préface de Narcisse, Emile, Contrat social, Gouvernement de Pologne,* etc. ; il conclut assez naturellement à l'impossiblité de concilier tout cela : Rousseau sociologue, et qui est anarchiste, Rousseau anarchiste et qui est politique autoritaire, et... « ultra-archiste ».

Un autre critique qui a été manifestement inquiet de quelque chose d'incohérent est M. Bourgoin, qui dans la *Revue de Métaphysique et de Morale* du 1ᵉʳ mai 1912 (Numéro du bicentenaire) souligne « Deux tendances de Rousseau », — à savoir : analyse de la personne morale et du jeu des passions (point de départ dans les aspirations individualistes), et philosophie qui cherche les principes de l'organisation politique (point de départ dans les dispositions de sociabilité). Malheureusement l'auteur, qui depuis 1897 s'occupait de la politique de Rousseau, mourut sans développer l'idée exprimée dans ces quelques pages.

On lira avec profit sur ce sujet un long travail de Paul Sackmann dans le *Herrig's Archiv,* de 1913 : c'est-à-dire publié, notons-le, aussitôt après les années du bi-centenaire où Rousseau avait été beaucoup discuté, et souvent dans l'esprit systématique de la critique moderne (comme Bourgoin) : « Das Rousseau Problem und seine neueste Loesungen. » Le « problème » dont parle l'auteur est justement celui de la réconciliation des éléments divers de l'œuvre de Rousseau ; et on voit qu'en effet tous les derniers venus ont trouvé quelque chose à réconcilier chez le philosophe de Genève : Boutroux, Hœffding, Bosanquet, Parodi, Bouvier, Delbos, et y compris M. Sackmann lui-même. Chez Boutroux c'est l'individu et l'émotion d'une part, et la société et l'intelligence de l'autre ; chez Hoeffding, c'est le sentiment du relatif en moi, et celui de l'absolu en moi, etc.

Signalons aussi le volume plus récent de L. Proal, *La Psychologie de J.-J. Rousseau* (Alcan 1923) ; l'auteur est un homme qui ne se pose pas en étudiant des doctrines de Rousseau, et qui n'a pas lu tous les commentaires divers produisant une impression de confusion terrible. Mais, étudiant surtout la personnalité de Rousseau, ce qui le frappe, lui encore, ce psychologue, c'est justement cette constante coexistence dans la *pensée* de Rousseau, de thèses apparemment incompatibles, et que Rousseau défend avec le même enthousiasme. Il en fait une longue énumération (entre autres p. 292-300) ; et il mentionne une lettre dans laquelle Rousseau, en réponse à des indications de contradictions déconcertantes que lui faisait son ami d'Escherny, s'empresse de lui en citer d'autres encore (1).

Nous avons enfin, à l'appui de notre dire, les études pénétrantes de M. Lanson, son chapitre sur Rousseau dans son *Histoire de la Littérature Française*, son article « Rousseau » dans la *Grande Encyclopédie* (1900), et celui sur l' « Unité de la Pensée de J.-J. Rousseau » dans les *Annales Rousseau* (VIII, 1912). Ce dernier titre, à lui seul, est significatif ; elle n'est pas évidente certes, cette unité de l'œuvre de Rousseau, puisque 150 ans après sa mort, il faut qu'un esprit comme celui de M. Lanson en fasse un objet de recherche. Et d'ailleurs celui-ci nous avertit d'emblée qu'il ne peut plus prendre le mot « *unité* de la pensée de Rousseau » dans le sens qu'il avait cru pouvoir lui donner encore en 1900 ; qu'il reconnaît devoir s'essayer « moins à faire apparaître un Rousseau logique qu'un Rousseau vrai ». En somme, dit-il, il y a contradiction indiscutable, mais elle est entre l'homme Rousseau et l'œuvre de l'écrivain ; et quant à cette dernière, il souligne l'existence d'oscillations constantes de l'émotion à l'intelligence, et *vice-versa*, un rythme habituel de sa pensée (2). Vers la fin de

---

(1) A vrai dire, nous ne savons où M. Proal a vu cette lettre. La note de p. 299 renvoie à Hachette III, 341, où Rousseau discute ses contradictions avec M. de Beaumont.

(2) M. Faguet avait relevé ce trait lui aussi : et il est en effet frappant dès qu'on y regarde de près. Voici la phrase qui termine l'article de M. Lanson ; nous tenons à la signaler, car il y souligne un point fort important pour l'interprétation que nous allons essayer [mais nous voyons quelque chose de bien plus grave chez Rousseau que la contradiction seulement entre l'homme et l'écrivain] : « Ce contraste de l'œuvre et de l'homme qu'on appelle contradiction si l'on veut, il ne faut pas essayer de voiler cela, car cela, c'est Rousseau même ».

l'article, M. Lanson se demande si « plus d'un lecteur ne pense pas que j'ai moins résolu que confirmé en les expliquant, quelques-unes des contradictions qu'on reproche à Rousseau, et les plus importantes. »

Il y a là des indices que nous devons méditer après les avoir recueillis. Sans doute, il était extrêmement naturel de chercher à ramener l'unité logique dans l'œuvre d'un écrivain — surtout d'un écriavin philosophe ; et on comprend bien que pendant longtemps — un siècle et demi — on n'ait pas résisté à la tentation d'aller même jusqu'à mutiler l'œuvre de Rousseau pour arriver à chef. Mais puisque aujourd'hui tant d'échecs en ont prouvé la futilité, pourquoi persister dans ces efforts ? Après tout, rien ne nous force à admettre *a priori* qu'il existe un système philosophique et logique de Rousseau qu'on puisse reconstituer de toutes pièces. Il semble plutôt que si c'est là la condition *sine qua non* de comprendre Rousseau, il faut d'emblée y renoncer.

Ce serait trop commode, d'autre part, si, de ces aveux, on allait conclure qu'il faut renoncer à expliquer Rousseau, ou qu'il faille l'étudier seulement comme un frivole dispensateur d'esprit sur les problèmes de son âge. Non certes ! Qu'un gratte-papier de troisième ou quatrième ordre se contredise sur des propositions fondamentales, peut ne nous importer en aucune façon. Mais Rousseau est Rousseau, et quoique vivant à l'âge du suffrage universel, nous n'en sommes tout de même pas encore à ce point que de peser ses incohérences dans la même balance que celles des Bouvard et Pécuchet. Et d'ailleurs la critique moderne ne nous impose que cette seule conclusion : Qu'on avait cherché sur une mauvaise piste en s'efforçant de ramener la pensée de Rousseau à l'unité philosophique, mais nullement qu'il n'y ait rien à trouver par ailleurs. De fait, cette existence simultanée de théories incompatibles, n'est-elle pas elle-même un problème — qui n'est pas uniquement d'ordre logique, mais psychologique aussi bien ? La présence de théories inconciliables dans un esprit ou dans une œuvre ne signifie point que ces théories ne puissent entrer en rapport les unes avec les autres. L'eau et le feu, peut-on dire, sont incompatibles ; cependant l'eau et le feu peuvent être mis en rapport, même si l'un doit à la suite de relations établies, exterminer l'autre ; les savants étudient avec profit ces relations. De même pour la pensée de Rousseau ; elle peut contenir des éléments hétérogènes, mais cela ne nous dispense pas d'étudier les rapports de ceux-ci. Au contraire : il doit y avoir sûrement une raison suffisante pour expliquer cette cohabitation — cette intime et hostile cohabitation. Et le fait qu'un écrivain qui offre une morale trahissant des tendances en sens nettement opposé, ait justement été l'un des penseurs les plus influents dans l'histoire, nous pousse à nous demander si la présence de ces conflits fonciers ne constituerait pas peut-être le problème tout entier de Rousseau.

C'est l'examen de ces questions dans notre IIᵒ — et principale — Partie dont nous nous autorisons pour justifier notre titre : *Essai d'interprétation nouvelle.*

*
* *

Résumons tout cela :

Rousseau, selon les termes de l'étude si connue de M. de Voguë dans la *Revue des Deux Mondes* (1895) « pèse d'un poids prodigieux sur tout notre établissement intellectuel » : — voilà le fait.

Pourquoi Rousseau, malgré les attaques sauvages dont il a été l'objet, ne veut-il pas mourir ? — Voilà le problème.

L'explication de Rousseau par le « style enchanteur » n'en est pas une ; celle par la « personnalité » évite le problème, ou si on veut, le recule ; celle de Rousseau « novateur » ne se soutient plus, — et d'ailleurs, supposé qu'elle tînt pour le XVIIIᵉ siècle, elle ne rend pas compte de l'intérêt porté à Rousseau au XXᵉ.

D'autre part, l'examen auquel nous venons de nous livrer sur la nature des discussions suscitées par l'œuvre de Rousseau a dirigé notre attention sur deux points :

1º On a tenu relativement peu compte dans le passé des conditions sociales et psychologiques prévalant au moment où il parut, — et qui ont continué à prévaloir depuis. Peser avec soin l'importance de ce facteur, ce sera l'objet de notre premier effort (*Première Partie*).

2º Nous tournant ensuite vers l'œuvre philosophique de Rousseau, nous nous rendons compte que les exposés de sa pensée offerts par les commentateurs les plus divers, et les plus dignes de confiance aussi, trahissent l'existence d'un conflit entre éléments essentiels, — c'est-à-dire condamnent d'emblée la tentation de chercher chez Rousseau un ensemble philosophique cohérent : Chercher à démêler la nature et l'étendue de ce manque de cohésion philosophique, le sens qu'il peut avoir, examiner si ce ne serait pas là ce qui donne à l'œuvre de Rosseau son caractère propre [et essentiel, et important, ce sera l'objet de notre second et plus important effort (*Seconde Partie*).

PREMIÈRE PARTIE

LE PROBLÈME

> Un succès prouve toujours quelque-
> chose : Qu'il s'est rencontré à un certain
> moment des concordances entre une
> œuvre et un groupe.
>
> F. BALDENSPERGER, (*La littérature*
> p. 203).

CHAPITRE PREMIER

L'AVÈNEMENT DU ROMANTISME AU SIÈCLE DE ROUSSEAU

1. Le problème : comment concilier les aspirations romantiques de tout *moi* humain et les nécessités d'une discipline sociale, commence à se poser dès le moyen âge. Discipline ecclésiastique. 2. Première tentative d'affranchissement, renaissance. 3. Suivie de réaction violente ; siècle de Louis XIV. 4. Le problème romantique se pose formidablement une seconde fois au XVIIIe siècle, et Rousseau va le sentir et l'exprimer profondément.

Et d'abord ré-examinons attentivement quelles sont les conditions sociales et psychologiques prévalant au moment où va paraître Rousseau, c'est-à-dire à quel moment précis de l'évolution de la pensée humaine il a accompli son œuvre.

Il paraîtra peut-être pédant de remonter, comme nous allons le faire, jusqu'à l'aube de l'ère chrétienne. Qu'on ne nous juge pas avant d'avoir lu. Un problème clairement saisi est à moitié résolu ; et en donnant quelque étendue à cette partie de notre étude, nous pourrons sensiblement abréger les suivantes.

§ 1. L'Empire romain s'était écroulé avec fracas, entraînant dans sa chute une civilisation qui l'avait créé et puis ruiné.

L'ordre social repose sur un renoncement de l'homme à satisfaire tous ses désirs ; ce renoncement (qui d'ailleurs comporte des degrés différents suivant la position sociale) peut être volontaire ou contraint.

La Rome impériale s'était élevée sur le principe de la con-

trainte ; par la force les nations étrangères avaient été con-
quises, les classes inférieures soumises.

Or, les peuples ont une dose considérable, mais pourtant
limitée, de patience ; les aristocrates romains avaient dépassé
la mesure ; leur prestige avait déjà été diminué par leur ardeur à goûter tous les plaisirs ; ils avaient laissé toute honte.
Le peuple se souvint alors que la nature chez un esclave et
chez un maître est la même; il devint plus conscient à la fois de
ses souffrances et de ses droits ; il rechercha à son tour la jouissance. Après tout, les privilèges des riches sont une concession
des peuples, puisque les peuples par le seul empire du nombre
détiennent toujours la force ; — ce raisonnement put se faire
sans qu'un philosophe vînt le formuler.

Le résultat avait été une désorganisation générale ; les
maîtres, énervés du reste par leur vie de réjouissances inces-
santes devaient céder aux aventuriers déterminés sortant souvent des basses classes ; ils cédaient beaucoup pour ne pas
perdre tout ; en conséquence les parvenus réclamaient des
joies avec toujours plus d'effronteries ; tous les égoïsmes
étaient lâchés, c'était l'anarchie.

Les Barbares en profitèrent ; Rome devint leur proie. Et
l'anarchie s'augmenta alors des égoïsmes sauvages des nouveaux venus ; un état de guerre incessant n''était pas fait
pour arrêter ce déploiement sans frein de tous les appétits.

Mais c'est de cet état de « barbarie » que devait naturellement sortir l'aspiration, de plus en plus forte, à un retour
d'ordre à tout prix. C'est Rome encore une fois qui va prendre
la direction des destinées des peuples. Elle a perdu le prestige
des armes, mais elle conserve, jusque dans les défaites, celui
d'un plus grand développement de l'esprit. Si les barbares
ont eu le bon sens de l'admettre et de céder devant cette puissance plus nécessaire que la force dans l'organisation des sociétés, les anciens maîtres du monde profitèrent des leçons de
la chute de l'empire. Tout compte fait, ce fut avec une rapi-
dité et une intelligence surprenantes que les chefs allaient
agir.

La tâche était formidable, mais elle était claire : il fallait arrêter ce déchaînement de la nature humaine, mâter ces individualités qui n'étaient pas seulement violentes, mais d'une essence inférieure — puisqu'elles étaient faites de passions encore sauvages et des passions exaspérées de classes longtemps réprimées.

Or, une religion nouvelle venait de paraître qui pouvait servir admirablement à la réalisation du but poursuivi — si on réussissait à la faire accepter au peuple à la place des anciens dieux : La religion du Christ, d'une part, promettait le bonheur à tous ; et elle pouvait le faire avec assurance puisque le bonheur ainsi promis ne dépendait pas des contingences du monde et ne devait se réaliser qu'après la vie. D'autre part, et surtout, pour l'obtenir, ce bonheur, il fallait mortifier sa chair, contraindre ses désirs et condamner la jouissance terrestre ; en un mot il fallait nier la nature. Or, un moyen de nier la nature, d'enchaîner les passions, de réfréner les égoïsmes, c'était justement ce qu'on cherchait pour assurer l'ordre dans la société démoralisée.

Après avoir donc combattu ce culte d'un genre nouveau qui attirait — parce qu'il assurait à tous le bonheur jusqu'ici réservé à quelques-uns, et qui même avait créé un *imperium in imperio* — les intelligents s'avisèrent de sa valeur sociale pourvu qu'il fût mis adroitement à contribution.

Ce fut une grande habileté de la part de ces premiers maîtres chrétiens en occident, d'abord, de faire abandonner la forme du Christianisme mystique et rêveur de l'Orient, du Christianisme qui prêchait le retour messianique immédiat (croyance d'ailleurs assez compromise par l'attente vaine de longues années) ; et ensuite, sans abandonner l'idée du Royaume céleste où tous les déshérités de ce monde trouveraient un jour la compensation de leurs privations, de faire servir le Christianisme en même temps, et avant tout, à un Royaume de Dieu sur la terre.

En effet, les croyances à ces deux Royaumes de Dieu —

céleste et terrestre — ne sont pas incompatibles comme l'avait cru le chrétien primitif ou oriental (1).

Pour celui-ci en effet la vie ascétique avait été la seule qui importât dans le monde ; l'ordre social lui était pour le moins indifférent ; et, en un sens, le désordre était même préférable puisque, plus la vie était mauvaise, plus il avait d'occasion de souffrir et mériter le bonheur à venir. Pour le chrétien posté-rieur, ou occidental, d'autre part, — celui dont il s'agira sur-tout ici — la vie ascétique devenait au fond essentiellement un moyen de dompter ses désirs ; par elle sera assuré à la so-ciété l'ordre, fondement de la sécurité et du bonheur ; mais d'ailleurs, indirectement, elle demeure toujours un moyen pour obtenir au ciel le dédommagement de privations s'il fallait ici-bas endurer encore ; — aux premiers siècles du catholi-cisme sur tout, il n'était pas superflu de pouvoir compter sur cette suprême compensation. C'est le sens de la formule astu-cieuse de Montesquieu : « Chose admirable, la religion chré-tienne qui ne semble avoir d'objet que la félicité dans l'autre vie, fait encore notre bonheur dans celle-ci » (*Esprit des Lois*, XXIV, 23).

Les nouveaux législateurs du moyen age, papes, évêques, presbytres, comprirent qu'il fallait user des grands moyens dans cette lutte contre les appétits humains, contre « la na-ture ».

Il est toujours plus facile de renoncer que de se modérer ; mais c'est le cas plus particulièrement quand il s'agit d'hommes frustes tels que les vainqueurs de Rome ; raisonner avec des loups dévorants, leur demander de bien vouloir, dans l'intérêt de chacun, modérer leurs passions, eût été aussi naïf que futile ; il était donc opportun, sans faire aucune distinction entre jouissances légitimes et illégitimes, petites ou grandes, de déclarer mauvaise *toute* jouissance. Donc Rome affirma son idéal ascétique.

(1) Nous n'examinons pas d'ailleurs si Jésus-Christ avait été bien compris en ceci.

Rome ne laissa aucun doute théorique sur la nature condamnable de toute jouissance terrestre. Sur le mot du Christ : « Malheur à vous qui riez, car vous pleurerez », saint Basile fonde sa thèse qu'il n'est permis de rire en aucune façon (*Oudépoté Kath'olou*). Et saint Amboise, après lui, s'étonne qu'on puisse chercher des occasions de rire : « Et nos ridendi materiam requirimus, ut hic ridentes, illic fleamus ». Saint Augustin met en doute si l'on ose même laisser, dans les églises, s'élever un chant harmonieux, — celui-ci procure de la jouissance.

Dans la vie journalière, l'Eglise devisa toutes les manières possibles de mortifier la chair, d'étouffer la voix des désirs ; elle créa couvents et monastères ; elle glorifia le martyre, forme extrême de renoncement, inutile en soi, mais excellent exemple montrant la possibilité de la victoire absolue sur soi-même (1); et tout cela du reste, au risque de réactions féroces et périodiques de sensualité et de sauvagerie.

L'un des moyens les plus efficaces dont l'Eglise se servit pour souligner sa doctrine de la lutte à mort contre la nature, fut la peur de l'enfer. Elle remisa provisoirement à l'arrière-plan le Dieu d'amour du Christ, qui était bon pour quelques doux mystiques d'Orient mais point pour les descendants des hordes barbares, et elle établit sur le trône de l'agneau immolé pour une humanité tourmentée d'infini, Satan le tortureur des âmes sensuelles.

Pour consacrer l'autorité de sa morale ascétique, l'Eglise eut encore la précaution — point inutile certes — de se pour-

---

(1) C'est ce que les révélations de l'érudition mettent en lumière tous les jours davantage. Voir p. ex. G. HERZOG, *La Ste-Vierge dans l'Histoire* (Nourry, 1908) d'où ressort clairement que le culte de la Vierge n'a été développé qu'en vue de pouvoir prêcher mieux l'idéal ascétique de la virginité (dans ce but on a faussé des textes, renié d'anciennes traditions, etc.) Herzog résume ainsi sa minutieuse enquête : « Le dogme de la naissance virginale du Christ doit son origine aux idées docètes, mais il ne s'est imposé à la conscience chrétienne que le jour où il a brisé avec ces idées et s'est mis sous le patronage de l'ascétisme » (162).

voir d'une philosophie d'un genre nouveau, la philosophie scolastique où la pensée est la servante de la théologie (*ancilla theologiæ*), la théologie elle-même étant, comme nous venons de le
rappeler, la servante d'une Eglise soucieuse d'une moralité terrestre. S'appuyant sur saint Paul qui disait que l'Evangile
est « folie pour les païens », elle prêche hardiment qu'il faut
croire et pas raisonner, car tout ce qui raisonnablement semblerait bon à l'homme est réellement mauvais. Anselme (1033-
1109) formulait son *fides præcedit intellectun* et son *credo ut
intelligam*, qu'on traduisait encore par *credo etsi absurdum*
et *credo quia absurdum* (1). Et en effet, du point de vue social
cette attitude se justifiait : après cela est-il opportun de discuter si l'Eglise ment, trompe, s'abuse elle-même ? Là n'est
pas la question : l'œuvre civilisatrice, tel est l'enjeu de la gi-
gantesque entreprise de persuader aux hommes de nier leur
propre nature (2). Et on ne saurait assez le souligner pour
faire bien comprendre ici le point de vue de l'Eglise, — qui
peut être le point de vue d'ailleurs de penseurs en dehors de
l'Eglise. Sans doute, si la vérité philosophique est d'accord
avec la nécessité morale et sociale, c'est mieux ; mais s'il y a
conflit c'est la vérité philosophique qui doit céder le pas devant
la nécessité morale, ou comme on l'appelle parfois, la « vérité »
morale (3).

L'Eglise du moyen-âge a agi d'ailleurs avec une clairvoyance
admirable. Nos savants actuels, avec leurs petites machines,

---

(1) Pour la masse des fidèles l'*Imitation* avertissait éloquemment qu'un
examen des choses de la foi précipite dans l'abîme.

(2) Qu'on lise le beau volume posthume d'Achille Luchaire, *La Société française au temps de Philippe Auguste* (1912) qui montre si bien que l'Eglise de
ce temps, malgré ses tares, est la partie la plus saine, la plus éclairée, la plus
énergique de la société.

(3) Ce conflit semble inévitable ; il s'est continué en tout cas à travers les
siècles ; il vient encore de donner naissance à la théorie américaine du Pragmatisme. La justification du Pragmatisme au point de vue social, et son insuffisance philosophique ont été exposées dans notre volume *Anti-Pragmatisme.
Examen des droits respectifs des l'aristocratie intellectuelle et de la démocratie sociale*. Alcan, 1909. (Surtout Partie II, ch. II, et Partie III, ch. I).

leurs mensurations et pesages des phénomènes psychiques, sont des enfants à côté des prodiges de pénétration qu'étaient ces docteurs — qui, il faut le reconnaître, avaient à leur disposition l'instrument le plus efficace pour leur travail, la confession. Tout en l'écrasant et en tonnant ouvertement contre elle, le prêtre savait bien que la nature humaine était irrépressible ; il avait soin de ne pas attendre l'impossible. Les concessions s'imposaient ; d'abord il établit la pénitence en sorte que les conséquences du péché ne fussent pas absolues, et qu'il puisse retenir le pécheur sous son contrôle. Mais on alla bien plus loin encore. La morale ecclésiastique, en effet, déclara supérieure la vie de renoncement complète, mais elle ne condamna point, par exemple, le mariage ; elle fit même de celui-ci un sacrement, car de cette façon le prêtre y exercerait haute surveillance. Elle parla au nom du Prince de la Paix, mais elle ne supprimait pas les hommes de guerre ; il en fallait *de bons* pour ne pas être réduit par *les mauvais* ; il en fallait pour soumettre les peuples non-chrétiens ; on ne persuadait pas Wittekind par les douces rêveries des Pères du désert, mais on l'acculait devant le dilemme : « le Christianisme ou la mort» ; et le Charlemagne de l'Eglise ne fut pas le grand empereur chrétien « malgré que », mais bien « parce que » il avait passé au fil de l'épée tout les habitants de Saragosse, vieillards, femmes et enfants compris, qui refusaient le baptême.

§ 2. Passons au second acte.

Les migrations des peuples avaient cessé ; les grandes conquêtes prirent fin, car il n'y avait plus en Europe de pays à conquérir au Christianisme. On essaya bien l'Asie, mais les Croisades échouèrent. Restaient encore, pour troubler la paix, les luttes entre vassaux et suzerains, entre princes et barons ; elles éclataient à la moindre occasion ; mais comparé à l'anarchie d'autrefois, il y avait presque de l'ordre. Il y avait en tout cas des heures de répit, et la nature humaine n'en demandait pas davantage pour manifester des velléités de s'émanciper de nouveau. Aux heures toutes sombres des bouleversements incessants des premiers siècles de notre ère, on avait accepté avec joie les promesses d'un bonheur futur puisqu'il ne pouvait tout de même pas être question d'un bonheur présent ; dès qu'une tranquillité relative s'établit et apporta avec elle des occasions de se réjouir, on ne les refusa pas volontiers.

On va assister donc à une longue période de lutte entre « l'esprit du siècle » qui veut s'affirmer de plus en plus, et l'Eglise qui ne veut pas perdre son prestige. Nulle part ces tentatives d'émancipation, et les tentatives de répression qu'on leur oppose jusqu'au jour de la grande crise du XVIᵉ siècle, ne peuvent être suivies aussi clairement que dans l'histoire de la littérature.

Les premiers monuments littéraires avaient été avant tout religieux. La *Cantilène de Ste-Eulalie*, le *Poème de la Passion*, la *Vie de St-Léger*, *St-Alexis*, etc., avaient célébré le martyre et le renoncement au monde en termes non équivoques. Les premières épopées avaient ensuite montré que les plus nobles subissaient eux aussi cette obligation de renoncer à satisfaire leurs ambitions personnelles ; ayant plus de puissance, ils avaient plus de devoirs encore que les autres à prouver leur soumission à Dieu ; leurs épées, ils les avaient mises au service de l'Eglise pour la conquête du Christianisme ; la femme, qui risquait par ses charmes de détourner le baron de sa morale de renoncement, brillait le plus souvent par son absence ; l'épisode de la belle Aude, dans la *Chanson de Roland*, tenait en quelques vers.

Le premier souffle d'émancipation vis-à-vis de l'Eglise fut introduit par les légendes dites celtiques ; celles-ci ramenaient l'idée païenne des joies de vivre ; elles substituaient le goût des aventures à la guerre sainte et aux recueillements monastiques, l'amour de la femme à l'amour de Dieu, et en un mot le bonheur terrestre aux félicités paradisiaques. Les poètes, sous la pression de l'Eglise, avaient beau employer un langage dévot, et parsemer leurs épopées d'épisodes empruntés de la bible, de personnages pieux, de cérémonies catholiques, ils avaient beau recréer entièrement Parsival, et Gauvain, et Lancelot, et même faire de Merlin une sorte de « Satan chrétien », tout fut en vain ; les amants, Tristan et Yseut, jetés

dans les bras l'un de l'autre par le philtre fatal et symbolique,
émergeaient triomphants. Tôt après, laissant la note tragique,
c'était Nicolette arborant le bonnet phrygien gaiment et
doucement, et Aucassin osant des sarcasmes contre le paradis
des mendiants et des éclopés, où ne serait pas Nicolette, sa
« très douce amie ». Enfin l'accueil empressé fait par l'Europe
entière au *Roman de la Rose*, lequel formulait minutieusement
le code de l'amour, témoignait mieux que nulle autre chose
du terrain perdu par les apôtres de l'ascétisme monacal.

Une autre tendance à l'émancipation se rattachait à l'éveil
de la conscience sociale du peuple. Déjà des traits de satire
contre la noblesse et le clergé — qui, *au nom de Dieu*, écra-
saient les petits et les humbles — avaient paru dans les fa-
bliaux ; Wace, dans son *Histoire des Normands*, entonnait
ce qu'on a justement appelé la « *Marseillaise* du moyen âge » ;
et au XIIIe siècle la grande épopée de *Renart* venait prendre
place à côté du *Roman de la Rose* pour affirmer que l'on n'était
plus disposé à suivre Rome, si celle-ci demandait le renoncement absolu comme la seule morale sociale.

En même temps, des velléités lyriques se manifestaient ;
des poètes comme Rutebeuf, Villon, Charles d'Orléans, obéissant à l'impulsion naturelle, faisaient entendre des accents personnels — assez minces souvent, mais point négligeables
puisque les petits ruisseaux font les grands fleuves.

En face de cette situation, que fait l'Eglise ? — Elle comprend que les conditions de la vie ont cessé d'être favorables à
des doctrines de renoncement trop sévères ; une opposition
inflexible compromettrait toute son œuvre : chercher seulement à enrayer le mouvement, céder le moins possible pour ne
pas perdre tout — telle sera sa tactique en littérature comme
dans les autres domaines. Son action était demeurée puissante
encore et pouvait être sauvegardée. L'Eglise s'y employa et
la littérature s'y prêta : Chrétien de Troyes avait commencé
par écrire le poème de la fatalité païenne dans *Tristan et
Iseut*, il devait finir par un *Perceval* chrétien ; en même temps
l'Eglise autorisait dans ses cathédrales l'usage des mélodies de
chansons populaires pour retenir ceux qui se lassaient des

mélopées graves et solennelles des siècles antérieurs ; et surtout elle avait créé le théâtre : faisant fond sur la passion du peuple pour le spectacle, elle cherchait à répandre par la scène son enseignement de la nécessité de dompter la nature et ses procédés de terrifier le pécheur par des visions de jugement et d'enfer. Malheureusement le terrain était fort glissant, une concession en entraînait une autre, et l'on sait assez comment la petite farce d'intermèdes innocents en vint graduellement à envahir la scène jusqu'à en chasser les solennels Mystères.

Il faut ajouter que, chose bizarre à première vue, au sein de l'Eglise même, on vit des docteurs assez dépourvus de sens pratique et assez étrangers aux réalités de la vie pour ne pas comprendre l'idée profondément morale qui avait dicté la philosophie scolastique, la *Philosophia, ancilla theologiæ* ; ils prétendirent revenir au *Intellectus præcedit fidem* ; en d'autres termes, à l'idée qu'une doctrine vraie du point de vue de la raison en soi importe plus qu'une doctrine utile au point de vue social. De cette façon combattant la doctrine des deux vérités, ils minaient les bases de la foi, et toute l'œuvre civilisatrice de l'Eglise. Tel, Abélard (1097-1142) : tel, surtout, deux siècles plus tard, Guillaume d'Occam (+ 1347). L'Eglise devait réprimer ces natures romanesques, éprises d'une vérité socialement désintéressée et dès lors moralement dangereuse, ces esprits naïfs et sublimes qui auraient pu séduire s'ils n'étaient frappés des foudres de l'excommunication (1).

---

(1) Cependant le plus sûr moyen de les confondre était de les attaquer sut leur propre terrain de la dialectique. Thomas d'Aquin (1224-1274) les avair écrasés sous sa *Somme* qui réalisait à peu près le programme suivant : d'une part concentrer les discussions des docteurs autant que possible sur des questions en soi indiscutables, et d'ailleurs sans importance pratique (*Trinité, Nature des Anges, Essence de la Divinité,* etc.), et par là détourner la pensée spéculative du problème des rapports de la vérité philosophique et de la vérité sociale ou religieuse ; d'autre part, pousser la discussion des dogmes relatifs au salut jusqu'à la subtilité ; et de cette façon, la raison étant embarrassée dans ses propres filets, il fallait en sortir par quelque « autorité », celle des Ecritures interprétées par l'Eglise, et celle de la tradition catholique. Le but, jamais perdu de vue,

L'Eglise devait, pour conserver son prestige dans les masses, sévir aussi lorsque des groupes sociaux cessaient de reconnaître son autorité. Contre les hérétiques, comme autrefois contre les infidèles, elle avait recours au bras séculier. Elle le fit dès le XIIIᵉ siècle contre les Albigeois, précurseurs de Jean Huss, en Bohême, et des Huguenots. Certes l'Eglise ne pouvait accuser ces réfractaires de ne pas pratiquer la morale du renoncement chrétien, puisque ceux-ci la pratiquaient plus rigoureusement ; mais ils voulaient le faire à leur manière, selon des doctrines à eux. Or, si on eût permis aux uns (supposé même que ce fussent des bons) de s'affranchir de la tutelle de l'Eglise, que dirait-on aux autres (les libertins) qui rechercheraient l'affranchissement dans des intentions néfastes pour la société ? A juste titre — de ce point de vue — l'Eglise considérait que les sectaires de l'indépendance l'empêchaient de remplir sa mission civilisatrice. Malgré la part indiscutable de justesse contenue dans cette attitude, la théorie nuisait au prestige de l'Eglise dès l'instant où les hommes montraient des velléités de raisonner les choses. Leur intelligence ne comprenait ni la valeur de la discipline ascétique, ni les circonstances sociales qui avaient conduit là.

Et l'on comprend que cela créait une situation très délicate. L'Eglise pouvait-elle dire aux hommes que l'ascétisme et la discipline n'étaient pas tant un ordre divin, une épreuve pour se montrer digne du royaume de Dieu dans le ciel, qu'un moyen de réaliser un royaume de Dieu sur la terre ? Impossible ; c'eût été d'une part rendre la bride à l'homme de la passion, le rejeter dans la poursuite de plaisirs grossiers et temporaires ; c'était toute l'œuvre de civilisation perdue. C'eût été d'autre part, pour l'Eglise, ruiner son propre crédit que de dire : Nous vous avons menti, — pour votre bien, mais nous vous avons menti. L'Eglise relégua donc au second plan son souci de bonheur présent des hommes, et elle se commit de

était de rendre à l'Eglise le prestige nécessaire pour réaliser son programme : mâter la nature humaine pour établir autant que possible un royaume de Dieu sur la terre.

plus en plus à la morale du renoncement. Se mentait-elle à elle-même, ou crut-elle sincèrement désormais à la seule morale de l'ascétisme présent et plus à la valeur de la vertu comme d'une sagesse mondaine ? Evidemment ici on ne peut plus parler de l'Eglise, comme un tout, mais seulement des représentants individuels de l'Eglise. Et il est probable qu'il y en eut toujours, parmi ceux-ci, qui comprirent la vérité et crurent à l'Eglise comme un moyen social de rendre les hommes heureux ici-bas, — qui comprirent aussi la nécessité du silence ; mais il y en eut d'autres qui acceptèrent la foi toute dictée, et adhérèrent sans examen à la morale du renoncement aux joies terrestres en vue du royaume de Dieu après cette vie. Il y a le troupeau des prêtres comme il y a le troupeau des fidèles laïques, seulement il est plus petit.

Cependant tous ces souffles épars que nous venons d'évoquer (thèmes païens dans la littérature populaire, satires sociales, éveil du sentiment de la personnalité dans le lyrisme des poètes, théologiens qui opposent la vérité en soi à la vérité pragmatique) se combinaient et préparaient la tempête qui ne pouvait tarder à éclater.

Justement la société féodale venait de s'abîmer dans la Guerre de Cent Ans ; l'Eglise était affaiblie de toute la déchéance des barons, ses alliés séculaires. Alors survint l'accident qui contribua à rendre presque désespérée la situation menaçant l'édifice moral de l'Eglise : la prise de Constantinople par les Turcs (1453), qui eut comme contre-coup la révélation des chefs-d'œuvres de l'art païen. On s'enivra de la philosophie de l'antiquité ; François Ier, en fondant le Collège Royal de France (1529), encouragea la passion pour cette civilisation classique que l'Eglise avait cru supplanter à jamais. Les poètes allaient imiter Théocrite et Virgile, car, ce qu'on cherchait dans l'antiquité (il convient de le souligner spécialement, puisque nous allons nous occuper de Rousseau) ce n'était pas l'ordre sévère des républiques de Sparte et de Rome, ou même les gloires militaires de l'empire des Césars, c'était l'émancipation de la pensée, osons le dire, c'était s'affranchir du Chris-

tianisme ; c'était l'idéal païen de la jouissance de la vie, —
c'était l'abbaye de Thélème dont la devise était : « Fais ce que
voudras ! » Rabelais brossait une esquisse solide de la révolution rêvée : satisfaire les aspirations naturelles de notre *moi*
et non les nier, rire et non pleurer, élever l'homme pour la vie
et non pour la mort. Tout cela était le pays d'Utopie sans
doute, mais une utopie dont chacun pouvait bien voir qu'elle
n'était point tout à fait irréalisable. « On en vendit — dit
l'auteur en parlant de son *Gargantua* — davantage en un
mois que de Bibles en neuf ans ». Et tantôt, Montaigne
allait venir qui, analysant les idées et les opinions de son
temps, saperait par la base l'édifice des croyances religieuses
et morales devenues traditionnelles.

Un mot très imporant sur Calvin — dont nous aurons à re-
parler à propos de Rousseau. Il ne collabora que très indirectement et *contre sa volonté* au mouvement de la Renaissance
et de l'affranchissement des esprits dans le sens que nous
avons indiqué. Il voulait discréditer Rome, mais c'était pour
poursuivre le même but qu'elle : écraser la nature humaine, nier
le *moi*. De fait, il allait plus loin que Rome dans sa morale de
renoncement austère ; le catholicisme avait toujours fait
des concessions à la faiblesse humaine, même quand il prétendait être impitoyable ; Calvin refusa toute concession ;
il ne voulut voir que la société mauvaise profondément, et que
les remèdes radicaux de la négation absolue de la nature. Sa
seule originalité — et elle compte chez un précurseur de Rousseau — consista à avoir substitué à l'Eglise et au prêtre, la
conscience morale individuelle. Or, c'est en se basant sur cet
élément d'individualisme qu'on a dit parfois (Dide, Faguet, etc.)
que Calvin avait été un précurseur de Rousseau, — et on
ajoute : par Rousseau il a été un précurseur de l'individualisme
romantique. Il y a dans cette dernière affirmation une confusion étrange d'éléments entièrement disparates dans la pensée
de Rousseau, — confusion qui est concevable chez des gens
non habitués aux distinctions philosophiques, mais non chez
des écrivains de profession. Oui, c'est bien au nom d'un *moi*
— cette conscience individuelle — que Calvin attaque Rome,

mais c'est un *moi* qui ne s'affirme que pour nier la nature humaine avec plus d'intransigeance que ne le demandait l'Eglise et le prêtre ; et ainsi, le Calvinisme, loin d'être un mouvement de retour romantique aux droits du *moi* naturel (comme l'avait voulu Rabelais) est un retour seulement aux devoirs du *moi*, soit, au Christianisme intransigeant de la première Rome catholique. Calvin exécrait Rabelais, et Rabelais dénonçait Calvin comme un imposteur : rien de plus naturel.

Calvin était d'accord avec Thérèse d'Avila, réformatrice des Carmélites au xvie siècle : « Ou souffrir, ou mourir », — qui est également la morale de volonté anti-passionnelle que reprendra (quoique indépendamment de préoccupation religieuse) Corneille pour ses héros.

Dans le domaine de la pensée catholique, le xvie siècle continuera les efforts des siècles précédents : enrayer les recherches de la vérité tout court au profit de la vérité ecclésiastique, c'est-à-dire de la philosophie de la vie anti-naturelle. Ce fut pour empêcher la diffusion de doctrines contraires à la foi que le Concile de Trente (1545-63) nomma une commission chargée de préparer un catalogue de livres prohibés (*Index librorum prohibitorum*). Et Philippe II, roi d'Espagne, décrétait peine de mort contre tout vendeur, acheteur ou seulement lecteur d'un livre mis à l'Index (1558) ; et avec le pape Paul IV, il regardait le *saint* office de l'Inquisition comme le seul moyen de maintenir l'autorité de l'Eglise. Le supplice du dominicain Giordano Bruno à Rome, en 1600, et le procès de Galilée en 1633, montrent qu'il ne s'agissait pas de mots seulement.

Résumons : contre la tradition morale catholique de renoncement, renforcée à l'heure du danger par le protestantisme, le xvie siècle nous fait assister à un grand mouvement d'idées révolutionnaires. Tout y contribue : le mécontentement des esprits à l'endroit des classes dirigeantes, la Renaissance des lettres et des arts favorisée par la connaissance des œuvres de l'antiquité, une grande curiosité scientifique, l'invention de l'imprimerie, etc.

La révolution était prête dans les esprits, semble-t-il — *elle ne descendit pas dans la sphère des réalités.*

§ 3. Nous arrivons au IIIe acte.

Dix siècles de discipline ecclésiastique ne se nient pas en un jour. D'ailleurs, réaliser les aspirations du moment, c'était retourner aux conditions qui avaient amené la chute de la société antique, et comme elle n'avait pas pu vivre sous ces conditions-là une première fois, le pouvait-elle davantage une seconde ? En d'autres termes : les peuples étaient-ils mûrs pour une conception *naturaliste* — on dira un jour *romantique* —de la vie ? Pour se contraindre sur la pente des passions et de l'anarchie, il faudrait, à défaut de l'autorité politique ou religieuse, au moins la raison ; cette raison, les peuples ne la possédaient point (1)

C'est ce dont on s'avisa à temps. Nous disons « on », car il serait difficile d'indiquer exactement par qui ce mouvement de machine-arrière fut déterminé ; il fut le résultat d'une quantité de mesures partielles qu'on prit sur mille points menacés, et inspirées par une commune nécessité ; — car il semble y avoir dans l'humanité une sorte d'instinct de préservation qui lui permet toujours de se reprendre avant qu'il soit trop tard. L'Eglise surtout, devant le danger, se ressaisit ; elle vit bien que le Calvinisme devait son ascendant sur tant d'esprits, au sérieux moral de ses chefs, et elle avait commencé par appliquer chez elle-même l'œuvre de la réforme.

On sait comment, unissant une fois de plus les forces du trône et de l'autel, les hommes politiques du grand siècle réussirent dans leur œuvre réactionnaire et nécessaire de discipline, c'est-à-dire surent faire rendre à la philosophie et morale anti-naturelles — condition de l'ordre social — la place que la philosophie naturelle ou amorale de la Renaissance avait menacé d'y substituer. Il y eut de fortes ombres au tableau, mais leur époque fut une époque d'ordre. En somme, l'esprit absolutiste du XVIIe siècle est une suite nécessaire de

(1) Remarquons que le problème était tout autre que dans l'antiquité. La « société » grecque et romaine était celle d'une élite ; la masse était formée d'esclaves dont les passions étaient contraintes par l'organisation politique. Le Christianisme avait changé cela ; le peuple était humble, bas, opprimé, mais tous étaient égaux devant Dieu et l'Eglise.

l'esprit du xvie ; il était dans la logique des choses qu'on substituât à un esprit de liberté dangereux, un esprit énergiquement réactionnaire, qu'aux théories de l'émancipation du *moi* on opposât celle de la contrainte du *moi*.

De sorte que le xvie siècle — du point de vue impersonnel de l'histoire — ne nous apparaît plus aujourd'hui que comme une saturnale intellectuelle un peu prolongée, où on s'était abandonné à un rêve de libération de la contrainte plusieurs fois séculaire imposée par la pensée ecclésiastique. Un violent coup de barre à droite empêcha ces aspirations a-morales de descendre dans le domaine des réalités, et prévint le renouvellement d'un effondrement comme la chute de la Rome impériale.

Dans le domaine de la pensée, la transition s'opéra sans choc trop violent. Comme on avait essayé (aux xiie et xiiie siècles) d'écouler les velléités de mondanité des légendes celtiques dans des histoires teintées d'apparences chrétiennes (sans tout à fait y réussir du reste) on écoula quatre siècles plus tard de nouveau, pour en être débarrassé dans le domaine de la vie réelle, l'esprit de la Renaissance philosophique et antireligieuse dans la littérature ; — et on réussit cette fois fort bien. En effet toute la littérature du siècle classique français est, au fond, d'essence chrétienne ; mais elle porte un masque païen. Les héros austères de Corneille et de Fénelon — on a souvent souligné le fait, on peut encore l'expliquer — chez qui les désirs du *moi* sont toujours niés au profit de notions morales (pas simplement politiques, comme chez Spartiates et Romains) portent des noms grecs et latins et sont placés dans un décor antique ; Racine expose mais déplore l'empire de la passion chez les hommes ; Molière et La Bruyère ont déjà, c'est vrai, le procédé de l'analyse du xviiie siècle, mais ils s'en servent dans l'esprit du xviie, c'est-à-dire précisément pour moraliser. Et La Rochefoucauld se place lui-même sur le terrain du renoncement chrétien pour formuler son réquisitoire : si quelque acte de vertu procure une jouissance, la vertu est absente ; vous posez pour le désintéressement, mais vous ne souffrez pas véritablement par la vertu ; donc vous êtes hypocrite. Limpide, de ce point de vue de morale chrétienne, est le fameux roman de Mme de La Fayette, *La Princesse de Clèves*.

Il ne faut pas oublier que celui qui, par excellence, représente l'esprit du XVIIe siècle — sans le dissimuler sous le volontarisme des Romains, comme Corneille, ou sous les discussions de la grâce, comme Racine — c'est Bossuet. Rappelons seulement comment dans ses *Maximes et Réflexions sur la Comédie* il s'opposera à la représentation de passions rendues agréables par l'art, car les rendre agréables ainsi, c'est les rendre aimables, et il est défendu de les aimer.

Et au point de vue strictement philosophique c'est, encore mieux que Bossuet, Pascal voulant démontrer que le christianisme est supérieur à toute autre religion, car il est « la seule religion contre la nature » (p.605, de l'éd. Brunschvicg) (1). Et en face du rationalisme relevant la tête avec Gassendi et Descartes, il foit le spectre de l'hérésie d'Abélard et de G. d'Occam ; il s'écrie en face des novateurs dangereux : « Taisez-vous, raison imbécile... », car la raison voudra se refuser à sanctionner une religion contre la nature.

Le grand combat de Pascal a du reste été celui contre les Jésuites, lesquels par leurs concessions à l'esprit de mondanité reniaient la morale anti-naturelle de ce christianisme dont ils se disaient les représentants.

Remarquons que c'est par une de ces anomalies dues à la complexité des problèmes du monde que Bossuet, le sévère tanceur de la cour du grand roi, s'est trouvé dans un camp opposé à celui de Pascal, et dans celui des Jésuites. Défendant l'austérité chrétienne comme les Jansénistes, il ne combat chez eux que les dissidents théologiques ; qui mettant la désunion dans l'Eglise (comme le font les Protestants) compromettent l'influence de celle-ci ; mais par le fait de combattre les Jansénistes, voici Bossuet rangé avec les Jésuites dont

---

(1) « O mon Dieu, rendez-moi incapable de jouir du monde, soit par faiblesse du corps, soit par zèle de charité, pour ne jouir que de vous seul. » (*Prière pour le bon usage des maladies.*)

cependant il doit condamner l'indulgence aux plaisirs du monde (1).

Nous relevons tout cela, car la lutte entre l'esprit janséniste (anti-nature) et l'esprit jésuite (concession à la nature) n'est qu'une escarmouche préludant au grand combat du XVIIIe siècle; et que là, on verra — par un nouveau jeu de combinaisons bizarres — les Jésuites et les « Philosophes » prêchant la même indulgence à la nature, et qui devraient donc maintenant être dans le même camp, mais qui, se trouvent en fait dans des camps opposés. Cette opposition de fait, qui est tellement contre la logique des choses, a pour explication une rivalité toute pratique sur terrain des influences sociales et politiques auxquelles aspirent à la fois les deux groupes de moralistes indulgents à la nature.

La Renaissance ne s'est vraiment un peu continuée au XVIIe siècle selon l'esprit, que dans la littérature précieuse ; celle-ci était bien d'inspiration païenne ; et encore il était entendu que les vers et les romans précieux n'étaient que joués. La quatrième *Maxime* dit expressément qu'il s'agit de « donner plus à l'imagination à l'égard du plaisir qu'à la vérité, et cela par ce principe de morale que l'imagination ne peut pécher réellement. »

§ 4. IVe acte.

Si le mouvement de la Renaissance, au point de vue social, n'avait pu — et n'avait dû — aboutir, il avait été cependant une première levée en masse contre la morale anti-naturelle de l'Eglise ; à qui savait entendre le langage des événements, ce mouvement disait : « L'humanité n'a pas encore renoncé aux aspirations du *moi* ; et, après tout, si les circonstances ne sont pas favorables aujourd'hui à un retour, les circonstances ne peuvent-elles pas changer ? »

---

(1) Notre assertion est curieusement confirmée par l'abbé Bremond, qui, de son point de vue de Christianisme dévot et mystique range dans une même classe Bossuet et Jansénistes — en face des Jésuites. On observera cependant que, pour lui, les Jésuites représentent le Christianisme vrai, et les Jansénistes et Bossuet le faux (Cf. *L'humanisme dévot*, p. 215-16).

Elles changèrent en effet au cours du XVIIIe siècle.

L'Eglise avait triomphé de la Réforme ; la France avait réalisé son unité nationale ; les conditions d'un état social stable étaient rétablies. Et ce fut précisément ce sentiment de la sécurité reconquise qui, secondé par les inconstances historiques, va remettre au cœur des hommes ce qu'on a appelé le « virus romantique ». L'équilibre va se rompre de nouveau — et les choses iront fort bien cette fois, puisque le Romantisme *sera*.

Observons d'abord qu'il y avait, en comparant l'état des esprits à ce moment de l'évolution de la civilisation chrétienne et celui qui prévalait au moyen âge, une différence importante : le clergé, tout en réclamant et recommandant (du point de vue purement social) le renoncement du chrétien, était devenu beaucoup moins absolu dans ses exigences ; non seulement il le devait, pour ne pas affaroucher ceux qui avaient encore des visées d'émancipation telles qu'au XVIe siècle, mais il le pouvait grâce aux progrès de civilisation déjà obtenus ; les contemporains de Bossuet étaient encore humains, mais ils n'étaient plus des barbares, et il y avait déjà là une justification à la tendance générale des esprits à se libérer du joug religieux et social qu'on leur imposait. Renan l'a dit, avec son sens pénétrant des choses :

> « L'abstinence et la mortification sont des vertus de barbares
> « et d'hommes matériels qui sujets à de grossiers appétits ne
> « trouvent rien de plus héroïque que d'y résister ; aussi sont-elles
> « surtout prisées dans les pays sensuels. Aux yeux d'hommes
> « grossiers, un homme qui jeûne, qui se flagelle, qui est chaste, qui
> « passe sa vie sur une colonne est l'idéal de la vertu. Car lui, le
> « barbare, est gourmand et il sent fort bien qu'il lui en coûterait
> « beaucoup s'il fallait vivre de la sorte. Mais pour nous un tel
> « homme n'est pas vertueux, car ces jouissances de la bouche et
> « des sens n'étant rien pour nous, nous ne trouvons pas qu'il y
> « ait du mérite à s'en priver... Platon était moins mortifié que
> « Dominique Loricat et apparemment plus spiritualiste. Les
> « catholiques prétendent quelquefois que la désuétude où sont
> « tombées les abstinences du moyen-âge accusent notre sensua-
> « lité ; mais tout au contraire, c'est par suite des progrès de l'esprit
> « que ces pratiques sont devenues insignifiantes et surannées »
> (*Avenir de la Science*, p. 404-5).

Il y avait, ensuite, que l'histoire des siècles précédant la Renaissance, se répéta. Les chefs responsables des peuples, clergé et magistrats politiques, au lieu de veiller à la situation toujours menacée — puisqu'elle reposait sur une contrainte des dispositions naturelles de l'homme, c'est-à-dire des dispositions qui ne demandaient qu'à briser toute entrave — ne songèrent qu'à profiter de la sécurité reconquise grâce aux Richelieu, Mazarin et Louis XIV, et des avantages des classes dirigeantes. Pendant quelques temps, les splendeurs du grand règne avaient continué à éblouir ; mais déjà lorsque Louis XIV se transporta avec toute sa cour à Versailles, le peuple de Paris se trouva livré à ses réflexions ; sous Louis XV et la Régence, les choses empirèrent. Des guerres continuelles pesaient sur la France, entre autres celle de Sept Ans qui ne devait rien lui rapporter. Si le commerce était prospère, les paysans étaient acculés à une noire misère ; la tentative de Law de relever la situation financière avait pitoyablement échoué ; et il n'était partout question que des dépenses folles des favorites. Les plus patients et plus sots étaient amenés à réfléchir : « La soumission aux privilégiés de la fortune, ou la contrainte de soi-même, ne sont-elles pas naïveté et folie ? » Et comment une nation intelligente, dans de telles conditions, ne serait-elle pas accessible à des idées sociales nouvelles où l'individualisme relèverait la tête ?

La pensée philosophique allait venir appuyer de son influence ces rêves d'émancipation, et aider à les formuler en termes précis. Il y avait en vérité un danger à posséder, à une époque aussi développée intellectuellement que le xviie siècle, un code arrêté de toutes les opinions autorisées — morales, politiques, religieuses. Aucune question pratique n'étant pour ainsi dire discutable, un philosophe appliquerait nécessairement les ressources de ses talents ailleurs, à des questions de logique par exemple, ou de psychologie. Or, il se trouvait que ces questions n'étaient théoriques qu'en apparence ; et qu'au contraire, plus elles étaient abstraites — pourvu qu'elles ne fussent pas métaphysiques — plus elles étaient fondamentales réellement pour l'appréciation de la valeur des croyances phi-

losophiques ou religieuses, morales ou politiques existantes.
En effet, il est impossible de scruter les domaines de la théorie
de la connaissance sans arriver à des conclusions précises sur
ce qu'on peut et ce qu'on ne peut pas croire et penser (psychologiquement et logiquement) ; la raison n'est pas libre de ne
pas tirer certaines conséquences de certaines prémisses ; ainsi,
un penseur qui aurait cherché seulement la vérité en soi, la
vérité philosophique pure, devait, consciemment ou inconsciemment, préparer des instruments dangereux pour la morale
chrétienne, puisque, nous l'avons vu, le critère pour les doctrines morales de l'église n'était pas la vérité, mais l'utilité
sociale.

Ce fut justement ce qui arriva avec Descartes. En formulant
sa méthode pour trouver la vérité, et par là en affirmant implicitement que le vrai est, partout et toujours, l'essentiel, il
renouvelait l'hérésie d'Abélard et de Guillaume d'Occam qui
avaient voulu substituer le *intellectus precedit fidem* au *credo etsi
absurdum*. Le critère philosophique en effet n'étant plus l'utilité mais la vérité, l'homme réfléchi se trouva devant cette question : « Puisque la doctrine de l'Eglise, demandant le sacrifice
de mon avantage personnel n'est pas *vraie* peut-être, pourquoi
continuer à pratiquer une morale de renoncement ; que m'importe la société ? »

En réalité, en ce qui concerne la fameuse « méthode », Descartes rétablissait simplement la méthode rationnelle, aussi
vieille que le monde, mais subtilisée par la scolastique ; cette
méthode cependant était si bien tombée en désuétude qu'on
l'avait oubliée et qu'elle pouvait *paraître* nouvelle. D'autre part
— et voici le *hic* —Descartes ne fut jamais lui-même dans cette
disposition d'esprit ; il semble que c'était au contraire dans le
but d'établir morale et religion sur des bases plus solides que
la tradition, qu'il se mit à réfléchir sur les problèmes de la
métaphysique. Il se trouva, en effet, lorsque Descartes mit à
l'épreuve sa méthode dans ce domaine spécial de la morale et
de la théologie, qu'elle le conduisait ailleurs qu'il n'avait pensé.
Alors *il lui faussa compagnie* ; c'est-à-dire qu'il cessa absolument d'appliquer sa méthode scientifique hardie, *mais en*

assurant qu'il l'appliquait encore (et nous ne disons point qu'il était de mauvaise foi, c'est là un problème très délicat) : il trouva moyen de formuler des idées anciennes et conservatrices. En fait, la « philosophie » de Descartes pèche constamment contre son critère de la vérité : « ne rien accepter pour vrai qui ne s'imposât point avec évidence à l'esprit ». Ainsi l'argument ontologique de l'existence de Dieu : parce que j'ai en moi l'idée auguste d'un Etre absolu, il ne s'impose pas à ma raison que cette idée doive avoir été déposée là par l'Etre absolu lui-même ; on conçoit très bien que cette idée ne soit que le produit de mon propre intellect (la théologie de Strauss au XIXe siècle repose tout entière sur cette idée que l'homme a créé Dieu à son image). Ailleurs, passer de cette affirmation que Dieu me donne la sensation d'avoir un corps, à cette autre que mon corps existe réellement puisque sans cela Dieu me tromperait, est une pétition de principe — que Dieu est véridique. Et prouver que Dieu est véridique en disant que la qualité d'être véridique est nécessairement impliquée dans la notion de Dieu, est encore, du point de vue de la méthode de Descartes, purement gratuit ; en réalité l'argument que Descartes suggère est que si Dieu n'est pas véridique, Dieu serait méprisable à l'homme, qui ne pourrait l'adorer ; mais de là à dire que Dieu *est* véridique au sens humain du mot, il y a loin... De fil en aiguille Descartes rétablit le Dieu de justice de l'Eglise, l'immortalité de l'âme, la liberté, qui ne sont que des postulats pratiques de la vie morale telle que, avec l'Eglise, il conçoit celle-ci. Quand Vinet s'écrie parlant de la méthode de Descartes : « On se demande comment tant de liberté a pu exister dans un siècle d'autorité », il oublie que « l'autorité » ne songe à juger que les conséquences, et que du moment que Descartes formule des conclusions orthodoxes en matière de religion et de morale, « l'autorité » s'occupe peu de la façon dont il y arrive. C'est ce qui explique comment Bossuet, Fénelon et autres ont pu être « cartésiens » ; ils l'étaient en morale et en métaphysique, sans l'être en ce qui est l'essentiel, la méthode (1).

(1) On demandera comment alors l'autorité philosophique de Descartes

Cependant cette façon d'échapper aux conséquences de ses prémisses ne pouvait durer. Déjà Bayle, esprit avisé, s'était tôt aperçu que Descartes n'était pas arrivé par la saine logique à ses idées de métaphysiques, et que les «libertins», ou tout esprit réfléchi, ne pouvaient manquer de s'en apercevoir bientôt ; — ce qui était inquiétant pour la cause de l'Eglise. Aussi peu disposé cependant que Descartes à retourner à la méthode de la scolastique, et aussi soucieux que lui des intérêts de la morale traditionelle, il adopta une autre tactique — mais bien plus dangereuse encore : il tira des conséquences de la méthode rationnelle, et eut le courage de proclamer hautement qu'elle n'aboutissait pas à la métaphysique de Descartes et de l'Eglise ; et la conclusion qu'il en tira, lui, était que la raison livrée à elle-même ne conduit nulle part, mais que comme nous voulons à tout prix une vérité, il fallait chercher dans la Révélation une base à la doctrine de renoncement.

Le XVIIIe siècle allait profiter de la dialectique de Bayle ; il adopta, de l'œuvre de celui-ci, la partie de logique qui était destructrice des croyances traditionnelles, tout en repoussant franchement la tentative (pragmatique) de reconstruire par l'argument de la Révélation qui servait à sauvegarder le Christianisme anti-nature. Pour prouver qu'il s'agit réellement bien pour les « philosophes » du XVIIIe siècle de se libérer de l'ascétisme chrétien, de la « religion contre la nature » de Pascal, il suffit de rappeler ces mots de Diderot, dans l'article « Philosophe », de *l'Encyclopédie* : « Notre « philosophe » ne se croit pas en exil dans ce monde ; il ne croit point être en pays ennemi ; il veut jouir en sage économe des biens que la nature lui offre...»

Et Voltaire qui ne vit pas — et n'eût pas voulu voir 1789, — ne se trompait pas quand il écrivait le 17 juin 1771 à un Allemand : « Il s'est fait dans les esprits une plus grande révolu-

---

s'était établie puisqu'il tirait d'une méthode scientifique des conclusions métaphysiques douteuses. La réponse est facile : Descartes avait employé sa méthode dans le domaine de la mathématique et de la physique ; et là il avait fait merveille ; c'était incontestable ; sa réputation de métaphysicien est basée sur ses succès de physicien : il avait raison là, c'était une *présomption* en sa faveur ici.

tion qu'au xvi⁰ siècle. Celle du xvi⁰ siècle a été turbulente, la nôtre est tranquille ».

Une autre cause encore qui favorisa la tendance et dès lors le désir d'affranchissement du joug de la morale anti-nature de l'Eglise, se trouve dans les récits des voyageurs et des explorateurs de contrées non civilisées. Il a été clairement démontré (entre autres par G. Atkinson) que ces récits étaient loin d'être toujours simplement objectifs ; beaucoup — et parfois les plus lus — étaient arrangés en sorte de propager certaines idées : les récits objectifs de voyage avaient suggéré l'idée des récits cuisinés, sinon tout entiers inventés. Quoique souvent dus à la plume d'hommes ayant des visées opposées, l'effet de tous agit dans le même sens : les uns — récits des missionnaires — faisaient honte aux chrétiens, des désintéressements vertueux trouvés chez des sauvages ; les autres — récits des penseurs indépendants, comme jadis Montaigne — soulignant la douceur des mœurs des hommes de la nature malgré des coutumes ou formes de cultes souvent repoussantes ou cruelles, et concluant que la discipline chrétienne était inutile, sinon nuisible, pour les mœurs et le bonheur des peuples. Déjà Bayle avait soutenu que, théoriquement, une société était possible sans Dieu — et il avait provoqué relativement peu de scandale ; ces récits servirent de preuve par les faits, que non seulement la morale ne dépend pas de l'Eglise, mais que la morale naturelle, dont l'idéal ascétique était absent, rendait les hommes heureux. On ne voyait pas du reste comment Dieu, s'il était bon, pouvait ne pas préférer cette morale de bonheur pour les hommes (comme Rabelais l'avait suggéré déjà).

Ajoutons que la « littérature sauvage » fut une des sources d'inspiration de la littérature sentimentale qui allait s'affirmer dans tous les domaines (roman, théâtre, poésie), c'est-à-dire celle qui engageait l'homme à écouter la voix de ses sentiments et aspirations spontanés plutôt que de se soumettre à la répression chrétienne.

Enfin le dernier facteur que nous mentionnerons — et parallèle à celui que nous venons d'indiquer — qui favorisa la réaction contre la morale anti-naturelle de l'Eglise, est celui

de la découverte de l'Angleterre. Des relations autres que
guerrières s'étaient établies entre ce pays et le continent, dès
le XVIIᵉ siècle ; beaucoup d'Anglais traversaient la Manche
pour venir en France dont le prestige en Europe était alors
si grand. Ils venaient chercher des idées ; mais ils en apportaient aussi. Il est vrai qu'il y eut aussi pas mal de Français
qui passaient en Angleterre, mais c'étaient des exilés ; les
Huguenots ne revenaient pas au pays, et leur influence fut
limitée. Au XVIIIᵉ siècle, on passa la Manche plus sonvent, et
il était rare qu'on ne revînt pas émerveillé de l'Angleterre.
Les Français apprenaient à connaître un peuple qui était libre
de tant de contraintes pesant sur leur pays — contraintes politiques, religieuses, morales. Sans doute cette vie libre était en
grande partie le résultat de circonstances favorables. Protégés
dans leur île contre des ennemis du dehors, les rois n'étaient
pas dans la nécessité de maintenir une discipline nationale
aussi sévère que Richelieu et Mazarin ; et le clergé, allié du
pouvoir séculaire, de son côté, ne voyait pas de raison pour in-
disposer inutilement les sujets en réclamant une soumission
si absolue à son contrôle. Tout cela avait eu sa répercussion
sur la vie en général : les inclinations naturelles étant moins
comprimées, l'esprit individualiste s'était développé — et ce
fut ce spectacle de gens libres qui éveilla chez les Français
des aspirations romantiques : on pouvait donc céder aux
appels de la nature, et le système social ne s'écroulait pas ;
au contraire la nation en était plus heureuse et plus prospère.
Comme on avait dit : les sauvages sont bons quoique —et peut-
être parce que — non chrétiens ; on dit : les Anglais sont heureux quoique — et peut-être parce que — non policés et non-
catholiques. Pourquoi ne pas l'être comme eux ?

On vanta d'ailleurs chez les Anglais, comme chez les sauvages, l'indulgence aux émotions spontanées du cœur, le sentimentalisme. Et quoique l'imitation de cette tendance prît
en France la forme ridicule du « bourgeois » et du « larmoyant »,
on n'y reconnut pas moins, au fond, la base de tout le reste :
la prétention de vivre son *moi*, et non de le nier ; le héros cor-
nélien — si chrétien dans sa conception du devoir — cédait

la place, dans la faveur publique, au bourgeois de Diderot et de
Nivelle de la Chaussée.

Notre chapitre se résume donc en ceci : Les problèmes sociaux et moraux dans le demi siècle qui précède la Révolution
étaient posés depuis longtemps ; dès que le christianisme avait
eu la puissance de faire triompher son idéal ascétique, c'est-à-
dire de renoncement aux jouissances du monde, la nature humaine protesta. Ce conflit entre « l'esprit du siècle » et « l'esprit chrétien » avait pris un caractère menaçant au xvi⁰ siècle.
Une réaction vigoureuse au nom des idées de la tradition avait
cependant, au xvii⁰ siècle, étouffé temporairement ces velléités
d'émancipation. Elles reparurent plus fortes au xviii⁰ ; et
nous voyons alors que, inconscients du sens historique des
mœurs chrétiennes, incapables d'apprécier les motifs qui
en auraient justifié peut-être encore l'existence et n'en compre-
nant que les abus et les déformations, les penseurs se sentirent
saisis d'un profond désir de secouer la morale ecclésiastique
de renoncement ; ils ne voyaient dans celle-ci que l'homme
condamné à la souffrance, à la résignation, à la *vertu* ; ils as-
piraient à céder aux sollicitations du cœur, de la « nature »,
et de ce qui leur semblait « raisonnable ».

Les réclamations des écrivains gagnaient accès dans les
cœurs d'autant plus aisément que les conditions sociales,
loin de s'améliorer depuis la mort de Louis XIV, allaient en
empirant : d'une part, l'abîme entre des privilégiés de ce
monde et des opprimés était plus profond, — le luxe inso-
lent des grands narguait la misère du peuple plus que jamais ;
et d'ailleurs l'idéal médiéval de la souffrance qui serait bonne,
avait perdu prise sur les esprits presque complètement ;
d'autre part, les désirs d'émancipation devinrent plus irré-
sistibles parce que les pouvoirs établis, sentant justement le
danger de la révolte, voulurent au lieu de faire des concessions utiles, essayer de la conjurer en usant des moyens de
contrainte que l'organisation sociale leur donnait ; ces tentatives de réduction par la force exaspérèrent les aspirations
des victimes.

Rousseau paraît alors ; et l'on voit bien que si les problèmes qui ont préoccupé Rousseau et son temps n'étaient pas nouveaux — loin de là — les circonstances l'étaient bien réellement. Rousseau parut au moment d'une irrésistible poussée dans le va-et-vient du « rythme psychologique » des peuples — comme l'aurait appelé M. Cazamian. Il paraît au moment où une puissante onde romantique (ou d'affranchissement moral) succédait à une longue onde classique (ou de discipline morale) ; et au moment où cette onde parvenait au sommet de sa courbe et était sur le point de déferler dans un mouvement de descente vertigineuse.

Un mot. Nous avons parlé du Christianisme spécifiquement dans le sens de doctrine de renoncement moral dirigée contre les dispositions naturelles. C'est là, croyons-nous, le côté du christianisme qui importe réellement. Sa morale de renoncement est sertie, c'est vrai, dans un vaste corps de doctrines métaphysiques et croyances religieuses ; mais, de celles-ci, les unes sont d'un ordre sentimental qui peut revêtir un caractère a-pragmatique, et qui quoique constituant un grand mouvement de pensée séculaire, demeurent proprement en dehors ou au-dessus du problème fondamental ; les autres sont, comme nous avons essayé de le montrer dans les pages précédentes, des dogmes requis directement ou indirectement par les théologiens moralistes pour accréditer et soutenir leur code civilisateur et leurs préceptes de renoncement. Or, nous avons bien conscience que la conception du christianisme comme simple doctrine morale anti-nature peut paraître archaïque et étrange ici, surtout à l'heure actuelle où l'abbé Henri Bremond, successeur des Fénelon et des François de Sales, remet en honneur avec tant de grâce et d'érudition le christianisme souriant. La question est de savoir qui, de lui ou de nous, est dans la tradition. Ces modernes — car l'abbé Bremond n'est pas le seul — ont-ils le droit d'être infidèles à la tradition catholique de l'excellence de la souffrance en soi, du renoncement sur la terre, de la valeur du martyre, etc. et de s'appeler encore catholiques ? Leur attitude, en effet, est très différente de celle du clergé du moyen âge, qui pour des raisons pratiques et psychologiques, en vertu de la faiblesse humaine, autorisaient, à part eux, des entorses aux principes, *mais* gardaient rigoureusement ceux-ci. Non, cette tendance actuelle de christianisme eudaimoniste — condamnée autrefois en tout cas chez Fénelon sinon chez François de Sales — et que l'abbé Bremond est obligé d'aller déterrer dans un tas de vieux bouquins et manuscrits qui sommeillaient, avec l'assentiment de l'Église, sous la poussière d'un oubli profond, est une preuve de la justesse de notre conception des choses. C'est le fait qu'on sent qu'en dernière analyse le christianisme doit pour vivre viser au bonheur en général (dans ce monde comme ailleurs), qui a inspiré cette forme si peu orthodoxe quoique prétendant l'être si fort. Et justement, les Bremond et les Montherlant, les Masson et les Giraud et toute cette marée montante de catholiques actuels cessent de prendre à l'égard du romantisme et de Rousseau cette attitude hostile qui était de tradition dans l'Église, et même les traitent avec singulièrement d'égard ; s'ils le font c'est qu'ils sentent chez lui un allié possible pour ce christianisme eudaimoniste analogue au leur et si différent de celui de saint Paul, de saint Augustin, de Bossuet, de Pascal, etc. (1).

Qu'on suive du reste les polémiques passionnées sur Rousseau chez les catholiques de toutes nuances au cours de ces 25 ou 30 dernières années, on verra bien que le débat s'oriente de plus en plus vers le problème pragmatique : Les idées de Rousseau sont-elle bonnes pour le bien-être social, ou lui sont-elles funestes ? non pas : sont-elles vraies ? Les Lemaitre, les Barrès, les Maurras, les Bourget, les Carrère, les Maritain, etc. n'ont voulu voir du romantisme et de Rousseau que leur effet d'anarchie sociale.

NOTE. — Nous aurons à examiner ce point au sujet de la *Profession de foi du Vicaire savoyard* — P.-M. MASSON dans son ouvrage sur la *Religion de Rousseau* appuie essentiellement sur la religion sentimentale de Rousseau.

(1) Ce problème fort intéressant mérite une étude à part ; nous en avons donné quelques éléments dans une petite publication récente : *La pensée religieuse de Rousseau et ses récents interprètes* (Alcan, 1927, 52 p.)

CHAPITRE II

ROUSSEAU DEVANT SON SIÈCLE
LE CONFLIT CHEZ L'HOMME ROUSSEAU

1. Rousseau romantique et Rousseau romain.

De très bonne heure, deux dispositions en sens contraire se manifestent chez l'enfant : l'une résultant des soins donnés à un être né très frêle et que l'on choie ; les souffrances intensifient la conscience du *moi* et la sensibilité qui constitueront une *nature romantique* ; l'autre sera le résultat de l'atmosphère calviniste de Genève et de lectures abondantes de Plutarque qui constituera ce qu'il a appelé lui-même une « *âme romaine* ».

2. Rousseau romantique.

A 11 ans, Rousseau est seul au monde. Tout concourt à affaiblir les aspirations romaines et accentuer au contraire le romantisme. La vie est sévère ; il s'étonne, puis se révolte, et quitte Genève. Son manque d'expérience et sa difficulté à comprendre les leçons de la vie en Italie, les bontés de Mme de Warens, son instruction décousue, sa gaucherie à Paris, ne font qu'exaspérer son *moi*. En même temps tout cela a accumulé en lui un profond dégoût de la vie de bohème et des mensonges sociaux — ce qui par contraste, le rejette aux idées « romaines ». La crise de Vincennes est à la porte.

NOTE sur Rousseau et la Psychiâtrie.

I. — ROUSSEAU ROMANTIQUE ET ROUSSEAU ROMAIN

Il nous faut maintenant reprendre le sujet complémentaire à celui du chapitre précédent, c'est-à-dire faire voir que Rousseau était particulièrement préparé à sentir ces problèmes. Nous disons *reprendre*, car certes nous n'avons pas la naïveté de prétendre ici à aucune originalité ; l'assertion, et si l'on

veut la démonstration, a été faite maintes fois que les conditions dans lesquelles naquit et vécut le Rousseau des premières années furent telles qu'elles ont contribué à le prédispo-
ser à sentir plus qu'un autre les problèmes du temps. En vertu
cependant de l'exposé de notre premier chapitre, nous pouvons
examiner ces conditions sous une forme à la fois plus large et
plus définie.

On s'appuie généralement sur tels antécédents dans la vie
de Rousseau, ou sur tels traits de caractère ; — et on le fait
selon que soi-même on veut appuyer sur tel côté de la pensée
de Rousseau ou sur tel autre ; sur son romantisme par exemple
(Lasserre, Seillière, Babbitt), ou sur son puritanisme (Dide,
Valette) ; ou, quand on tient compte à la fois de tendances
diverses de son esprit, cela a été simplement pour les juxtapo-
ser, et souligner peut-être l'interne incohérence, mais en ren-
voyant dos à dos les différentes personnalités et en disant :
malgré cela Rousseau a agi sur son temps (Faguet). Nous es-
timons, nous, que l'on ne procède point ainsi de la bonne manière, et nous ne ferons pas d'efforts particuliers pour trouver
chez Rousseau une personnalité simple, ou harmonieuse dans
la complexité. Si ce que nous apprenons de lui manifeste quelque unité, fort bien ; mais en cas contraire nous ne chercherons
pas à aller contre la réalité, imaginant que c'est notre devoir
de créer cette unité où elle n'existe pas. Et même, puisque nous
sommes disposés d'emblée à voir en Rousseau un esprit ouvert
aux courants d'idées divers de son siècle, nous considèrerons
comme plutôt naturel de trouver un esprit marqué lui-même
de ces tendances différentes.

Puisque nous parlons psychologie il sera opportum de prévenir d'ailleurs en passant un autre malentendu. D'éléments
disparates, peut-être violemment contradictoires, il ne faut pas
conclure nécessairement à infériorité ou monstruosité. Dans
son volume massif *J.-J. Rousseau* — déjà cité — M. Seillière
a fait de l'homme de Genève un portrait sombre et repoussant,
et présentant les pires tares et les pires marques de dégénéres-
cence. Si on ne sentait quelqu'un qui déteste les idées de Rous-

seau, il y aurait lieu de s'indigner ; mais les traits qui pourraient être justes chez M. Seillière trahiraient aussi bien simplement une nature variée et qui vibre à tous les souffles. D'ailleurs
les recherches de psychologie moderne ne tendent-elles pas
vers cette constatation que l'homme est le plus souvent un
composé d'éléments hétérogènes, fréquemment et bizarrement
en lutte les uns avec les autres. Et nous sommes tentés de
mettre en regard de l'affreuse grimace de Rousseau dessinée
par M. Seillière les réflexions d'un psychologue moderne,
P. Mendousse, qui dans l'*Ame de l'adolescent* (Alcan), écrit :

« Peut-être ne serait-il pas excessif d'affirmer que tout adolescent normal doit présenter dans sa mentalité un mélange de génie
et de folie, et peut-être y a-t-il lieu de craindre pour la vitalité d'un
grand garçon trop bien équilibré. La genèse d'une vitalité morale,
maîtresse d'elle-même, implique comme sa principale condition
un appel constant aux virtualités émotives ».

... Du reste, qu'on nous pardonne cette citation à l'adresse
de tant des commentateurs chagrins de Rousseau ; si nous ne
croyons pas, comme M. Seillière, que Rousseau ait été un
monstre, nous ne croyons pas davantage que le manque d'équilibre mental soit le chemin nécessaire pour la virilité morale.

Un autre point encore sur lequel nous désirons attirer l'attention, c'est que nous ne nous contenterons pas de l'explication
par l'hérédité pour la psychologie de l'homme Rousseau.

Et sans doute, il ne peut être question de nier dogmatiquement l'hérédité au moins physiologique — comme le
faisait Helvétius du temps de Rousseau ; et Ribot (*Hérédité
psychologique*) a le droit de dire : puisque nous savons absolument qu'il y a influence de nos sensations sur nos sentiments
et sur nos émotions, partant sur nos pensées mêmes, il est
impossible de nier l'hérédité psychologique. Mais d'abord,
fort souvent au moins, on attribue à ce facteur de l'hérédité des
choses qu'il n'est nullement nécessaire de lui attribuer ; par
exemple, des effets de simple imitation consciente ou inconsciente de l'entourage immédiat. Qui dira, dans une famille

de musiciens, ce qui est hérédité et ce qui est imitation et admiration des parents ? et pourquoi ne pas dire que le métier
d'horloger peut être héréditaire comme la vocation musicale ?

En outre, et surtout, du point de vue qui nous intéresse ici,
l'hérédité n'est pas une explication. Que vous disiez : « tel trait
de caractère est là, parce qu'il est là », ou : « tel trait est là
parce qu'il était chez son père et chez sa mère », en quoi *com-
prendrez*-vous mieux ? En tout cas, tandis que les éléments
hérités — car encore un coup nous ne voulons pas nier qu'il y
en ait — échappent à notre emprise, il y a toujours, à côté, une
part du *moi* que nous n'avons pas à accepter comme un *x*, et
qui est susceptible d'analyse et de compréhension. Il y a plus ;
il est certain que plus un individu est supérieurement organisé,
plus les dispositions innées ou éléments hérités, seront suscep-
tibles de modifications, — car il sera plus sensible à toute modification par les événements. En d'autres termes, plus on a
affaire à un humain d'une mentalité accusée et supérieure —
comme Rousseau — plus le facteur d'hérédité diminue d'importance dans la formation du *moi* ; et dès lors, plus on peut
tenir compte des contingences pour expliquer son être psychique (1).

(1) Nous savons bien que Rousseau a été le tout premier à recourir à l'hérédité
pour expliquer ce qu'il pensait être un trait fondamental de son être, son romantisme. Il dit de ses parents : « Leurs amours avaient commencé presque
avant leur vie ; dès l'âge de 8 à 9 ans ils se promenaient ensemble tous les soirs
sur la Treille ; à 10 ans, ils ne pouvaient plus se quitter. Tous deux, nés tendres
et sensibles, n'attendaient que le moment de trouver dans un autre la même
disposition... Le sort qui semblait contrarier leur passion ne fit que l'animer. Le
jeune amant, ne pouvant obtenir sa maîtresse, se consumait de douleur ; elle
lui conseilla de voyager pour l'oublier. Il voyagea sans fruit et revint plus amoureux que jamais... » (VIII, 2). Cela semblait être dans la famille : « Gabriel Bernard, frère de ma mère, devint amoureux d'une des sœurs de mon père ;
mais elle ne consentit à l'épouser qu'à condition que son frère épouserait la
sœur ». Et Rousseau conclut : « Tels furent les auteurs de mes jours. De tous les
dons que le ciel leur avait départis, un cœur sensible est le seul qu'ils me laissèrent » (3). *Mais*, d'abord, on sait aujourd'hui que Rousseau s'est mépris sur
mainte chose concernant sa parenté. (Le romantique double mariage d'une
sœur Bernard avec un frère Rousseau et d'un frère Bernard avec une sœur
Rousseau, qui aurait eu lieu le même jour est une « histoire » ; une des

Essayons donc, en prenant le caractère de Rousseau comme un effet avant de le prendre comme une cause, et en nous abstenant de demander aucun secours à l'explication par l'hérédité, à quoi nous arriverons. Et si nous n'expliquons pas tout, ce que nous obtiendrons sera du moins une vraie explication, sera solide et utilisable.

§ 1. Partons de cette simple donnée : « Je naquis infirme et malade » (2) (1) ; et plus bas : « J'étais né presque mourant, on espérait peu me conserver » (3).

Chez un être souffrant, la conscience du *moi* s'éveille tôt. Un enfant ne réfléchit guère qu'il existe avant que cette réflexion s'impose à lui ; et c'est la souffrance qui est l'occasion de l'éveil de la conscience (2) du *moi* ; naturellement, l'enfant pensera alors à la cessation de la souffrance. Et plus la souffrance est prolongée, ou fréquente, ou forte, plus la conscience du *moi* devient intense ; plus aussi l'enfant pense à ce qui est, en ce moment de l'existence, la seule forme concevable du bonheur, l'absence de souffrance. C'est dire que l'intelligence se développe en conséquence de la conscience du *moi*, et presque simultanément avec elle. C'est dire encore qu'un enfant bien portant sera moins intelligent en général qu'un enfant débile. D'ailleurs, le premier sera confirmé toujours davantage dans l'inconscience ou positivisme initiaux qui ne favorisent point la réflexion ; tandis que le second porte en lui les germes d'une imagination qui de négative deviendra positive et romantique : il rêvera bientôt dans un monde romantique un *moi* romantique. (Il est bien entendu d'ailleurs que les cir-

tantes dont Rousseau dit qu'elle fut toute sage et vertueuse, fauta avant le mariage) ; ensuite, on n'a pas épuisé Rousseau quand on a dit qu'il était romantique ; enfin Rousseau lui-même sera loin d'ignorer dans la suite des *Confessions* les actions des contingences sur la formation de son être ; on le verra tout à l'heure.

(1) Les chiffres entre parenthèses indiquent les pages du volume VIII des *Œuvres* de Rousseau, édition Hachette. C'est le premier volume des *Confessions*.

(2) Pour être bien sûr de n'être pas mal compris — le langage de la psychologie étant si peu précis — il faudrait dire la *conscience consciente du moi*.

constances peuvent donner l'occasion au bien portant de se rattraper plus tard intellectuellement ; mais généralement l'autre garde son avance ; un homme heureux développe rarement son intelligence).

Sans doute les premières souffrances sont toutes physiques ; mais cela n'importe pas à une période de la vie où le bien-être physique peut seul compter ; pourtant les souffrances physiques, chez l'être dont l'intelligence est éveillée maintenant, vont entraîner tantôt à leur suite des souffrances nettement morales : le faible, si même il n'est pas écrasé dès l'enfance par des forts (parents grossiers, camarades inconsciemment cruels), comprend son infériorité ; il est exposé à des maux inconnus aux forts ; ceux-ci ont des joies auxquelles il ne peut aspirer ; et il se sent mal préparé à la lutte pour la vie ; la révolte est inutile pour un être faible ; l'idée du destin s'impose à son esprit ; il se résigne de cette résignation triste et touchante qui est devenue une des caractéristiques du romantisme. (C'est cet élément de souffrance qui le distingue du romanesque.)

Nous venons de définir le cas de Rousseau, « né presque mourant » : « Je sentis avant de penser, c'est le sort commun de l'humanité, je l'éprouvai plus qu'un autre » (3), dit-il parlant de sa première enfance. « Sentir » c'est vague, « souffrir » serait suffisant et en même temps plus révélateur. Rousseau, comme tous les analyseurs de caractères de nos jours, emploie « sentir » pour « comprendre », et réserve le mot « comprendre » pour « comprendre qu'on comprend ».

Écartons ici une objection possible. D'après certains médecins, Rousseau aurait été un malade imaginaire (il ne s'agit pas ici de la question de la folie, mais uniquement des maux physiques). Psychologiquement parlant, cela ne fait pas grande différence. Naturellement, cela ne peut s'appliquer à la première enfance ; un enfant doit avoir éprouvé la souffrance avant de pouvoir l'imaginer ; il faut même déjà un développement psychologique considérable pour être malade imaginaire. Et, plus tard, qu'un homme soit malade ou qu'il se croie malade, les résultats pour la formation du caractère sont les mêmes.

Dugas, dont la petite étude sur *la Timidité* (Alcan. 5ᵉ éd., 1910) devrait être méditée par quiconque s'occupe de Rousseau — on éviterait ainsi ces superficielles condamnations de sa personne si fréquentes sous les meilleures plumes — avait déjà noté ces divers rapports psychologiques, seulement il les appliquait au caractère tout fait : « L'excès de sensibilité développe en lui une clairvoyance aiguë » (p. 55). On le voit, Dugas part de l'idée que la sensibilité est innée; ce n'est pas nécessaire ; seule la faculté de sentir est là ; la sensibilité (ou hypertrophie de la faculté de sentir) est développée graduellement par la cause externe de la souffrance. Dugas décrit plus bas, de la même manière que nous, l'intervention de l'imagination. « Il [un caractère comme celui de Rousseau] se crée une société idéale, celle des livres, qui lui renvoient l'écho agrandi de tous ses sentiments si subtils qu'ils soient, si romanesques qu'il les juge lui-même » (p. 95). Pas n'est besoin toujours d'attendre les livres ; mais ceux-ci sans doute concourent à développer l'imagination une fois qu'elle a pris son essor ; nous verrons, à propos de Rousseau, combien cela se vérifie. Enfin, Dugas remonte aux origines de ce que nous avons appelé la tristesse romantique, en disant : « Il croit à la trahison comme il croit à l'amitié ; sans ombres de preuve, sur la foi d'apparences souvent trompeuses : un regard effrayant surpris dans les yeux d'un ennemi imaginaire lui révèle toute une suite de machinations et de complots » (p. 58). Cela se rapporte à l'adulte ; mais l'enfant déforme tout autant la réalité.

Un enfant qui souffre et qui s'est une fois rendu comtpe de sa souffrance, n'en reste pas là. Partant de la sienne, il comprend la souffrance d'autrui et y compatit. Son intelligence éveillée l'entraîne naturellement. Et c'est uniquement une affaire d'intelligence. En effet, pourquoi, ou plutôt comment, le bien portant ou l'heureux sympathiserait-il avec une souffrance qu'il ne connaît pas ? Au contraire, comment le souffrant ne sympathiserait-il pas ? Alors, l'enfant ressentant la souffrance non seulement pour lui, mais pour tous ceux dont le sort est pareil au sien, sa tristesse et son romantisme s'accroît de toute la grandeur des souffrances des autres ; il rêve un monde dont ces choses soient absentes pour ses semblables comme pour lui ; et, en tant que cela dépend de lui, il cherche même à réaliser cet idéal.

Nombre de scènes des jeunes années de Rousseau trahissent en lui ces dispositions. Un jour son frère est rudement châtié par son père : « Je me jetai impétueusement entre-deux, l'embrassant étroitement. Je le couvris ainsi de mon corps, recevant les coups qui lui étaient portés... » (4). Revenu à Genève, de Bossey où il avait été en pension avec son cousin Bernard (1), il défend ce dernier plus chétif que lui contre les gamins de la rue. « Me voilà déjà redresseur de tort » (17) ; il avait douze ans. Il aime mieux souffrir en silence que de causer de la souffrance en dénonçant un camarade qui lui écrase les doigts entre deux cylindres de machine et un autre qui manque de le tuer d'un coup de maillet sur la tête (4e *Rêverie*). Et son imagination s'exalte jusqu'à prendre le moyen pour le but, à voir dans la souffrance une vertu en soi ; ainsi quand il imite Scévola en mettant sa main sur un réchaud brûlant (4).

Tout enfant est faible, donc tout enfant souffre ; donc son intelligence est tôt éveillée ; donc tout enfant est bon ; donc tout enfant est romantique. Et ce serait le cas surtout des petites filles, plus frêles que les garçons, et d'enfants de pauvres plus que d'enfants de riches — sauf le cas de maladie où la différence est réduite. Cependant, les impressions d'enfance sont fugitives ; le sens de la force, faisant oublier la souffrance, efface le sens de la pitié ; chez l'homme généralement, et chez la femme qui est heureuse dans le monde, aussi.

Tel ne fut pas le cas pour Rousseau. « Je l'éprouvai [le sort commun de l'humanité] plus qu'un autre » ; ce qui signifie pour nous : j'eus plus d'inclinations romantiques qu'un autre enfant. Comment peut-il dire cela ? En raison de ce fait que

---

(1) Le père de Rousseau avait, à la suite d'une querelle, quitté Genève pour se soustraire à la condamnation prononcée par les tribunaux.

non seulement il fut plus maladif que maint enfant (1), mais il fut élevé avec une tendresse extrême. On le soigne ; on le dorlotte ; on l'empêche de mourir. Il avait perdu sa mère en naissant ; une tante, dit-il « femme aimable et sage, prit si grand soin de moi qu'elle me sauva... chère tante, je vous pardonne de m'avoir fait vivre » (3). Et souvenons-nous que les soins non naturels de la tante, ou de l'étrangère — « ma mie Jacqueline » — ont presque nécessairement, surtout quand il s'agit d'enfant chétif, quelque chose d'artificiel ; c'est la femme qui joue à la mère sans l'être et qui force les gestes. Rousseau répète cent fois les soins extraordinaires dont il fut l'objet : « J'avais un frère plus âgé que moi de sept ans, l'extrême affection qu'on avait pour moi le faisait un peu négliger » (4) ; « les enfants de rois ne sauraient être soignés avec plus de zèle que je ne le fus pendant mes premiers ans » (5) ; « mes volontés étaient si peu excitées et si peu contrariées qu'il ne me venait pas dans l'esprit d'en avoir. Je puis jurer que, jusqu'à mon asservissement sous un maître, je n'ai jamais su ce qu'était une fantaisie » (5 et cf. p. 42) ; etc. Rien de plus propre à développer, chez un enfant délicat déjà et sensible, plus de délicatesse encore et plus de sensibilité ; plus de souffrances morales et plus de romantisme. Il en est de la sensibilité comme des muscles, qu'on développe en les exerçant.

Qui ne se rappelle, au premier livre des *Confessions*, l'histoire de Bossey, quand, accusé d'avoir cassé un peigne, Rousseau est injustement et brutalement châtié. Cinquante ans après, il en est tout ému encore.

« La douleur du corps, quoique vive, m'était peu sensible ; je ne sentais que l'indignation, la rage, le désespoir. Mon cousin, dans un cas à peu près semblable, et qu'on avait puni d'une faute involontaire comme d'un acte prémédité, se mettait en fureur à mon exemple et se montait pour ainsi dire à mon unisson. Tous deux, dans le même lit, nous nous embrassions avec des transports con-

---

(1) Il parle ailleurs de « robuste constitution » (VIII, 256), mais c'est de plus tard qu'il s'agit, et nous allons justement voir comment, malgré cela, il resta, lui, sensible.

vulsifs, nous étouffions ; et, quand nos jeunes cœurs un peu soula-
gés pouvaient exhaler leur colère, nous nous levions sur notre séant
et nous nous mettions tous deux à crier cent fois de toute notre force :
Carnifex ! Carnifex ! Carnifex ! Je sens en écrivant ceci que mon
pouls s'élève encore ; ces moments me seront toujours présents,
quand je vivrais mille ans » (12).

Et, quelques lignes plus bas, il établit lui-même la relation
de son caractère une fois formé et de ses écrits avec ces impressions d'enfance, montrant comment sa pitié ne resta pas
égoïste, mais s'étendit à tout ce qui souffrait autour de lui, « se
détacha de tout intérêt personnel » :

« Quand je lis les cruautés d'un tyran féroce, les subtiles noirceurs
d'un fourbe de prêtre, je partirais volontiers pour aller poignarder
ces misérables, dussé-je cent fois y périr. Je me suis souvent mis
en nage à poursuivre à la course ou à coups de pierre un coq, une
vache, un chien, un animal que j'en voyais tourmenter un autre,
uniquement parce qu'il se sentait le plus fort, Ce mouvement peut
m'être naturel et je crois qu'il l'est ; mais le souvenir profond de la
première injustice que j'ai soufferte y fut trop longtemps et trop
fortement lié pour ne l'avoir pas beaucoup renforcé » (12).

Ici une remarque importante. On a accusé Rousseau de s'être
rendu meilleur qu'il n'était. Cela n'est nullement nécessaire.
Tout revient au contraire, quand on part des données mêmes
livrées par Rousseau, à une aspiration profonde et banale à
être heureux ; en effet, en cultivant le *moi* de l'enfant et en
développant sa sensibilité, comme nous l'avons vu, son entourage a rendu Rousseau tel que son bonheur ne peut être atteint
qu'à la condition du bonheur de tous les hommes. Cette condition, qui a l'air si généreuse, est d'une si fantastique prétention, elle met le bonheur à un prix si exorbitant, étant donné
les circonstances du monde réel, que l'on voit bien que Rousseau n'a pas abandonné son romantisme, son *moi*, en devenant
humanitaire. Rousseau a connu cette faiblesse, et disons, si on
veut employer un gros mot, cette lâcheté de beaucoup de gens
qui préfèrent ignorer la misère ; non pas pour ne pas la
secourir, mais pour ne pas en souffrir. « C'est parce qu'il aime

les hommes qu'il les fuit, car il souffre moins de leurs maux quand il ne les voit pas. » (Vallette, *Rousseau Genevois*, p. 361.) Et si, sans doute, Rousseau, pas plus que ceux qui ont interprété contre lui les *Confessions*, n'a présenté son cas avec toute la clarté désirable, s'il a cru peut-être parfois à une réelle bonté morale en lui, alors qu'il recherchait simplement au fond ce qui lui était le plus agréable, il ne manque pas de passages où lui-même reconnaît qu'il a été « bon » parce qu'il avait des raisons pour ne pas être mauvais (1) ; et, en tous cas, lui-même nous fournit tous les éléments de la démonstration que, s'il est magnanime, il n'a aucun mérite à être ce que les circonstances l'ont fait.

Rousseau a non seulement une sympathie violente pour ceux qui souffrent, mais, en vertu des mêmes dispositions appliquées avec conscience, il manifeste en même temps une indulgence extraordinaire pour ceux qui sont obligés de faire souffrir — car, selon lui, ils doivent souffrir de faire souffrir. Comme enfant déjà, il était plus affligé « de déplaire que d'être puni » (8) ; et, plus tard, il poussa toujours plus avant cette intelligence subtile de la recherche du bien-être, étendant le manteau de l'indulgence sur ceux qui par paresse ou incurie font du tort aux autres ; surtout si l'autre c'est lui, il excuse toujours, songeant à la souffrance que représenterait pour certains la lutte contre la paresse ou la nature. Ainsi, après avoir raconté les efforts vraiment trop sommaires de son père pour le retrouver quand, enfant, il s'était enfui de Genève, Rousseau conclut :

« Mon père n'était pas seulement un homme d'honneur..., il était bon père, surtout pour moi. Il m'aimait très tendrement ; mais il

---

(1) Voir entre autres la 6e *Rêverie*, dont le texte est dans ces mots : « Je sais et je sens que faire du bien est le plus vrai bonheur que le cœur humain puisse goûter. » (IX, 366.) On y lit aussi (p. 371) : « Si j'eusse été le possesseur de l'anneau de Gygès, il m'eût tiré de la dépendance des hommes et les eût mis dans la mienne... Maître de contenter mes désirs... qu'aurais-je pu désirer avec quelque suite ? Une seule chose : c'eût été de voir tous les cœurs contents ; l'aspect de la félicité publique eût pu seul toucher mon cœur d'un sentiment permanent, et l'ardent désir d'y concourir eût été ma plus constante passion. »

aimait aussi ses plaisirs... [ce qui] ralentissait quelquefois son zèle qu'il eût poussé plus loin sans cela » (37-38).

Plus déconcertante encore est sa sympathie pour tous ceux qui jouissent, même en trichant, à ses propres dépens. Quand il apprend que Claude Anet est l'amant de « Maman », comme lui, il décrit ainsi ses sentiments :

« Au lieu de prendre en aversion celui qui me l'avait soufflée, je sentis réellement s'étendre à lui l'attachement que j'avais pour elle. Je désirais sur toute chose qu'elle fût heureuse et, puisqu'elle avait besoin de lui pour l'être, j'étais content qu'il fût heureux aussi » (126).

Et quand Vintzenried le chasse tout à fait du cœur de Mme de Warens, Rousseau se résigne à son sort, et :

« Le premier fruit de cette disposition si désintéressée fut d'écarter de mon cœur tout sentiment de haine et d'envie contre celui qui m'avait supplanté : je voulus au contraire, et je voulus sincèrement, m'attacher à ce jeune homme, travailler à son éducation, lui faire sentir son bonheur, l'en rendre digne s'il était possible » (189).

Aussi l'a-t-on accusé de manque de fierté et d'absence totale de sens moral. Si on veut ; seulement il faudrait pourtant tenir compte alors de ce fait qu'il n'est pas immoral à son profit ; c'est au profit des autres et *à ses propres dépens* ; et il est un peu ridicule d'accuser un homme qui est différemment et réellement plus moral que les autres (si moral signifie désintéressé) de ne l'être pas du tout ; son immoralité consiste à ne pas réclamer ce qui, aux yeux des hommes ordinaires, constituerait des droits ; ce n'est pas de l'immoralité, c'est de l'hypermoralité.

Il reste d'ailleurs toujours vrai aussi que cette hypermoralité était plus agréable à Rousseau même que la moralité courante, puisqu'il souffre vraiment plus de la souffrance ou de la privation d'autrui que de la sienne propre ; mais cela ne change rien au fait que le monde a mauvaise grâce à lui reprocher ces dispositions-là.

Cette préoccupation de la souffrance humaine chez Rousseau est confirmée dans le 2ᵉ *Discours*, en 1753. Il se demande quelles sont les dispositions fondamentales de l'être humain avant le développement de la raison (c'est-à-dire simplement les dispositions absolument fondamentales) ; il répond en s'interrogeant lui-même : 1º l'instinct de conservation ; 2º la répugnance « à voir périr ou souffrir tout être sensible et principalement son semblable » (I, 81, cf. 98-9, 109-110, 113) ; et, dans sa réponse à Ch. Bonnet (Philopolis), qui lui demandait comment il se fait, si l'homme est naturellement bon, que la populace se repaît avec tant d'avidité du spectacle d'un malheureux expiant sur la roue », ce mot bien Rousseauesque : « La pitié est un sentiment si délicieux qu'il n'est pas étonnant qu'on cherche à l'éprouver » (I, 157) (1).

Une circonstance particulière contribua encore à enfoncer Rousseau dans ses dispositions romantiques. On pourvut abondamment l'esprit de l'enfant des éléments nécessaires pour pousser son imagination à substituer au monde de la réalité un monde de rêves. Son père s'était chargé de cela. Déjà il avait mis aux champs cette imagination de Jean-Jacques, en s'abandonnant à ses douleurs d'une façon si théâtrale à propos de la mère de l'enfant : « Quand il me disait Jean-Jacques parlons de ta mère, je lui disais : Eh bien ! mon père, nous allons donc pleurer ! Et ce mot seul lui tirait déjà des larmes » (3). Sans doute un enfant peut toujours pâtir de l'absence d'une mère, mais comment en souffrirait-il puisqu'il ignore ce qu'est une mère ; dites-lui cependant qu'il est privé d'un bien inestimable, il n'a pas de raison pour en douter, il s'en forme une image idéale à sa façon, et il s'afflige.

Mais le père fit mieux encore ; il apprit à lire à l'enfant dans les romans — les romans de la bibliothèque de sa mère : « Nous

(1) Il dit évidemment le contraire de ce qu'il veut, car, exprimée ainsi, la phrase contredirait sa thèse de « la répugnance à voir souffrir » ; mais, si l'argument est détestable, le sentiment subjectif qui l'a inspiré est très clair : comment résister au sentiment de la pitié, comment cet empressement de témoigner sa sympathie au pauvre roué ne se manifesterait-il pas C'est pour plaindre le supplicié, non pour le moquer, qu'on va « avec tant d'avidité » au « spectacle ».

lisions tour à tour, sans relâche, et passions des nuits à cette occupation » (3). Quels étaient ces romans ? Nous le savons par les indications de Rousseau ; c'était l'*Astrée* et les grands romans « précieux » du XVIIe siècle, encore à la mode au début du XVIIIe siècle. Il faisait allusion directement au *Grand Cyrus* (1644-1653) de Mlle de Scudéry, à *Cassandre* (1542) et à *Cléopâtre* (1647) de la Calprenède.

« En peu de temps j'acquis, par cette dangereuse méthode, non seulement une extrême facilité à lire et à m'entendre, mais une intelligence unique à mon âge sur les passions... Les émotions confuses, que j'éprouvai coup sur coup, n'altéraient point la raison que je n'avais pas encore ; mais elles m'en formèrent une d'une autre trempe et me donnèrent de la vie humaine des notions bizarres et romanesques, dont l'expérience et la réflexion n'ont jamais bien pu me guérir » (3-4).

Naturellement, Rousseau étant enfant, ces sentiments affectés et ces préciosités de l'amour ne lui apparaissaient pas sous leur forme creuse et vaine ; il croyait à leur sincérité, il s'échauffait à ces scènes de passion artificielles. C'est là un phénomène qui n'a rien d'extraordinaire, même chez des adultes. Ainsi, lorsque, le 2 octobre 1762, l'*Orphée* de Glück fut pour la première fois représenté à la cour de Vienne, il fut applaudi, mais personne ne se douta jusqu'à quelque temps après l'événement que c'était une œuvre révolutionnaire. C'est que la révolution consistait en ceci : substituer des sentiments sincères à des sentiments artificiels ; comme les seconds imitent les premiers, et que les premiers sont les modèles des seconds rien de plus facile pour un public ordinaire de prendre les uns pour les autres ; les auditeurs de Glück à la cour de Vienne se trouvant en présence de sentiments sincères les ont pris pour des sentiments artificiels, car c'est ce qu'ils demandaient de l'art, comme *vice versa* une personne simple, même de nos jours, goûtera l'*Astrée* ou les sentimentalités de Métastase et des Italiens de l'époque, car ils n'ont pas l'idée d'y chercher des contrefaçons (1).

(1) La confusion était d'autant plus facile qu'*Orphée et Euridice* était un thème mythologique, exactement comme ceux qui servaient de prétexte aux

Cette illusion dura chez Rousseau jusqu'après la vingtième année ; il raconte qu'à l'époque de son deuxième passage à Lyon (1731), Mlle du Châtelet lui donna à lire *Gil Blas* : « Je le lus avec plaisir, mais je n'étais pas encore mûr pour ces sortes de lectures ; il me fallait des romans à grands sentiments » (121). Dans la deuxième *Préface* à la *Nouvelle Héloïse*, il déclare ne pas écrire pour de « nouveaux Céladons » — c'est qu'alors il s'était donc avisé de la différence.

§ 2. Mais en même temps qu'il subissait les différentes influences que nous avons dites, et qui ne pouvaient pas ne point former une nature d'un romantisme exalté, il en subissait d'autres en sens directement contraire. Tout, autour de lui, dès qu'il franchissait le seuil de la maison paternelle, prêchait précisément la contrainte des passions et le renoncement aux jouissances de la vie, les dangers mortels de l'imagination romanesque ; en un mot, la négation du *moi* comme l'idéal d'une belle vie.

Calvin avait voulu que le véritable souverain de Genève fut Dieu ; il avait soumis le pouvoir temporel au pouvoir spirituel; et les pasteurs étaient les ministres du Tout-Puissant, c'est-à-dire les interprètes de la Révélation, les docteurs de la loi.

Une organisation pareille avait été le rêve de l'Église catholique, rêve que justement la Renaissance ébranlait au xvie siècle ; mais Calvin (avec cette différence purement formelle qu'il demandait à la Bible seule des arguments pour étayer sa politique et sa morale, au lieu de s'appuyer en même temps sur la tradition ecclésiastique) avait pu rétablir dans une petite ville ce que les papes ne réussissaient plus à maintenir dans le monde si ce n'est au prix de concessions équivalant à la consommation d'un lent suicide. Pour étouffer les résistances, il

---

opéras conventionnels de l'époque. Et ajoutons qu'il n'est pas improbable que le succès du *Devin de village* de Rousseau fut dû à un malentendu de cette sorte : c'était une pastorale sincère opposée à la pastorale artificielle ; Rousseau songeait à la première, alors que les courtisans — pères de ceux qui allaient jouer encore aux bergers et bergères au *Hameau* de Versailles avec Marie-Antoinette — applaudirent la seconde.

avait eu recours sans hésiter aux moyens violents de l'époque :
Castellion, le directeur du Collège de Genève fondé par Calvin
fut « démis du ministère » pour protestations contre le système
Césareo papiste » (1544) ; Arneaux, contestant à Calvin son rôle
d' « interprète de Dieu » dut pour pénitence « faire le tour de la
ville en chemise, tête nue, une torche allumée à la main et se
rendre ensuite devant le tribunal, crier merci à Dieu et à la
justice... » (1546). Bolsec, Gribaldo, Téliot, Letourneau furent
bannis comme hérétiques ; Narbert eut la langue percée d'un
fer rouge pour avoir proféré des injures contre Calvin et ses
ministres ; Gruet attaquant la législation eut la tête tranchée
et clouée au gibet à titre d'exemple (1547) ; Mounet et d'Ar-
gilières furent condamnés à mort pour hérésie, et en 1553 ce
fut le tour de Servet, brûlé pour avoir cherché à renverser les
« vrais fondements » de la religion chrétienne, et s'être « dressé
contre la majesté divine et la sainte Trinité (1) ». C'est Bèze
qui devait prononcer le mot si curieux à première vue dans la
bouche d'un protestant : *libertas conscientiæ, diabolicum
dogma*, et au collège de Genève, les écoliers devaient, avant
d'être inscrits, jurer qu'ils détestaient les erreurs renouvelées
par Servet et ses complices.

Le dogme si rigidement imposé était la base de la morale ; il
s'agissait de faire prévaloir le principe du Christianisme historique : le renoncement à la vie était la condition du salut. « Ils
firent revivre », écrit Dide (d'ailleurs empêché par ses préjugés
anti-protestants de saisir le sens des faits qu'il expose) « en
l'aggravant, l'ancien régime disciplinaire que l'ancienne autorité épiscopale avait établi, mais qu'elle avait laissé tomber
en désuétude. Ils retinrent du passé ce qu'il avait... d'inquisito-
rial et y ajoutèrent de nouvelles tracasseries [lisez contraintes].
Tous les actes de la vie furent soumis à la censure théologique... »

On proposa (1546) la suppression des tavernes, pour les

---

(1) Voir Choisy, *Théocratie à Genève au temps de Calvin* (1899) ; aussi Dide,
J.-J. Rousseau, le Protestantisme et la Révolution française (1911) ; G. Goyau,
Une Ville-Eglise, Genève 1535-1907. (2 vol. 1919).

remplacer par quatre « abbayes » présidées par des syndics et
le lieutenant ; l'hôte ne donnerait à manger et à boire qu'à ceux
qui feraient prière avant et après avoir mangé, les jeux seraient interdits, mais une bible serait là pour ceux qui vou-
draient y lire (la tentative du reste dut être abandonnée après
six mois). Après l'échauffourée de 1556 qui mit en péril la
théocratie calviniste, et où sept conspirateurs furent bannis et
sept exécutés, le système disciplinaire fut renforcé ; entre
autres on demanda la punition des personnes qui, après que la
Cène leur avait été refusée (une des peines les plus fréquemment prononcées) ne se souciaient pas de la redemander.
L'exécution de toutes les peines appartenait au pouvoir temporel, mais les sentences étaient prononcées par le « Consistoire » composé des ministres et de douze laïques. Ceux-ci, les
anciens, étaient choisis dans différents quartiers et faisaient
rapport tous les jeudis ; ils se censuraient entre eux, et cette
censure était faite régulièrement avant d'aller à la Table sainte.

A la fin du XVIIᵉ siècle, il est vrai, il y eut de légers adou-
cissements. Cependant Valette (*Rousseau Genevois*) trace un
tableau de Genève à la veille de la naissance de Rousseau qui
suffit à montrer que l'empreinte de Calvin était encore très
fortement marquée. C'était alors une petite ville de 18.500 habitants (environ 5.000 de plus qu'au temps de Calvin), dont
97 papistes, tant nourrices que familles savoyardes séjour-
nant avec permission, ce qui est un progrès sur le XVIᵉ siècle où
tout le monde doit être « instruit dans la foi » sous peine de
bannissement.

Quoiqu'on fût moins strict sur la question du dogme, cependant pour être citoyen il fallait adopter le *credo* du Consistoire (1). Le culte des domestiques qui avait lieu à 5 heures du
matin le dimanche au XVIᵉ siècle, à lieu maintenant à 7 heures.
Du reste, chacun se rend au temple au moins deux fois sur
quatre chaque sabat, et le jeudi. Les portes de la ville sont

---

(1) Lorsque Rousseau, en 1754, reprit la foi protestante, il reçut une instruction religieuse et dut faire sa profession de foi calviniste avant de rentrer dans
ses droits de citoyen qu'il avait perdus en se faisant catholique (VIII, 280).

fermées, les échopes closes, et des chaînes sont tendues autour
des temples durant le service. Les ordonnances somptuaires
demeuraient ce qu'elles avaient été, elles réglaient, dit Vallette,
« jusqu'aux manifestations de générosité, du deuil des particuliers, prescrivant la longueur des crêpes... » Si l'usage des
carrosses n'est plus puni, il est encore vu de mauvais œil. La loi
pénale, durant tout le cours du XVII\e siècle, « outre le luxe »,
punissait sévèrement le blasphème, le suicide, le duel, la fai-
néantise, la mendicité ; les ivrognes sont enfermés et exposés
dans une cage de fer au Molard. La prostituée, femme ou fille,
est liée et menée au port de Longemalle et là noyée et submer-
gée. L'adultère, quand il n'est pas puni de mort ou de détention,
conduit tout au moins à l'amende et au carcan » (*Ibid.*, p. 13).

Au début du XVIII\e siècle, de nouveaux édits somptuaires
sont décrétés ; et en 1710 des ordonnances sévères sont
publiées contre les joueurs et renouvelées en 1718 ; les masques
et les travestissements, de même que le théâtre sont prohibés ;
et la danse est vue de mauvais œil. Et M. Ritter (*Famille et
jeunesse de Rousseau*, p. 55) remarque : « L'hypocrisie qui
semble le fruit naturel d'un régime semblable était elle-même
impossible : la ville était si petite qu'elle n'offrait point de retraite où se cacher. Il fallait être vertueux ou s'en aller... (1) ».

Rousseau était né en 1712, il connut donc ce régime où la
moindre velléité d'individualisme était impitoyablement ré-
primée ; les premiers « cercles » ou clubs s'ouvrirent à Genève
en 1734, six ans après le départ de Rousseau. Mais si les réminiscences des institutions de sa ville natale sont innombrables
dans ses écrits, et son admiration fort grande quand il discute

----

(1) Le grand-père de Rousseau avait été « dizenier », sorte de magistrat subal-
terne qui tenait un registre des gens de son quartier et veillait à ce que les
« bourgeois et habitants se gouvernassent honnêtement en leurs ménages » ; il fut
destitué en 1707, « ayant — dit M. RITTER, p. 73 — montré quelque faiblesse ».
La mère de Rousseau avait eu affaire au Consistoire à trois reprises (pour avoir
joué aux cartes, pour avoir reçu la visite d'un homme de trente-six ans, pour
être allée voir jouer la comédie, travestie en paysanne) (*Ibid.*, p. 91-97, 146). Le
père de Rousseau dut s'enfuir, ou préféra s'enfuir, pour échapper aux rigueurs
de la loi (*Ibid.*, p. 113).

les lois et les mœurs calvinistes, on est surpris d'abord, lorsqu'on se rapporte aux *Confessions*, de trouver que c'est à peine si quelques phrases ici et là trahissent le souvenir de l'esprit austère de ce milieu.

Voici, ce qu'en cherchant bien on peut trouver : « Jamais une seule fois jusqu'à la sortie de la maison paternelle [à onze ans] on ne m'a laissé courir seul dans la rue ou avec les autres enfants » (5). Chez les Lambercier, où il est en pension avec son cousin, il note leur peu de sévérité, contrastant probablement avec ce qu'il aurait été naturel d'attendre : « M. Lambercier était un homme fort raisonnable, qui sans négliger notre instruction ne nous chargeait point de devoirs extrêmes » (7) ; et « Mlle Lambercier ne manquait pas, au besoin, de sévérité, non plus que son frère » (8) ; « Si jamais éducation fut modeste et chaste, ce fut assurément celle que j'ai reçue... », et il décrit (p. 9-10) l'horreur pour ainsi dire sacrée qu'on lui inspirait à lui, qui naturellement n'y entendait rien à cet âge, pour les choses sexuelles. Ce fut pendant les quelques mois qu'il demeura chez son oncle Bernard, au retour de Bossey, qu'il sentit le plus directement cette influence de milieu spécifiquement genevois ; la mère de son cousin était « une dévote un peu piétiste » (16) ; « On délibérait si on me ferait horloger, procureur ou ministre. J'aimais mieux être ministre, car je trouvais bien beau de prêcher » (16) ; « Mon oncle Bernard ayant lu un jour dans la famille un très beau sermon de sa façon, nous nous mîmes [mon cousin et moi] à composer des sermons » (16). On voit que c'est assez maigre comme récolte.

Cependant Rousseau enfant communia avec l'esprit de Genève d'une autre façon. Vallette s'inspirant des *Confessions* et de la *Dédicace du deuxième discours*, et s'aidant de documents de l'époque, a évoqué d'une façon très vivante, le tableau d'un maître horloger de Genève au XVIIIe siècle (p. 20-24). A la fois ouvrier et petit patron, Isaac Rousseau, père de Jean-Jacques, doit se soumettre aux mille observances de sa corporation dans la façon d'exercer son métier, d'acheter ses matières brutes et d'écouler ses produits, comme dans la vie privée il est soumis aux mille exigences de la loi calviniste. Pourtant « membre du souverain » nominalement, il discute de tout, lit de tout, peut-être se dédommageant ainsi de la maigre part qui lui revient en réalité dans le gouvernement des affaires. Aux outils de son père, Jean-Jacques voyait mêlés des volumes de Tacite, Grotius, Plutarque ; dès l'âge de sept ans il les ouvrait, et pour autant qu'il pouvait comprendre, son imagination s'exaltait à la lecture des grandes vertus romaines, comme il s'était exalté à la lecture des romans sentimentaux du XVIIᵉ siècle : « Plutarque surtout devint ma lecture favorite. Le plaisir que je prenais à le relire sans cesse me guérit un peu des romans ; et je préférai bientôt Agésilas, Brutus, Aristide, à Orondate, Artamène et Juba » (4, cf. IX, 206). Cette admiration pour les Romains (1) était demeurée traditionnelle dès l'aube des temps chrétiens.

Les causes qui l'inspirèrent ne furent du reste pas toujours les mêmes. D'abord pendant des siècles après les invasions barbares, jusqu'à Charlemagne et même jusqu'à Charles-Quint, c'était le grand empire des Césars qui avait hanté l'imagination des chefs de peuples. Mais ce rêve une fois abandonné, la fascination exercée par la Rome antique ne cessa point, seulement on admira autre chose. On admira, comme Amyot y encourageait par ses traductions de Plutarque, et comme Montaigne et maint autre, les grandes vertus patriotiques : le désintéressement, le contrôle des passions, la négation du moi. Le XVIIᵉ siècle surenchérit et poussa l'enthousiasme jusqu'aux dernières limites, avec Corneille, avec Balzac et les « Précieuses » même (voir La Couronne de Julie), avec les Jansénistes, avec Fénelon, qui les citait et les offrait directement comme modèles aux ministres de l'Évangile, avec Bossuet qui les exaltait dans son Histoire universelle, eux chez qui les pères n'élevant pas assez sévèrement leurs enfants « étaient appelés en justice par les magistrats et jugés coupables d'un attentat envers le public ».

(1) Nous disons tout court « les Romains », quoique Rousseau, à l'exemple de tant d'autres, songeât en même temps aux Grecs des petites républiques, aux Spartiates surtout, aux Grecs héroïques, aux Grecs romains, si on peut ainsi dire.

En d'autres termes les Romains étaient dès le XVIᵉ siècle les modèles les plus parfaits de l'abnégation, de l'austérité, de l'ascétisme chrétien ; l'éloge des Romains, sous la plume de Corneille et de Bossuet, n'était qu'une forme de l'éloge de la morale chrétienne.

Il en était de même chez les Genevois ; leur culte pour les Romains devait être plus complet même, puisque les vertus calvinistes prétendaient surpasser encore les vertus catholiques. Et quand, au XVIIIᵉ siècle, l'admiration pour les Romains commençait à n'être déjà plus en France qu'une tradition, et que même certains écrivains dirigeaient contre leur morne austérité des attaques non dissimulées, à Genève, au contraire, le prestige des farouches représentants de la vertu antique ne subit guère de recul ; la « vertu romaine » n'était qu'une autre expression pour « vertu calviniste », et Rousseau, à travers les Romains pour lesquels il professa une admiration si profonde comme enfant déjà, admirait bien l'esprit de Genève même (1).

Les échos de l'admiration de Rousseau pour les Romains fourmillent dans les *Confessions* et ailleurs. Sans doute, à l'époque de l'enfance elle fut forcément platonique, puisqu'un enfant ne peut guère espérer encore faire œuvre de Romain. Il entend bien lui-même comme plaisanterie des passages comme : « Deux ans passés au village [de Bossey] adoucirent un peu mon âpreté romaine » (7) ; « Jusque-là j'avais eu des accès d'orgueil par intervalle quand j'étais Aristide ou Brutus », dit-il plus bas ; mais lorsqu'il eut construit un aqueduc, chose utile, il vit la vanité de la gloire (car il est porté à confondre à cet âge la « gloire » et la « vertu »), « à dix ans j'en jugeais mieux que César à trente » (15). L'épisode du réchaud, quand il imite le geste de Scévola, est une pittoresque illustration de son en-

---

(1) Il est remarquable que l'écrivain français avec lequel Rousseau eut le plus de points de contact une fois qu'il fut devenu l'auteur vertueux des *Discours,* du *Contrat social* et de la *Nouvelle Héloïse*, c'est Bossuet, comme d'autre part l'écrivain du XVIᵉ siècle avec lequel Bossuet a le plus d'affinités, lorsqu'on considère l'esprit et non la lettre, c'est Calvin.

thousiasme de garçon (4). On se souvient de son exclamation au Pont du Gard : « Que ne suis-je né Romain ! » (183) et son imagination travaille si bien qu'elle lui fait oublier ses amours avec Mme de Larnage.

Et sans doute encore, Rousseau s'est souvent mépris lui-même sur le sens de certains actes, chez les autres ou chez lui, en leur attribuant un mobile romain, alors qu'au contraire il s'agissait d'un mobile tout romantique. Déjà bien avant de se mettre aux *Confessions*, dans sa lettre à Tronchin (27 nov. 1758), il disait : « A douze ans j'étais un Romain. » Mais par où l'était-il ? Ses exaltations sentimentales semblent prouver qu'il était plutôt le contraire. Les Romains, tels que les admire le monde, sont des hommes toujours maîtres d'eux-mêmes, contrôlant leurs passions, et par là capables d'actions désintéressées ; mais les velléités « héroïques » des jeunes années de Rousseau venaient justement, nous l'avons vu, de ce qu'il ne pouvait contrôler ses sentiments ; il croit naïvement qu'il rêve de grands sacrifices, quand en réalité il songe seulement à écarter la souffrance des autres parce qu'elle lui fait mal ; lorsqu'après la lecture de Plutarque, il s'imaginait allant poignarder des tyrans ou lorsqu'il s'époumonnait à la poursuite des chiens molestant des poules, il obéit donc à un mouvement de passion, il succombe à sa grande impressionnabilité. C'était anti-genevois et anti-romain, car il en était de Genève comme de Rome ; la sentimentalité y était considérée comme coupable. Comme pour les inquisiteurs d'Espagne, comme pour les puritains de la Nouvelle-Angleterre, la pitié était une faiblesse odieuse au Tout-Puissant.

Une des causes qui contribua le plus à faire admirer Calvin dans sa ville, ce fut son imperméabilité à toute espèce de partialités. Cela se voit en particulier dans la longue affaire des « Perrinistes ». Des membres de la famille de Perrin, grand ami de Calvin, avaient été punis pour conduite frivole (danse surtout) ; ils avaient compté sur l'impunité, à cause de leur position sociale. Calvin refusa absolument d'épargner ses amis. Perrin irrité se mit alors à la tête des « anti-disciplinaires », mais Calvin, tout en conservant avec lui des rapports d'amitié,

le combattit impitoyablement (CHOISY, *loc. cit.*, p. 81). Autre
exemple après la mort de Calvin : en 1632, un Nicolas Antoine,
ancien régent du collège, puis pasteur à Divonne, fût brûlé
à Genève pour hérésie, accusé d'arianisme comme Servet,
soixante-dix-neuf ans auparavant ; Antoine était un exalté,
on le reconnut fou ; mais loin que cette folie émut la pitié des
juges, ils se défendirent de toute faiblesse de cette sorte, et
déclarèrent que la folie était un châtiment de Dieu ; ils étaient
sûrs du reste « d'être approuvés de toute la chrétienté à l'exception des anabaptistes et des libertins » ; et voici leur argument :
« Maintenant, si vous lui faites grâce parce qu'il est fou, vous devez absoudre les adultères qui cèdent à la force de leur penchant, laisser en liberté les meurtriers qui sont emportés par la
colère, épargner les voleurs pour qui le bien d'autrui a d'irré-
sistibles attraits » (GABEREL, *Egl. de Genève*, II, 29).

Mais même si Rousseau s'est mépris parfois sur ses propres
sentiments, et a pris pour du volontarisme romain ce qui
n'était que de la sensiblerie romantique, il reste cependant
que la « vertu romaine » — qu'il confond avec l'abnégation
chrétienne — exerce sur lui une fascination extraordinaire ;
que même s'il n'a jamais été lui-même un « romain », il a vu là
un idéal à réaliser comme en témoigneront abondamment ses
écrits.

§ 3. De ce qui précède il faut retenir ceci : Dès la plus tendre
enfance un conflit existe virtuellement dans l'âme de Rousseau ;
il sera sollicité par deux tendances morales qui vont en sens
exactement contraires ; l'une qui l'engage à s'abandonner aux
sollicitations de son *moi*, et elle créera ce que nous appellerons le Rousseau romantique ; l'autre qui l'engagera à résister
et elle créera ce que nous appellerons le Rousseau romain ou
calviniste.

Le lecteur a déjà reconnu que ces deux tendances morales
sont celles aussi qui se disputaient l'empire de la société au
XVIIIᵉ siècle, l'une progressive et libertaire, — *romantique* ;
l'autre traditionaliste, austère, christiano-romaine ou calviniste, — en terme littéraire, *classique*. Et ainsi nous compre-

nons pourquoi — par prédestination en quelque sorte — Rousseau fut plus sensible qu'aucun autre aux grands problèmes de ses contemporains ; pourquoi plutôt que Buffon, Montesquieu et Voltaire, il exercera l'action que nous savons ; ou, si l'on veut, comment il pourra être le plus éloquent, celui dont on a dit : « Il a tout enflammé ».

Voilà le point de départ. Et, à vrai dire, nous pourrions nous en tenir là et aborder tout de suite l'œuvre philosophique de Rousseau. Suivons cependant pendant quelques instants chez le Rousseau s'avançant dans la vie, ce qui va advenir de ces deux tendances en germe dans l'âme de l'enfant : L'une d'elle va-t-elle triompher au dépens de l'autre ? Si oui, laquelle ? Si non, que va-t-il se passer. On verra comment d'une manière extrêmement frappante l'œuvre de prédestination va continuer ; comment la vie s'est appliquée pour ainsi dire à développer jusqu'au tréfond, tantôt un romantisme exalté, tantôt un calvinisme austère, comment donc fut rendue de plus en plus aiguë l'emprise du conflit auquel Rousseau ne réussira jamais à se soustraire entièrement — au moins dans son œuvre écrite.

II. — Rousseau romantique

§ 1. Un Genevois, même disposé romantiquement, — et nous sommes disposés ainsi en naissant — peut accepter l'influence calviniste ou romaine, et acquérir pour ainsi dire une seconde nature superposée à la première. Il faut pour cela que les circonstances n'aient pas intensifié son sentiment du *moi* d'une façon anormale ; et aussi qu'il n'ait pas à pâtir trop sévèrement, quand il grandit, d'une discipline rigoureuse. Rousseau n'acquit pas cette seconde nature : son *moi* avait été anormalement intensifié d'abord ; une phase de discipline trop écœurante suivit.

A onze ans la vie impitoyable était là pour lui. N'ayant plus de maison paternelle — son père avait quitté Genève pour

Nyon en suite de difficultés judiciaires — il doit se préparer à
gagner son pain. Après quelques mois encore de belle enfance
insouciante à Bossey et chez l'oncle Bernard, il vivra chez des
patrons selon la coutume de l'époque :

« L'on me mit (1725) chez M. Masseron, greffier de la ville, pour
apprendre de lui, comme disait M. Bernard, l'utile métier de *gra-*
pignan... L'occupation me paraissait ennuyeuse, insupportable ;
l'assiduité, l'assujettissement achevèrent de m'en dégoûter, et je
n'entrais au greffe qu'avec une terreur qui croissait de jour en jour ».
(19).

Le greffier rendait à son élève le mépris que celui-ci lui témoignait ; il l'appelait un « âne » ; et Rousseau, renvoyé « igno-
minieusement pour son ineptie » fut placé ensuite en apprentissage chez un graveur. Ce fut pire encore :

« Mon maître M. Ducommun, était un jeune homme rustre et
violent, qui vint à bout, en très peu de temps de ternir tout l'éclat
de mon enfance, d'abrutir mon caractère aimant et vif, et de me réduire par l'esprit ainsi que par la fortune, à mon véritable état
d'apprenti. Mon latin, mes antiquités, mon histoire, tout fut pour
longtemps oublié ; je ne me souvenais pas même qu'il y eût des
Romains au monde. Mon père, quand j'allais le voir, ne trouvait
plus en moi son idole ; je n'étais plus pour les dames le galant Jean-
Jacques » (20).

Qu'était-il arrivé ? Lorsque l'enfant, habitué à s'abandonner à ses désirs, est morigéné, son premier mouvement est la
surprise plus que la révolte. Il croit d'abord à un malentendu.
Il ressent profondément ce que Dugas (*ouvr. cité*, pp. 5, 140)
appelle « l'incoordination psychologique », c'est-à-dire le
manque d'accord entre le *moi* et son milieu. Il est désemparé ;
il cesse d'agir spontanément selon l'inclination naturelle ;
Il devient inquiet, prudent, et il souffre. Or dit Dugas (p. 104) :
« Une sensibilité fine, nuancée, ne veut pas se traduire et ne
veut pas se trahir : elle se fait donc voilée et discrète, ou elle
se dérobe entièrement et se déguise... On ne peut dire que le
timide soit réservé ou secret ; il se fait volontiers connaître,

mais il ne veut pas qu'on le méconnaisse » ; et dans ce cas « la
timidité n'est pas seulement une mauvaise honte, elle est encore une sorte de prudence». Rousseau nous en fournit lui-même
deux bons exemples. Voici avant « l'incoordination psychologique ». Un soir, pour quelque espièglerie, on l'envoie coucher
sans souper ; il salue tout le monde, puis :

« Quand la ronde fut faite, lorgnant du coin de l'œil ce rôti qui
avait si bonne mine et qui sentait si bon, je ne pus m'abstenir de
lui faire aussi une révérence et de lui dire d'un air piteux : *Adieu,
rôti* » (21).

Cette saillie lui fit pardonner, il soupa : « Peut-être eut-elle
eu le même bonheur chez mon maître, mais il est sûr qu'elle ne
m'y serait pas venue ».

Autre exemple. Rousseau, après que « l'incoordination psychologique » se fut produite :

« Mille fois durant mon apprentissage et depuis, je suis sorti dans
le dessein d'acheter quelques friandises. J'approche de la boutique
d'un patissier, j'aperçois des femmes au comptoir ; je crois déjà
les voir rire et se moquer entre elles du petit gourmand. Je passe
devant une fruitière, je lorgne de l'œil les belles poires, leur parfum
me tente ; deux ou trois jeunes gens tout près de là me regardent ;
un homme qui me connaît est devant sa boutique ; je vois de loin
venir une fille ; n'est-ce point la servante de la maison : ma vue
courte me fait mille illusions. Je prends tout ce qui passe pour des
gens de ma connaissance ; partout je suis intimidé, retenu par
quelque obstacle » (24 à 5) (1).

---

(1) Il ne sera pas inutile de rappeler ici que du reste la timidité, ou le sens
de « l'incoordination psychologique » n'est nullement un signe d'infériorité.
Plutôt le contraire ; elle témoigne d'une perspicacité aiguë des différences indi-
viduelles et de leurs conséquences ; elle est donc un signe d'intelligence ; Dugas
n'a pas tort quand il prétend qu'un homme qui n'est pas timide est un sot.
Cette peur d'entrer dans un magasin se rencontre très fréquemment chez des
intellectuels. Carlyle en est un exemple frappant : « la seule pensée d'entrer
dans une boutique le rendait malheureux... l'idée de commander un habit et
de s'acheter des gants l'anéantissait. La pensée de partir après son mariage
seul avec sa femme lui paraissait purement et simplement inadmissible » (cité
Dugas p. 117 ; cf. pour Daudet, p. 165). On trouvera les angoisses d'une âme

Les choses ne s'arrêtent pas là. Lui, devenu si timide et farouche déjà, on l'accuse pour les plus innocentes actions ; ses regards inquiets ne trahissaient-ils pas comme une continuelle mauvaise conscience ? Un jour, il s'était amusé à graver pour lui et ses camarades, des jetons ; mais le maître le surprend, et prétendant qu'il s'essaye à fabriquer de la fausse monnaie, le roue de coups (20) ; alors, il se résigne au moyen qui lui est seul laissé pour sauver quelques joies à son pauvre *moi*.

D'une part, il va adopter la dissimulation comme principe de vie ou de morale. « La timidité, comme le dit encore Dugas, est liée directement à la sincérité et indirectement au mensonge ; le timide veut être vrai, et ne sait être que faux » (p. 113). Jean-Jacques étant arrivé à la conclusion que la société est un état de guerre entre les individus, et sachant qu'il n'était pas physiquement le plus fort, il luttera de l'arme des faibles : il mentira, il rusera, il volera. Et l'entourage qui est le sien le pousse toujours plus avant dans cette voie : pour satisfaire sa gourmandise d'enfant, il dérobe des pommes ; il est surpris ; il reçoit le châtiment ordinaire ; — et il s'en fait un argument pour continuer :

« A force d'essuyer de mauvais traitements, je devins moins sensible ; ils me parurent enfin une sorte de compensation du vol, qui me mettait en droit de le continuer. Au lieu de retourner les yeux en arrière et de regarder la punition, je les portais en avant et je regardais la vengeance, je jugeais que me battre comme fripon, c'était m'autoriser à l'être » (23).

Bref, les circonstances de la vie du jeune Rousseau exaspèrent simplement le romantisme qui est au fonds de l'âme

timorée exprimée dans des termes qui rappellent singulièrement ceux de Rousseau dans une lettre de Jules Laforgues (LÉAUTAUD et VAN BEVER, *Poètes d'aujourd'hui*, vol. I page 126). Et encore mieux, CHATEAUBRIAND, *Mémoires d'outre Tombe*, Chap. « Ma vie solitaire à Paris » : « Quand la nuit approchait, j'allais à quelques spectacles, le désert de la foule me plaisait, quoiqu'il m'en coûtat toujours un peu de prendre mon billet à la porte et de me mêler aux hommes ».

de tout homme. Il sent de profondes velléités d'affirmer opi-
niâtrement son *moi* en face de la société. Il n'avait pas en
lui (et ce n'était pas sa faute) l'étoffe d'un austère Romain ;
ou, s'il l'avait eue tout comme d'autres, son enfance douillette
en plein Genève, l'avait considérablement endommagée.

D'autre part, la fascination pour la vertu romaine ne s'effa-
cera jamais complètement ; mais elle demeurera pour le moment comme enveloppée d'un nuage ; le Romain est maintenant dans la pensée de Rousseau simplement celui qui a une
forte volonté, et il ne songe pas même à distinguer, selon que
cette volonté sert à se vaincre soit-même (Caton-Brutus-Fabri-
cius) ou à vaincre le monde à son profit (César) ; et parfois il
choisit Caton et parfois César comme le type du Romain ad-
miré. Nous avons justement aux pages des *Confessions* relatives à cette période de sa vie un curieux exemple :

« Il faut, dit Rousseau, que malgré l'éducation la plus honnête,
j'eusse eu un grand penchant à dégénérer ; car cela se fit très rapidement, sans la moindre peine, et jamais César si précoce ne devint
si promptement Laridon » (20).

Or César montant au Capitole, et Jean-Jacques roué de
coups par Ducommun sont deux événements d'origine aussi
romantique l'un que l'autre ; seulement, ici le moi a été vaincu
par la société, là la société a cédé devant le *moi*. César, du
point de vue de la vertu, est le moins Romain des Romains ;
l'excuse de Rousseau si s'en est une, serait que Lafontaine
avait fait la confusion avant lui (1).

(1) La façon lâche dont Rousseau emploie ces mots « Romains », et César
en particulier, ressort bien de ce fait que César ici considéré comme un héros
véritable, était dans l'épisode de l'aqueduc (quelques pages avant seulement)
un exemple du contraire : « Avoir pu construire un acqueduc me paraissait le
suprême degré de la gloire... A dix ans j'en jugeais mieux que César à 30 ».
Rappelons à propos de cette confusion entre le Romain Caton ou Brutus et le
Romain César — qui est fréquente dans les *Confessions* — ce que uuos avons
dit tout à l'heure, à savoir que parfois Rousseau interprète des exaltations
purement romantiques comme s'il s'agissait de vrais enthousiasmes pour la
vertu et la justice.

Rousseau ne « dégénéra » pas en réalité, car il n'avait jamais plané. Mais, on peut bien y insister à sa décharge puisqu'il s'accuse lui-même : c'est à *cause de* son éducation et non *malgré* elle qu'il était devenu Laridon — par suite de cette éducation qui avait donné à son *moi* une importance très grande, et à force de soins, énervé sa virilité :

« Accoutumé à une égalité parfaite avec mes supérieurs dans la manière de vivre, à ne pas connaître un plaisir qui ne fût à ma portée, à ne pas voir un met dont je n'eusse ma part, à n'avoir pas un désir que je ne témoignasse, à mettre enfin tous les mouvements de mon cœur sur mes lèvres, qu'on juge de ce que je dus devenir dans une maison où je n'osais pas ouvrir la bouche, où il fallait sortir de table au tiers du repas, et de la chambre aussitôt que je n'y avais rien à faire ; où sans cesse enchaîné à mon travail je ne voyais qu'objets de jouissance pour d'autres et de privations pour moi seul ; où l'image de la liberté du maître et des compagnons augmentait le poids de mon assujettissement » (20 à 21).

C'est là le seul Rousseau qui vit dans ces années d'enfance : plutôt pas mauvais que bon, romantiquement passif, et non romainement discipliné.

§ 2. Nous arrivons ainsi à la suprême manifestation de ce désarroi à base romantique. Le *moi* du timide romantique, dit toujours Dugas, ne se contraint pas parce qu'il veut mais parce qu'il doit ; or, cette contrainte doublée de ressentiment l'irrite et l'épuise tout à la fois ; le moment arrive où le *moi* ne se contient plus : « Ces sentiments longtemps comprimés se déchaînent ; il a laissé par exemple s'accumuler en son cœur une sourde colère contre une personne ; un jour cette colère éclate pour un motif futile ; elle paraît injustifiée ; elle est naturelle pourtant, et aurait pu être prévue » (128). Puis, le timide se reprend, se rend compte d'avoir compromis ses chances de bonheur, si pauvres déjà, et tombe dans l'abattement ; il se contient jusqu'à nouvelle explosion ; se reprend encore, et ainsi de suite...Il paraît fantasque, incompréhensible aux autres, et le paraît d'autant plus qu'il est plus fidèle à lui même et à son caractère » (129) (1).

(1) Cf. Un passage des *Confessions* VIII, 24, 2e al.

« J'atteignis, dit Rousseau, ma seizième année, inquiet, mécontent de tout et de moi, sans goût de mon état, sans plaisir de mon âge, dévoré de désir dont j'ignorais l'objet, pleurant sans sujet de larmes, soupirant sans savoir de quoi, enfin caressant tendrement mes chimères faute de rien voir autour de moi qui les valût » (28).

Personne n'ignore le coup de tête enfin, dont les conséquences vont être si considérables : Rousseau aimait, le dimanche, à sortir de la ville enfermée dans d'étroites fortifications. Il allait dans la campagne avec des camarades, quoiqu'il eut même à leur égard la méfiance du rêveur (« je leur aurais volontiers échappé si j'avais pu » (28). Au coucher du soleil les portes étaient fermées, et les retardataires devaient attendre jusqu'au lendemain pour rentrer. Rousseau fut surpris deux fois, et au retour chez Ducommun, battu. Surpris une troisième fois, il décide de ne pas s'exposer au châtiment certain, et du reste promis ; et de quitter Genève. Cette décision fut non pas « un caprice du moment », mais le résultat de quatre ou cinq ans de contrainte, qui n'ont pas réduit à capitulation son *moi*. Sans doute Rousseau eut un moment de terreur quand courant à perdre haleine il vit le pont se lever : « Dans le premier transport de ma douleur, je me jetai sur glacis et mordis la terre » (28). Il éprouva une sorte de terreur animale à la première pensée qui se présenta à lui, — être battu ; mais avec cela même se présente la misère de sa vie comparée à ses rêves romantiques, et de ce contraste jaillit l'idée du salut (1) : Quelle occasion d'arracher son *moi* étriqué à des conditions intolérables : Il n'est pas étonnant qu'il accueillit facilement l'idée de quitter Genève pour toujours ; le sentiment de la liberté lui fit compter pour rien les perspectives

(1) DUCROS (*Jean-Jacques Rousseau de Genève à l'Hermitage*, p. 35) nous paraît avoir mal compris le caractère de Rousseau, enfant ; surtout ici, quand il dit que Rousseau après avoir conté dramatiquement la douleur de ne pouvoir rentrer à Genève, se *trahit* aussitôt après en nous racontant « sa joie d'aller à l'aventure et d'entrer comme il dit dans le vaste espace du monde, libre enfin et maître de lui ». Il ne se *trahit* pas du tout ; la succession des deux sentiments contraires est parfaitement concevable ; et même, dans les circonstances où Rousseau se trouvait, normale.

de la faim et de la misère matérielle — qu'il ne pouvait du reste envisager dans leur réelle horreur, n'en ayant jamais fait l'expérience.

Chacun a présentes à la mémoire les pages écrites quarante ans plus tard, toutes palpitantes encore d'émotion communicative, où il évoque ces heures de résurrection glorieuses :

« L'indépendance que je croyais avoir acquise était le seul sentiment qui m'affectait. Libre et maître de moi-même, je croyais pouvoir tout faire, atteindre à tout ; je n'avais qu'à m'élancer pour m'élever et voler dans les airs. J'entrais avec sécurité dans le vaste espace du monde ; mon mérite allait le remplir ; à chaque pas j'allais trouver des destins, des trésors, des aventures, des amis prêts à me servir, des maîtresses empressées à me plaire ; en me montrant, j'allais occuper de moi l'univers ; non pas pourtant l'univers tout entier, je l'en dispensais en quelque sorte, il ne m'en fallait pas tant ; une société charmante me suffisait sans m'embarrasser du reste. Ma modération m'inscrivait dans une sphère étroite, mais délicieusement choisie, où j'étais assuré de régner. Un seul château bornerait mon ambition : favori du seigneur et de la dame, amant de la demoiselle, ami du frère et protecteur des voisins, j'étais content ; il ne m'en fallait pas davantage » (30).

En quittant Genève, il s'enlevait pour longtemps, sinon pour toujours, l'occasion de devenir romano-genevois, et la destinée semblait écarter le dernier obstacle à la victoire complète du *moi* romantique.

Il passa les premiers jours à savourer la volupté de la liberté reconquise ; il demeure chez des paysans de sa connaissance, laissant vivre son *moi*. Il va frapper chez le curé de Confignon pour voir « comment étaient faits les descendants des gentils hommes de la cuillier !» (30). Le curé l'envoie à Annecy, chez Mme de Warens ; il pouvait y aller en un jour ; il en met trois, flânant, chantant sous les fenêtres des châteaux où devait demeurer sûrement quelque belle, et « fort surpris après s'être longtemps époumonné, de ne voir ni dames, ni demoiselles qu'attirât la beauté de sa voix ou le sel de ses chansons » (32). Il trouve exactement ce qu'il cherchait sous la forme de Mme de Warens ; il s'attendait à une vieille dévote, sorte de Tante Bernard catholique, et il se trouve face à face avec « un visage pétri de grâces, de beaux yeux pleins de douceur, un teint éblouissant, le contour d'une gorge enchanteresse » (33). Il s'étonne « comment en approchant pour la première fois d'une dame aimable, polie, éblouissante, d'un état supérieur au mien » il n'éprouve « pas un moment de timidité ou de gêne » (35). C'est que son romantisme a toujours consisté à ne vouloir connaître la différence entre le rêve et la réalité ; toute bonne fortune est un simple dû de la destinée ; toute fortune contraire le déconcerte et le désarçonne. Tout est si bien allé jusque là, qu'il est fort encouragé à pratiquer encore l'insouciance romantique. Sur un seul point, il est intraitable : il ne retournera pas à Genève, le pays de la contrainte ; l'éloquence de Mᵐᵉ de Warens elle-même échoue devant cette proposition contre nature. Rousseau adopte la ligne de moindre résistance : Mᵐᵉ de Warens lui propose de se faire catholique ; il ira à Turin ; que lui importe ? Elle arrange tout, on trouve les bonnes volontés nécessaires pour gagner un prosélyte à l'Eglise — c'est-à-dire l'argent pour couvrir les frais du voyage. Il dit bien : « Je trouvais toutes ces charités bien dures ; j'avais le cœur serré ; je ne disais rien » (37) ; mais pas le plus petit effort de volonté : « agir contre mon penchant me fut toujours impossible » ; il n'est, pour le moment, pas romain pour un sou, et n'a pas envie de l'être. Du reste, ces scrupules sont vite oubliés. « Le voyage de Turin flattait ma manie ambulante, qui déjà commençait à se déclarer » (37) (1).

« Je m'acheminais gaiement avec mon dévot guide et sa sémillante compagne (rencontrés à Annecy, chez sa bienfaitrice et faisant la

(1) On a cru devoir attribuer le goût des voyages chez Rousseau à une maladie spéciale, la « dromomanie », comme on attribuait son romantisme à l'hérédité. Il nous semble que c'est ici encore substituer un mot à une explication : la dromomanie explique les vagabondages de Rousseau comme la *virtus dormitiva* l'influence de l'opium. Il est bien plus simple de voir dans la « manie ambulante » de Rousseau un effet de son désir de se soustraire aux contraintes sociales auxquelles il n'a jamais pu se faire » (Cf. *Chronique médicale*, 1ᵉʳ mars 1910 : « La Dromomanie de Rousseau », par le Dʳ Régis, prof. de psychiâtrie à Bordeaux).

même route). Nul accident ne troubla mon voyage. J'étais dans la plus heureuse situation de corps et d'esprit où j'aie été de mes jours » (39).

Comme il y a plus loin d'Annecy à Turin que de Genève à Annecy, il y avait plus de temps pour les rêves : « Les jeunes désirs, l'espoir enchanteur, les brillants projets remplissaient mon âme » (39-40) (1).

Le voilà à l'Hospice des catéchumènes pour y recevoir son instruction dans la foi catholique. Quand il en est congédié, il a un mauvais moment ; il décrit la scène de sortie de l'hospice, la collecte qui rapporte un peu plus de vingt francs, la recommandation de vivre en bon chrétien, puis comment « on ferma la porte sur moi, et tout disparut » (48).

« Il est aisé de juger quelle brusque révolution dut se faire dans mes idées, lorsque de mes brillants projets de fortune, je me vis tomber dans la plus complète misère, et qu'après avoir délibéré le matin sur le palais que j'habiterais, je me vis le soir réduit à coucher dans la rue » (48).

Mais cela ne dura que l'instant d'y penser. Exactement la même scène se reproduisit que celle qu'il avait décrite à propos de son adieu à Genève : le sentiment romantique de l'indépendance prévaut :

« On croit que je commençai par me livrer à un désespoir d'autant plus cruel que le regret de mes fautes devait s'irriter en me reprochant que tout mon malheur était mon ouvrage. Rien de tout cela. Je venais pour la première fois de ma vie d'être enfermé pendant plus de deux mois ; le premier sentiment que je goûtai fut celui de la liberté que j'avais recouvrée » (48-9) (2).

---

(2) Rousseau dit que le voyage dura 7 ou 8 jours ; M. Ritter prouve qu'il en dura 20 (*ouvr. cité*, p. 196).

(1) On a longtemps adopté comme date de la sortie de l'Hospice, le 23 août. MASSON (*Rev. Hist. litt.* Janv. 1914) semble certainement avoir raison quand il dit qu'il faut lire sur le régistre de l'Hospice, 23 *avril*, ce qui ramènerait à moins de deux semaines, ce séjour de « deux mois », — du 12 au 23 avril. Ce-

Et il fit « pour cinq ou six sous un des bons dîners que j'aie fait de mes jours » (49). En vain la vie essaie-t-elle de le corriger, car ses besoins sont fort modestes ; cela ne veut pas dire qu'il était romain, mais juste le contraire : il l'a dit ailleurs, il pèse les jouissances de certains biens et la peine de se les procurer ; et il choisit la privation qui lui coûte le moins ; ce n'est pas de l'héroïsme, c'est de la paresse ; comme chez tout romantique intelligent, ses grands besoins sont des désirs de luxe. Il logera donc à un sou la nuit, couchant dans la même chambre avec une famille de cinq ou six enfants et une bande de « domestiques hors de service » ; *mais* il entend chaque jour de la belle musique à la messe du roi, guettant en même temps dans la suite de celui-ci « quelque jeune princesse qui méritât son hommage et avec laquelle je pusse faire un roman » (50).

Quand son pécule est épuisé, il va de porte en porte offrant pour presque rien ses services de graveur ; et quand il pourrait être sur le point de se décourager, quelque coup du sort le raffermit dans son romantisme impénitent. Un jour, il arrive chez le délicieuse Mme Basile ; et il ébauche avec elle la plus poétique des idylles ; celle-ci finit par une humiliante expulsion sur l'ordre d'un mari bourru ; mais il avait pu un matin la regarder tout à son aise, et son imagination avait fait le reste ; à cinquante ans il écrivait encore :

« De mes jours je n'eus un si doux moment... Rien de tout ce que m'a fait sentir la possession des femmes ne vaut les deux minutes que j'ai passées à ses pieds sans même oser toucher à sa robe » (53).

De temps à autre quelques gros nuages venaient à la vérité obscurcir ce ciel serein, mais si leur passage laissait un souvenir au fond de son cœur, il ne prendra conscience de long-

pendant cela soulève une assez grosse difficulté : comment trouver place en quelques jours pour tant d'événements ? Le sage M. Ritter pense qu'il doit y avoir malentendu, et suggère (*Annales Rousseau,*) que la date du 23 avril est celle de l'abjuration ou de quelque autre événement du séjour à l'Hospice sans être pour cela la date de sortie.

temps encore de leur effet psychologique sur la formation de
son être.

Un jour, une « dame de condition » avait demandé à le voir ;
et il avait reçu la nouvelle comme on peut s'y attendre : « A
ce mot, je me crus tout de bon dans les hautes aventures ;
car j'en revenais toujours là » (56). Mais il avait fallu déchan-
ter encore ; il s'agissait d'une place de valet. Du moins serait-
il un « favori » ; non, il fut « le valet des valets » de Mme de Vercellis. Peu de temps après, Mme de Vercellis meurt ; et après
avoir été sur le pavé pour quelques semaines, Rousseau entre
chez « le chef de l'illustre maison de Solar », — comme laquais
encore : « Quoi ! toujours laquais ! me dis-je en moi-même
avec un dépit amer » (64). Un roman muet esquissé avec
Mlle de Breil (65-7), la fille de son auguste maître, le distrait un
instant ; mais au premier succès, il est si ému qu'il répand le
contenu d'une carafe d'eau sur la robe de sa dulcinée, et tout
fut fini. Quant aux leçons de l'abbé de Gouvon (aussi de la famille), il avait alors trop peu la faculté de l'effort continu
pour s'y plaire. On fut pourtant très bon pour lui ; c'était bien
autre chose qu'aux jours de Masseron et de Ducommun : mais
même cela était trop pour lui maintenant : « Des vues éloignées
ont rarement assez de force pour me faire agir. L'incertitude
de l'avenir m'a toujours fait regarder les projets de longue
exécution comme des leurres de dupes » (103). Il avait retrouvé
à Turin, un Genevois, un ancien camarade d'apprentissage,
alors un vagabond, gai, insouciant, débrouillard, qui le fascina.
Le « bouffon Bâcle » devint pour lui l'incarnation de la vie
libre, et il fit irruption dans la vie de Rousseau. Un jour
Bâcle annonce son départ pour Genève : pourquoi, lui,
Rousseau — puisque le chemin de Genève passe par Annecy
— n'irait-il pas chez Mme de Warens ? Quarante années plus
tard, dans les *Confessions*, il fit son « peccavi », mais au moment même, il se sent dans les meilleures dispositions, —
comme lorsqu'il avait quitté Genève, comme lorsqu'il était
sorti de l'Hospice à Turin :

« Je pars avec ma fontaine (1) et mon ami bâcle, la bourse légèrement garnie, mais le cœur saturé de joie et ne songeant qu'à jouir
de cette ambulante félicité à laquelle j'avais tout à coup borné mes
brillantes ambitions » (71).

Le destin était contre — ou avec — lui ; *contre*, si on considère qu'il l'enfonçait dans son romantisme funeste ; *avec*, si
on considère qu'un jour, quand la réaction viendra, elle sera
d'autant plus décisive. Il avait craint l'accueil de Mme de Warens ; elle le reçut de façon à lui faire presque croire qu'il avait
agi sagement. Comme punition, elle le prend chez elle, c'est-à-
dire qu'il vivra à l'abri de souci du pain quotidien, près d'une
femme si aimable qu'elle ne savait contrecarrer aucun de ses
désirs. La morale du renoncement est inconnue chez la
bonne dame d'Annecy ; de même que celle de la prévoyance :
« D'autant plus que n'étant point encore dans l'étroite confi-
dence de ses affaires, je les supposais en état d'aller toujours
sur le même pied » (74) ; et que « la prévoyance a toujours
gâté chez moi la jouissance ». Dans ces conditions, on comprend
que Rousseau se garda bien d'évoquer le souvenir des Romains.

« Dès les premiers jours la familiarité la plus douce s'établit entre
nous au même degré où elle a continué tout le reste de sa vie.
Petit fut mon nom ! Maman fut le sien ; et toujours nous de-
meurâmes *Petit* et *Maman,* même quand le nombre des années en
eut presque effacé la différence entre nous... Elle fut pour moi la
plus tendre des mères qui jamais ne chercha son plaisir, mais toujours mon bien ; et si les sens entrèrent dans mon attachement
pour elle, ce n'était pas pour en changer la nature, mais pour le
rendre seulement plus exquis, pour m'enivrer du charme d'avoir
une maman jeune et jolie qu'il m'était délicieux de carresser...
Je n'avais ni transports ni désirs auprès d'elle ; j'étais dans un calme
ravissant, jouissant sans savoir de quoi. J'aurais ainsi passé ma
vie et même l'éternité sans m'ennuyer un seul instant... je ne me sou

(1) Une fontaine de Héron, instrument de physique que lui avait donné
l'abbé Gouvon, et qu'il comptait exhiber en voyage pour de l'argent. Anatole
France dans son *Petit Pierre,* raconte que de son temps encore les enfants
jouaient avec des fontaines de Héron.

viens pas de m'être élancé jamais dans l'avenir avec plus de force
et d'illusion que je fis alors ; et ce qui m'a frappé le plus dans le
souvenir de cette rêverie quand elle s'est réalisée, c'est d'avoir
retrouvé des objets tels exactement que je les avais imaginés »
(74-5).

Rêves romantiques naturellement ! Il semblait revenu aux
jours d'enfance à Genève. Pendant tout ce temps, pas un
coup de tête ; — pourquoi en ferait-il puisque tout était
bien ?

Une inquiétude cependant — c'était toute l'expérience
du monde qu'il avait faite sienne : « Cette vie était trop douce
pour pouvoir durer » (78) ; du reste, Mme de Warens « bâtissait
pour ma fortune force projets dont je me serais bien passé ».
Encore, Rousseau n'avait guère à prendre de ces plans que ce
qu'il voulait. M. d'Aubonne, « homme de beaucoup d'esprit »
— comme Masseron, le greffier — déclare l'enfant « incapable », pouvant tout au plus devenir curé de village. Rousseau dut aller au séminaire des Lazaristes, à Annecy. « J'allai
comme j'aurais été au supplice » (82). Il y alla, mais il n'y fit
rien ; sauf pourtant ce qu'il n'aurait pas dû, de la musique.
Les bonnes heures sont toujours celles de ses visites à Mme de
Warens. Rousseau pense que, s'il faut travailler dans la vie,
la musique ne sera pas le choix le plus désagréable ; sans peine,
il obtient consentement et s'en va demeurer chez le maître de
musique de la cathédrale. Il essaie pendant un hiver d'apprendre la musique, il est moins malheureux qu'au séminaire : « la maîtrise n'étant du reste qu'à vingt pas de la maison
de maman, nous étions chez elle en un moment, et nous y
soupions souvent ensemble » (86).

§ 3. C'est ici qu'il faut placer la grande borne ; ici que
Rousseau va commencer à connaître le revers de la médaille
romantique.

Un jour, il est dépêché par Mme de Warens pour accompa-
gner jusqu'à Lyon, le maître de musique. Celui-ci était en
rupture de ban avec ses supérieurs, et avait décidé de les

planter là tout soudainement en pleine semaine sainte. Il
semble évident que Mme de Warens profita de l'incident pour
éloigner Rousseau pendant quelques jours ou heures, et pour
réaliser un projet dont elle ne voulait s'ouvrir à lui. Elle fila
mystérieusement sur Paris (pour quelque mission diploma-
tique, dit M. Benedetto). A son retour de Lyon, Rousseau ne
peut donc aller à la maîtrise qui est abandonnée, ni chez
Mme de Warens laquelle est absente. Il était trop mal habitué pour faire face à la situation ; son attitude est toute
passive ; une seule possibilité se présente à son esprit, attendre
le retour de maman. Entre temps, il va retrouver un certain
« Venture de Villeneuve », un aventurier qui un jour s'était
présenté chez son maître et qui, par son assurance, sa faconde,
avait fasciné Jean-Jacques. Venture occupe une misérable
chambre chez un cordonnier, Rousseau ira partager ce logis. Sauf pour l'épisode romantique de l'idylle des cerises
(1er juillet) ces semaines d'attente vaine furent, on le conçoit,
démoralisantes. Trois mois se sont écoulés... Rousseau finit par
accepter l'arrangement, fait pour lui, de raccompagner chez
elle, la Merceret, une des servantes de Mme de Warens, qui,
sa maîtresse ne revenant pas, rentrera chez ses parents à Fri-
bourg. Mais après, que va-t-il faire ? Où va-t-il se diriger ?
Il n'en sait rien ; vaguement du côté de la Savoie. C'est toujours un but, et un moyen de passer quelques jours. Les pages
extrêmement alertes de Rousseau relatives à cette période
font oublier la misère noire dans laquelle il vécut, et ses profonds découragements. Il faut bien lire entre les lignes de ces
récits charmants où il se représente égaré à Moudon, hébergé
par un aubergiste excellent lui faisant crédit ; puis, admirant
à Lausanne « ce beau lac qu'on voit là dans sa plus grande
étendue » ; puis, voulant, sans y réussir le moins du monde,
payer d'audace et s'improviser maître de musique. Il faut
surtout deviner le pauvre garçon, dans des pays absolument
étrangers, sans ressources, sans moyens de s'en procurer, —
et sans vraiment que ce soit sa faute puisque son éducation
d'abord, les conditions de son existence ensuite n'ont fait de
lui qu'un rêveur sans volonté, et une épave humaine ayant

besoin avant tout de protection et d'affection. Il faut le deviner quand, dans sa détresse et dans son sincère désir de
vivre honorablement en gagnant quelque argent, il s'est si
ridiculement compromis dans sa tentative de concert. Ecrasé,
moqué, dégoûté, impuissant, il « lâche la bonde à ses larmes »
devant un homme à lui parfaitement inconnu, auquel il a
tout confessé. Il faut le deviner dans son désarroi, invoquant
comme en prière, le souvenir de celle qui fut sa providence :
« Je ne cessais de penser à elle, et de désirer de la retrouver,
non seulement pour le besoin de ma subsistance, mais bien
plus pour le besoin de mon cœur » (106). Il s'en va à pied à
Vevey, la patrie de Mme de Warens. « Dans ce voyage, je
m'attendrissais, je soupirais et pleurais comme un enfant.
Combien de fois, m'arrêtant pour pleurer à mon aise, assis
sur une grosse pierre, je me suis amusé à voir couler mes
larmes dans l'eau » (108). Il faut le deviner, à Neuchâtel,
essayant la même vie « d'artiste » qu'à Lausanne, c'est-à-dire
courant le cachet, mais écrivant à son père (irrité de sa conversion au catholicisme) cette lettre désespérée dans laquelle il
demande que « l'indignation fasse place à la pitié », car « ses
yeux (de père) se chargeraient de larmes » s'il concevait le
dénuement du « fils malheureux », (X, 1-2). Il faut le comprendre enfin, quand il s'embarque dans sa folle aventure du
faux archimandrite, lequel prétendait quêter pour délivrer
les chrétiens esclaves des Turcs, et quand se sachant complice
de la fraude, il se jette aux pieds de l'ambassadeur de France
à Soleure « lâchant de nouveau la bonde »... Après cette série
noire, une éclaircie dans son ciel. Grâce à la bonté de l'ambassadeur, il est remis sur pieds ; muni de lettres et d'argent, il
reprend courage et part pour Paris. Les récentes expériences
ne seront pas perdues pour toujours ; elles compteront plus
tard pour leur bonne part à établir le bilan du passé ; elles
s'ajouteront à celles de la vie de laquais à Turin ; mais sous
l'effet de ce bienfaisant changement de fortune, le romantique
optimiste est, pour l'instant, ressuscité tout entier. « Je mis
à ce voyage une quinzaine de jours que je peux compter parmi les plus heureux de ma vie... Mes douces chimères me te-

naient compagnie, et jamais la chaleur de mon imagination n'en enfanta de plus magnifiques » (112). Il hésitait entre la gloire militaire (il avait une lettre pour un officier) et une douce vie de campagne.

Mais Paris lui réservait de nouvelles désillusions ; d'abord Paris, la ville de ses rêves magnifiques, ville de palais et de marbre et d'or, a de sales rues puantes, de vilaines maisons lépreuses, des mendiants... ; il y entre par un des quartiers les plus malpropres. Et puis, surtout, la place de gouverneur du neveu de M. Goddard est impossible — elle lui rappelle les jours humiliants d'Italie. Aussi, dès qu'une dame lui apprend que sa protectrice va rentrer en Savoie, il part ; et l'écœurement des quelques semaines à Paris, lui procure par contraste une nouvelle période d'exaltation romantique ; un supplément d'argent de l'ambassadeur de Soleure, rend plus facile son voyage : « L'éloignement de tout ce qui me fait sentir ma dépendance... me jette en quelque sorte dans l'immensité des êtres, pour les combiner, les choisir, me les approprier à mon gré et sans crainte. Je dispose en maître de la nature entière et [il s'égare plusieurs fois,] j'eusse été fâché d'aller plus droit, car sentant qu'à Lyon j'allais me retrouver sur la terre, j'aurais voulu n'y arriver jamais » (115). Là, attendant des nouvelles de maman, il passe quelques jours sans argent, mais pas inquiet. Il apprend que Mme de Warens s'est fixée à Chambéry et qu'elle l'attend ; elle lui envoie même de l'argent pour continuer sa route : « Je goûtais d'avance, mais sans ivresse, le plaisir de vivre auprès d'elle ; je m'y étais toujours attendu ; c'était comme s'il ne m'était rien arrivé de nouveau » (122). On le voit allant reprendre sa quiète vie romantique d'autrefois.

Toutefois les espoirs de retour à l'ère de rêves devront être de plus en plus abandonnés ; de plus en plus les déceptions lui infligeront les rudes leçons de la vie. D'abord à Chambéry, ce n'est plus la campagne comme à Annecy, mais la maison sombre du quartier archi-peuplé qui entoure la cathédrale. Et puis, il fallut travailler. Mme de Warens avait trouvé pour lui une place parmi les employés au cadastre du roi Victor-Amédée (1). Rousseau dit lui-même : « Cette uniformité (de vie) était précisément ce dont j'avais le plus grand besoin pour achever de former mon caractère que des troubles continuels empêchaient de fixer » (127). Mais il ne se disciplina pas. Après quelques semaines, le travail étant devenu routine, il céda à toutes sortes d'enthousiasmes ; — pas plutôt était-il vraiment plongé dans un genre d'occupation qu'il en était fatigué ; ce furent d'abord les mathématiques ; puis le dessin du bureau le conduisit à goûter la peinture ; il s'y abandonna tellement qu'on « était obligé de l'en arracher ». Puis « la musique absorba tout le reste », — d'autant plus qu'il pouvait s'y livrer avec maman. A quelque temps de là, la guerre éclata (1733), l'armée française passa par la Suisse pour aller dans le Milanais ; il n'en fallut pas plus pour passionner Jean-Jacques pour la politique et pour la France. Cette lubie un peu passée, il revient à la musique ; « les opéras de Rameau commençaient à faire du bruit » (131) ; il se procure le *Traité de l'harmonie* ; il le dévore. Et voici qu'arrive à Chambéry un organiste, « bon musicien, et qui accompagnait très bien du clavecin » ; Rousseau et lui sont inséparables ; on propose des concerts chez maman, — maman ne résiste pas ; Rousseau « ni nuit, ni jour » ne s'occupe d'autre chose ; en rapport avec cela, de petits soupers « très gais, très agréables ; on y disait le mot et la chose ; on y chantait des duos ; j'étais à mon aise, j'avais de l'esprit, des saillies » (132). Est-ce la mélancolie et la monotonie du travail de bureau ou autre chose ; en tous cas Rousseau tombe malade, et c'est un prétexte pour abandonner le cadastre. Il se met alors à donner des leçons de musique. Ce n'était qu'un pis aller ; cette vie sans base — et sans qu'il s'en aperçut toujours — le minait moralement et physiquement.

Ce n'est pas tout ; il va être frappé dans ses plus chères affections, dans la personne qui pour lui comptait seule ; il dé-

(1) Rousseau explique que le roi, voyant sa dynastie menacée, voulut avant d'abandonner son royaume, en exploiter toutes les richesses, l'épuiser en quelque sorte ; en vue de cela, ce travail de cadastre.

couvre un profond désordre moral chez Mme de Warens, la
femme qu'à l'égale d'une mère, il aimait ; car, même s'il avait
dans le passé aperçu en elle quelques faiblesses, il avait fermé
les yeux. On se souvient des pages navrantes des *Confessions* :
ses dames de Chambéry avaient voulu « déniaiser » leur professeur de musique ; Mme de Warens, pour le protéger, trouve
l'étrange moyen de s'y employer elle-même ; et puis Rousseau apprend bientôt que Claude Anet jouit des mêmes privilèges que lui.

Quelques mois après (1734) nouvelle catastrophe. Claude
Anet meurt subitement, lui qui constituait l'élément stable
de la petite communauté. A l'anarchie morale de la maison
succède l'anarchie économique. Rousseau essaye bien de
prendre la place d'Anet, mais lui-même s'en sent incapable,
et on ne le prend pas au sérieux. On avise, sans conviction, des
remèdes qui ne sont que des expédients ; la musique, par
exemple. Rousseau fit un jour une équipée à Besançon pour
étudier avec l'abbé Blanchard ; une aventure de douane, la
confiscation de son bagage (148-9), et le départ de l'abbé
Blanchard pour Paris peu après, firent échouer ce projet ; et
on n'y pensa plus. La seule chose qui devait servir Rousseau
plus tard, ce fut celle dont il l'attendait le moins, à savoir les
abondantes lectures que son oisiveté lui permettait ; il se pas-
sionna tour à tour pour les différentes sciences, (c'est ainsi
qu'il fit sa fameuse expérience avec de l'encre de sympathie
qui manqua l'aveugler) ; il tomba gravement malade et s'a-
bandonna au luxe délicieux de se faire rappeler à la vie par
maman. C'est à cette maladie que nous devons l'idylle des
Charmettes. Il fallait sortir des vieux murs de Chambéry
pour vivre à la campagne, de grand air et de laitage ; malade
et garde-malade louèrent aux portes de la ville la petite maison qui est devenue un grand lieu de pèlerinage : « Ainsi cou-
lèrent mes jours heureux, et d'autant plus heureux que n'apercevant rien qui dût les troubler, je n'envisageais en effet leur
fin qu'avec la mienne » (175) (1). Il ne mourut pas ; mais son

(1) A cause de quelques difficultés de dates, on a voulu contester le caractère

romantisme mourut. Les Charmettes sont le suprême adieu
de Rousseau au romantisme. La guérison revenue, ce fut la
même vie d'expédients — mais pire. Rousseau assistait impuissant à la débâcle financière de Mme de Warens. Un jour,
il va à Genève recueillir le petit héritage de sa mère, car il est
maintenant majeur : « J'en mis quelque partie en livres, et je
volai porter le reste aux pieds de maman » (176) : — c'était
une goutte d'eau dans l'océan. Rousseau se réfugie de plus en
plus dans le travail, lequel du reste ne le protège pas toujours
des folies ; il s'était mis à l'étude de la médecine, et bientôt il
s'imagina avoir un polype au cœur. Il part pour Montpellier
dans l'idée de se faire soigner ; en route, il rencontre une
femme piquante, Mme de Larnage, à qui il doit « de ne pas mourir sans avoir connu le plaisir » (181); — flamme éteinte presqu'aussitôt qu'allumée, et qui par le souvenir allait se transformer en dégoût devant la futilité de l'existence. Quand il
revint de Montpellier, après cinq ou six semaines, il trouve
l'œuvre de ruine beaucoup plus avancée qu'avant son départ : Mme de Warens s'était abandonnée, en désespérée, à
un jeune Vaudois plein d'entrain et de faconde, un certain
Vintzenried qui peut-être sauverait la situation. Crut-elle
vraiment en Vintzenried, ou voulut-elle se donner l'illusion
d'y croire ? — Cette seconde interprétation paraît la plus probable, car son attitude envers Rousseau s'explique bien alors.
Elle sait celui-ci assez intelligent pour deviner « le chevalier
de Courtilles » — *Taleralatalera* comme il l'eût bientôt sur-
nommé ; la présence de Rousseau dans la maison constituait
ainsi un constant trouble-fête à ses tentatives de s'aveugler
elle-même, de ne pas voir le gouffre ouvert à ses pieds ; elle
préférait éloigner ce témoin inquiétant, et sans doute dans
cette intention, expédiait Jean-Jacques vivre seul aux Charmettes la plupart du temps.

historique du séjour aux Charmettes — voire tout simplement le traiter de
fiction. Cela nous paraît une folle concession au dieu d'une soi-disante érudition.
Nous avons présenté quelques observations sur ce petit problème dans la *Revue
d'Histoire litt. de la France*, 1928 (n° de janv-mars).

Les mois qui précèdent le départ pour Paris ne sont que des mois d'agonie morale où Rousseau chercha à se raccrocher désespérément à son passé romantique. Mais il tombe de déception en déception. Ses lettres sont celles d'un pauvre naufragé qui par moments ne demande qu'à se noyer. Une tentative de préceptorat à Lyon a échoué ; il commet, victime de sa timidité et de sa nonchalance, les plus naïves sottises, — telles que faire la cour à Mme de Mably, et faire usage illégitimement de la cave de son bienveillant patron. Tout s'écroule autour de lui. Dans l'immensité de son abattement, il essaie une dernière fois d'aller à Chambéry, chez maman. Il savait certainement d'avance que les choses n'iraient point mieux, mais il ne se connaissait plus... (1) Il repart presque aussitôt pour Paris, non pas qu'il ait davantage confiance en son étoile, mais parce qu'il ne sait rien d'autre : il avait inventé un système de notation musicale, et il avait écrit une comédie, — et c'était tout. Il faut se garder de se moquer de lui ou de le juger ; il n'est pas responsable de son éducation et de sa destinée ; il ne dépendait pas de lui d'acquérir un autre caractère ; et il fut dans ces années-là le plus malheureux des hommes.

§ 4. Il arrive à Paris en 1742, avec 15 louis dans sa poche, et la mort dans l'âme. Pour la première fois il ne parle pas d'un voyage au gai soleil de l'insouciance. Il n'a plus de foyer derrière lui auquel il puisse retourner en cas de nécessité ; la jeunesse commence à passer... et les sept années qui suivent vont constituer une nouvelle série de désenchantements. Il est balloté dans tous les sens et à tous les hasards des rencontres et des événements, ne sachant ni profiter de la bonne fortune, ni vaincre la mauvaise, et agissant en toutes choses de la façon

---

(1) Recommandons ici la lecture de l'article de Mme Noëlle Roger dans la *Revue des Deux Mondes*, du 1er oct. 1924, sur cette phase de la vie de Rousseau et le drame des Charmettes. Sauf qu'elle est empreinte d'une sévérité excessive par moments pour Mme de Warens, cette étude révèle une pénétration psychologique remarquable.

la plus déconcertante aux yeux d'un homme qui aurait au moindre degré le sens de la vie pratique. L'Académie des Sciences, à laquelle il avait présenté son système de notation musicale, lui avait fait l'aumône de quelques bonnes paroles et l'avait renvoyé. Ne voyant pas d'issue à sa situation, il s'enferme cependant trois mois pour retravailler un système qu'il reconnaît lui-même maintenant — éclairé par la critique de Rameau — peu viable ; pis encore, il n'a pas de quoi vivre, et il engloutit le reste de son pécule pour payer les frais d'impression de son mémoire ; et il donne des leçons à une Américaine pour obtenir un succès qui ne pouvait que rester ignoré. Bref, il est complètement désemparé. Il avait d'excellentes lettres de recommandation ; il ne s'en sert pas : « L'extrême besoin que j'avais qu'on pensât à moi était précisément ce qui m'ôtait le courage de me montrer, et la nécessité de faire des visites me les rendait insupportables, au point que je cessai même de voir les académiciens et autres gens de lettres avec lesquels j'étais déjà faufilé » (202). Le père Castel lui conseille de lâcher musiciens et savants : « Changez de corde, et voyez les femmes » (203). Il commence, avec sa maladresse coutumière, par Mme Dupin, qui le « reçut à sa toilette. Elle avait les bras nus, les cheveux épars, son peignoir mal arrangé » — il tombe amoureux. Pourtant on lui pardonne et il reste même attaché à la maison comme précepteur intérimaire de M. de Francueil, fils de M. et beau-fils de Mme Dupin. Puis, après une maladie, il abandonne, et reprend son idée de musique ; pendant sa convalescence, il projette l'opéra des *Muses galantes*. Tout cela n'aboutit à rien. Cependant les « femmes » veillaient ; elles lui procurent la place de secrétaire de M. Montaigu, ambassadeur de France à Venise. Ce sera une diversion. L'Italie l'enchante, Venise, ville de plaisir surtout ; plus tard, quand banni de l'île de Saint-Pierre il ne sait où aller, c'est à Venise qu'il pense entre autres : musique, femmes, tout lui sourit. Mais cela encore devait finir misérablement, et sans qu'on puisse, semble-t-il, trop blâmer Rousseau. Que faire ? Paris encore ? Non ; il veut aller à Genève, attendre... quoi ? « Qu'un meilleur sort, écartant les obstacles pût me réunir à ma pauvre maman »

(229). Après tout, quelques semaines plus tard, il se retrouve à Paris quand même, où on lui donne à entendre — à propos de l'équipée de Venise — qu'un homme de sa condition doit être plus soumis aux grands de ce monde et plus pratique... Il se consolera maintenant de ses déboires, par son amour de pitié pour Thérèse Levasseur, pauvre servante, bousculée dans le monde comme lui et moins apte encore à se défendre, — qu'il peut comprendre et qui peut le comprendre. Rien n'est plus naturel que cette liaison à cette heure de la vie de Rousseau ; dégoûté des hommes, il se sent à l'aise avec des gens sans malice ; il peut être pris au pied de la lettre quand il écrit : « Il me fallait à la place de l'ambition éteinte, un sentiment qui remplît mon cœur. Il fallait pour tout dire un successeur à maman puisque je ne devais plus vivre avec elle ; il me fallait quelqu'un qui vécut avec son élève et en qui je trouvasse la simplicité, la docilité de cœur qu'elle avait trouvée en moi » (235).

Et Rousseau s'y abandonne, à ce pauvre bonheur, et malgré le dénuement dans lequel il était, il raconte encore : « Je vivais avec ma Thérèse aussi agréablement qu'avec le plus beau génie de l'univers... Cette douce intimité me tenait lieu de tout : l'avenir ne me touchait plus ou ne me touchait que comme le présent prolongé ; je ne désirais rien que d'en assurer la durée. Cet attachement me rendit tout autre dissipation superflue et insipide » (236).

Rousseau parle ainsi plus de vingt ans après. Qu'on mesure la chute : il en est à oublier l'idylle des Charmettes par l'idylle quasi-crapuleuse de l'Hôtel Saint-Quentin. Et quoi pour le sortir de cette situation ? Des insuccès continuels. *Les Muses galantes* ne sont pas agréées ; *les Fêtes de Ramire* (opéra de Rameau qu'on avait chargé Rousseau de retoucher) non plus ; la comédie de *Narcisse* eut encore le même sort (1). En attendant, il a charge d'une famille de sept ou huit personnes qu'il s'est mise sur les bras par ses relations avec Thérèse. Il accepte de faire de la chimie avec M. de Francueil. Au retour de Che-

---

(1) Elle sera représentée, mais beaucoup plus tard, en 1752.

nonceaux (où il était avec la famille de son élève) il trouve
Thérèse prête à lui donner un enfant ; on sait ce qu'il en fit,
ainsi que des suivants : il les mit à l'hospice des enfants trouvés. Nous n'allons pas discuter à nouveau cette affaire. Que
ceux qui, se plaçant par l'imagination dans les circonstances
où se trouvait Rousseau, eussent fait autrement lui jettent la
première pierre. (1)

Note sur Rousseau et la psychiâtrie. — Nous ne reviendrons
guère sur la psychologie de Rousseau ; il n'y aura pas lieu de la
faire pour le but que nous nous proposons, c'est-à-dire étudier sa
pensée. Il convient d'autre part, étant donné le rôle que nous assi-
gnons naturellement à sa personne dans la formation de cette
pensée, et étant donné les polémiques sans cesse renouvelées autour
de l'œuvre et qui si souvent prennent pour point de départ sa personne, de nous expliquer sur le problème qu'on a souvent appelé
celui de la folie de Jean-Jacques Rousseau.

Il en est, comme Lemaître, qui ont exploité, non sans hypocrisie,
cette note pour dire : Rousseau est un malade ; il faut le plaindre ;
mais ses opinions ne comptent pas. Il en est qui ont brandi le fouet
de l'indignation, comme Seillière, et qui l'ont déclaré un méchant
homme, et ont continué au détriment de Rousseau les enquêtes
du genre Lombroso pour l'homme criminel — annulant du reste
ces anathèmes puisqu'on n'anathématise pas un non-responsable.
Il en est qui, comme Babbit, ont joué à la vertu offensée et ont fait
de Rousseau un dépravé. Louis Proal vint à propos. Il y a dans son
livre sur le tempérament et le caractère de Rousseau (*La Psychologie de Jean-Jacques Rousseau*, Alcan 1923) — avec peut-être
parfois trop de mots savants — beaucoup de bon sens, beaucoup
aussi de citations intéressantes empruntées à des autorités médi-
cales.

(1) Rousseau a évidemment exprimé toute la vérité quand il a écrit : « Je
m'y déterminai gaillardement et sans le moindre scrupule », et : « Je formai
ma façon de penser sur celle que je voyais en règne chez des gens très aimables
et dans le fond très honnêtes » (244). Plus tard, dans les *Confessions* (et déjà
dans l'*Emile*) Rousseau a pris simultanément avec l'attitude que nous venons
de rappeler, une autre attitude inconciliable avec celle-là, et où il se blâme ; or,
ou bien, il pouvait agir autrement et alors ses explications de l'état d'esprit
qui le fit agir sont fausses et inutiles, ou bien il ne pouvait ne pas agir ainsi et
alors ses blâmes et ses remords sont superflus ; il a pu y avoir regrets, mais non
pas remords.

Or, M. Proal écrit : « Rousseau n'a pas été seulement dans un état voisin de la folie, il a franchi la frontière qui sépare le génie de la folie » (p. 310). Cela cependant n'a, en soi, rien de choquant ; car d'abord, on sent d'emblée que l'auteur n'est pas animé de la fureur anti-rousseauiste d'un Seillière (que, soit dit en passant, il ne nomme même pas quand bien même il publie deux ans après). C'est ensuite, on le sent bien, plus que toute autre chose une affaire de définition ; car voici un collègue de M. Proal, le Dʳ Régis de l'université de Bordeaux, qui dans une revue médicale, et traitant de Rousseau dans un esprit assez pareillement pondéré, écrira, lui : « L'auteur d'*Emile* ne fut jamais un fou. Bien que tourmenté par des craintes et des soupçons imaginaires, bien qu'ayant obéi à des idées fausses, au point d'accomplir parfois des actes déraisonnables, il n'a jamais franchi cette ligne de démarcation difficile à préciser, mais réelle, qui sépare l'inquiétude, la suspicion outrée, l'exaltation et même certains délires élémentaires, de la vraie insanité ». Il y a eu « trouble mental », Rousseau est un « persécuté mélancolique ». (*Chronique médicale*, 1ᵉʳ juillet, 1890). Et du reste ce Rousseau « fou » est, chez M. Proal, en compagnie assez honorable ; à savoir Socrate, Lucrèce, Le Tasse, Pascal, Bernardin de Saint-Pierre, Strindberg, les Prophètes d'Israël, Luther et les réformateurs religieux, Mahomet et d'autres fondateurs de religion (p. 402, et ss). M. Proal place Rousseau dans une société de génies (p. 308, et ss.) ; ce qui l'intéresse, « c'est cette coexistence du génie et de la folie », avait-il dit aux premières pages de son livre. Il explique ailleurs que le mot *dégénéré* qu'il finit par adopter, avec le Dʳ Magnant, pour caractériser Rouseau (p. 254), ne doit pas être pris dans le sens que ce terme a dans la vie de tous les jours ; il s'agit simplement d'une disposition (ici sensibilité) qui est très forte, se manifeste souvent au dépend d'autres.

C'est fort intéressant ; mais c'est ici qu'on se prend à réfléchir. On ne voit pas que tant d'érudition nous éclaire beaucoup. Involontairement on pense à Molière... « Et voilà ce qui fait que votre fille est muette ». Voici par exemple un passage : « Les biographes de Rousseau ne sont pas d'accord sur la nature de son nervosisme. Le Dʳ Régis, le Dʳ Moebius et Faguet concluent à la neurasthénie, le Dʳ Pierre Janet à la psychasténie, les philosophes Renouvier et Espinas à l'hystérie. Le Dʳ Magnan, dont le diagnostic était réputé infaillible, et le Dʳ Sérieux, l'un de ses meilleurs élèves, le Dʳ Briand, médecin en chef de l'asile de Sainte-Anne, placent Rousseau, dans la catégorie des dégénérés supérieurs, ils voient en lui le type de déséquilibré de la sensibilité avec tendances paranoiaques, caractérisées par l'orgueil et la défiance ; c'est un tempérament morbide dont l'exagération réalise le délire de persécution à base d'interprétation. »

(p. 254)... Et plus loin : « A la précision trompeuse de ces diagnos-
tics : Hystérie, psychasténie, neurasthénie, il faut donc préférer
celle de dégénéré supérieur, dont la déséquilibration constitution-
nelle est caractérisée avant tout par un développement anormal
de la sensibilité ». (p. 256). Va pour « dégénéré supérieur dont... » ;
mais encore là il y aura tant de qualifications, de réserves ; de définitions et explications, qu'on ne voit personne qui ne puisse être
considéré comme fou, dément ou aliéné si Rousseau doit être ainsi
caractérisé : il n'est pas fou, car fou signifie cela... ; il n'est pas dément, car dément signifie cela ; il n'est pas aliéné, car aliéné signifie cela ; d'autre part il *est* « dégénéré », mais « dégénéré » ne signifie pas ce qu'on pense ; il est paranoiaque, mais paranoiaque
dans tel et tel sens ; il y a chez lui de la psychose, mais psychose
n'est pas ce qu'entend le docteur X... Et que serait-ce si l'on venait
encore à la physiologie du cas ? — On en arrive alors au « calvaire
urinaire » des docteurs Poncet et Le Riche (p. 318). Et partout on
nous effraye de ces gros mots : Rousseau n'est pas seulement timide,
il est *phobique*. Il avait la phobie verbale, la phobie urinaire, la phobie des ténèbres : et « une figure cachée sous un drap blanc lui donnait des convulsions dans son enfance... » (289) Ailleurs : « Il écrit à
Saint-Germain, en 1770 : *Je doute qu'aucun homme ait jamais eu
une jeunesse plus chaste que la mienne*, et cependant il avait des
aberrations sexuelles : le masochisme et l'exhibitionisme » (p. 304).

Au point de départ de tant de discussions subtiles et n'aboutissant à rien, il y a, nous semble-t-il, toujours l'idée que l'homme normal existe, — ce qui n'est pas le cas. Et si l'homme normal n'existe
pas, ou en grande exception, pourquoi juger Rousseau sur la mesure
de l'abstrait alors qu'on ne fait jamais cela avec d'autres ? Rousseau est très humain, parce qu'il a justement ces faiblesses de tous
les humains. Le langage de tous les jours va très bien pour dire que
Rousseau est simplement un être très sensible ; de là ses caractéristiques, son tempérament, ses « crimes », ses malheurs. Qu'on lise
les pages 260 et suivantes où Proal définit le sensible Rousseau
allant, en vertu de cette sensibilité, tantôt très haut et tantôt très
bas, et qu'on nous dise si ces mots ne s'appliquent pas à tant de
gens que nous connaissons et pour lesquels nous ne songeons point
toujours à l'intervention du médecin (1).

Que ceci ne nous empêche pas de reconnaître la valeur de l'étude
de M. Proal et — c'est trop rare pour ne pas le souligner — de son opinion sans fanatisme. Il a su résumer lui-même son opinion dans un
langage parfaitement accessible au commun des mortels, quand il
a défini le cas Rousseau de la façon suivante : « Déséquilibration

_____

(1) Qu'on voie encore pp. 7, 9 ; 27-28 ; 43 ; 271-285, 289, 382 ssq, 423, 437.

mentale qui ne l'a pas empêché d'écrire des chef-d'œuvres, et qui a fini par déterminer un délire patiel » (p. 23)... Mais, réduit à cela, tout ce problème de la folie de Rousseau signifie en vérité peu de chose (1).

(1) Veut-on un cas où il est possible de voir l'*abime* entre l'être normal et la folie caractérisée : qu'on prenne alors celui de Maupassant ; le livre de Georges NORMANDY, *La fin de Maupassant* (A. Michel, 1927) surtout dans ses derniers chapitres, est effrayant. Qui oserait, ayant lu cela, employer un terme commun pour deux cas aussi différents que le jour et la nuit ?

LE CONFLIT CHEZ ROUSSEAU
L'ÉCRIVAIN

> Son cœur et sa raison seront incessam-
> ment en guerre.
> Rousseau (*Nouvelle Héloïse*, I, 26).

CHAPITRE PREMIER

ROUSSEAU ET LES ROMAINS
DISCOURS SUR LES SCIENCES ET LES ARTS

Rousseau, désabusé de la vie « romantique », se reprend d'un grand enthousiasme pour la *vertu*. Le *Premier Discours* est un hymne à la vertu. Trois notions de vertu : *vertu romaine* de désintéressement ; *vertu d'innocence* ; *vertu de sagesse* ou philosophique. Rousseau exalte la vertu romaine — qu'il ne distingue pas de la vertu des chrétiens et qui vaut par le renoncement à toute prétention d'avantages personnels ou romantiques.

Note sur l'originalité du Paradoxe.

§ **1**. Donc Rousseau, épave humaine quand il arrive à Paris en 1742, l'est plus encore sept ans après, en 1749. Il approche de la quarantaine ; la jeunesse s'est évanouie pour de bon ; comme carrière, il n'a derrière lui qu'un gaspillage de talents et de forces ; comme vie personnelle, c'est un éparpillement de sa personne dans le monde flottant des lettres, et en marge, une existence de fortune au milieu de la tribu Levasseur. Les heures de joie ne sont que de courts répits dans d'interminables phases de désillusion. Y avait-il un moyen de s'affranchir de ce marasme, d'échapper à cette vie sans base et sans but ? Si un jour la question se formulait nettement à l'esprit, surtout à l'esprit d'un homme qui connaissait Genève, la ville d'ordre, de décence, de discipline, une réponse s'offrait aussitôt. Rousseau était bien mûr pour un retour sur lui-même ; et Rousseau était resté aussi impressionnable que dans l'enfance ; il ne fallait pour ainsi dire que presser sur un bouton.

On sait comment cela arriva : Dans sa vie de bohême, Rousseau s'était beaucoup attaché au plus bohème d'entre les hommes de lettres de l'époque, Diderot ; celui-ci, un jour, est emprisonné dans le donjon de Vincennes pour sa très libre *Lettre sur les aveugles* (fin juillet, 1749). Rousseau s'en émut à un point extraordinaire ; « la tête faillit m'en tourner », dit-il ; il écrit à Mme de Pompadour demandant comme une grâce d'être enfermé avec Diderot ; si sa captivité « eût duré quelques jours encore avec la même rigueur, je crois que je serais mort au pied du malheureux donjon » (VIII, 247). Diderot ayant été transféré du donjon au château, il put se promener dans le parc, et put recevoir ses amis. Rousseau y courut, et lorsqu'il arrive : « Moment inexprimable... je ne fis qu'un saut, un cri ; je collais mon visage sur le sien, je le serrais étroitement sans lui parler autrement que par mes pleurs et mes sanglots ; j'étouffais de tendresse et de joie » (248). Comment s'empêcher — en passant — de comparer cet état d'exaltation avec la sérénité de Rousseau aux Charmettes (1), avec les « moments paisibles qui lui ont donné le droit de dire qu'il avait vécu », et dont il regrette « l'aimable cours ».

Aujourd'hui l'équilibre n'existait plus ; il semblait que chaque parcelle de bonheur fût si rare qu'elle devait provoquer de vraies crises de sentimentalité. Rousseau continue ses visites, tous les deux jours au moins ; c'était à deux lieues de

---

(1) « Comment ferai-je pour prolonger à mon gré ce récit si touchant et si simple, pour redire toujours les mêmes choses, et n'ennuyer pas plus mes lecteurs en les répétant que je ne m'ennuyais moi-même en les recommençant sans cesse ? Encore si tout cela consistait en faits, en actions, en paroles, je pourrais le décrire et le rendre en quelque façon : mais comment dire ce qui n'était ni dit, ni fait, ni pensé même, mais goûté, mais senti, sans que je puisse énoncer d'autre objet de mon bonheur que ce sentiment même ? Je me levais avec le soleil, et j'étais heureux ; je me promenais, et j'étais heureux ; je me promenais, et j'étais heureux ; je voyais maman, et j'étais heureux, je la quittais et j'étais heureux ; je parcourais les bois, les côteaux, j'errais dans les vallons, je lisais, j'étais oisif ; je travaillais au jardin, je cueillais les fruits, j'aidais au ménage, et le bonheur me suivait partout : il n'était dans aucune chose assignable, il était tout en moi-même, il ne pouvait me quitter un seul instant ». (*Confessions*, Livre VI).

Paris ; il allait à pied n'ayant pas de quoi payer un fiacre.
C'est à un de ces voyages qu'il fut frappé d'une vision. Il
avait lu dans un journal un programme de concours proposé
par l'Académie de Dijon : « Si le progrès des Sciences et des Arts
a contribué à épurer les mœurs » (249) (1). La façon de formuler cette demande, — et surtout la façon de la lire — locali-
sait pour ainsi dire le problème qui vaguement, depuis longtemps, sollicitait Rousseau et le travaillait : C'était depuis
qu'il était entré complètement en contact avec la « civilisation », avec les lettres et les arts » qu'il se sentait dans le monde
comme une plante déracinée, que la vie lui paraissait sans noblesse et sans prix. Il le comprenait tout à coup. Et qui plus est,
ce problème, ce n'était pas seulement le sien ; c'était celui
de tous. Que voyait-il en effet, tout autour de lui que misère
morale ou mensonger bonheur ? Le monde était malade,
comme lui était malade. C'était donc qu'on prenait pour bon ce
qui était réellement mauvais. Non, « les sciences et les arts »
n'épurent rien ; ils corrompent plutôt :

« Si jamais quelque chose a ressemblé à une inspiration, c'est le
mouvement qui se fit en moi à cette lecture : tout à coup je me sens
l'esprit ébloui de mille lumières ; des foules d'idées vives s'y présentent à la fois avec une force et une confusion qui me jeta dans
un trouble inexprimable ; je sens ma tête prise par un étourdisse-
ment semblable à l'ivresse... Je me laissai tomber sous un des
arbres de l'avenue... Si j'avais pu écrire le quart de ce que j'ai vu
et senti sous cet arbre, avec quelle clarté j'aurais fait voir toute
les contradictions du système social ! » (X, 301) (2).

(1) La question telle que posée dans le *Mercure* d'octobre (donc ce n'était
pas en été comme le pensait plus tard Rousseau) était : « Si le rétablissement des
sciences et des arts a contribué à épurer les mœurs ». On entendait donc réellement une discussion de la Renaissance. Rousseau en rédigeant la chose «... a
contribué *à corrompre et* à épurer les mœurs... » en a fait un sujet beaucoup plus
général.

(2) Rousseau ajoute : « Avec quelle force j'aurais exposé tous les abus de nos
institutions ! Avec quelle simplicité j'aurais démontré que l'homme est naturellement bon et que c'est par ces institutions seules que les hommes deviennent méchants ». Mais ceci est déjà le sujet du *Second Discours* ; cette
phrase écrite dix-sept ans au moins après, est donc une anticipation.

Et qu'est-ce que Rousseau trouve de plus entièrement opposé à ce qui l'a trompé, à ce qui trompe le monde ? C'est la vieille vertu calviniste et romaine, cette vertu honnie dans cette société surtout où se mouvaient les philosophes et les gens du monde ; les vilenies, les bassesses pour « jouir » du monde, et ces nausées après des jouissances empoisonnées et du reste sans distinction, on ne les connaissait pas chez les Romains de la république et à Genève. Donc, de même que par dégoût de la discipline absurde et cruelle des Masseron et des Ducommun, il s'était vingt ans avant jeté à corps perdu dans le « romantisme » qu'il considérait comme une dé-livrance de la contrainte de son pauvre *moi*, maintenant avec le même emportement, comme après une longue nostalgie, et en homme qui a réfléchi, il se rejette avec grand espoir dans la vertu romaine. A l'épisode tragique de la fuite de Genève (en 1728) correspond exactement au point de vue psy-chologique, l'illumination de la route de Vincennes (1749). Les deux événements sont aussi soudains l'un que l'autre, mais en même temps aussi fatals l'un que l'autre, — résultats tous deux d'un long et profond travail de préparation inté-rieur.

Or, ces Romains et ces Calvinistes, sur quoi voulaient-ils fonder leur vie peut-être austère, mais qui satisfait des aspi-rations profondes et durables ?

On peut le dire en un mot : *La vertu.*

§ **2**. Le *Premier Discours* en effet est tout entier un hymne à la vertu.

Rousseau adresse son discours aux membres de l'Académie de Dijon : « C'est la *vertu* que je défends devant les hommes *vertueux* » (1) ! Et en quoi va consister ce qu'on a appelé le paradoxe de Rousseau ? C'est que les « peuples policés »,

---

(1) Nous citons toujours d'après l'édition Hachette des *Œuvres de Rousseau*. Sauf indication contraire, il s'agit du volume I ; le chiffre indiqué est celui de la page.

ceux qui ont « cette douceur de caractère et cette urbanité de mœurs qui rendent... le commerce si liant et si facile, ont les apparences de toutes les *vertus*, sans en avoir aucune (p. 3) ». La « décence » n'est point nécessairement la *vertu*, et une « grande pompe » n'accompagne guère la *vertu*, et la « parure » est étrangère à la *vertu* (4). « A mesure que leur lumière [des sciences et des arts] s'élevait à l'horizon », on a vu « la *vertu* s'enfuir » ; et cela est ainsi « dans tous les temps et tous les lieux (5) ». Ce qu'il faut conquérir, c'est les *vertus* d'un « petit nombre de peuples... préservés de cette contagion des vaines connaissances » (6). « Rome, [qui fut] jadis le temple de la *vertu*, devient le théâtre du crime » (6). Qu'est-ce qui fait qu'on peut appeler Sparte une « république de demi-dieux » ? C'est que les *vertus* de ses citoyens « semblaient supérieures à l'humanité » (7) ; « là, disaient les autres peuples, les hommes naissent *vertueux* et l'air même du pays semble inspirer la *vertu* » (7-8). Socrate à Athènes et Caton à Rome déchaînaient leur éloquence contre les « artificieux et subtils qui séduisaient la *vertu* », et ils nous ont laissé à tous « l'exemple et la mémoire de leur *vertu*, (8). Que regrette « la grande âme » de Fabricius ? « Les toits de chaume de ces foyers rustiques qu'habitaient jadis la modération et la *vertu* » (8), et il termine son apostrophe : « Le seul talent digne de Rome est celui de conquérir et d'y faire régner la *vertu*. Quand Cinéas prit notre sénat pour une assemblée de rois... que vit-il donc de si majestueux ? O citoyens ! Il vit un plus beau spectacle que ne donneront jamais vos richesses, ni tous vos arts, le plus beau spectacle qui ait jamais paru sous le ciel : l'assemblée de deux cents hommes *vertueux*, dignes de commander à Rome et de gouverner la terre » (9). Bref, que prouve l'exemple de Rome ? que la science et la *vertu* seraient « incompatibles ».

Et pourquoi, se demande Rousseau dans la 2e partie, les sciences et les arts sont-ils vains ? C'est qu'ils doivent leur naissance à nos vices : « Nous serions moins en doute sur leurs avantages s'ils la devaient à nos *vertus* » (10). Les « funestes paradoxes » de « vains et futiles déclamateurs » « sapent les fondements de la foi et anéantissent la *vertu* » (11). On parle de luxe et de confort : question bien secondaire, car que deviendra la *vertu* quand il faudra s'enrichir à quelque prix que ce soit (12) ? » La réelle question pour les empires est de savoir s'il importe plus « d'être brillants et momentanés, ou *vertueux et durables* » (12-13). Pourquoi se plaît-on « à se rappeler l'image et la simplicité des premiers temps » ? C'est que les hommes étaient « innocents et *vertueux* » (14). En quoi les « commodités de la vie » sont-elles funestes aux états ? c'est que le « vrai courage s'énerve et les *vertus* militaires s'évanouissent » (14). Les Romains l'avouent, les Spartiates avaient prévenu ce malheur par les institutions ; le fait qu'on s'arrête à « la distinction des talents » aboutit « à l'avilissement des *vertus* » (16). « Les récompenses sont prodiguées au bel esprit et la *vertu* reste sans honneurs » (16) ; et le sage court après la gloire alors que la *vertu* n'a plus pour lui aucun avantage : sur quoi, arrivent les philosophes qui « prétendent (que) tout est en représentations... qu'il n'y a ni *vertus*, ni vices » (18). Et le discours finit sur cette invocation : « *O vertu*, science sublime des âmes simples... Voilà la véritable philosophie, sachons nous en contenter ; et sans envier la gloire de ces hommes célèbres qui s'immortalisent dans la république des lettres, tâchons de mettre entre eux et nous cette distinction glorieuse qu'on remarquait jadis entre deux grands peuples ; que l'un savait bien dire, et l'autre bien faire » (20).

Si quelqu'un se plaisait, même après cela, à mal comprendre Rousseau, celui-ci s'expliquait encore dans les discussions qui suivirent la publication du *Discours*. On lui objecte qu'on enseigne aux jeunes gens beaucoup de choses qui leur servent à goûter la vie plus tard ; il répond : « Je ne vois point le rapport avec les devoirs des citoyens dont il faut commencer par les instruire » (25). Il veut bien reconnaître qu'on a fait « un grand nombre d'inventions utiles qui ont ajouté aux charmes et aux commodités de la vie » ; mais « considérons... toutes ces connaissances par rapport aux mœurs » (48). Ou plus loin : « Si quelque chose peut compenser la ruine des mœurs, je suis prêt à convenir que les sciences font plus de bien que de mal » (52). Ou encore : « Je vois qu'on me parle toujours de fortune et de grandeur. Je parlais, moi, de mœurs et de *vertu* » (52) (1). « Que ne donneraient-ils point [mes adversaires] pour que cette malheureuse Sparte n'eût jamais existé !... C'est une terrible chose qu'au milieu de cette fameuse Grèce qui ne devait, dit-on, sa *vertu* qu'à la philosophie, l'Etat où la *vertu* a été la plus pure et a duré le plus longtemps ait été précisément celui où il n'y avait point de philosophes ! » (56).

Mais que faut-il entendre par *vertu* ? Aucun des passages cités ne nous le laisse certainement deviner, et Rousseau, s'autorisant sans doute de ce que « les principes de la vertu sont gravés dans tous les cœurs » (20), croit pouvoir s'abstenir de toute explication. Cette attitude peut être possible pour certains écrits de morale courante où le mot serait assez explicite par le contexte ; mais quand il s'agit d'une œuvre philosophique où le terme *vertu* revient une dizaine de fois à chaque page. c'est illégitime. Que ce soit du reste gravé au cœur de chacun, ou que ce ne le soit pas, est indifférent ; car, de deux choses l'une : ou bien la notion de vertu est réellement indéfinissable, n'est pas intellectuellement saisissable, est arationnelle, et alors que faire de cet x dans une discussion philosophique qui est rationnelle ou qui n'est pas ? ; ou bien elle est définissable, et rationnelle et acceptable dans la discussion, et alors il est indispensable que la signification exacte soit indiquée.

Le mot vertu a acquis au cours de l'histoire de la pensée trois sens fort distincts, fort différents, incompatibles même, Récapitulons-les.

Il y a d'abord la conception grecque ou classique : La vertu est un moyen de bonheur, celui que Socrate et Platon, et tous les philosophes antiques après eux, prêchaient ; la vertu, c'est la sagesse morale. Il ne faut pas renoncer aux passions, à un raffinement de la vie parce que le plaisir, ou le luxe en soi sont

(1) C'est vrai qu'on déplaçait ainsi la question. Par exemple Bordes : « Je suppose que tous les Etats dont la Grèce était composée eussent suivi les mêmes lois que Sparte, que nous resterait-il de cette contrée si célèbre »? (56)

des maux, mais parce que ceux-ci pourraient, si nous y cédons trop, procurer plus de maux que de jouissance par les conséquences qui y sont attachées ; nous ne devons y renoncer que lorsque, en ce faisant, nous sommes certains d'augmenter la somme totale du bonheur. On faisait la théorie de cette vertu-là, du point de vue positif, c'est-à-dire en parlant davantage de goûter autant de joie que possible (morale épicurienne), ou du point de vue négatif, c'est-à-dire en parlant davantage de supporter la privation autant que possible (la morale stoïcienne) : le but proposé était, en somme, le même. Cette ordonnance sage de la vie n'était certes pas apportée au monde en naissant ; au contraire ; comme disait Montaigne : « Il n'est science si ardue que savoir vivre cette vie » ; en effet, il fallait connaître bien des choses, et même posséder des connaissances physiologiques n'était pas inutile ; cette vertu *s'apprenait* ; et une fois qu'on savait comment être heureux, et à l'heure au moins où l'esprit était parfaitement clair, on pratiquait naturellement la vertu, puisque personne ne choisit d'être malheureux ; le vice, c'est de l'ignorance ; la faute, c'est une erreur au fond ; et c'est en partant de là que Socrate formulait son : « Personne n'est méchant volontairement ». Il s'était formé une sorte de code moral théorique : depuis Platon on distinguait toujours plus ou moins les mêmes quatre vertus fondamentales, sagesse (intelligence), courage, tempérance, et justice (qu'il faut se garder d'interpréter dans le sens chrétien). Pratiquer ces vertus, c'est pratiquer le bonheur.

Il faut ajouter ici cette remarque : nous venons de définir la vertu pure du philosophe ; mais il y a, à côté de cela, la vertu du citoyen ordinaire. La vertu politique (au sens aristotélien de sociale) repose sur cette fiction que le citoyen est là pour l'Etat — non le contraire. Comme il n'est réservé qu'à un petit nombre de comprendre et d'apprendre la science ou philosophie de la vertu, la masse de la communauté sociale reçoit du législateur et du philosophe une morale d'autorité qu'il n'y a qu'à pratiquer. Grâce à la sagesse et à l'astuce des philosophes, les citoyens, croyant à ce devoir de se sacrifier pour l'Etat, s'exaltent pour celui-ci. On sait comment en

Grèce et à Rome, de cette façon ils travaillaient réellement à leur propre bonheur. Si on n'avait pas recours à ce stratagème et qu'on leur permît de savoir qu'on n'avait en vue que leur propre avantage, chacun penserait qu'il peut bien le poursuivre à sa façon, et ce serait le règne de l'anarchie (1).

Il y a ensuite la conception chrétienne de la vertu — dont nous avons parlé abondamment au chapitre I de notre première partie. Ici le bonheur naturel (ou terrestre) ne compte pas ; il n'est plus question d'une sage administration de nos facultés de jouissance, c'est-à-dire qu'il ne faut pas renoncer seulement à certaines jouissances naturelles pour en gagner un plus grand nombre d'autres par ailleurs, ou pour éviter la douleur conséquente ; les jouissances naturelles (ou terrestres) sont déclarées mauvaises par elles-mêmes et la vertu consiste à y renoncer : bref, il faut les supprimer, non les ordonner.

Sans doute la vertu chrétienne, le renoncement terrestre, est peut-être récompensé après cette vie, mais l'essentiel pour notre morale ici-bas reste ceci : les jouissances naturelles sont mauvaises, la jouissance naturelle c'est le péché ; et comme l'homme suivrait spontanément la voix de la nature, le péché est inné, « originel », et la vertu c'est la négation de la nature, ou du *moi*. « La vraie et unique vertu est de se haïr, car on est haïssable par sa concupiscence », comme dit Pascal (*Pensées*, *XXIV*, 39 *bis*), et : « Les passions dominées sont des vertus » (*ibid.*, *XXV*, 104).

La vertu ainsi comprise ne demande pas une sagesse particulière, ni à être apprise, comme chez les Grecs ; il suffit de

---

(1) Les philosophes eux-mêmes surtout les Romains, moins pénétrants que les Grecs, ont souvent perdu de vue la vraie base de leur vertu, et ont pris le moyen (lutte contre les appétits dangereux et contre la fortune) pour le but. Ainsi Sénèque, dans la fameuse apostrophe finale de son *De Providentiâ* à ceux qui se plaignent du tribut que l'homme doit payer au renoncement et à la souffrance : la fortune a essayé en vain le feu contre Mucius, la pauvreté contre Fabricius, l'exil contre Rutilius, la torture contre Regulus, le poison contre Socrate, la mort contre Caton...

savoir qu'on est mauvais dès qu'on jouit ; il est facile dès lors
de parler de conscience morale innée.

Enfin il y a une troisième conception de vertu où celle-ci
est assimilée à l'innocence. La vertu est un moyen de bonheur
comme dans la première espèce considérée ; mais il ne s'agit
ni de nier la nature, comme dans la vertu chrétienne, ni de la
développer avec sagesse, comme dans la vertu grecque ; il
s'agit de s'en tenir à la seule jouissance résultant de la satisfaction des désirs de la nature — de la nature telle qu'elle est
chez l'être primitif ou chez l'enfant, avant qu'elle se soit con-
pliquée des éléments que l'intelligence, ou disons la civilisation, a pu suggérer d'y ajouter ; tout développement de cette
sorte est considéré comme funeste ou dangereux au bonheur.
La vertu-innocence est réinventée à toutes les époques de civilisation avancée ; les philosophes arrivent toujours à la proposer après que l'on a laissé libre cours à la nature, c'est-à-dire
aux passions, et après que le dégoût ou la déception ont suc-
cédé à la satisfaction des plus subtiles aspirations de bonheur.
C'est un fait que l'habitude tue la jouissance ; et quand un
peuple s'est jeté dans la voie des plaisirs raffinés, en suite de
puissance économique ou matérielle, le résultat est presque
inévitable que pour obtenir de nouvelles jouissances, il faut
reculer les limites de la nature jusqu'au dernier point ; alors, la
faculté des plaisirs étant épuisée, on ne voit plus de jouissance
possible que pour ceux qui n'ont pas été rassasiés : la conclusion s'impose, il faut empêcher les simples de se « civiliser », et
engager ceux qui le sont à agir comme s'ils ne l'étaient pas.
On conçoit donc cette station à la nature primitive, ou ce retour à la nature primitive, comme la vertu — vertu entendue
dans le sens de moyen de bonheur terrestre, comme dans la
vertu-sagesse des Grecs. Sans parler même de la légende du
paradis chez les peuples de la bible, on connaît les rêves d'âges
d'or en Grèce et à Rome nés dans les temps des plus furieux
déchaînements d'appétits et des plus raffinés désirs. Sans
doute pourrait-on dire que la vertu innocence est, en un sens,
une application extrême de la vertu grecque : la suprême sa-

gesse, c'est de ne jamais céder à la passion, car l'homme est trop faible pour être mesuré. Mais cette différence de quantité est en même temps une différence de qualité : comme la vertu grecque consiste à cultiver la sagesse dans la passion, et que la vertu-innocence (prévenant ce développement de la passion jusqu'au degré où la sagesse doit intervenir) consiste à cultiver la bêtise — au sens étymologique — il ne saurait y avoir confusion des deux.

On voit l'incompatibilité de ces trois notions de vertu : vertu-sagesse, vertu-renoncement et vertu-innocence. Si on propose la vertu du renoncement au bonheur terrestre, on exclut vertu-sagesse et vertu-innocence, qui toutes les deux visent à ce bonheur précisément. Et vertu-sagesse et vertu-innocence s'excluent à leur tour réciproquement, puisque la première suppose l'ordonnance de la nature humaine dans l'état de civilisation, et que la seconde défend même de développer la nature primitive pour n'avoir pas la tâche impossible de l'ordonner. Donc, tout philosophe doit choisir l'une d'entre elles à l'exclusion des autres.

Evidemment, la question doit se poser : à laquelle de ces trois notions de vertu Rousseau pense-t-il dans son *Discours* ? La réponse, il faut le reconnaître ne s'impose pas à première vue. Il n'y a même pas de doute que toutes les trois se trouvent *à la fois* dans ces pages.

C'est la vertu-sagesse, quand, à des adversaires qui lui reprocheraient, en condamnant les sciences et les arts, de provoquer cette oisiveté qu'il déclare lui-même si fatale, Rousseau répond : « Je sais qu'il faut occuper les enfants et que l'oisiveté est pour eux le danger le plus à craindre. Que faut-il donc qu'ils apprennent ? Voilà certes une belle question. Qu'ils apprennent ce qu'ils doivent faire étant hommes, et non ce qu'ils doivent oublier » (15). C'est la sagesse de la vie des philosophes grecs, puisque, si, comme il est dit ailleurs, les principes de la vertu étaient « gravés dans tous les cœurs » (20), il ne serait pas besoin de les « apprendre ». Ou c'est encore la vertu-sagesse, à la fin du Discours, quand Rousseau semble si fort se

contredire en déclarant qu'il ne faut pas bannir cette science
si néfaste, et que les rois s'honoreront en l'honorant et qu'il
écrit : « Mais tant que la puissance sera seule d'un côté, les
lumières et la sagesse seules d'un autre, les savants penseront
rarement de grandes choses, les princes en feront plus rarement de belles, et les peuples continueront d'être vils, corrompus et malheureux » (19). C'est elle encore quand, dans le
Discours sur la vertu la plus nécessaire aux héros, de 1751, où
il a cherché à se mettre au clair avec lui, sans du reste y réussir
— il appelle plus tard ce discours un « torchecul » — il dit
par exemple : « L'âme la plus pure peut s'égarer dans la route
même du bien, si l'esprit et la raison ne la guident » (163).

C'est la vertu-innocence, quand Rousseau parle de la civilisation qui a fait « fuir la vertu » (5-6), et des peuples « préservés
de cette contagion vaine des connaissances qui favorisent
l'hypocrisie de la vertu » (6). L'erreur, dit-il ailleurs, a été de
sortir « de l'heureuse ignorance où la sagesse éternelle nous
avait placés » (9) ; le temps des hommes « innocents et vertueux » n'est plus (14) ; il n'y a plus de vertueux citoyens,
sauf peut-être quelques-uns « dispersés dans nos campagnes
abandonnées » (17). Les hommes sages lèveront les mains au
ciel et diront : « Dieu tout puissant, toi qui tiens dans tes
mains les esprits, délivre-nous des lumières et des funestes
arts de nos pères et rends-nous l'ignorance et la pauvreté, les
seuls biens qui puissent faire notre bonheur et qui sont précieux devant toi » (18).

Enfin, c'est la vertu-renoncement, c'est-à-dire la vertu ayant
son but en soi en ce qui concerne cette vie et indifférente aux
avantages de celui qui la réalise, lorsque, par exemple, opposant les « commodités de la vie » et les « arts » d'une part, au
« vrai courage » et aux « vertus militaires » de l'autre (14),
Rousseau blâme les premiers, agréables dans leurs effets, et
exalte les seconds, où l'on se prive sans compensation. Ou
lorsque, sans vouloir même prendre en considération la question de savoir si on est plus heureux dans la civilisation quand
on « s'amuse à des occupations oisives et sédentaires », il ne
regrette que ceci : qu'on « amollit » et « effémine les courages »

(14) — comme si le courage n'était pas seulement un moyen, mais un but. C'est la vertu -renoncement encore quand, dans sa réponse à Bordes, lequel avait attaqué le *Discours*, il écrit sans hésiter : « Tout est source de mal au delà du nécessaire physique » (65) ; ainsi le bien, c'est se priver de tout ce qui est plus qu'exister, de tout ce qui pourrait être agréable. C'est la vertu-renoncement toujours dans des affirmations comme celle-ci, qu'il importe plus aux peuples d'être « vertueux et durables » que « brillants et momentanés » (12-13) : « vertueux » opposé à « brillant » peut signifier seulement : renoncement opposé à jouissance ; donc, entre ces deux alternatives, être heureux momentanément et n'être pas heureux du tout, c'est la seconde qu'il faut choisir ; à un plaisir même court la vertu oppose comme supérieur un long ennui. Un homme plaidait auprès de Richelieu en disant : « Il faut bien vivre, monseigneur ! » et le cardinal avait répondu : « Je n'en vois pas la nécessité. » Rousseau, contemplant la vie du point de vue de la vertu, ne voit pas la nécessité de jouir — car on ne saurait pourtant admettre que l'existence par elle-même soit une jouissance.

De ces trois conceptions de la vertu donc, laquelle Rousseau entend-il vraiment ?

A juger selon la lettre, il semblerait que Rousseau entend le plus souvent défendre la vertu comme moyen de bonheur, soit la vertu-sagesse, soit la vertu-innocence, tandis que les passages où il défend la vertu-renoncement sont moins exploités, sinon plus rares. D'autre part, il ne faudrait pas conclure, parce que l'auteur n'a pas su dégager la vertu-renoncement aussi nettement que peut-être les deux autres, celle-ci n'en soit pas, après tout, la plus importante dans sa penée. En réalité, il n'y a pas de doute pour nous que tel soit le cas en effet.

Remarquons d'abord que ce peut être justement parce que c'est la plus naturelle à la pensée, que l'auteur semble moins soucieux de la définir ; elle est celle qu'il est le moins nécessaire d'expliquer, car elle est la notion courante : celle de privation, de condamnation de la jouissance. L'abbé Morelly,

dans son fameux *Code de la nature* (1755), fonde sa théorie de la
nécessité d'une réforme sociale sur ceci que les penseurs ont
jusqu'alors erré, parce qu'ils partaient de ce principe faux :
« L'homme naît vicieux et méchant » : C'est-à-dire que tous
les penseurs partent de ceci, pour ainsi dire *a priori*, qu'en
suivant sa nature l'homme pèche et qu'il est vertueux en
renonçant au péché, c'est-à-dire à ses désirs naturels ; c'est
la théorie chrétienne de la vertu (1).

C'était bien ainsi que l'entendaient tous ces « libertins »
dont les théories commencèrent à s'affirmer au XVIᵉ siècle,
et que Saint-Evremond a si bien résumées dans ce mot :
« Trouvez bon que les délicats nomment plaisir ce que les gens
rudes et grossiers ont nommé vice, et ne composez pas votre
vertu des vieux sentiments qu'un naturel sauvage avait ins-
pirés aux premiers hommes » (2). Pour ces gens-là, selon le mot
de l'abbé Bernier, « l'abstinence des plaisirs est un grand péché ».
C'était l'attitude que le parti des philosophes cherchait à
répandre.

(1) Cette vertu, à tort nous l'avons vu, on l'a assimilée à la vertu politique,
c'est-à-dire celle où le citoyen auquel on demande certaines privations au nom
de son pays gagne lui-même à ce sacrifice, puisqu'il assure l'ordre social
dont il est le premier à profiter ; la vertu chrétienne seule signifiait bien réellement renoncement à toute jouissance terrestre : le fait qu'il y a renoncement
dans les deux cas suffit, chez des esprits peu soucieux de précision, pour les
confondre. Si, cette confusion, les chrétiens comme Fénelon et Bossuet la faisaient, on ne saurait trop reprocher aux auteurs profanes, Gassendi, Bernier,
Saint-Evremont — pour ne pas dire Bayle — de les avoir confondues dans une
commune réprobation. Aux yeux de ces derniers cette vertu romaine ou lacédé-
monienne n'était point admirable, car ces peuples d'abord étaient pauvres et
« il faudrait être bien bon si on leur faisait un mérite de leur frugalité » (Bayle,
Rép. aux questions d'un provincial, ch. XI) ; et, plus tard, souvent la frugalité
des Romains était fort intéressée : la république l'avait recommandée par prudence politique, et dès lors les ambitieux affichaient la pauvreté pour mériter
les fonctions publiques. (Cf. Saint-Evremond. *Réflexions sur les différents génies
du peuple romain* I, p. 157.)

(2) Ce n'était pas le « naturel sauvage » qui avait inspiré ces idées de la
supériorité de la privation, mais le christianisme ; cette théorie de Saint-Evremond, et autres, montre combien déjà était effacé même chez des intelligences
cultivées, le sens réel de la civilisation du moyen âge.

Le débat avait donc été ramené graduellement et réduit à
cette proposition élémentaire : La vertu consiste-t-elle dans
la jouissance des choses du monde, ou dans le renoncement ?
Les libertins et les philosophes défendaient la première proposition. Rousseau, acceptant lui aussi leur critère (jouissance approuvée ou réprouvée) et flétrissant les « commodités
de la vie », « les arts », « le luxe », « la gloire »... « images de tous
les égarements du cœur et de la raison » (16), prenait la défense du point de vue exactement opposé. On ne voit pas vraiment comment, si on veut rester conséquent dans l'interprétation du *Premier Discours* on peut y voir autre chose qu'un
plaidoyer pour la *vertu de renoncement*.

§ **3.** Ceci dit, il faut maintenant considérer les raisons qui
ont fait que cette vertu de renoncement n'ait pas inspiré d'une
façon conséquente toute la discussion du *Premier Discours* ;
puisque, nous l'avons vu, les paroles de Rousseau sont loin
d'être toujours en accord avec cette idée fondamentale. Nous
nous excusons de tant de discussions, mais s'il dépend bien
de nous de rendre les choses claires, il est hors de notre pouvoir de les rendre simples.

D'abord, il faut rappeler que la conception chrétienne de la
vertu n'était pas demeurée de tous points conséquente ;
l'idéal ascétique avait été mitigé ; on rachètait par telles
pratiques purement formelles (jeûnes, prières, retraites, dons
en argent) un peu de droits à des jouissances terrestres : c'était
entré de plus en plus dans les mœurs. Les prélats chrétiens
les plus austères éprouvaient une certaine pudeur à insister
sur la théorie du péché originel, c'est-à-dire sur l'affirmation
de la nature absolument mauvaise de l'homme, et sur la condamnation du plaisir ; ils voyaient le grand risque de détourner
d'eux les fils d'un siècle manifestant de fortes tendances
d'affranchissement ; ils étaient donc disposés à pactiser, cherchant seulement le moyen de pouvoir continuer à prêcher une
discipline morale. Et Rousseau n'a pu manquer d'être jusqu'à
un certain point affecté par cette notion moins rigoureuse, et
même d'être tenté par la perspective de gagner des approba-

tions pour son *Discours* en laissant entrevoir une vertu pas exclusivement sévère. Cela d'autant plus que justement les théories « libertines » ou « philosophiques » s'étaient enrichies récemment de nouveaux arguments. A l'argument que la jouissance développe l'amour du superflu, et que celui-ci favorise la chasse à la richesse qui signifie écrasement des petits et misère sans fin dans le monde, l'école nouvelle des économistes osait répondre : ce n'est qu'apparence ; car si vous bannissez les arts, les plaisirs, les richesses, vous verrez la société s'écrouler ; la soif de jouissance des riches procure du travail, donc de l'argent, donc de la nourriture aux pauvres (1). Tout en considérant comme parfaitement dangereux les économistes, et les attaquant directement dans son *Discours*, Rousseau sentait la sagesse de ne pas opposer à une théorie morale qui avait *tout* pour la recommander, un évangile de la vertu qui n'avait *rien* pour cela. On pouvait peut-être humaniser un brin.

Mais ce qui devait surtout compromettre en une certaine mesure l'unité interne du *Discours* c'était que, on s'en souvient, Rousseau était lui-même au fond, de dispositions très romantiques, — et si l'exaltation éprouvée sous « l'arbre de Vincennes » persiste tout au travers du *Discours* (et même dans les réponses aux réfutations qui arrivèrent nombreuses), il fallait s'attendre à ce qu'aux heures où il est forcé de sou-

---

(1) C'est en Angleterre, d'abord, qu'on eut, comme si souvent, le courage d'être explicite. Le titre même du célèbre opuscule de Mandeville (2e édition, 1714) est déjà très clair : *La fable des abeilles, ou les vices privés font la prospérité publique* (*The Fable of the Bees, or Private vices publick benefits*). Les abeilles — à la manière des hommes — se préoccupent beaucoup de vertu ; elles attaquent avec zèle les vices les unes des autres, et demandent à Jupiter de leur envoyer la vertu. Jupiter les entend et les rend vertueuses et frugales ; aussitôt toute industrie cesse, la ruche devient pauvre, sans moyen de défense, et finalement se disperse. Conclusion : rien de plus néfaste que la vertu de renoncement. Melon, dans ses *Essais politiques sur le commerce* (1734) développa en France ces idées, et Voltaire, par le charmant badinage du *Mondain* (1736) donna à cette façon de voir toute sa séduction. Voir aussi Montesquieu, *Lettres Persanes*, 106. En Angleterre, Hume dans un *Essai sur le luxe* cherche à établir qu'il n'y a pas de lien nécessaire entre corruption des mœurs et luxe ; Formey défendit la même thèse contre le *Premier Discours* de Rousseau (Cf. Baudouin, *J.-J. Rousseau*, I, 147).

peser sa pensée pour la mettre en termes d'arguments rationnels, il résiste mal parfois à la tentation de glisser de la notion
de rigide vertu-renoncement à l'une des deux notions de vertu-
sagesse ou de vertu-innocence où le bonheur terrestre n'est
pas condamné, bref de laisser le sentiment par moments l'emporter sur la logique, et en somme de composer. En sorte que
s'il blâme toujours le développement de talents agréables (17)
il ne peut s'empêcher de louer celui des « talents utiles », —
utiles pas seulement pour être bon dans le monde, mais pour
y être heureux. Ainsi au fond, tout en partant en guerre avec
fracas contre les nouveaux hédonistes (« les anciens politiques
parlaient sans cesse de mœurs et de vertus, les nôtres ne
parlent que de commerce et d'argent », 12), Rousseau se rend
assez à leurs sollicitations.

Reconnaissons que la concession est grave, car enfin la distinction suggérée entre les talents « agréables » qu'il ne faut
pas développer, et les talents « utiles » qui sont légitimes, est
fort subtile : dès que la vertu conduit au bonheur, ce n'est
plus une vertu de renoncement. La vertu hédoniste est donc
une intruse dans le *Premier Discours* de Rousseau dont la
définition du luxe (tout à fait conséquente avec sa pensée)
est : « tout est source de mal au delà du nécessaire physique »
(I, 65) (I). Rousseau s'est leurré lui-même quand il a cru
pouvoir tout simplement et impunément introduire la notion
de bonheur. Notons qu'il a déclaré lui-même que la « Prosopo-
sée » — vertueuse — de Fabricius était le morceau central de
son *Discours*, le seul qui appartint à l'inspiration originale et
qui était resté intact (X, 301-2). Or, où serait le mérite de Fabricius si, connaissant les passions, le luxe, les sciences, les arts
comme des sources de maux, il les eût repoussés ? En quoi consisterait sa « grande âme » si sa rusticité, sa frugalité, sa modération, son toit de chaume le rendaient parfaitement heureux ?
Il est évident que Fabricius n'est méritant et vertueux que si

(1) Définition en accord avec celle de Mandeville : Luxe = tout ce qui n'est
pas absolument nécessaire à la subsistance de l'homme (*Fable des Abeilles*,
Remarque L).

ces objets de jouissance sont bons et agréables, et s'il s'en prive parce que la vertu consiste justement dans cette privation (1). Cela reste la grande chose en effet dans ce *Premier Discours*.

Rousseau est vacillant, nous l'avons reconnu, sur ce qu'est un homme vertueux ; mais il ne l'est pas du tout pour définir celui qui n'est *pas vertueux*. N'est pas vertueux quiconque cède à la passion, à ses désirs de jouissance. Rien n'est plus erroné que de faire du Rousseau du *Premier Discours* un champion de la doctrine du bon sauvage, c'est-à-dire de la doctrine que cet homme est vertueux qui répond aux suggestions de la nature ; c'est le contraire qui est vrai. Ses anathèmes vont justement à tous ces peuples qui ont cédé à cette voix de la nature. Quand il reproche aux Romains leur débauche et leur obscénité (6), qu'est-ce sinon blâmer les Romains d'avoir cédé à la nature, au lieu de lui résister comme on l'avait fait à Rome quelque temps grâce à des lois sévères condamnant les penchants personnels au nom d'un état impersonnel ? Quand il reproche à Athènes ce luxe et ces arts qui l'ont finalement rendue esclave de Rome, qu'est-ce sinon blâmer les Athéniens d'avoir cédé au besoin naturel de jouissance, et même d'avoir élargi ces moyens de jouissances et reculé les limites de la nature ? Quand il reproche à Constantinople à la fois le luxe et la débauche, et tous les crimes, vol, assassinat, fornication, qu'est-ce encore que la nature ? Voler ce dont on a besoin ou seulement envie, tuer celui qui occupe une position que vous ambitionnez, cultiver le plaisir sous toutes ses formes, c'est la nature toujours. Et même dissimuler sous des appa-

---

(1) Ailleurs, Rousseau déclare en outre que son *Discours* ne l'avait plus satisfait après quelque temps ; il lui avait fait subir quelques modifications de fond ; puis, s'étant ravisé, il avait à peu près rétabli le texte primitif, y laissant seulement « quelques notes » et « deux additions faciles à reconnaître » (2). Ces passages « faciles à reconnaître » pourraient bien être ceux où il contredit (lui, pensait peut-être qu'il ne faisait qu'atténuer) la « vertu romaine » de la prosopopée ; tel est particulièrement le passage sur les hommes « innocents et vertueux » qui commence ainsi : « On ne peut réfléchir sur les mœurs qu'on ne se plaise à se rappeler l'image de la simplicité des premiers temps... » (p. 13-14).

rences trompeuses la poursuite du plaisir et de la joie lorsque la société et le prochain vous empêcheront d'y parvenir, « cultiver les apparences de toutes les vertus sans en avoir aucune » comme s'exprime Rousseau, c'est la nature encore. *Vice-versâ*, ceux que Rousseau oppose comme exemples de vertus aux peuples « corrompus » que nous venons de rappeler, ces admirables Spartiates, ces Romains, ce sont les peuples qui ont réfréné victorieusement le développement en eux des penchants naturels. Tout ceci est la morale chrétienne pour laquelle, sous le nom de morale romaine, Rousseau emploie son éloquence ; c'est la morale *anti*-naturelle ; cela saute aux yeux dès qu'on considère le *Premier Discours* sans y mêler des notions que Rousseau développera peut-être plus tard, dans le *Second Discours*, mais qui pour le moment lui sont encore étrangères (— et sur ce point le *Second Discours* sera justement en opposition catégorique avec le premier).

Il suffit d'y réfléchir pour voir que cette morale chrétienne ou romaine exclut *particulièrement* la théorie de la bonté naturelle de l'homme. Il n'en pourrait être question chez Rousseau dans l'ordre d'idées où il se mouvait alors : pourquoi ses anathèmes si tout ce qu'on combat n'est pas mauvais ? Rousseau avait adopté dans son *Premier Discours* la théorie traditionnelle et théologique dont parle l'abbé Morelly pour l'attaque : « L'homme naît vicieux et méchant », — et seul un préjugé opiniâtre a rendu aveugle à ce fait la critique moderne. Sans prendre la peine de réfléchir, on a prêté à Rousseau un raisonnement qui au premier abord paraissait assez logique : « L'homme civilisé est mauvais, n'est-ce pas dire que l'homme non-civilisé doit être bon ? » Mais Rousseau a expressément écarté ce raisonnement et prétend vouloir dire exactement ceci : La civilisation a rendu l'homme pire, mais ce n'est pas dire qu'il ait autrefois été bon. Voici ses termes : « Les hommes sont pervers, ils seraient pires encore s'ils avaient eu le malheur de naître savants » (10) ; c'est-à-dire que ce n'est pas la civilisation qui les a corrompus, la civilisation leur a seulement donné un moyen d'exercer avec plus de succès cette perversité originelle. Et ailleurs : « La nature humaine au fond n'était pas

meilleure », seulement « les hommes trouvaient leur sécurité
dans la facilité de se pénétrer réciproquement ; et cet avantage, dont nous ne sentons plus le prix, leur épargnait bien des
vices » (4). Dans la discussion qui suivra la publication du
Discours, Rousseau ne parlera pas moins clairement : «M. Gautier prend la peine de m'apprendre qu'il y a des peuples vicieux qui ne sont pas savants, et je m'étais déjà bien douté que
les Calmoucks, les Bédouins, les Cafres n'étaient pas des prodiges de vertu et d'érudition » (24). En 1752 encore, dans la *Préface de Narcisse*, on lit : « Quand j'ai dit que les mœurs s'étaient
corrompues, je n'ai pas prétendu que celles de nos aïeux
fussent bonnes, mais seulement que les nôtres étaient encore
pires » (V. 103) (1). Tout cela c'est la doctrine chrétienne de
l'homme mauvais, proie du péché originel ; l'homme naturel
doit être vaincu par la vertu ; c'est la doctrine commune aux
catholiques austères (saint Augustin et les Jansénistes) et aux
protestants (Luthériens et Calvinistes), cette doctrine reprise encore au commencement du xixe siècle avec une si
audacieuse logique par Joseph de Maistre : « Le péché originel
[défini par lui : la *capacité de commetrre tous les crimes*] qui
explique tout et sans lequel on n'explique rien « (*Soirées de
Saint-Pétersbourg*, 2e Entretien). La preuve scientifique que
nous en sommes tous atteints est « que tout être qui a la faculté de se propager ne saurait produire qu'un être semblable
à lui » (2). Et c'est cette doctrine que Rousseau sent se réveiller

(1) On verrait dans des écrits antérieurs au *Premier Discours* même, que
Rousseau ne songeait point d'abord à ce que nous avons appelé vertu innocence. En lisant attentivement, par exemple sa tragédie *La découverte du
Nouveau monde* (V, 187), on verra qu'il adopta bien jusqu'à un certain point
l'idée courante déjà de la bonté des sauvages, mais il ne l'oppose nullement à la
perversité des civilisés ; c'est-à-dire qu'il y a autant de perversité chez les sauvages que chez les civilisés, et autant de bonté chez les uns que chez les autres.
Si on voulait établir une différence, on verrait les sauvages plus braves mais non
meilleurs.

(2) La seule atténuation à sa vérité consiste en ceci : « Il faut bien observer qu'il
y a, entre l'homme infirme et l'homme malade, la même différence qui a lieu
entre l'homme vicieux et l'homme coupable ». D'ailleurs De Maistre a tort
quand il croit que Rousseau a *toujours* été l'adversaire de cette doctrine du

en lui, le jour où il se met à comparer du point de vue pratique
les résultats de la théorie de la nature chez les philosophes
et contemporains des grandes villes, avec la théorie sociale
que Genève lui avait fait connaître : l'homme naturel, non réfréné par la religion et la conscience, est méchant, hypocrite,
pervers, et l'une des grandes fautes de la civilisation des
sciences et des arts, est qu'elle « sape les fondements de la foi
et anéantit la vertu » (11). C'est ce que nous avons nommé la
tendance romaine, qui s'affirme en face de la *tendance romantique*, laquelle avait eu si longtemps le champ libre dans l'esprit de Rousseau. Et plus Rousseau s'était abandonné au romantisme dans sa vie, plus, par réaction à moitié inconsciente.
il se jetait farouche dans les tirades romaines : à tout prix
disciplinez, réfrénez, niez la nature et les instincts, — dit-il
maintenant.

Note sur l'originalité du paradoxe. — On a discuté à qui appartenait réellement l'idée du « paradoxe » — que la civilisation à laquelle l'homme s'était passivement abandonné, était mauvaise.
Surtout on a prétendu que Diderot avait été le premier à le suggérer : « L'affirmative — aurait-il dit — c'est le pont aux ânes !
tandis que le parti contraire présente à la philosophie et à l'éloquence un champ nouveau riche et fécond. — Vous avez raison,
me dit Rousseau, je suivrai votre conseil » (Marmontel, *Mémoires*,
ch. VIII). Rousseau lui, rapporte seulement que Diderot encouragea son ami lorsque celui-ci eut proposé la thèse du « paradoxe »
(VIII, 249-51 ; IX, 213-4 ; X, 301-2). C'est une querelle sans importance. Le fait à constater c'est que Rousseau était mûr pour la
crise. Si la question de l'Académie de Dijon n'eût pas été le petit
événement qui déclancha, autre chose se fût tôt présenté. Mais
même si la question n'avait pas déclanché Rousseau, et que ce fût
en effet Diderot qui eût incité Rousseau par une boutade, — qu'est-
ce à dire encore ? D'abord, ceci demeure que Diderot n'a rien fait
de son idée, et il l'a même à l'occasion combattue, tandis que Rousseau — et c'est l'essentiel — en a saisi la valeur, l'a adoptée, l'a

péché, avec ses « sauvages » qui « ont fait dire tant d'extravagances et qui ont
servi de texte éternel à J.-J. Rousseau, l'un des plus dangereux sophistes de son
siècle, et cependant le plus dépourvu de véritable science, de sagacité et surtout
de profondeur ; avec une profondeur apparente qui est toute dans les mots ».

faite sienne. Ou bien, il faudrait établir que Diderot se rendait compte qu'un Rousseau inconnu allait sortir de son geste : Qui voudrait essayer de prouver cela ? Et ajoutons encore ceci : si Diderot avait soupçonné quel abîme le courant d'idées contenu dans le *Premier Discours* allait creuser entre Rousseau et les Encyclopédistes, il se fût certainement bien gardé de précipiter l'orage. Car quand même on porte généralement à plus tard la date de la rupture, et si Rousseau lui-même n'en eut conscience que plus tard, nous avons bien dans le *Premier Discours* le point de départ de la brouille future.

Pour qui tiendrait à étudier de plus près la question, il pourra consulter, par exemple E. Ritter, *Zeitschrift für Französische Sprache und Literatur*, Vol. XI, 1, republié *Annales Rousseau*, XVI ; Brockerhoff, *Rousseau*, 1, 489-90 ; II, 293-5, 307 ; Baudouin... et d'autres biographes. Plus récemment Ducros, *Rousseau, de Genève à l'Ermitage* (Paris 1910, p. 167, 178 ss.), qui oppose le témoignage de Diderot lui-même aux allégations de ceux qui feraient de celui-ci l'auteur du paradoxe ; d'autre part, ce même témoignage trahirait la raison qu'aurait pu avoir Diderot en écrivant (*Essai sur les règnes de Claude et Néron*, § 66) un récit différent de celui qu'il avait fait oralement bien des années avant. Voir aussi Plan, *Rousseau jugé par les Gazettes de son temps* (Paris, 1912, p. 128). Après avoir quasi-sommeillé pendant quelques années, la question a été reprise par F. Vézinet, lequel dans un article de la *Revue d'histoire littéraire de France*, « Rousseau ou Diderot » (Avril-Juin, 1924 — repris et un peu augmenté dans le petit volume *Autour de Voltaire*, Champion, 1925, p. 121-141) écarte Diderot.

Faguet nous semble avoir bien résumé la situation dans sa *Vie de Rousseau* (Soc. d'impr. 1911) : « La question ne mérite pas dix lignes d'examen, tant ces diverses versions sont conciliables : Rousseau est intéressé par la question qui ne l'intéresserait pas si déjà il ne penchait pour le paradoxe ». M. Gran a étudié la chose du point de vue psychologique et arrive justement à la même conclusion : la « crise » se préparait de longue date, elle n'a fait qu'éclater en 1749; Rousseau aurait eu alors une sorte d'illumination comparable aux crises de conversions religieuses. L'article de Gran sur la « Crise de Vincennes » se trouve dans les *Annales Rousseau*, Vol. VII, et a été repris dans son livre sur *Rousseau*. Enfin citons encore E. Champion dont le point de vue, exposé dans *Rousseau et la Révolution Française*, Paris, 1909, ch. IV, est celui qui s'accorde le plus avec le nôtre. Pour lui, Rousseau est d'abord foncièrement genevois de nature ; il est alors converti par Mme de Warens au point de vue que nous avons appelé « romantique » ; et au *Premier Discours* il se re-convertit au calvinisme. Mais, sans compter que la notion de calvinisme n'est pas, pour nous, tout-à-fait ce qu'elle est pour Champion ; nous ne concevons pas de même non plus la place du *Discours* dans l'œuvre ; selon nous la pensée de Rousseau n'a pas été depuis, un simple prolongement de ce « calvinisme » retrouvé.

CHAPITRE II

ROUSSEAU ET LES SAUVAGES. DISCOURS SUR L'INÉGALITÉ

1. Rousseau conscient de la complexité des problèmes qu'il a soulevés. Incertitudes dans la conduite de sa vie et dans sa pensée philosophique.
2. Il abandonne l'idéal de l'austérité et la vertu romaine, et pense trouver dans la vertu d'innocence des sauvages une solution au problème du bonheur. Il rejette la doctrine chrétienne de l'homme naturellement mauvais.
3. En réalité Rousseau n'a jamais prouvé que l'homme de la nature soit bon, mais seulement qu'il n'est pas mauvais ; mais il n'est malheureusement pas conscient de cette distinction. Trois sens du mot *bonté* dont Rousseau n'a que faire (*bonté chrétienne de discipline*, *bonté sentimentale de désintéressement* sans sens aucun, *bonté eudaimoniste* qui n'est pas à proprement de la bonté étant naïvement intéressée).
4. Encore moins qu'il n'a prouvé que l'homme est naturellement bon, Rousseau n'a prouvé que l'homme est naturellement heureux ; celui-ci est seulement non malheureux à l'état sauvage. D'où résulte que Rousseau est justifié en récusant l'accusation qu'il prêche le retour à l'état de nature.
5. Tout ceci conduit à une nouvelle conception de « bonté » et de — « vertu ».

§ 1. Rousseau s'étant précipité de l'extrême romantisme de sa jeunesse dans l'extrême vertu qui est celle d'un renoncement absolu, il s'enferra — de par sa propre éloquence — sur cette notion.

Il essaya de tenir ferme dans la discussion qui suivit, et les nombreuses réfutations de son premier discours servirent en partie à le confirmer dans sa position extrême.

Pourtant quelque chose en lui protestait. Ses propres arguments ne l'avaient pas converti. Cela se voit d'abord dans sa vie. Quand il écrivait dans ses *Confessions* que sa conversion

datait du jour où il lut sur la route de Vincennes la question de
l'Académie de Dijon : *Si le progrès des sciences et des arts a
contribué à épurer les mœurs*, (« A l'instant de cette lecture, je
vis un autre univers et je devins un autre homme », VIII, 249),
cela signifiait simplement : Je me sentis disposé à considérer
le monde d'un point de vue philosophique nouveau ; car il
nous dit lui-même qu'une fois le *Discours* écrit et envoyé à
Dijon, il oublie tout, et qu'il faut la nouvelle (en juillet de
l'année suivante) qu'il a gagné le prix pour ramener son attention à des dispositions de réforme dans le domaine de la vie
pratique : « Cette nouvelle réveilla toutes les idées qui me
l'avaient dicté, les anima d'une nouvelle force, et acheva de
mettre en fermentation dans mon cœur ce premier levain
d'héroïsme et de vertu que mon père, et ma patrie, et Plutarque y avaient mis dans mon enfance ». Ce n'est pas tout ;
même alors : « La mauvaise honte et la crainte des sifflets
m'empêchèrent de me conduire d'abord sur ces principes et de
rompre brusquement en visière avec mon siècle » ; mais « j'en
eus dès lors la volonté décidée » (252-3). Un an s'écoula encore,
et il fallut le prodigieux succès du *Discours imprimé* auprès du
public — qui avait entrevu dans ce pamphlet quelque importante vérité — pour ramener pour de bon l'attention de l'auteur sur sa propre œuvre et rafraîchir ses résolutions. Et alors
encore la lutte n'était point égale entre la « volonté », n'importe combien « décidée » de Rousseau, et les habitudes romantiques ; il ne put se résoudre à abandonner que graduellement
sa vie de bohême. C'est ainsi qu'il met encore trois enfants à
l'hospice (VIII, 254) ; qu'il fréquenta toujours ses anciens
amis, et fit à l'occasion la fête avec eux (épisode de la fille
Kluepfel, 251-2). Ajoutons qu'il s'était laissé entraîner dans la
Querelle sur la musique italienne ; la *Lettre* de Grimm *sur Om-
phale* est d'avril 1752 ; la *Lettre sur la musique française* qui
souleva une nouvelle tempête, est de novembre 1753 ; et entre
les deux se place la composition et les représentations du
Devin du village (printemps 1752 et automne 1753) ; enfin en
novembre la répétition des *Muses galantes* chez M. de la Pope-
linière. En somme, Rousseau continuait à essayer de vivre par

la musique. Il laisse aussi jouer, en 1752, une comédie *Nar-cisse* — qui fut, du reste, un échec (275-6). Seul le métier de copiste pourrait être considéré comme un premier pas vers la réforme, — peut-être (257). Tout cela est simplement humain et ceux qui refusent d'en tenir compte manquent de perspicacité psychologique. Cette lenteur à réaliser ses beaux projets réfute en même temps ceux qui prétendent que Rousseau a voulu jouer un rôle, et attirer l'attention ; il aurait bien mal joué sa pièce après avoir si gauchement dressé son tréteau.

Cette longue hésitation est manifeste aussi dans sa pensée. Car il n'avait pas attendu d'écrire les *Confessions* pour se rendre compte que « cet ouvrage — le *Premier Discours* — plein de chaleur et de force, manque absolument de logique et d'ordre » (250). Et on peut l'en croire quand il écrit : « Toute cette polémique (au sujet du *Premier Discours*) m'occupait beaucoup » (260) (1). Il y a d'ailleurs, entre le *Premier Discours*, et ce qu'on appelle assez improprement le *Second Discours*, une série d'écrits secondaires — par exemple le *Discours sur la vertu la plus nécessaire aux héros* (1751) et la *Préface à Narcisse* (1752). Cette polémique l'occupait parce qu'il n'était pas satisfait ; forcé de sonder ses idées, de les creuser, il les trouve frustes, souvent incohérentes ; et en fait, il les transforme au cours de ces discussions, beaucoup plus qu'il n'en est lui-même conscient.

(1) En novembre 1750, le *Mercure* donne une analyse du *Discours*, avec commentaires ; y revient en janvier et en juin 1751. Rousseau répond le même mois. Bordes, à Lyon, attaque le Discours. En septembre, le Roi de Pologne publie sa réfutation dans le *Mercure* ; et en octobre, Rousseau répond et au roi de Pologne, et à Grimm, et à Gauthier. En décembre, le *Mercure* publie la réfutation de Bordes. En avril 1752, réponse de Rousseau à Bordes. Ce même printemps, réponse de Rousseau à un autre adversaire. En août, Bordes lit une *Apologie des Sciences et des Arts* devant l'Académie de Lyon. En décembre, Rousseau compose la *Préface à Narcisse*. En été 1753, Rousseau commence une réponse à la seconde réfutation de Bordes... En novembre, le *Mercure* publie le sujet du concours qui donnera lieu au *Second Discours*.

En effet, Rousseau n'était plus du tout au même point, philosophiquement parlant, que quand il avait écrit le *Premier Discours*, lorsque quatre ans plus tard, il lut dans le *Mercure*, le nouveau sujet de concours de l'Académie de Dijon : *Quelle est la source de l'origine de l'inégalité des conditions parmi les hommes, et si elle est autorisée par la loi naturelle ?* Il était encore en pleine querelle sur la musique française, mais il semble qu'il fut alors ressaisi tout entier par cet ordre d'idées — comme la première fois : là était la sollicitation impérieuse de sa pensée ; et il fait son fameux séjour d'une semaine dans la Forêt de Saint-Germain pour méditer sa réponse.

Pour méditer à mon aise ce grand sujet, je fis à Saint-Germain un voyage de sept ou huit jours, avec Thérèse, notre hôtesse, qui était bonne femme, et une de ses amies. Je compte cette promenade pour une des plus agréables de ma vie. Il faisait très beau ; ces bonnes femmes se chargèrent des soins et de la dépense ; Thérèse s'amusait avec elles ; et moi, sans souci de rien, je venais m'égayer sans gêne aux heures du repas. Tout le reste du jour, enfoncé dans la forêt, j'y cherchais, j'y trouvais l'image des premiers temps dont je retraçais fidèlement l'histoire ; je faisais main basse sur les petits mensonges des hommes ; j'osai dévoiler à nu leur nature, suivre le progrès du temps et des choses qui l'ont défigurée, et comparant l'homme de l'homme avec l'homme naturel, leur montrer dans leur perfectionnement prétendu, la véritable source de ses misères. Mon âme exaltée par ces contemplations sublimes, s'élevait auprès de la Divinité ; et voyant de là mes semblables suivre, dans l'aveugle route de leurs préjugés, celle de leurs erreurs, de leurs malheurs, de leurs crimes, je leur criais d'une voix faible qu'ils ne pouvaient entendre : « Insensés, qui vous plaignez sans cesse de la nature, apprenez que tous vos maux viennent de vous ! » (VIII, 276-77)

C'est ainsi que Rousseau voit son *Discours* en 1765. Il semble ne sentir aucune solution de continuité d'avec son premier. Quant à nous, reportons-nous au *Discours* lui-même de 1754 — ce sera plus sûr. Et d'abord, résumons-le :

Pour organiser la vie de la façon la plus favorable à l'homme, il faut chercher « ce qui convient le mieux à sa constitution » (II, p. 81) ; pour savoir ce qui convient le mieux à sa constitution, il faut étudier ce que la nature l'a fait. Rousseau annonce avoir discerné en l'homme deux principes antérieurs à l'âge de raison ou social, donc deux principes naturels ou innés : l'instinct de la conservation, lequel « nous intéresse ardemment à notre bien-être », et l'instinct de la pitié, ou « répugnance à voir périr ou souffrir tout être sensible et principalement nos semblables » (81).

Cela dit en manière de Préface, Rousseau arrive à son sujet de l'inégalité, tenant pour entendu par avance que l'inégalité est la cause des malheurs sociaux. Et il pose sa thèse que nous résumons ainsi : Il y a deux sortes d'inégalités, l'inégalité physique et naturelle, et l'inégalité morale et sociale : la première n'est pas un obstacle au bonheur ; la seconde, quand elle existe est la mère de toutes les souffrances et de toutes les misères (1). *L'inégalité physique et naturelle* existe toujours ; il y a en elle une source *possible* de conflits et de misères ; cependant dans l'état de nature — tel que l'entend Rousseau, c'est-à-dire avant que les hommes vécussent en société — cette inégalité a très peu d'importance, parce que le supérieur n'a aucun avantage à s'en prévaloir : la seule jouissance que l'homme connaisse est alors physique ; or, il y a dans la nature de quoi le satisfaire (nourriture et amour) tant que l'homme veut et quand il veut. Mais l'homme sortira de cet état de nature, et arrivera, par l'intelligence de certaines possibilités dans la vie à l'idée de fonder une société qui sera basée sur la propriété ; alors seulement les forts, pour l'établir, useront contre les faibles des avantages que leur donne leur supériorité, et du reste se disputeront entre eux ; les conflits et les misères cesseront donc d'être des possibilités pour devenir des réalités : l'inégalité physique et naturelle sera devenue *inégalité morale et politique*.

Reprenons avec Rousseau certains développements impor-

----

(1) Rousseau répond à une question, on se le rappelle : « Quelle est la source de l'inégalité des conditions parmi les hommes, si elle est autorisée par la loi naturelle ? »

tants pour bien apprécier l'esprit du *Discours*. Dans la Première Partie il s'attache à décrire longuement cet état de nature où l'inégalité physique et naturelle n'a pas d'effets dé-
sastreux, ne peut en avoir, — et où, par conséquent, l'humanité est à l'abri de luttes ou de souffrances. L'homme se distingue déjà des animaux par la raison ; toutefois celle-ci constitue non une supériorité, mais une simple compensation à
des avantages que les animaux auraient autrement sur lui ;
elle lui fournit seulement des armes artificielles rendant égale
la lutte avec les plus forts et les plus rapides que lui : « Les
hommes... observent, imitent leur industrie et s'élèvent [!]
ainsi jusqu'à l'instinct des bêtes » (85) : c'est là un état tout-à-
fait enviable ; d'abord l'homme est robuste, ce qui n'est pas
un mince avantage, et puis il n'a pas un désir qui ne soit satisfait (91).

« Son imagination ne lui permet rien ; son cœur ne lui demande
rien. Ses modiques besoins se trouvent aisément sous sa main, et il
est si loin du degré de connaissances nécessaires pour désirer d'en
acquérir de plus grandes qu'il ne peut avoir ni prévoyance, ni curiosité (91) ».

Il n'a pas d'avantages à cultiver sa force :

« J'entends toujours répéter que les plus forts opprimeront les
faibles. Mais qu'on m'explique ce qu'on veut dire par ce mot d'oppression... Un homme pourra bien s'emparer des fruits qu'un autre a
cueillis, du gibier qu'il a tué, de l'antre qui lui servait d'asile...
[mais] si l'on me chasse d'un arbre, j'en suis quitte pour aller à un
autre ; si l'on me tourmente dans un lieu, qui m'empêche de passer
ailleurs ? » (104). [Quant à me réduire en servitude :] « il faut qu'il
(le fort) se résolve à ne pas me perdre de vue un seul instant, à me
tenir lié avec un très grand soin durant son sommeil de peur que je
ne lui échappe ou que je ne le tue, c'est-à-dire qu'il est obligé de
s'exposer volontairement à une peine beaucoup plus grande que
celle qu'il veut éviter [chercher lui-même sa subsistance qui est
abondante partout] » (104).

L'homme ne s'astreindra pas « à un travail pénible » ; ce
serait sot, par exemple, de cultiver un champ puisque la

nourriture ne manque nulle part ; [Rousseau ne parle encore
que de l'homme vivant des régions où la nature le nourrit
toute l'année de ses fruits] et si elle devait manquer,
ce serait sot encore puisque la société n'existant pas et la
terre n'étant à personne, il serait « sûr de ne pas recueillir
le prix » de son labeur (92). L'amour n'est pas davantage
une occasion de conflit, car l'amour physique seul existe ;
« il est facile de voir que le moral de l'amour est un sentiment
factice né de l'usage de la société », et « il est fondé sur certaines
notions du mérite ou de la beauté qu'un sauvage n'est point
en état d'avoir » (101) ; « toute femme est bonne pour lui » ;
et il n'en manque pas. Il n'est pas jusqu'à la connaissance de
la mort et de ses terreurs « qui ne lui soit inconnue » (91). Et
Rousseau conclut :

> « Je sais bien qu'on nous répète sans cesse que rien n'eût été plus
> misérable que l'homme en cet état... Or, je voudrais bien qu'on
> m'expliquât quel peut être le genre de misère d'un homme libre,
> dont le cœur est en paix, et le corps en santé » (97).

Rousseau appuie sur un second point très fortement ; c'est
que la nature rend l'homme *in*sociable. Si elle avait voulu qu'il
formât une société, elle aurait rendu entre l'état de nature et
l'état de société le passage facile ; elle a mis, au contraire, tous
les empêchements pour que cette raison (dont elle avait besoin seulement pour mettre l'homme à même de se défendre
contre des animaux supérieurs à lui par l'instinct) n'aboutît
pas au lien social. L'exemple le plus frappant, c'est les obstacle
quasi-insurmontables qu'elle a mis à la formation du langage, qui est naturellement une des premières conditions pour
l'existence d'une société au sens humain du mot. Rousseau
tire un parti admirable des idées de son ami Condillac sur les
langues :

> « La première difficulté qui se présente est d'imaginer comment
> elles purent devenir nécessaires. Car, les hommes n'ayant nulle
> correspondance entre eux, ni aucun besoin d'en avoir, on ne con-
> çoit ni la nécessité de cette invention, ni sa possibilité, si elle ne fut
> pas indispensable » (93). [Autre difficulté] « pire encore que la pré-

cédente : si les hommes ont eu besoin de la parole pour apprendre à penser, ils ont eu plus besoin encore de savoir penser pour trouver l'art de la parole » (94). [En effet,] « le premier langage de l'homme, le langage le plus universel, le plus énergique, et le seul dont il eût besoin avant qu'il fallût persuader des hommes assemblés, est le cri de la nature ».

On s'avisa un jour de lui substituer les articulations de la voix, mais cette substitution :

« Ne peut se faire que d'un commun consentement et d'une manière assez difficile à pratiquer pour des hommes dont les organes grossiers n'avaient encore aucun exercice, et plus difficile encore à concevoir en elle-même puisque cet accord dut être motivé, et que la parole paraît avoir été fort nécessaire pour établir l'usage de la parole » (94-5)... « Je m'arrête à ces premiers pas, et je supplie mes juges de suspendre ici leur lecture pour considérer, sur l'invention des seuls substantifs physiques, c'est-à-dire sur la partie de la langue la plus facile à trouver, le chemin qui lui reste à faire pour exprimer toutes les pensées des hommes, pour prendre une forme constante pour pouvoir être parlée en public, et influer sur la société ; je les supplie de réfléchir à ce qu'il a fallu de temps et de connaissances pour trouver les nombres, les mots abstraits, les aoristes, et tous les temps de verbes, les particules, la syntaxe, lier les propositions, les raisonnements et former toute la logique du discours... » (96). [Et] « quoiqu'il en soit de ces origines, on voit du moins au peu de soin qu'a pris la nature de rapprocher les hommes par des besoins mutuels et de leur faciliter l'usage de la parole, combien elle a peu préparé leur sociabilité, et combien elle a peu mis du sien dans tout ce qu'ils ont fait pour en établir les liens » (96).

Ainsi, seuls des « hasards » ont contribué à cette évolution de l'état de nature à l'état social :

« *La perfectibilité* (1), les vertus sociales, et les autres facultés que l'homme naturel avait reçues en puissance ne pouvaient ja-

---

(1) C'est Rousseau qui souligne (ici et p. 90), sans doute parce qu'il se demande s'il ne devrait pas employer ce terme dans un sens ironique, étant donné sa thèse et puisqu'il attaque la société « perfectionnée ». Nous examinerons la question plus bas.

mais se développer d'elles-mêmes,... elles avaient besoin pour cela du concours fortuit de plusieurs causes étrangères qui pouvaient ne jamais naître, et sans lesquelles il fût demeuré éternellement dans sa condition primitive » (104).

Ce sera l'objet de la IIᵉ partie de « considérer et rapprocher les différents hasards qui ont pu perfectionner la raison humaine en détériorant l'espèce, rendu un être méchant en le rendant sensible » (104) (1).

La IIᵉ partie commence par un coup de trompette :

« Le premier qui, ayant enclos un terrain, s'avisa de dire *Ceci est à moi*, et trouva des gens assez simples pour le croire, fut le vrai fondateur de la société civile. Que de crimes, de guerres, de meurtres, que de misères et d'horreurs n'eût point épargnés au genre humain celui qui arrachant les pieux ou comblant le fossé, eût crié à ses semblables : Gardez-vous d'écouter cet imposteur, vous êtes perdus si vous oubliez que les fruits sont à tous et que la terre n'est à personne » (105).

Ceci dit, Rousseau revient à son histoire psychologique de l'humanité, c'est-à-dire à l'exposé des « hasards » qui ont arraché les hommes à l'état de nature.

Première étape de sortie de l'état de nature primitive, ou purement animale

Les hommes vivaient maintenant sous des climats différents et certains sont obligés d'user de leur intelligence plus qu'au « premier état de nature » pour vaincre les difficultés de l'existence ; ils réinventèrent le feu pour se chauffer, le vêtement dans le même but ; ceux des bords de la mer et des fleuves inventèrent la ligne et le hameçon ; ceux des forêts, les arcs et les flèches (106) ; Rousseau dit que l'homme arrive « presque sans y songer » à quelque sorte de réflexion ou plu-

---

(1) Nous noterons plus bas que « méchanceté » n'a rien à faire avec bonheur. C'est « sot » qu'il est devenu, et pas méchant.

tôt à « une prudence machinale ». Mais aussi, l'homme ne peut manquer de concevoir quelque fierté de ses inventions et de se sentir supérieur aux animaux : et le voilà prêt pour un premier mouvement d'orgueil, ce qui le « préparait de loin » à aspirer au premier rang social *parmi ses semblables.*

Son intelligence ne s'arrête pas là ; il comprend quand il y a avantage à s'associer avec ses semblables, et quand il doit plutôt agir seul ; le langage se développe quelque peu à ce moment, assurant le progrès de la sociabilité.

Cependant, à côté de ces mauvais germes, il s'en développe d'autres, qui sont au bas mot, moins condamnables. L'industrie naît ; on apprend à connaître les joies du confort, à ne pas dépendre du présent toujours ; on construit des huttes : « Ce fut l'époque d'une première révolution qui forma l'établissement et la distinction des familles et qui introduisit une sorte de propriété » (107) ; de là encore « peut être naquirent déjà bien des querelles et des combats ». Mais aussi l'habitude de vivre ensemble fit naître les plus doux sentiments qui soient connus des hommes, l'amour conjugal et l'amour paternel » (108). Et l'homme perd de sa « férocité ».

Rousseau continue ainsi — il faut le dire, avec plus d'éloquence que de système — le récit de cette triple évolution :

1. L'industrie, qui ouvre à l'homme des horizons nouveaux de jouissance, et la division du travail rendue possible par la vie en commun.

2. Possibilité de s'abandonner aux sentiments doux de ce qu'on nomme famille ; et, la parole se développant, l'amour d'homme à femme, « sentiment doux et tendre, s'insinue dans l'âme » (109). Et le besoin de plaire en général fait naître les arts, chant, danse, jeux athlétiques, éloquence.

3. Les dangers qui, cependant, se pressent sur les pas de ces acquisitions séduisantes ; d'abord le luxe d'un jour devient le besoin du lendemain, et « la privation en devient bientôt plus cruelle que la privation n'en était douce » (108) ; l'habitude du confort et du luxe amollit corps et esprit ; ensuite, quand il y a contrariété dans l'amour, ce plus tendre des sentiments, la jalousie et la discorde s'ensuivent, avec tout un cortège de

maux ; de même pour le développement des arts d'agrément ; les hommes se comparent entre eux, cela amène — « premier pas vers l'inégalité » — vanité et mépris d'un côté, honte et envie de l'autre. Enfin, cela entame le sentiment de pitié naturelle.

C'est cependant ici que Rousseau entrevoit une période, dans le développement social, où les bienfaits du développement intellectuel (par l'industrie) ont porté des fruits vraiment désirables, tandis que les maux ne se sont pas encore manifestés ; ou, au moins, où la prépondérance est aux premiers sur les seconds. C'est *l'âge d'or* de l'Humanité, « ce période du développement des facultés humaines, tenant un juste milieu entre l'indolence de l'état primitif et la pétulante activité de notre amour-propre, dut être l'époque la plus heureuse et la plus durable » (110) — la plus durable, puisque tous les sauvages y sont restés, et par conséquent celle indiquée par la nature comme la plus propre à l'homme.

Notons toutefois que Rousseau caractérise nettement cette période comme étant d'un équilibre instable ; même si cet état est prolongé chez beaucoup d'hommes, il demeurera sans cesse à la merci d'un accident. A la vérité, l'accident est fatal peut-on dire, puisque l'intelligence est ce qui distingue l'homme de l'animal et que le « hasard » se manifeste à la suite d'un acte d'intelligence, lequel acte se manifeste à son tour devant un phénomène point du tout extraordinaire dans le cours des événements. Rousseau le reconnaît puisqu'il écrit : « Il y a grande apparence qu'alors les choses en étaient déjà venues au point de ne pouvoir plus durer comme elles étaient [dans l'état de nature] », (105 ; voir aussi 110). En d'autres termes, Rousseau admet que ce serait un accident si « l'accident » ne se produisait pas.

Ceci d'ailleurs n'a pas d'importance dans la compréhension générale du *Second Discours*, sauf que peut-être cela décharge Rousseau d'avance de l'objection facile et banale (de Voltaire par exemple) qu'il aurait proposé, lui, de retourner à l'état de nature : si, en effet, l'évolution est fatale pour l'homme se trouvant à cette étape de son développement, ce serait

absurde d'y retourner puisque ce serait pour en sortir fatalement de nouveau.

Deuxième Etape : *La catastrophe se consomme*

Quelques mots suffisent à résumer la fin du *Discours*.

Après la description de l'âge d'or, Rousseau reprend le
récit de l'évolution ; et quoique les facteurs qui ont contribué
à la descente fatale soient plusieurs, parmi les « hasards » il en
est un qu'il regarde comme particulièrement « funeste » ; celui
qui précipite la catastrophe, c'est *l'invention de la métallurgie
et de l'agriculture.* Par *quel* hasard les hommes sont arrivés à
l'idée de travailler le fer, pour en faire des instruments ara-
toires, lesquels permirent les provisions de pain, et indirectement de créer le loisir et l'occasion du luxe, et l'écrasement du
faible, nous ne savons ; mais ce que nous savons, c'est que
cette découverte — évitable ou fatale — fit comprendre à
l'homme comme jamais encore la possibilité de la richesse
et fut suivie bien vite de l'envie d'accumuler, de posséder.
Ajoutez que :

« Dès qu'un homme eut besoin du secours d'un autre, dès qu'on
s'aperçut qu'il était utile à un seul d'avoir des provisions pour
deux, l'égalité disparut, la propriété s'introduisit, le travail devint
nécessaire, et les vastes forêts se changèrent en campagnes riantes,
qu'il fallut arroser de la sueur des hommes, et dans lesquelles on
vit bientôt l'esclavage et la misère germer et croître avec les
moissons » (110).

« Voilà donc toutes nos facultés développées » (112) ; c'est-
à-dire l'homme est esclave de ses ambitions, et la voix de la
pitié naturelle au cœur de chaque individu est étouffée par les
« passions effrénées de tous » (113-14). La reconnaissance de
la propriété du sol semble avoir été le coup de grâce :

« De la culture des terres s'ensuivit nécessairement leur
partage, et de la propriété une fois reconnue, les premières
règles de justice » (112) (1). Ainsi le *droit civil* remplaça le *droit*

---

(1) Rousseau ici ne souligne pas « justice » comme il avait souligné « perfectibilité », — c'est cependant bien sûr qu'ici aussi on peut se demander s'il ne
s'agit pas de « règles d'injustices ».

de nature. Les riches eurent l'idée de fonder *l'État* pour assurer la conservation de leurs propriétés, et firent usage de rusés discours, disant :

« Unissons-nous pour garantir de l'oppression les faibles » ; ce qui signifiait : unissons-nous pour ratifier la propriété de chacun, donc du riche comme du pauvre. (114-15). [Et les hommes crurent à ces fallacieuses paroles] : « Tous coururent au devant de leurs fers, croyant assurer leur liberté » (115) ; [et] « les sages même virent qu'il fallait se résoudre à sacrifier une partie de leur liberté à la conservation de l'autre comme un blessé se fait couper le doigt pour sauver le reste du corps » (115).

Enfin, pour compléter la misère universelle, les États se dressent contre d'autres États :

« Les corps politiques, restant ainsi entre eux dans l'état de nature, se ressentirent bientôt des inconvénients qui avaient forcé les particuliers d'en sortir, et cet état devint encore plus funeste entre ces grands corps qu'il ne l'avait été auparavant entre les individus. De là sortirent les guerres nationales, les batailles, les meurtres, les représailles qui font frémir la nature et choquent la raison, et tous ces préjugés horribles qui placent au rang des vertus l'honneur de répandre le sang humain. Les plus honnêtes gens apprirent à compter parmi leurs devoirs celui d'égorger leurs semblables, on vit enfin les hommes se massacrer par milliers sans savoir pourquoi ; et il se commettait plus de meurtres en un seul jour de combat, et plus d'horreurs à la prise d'une seule ville qu'il ne s'en était commis dans l'état de nature durant des siècles entiers, sur toute la surface de la terre » (115-6).

§ 2. Il y a, on l'a vu, dans tout ce *Second Discours*, une atmosphère de pessimisme incontestable : Aux yeux de Rousseau, les maux de la civilisation l'emportent de beaucoup sur les avantages, les premiers étouffant les seconds ; et, qui plus est, les gains les plus indiscutables (les arts, les doux sentiments de la famille et de l'amour) à leur tour entraînent à leur suite les pires des maux (jalousie, ambition, ou simple désir de se distinguer). Et c'est cette conclusion justement, qui fit voir dans le *Second Discours* sur l'origine de l'inégalité un écrit parent du *Discours sur les Sciences et les Arts,* — voire

comme un fondement philosophique au pessimisme exprimé
dans le premier écrit. Dans l'un comme dans l'autre, Rousseau
fulmine contre les maux de la civilisation. Et, ce qu'on ne
peut tout à fait nier, Rousseau ne voit pas les choses autrement ; il a en effet lui-même, plus d'une fois, affirmé la communauté d'inspiration des deux Discours.

ET CEPENDANT, IL Y A MALENTENDU : il y a là une erreur
évidente dès qu'on descend des apparences aux réalités. Il y
a, en fait, opposition radicale entre les deux discours. Dans
le premier, Rousseau avait fait un plaidoyer pour la vertu, la
vertu qui signifiait victoire sur nos passions et renoncement
aux jouissances de l'existence, la vertu chose sainte en elle-
même. Or, il apparaît dès la préface du *Second Discours*, que
l'idéal de la vertu de renoncement n'est plus du tout la préoccupation première de Rousseau : tout au contraire, le bonheur
comme but de l'existence est accepté dès les premières pages.
Rousseau parle comme s'il n'avait jamais parlé d'autre but
que de « défendre la cause de l'humanité » ; comme s'il n'avait
jamais exalté la beauté de la vertu ; bref comme s'il n'avait
jamais écrit le *Premier Discours*. Quand il pose comme premier principe, naturel et légitime, déposé au cœur de chaque
homme, « un intérêt ardent à son bien-être » ; quand, sans
s'étonner, il laisse se glisser dans son texte des paroles comme :
« L'amour du bien-être est le seul mobile des actions des
hommes » (107), il ne s'aperçoit même pas qu'il parle un langage surprenant pour des lecteurs de son *Premiers Discours* (1).
Plus tard, d'ailleurs, il l'a compris et même assez tôt, car il
s'indigne contre Voltaire l'accusant d'être indifférent à la
félicité des hommes : « Vous avez qualifié de livre contre le
genre humain un écrit qui plaide la cause du genre humain
contre lui-même » (août 1756). La chose est celle-ci : Dans
le *Premier Discours*, Rousseau croyait que le but de la vie

---

(1) Thèse qu'il répètera de plus en plus souvent à mesure qu'il s'affermira
dans une philosophie romantique. Voir par exemple *Emile*, II (Vol. 11, 60),
ou III Vol. II, 137) ; *Lettre à M. de Beaumont* (Vol. III, 64) : L'unique passion
qui naisse avec l'homme, savoir l'amour de soi... » ; etc.

est le renoncement pour la vertu ; dans le *Second Discours,* il a tout simplement cessé de croire au renoncement à la vie.

Certes cette attitude vis-à-vis de la vie — que le bonheur est le but de l'existence et que nous définissons comme l'attitude « romantique » — n'a rien d'extraordinaire ; et c'est bien la vertu puritaine ou calviniste qui n'est *pas* naturelle. Mais cela n'écarte pas le fait que Rousseau avait, au moment du *Discours sur les Sciences et les Arts* adopté la première, celle prévalant dans le monde depuis la victoire des idées chrétiennes. Et nous savons d'ailleurs que c'était seulement dans un accès de réaction exaltée que Rousseau avait passé de ses rêves romantiques amèrement déçus à la défense de la vertu traditionnelle romaine ou puritaine.

Il ne saurait être indifférent de comprendre comment Rousseau est ensuite repassé au romantisme ; cela, le corps du *Second Discours* nous le révèle — et ce sera naturellement un romantisme d'une nuance nouvelle, un romantisme moins primesautier que celui d'avant 1749.

Et d'abord, il est normal qu'en quatre années bien des choses prennent un aspect nouveau ; les conséquences des théories embrassées fanatiquement apparaissent, et malgré qu'on en ait, battent en brèche celles-ci. Or, la vertu puritaine, Rousseau l'avait inconsciemment compris maintenant, n'a de sens qu'avec une théologie qui justifie le renoncement aux jouissances naturelles (par une attente de jouissances surnaturelles après la vie). Se priver sans motif aucun est d'un sot ; il faut une raison suffisante. Mais Rousseau n'avait jamais voulu de théologie ; au moins il n'en avait jamais été question dans ses écrits jusqu'alors. Quel sens y aurait-il eu dans ces conditions, à conserver les notions théologiques de la vertu qu'on trouve chez un Bossuet ou un Calvin, de conserver le renoncement aux jouissances naturelles, dans un système de morale où, cependant, aucune place n'était faite au dogme chrétien d'immortalité ? Et pire que cela : Rousseau se rendait compte — sans qu'il l'ait jamais formulé du reste, sans même peut-être qu'il en ait jamais eu lui-même clairement conscience — qu'il avait glissé à tort sa vertu *chrétienne* aux Romains dans le *Premier Discours*. C'était là encore une grave confusion ; car, si les vrais Romains étaient des gens admirables par la façon dont ils savaient contrôler leur *moi*, ils ne songeaient pas à une vertu de renoncement dans le sens chrétien ; ils gagnaient à cette discipline de leurs appétits ; les privations d'un côté se retrouvaient en gains plus grands de l'autre ; et ils ne devaient « renoncer », s'ils étaient raisonnables, qu'autant que cela leur profitait. C'était une vertu pragmatique, politique si on veut, une variété de ce que nous avons appelé vertu-sagesse. Les Fabricius et les Caton de Rousseau, au contraire, s'abstenant *pour rien* on ne comprend plus ; ce sont des âmes fortes encore, mais ce ne sont pas des âmes sages ; et une âme forte et non sage, est-elle réellement une grande âme ?

Et plus tard on verra, quand Rousseau sera amené aux grandes discussions théologiques de la *Profession de foi*, que le côté inhumain d'une religion qui n'accorde le bonheur futur à l'homme qu'au prix de souffrances préalables sera justement une des choses qui lui dictera souvent son attitude hostile vis-à-vis du christianisme traditionnel, catholique ou protestant.

Nous n'en sommes pas encore là. Dès maintenant, cependant, Rousseau se trouve, de par la matière qu'il traite, devant un dogme très anti-romantique de la philosophie chrétienne, le dogme de l'homme naturellement mauvais, ou du péché originel. Au nom de ce dogme on prétendait barrer l'homme du bonheur : Si la souffrance et le mal existent dans le monde, ce n'est pas Dieu qu'on peut en rendre responsable, c'est que l'homme est mauvais ; comme il est mauvais, ce qu'il aime sera le mal ; et comme il aime la jouissance, le bonheur du monde, cette jouissance et ce bonheur du monde seront mauvais ; et la vertu consistera à lutter contre ces jouissances, à s'en priver, à renoncer. Or ce dogme du péché originel (notion contraire à toute justice puisqu'elle montrait l'homme souffrant pour un péché qu'il n'avait pas commis, mais dogme auquel on avait été acculé pour arriver à décharger Dieu, et qui était à la base de toute morale chrétienne depuis le moyen âge) (1), Rousseau, nous l'avons vu, l'avait adopté dans son *Premier Discours*. Il l'avait adoptée, cette idée de la « perversité » de l'homme. non pas avec grande décision, ni même très explicitement ; mais elle était pour lui un postulat : seule une théorie qui commandait à l'homme de lutter contre une nature pécheresse justifiait son enthousiasme pour la vertu de renoncement, la vertu qui a comme objet l'expiation.

Mais maintenant qu'il a changé son point de départ, et qu'il veut clairement que l'homme cherche son bonheur dans le monde, c'est autre chose : une théorie qui implicitement condamne le bonheur dans le monde n'est plus son fait : non seulement il n'en a plus besoin, mais elle est une pierre d'achoppement.

Ajoutons que Rousseau n'est pas encore disposé (comme il le sera six ans plus tard dans la *Profession de foi* et dans le *Contrat social*) à s'incliner devant certains mystères du dogme ; il ne voit, pour l'heure, que l'obstacle à son évangile du bonheur dans ce dogme de l'homme mauvais par nature ; c'est avec la fougue coutumière du nouveau prosélyte qu'il fonce sur cette croyance, et qu'il en exploite à l'avantage de sa théorie, le côté révoltant.

Et c'est ainsi qu'il est amené à se rapprocher de cette philosophie qui s'élaborait tout autour de lui, que la nature n'est pas mauvaise ; c'est ainsi qu'il se rapproche de ces « philosophes » qui, exaltant le bon sauvage, récusaient en même temps avec vigueur le dogme ecclésiastique de la perversité originelle.

§ **3.** Il faut être ici d'une prudence extrême quant à l'emploi des termes et leur sens précis : on rattache communément les idées que nous venons de rappeler, au nom de Rousseau

---

(1) Dire seulement que l'homme est *faible* et que le monde est un lieu d'épreuve ne suffisait pas ; car pourquoi soumettre l'homme à cette épreuve ? pourquoi ne pas le rendre heureux sans ces cruelles épreuves ? Seul l'homme *mauvais* permettait de conserver le Dieu puissant et bon. Ces questions seront reprises à propos de la **Profession de foi** de l'*Emile*.

que l'homme était naturellement bon. Mais ce qui est malheureusement vrai aussi, c'est que si Rousseau a été identifié avec l'idée de la bonté de l'homme naturel, il n'est pas innocent du malentendu. Il a, *après coup, cru avoir prouvé* la bonté naturelle dans le *Second Discours* ; il l'a constamment prétendu dans ses écrits postérieurs, et en vérité il est mort avec la conviction que, s'il était une chose qu'il avait prouvée, c'était celle-ci. Nous défions cependant de trouver, dans le texte même du *Second Discours*, un mot qui signifie que l'homme naturel est positivement bon dans le sens de désintéressé. On trouve l'idée dans la note *i*, — note très importante, mais certainement postérieure au *Discours* (voir vol. VIII, 71). Quand Rousseau était en plein dans son argumentation, il a parfaitement conservé son sang froid sur ce point, et n'a jamais glissé de la notion de l'Homme *pas mauvais* par nature à celle de l'homme positivement *bon* par nature.

Nous avons fait longuement cette démonstration appuyée sur les textes dans la *Revue du Dix-Huitième siècle*, oct.-déc. 1913, pp. 435-447 ; nous ne la reproduirons pas ; en voici cependant la conclusion : « Dans le *Premier Discours*, Rousseau considère la vertu comme une lutte contre les penchants naturels de l'homme, affirmant implicitement que l'homme est naturellement mauvais.

Dans le *Second Discours*, amené par ses attaques contre la civilisation à exalter, par contraste avec l'œuvre de l'homme social, celle de la nature, il ne peut admettre que cette nature soit responsable de la perversité humaine ; l'homme est devenu méchant, il n'était à l'origine « pas méchant ».

Dans les « Notes » au *Second Discours*, oubliant la nuance capitale et qu'il avait soulignée lui-même, entre « pas méchant » et « bon », il déclare avoir démontré que l'homme est naturellement bon.

Puis, toujours plus pénétré de la corruption de l'homme social, et aussi, poussant toujours plus loin ses théories relatives à la bonté de l'œuvre de la nature, il affirme (naturellement avec toujours plus de conviction) que l'homme, œuvre de cette nature, est « bon » au fond (*Emile* et *Nouvelle Héloïse*).

Et quand, au soir de la vie, il fait une revue solennelle de son œuvre, il lui semble voir dans la théorie de la bonté originelle de l'homme le « grand principe » de toute sa pensée...

Mais alors, si l'idée de la bonté originelle de l'homme est une

thèse doublement accessoire d'une théorie complètement indifférente à la pensée fondamentale de Rousseau dans le *Second Discours* — et d'ailleurs dans toute son œuvre subséquente — nous
avons le droit de conclure qu'elle a accaparé dans les discussions
sur la pensée de Rousseau une place — la première de toutes —
qui ne lui appartient en aucune façon...

Il valait la peine de faire toute cette démonstration puisque la
critique a toujours suivi Rousseau en affirmant avec lui que la
croyance à la bonté originelle était le fondement de l'édifice...
On se moquerait de nous si nous voulions le prouver ; on rencon-
trerait en effet, difficilement un commentateur qui n'ait *pas*
accepté la proposition : Rousseau a entendu prouver que l'homme
est naturellement bon... Nous ne citerons qu'un seul nom, celui
de M. Lanson, le plus pénétrant parmi les critiques récents, celui
qui, sans écrire un livre, a cependant écrit la plus admirable étude
qui soit sur Rousseau, et qui n'a pas plus que les autres évité
l'écueil, — ce qui équivaut à dire, qu'à moins de faire une étude
spéciale sur ce point, l'erreur est inévitable : « La nature, dit
Lanson dans son *Histoire de la littérature française*, avait fait
l'homme bon et la société l'a fait méchant ; la nature a fait l'homme
libre et la société l'a fait esclave ; la nature a fait l'homme heureux
et la société l'a fait misérable. Trois propositions liées... Là-dessus
se fonde tout le système. » Comme Rousseau (ainsi dans le dernier
passage que nous avons de lui sur ce point, IIIᵉ dialogue, vol. IX,
287 : « La nature a fait l'homme heureux et bon »), Lanson réunit
sur le même plan « heureux » et « bon » ; il ne tient pas compte du
fait que ces deux notions s'excluent, ou tout au moins que la
première (heureux) rend la seconde (bon) superflue (1) ; la nature
ayant fait l'homme heureux, il n'y aurait en effet aucune raison
de le faire « bon » par-dessus le marché, puisque déjà l'homme
n'avait pas de motif pour être méchant. Rousseau lui-même l'a
dit : « La mauvaise action dépend de l'intention de nuire » (II, 60) ;
or l'homme ne peut vouloir nuire que pour se procurer du bonheur.
« L'amour de soi est la seule passion naturelle à l'homme » (II, 60) ;
mais alors, s'il *est* heureux, quelle bonté y aurait-il à ne pas nuire ?
Il ne s'agit donc pas ici de « bonté », mais tout au plus de « non-
méchanceté ». Et en effet, Lanson comme Rousseau, dit « homme
bon » et définit « homme non-méchant » ou « innocent » : « Dans
l'état naturel, l'homme est bon : comment serait-il mauvais puisque

---

(1) Car Rousseau se meut dans le monde seul ; le bonheur dans l'autre monde
comme récompense de la vertu dans celui-ci ne compte pas dans la façon dont
il pose le problème. Nous l'avons abondamment expliqué ailleurs.

ni la moralité, ni la loi n'existent ? [Mais, justement, la même chose s'applique à « bon » : « Comment serait-il *bon* puisque ni la moralité ni la loi n'existent ? »] Il ne pèche pas contre la règle puisqu'il n'y a pas de règle [mais justement il *n'obéit* pas à la règle puisqu'il n'y a pas de règle]. Il est égoïste [donc pas *bon* — « l'homme naturel est bon » — ou alors, « égoïste » est synonyme de « bon »] ; il suit l'instinct qui lui dicte de conserver son être. Il est innocent [!] comme l'animal. Il satisfait son besoin ; il ne *veut* de mal à personne [mais pas de bien non plus] : Au delà de son besoin, il ne prend rien... »

Venons à la troisième notion de « bonté » ; — et celle-ci rentre déjà jusqu'à un certain point dans les préoccupations de Rousseau. Le vocabulaire, en effet, est complaisant ; il permet d'employer le mot bon — et partant celui de vertueux — dans les sens non seulement différents, mais selon le point de vue entièrement opposés. Ne dit-on pas, en effet, de l'action d'un homme qu'elle est *bonne* parce qu'il a résisté à son désir de satisfaire son propre besoin de bonheur et a cultivé une vertu de renoncement, ou qu'elle est *bonne* parce qu'elle lui a *donné* justement ce bonheur personnel, — en cultivant son esprit, en réalisant de belles ambitions, ou tout simplement en affermissant sa santé et jouissant de la vie de toute manière ? Le contexte indique généralement d'une façon suffisante de laquelle des *bontés* il s'agit. Or, donc Rousseau, quand il a prétendu avoir démontré que l'homme était naturellement bon, l'a-t-il voulu peut être dans ce dernier sens ? Certainement non ! Rousseau n'a pu entendre cette bonté là encore non plus que celle de vertu de renoncement ou de bonté désintéressée des philosophes amis des sauvages car celui qui possède cette bonté serait heureux ; — or, il présente l'homme naturel comme *non-malheureux*, mais jamais comme *heureux*, — et la nuance est aussi importante que celle entre l'homme bon et l'homme non-mauvais.

§ **4.** Et ceci nous ramène à ce qu'il y a *d'autre* dans le *Second Discours*, — à savoir que Rousseau est maintenant préoccupé du bonheur de l'homme, bonheur de l'homme sur la terre, et auquel il était parfaitement indifférent dans le *Premier Discours* où la vertu pour la vertu était seule honorée.

C'est cette nouvelle conception philosophique qui va alors suggérer une quatrième idée de « bonté », plus complexe que les autres, mais qui sera celle de Rousseau ; celle qui se dégage de dessous un vaste amas de discussions. Nous disons *se dégage*, car Rousseau n'est pas parvenu à exprimer jamais proprement, nettement, la pensée qu'il sentait agir en lui.

Donc (nous reportant à notre résumé), examinons cette distinction si importante : que Rousseau n'a pas présenté l'homme primitif comme *heureux*, mais seulement comme *non-malheureux*.

Rousseau n'a pas décrit l'homme primitif comme heureux, car le bonheur n'est pas à sa portée ; et le non-malheur, qui seul peut être sien, est aussi le sort de l'animal. Il faut d'abord que l'homme soit sorti de l'état de nature pour que l'industrie lui apprenne à connaître les joies du confort, et que l'habitude de vivre ensemble « fasse naître le plus doux sentiment », amour de famille, puis amour entre homme et femme ; dans l'amour physique du sauvage, il n'y a point ce que Rousseau appelle « amour qui servira la beauté » (104).

Les mots mêmes que Rousseau est obligé d'employer sont révélateurs, tels *perfectibilité, vertus sociales* du primitif :

« La perfectibilité, les vertus sociales, et les autres facultés que l'homme naturel avait reçues en puissance ne pouvaient jamais se développer d'elles-mêmes... » (104) : *reçues en puissance...* il fallait *sortir* de l'état de nature pour en connaître la réalité.

Même dans son passage le plus affirmatif, il n'est question que d'un bonheur négatif entièrement ; c'est le non-malheur qu'il décrit :

Je sais bien qu'on nous répète sans cesse que rien n'eût été si misérable que l'homme dans cet état ; et s'il est vrai, comme je crois l'avoir prouvé, qu'il n'eût pu qu'après bien des siècles avoir le désir et l'occasion d'en sortir, ce serait un procès à faire à la nature et non à celui qu'elle aurait ainsi constitué. Mais si j'entends bien ce terme de *misérable*, c'est un mot qui n'a aucun sens, ou qui

ne signifie qu'une privation douloureuse, et la souffrance du corps
ou de l'âme : or, je voudrais bien qu'on m'expliquât quel peut être
le genre de misère d'un être libre dont le cœur est en paix et le corps
en santé (97).

Nous remarquons, à la vérité, que Rousseau nie dans la
seconde partie de ce passage sa propre théorie que la possibilité du bonheur n'existe qu'après la sortie de l'état sauvage
ou naturel ; mais c'est simplement que *pour le moment* (nous
verrons tout à l'heure pourquoi) cette théorie l'embarrasse
beaucoup ; et c'est logiquement que partout ailleurs il s'en
tient à elle. Il la réaffirme par exemple dans la *Lettre sur les
Spectacles* : « L'homme n'est ni un chien, ni un loup. Il ne faut
qu'établir dans son espèce les premiers rapports de la société
pour donner à ses sentiments une moralité toujours inconnue
aux bêtes ... » (vol. II, 236). Elle revient dans la première
ébauche du *Contrat social* (qui ne doit pas être très postérieure
au *Second Discours*) : « L'heureuse vie de l'âge d'or... insensible aux stupides hommes des premiers temps » (Ed. Dreyfus-
Brisac, p. 248). Il ne la lâchera pas, et on peut résumer sa
pensée sur ce point par la phrase suivante tirée de la *Lettre à
M. de Beaumont*. « Dans cet état (de nature), l'homme ne connaît que lui ; il ne voit son bien-être opposé ni conforme à
celui de personne ; il ne hait ni n'aime rien ; borné au seul
instinct physique, il est nul, il est bête » (vol. III, 65).

Et c'est ici, nous le répétons, — et on va s'en apercevoir
de plus en plus à mesure que nous verrons la pensée de Rousseau se développer — que l'on devra chercher dorénavant le
point de départ de ses efforts pour constituer la philosophie
pragmatique qui était son rêve : L'homme pour connaître le
bonheur *doit sortir* de l'état de nature ; — ce qui va avoir,
comme corollaire, le changement de la thèse de l'état social
mauvais en celle, bien différente, d'un état social simplement
très dangereux.

Mais, hélas ! ici comme tout à l'heure, Rousseau s'est ensuite
souvent mépris sur ce qu'il avait réellement établi. Comme il
a étourdiment affirmé dans ses écrits postérieurs qu'il avait

démontré que l'homme était non seulement *non-mauvais*, mais positivement *bon* ; ainsi il a cru après coup avoir démontré que l'homme primitif avait été *heureux*, alors que la démonstration avait porté sur ce point seulement qu'il n'était *pas malheureux*. De ces deux regrettables confusions il faut avouer que celle-ci est la plus persistante et la plus grave ; elle crée des malentendus constants. Car, voici, les périodes « vertueuses » du *Premier Discours* sonnaient encore aux oreilles de Rousseau pendant qu'il écrivait le *Second* ; il avait été si fasciné par ce rôle, plus digne semble-t-il d'abord, d'apôtre de la vertu romaine, que celui de défenseur d'une chose aussi commune et ayant si peu besoin d'avocat qu'une « vertu » qui assurait la jouissance des biens du monde. Ainsi, profitant de l'équivoque du mot *bon* indiquée tout à l'heure (bon dans le sens désintéressé et bon dans le sens intéressé), il pouvait glisser des idées de bonté dans le sens de vertu romaine au milieu de démonstrations concernant la bonté dans le sens du profitable au bonheur ; et il a pu, sans que ni lui ni ses lecteurs souvent s'aperçussent du malentendu, continuer à se croire le prophète en quelque sorte inspiré de la vertu du *Premier Discours*.

Il en résulte que dans tout cet écrit, ce dualisme déconcertant, cette coexistence des deux tendances calvinistes et romantiques (l'homme n'a pas droit au bonheur, et le droit reconnu au bonheur), là où la seconde seule est conséquente avec le fond même de l'ouvrage ; et non seulement l'idéal calviniste ou romain du *Premier Discours* n'a pas disparu de l'horizon de la pensée de l'auteur, non seulement on voit cet idéal essayant sans cesse de pénétrer de nouveau dans la place, mais toute la disposition du *Second Discours* est telle que la vertu romaine est favorisée au dépens de la vertu romantique.

Mais alors puisque Rousseau a déclaré l'homme primitif incapable de bonheur, « stupide », et plus tard « nul » et « bête » ; et puisque d'ailleurs on chercherait en vain dans le *Second Discours* la description de l'homme des premiers âges que la postérité prête à Rousseau, comment Rousseau a-t-il pu donner aux autres — et à lui-même — l'impression qu'il avait décrit en son homme de la nature un être heureux ?

Voici l'explication :

Rousseau distingue deux âges, celui de l'état de nature, et celui de l'état social, correspondant à la première partie de son ouvrage (p. 84-105) et à la seconde partie (p. 105-126). Et le premier est bon — ou pas mauvais ; le second est positivement mauvais. D'autre part, Rousseau place son âge d'or avant l'état social, *mais* pas tout à fait au début des temps ; l'homme a dû sortir de l'état des besoins purement physiques pour arriver à une conception de besoins d'un autre ordre et réellement supérieurs. Et aussi, il n'a pas passé brusquement d'un état à l'autre ; et même, Rousseau décrit longuement une période de transition ; et c'est avant cette période que l'homme était sauvage, et après qu'il était social. Cela fait donc, en réalité *trois* âges : 1º état de nature ; 2º âge d'or ; 3º état social ; c'est-à-dire qu'il y a véritablement pour *un* état social, *deux* soi-disant états de nature. Or, comme Rousseau ne prétend parler que de deux âges en tout, il peut donc rattacher, — en vérité selon le besoin, — la période de bonheur soit avec le premier âge (en prolongeant celui-ci jusqu'après l'acquisition de la puissance du bonheur), soit avec le second âge (en reculant celui-ci jusqu'au moment où l'homme est sorti de l'état de nature) ; l'âge d'or est un état intermédiaire : si l'état de nature cesse avant l'état intermédiaire, l'état de nature ne contient pas ce bel âge d'or que Rousseau peut opposer à l'état social ; d'autre part, si l'état de nature est conçu comme s'étendant jusqu'après la période intermédiaire de façon à comprendre l'âge d'or, alors toute la première partie du *Second Discours* dont nous venons de donner l'analyse et qui peint l'homme comme digne d'envie (simplement parce qu'il est non malheureux, humainement parlant), est absolument non-avenue, puisqu'elle ne décrit pas l'âge d'or.

Selon la logique des choses, la période du bonheur va clairement avec le second âge — social — puisqu'au premier âge l'homme est incapable des jouissances qui sont celles de la période de bonheur.

Mais alors, que devient l'opposition du premier âge *excellent* et du second âge *mauvais*, que l'on a toujours — Rousseau compris — regardé comme le grand thème du *Second Discours* ? Évidemment, c'est un leurre, et l'opposition n'est pas entre Première Partie (état naturel), et Seconde Partie (état social), mais entre première période (âge d'or) et seconde période (état social) de la Seconde Partie. Et la Première Partie est un hors-d'œuvre. Rousseau va-t-il l'abandonner cependant. Nous savons que non. Et nous comprenons aussi pourquoi. La Première Partie qui est un hors-d'œuvre au point de vue de la question du bonheur — qui est le sujet propre du *Discours* — peut se justifier si on tient compte de la bonté dans le sens de vertu romaine, cette bonté romaine à laquelle Rousseau (contre toute logique) donne, en fait, tant de place : L'homme à l'âge ancien où les passions corruptrices n'existent pas (car elles ne se sont pas développées) peut être opposé à l'homme qui est sorti de cet état et où se sont développées les fatales dispositions aboutissant à la corruption de l'état social. Sans doute, logiquement parlant, la non-vertu de l'homme social ne peut être mise en contraste avec la vertu romaine, mais avec une vertu seulement d'innocence ; Rousseau, cependant, n'en est pas à une confusion de plus ou de moins ; pas plus qu'il n'a distingué entre bon et non-méchant, et entre heureux et non-malheureux, il ne distingue — ou il oubliera de distinguer — entre vertu de renoncement et vertu d'innocence. Donc, de ce point de vue-là (qui est, du reste, une intrusion), Rousseau peut, en quelque sorte, opposer en effet Première Partie et Seconde Partie, arrêtant la première dès avant les premiers pas de la sortie de l'état de nature, et il n'a que deux âges.

Mais Rousseau sent si bien lui-même au fond que la question de bonheur, seule en cause, élimine logiquement sa Première Partie relative à la vertu d'innocence (corrélative non de bonheur, mais seulement de non-malheur), qu'il fait bien rentrer la description de son âge d'or, où déjà l'homme est devenu capable de bonheur positif, dans la Seconde Partie (après p. 105) (1). Par contre, alors là, il ne distingue par aucun signe extérieur (chapitre nouveau, ou paragraphe nouveau) les deux périodes qui sont en réelle opposition : l'âge d'or et l'état social.

Un fait qui montrerait encore que Rousseau est certes dupe de lui-même — par cette intrusion constante des notions de vertu et de renoncement du *Premier Discours* dans celles de bonheur du *Second* — c'est la façon dont il place aux premières lignes de sa Seconde Partie ce coup de trompette sur la propriété (« Le premier qui, ayant encos un terrain, s'avisa de dire : Ceci est à moi... ») Cela *paraît* marquer une limite, mais le coup de trompette est sonné d'avance... Le long développement de la sortie de l'état de nature à l'aboutissement à la propriété, à la justice sociale, etc., logiquement doit précéder ; mais ce coup de trompette est mis là comme une solennelle division, comme si là était le point de séparation : c'est un trompe-l'œil, mi-innocent, mi-habile.

Et il y a eu comme une sorte de fatalité qui a confirmé Rousseau dans cette malheureuse fausse position ; l'équivoque, en effet, lui fournit des passages de son texte répondant triomphalement à tous ses critiques, hédonistes aussi bien qu'ascétistes ; et alors ayant réponse à tout, il y a juste ce qu'il faut pour *ne pas* lui suggérer la nécessité de changer son attitude et devenir conséquent. Il veut établir, en effet, que l'état social est détestable, et il ajoute qu'il faudrait y substituer l'état de nature : c'est bien. Mais à ceux qui lui opposent que l'état de nature n'est pas si enviable que cela du point de vue du bonheur, il répond : Mais non ; je ne l'ai pas prétendu, — et il en appelle aux passages où il établit que l'homme n'arrive à l'âge d'or qu'une fois *sorti* du premier état de nature, et que ce premier état de nature n'est qu'indifférent. Et à ceux qui lui opposent que l'état social comporte des éléments de jouissance réelle et ne représenta pas

---

(1) Il reprend ceci *Lettre à M. Beaumont*, VIII, p. 50.

seulement la misère, il répond : Mais, sans doute, je n'ai
jamais contredit cela, — et il invoque les passages relatifs
au second état de nature (celui de l'âge d'or) où il a montré
que le développement de la raison qui a conduit à l'état social
est le même, après tout, que celui qui a conduit à l'âge d'or.

Qui sait ? Rousseau fut si aveuglément épris de ce mot de
vertu jusqu'à la fin de sa vie que, peut-être, s'il se fût un jour
rendu compte qu'il parlait bourgeoisement de bonheur quand
il croyait parler de vertu romaine, il eût, du coup, pris en
horreur son romantisme. Il est bien sûr, du reste, que cette
confusion de vertu sauvage et vertu romaine n'est pas particulière à Rousseau ; seulement elle est particulièrement
importante à signaler chez lui à cause des conséquences pour
l'intelligence de sa pensée générale. Mais, par exemple, cette
confusion était courante dès le XVIIe siècle chez les Jésuites.
Ceux-ci, comme Rousseau, donnent en exemple à leurs contemporains chrétiens, les sauvages, après avoir auparavant
proposé comme modèles les austères citoyens des républiques
de Rome et de Sparte ; les Pères étaient si loin de songer à la
différence que nous avons rappelée entre vertu et innocence,
entre anti-passionnel et a-passionnel, que tout en opérant
eux-mêmes le rapprochement, en plaçant eux-mêmes côte à
côte les termes différents, ils sont restés inconscients de la
confusion. Lichtenberger écrit à leur propos :

« Nourris dans l'admiration de l'antiquité classique, ils [les Jé-
suites] voient dans les usages des sauvages, des analogies avec ceux
des vieux Grecs ; ils leur supposent une communauté d'origine et
louent chez eux les qualités que leurs maîtres leur avaient appris à
admirer dans la Sparte de Lycurgue. Ecoutez ce que dit le Père
Lafitau des sauvages américains. Il les trouve extraordinairement
analogues (par des raisons fort naïves d'ailleurs) aux Hellènes
primitifs et suppose d'anciennes migrations pour expliquer ce
phénomène. S'ils ne sont pas sans défauts, ils ont l'esprit bon »
(*Socialisme au XVIIIe siècle*, p. 58-9) (1).

(1) On avait signalé déjà sans doute le fait que Rousseau ne place pas son
âge d'or dans l'état de nature proprement dit, mais dans une phase transi-
toire entre cet état et l'état social ; et aussi par conséquent, que Rousseau

En résumé, l'âge social est opposé tantôt à l'état de nature (pour vertu), tantôt à âge d'or (pour bonheur)

Voilà donc, selon nous, comment il faut schématiser le *Second Discours*.

ÉTAT DE NATURE. — Sans intérêt pour la thèse de Rousseau puisque le bonheur y est étranger ; l'homme ne connaît celui-ci ni pour le posséder ni pour le désirer ; cette partie de l'écrit ne serait justifiée qu'à titre d'introduction brève ; elle est élevée cependant à la dignité d'une des deux grandes Parties du *Discours* ; et la cause en est, d'une part, la vieille tendresse de Rousseau pour la vertu romaine, et parce que non-corruption de l'homme à l'état sauvage a été légèrement assimilée à excellence morale ; d'autre part, parce que, grâce à une non moins grande inconséquence, on a opposé à la misère de l'homme civilisé, l'état d'animale sérénité de l'homme naturel. *L'homme n'est ni heureux ni malheureux.*

ÂGE D'OR. — L'homme a maintenant acquis (par l'emploi de l'intelligence, industrie, etc., etc.) la faculté d'être heureux ; cependant l'évolution est arrêtée avant que des ambitions, des jalousies et des inimitiés de toutes sortes — dont la possibilité se développe concurremment avec la faculté de bonheur — aient fait pencher la balance du côté des maux. *L'homme est heureux.*

ÉTAT SOCIAL. — Les « funestes hasards » ont achevé le développement jusqu'au point où la balance des maux l'emporte de façon grave sur les biens. *L'homme est malheureux.*

---

n'admirait pas entièrement l'état anti-social. Ainsi E. Champion dans son *J.-J. Rousseau et la Révolution française* : « Par certains côtés son éloge [de l'état naturel] est une satire presque aussi sombre que celle qu'il fait de l'état social : L'homme sauvage n'a pas de vices, mais pas davantage de vertus ; ni bon ni mauvais, il est nul, il est bête, ne pense, n'aime, ni ne hait, n'a ni droit ni devoir... » (p. 51) ; et en *note* : « Je complète ce que dit Rousseau dans le *Discours* par le commentaire qu'il en fait dans sa *Lettre à l'Archevêque de Paris* (VIII, 50). Il ne croit bon que l'état intermédiaire entre l'état de nature et le troisième état ». Mais si on l'avait signalé on n'en avait sauf erreur vu encore la portée.

§ **5.** Maintenant ceci amène à une question : L'homme est-il condamné à rester malheureux en suite des « funestes hasards » ? Est-il nécessaire que les inconvénients de la civilisation l'emportent sur les avantages — *toujours* ? Le *Second Discours* ne répond pas absolument que c'est nécessaire, et même il admet qu'à côté de tous les maux, des biens sont résultés de la sortie de l'état de nature. Rousseau décrit ceux-ci en termes parfois enchanteurs ; c'est quelque chose, et laisse entrevoir la quatrième notion de « bonté » — celle que du fond de son être, cherche Rousseau. Ce que le *Second Discours* donne à entendre clairement en tous cas, c'est que la cause des misères de l'état social (à distinguer des causes de bonheur positif) est *la passion*.

Or, on voit tout de suite deux moyens de se débarrasser de la cause du mal : A) un retour à l'état de nature où l'homme n'était pas encore livré à ses passions, n'en connaissait pas les misères. B) pour l'homme dans l'état social, la suppression de la passion par la volonté.

A) *Le retour à l'état de nature*, à cause des violentes diatribes de Rousseau contre l'état social, se présente spontanément à l'esprit comme le moyen en quelque sorte infaillible ; et les lecteurs se sont presque toujours arrêtés à cette solution, la considérant comme implicitement contenue dans le corps du *Discours*. Voltaire le premier dans sa fameuse lettre : (« J'ai reçu, monsieur, votre nouveau livre... On n'a jamais employé tant d'esprit à nous rendre bêtes ; il prend envie de marcher à quatre pattes quand on lit votre ouvrage... » — 30 août, 1756) : si les choses sont comme Rousseau les dépeint, l'homme n'a qu'à reculer en arrière des soi-disant progrès pour annuler le mal. Mais Rousseau lui-même n'en veut absolument pas et semble refuser d'accepter les conclusions de ses prémisses. Il y résiste dès la conclusion du *Premier Discours* (17), où, par le fait qu'il a dénoncé les maux résultant des sciences et des arts, il pressent déjà que d'autres voudront lui prêter cette idée de retour ; on peut presque dire que dans la polémique qui suivit ce *Premier Discours* Rousseau fait porter tout son effort sur cette thèse : il ne faut pas abandonner cette civilisation que j'ai attaquée (voir surtout 34, 47-8, 52, etc.), Dans le *Second Discours*, la position est plus difficile.

Rousseau est visiblement embarrassé. Tantôt il explique que les hommes ne *peuvent* pas revenir en arrière : « Les peuples une fois accoutumés à des maîtres ne sont plus en état de s'en passer » (72) ; tantôt que les hommes ne *veulent* plus : « Quand une fois les coutumes se sont établies et les préjugés enracinés, c'est une entreprise dangereuse et vaine de vouloir les réformer ; le peuple ne peut même pas souffrir qu'on touche à ses maux pour les détruire, semblable à ces malades stupides et sans courage qui frémissent à l'aspect du médecin » (330) ; tantôt encore c'est que les bouleversements occasionnés par une réelle réforme seraient tels qu'il vaut mieux encore subir les maux actuels : « L'homme sauvage et l'homme policé diffèrent telle-ment par le fond du cœur et les inclinations que ce qui fait le bonheur suprême de l'un ferait le désespoir de l'autre » (125. cf. aussi 120-1 ; III, 364-5, V, 348-9). Qui ne voit que ce sont là seulement de mauvais prétextes ? Que les peuples ne puissent pas ou ne veuillent pas retourner, ou que des catastrophes for-midables soient à craindre en renonçant maintenant à l'ordre social établi, n'a proprement rien à voir avec la qestion de principe : s'il serait bon ou non de revenir à l'esprit de na-ture ?

L'embarras de Rousseau éclate plus complet encore quand s'étant relu, il rédige la fameuse *Note i*. Là, il se sent si bien acculé à la thèse du retour qu'il cède — malgré les textes du *Discours* proprement dit. Et il propose en propres termes, à ceux qui le peuvent, de retourner à la nature ; seulement, dit-il, moi et la plupart des hommes que je connais, ne le pou-vons pas. Citons ses paroles :

« Quoi donc, s'écrie-t-il d'abord, faut-il détruire les sociétés, anéantir le tien et le mien, et retourner vivre avec les ours ? Con-séquences à la manière de mes adversaires que j'aime autant pré-venir que de leur laisser la honte de la tirer ». [Et puis, au lieu de réfutation, on lit ceci :] « Vous qui pouvez... reprenez, puisqu'il dépend de vous, votre antique et première innocence, allez dans les bois perdre la vue et la mémoire des crimes de vos contemporains et ne craignez point d'avilir votre espèce en renonçant à ses lumières pour renoncer à ses vices » (138).

D'une autre manière encore cette *Note i* trahit l'embarras dans lequel se trouve Rousseau grâce à son insouciance de la précision dans l'emploi des termes : Il ne veut pas la vie présente (sociale), il ne veut pas vouloir la vie passée (de nature) il lui reste la vie à venir... et il ne l'écarte pas : mes adversaires veulent me faire croire que je dois conclure au retour à la vie passée ; je réponds : que ceux qui peuvent reprennent « l'antique et première innocence » ; mais quant à moi et « ceux qui sont convaincus que la voie divine appela tout le genre humain aux lumières et au bonheur des célestes intelligences » nous tâcherons de « *mériter le prix éternel* qu'ils en doivent attendre » (138). Il n'est pas besoin de dire que Rousseau renoncerait ainsi à l'idée même du *Second Discours* qui est d'atteindre au bonheur *terrestre*. Sauf dans cette page d'un mysticisme si curieux et si inattendu, il reste fidèle au point de vue romantique : bonheur *ici-bas* ; et c'est heureux pour lui qu'il ait relégué cette échappatoire dans une note où elle n'a pas été remarquée. Ajoutons que toute cette *Note i*, qui donc est en opposition avec le corps du *Discours*, l'est aussi avec les écrits postérieurs. Ainsi dans la *Préface à Narcisse* (un peu postérieure au *Second Discours*) Rousseau développe cette thèse : « quand le peuple est corrompu on ne revient pas en arrière » ; tout ce qu'on peut faire, c'est de « l'empêcher de devenir pire » (V. 108). Et il aboutit, au début du *Contrat social*, à cette déclaration : « L'ordre social est un droit *sacré* qui sert de base à tous les autres » (III, 306-7 ; cf. aussi V, 240 ; 348-9 ; VI, 389).

Lequel des deux Rousseau est en accord logique avec la pensée générale de l'auteur ? Celui qui *implicitement* demande le retour, ou celui qui *explicitement* récuse ? Il n'y a pas de doute : le Rousseau qui récuse. — Et cela *d'une part*, en vertu toujours de ce fait que dans la toute première partie du *Discours* il n'a pas prouvé que l'homme naturel est « heureux », mais seulement « non-malheureux », et que Rousseau aspire

et l'homme social par la pensée ; il n'y a pas en effet seulement
l'homme qui ne pense pas (sauvage — qui ne connaît pas de
maux) et l'homme qui pense (civilisé — qui connaît tous les
maux) ; car, une fois qu'il pense, l'homme peut encore penser
peu ou beaucoup, faux ou juste, mal ou bien. Il y a donc en
réalité trois termes : 1° l'homme qui ne pense pas (pas malheureux) ; 2° l'homme qui pense à moitié ou mal (malheureux) ;
3° l'homme qui pense bien (heureux).

Examinons de ce point de vue la phrase paradoxale de
Rousseau : « J'ose presque assurer que l'état de réflexion est
un état contre nature (lisons maintenant, un état de malheur),
et que l'homme qui pense est un animal dépravé (lisons maintenant, un animal misérable) » (87) (1). La thèse qui associe
l'être réfléchissant et l'être dépravé est juste, et nullement
paradoxale à l'esprit de Rousseau, si elle s'applique à l'homme
qui *commence* à réfléchir, c'est-à-dire qui réfléchit peu ou mal,
et qui est dépravé ou mauvais ou malheureux, comparé à
celui qui ne réfléchit pas du tout ; mais s'applique-t-elle aussi
à l'homme qui réfléchirait à fond ? celui qui, par le développement de la pensée, serait capable des jouissances réelles (propriété, affection, amour, sciences, arts), mais qui, par la même
réflexion, poussée plus loin, saurait éviter les dangers de l'état
social ? — Ce serait au moins à voir. Rousseau n'a donc pas
tort de s'arrêter à cette constatation et de faire valoir que
dans un certain sens, l'homme un jour est devenu malheureux
parce qu'il s'est mis à réfléchir ; car l'homme allait certainement au début, et même pour longtemps après, réfléchir très
gauchement ; — tout comme l'homme qui toucherait pour
la première fois un violon jouerait assurément fort mal.

Et cependant, Paganini est *devenu* un grand artiste. Nous
ne sachions pas que Rousseau l'eût jamais nié. Et on commence
donc à soupçonner ainsi qu'en prenant la peine d'aller de la
lettre du *Second Discours* à l'esprit, on verrait que Rousseau
a commencé à entrevoir que la cause du malheur des hommes
n'est pas leur perte de cette bonté naturelle, — qui n'existait

_____

(1) Par parenthèse, le « presque » est joli, il trahit bien le Rousseau paresseux.

même pas, mais leur manque de discernement en passant à l'état social. Même s'il est sans cesse encore victime du mot à sens multiple de « vertu », Rousseau ne pouvait, même dans le *Second Discours*, passer *toujours*, à côté de la notion de vertu raisonnable — celle-ci jouait en quelque sorte des coudes pour arriver au premier plan ; et la logique des choses amenait forcément Rousseau à l'indiquer ici et là de quelque manière : « Nous ne cherchons à connaître, dit-il par exemple (90), que parce que nous désirons de jouir ». Et dès le *Discours sur la vertu des héros* (1751) — si désespérément confus — on le surprend déclarant qu'il fallait abandonner le terrain de la bonté et la méchanceté au sens purement moral pour celui de sagesse et d'aveuglement : « Les hommes sont plus aveugles que méchants » (I, 166).

En résumé : On voit que si Rousseau avait rejeté les Romains pour les sauvages, c'est-à-dire rejeté la vertu qui excluait le bonheur pour revenir à un idéal pas du tout austère avec ce que nous avons appelé la vertu-innocence (laquelle garantit l'homme contre le malheur) il ne va pas cependant s'attarder à cette idylle morale qui ne répond que négativement à ses vœux. Et si d'autre part, il semble encore parfois incliné à se rapprocher plutôt de la vertu romaine, il ne peut en être vraiment question puisque celle-ci récuse le droit au bonheur dans ce monde qui est maintenant devenu son objectif. Il ne reviendra pas aux Romains, en effet, mais les Suisses vont — pour quelques mois au moins — paraître réaliser à ses yeux l'idéal de vie, ou ce qu'il appelle d'un nom toujours le même, la *vertu*.

CHAPITRE III

ROUSSEAU ET LES SUISSES
LETTRE SUR LES SPECTACLES

A

A. — 1. Ton austère de « vertu romaine ». Et cependant pas en accord avec la vertu du *Premier Discours*, ni en désaccord avec le romantisme du *Second*.

2. Différence fondamentale des opinions de Rousseau et de Bossuet sur le théâtre, malgré des apparences d'accord jusque dans les termes employés pour censurer les spectacles.

3. Différence des idées de Rousseau d'avec celles de D'Alembert et des « philosophes » ; ceux-ci adoptent sans autre que l'homme interprètera intelligemment les héros de théâtre ; Rousseau prend en considération la majorité du public qui interprètera de façon funeste à son « utilité », c'est-à-dire à son bonheur.

4. Même à supposer que le peuple comprenne les spectacles qu'on lui offre, le théâtre tel qu'il existe est funeste à l'homme — qui y cherche *naturellement* le fruit défendu.

5. Rousseau esquisse d'autres plaisirs que le théâtre, qui, ceux-ci seront légitimes par le fait qu'ils portent en eux le bonheur plus vrai et plus durable.

B. — Notions à élucider pour bien comprendre la philosophie morale de Rousseau ;

1. *La conscience morale* ou *sentiment moral inné* ; cette notion paraît l'éloigner des « philosophes » et le rapprocher du christianisme traditionnel ; la vérité est juste l'opposé ; mais Rousseau a contribué lui-même à créer la confusion sur ce point, car il a *appelé* ces notions « innées », et il a *démontré* qu'elles ne l'étaient pas. Sa conscience morale est d'essence rationaliste.

2. *Vivre selon la nature* signifie maintenant chez Rousseau non plus : selon la nature primitive, mais — dans l'état social — selon la nature de l'homme, laquelle comporte la raison, c'est-à-dire contrôle la passion romantique ; et il s'agit ici de *la* raison (dans le sens absolu du terme) qui est opposée chez Rousseau à la raison telle que développée par un groupe de philosophes du

XVIIIe siècle et qui *prétendaient* à faux avoir la raison parfaite. Donc sur ce terrain de la raison, le propre terrain choisi par eux, Rousseau se sépare des « philosophes ».

3. Conclusion.

(1) *NOTES sur deux points contestés.*

§ **1.** Ce qui frappe d'abord dans la *Lettre à D'Alembert*, c'est le retour au ton de l'austérité.

En vain Rousseau en parle-t-il avec attendrissement dans les *Confessions* (« Elle respirait une douceur d'âme qu'on sentait n'être point jouée ») ; le lecteur n'a vu généralement dans ces pages que Rousseau le censeur, le calviniste, le Genevois (1). Certains la considèrent comme la plus puritaine de ses œuvres. Et il faut bien que cette note soit bien accentuée puisque M. Seillière, qui ne veut voir en Rousseau qu'un romantique à tout crin, et est embarrassé toutes les fois qu'il le trouve proposant quelque discipline morale, dit de la *Lettre à D'Alembert* : « son œuvre la plus rationnelle de beaucoup en morale » ; mais que du reste, se hâte-t-il d'ajouter, « l'esprit de contradiction lui a dictée pour une part » (*A. Vinet,* 925, p. 96).

Le style de l'ouvrage incontestablement justifie jusqu'à un certain point cette impression des lecteurs contraire au sentiment de Rousseau ; il est, presque jusqu'aux toutes dernières pages, d'une sévérité qui rappelle le *Premier Discours.* L'article de D'Alembert (au Vol. V de l'*Encyclopédie,* 1757) conseillant d'établir un théâtre à Genève, contient, écrit Rousseau « le plus dangereux conseil qu'on pût nous donner » (179) : « il ne s'agit plus d'un vain babil de philosophie, mais d'une vérité de pratique importante à tout un peuple » (180). On propose de « réunir la sagesse de Lacédémone à la politesse d'Athènes » (178) : Or, c'est impossible, car « il s'agit de savoir, en effet, si la morale du théâtre est nécessairement relâchée, si les abus

---

(1) On ne voit guère que Faguet qui soit d'accord avec Rousseau, il l'appelle « la plus idyllique des œuvres de Rousseau » (*Vie de R.,* p. 264). C'est qu'il ne pense qu'à la dernière partie de la *Lettre.*

sont inévitables, si les inconvénients dérivent de la nature des choses... » (188). Rousseau répond *oui* à ces questions : *La moralité* de Genève serait dès lors le prix à payer pour l'établissement d'un théâtre dans la ville ; c'est un prix inacceptable ; il y a là un piège d'autant plus dangereux à éviter que, même sans la recommandation de D'Alembert, la jeunesse de Genève n'aurait que « trop de penchants » pour le théâtre ; en suivant ce conseil, elle croirait maintenant encore « rendre un service à la patrie et presque au genre humain ! Voilà le sujet de mes alarmes » (179). Et, s'il faut bien convenir que le théâtre français est « à peu près aussi parfait qu'il peut l'être », cependant « je demande quel profit *les mœurs* peuvent tirer de tout cela » (185) ; l'essentiel est « l'effet *moral* d'une tragédie » (196) ; or, sur la scène « le savoir, l'esprit, le courage ont seuls notre admiration, et toi, douce et modeste *vertu*, tu restes toujours sans honneur » (196) ; enfin, « plus la comédie est agréable et parfaite, plus son effet est *funeste aux mœurs* ». (199). Il continue, anathématisant après la tragédie la comédie :

> « Le plaisir même du comique est fondé sur un vice du cœur humain; c'est en suite de ce principe que plus la comédie est agréable et parfaite, plus son effet est funeste aux mœurs » (199).

On ne peut applaudir et rire avec le rusé et le méchant sans approuver, ou au moins accepter le mal qu'il fait. Et encore :

> « J'entends dire qu'il (Molière) attaque des vices ; mais je voudrais bien que l'on comparât ceux qu'il attaque avec ceux qu'il favorise. Quel est le plus blâmable d'un bourgeois sans esprit et vain qui fait sottement le gentilhomme, ou du gentilhomme qui le dupe ?... Quel est le plus criminel d'un paysan assez fou pour épouser une demoiselle, ou d'une femme qui cherche à déshonorer son époux ?... C'est un grand vice d'être avare et de prêter à usure ; mais n'en est-ce pas un plus grand encore à un fils de voler son père, de lui manquer de respect, de lui faire mille insultants reproches ?... Si la plaisanterie est excellente en est-elle moins punissable ?

Quant au *Misanthrope* (qu'on reconnaît unanimement pour son chef-d'œuvre), c'est comme le couronnement de toute cette action regrettable : « Voulant exposer à la risée publique tous les défauts opposés aux qualités de l'homme aimable, de l'homme de société, après avoir joué tant d'autres ridicules, il lui restait à jouer celui que le monde pardonne le moins, le ridicule de la vertu : C'est ce qu'il a fait dans le *Misanthrope* » (201).

Tel le langage de Rousseau.

Et cependant, dès qu'on examine de près ces phrases, il n'y a pas un mot qui signifie que le vice soit condamné en lui-même et non dans ses conséquences, et la vertu du renoncement recommandée pour sa valeur propre ; ou pas un mot qui irrécusablement condamne ce que nous avons nommé le romantisme, c'est-à-dire la légitimité de la recherche de la jouissance. Les expressions qui donnent cette impression d'austérité avec le plus de force apparente sont toujours qualifiés par le contexte.

Prenons par exemple ces mots à l'adresse de D'Alembert et des Philosophes : « S'il est vrai qu'il faille des amusements à l'homme, vous conviendrez au moins qu'ils ne sont permis qu'autant qu'ils sont nécessaires, et que tout amusement inutile est un mal pour un être dont la vie est si courte » (187). Lorsque des paroles d'un moraliste sévère comme celles que nous venons de rappeler tout à l'heure résonnent à vos oreilles, il est naturel peut-être qu'on soit porté à entendre « s'il est vrai qu'il faille des amusements... » comme signifiant « *S'il était même vrai que...* » interprétant que les amusements *sont* condamnables. Mais dans cette même phrase encore, Rousseau admet qu'il est de ces amusements qui peuvent être « nécessaires » ; et il admet aussi qu'on peut songer à des amusements *utiles*, il parle de la vie courte dont l'homme dispose, vie qu'il ne faut donc pas employer à des « amusements inutiles », — tout cela rend certain qu'il entend par sa phrase : « *parce qu'il est vrai* qu'il faut des amusements... » Et nous avons pour nous confirmer en ceci tout le *Second Discours* qui précède où Rousseau cherche le bonheur des hommes dans le monde ; et nous aurons enfin les dernières pages de la *Lettre à D'Alembert* elle-même qui développeront cette thèse — d'ailleurs formulée en toutes lettres dans une *Note,* une de ces *Notes* à la façon de Rousseau qui contient l'essentiel de sa pensée — du « Dieu juste et bienfaisant [qui]...veut que l'homme se délasse »(253-4).

Autre exemple : Rousseau discutant (dans une digression) les hommes frivoles « uniquement occupés de l'importante affaire d'amuser les femmes » (247). De quoi les blâme-t-il ? De manquer d'austérité ? Point, mais de ce qu'ils sont dupes de plaisirs mesquins et en négligent d'autres plus grands ; et il ajoute : « Il ne serait pas difficile de montrer qu'au lieu de gagner à ces usages. les femmes (mêmes) y perdent » (248) ; pour elles aussi il y a mieux comme jouissances que ces hommages constants des hommes.

Autre exemple : Peut-être eût-il été préférable et plus sage de ne pas parler religion du tout dans la *Lettre sur les Spectacles* ; mais Rousseau s'y est laissé entraîner, car D'Alembert, pour gagner la cause du théâtre, en avait parlé le premier. Après tout, disait celui-ci, le clergé « socinien » de Genève ne connaît déjà plus la morale austère du renoncement professé par l'église traditionnelle. Or Rousseau, en prenant le parti du clergé de Genève, peut sembler un instant prendre parti pour le calvinisme ; il réfute D'Alembert en disant que celui-ci suppose seulement d'après ouï-dire l'existence du socianisme à Genève, sans en rien savoir certainement ; et que du moment que les pasteurs ne se déclarent pas eux-mêmes sociniens, on n'a pas le droit de leur prêter cette croyance ; mais Rousseau s'arrête là ; et au contraire dans des passages tout voisins, le voici qui justement loue un Dieu qui veut le bonheur des hommes, même le bonheur terrestre ; lui, Rousseau, n'a aucune sympathie par exemple pour la doctrine des peines éternelles : « Je ne suis pas scandalisé que ceux qui servent un Dieu clément et juste, rejettent l'éternité des peines » (184). Et quant aux idées de tolérance et d'indifférence aux dogmes trouvées à Genève, elles le séduisent à tel point qu'il s'écrie : Et si c'est là du socianisme, « je vous remercie pour ma patrie de l'esprit de philosophie et d'humanité que vous reconnaissez dans son clergé » (185).

Donc l'idée de vertu renoncement *demeure périmée*. Rousseau n'y revient pas.

§ **2.** Il faut être sur ses gardes, et nous ne résistons pas au désir de montrer comme l'érudition moderne, qui s'est faite si naïvement l'esclave des textes (mais non des contextes !) a parfois égaré. On a souvent rapproché Rousseau de Bossuet (nous l'avons rappelé dans notre Introduction) ; et en effet la *Lettre sur les Spectacles* rappelle tellement les *Maximes et Réflexions sur la Comédie* qu'on en demeure confondu. Avec apparemment les mêmes arguments, souvent avec les mêmes termes que Rousseau, Bossuet a voulu réduire la question du théâtre à la « question des bonnes mœurs » (II). Comme le fera Rousseau, Bossuet affirme que le théâtre français — Corneille, Racine — est dans toute sa grande éloquence, « dangereux à la pudeur » ; et, de même que le fera Rousseau, Bossuet s'attaque aux « infâmies » de Molière et aux « fausses tendresses » de Quinault (III). Le nœud du problème semble être exactement le même chez les deux écrivains ; à savoir qu'un auteur, quoiqu'il en dise, écrit toujours, et *doit* toujours écrire ses pièces pour « exciter les passions » c'est-à-dire pour plaire ; et « si même elles manquent leur coup, les règles de l'art sont frustrées » (IV) ; or, « il faut toujours que les règles de la véritable vertu souffrent par quelque endroit pour donner au spectateur le plaisir qu'il cherche » (VI) ; enfin, c'est la séduction de l'amour au théâtre qui constitue le plus grand danger : « Mais il y paraît comme une noble faiblesse, comme la faiblesse des héros et des héroïnes » ; supposez même qu'on admette quelque chose de licite en amour, cependant « le licite loin d'empêcher son contraire, le provoque, et vous pouvez dire à coup sûr de tout ce qui excite le sensible dans les comédies les plus honnêtes, qu'il attaque secrètement la pudeur » (V), etc. (I).

(1) Malgré ces arguments si précisément les mêmes, nous ne voyons pas du

Eh bien, malgré tant d'analogies, il n'y en a pas moins entre les deux écrivains, divergence fondamentale ; car, s'ils reprochent les mêmes choses, c'est pour des motifs différents. Pour Bossuet, d'une part, et pour l'Eglise, la mondanité (qui signifie amour du monde) est mauvaise *en soi* ; tout « amusement » est autant de pris sur la part de Dieu ; Bossuet s'appuie volontiers sur cette idée de Platon : « qu'un homme sage avait honte de faire rire » (XXXII) ; et surtout, cela va de soi, il invoque l'autorité des Pères, pour lesquels « il était ordinaire de prendre à la lettre la parole de Notre Seigneur : *Malheur à vous qui riez, car vous pleurerez* » (XXXIII). Il citait aussi l'exemple de Saint-Augustin qui « met en doute s'il faut laisser dans les églises un chant harmonieux, ou s'il vaut mieux s'attacher à la sévère discipline de Saint-Athanase et de l'église d'Alexandrie dont la gravité souffrait à peine dans le chant ou plutôt la récitation des Psaumes de faibles inflexions » (XXI). Pour Rousseau d'autre part, la « mondanité » n'a rien de répréhensible en soi ; le plaisir, la jouissance sont légitimes, et Dieu même veut que « l'homme se délasse ».

Ceci est vrai : le ton de Rousseau est aussi sévère que celui de Bossuet ; il est plus sévère qu'il ne l'a jamais été. Mais voilà justement ce qui fait l'intérêt de cette nouvelle phase de la pensée de Rousseau. Dès qu'on se pose la question, il devient évident que la seule raison aux yeux de Rousseau pour condamner le théâtre, c'est que celui-ci constitue une jouissance dont les *effets* sont préjudiciables, très préjudiciables au bonheur de l'homme. Il ne prétend pas prouver davantage ; mais son enthousiasme pour cette cause, combinée avec la conscience de la force de la tentation du théâtre, lui inspire ses avertissements foudroyants. Une mère mettant son enfant en garde contre le feu ne plaisante point ; elle tance et menace

---

tout qu'il *faille* voir des emprunts de Rousseau à Bossuet. L'intelligence travaille partout de même, et suggère naturellement les mêmes raisonnements dans des conditions semblables. Brunet, dans son excellente édition de la *Lettre sur les Spectacles* (Hachette) n'est pas de cet avis, et pense que Rousseau a dû connaître Bossuet et s'en servir.

en proportion de son souci pour la sécurité de l'enfant. Ce souci du bonheur des hommes inspire à Rousseau même sévérité.

§ 3. Un petit fait aurait pu éveiller l'attention du lecteur sur cette différence, c'est qu'on va voir Rousseau substituer de plus en plus fréquemment le mot *utile* (qui a un ton plus rationnel) au mot *vertueux* qui conserve depuis l'avènement du Christianisme quelque chose de métaphysique. Il consacrera positivement ce terme dans *Emile* ; Que saura Émile, arrivé à l'âge de l'intelligence, à 12, 15-16 ans ? « Il ne s'agit pas de savoir ce qui est, mais seulement ce qui est utile... » ; « A quoi cela est-il bon ? Voilà désormais le mot sacré, le mot déterminant... ». Mais dès avant l'*Emile*, et de plus en plus, le mot *utile* servira à la discussion philosophique, tandis que le mot *vertu* sera réservé aux morceaux d'éloquence.

Comme pour le mot *bon*, Rousseau n'analyse pas du reste explicitement sa notion d'utile. Le lecteur doit d'après le contexte en déduire le sens : « utile à quoi ? » Bossuet lui-même eût pu arguer : Utile à la réalisation de l'idéal chrétien de renoncement. Et à vrai dire, on ne peut saisir le vrai sens du terme chez Rousseau à moins qu'on ne se souvienne du *Second Discours* ; Rousseau qui avait écrit ce Discours s'en souvenait, lui, mais le lecteur toujours superficiel ne s'en souvient guère qu'après être déjà bien avancé dans sa lecture. Aux premières pages, tout ce qu'on peut deviner c'est que les « amusements utiles » demandent du discernement, tandis que les amusements auxquels on s'abandonne sans discernement peuvent être non utiles, ou mauvais. Mais il n'y a pas de « Prosopopée à Fabricius » dans la *Lettre à D'Alembert* ; il n'y a pas de plaidoirie pour l'austérité des mœurs d'autrefois, et on finit par se rendre bien compte qu'il s'agit de l'utilité du théâtre pour le bonheur des hommes.

En somme, le nœud de la question, selon Rousseau, consiste en ceci : l'erreur des « Philosophes » comme d'Alembert ou Voltaire, c'est de juger le théâtre du point de vue de l'art seulement en négligeant l'effet moral sur les spectateurs.

Or, pour une petite élite de spectateurs, sans doute, pour des
gens cultivés, pour « l'honnête homme » des XVIIe et XVIIIe
siècles, les héros grecs et romains des tragédies sont simplement *intéressants* (telle Phèdre, tels Syphax, Agamemnon,
Horace, Œdipe) ; leurs « crimes » du reste, non seulement
s'expliquent, mais même, moralement parlant, s'excusent ;
car, placés dans des circonstances particulières où les avaient
forcés les dieux, symboles de la fatalité, ces héros, ont commis
en les détestant des actions néfastes ; ils méritent notre sympathie. L'idée d'une moralité des actions, de blâme ou de
louange, est absente ; ils nous intéressent davantage que le
commun des mortels simplement parce que les auteurs des
tragédies les ont choisis dans les milieux où la souffrance
des choses de l'esprit est plus grande, où les sentiments de
l'âme sont plus développés. *Mais* cette conception-là n'est
pas à la portée des spectateurs de nos théâtres modernes qui
ne sont pas familiers avec la philosophie fataliste de l'antiquité, — ni du reste avec aucune philosophie autre que celle
enseignée par l'Eglise, et qui est essentiellement une philosophie de responsabilité morale ; et même si cette conception
des choses (fatalité) était acceptable philosophiquement
parlant, et plus vraie que celle de l'Eglise, elle serait encore
absurde à étaler aux yeux des masses. Le théâtre grec visait
les citoyens, c'est-à-dire une élite ; le théâtre moderne *vise*
peut-être aussi une élite, mais il *atteint* la masse qui depuis
l'avènement du christianisme est au moins à demi affran-
chie de la servitude ; c'est-à-dire cette masse pour qui, par
suite de sa conscience chrétienne d'une responsabilité morale,
voit avec simplicité dans un « héros » littéraire un homme
dont les actions seraient à admirer, ou en tous cas un homme
avec qui — *a priori* pour ainsi dire — la notion de crime ne
saurait être associée ; autrement elle ne pourrait le considérer
comme un « héros ». Or aux yeux de Rousseau, cette masse
innombrable importe beaucoup plus que la petite élite au
nom de laquelle bataillent d'Alembert et Voltaire ; et Rousseau
s'identifiera avec cette grande majorité des spectateurs qui
voient dans les « êtres exceptionnels » dont les histoires les

fascinent comme elles fascinent le public d'élite, des héros
dont les actions peuvent être admirées, voire même sont à
imiter. Pour ces spectateurs-là, quand l'homme commet un
meurtre ce n'est pas un dieu qui a guidé sa main, mais c'est
la volonté qui a agi. Bref, lorsqu'on leur dira : « Voici un
héros », ils chercherront en cet homme un héros tel qu'ils
le conçoivent, eux ; non un héros de passion, ou de souffrance,
mais un héros d'action ; ils obéiront à la suggestion, ne
plaindront pas, mais admireront le parricide, le meurtrier,
l'incestueux. Leurs idées seront peut-être bouleversées, mais
puisque de grands écrivains affirment que ce sont là des
« héros », on acceptera d'autorité ce dogme.

Rousseau songe aux conséquences de ce formidable malentendu. Quel enfer sera le monde si les hommes se mettent
à agir en partant de la théorie que les êtres de meurtre et de
crime sont d'« intéressants » modèles ! Et d'ailleurs ce ne sont
pas seulement leurs victimes à qui il faut penser, mais aux
héros eux-mêmes dont l'existence sera un tissu de lamentables
tragédies, si, cultivant la philosophie de la fatalité, ils s'abandonnent à leurs passions.

Il n'est pas nécessaire du tout pour comprendre la thèse de
Rousseau d'adopter la morale que prêche l'Eglise (renoncement aux jouissances de la vie) ; la morale du bonheur sous
n'importe quelle forme entre en ligne de compte tout aussi
bien : la responsabilité morales des hommes de théâtre demeure puisqu'il y a toujours *action* morale sur le public
« Tout tire à conséquence pour les spectateurs » (199). Dès
lors, dit Rousseau, acceptez que la tragédie soit intéressante
concédez même qu'on puisse trouver des leçons de vertu,
dans certaines pièces — et Rousseau reste d'accord qu'il
existe par hasard des pièces de théâtre dont la morale est irré-
prochable — ce n'est pas assez ; encore faut-il que la majorité
des spectateurs conçoivent les choses ainsi ; cependant :

« Suivez la plupart des pièces du Théâtre Français ; vous trouverez presque dans toutes des monstres abominables et des actions
atroces, utile si l'on veut à donner de l'intérêt aux pièces et de l'exer-

cice aux vertus, mais dangereuses certainement en ce qu'elles accoutument les yeux du peuple à des horreurs qu'il ne devrait pas même connaître, et à des forfaits qu'il ne devrait pas supposer possibles » (199).

Or notons l'expression *les yeux du peuple* ; le danger c'est donc l'entendement imparfait, l'imbécillité si l'on veut, des masses. Par exemple, *Mahomet* ou *le Fanatisme* de Voltaire peut être pour quelques spectateurs intelligents, une pièce belle, morale même et utile ; mais par le fait qu'elle présente au peuple le fanatisme *triomphant*; — et par le seul fait que *Mahomet* est donné comme un « héros », c'est-à-dire après tout est un homme digne de faire le sujet d'une tragédie, — cette pièce est « dangereuse » ;

« Je crains bien ... qu'aux yeux des spectateurs, sa grandeur d'âme ne diminue beaucoup l'atrocité de ses crimes, et qu'une pareille pièce jouée devant des gens en état de choisir ne fit plus de Mahomet que de Zopire » (197).

Dans le domaine de la Comédie, la pensée vraie de Rousseau éclate bien plus lumineuse encore. Naturellement, car les maux signalés dans la Tragédie sont en très grande partie neutralisés par le fait que les personnages sont ainsi conçus que l'application de leur morale à nos circonstances de tous les jours ne s'impose pas trop à l'esprit. Ces princes et princesses, débitant des discours sublimes et abstraits dans des situations si exceptionnelles, ne sont pas nos frères ; ils rappellent encore trop les demi-dieux qu'ils étaient à l'origine. Dans la Comédie, il en est autrement. Ce sont des personnages empruntés à la vie de tous les jours qui sont mis à la scène, et l'effet pratique mauvais du théâtre ressort immédiatement. Voyez Molière, « des talents duquel je suis plus admirateur que personne » :

« Ses honnêtes gens ne sont que des gens qui parlent ; ses vicieux sont des gens qui agissent et que les brillants succès favorisent le plus souvent. Enfin l'honneur des applaudissements rarement pour le plus estimable, est presque toujours pour le plus adroit « (200).

Et Rousseau invite ceux qui oublient les victimes pour les adroits à oublier les adroits pour les victimes. Que « les sots sont victimes des méchants » est vrai dans la vie ; mais au théâtre c'est pire car ces choses sont mises « avec un air d'approbation » (200). Rappelons au moins quelques phrases du plaidoyer de Rousseau contre Molière :

> « Voyez comment, pour multiplier ses plaisanteries, cet homme trouble tout l'ordre de la société ; avec quel scandale il renverse tous les rapports les plus sacrés sur lesquels elle est fondée, comment il tourne en dérision les respectables droits des pères sur leurs enfants, des maris sur les femmes, des maîtres sur leurs serviteurs ! Il fait rire, il est vrai, et n'en devient que plus coupable en forçant par un charme invincible, les sages mêmes de se prêter à des railleries qui devraient attirer leur indignation. »

On a toujours appuyé — incité à la chose d'ailleurs par le mot de connotation austère de « vertu », brandi et par Molière et par Rousseau à propos d'Alceste — sur le mauvais côté dans la discussion du Misanthrope ; on a laissé dans l'ombre ce que Rousseau avait au fond bien souligné, qu'Alceste est un homme « qui aime ses semblables » : « Qu'est-ce que le Misanthrope de Molière ? C'est un homme de bien qui déteste les mœurs de son siècle et la méchanceté de ses contemporains ; qui, précisément parce qu'il aime ses semblables, hait en eux les maux qu'ils se font réciproquement et les vices dont ces maux sont l'ouvrage » (202). Sans doute, Alceste s'écrie qu'il hait *tous* les hommes :

> *Les uns parce qu'ils sont méchants,*
> *Et les autres pour être aux méchants complaisants.*

Mais, pour ces derniers, c'est façon de dire : il hait leur bêtise — dont ils ne peuvent rien — et plaint leur sort. Rousseau d'autre part, déteste Philinte qui par sa bonté *aveugle* contribue à augmenter la somme du malheur ; si le Misanthrope est colère et « méchant » parce qu'il hait les hommes, Philinte est doux et « bon » parce qu'il n'aime pas les hommes.

Rappelons à ce sujet, avant d'aller plus loin, le frappant passage relatif au *Légataire universel* :

« Osons le dire sans détour, qui de nous est assez sûr de lui pour
supporter la représentation d'une pareille comédie sans être de
moitié des tours qui s'y jouent ? Qui ne serait un peu fâché si le
filou venait à être surpris ou manquait son coup ?... Belle instruction pour la jeunesse [c'est-à-dire pour les esprits mal mûrs] que
celle où les hommes faits ont bien de la peine à se garantir de la séduction du vice ?... En vérité, pour savoir mettre un fripon sur la
scène, il faut un auteur bien honnête homme » (208).

Rousseau, en même temps qu'il traite en général de la
tragédie et de la comédie, consacre des pages très spéciales à
l'*amour* au théâtre. Car, justement il n'y a aucune passion qui
séduise et charme autant, et par conséquent qu'il soit plus
naturel aux auteurs soucieux de plaire, de porter à la scène.
Surtout récemment, depuis Molière et Corneille, on n'a guère
que des « romans sous le nom de pièces dramatiques ». L'amour
est une « passion dangereuse » (208-9).

Nous interprétons ainsi, en la résumant, l'argumentation
de l'auteur de la *Lettre sur les Spectacles* : L'amour est le règne
des femmes ; or ce règne est mauvais. La femme peut être une
préoccupation légitime, douce, très recommandable dans la
vie ; par le fait qu'elle ne peut être la seule préoccupation, il y a
possibilité d'excès et par le fait que la femme est si douce et si
absorbante, il y a même *probabilité* d'excès ; donc il y a urgence à contrôler particulièrement cette passion, urgence de
« vertu ». Rousseau introduit à plusieurs reprises de véritables
traités sur le rôle de la femme dans la société. Les femmes dans
l'amour « selon l'ordre naturel » résistent, c'est-à-dire que tout
en ne demandant qu'à céder, elles font valoir leurs avantages
elles exploitent leur domination ; elles rendent le mal plus
aigu. Et celle qui saura le mieux faire valoir ses charmes, la
femme qui sera la plus femme, et qui par conséquent sera la
plus dangereuse, aura le plus de pouvoir ; déjà, tandis que les

Anciens « confinaient leurs femmes dans la maison [Rousseau dit « par respect », — le motif importe peu] chez nous la femme la plus estimée est celle qui fait le plus de bruit » (210) : c'est non seulement la femme, mais la mauvaise femme, « la Dame de cour » qui est mise au premier rang : — faut-il que le théâtre y contribue encore ?

Un contre-coup néfaste de cet état de chose dans la société et au théâtre, est que les vieillards sont méprisés sur la scène ; en effet, où l'amour règne, il n'y a pas de place pour les plus sages, pour ceux qui ont pu acquérir l'expérience de la vie et entre les mains de qui on pourrait en sécurité remettre le soin du bien-être général.

Tout cela nous paraît aujourd'hui — et en fait paraissait à des contemporains comme Voltaire — un peu redondant ; mais il est bien certain qu'on lit mal quand on voit dans tout cela un Rousseau moraliste et chagrin ; il ne condamne pas l'amour, il ne peut le condamner puisque c'est un sentiment très doux, et qu'il veut que l'homme fasse usage de ses moyens de jouissance ; mais est-ce sa faute s'il y a péril ? « Le mal qu'on reproche au théâtre [on, c'est-à-dire moi, Rousseau] n'est pas précisément inspiré des passions criminelles [car, la tragédie surtout, est souvent tout à fait honnête, ainsi *Le Cid*] mais de disposer l'âme à des sentiments trop tendres qu'on satisfait ensuite au dépend de la vertu » (212), — de la « vertu », lisez « de l'ordre et du bonheur ».

« Quand il serait vrai qu'on ne peint au théâtre que des passions légitimes, s'en suit-il de là que les impressions en sont plus faibles, que les effets en sont moins dangereux ?... quand le patricien Manilius fut chassé du Sénat de Rome pour avoir donné un baiser à sa femme en présence de sa fille, à ne considérer cette action qu'en elle-même qu'avait-elle de répréhensible ? Rien sans doute ; elle annonçait même un sentiment louable. Mais les chastes feux de la mère en pouvaient inspirer d'impurs à la fille. C'était d'une action fort honnête faire un exemple de corruption. Voilà les effets du théâtre » (212).

Rousseau expose longuement, et de la façon la plus habile, le sujet de la Bérénice de Racine. Titus hésite entre son amour

pour une princesse étrangère et son devoir d'empereur lui in-
terdisant un tel mariage. Au début de la pièce on blâme la
faiblesse de Titus hésitant, il manque de virilité ; mais à la
fin de la pièce, Bérénice a été si touchante qu'on voudrait que
Titus sacrifiât la « vertu ». Le spectateur « finit par plaindre
cet homme sensible qu'il méprisait, par s'intéresser même à
cette passion dont il lui faisait un crime, par murmurer en
secret du sacrifice qu'il est forcé d'en faire aux lois de sa patrie » (213). Le public est du reste, parfaitement convaincu du
devoir de Titus ; mais

« Cela n'empêche pas que certaines passions satisfaites ne leur
semblent préférables à la vertu même, et que s'ils sont contents de
voir Titus vertueux et magnanime, ils ne le fussent encore plus de le
voir heureux et faible, ou du moins qu'ils ne consentissent volontiers à l'être à sa place... Tant il est vrai que les tableaux de l'amour
font toujours plus d'impresion que les maximes de la sagesse, et que
l'effet d'une tragédie est tout à fait indépendant de celui du dénouement » (214).

L'amour est irrésistible, car « on se dit malgré soi qu'un
sentiment si délicieux console de tout » (215). Et la tragédie
ne le cède en rien à la comédie dans la part qu'elle prend à
suggérer cette idée ; car précisément ce qui est si « dangereux »
c'est que ces images de l'amour, on ne les trouve dans la tragédie, qu'entre âmes honnêtes » (215) ; or, personne ne se croit
obligé d'être un héros, et c'est ainsi « qu'admirant l'amour
honnête on se livre à l'amour criminel » (215).

Il ne sera pas superflu de rappeler ici que cette considération
du public pas foncièrement intelligent entre les mains de qui la
civilisation met des armes dangereuses, lui était déjà apparue
à propos des théories développées dans son *premier Discours* ;
mais là comme ici, il avait manqué de se rendre compte que
c'était au fond son grand argument ; elle ne devint consciente
pour lui-même, pour ainsi dire qu'après coup ; il la mentionne
tout à la fin comme un correctif à certaines conclusions qu'on
pourrait lui prêter (qu'il voudrait revenir au temps où la civilisation n'existait pas)

« Que penserons-nous de ces compilateurs d'ouvrages qui ont indiscrètement brisé la porte des sciences et introduit dans le sanctuaire une populace indigne d'en approcher, tandis qu'il serait à à souhaiter que tous ceux qui ne pouvaient avancer loin dans la carrière des lettres eussent été rebutés dès l'entrée et fussent jetés dans les arts utiles à la société » (I, 19).

Et puis, dans la réfutation aux attaques, il ramène vigoureusement cette idée : « J'ai dit que la science convient à quelques grands génies, mais qu'elle est toujours nuisible aux peuples qui la cultivent » (26). Citons encore ceci : « La science est très bonne en soi ; cela est évident et il faudrait avoir renoncé au bon sens pour dire le contraire... Cependant ma conclusion était que, puisque les sciences font plus de mal aux mœurs que de bien à la société [c'est depuis le *Second Discours* seulement qu'il identifiera les deux choses] il eût été à désirer que les hommes s'y fussent livrés avec moins d'ardeur » (I, 31). Malheureusement le *Discours* est resté ce qu'il était — bien peu lisant les correctifs ajoutés dans les longues discussions qui suivirent, — c'est-à-dire susceptible de commentaires erronés, partant l'apparence du paradoxe, tout comme la *Lettre sur les Spectacles*. Dans la *Préface à Narcisse*, on trouve ces mots caractéristiques : « La science n'est point faite pour l'homme en général il s'égare sans cesse dans sa recherche, et s'il l'obtient quelquefois ce n'est presque jamais qu'à son préjudice » (V, 107). Enfin rappelons encore ce passage de la réponse de Rousseau à la lettre fameuse dans laquelle Voltaire avait essayé de ridiculiser le *Second Discours* (30 août 1756 : « il prend envie de marcher à quatre pattes quand on lit votre ouvrage ») : « Ce que nous ne savons point nous nuit beaucoup moins que ce que nous croyons savoir. »

§ 4. Mais Rousseau est un dialecticien de première force ; et s'il groupe presque toujours ses arguments selon un plan émotionnel plutôt que rationnel, cependant il n'en manque pas un. Supposé que le peuple fût à même d'entendre, dans le sens supérieur du terme, le théâtre sera-t-il « utile » ? — utile aux mœurs, utile au bonheur ? Non, car il se trouve que plus une

pièce est non-utile, voire plus elle est dangereuse, plus le peuple l'aime. Le premier objet du théâtre, pour le peuple c'est certainement l'amusement:

« Quant à l'espèce de spectacles [qui prévaudra] c'est nécessairement le plaisir qu'ils donnent et non leur utilité qui la détermine. Si l'utilité peut s'y trouver, à la bonheur ; mais l'objet principal est de plaire, et pourvu que le peuple s'amuse, cet objet est assez rempli » (188). [Donc] « Qu'on n'attribue pas au théâtre le pouvoir de changer les sentiments ni des mœurs, qu'il ne peut que suivre et embellir. Un auteur qui voudrait heurter le goût général composerait bientôt pour lui seul » (189) (1).

Les objections sont prévues :

I. Le théâtre enseigne la « vertu », même une vertu conduisant au bonheur, prétend-on parfois. Rousseau répond : a) Il n'est pas exact, comme on l'assure souvent, que la vertu soit toujours récompensée et le crime puni ; dans cette atmosphère particulière de « grandeur » où se meut la tragédie (et Rousseau entend généralement la tragédie française comme la meilleure du monde moderne) des scélérats comme des héros sont encensés, « témoins, Catilina, Mahomet, Atrée et beaucoup d'autres » (196). Atrée finit la tragédie qui porte son nom par ce vers :

> *Et je jouis enfin du prix de mes forfaits.*

(1) « Nous ne partageons pas, dira encore Rousseau, les affections (ou passions) de tous les personnages, il est vrai ; car, leurs intérêts étant opposés, il faut bien que l'auteur nous en fasse préférer quelques-uns ; autrement nous n'en prendrions point du tout ; *mais* loin de pouvoir choisir pour cela entre les passions qu'il veut nous faire aimer, l'auteur est forcé de choisir celles que *nous* aimons... A Londres, un drame intéresse en faisant haïr les Français ; à Tunis, la belle passion sera la piraterie ; à Messine, une vengeance bien savourée ; à Goa, l'honneur de brûler les Juifs. Qu'un auteur choque ces maximes, il pourra faire une fort belle pièce où l'on n'ira point » : il aura « manqué à la première loi de son art » (190-1).

Rousseau aurait pu citer les paroles de Molière lui-même, dans la *Critique de l'Ecole des Femmes*, Sc. VII : « Je voudrais bien savoir si la grande règle de toutes les règles n'est pas de plaire, et si une pièce de théâtre qui a attrapé son but n'a pas suivi le bon chemin ? » Et Racine dans la *Préface à Bérénice*, de même : « La principale règle est de plaire et de toucher : toutes les autres ne sont faites que pour parvenir à cette première ».

b) D'ailleurs, même lorsque les criminels sont punis, « ils sont présentés sous un aspect si favorable que tout l'intérêt est pour eux ». Le vertueux Caton est un pédant, Cicéron, le sauveur de la république est un rhéteur ; et d'autre part, « au forfait de brigands » d'un Catilina, on donne le coloris « des exploits d'un héros » ; et « on a peine à ne pas excuser » l'incestueuse Phèdre, l'empoisonneur Syphax, le meurtrier de sa sœur Horace, celui de sa fille Agamemnon, celui de sa mère Oreste » (199).

2. Autre objection : Les écrivains de théâtre ont peut-être échoué, mais ils ont *voulu* la moralité ; et dès lors le théâtre existant peut être condamné, mais pas le théâtre en soi. Ronsard déjà, dont toute l'œuvre consista longtemps à affranchir l'art de l'Eglise, affirmait que la tragédie et la comédie devraient être avant tout « didactiques et enseignantes ». Selon Corneille, il s'agira au théâtre de peindre la vertu et le vice tels qu'ils sont, et la vertu est certaine de gagner tous les cœurs, même malheureuse et le vice est certain d'être haï même triomphant ». Selon Racine « la scène devrait être une école où la vertu devrait être enseignée de même que dans les écoles de philosophie » (1)

Rousseau répond : Supposé encore que le théâtre soit utile et vertueux, et supposé que le public s'y rende, le théâtre alors ferait œuvre superflue : « Le théâtre, dit-on, dirigé comme il peut et comme il doit l'être rend la vertu aimable et le vice odieux ? » Mais, qu'est-il besoin de théâtre pour cela :

« Avant qu'il y eût des comédiens, n'aimait-on point les gens de bien, ne haïssait-on point les méchants ?... Le théâtre rend la vertu

---

(1) En Angleterre la même opinion prévalait. Le Docteur Johnson représente bien le point de vue anglo-saxon des siècles passés, lui qui choisissait jusqu'aux exemples de son dictionnaire avec l'idée de suggérer des pensées morales. Il considère que « le premier défaut de Shakespeare est celui qu'on peut reprocher à tous les livres des hommes. Il sacrifie la vertu à l'opportunité, et il est tellement plus préoccupé de plaire que d'instruire qu'il semble écrire sans aucun souci de la vertu... C'est toujours le devoir d'un auteur de rendre le monde meilleur » (Cf. Jusserand, *What to expect of Shakespeare* ; 1911).

aimable... Il opère un grand prodige de faire ce que la nature
et la raison font avant lui » (191).

C'est du « verbiage » que de nous faire accroire que le théâtre
nous fait « juger des êtres moraux autrement que nous en
jugeons nous-mêmes ». « Il n'y a point d'art pour produire cet
intérêt [pour la bonne morale], mais seulement pour s'en prévaloir » (192).

« Nos auteurs modernes (Destouches, Lachaussée, p. ex.) font
des pièces plus épurées (que Molière et Regnard)... qu'arrive-t-il ?
Qu'elles n'ont plus de vrai comique et ne produisent aucun effet.
Elles instruisent beaucoup si l'on veut, mais elles ennuient encore
davantage. Autant vaudrait aller au sermon. » (208).

3. Reprendra-t-on la thèse d'Aristote : « La tragédie mène
à la pitié par la terreur », c'est-à-dire qu'en exaltant la pitié,
on exerce en quelque sorte et développe ce sentiment ? Réponse : Telle qu'on pourrait exciter la pitié au théâtre, ce ne
serait « qu'une émotion passagère et vaine » puisqu'elle s'exerce
sur une non-réalité ; qui plus est, nous allons nous payer de
sentimentalité pour négliger l'action ; telle Messaline touchée
et pleurant en entendant Valérius Asiasticus implorant sa
grâce et qui cependant le fait exécuter ; ainsi, nous croirions
qu' « en donnant des pleurs à ces fictions [théâtrales]nous avons
satisfait à tous les droits de l'humanité sans avoir plus rien à
mettre du nôtre » (193) ; nous allons « pleurer », nous applau-
dire de nos « belles âmes » — et cela s'arrêtera là. Ou alors,
supposez que le crime soit puni et la vertu récompensée, ces
pièces nous transportent dans le domaine de l'imagination
pure, et on s'habitue à considérer la lutte entre la vertu et le
vice [Corneille, Racine] comme hors du domaine de la réalité,
c'est-à-dire comme étrangères à la vie.

La question étant donc : « Quel profit les mœurs peuvent
tirer du théâtre» (195), on peut déjà répondre, sans même examiner le théâtre de la réalité, que « le bien est nul » ; et déjà, que
plutôt le théâtre nous porte à l'indifférence au bien, ce qui est
assez grave. Alors reste « le mal », que positivemet le théâtre

pourrait faire : Il y en a ; il suffit d'étudier l'œuvre de nos écrivains.

Nous pouvons être très brefs sur d'autres dangers sociaux qui sont liés à la cause du théâtre, car il s'agit d'objections bien plus banales que les précédentes. Rousseau voit toujours les obstacles au bonheur.

Les goûts « de luxe, de parure, et de dissipation » (216), il les déplore non pas en tant que « vices » proprement dits, mais à cause de leurs suites : les soucis d'argent, les jalousies, les maladies, bref toutes sortes de misères. Et si déjà les personnages représentés sur la scène suggèrent des façons de vivre luxueusement et libertinement, les acteurs ajoutent encore au mal en agissant par le mauvais exemple de leurs mœurs privées (221-32). Rousseau insiste beaucoup sur ces dangers de la profession d'acteur qui ne peut être honnête : « Des spectacles et des mœurs voilà qui formerait vraiement un spectacle à voir » (221). L'immoralité des acteurs est universelle, sauf pour les Grecs chez lesquels le théâtre était un sacerdoce et où les femmes ne montaient jamais sur la scène ; il y a donc une cause universelle, cause facile à trouver.

« Qu'est-ce que le talent du comédien ? L'art de contrefaire, de revêtir un autre caractère que le sien, de paraître différent de ce qu'on est, de se passionner de sang-froid, de dire autre chose que ce qu'on pense aussi naturellement que si l'on le pensait réellement, et d'oublier enfin sa propre place à force de prendre celle d'autrui » (231).

Rousseau n'accusera pas l'acteur d'être précisément un trompeur, mais de cultiver pour tout métier le talent de tromper les hommes, et de s'exercer à des habitudes qui, ne pouvant être innocentes qu'au théâtre, ne servent partout ailleurs qu'à mal faire (231).

« Ces hommes si bien parés, si bien exercés au ton de la galanterie et aux accents de la passion n'abuseront-ils jamais de cet art pour séduire de jeunes personnes ? Partout la tentation de mal faire augmente avec la facilité ; et il faut que les comédiens soient plus

vertueux que les autres hommes s'ils ne sont plus corrompus »
(231) (2). [Et il conclut] : « Si tout cela tient à la profession du comédien, que ferons-nous, Monsieur, pour prévenir des effets inévitables ? Pour moi je ne vois qu'un seul moyen ; c'est d'ôter la
cause... défendre aux comédiens d'être vicieux, c'est défendre à
l'homme d'être malade » (240).

Il est d'ailleurs tout aussi impossible de prévenir les effets
d'exemples funestes sur la communauté dans une petite ville
comme Genève que dans une grande. Dans une petite ville,
les acteurs connaissent les magistrats, et il y aura des acceptions de personnes ; et les lois, si elles existent, ne seront pas
appliquées ; supposé même que le magistrat soit intègre, il y
aura toujours sa femme et ses enfants qui, n'étant pas responsables de faire observer la loi, favoriseront l'acteur.

« Quel homme osera s'opposer à ce torrent, si ce n'est peut-être
quelque ancien pasteur rigide qu'on n'écoutera point, et dont le
sens et la gravité passeront pour pédanteries chez une jeunesse in-
considérée ? » (261).

Tout ceci est de bonne psychologie. L'acteur par sa seule
présence et son exemple incite à la passion, laquelle est cause
de désordre, lequel chasse le bonheur de la sagesse.

*
* *

§ 5. Et, à la rigueur, dans tout ceci encore, les commentateurs qui s'en tiennent uniquement à la lettre des textes
pourraient essayer de soutenir que Rousseau marchait la main
dans la main avec Bossuet — puisque les effets du théâtre
tour à tour considérés, sont combattus comme étant mauvais
et par l'un et par l'autre : Ils sont mauvais comme contraires
à la vertu de renoncement, et ils sont mauvais aussi comme
allant à l'encontre du bonheur humain.

Ici cependant les chemins se séparent complétement ; ou
plutôt, le théâtre étant condamné comme amusement mondain, et amusement mondain étant du point de vue chrétien
condamnable en soi, la tâche de Bossuet est finie ; il n'y a rien

à ajouter. Pour Rousseau au contraire, qui ne nie pas du tout la légitimité du plaisir dans le monde, il reste quelque chose à faire ; en fait il reste l'essentiel à faire : il peut être constructif après avoir été destructif. N'y aurait-il pas, en effet, un amusement mondain qu'on pourrait substituer à celui du théâtre qui nuit à l'homme, un amusement qui — si l'homme s'avisait d'y recourir — le dédommagerait, et peut-être davantage? Rousseau répond : Certainement. Il y a dans la vie des jouissances qui, outre qu'elles ne sont pas dangereuses pour la morale et le bonheur, sont plus grandes, plus profondes, plus raffinées que ne pourraient jamais êtres celles du théâtre ; ou tout au moins, on en peut goûter d'aussi profondes et d'aussi raffinées sans avoir recours à cette machinerie compliquée du théâtre. Seulement, il faut les entendre. Comme la parure violente trahit l'esprit naïf, et la parure modeste trahit le goût, (c'est-à-dire au fond trahit une intelligence plus pénétrante qui voit déjà des beautés là où l'esprit fruste doit les suppléer par le criard), ainsi le théâtre trahit « un faux goût », sans tact, sans délicatesse, substitué mal à propos parmi nous à la solidité de la raison (254).

Et Rousseau donne des exemples de gens qui n'ont pas l'amusement des théâtres, et il démontre non pas qu'ils sont *meilleurs* sans théâtre, mais qu'ils sont *plus heureux* — ou, si on veut, qu'ils sont meilleurs en ce qu'ils sont plus heureux.

Il évoque les « montagnons » du Jura Neuchâtelois. Ces « heureux » qui n'ont pas du théâtre, sont libres de toute espèce d'impôts (et au XVIIIe siècle, on sait ce que cela signifiait) ; ils connaissent « les douceurs de la société » ; en hiver, ils sont « bien au chaud » ; ils ont de « jolies maisons » ; ils font « mille travaux amusants »; ils « lisent », et ils « savent raisonner avec esprit » ; ils « peignent » ; ils « chantent ». On observera que la musique, la lecture, la fabrication de « meubles élégants », etc. sont des occupations de luxe, d'oisiveté — ce qui prouve bien que l'oisiveté n'est pas condamnée par Rousseau comme on l'affirme volontiers en interprétant mal les invectives de Rousseau contre la classe oisive : *L'erreur* dans la façon d'occuper ses loisirs est le souci de Rousseau ; et on les occupe

mal quand on s'en sert pour préparer le malheur des autres
ou de soi-même.

Cela devient bien évident quand on considère la façon encore
dont Rousseau célèbre le « bonheur » des Genevois sans théâtre?
Il vante chez eux les « sociétés » ou « cercles » ou « coteries »
(244 ss) ; on s'y assemble pour des exercices d'armes, des
concours, des fêtes militaires, — ces assemblées « ayant pour
objet le plaisir et la joie » (244) : Dans ces locaux,

« Se rendent tous les après-midis ceux des associés que leurs
affaires ou leurs plaisirs ne retiennent point ailleurs. On s'y ras-
semble, et là, chacun se livrant sans gêne aux amusements de son
goût, on joue, on cause, on lit, on boit, on fume... souvent aussi
l'on va se promener ensemble... tels sont les amusements journa-
liers de la bourgeoisie de Genève » (245).

Il faut le reconnaître, Rousseau toujours fasciné par la
« vertu romaine », aux considérations légitimes, en mêle encore
d'étrangères dont le rapport au bonheur n'est pas clair — et
qui dès lors égarent le lecteur ; oubliant la distinction qu'il
a établie entre gens positivement heureux et gens simplement
non-malheureux, il s'abandonne à une fastidieuse énumération des maux que les Montagnons neuchâtelois ne connaissent
pas, — mais dont la suppression ne leur donneraient pas encore la joie de vivre. Supposé, dit-il, qu'on introduise le spectacle chez eux, qu'arrivera-t-il ? Il y aurait relâchement de
travail, premier préjudice ; augmentation de dépenses (pour
assister au spectacle), deuxième préjudice ; diminution de re-
cettes (en suite du relâchement de travail), troisième préjudice;
établissement d'impôts (pour subventionner le théâtre), quatrième préjudice ; introduction du luxe sous toutes ses formes,
cinquième préjudice ;... « tout le reste facile à concevoir » (220).

Il en est de même quand Rousseau parle de Genève ; il insiste trop sur la simple absence de soucis matériels. Il a des
phrases comme celles-ci : « Le peuple genevois ne se soutient
qu'à force de travail, et n'a le nécessaire qu'autant qu'il se refuse tout superflu » (240). — comme si, au point de vue du

bonheur, c'était en soi un signe de supériorité de se refuser le superflu.

« Il me semble que ce qui doit d'abord frapper tout étranger entrant à Genève, c'est l'air de vie et d'activité qu'il y voit régner. Tout s'occupe, tout est en mouvement, tout s'empresse à son travail et à ses affaires. Je ne crois pas que nulle autre aussi petite ville au monde offre un pareil spectacle. Visitez le quartier St-Gervais, toute l'horlogerie de l'Europe y apparaît rassemblée. Parcourez le Molard et les rues basses, un appareil de commerce en grand, des montagnes de ballots, de tonneaux confusément jetés, une odeur d'Inde et de droguerie vous font imaginer un port de mer » (241).

Ah ! si Rousseau montrait que le travail en soi est un plaisir, il serait d'accord avec le but de sa démonstration que Genève est heureuse ; or justement il ne le fait pas, mais plutôt il parle de l' « austère parcimonie », un des « trésors » des Genevois...

C'est encore le cas en partie quand il parle des Anglais dont les mœurs viennent de lui être révélées par Muralt ; il loue leur vie retirée et vertueuse, mais ne dit que la moitié de ce qu'il doit penser quand il écrit par exemple :

« Il n'y a point de bonnes mœurs pour les femmes hors d'une vie retirée et domestique ; si je dis que les paisibles soins de la famille et du ménage sont leur partage, que la dignité de leur sexe est dans la modestie, que la honte et la pudeur sont en elles-mêmes inséparables de l'honnêteté, que rechercher le regard des hommes c'est déjà se laisser corrompre et que toute femme qui se montre se déshonore : à l'instant va s'élever contre moi cette philosophie d'un jour qui naît et meurt dans le coin d'une grande ville et veut étouffer le cri de la nature, et la voix unanime du genre humain (233).

D'après cela on dirait vraiment que Rousseau se soucie des « bonnes mœurs » en elles-mêmes. C'est Rousseau retenu par des réminiscences calvinistes ou romaines ; en réalité, il n'est pas encore conscient pourquoi il admire les Anglais, et il ne le deviendra que dans *La Nouvelle Héloïse*. Comme Voltaire, comme Montesquieu, c'est le bonheur et non le puritanisme des Anglais qu'il enviera pour le monde.

*
* *

Par ailleurs, cependant, Rousseau est entraîné si bien dans
ces mêmes pages par son sujet du bonheur comme but à réaliser qu'il convient que le théâtre même ne doit être *a priori*
exclu. A ceux qui sont dans des conditions telles (et c'est le cas
des habitants des grandes villes) que l'existence de théâtres
fournit plus de joies directes que l'absence de théâtres n'en
pourrait fournir indirectement, qu'on le leur donne sans hésiter : « En certains lieux, ils [les spectacles] seront utiles... pour
distraire le peuple de ses misères, pour lui faire oublier ses
chefs [exploiteurs méchants, mais puissants] en voyant ses
baladins... ; [aussi] pour couvrir d'un vernis de procédés la
laideur du vice » ; et tout cela, en un mot, « pour que les mauvaises mœurs ne dégénèrent pas en brigandage » (221), c'est-à-
dire pour que malheur ne dégénère pas en malheur pire.

Mieux que cela, Rousseau entrevoit *à Genève même* un
théâtre non seulement non-mauvais, mais positivement utile.
Il s'expliquera, après avoir maudit l'esprit du théâtre existant
et en décrivant un théâtre idéal : celui-ci serait adapté à la
mentalité du peuple, et s'appliquerait à ne provoquer l'admiration que de « héros » excellents à imiter :

« Il n'est pas bon qu'on nous montre toutes sortes d'imitations,
mais seulement celles des choses honnêtes et qui convient à des
hommes libres. Il est sûr que des pièces tirées comme celles des
Grecs, des malheurs passés de la patrie ou des défauts présents du
peuple, pourraient offrir aux spectateurs des leçons utiles. Alors
quels seront les héros de nos tragédies ? Des Berthelier ? des Lé-
vrery ? [deux martyrs de la liberté politique genevoise] Ah !
dignes citoyens, vous fûtes des héros sans doute, mais votre obscurité vous avilit, vos noms communs déshonorent vos grandes
âmes, et nous ne sommes plus assez grands nous-mêmes pour vous
savoir admirés » (259-260).

Dans *la Nouvelle Héloïse*, Rousseau reviendra à la charge :
« Qu'on représente à Berne, à Zurich, à la Haye, l'ancienne
tyrannie de la maison d'Autriche, l'amour de la patrie et de la

liberté nous rendra ces pièces intéressantes : Mais qu'on me dise de quel usage sont ici les tragédies de Corneille, et ce qu'importe au peuple de Paris, Pompée ou Sertorius. » (IV, 172).(1).

Toutefois, notons-le bien, s'il admet des spectacles patriotiques, Rousseau ne veut pas entendre parler de « comédie » c'est-à-dire théâtre régulier « Quant à la comédie, il n'y faut pas songer ; elle causerait chez nous les plus affreux désordres»(260)

Par ailleurs, Rousseau va si loin dans ses concessions qu'il conçoit même telles tragédies classiques qu'avec un peu de remaniement on transformerait en spectacles acceptables ; c'est ainsi qu'il esquisse le plan d'une Bérénice idyllique dont le 5ᵉ acte serait à peu près seul à changer :

« Pour rendre cette vérité sensible imaginons un dénouement tout contraire à celui de l'auteur. Qu'après avoir mieux consulté son cœur, Titus ne voulant ni enfreindre les lois de Rome, ni vendre le bonheur à l'ambition, vienne avec des maximes opposées abdiquer l'empire aux pieds de Bérénice ; que pénétrée d'un si grand sacrifice, elle sente que son devoir serait de refuser la main de son grand amant, et que pourtant elle l'accepte ; que tous deux, enivrés des

(1) Il n'est pas inutile de rappeler que la Suisse depuis un certain nombre d'années a réalisé les vœux de Rousseau ; ses « Festspiele » et «pièces historiques» sont destinées justement à réchauffer le dévouement au sol natal ; et elles sont représentées sans le concours d'acteurs de profession. A l'étranger aussi, à mesure qu'on s'occupe davantage de cultiver la moralité des peuples tout en lui accordant le droit à la réjouissance, les théâtres du peuple se développent ; Bussang a été le premier et est encore le plus connu. Déjà la renaissance des Mystères et des Miracles selon la tradition du moyen âge était avancée lorsque la guerre éclata. Le théâtre pendant la guerre a souvent été un théâtre patriotique. Non seulement Rousseau n'aurait fait aucune objection à un théâtre animé d'un tel esprit, mais il l'aurait encouragé. Lui-même exigeait la présence des pauvres à un *bon théâtre* : « On me demandera qui force le pauvre d'aller aux spectacles. Je répondrai, premièrement ceux qui l'établissent et lui en donnent la tentation ; en second lieu sa pauvreté même qui, le condamnant à des travaux continuels, sans espoir de les voir finir, lui rend quelques délassements plus nécessaires pour les supporter... n'est-il pas cruel à celui qui travaille, de se priver des récréations des gens oisifs ?... Ce même amusement qui fournit un moyen d'économie aux riches [le pauvre paie les impôts pour le théâtre comme le riche] affaiblit doublement le pauvre soit par un surcroit de dépense, soit par moins de zèle au travail comme je l'ai ci-dessus expliqué » (255-6).

charmes de l'amour, de la paix, de l'innocence, et renonçant aux
vaines grandeurs prennent avec cette douce joie qu'inspirent les
vrais mouvements de la nature, le parti d'aller vivre heureux et
ignorés dans un coin de la terre, qu'une scène si touchante soit ani
mée des sentiments tendres et pathétiques que fournit la matière,
et que Racine eût si bien fait valoir... La pièce finissant ainsi, sera,
si l'on veut, moins bonne, moins instructive, moins conforme à
l'histoire ; mais en fera-t-elle moins de plaisir ? et les spectateurs
en sortiront-ils moins satisfaits ? (213-4)

Ou bien écoutons ceci :

« Thyeste est peut-être de tous ceux qu'on a mis sur notre théâtre
le plus sentant le goût antique (allusion à la théorie que la tragédie
doit éveiller la pitié). Ce n'est point un héros courageux, ce n'est
point un modèle de vertu ; on ne peut pas dire non plus que ce soit
un scélérat ; c'est un homme faible, et pourtant *intéressant par
cela seul qu'il est homme et malheureux.* Il me semble aussi que par
cela seul, le sentiment qu'il excite est extrêmement tendre et touchant ; car cet homme tient de bien près à chacun de nous au lieu
que l'héroïsme nous accable encore plus qu'il ne nous touche parce
qu'après tout nous n'y avons que faire. Ne serait-il pas à désirer
que nos sublimes auteurs daignassent descendre un peu de leur
continuelle élévation, et nous attendrir quelquefois pour la simple
humanité souffrante de peur que n'ayant de la pitié que pour des
héros malheureux, nous n'en ayons jamais pour personne » (98).

Par quelque détour on revient toujours à ceci : Rousseau ne
condamne pas le théâtre comme mondanité, mais comme
mondanité dangereuse au bonheur. Qu'en tous cas, si l'on veut
ou s'il faut des spectacles, on les choisisse plutôt moins séduisants, et plus utiles — car en fin de compte il y aura compensation pour le bonheur général et le peuple qui aura les spectacles plus utiles sera plus heureux que celui qui les a plus
séduisants. Mais il reste que le peuple le plus favorisé sera celui
qui saura remplacer le théâtre par des plaisirs à la fois plus
sûrs, et en fait supérieurs.

B

§ 1. On voit que Rousseau a bien continué à se mouvoir dans le sens de la vertu rationnelle — comme nous le laissons entrevoir dans les dernières pages consacrées au *Second Discours*. Celui-ci se résumait en ceci : L'homme n'est susceptible de jouissances supérieures à celles de l'animalité qu'en quittant l'état de nature ; il quitte l'état de nature par intelligence des choses ; *mais* la raison humaine n'est pas quelque chose d'absolu ; il n'y a pas seulement les êtres qui ne raisonnent pas, et les êtres qui raisonnent, mais parmi les êtres qui raisonnent il faut distinguer encore entre ceux qui raisonnent imparfaitement, et ceux qui raisonnent parfaitement.

Dans la *Lettre sur les Spectacles*, la chose se précise : Rousseau conçoit qu'un homme qui serait vraiment sage, saurait par la seule pensée, où est le bonheur, saurait le goûter sous sa forme la plus haute et saurait se le procurer ; et cet homme Rousseau l'appellerait « vertueux » ; — ce serait la vertu-sagesse de Socrate et Platon.

Ce qui l'empêche de voir clair en lui-même, ou en tous cas d'exposer avec toute la clarté désirable sa pensée, c'est que tout en faisant l'effort de se chercher — et parce qu'il doit faire cet effort —, il se laisse entraîner sans cesse à faire de la polémique ; on le voit sans cesse préoccupé à empêcher qu'on ne confonde sa pensée avec celle des autres surtout avec celle des « philosophes ».

Il y a du reste en effet, un certain nombre de notions assez délicates et qui toujours menacent de jeter la confusion dans les problèmes complexes, et Rousseau souvent est submergé. Ayant le bénéfice d'un siècle et demi de plus d'efforts philosophiques, nous devrions être à même de voir plus clair, de démêler l'écheveau et d'indiquer où Rousseau devait aboutir s'il avait développé conséquemment sa pensée. Parmi ces notions, il en est deux surtout qui ont contribué à obscurcir et embrouiller les problèmes, et nous voulons nous y arrêter.

*_*_

La première est celle de la *conscience morale*, ou ce *sentiment moral inné* auquel Rousseau recourt constamment, et qui, selon lui, inspire à l'homme qui veut s'y soumettre la conduite vertueuse qui conduit au bonheur. Mais ce sentiment moral ou cette conscience sont justement ce qu'invoquent les philosophes religieux ; et dès lors Rousseau a l'air de faire cause commune avec la morale chrétienne de renoncement et de rejeter une morale rationnelle. Et on ne peut nier qu'il n'y ait accord de forme avec la morale chrétienne ; ce sentiment moral exige une lutte contre la passion tout à fait comme la morale du bonheur dont Rousseau s'est fait le champion ; c'est un accord extérieur peut-être, mais c'est un accord. De plus, Rousseau *lui-même* associe son « sentiment moral » avec celui des chrétiens, et l'invoque avec eux contre les « philosophes » rationalistes ; dès lors, en approuvant la morale chrétienne il laisse penser (et pense par moments lui-même penser) qu'il adopte la philosophie chrétienne de renoncement aussi bien. Enfin cette assimilation du sentiment moral chez les chrétiens et chez Rousseau (confondant le moyen du renoncement et le but du renoncement), les « philosophes » n'ont pas manqué de l'affirmer *à leur tour*, et eux, considérant la conscience morale comme un trouble-fête pour quiconque cherche dans le monde le plaisir, ils croient devoir envelopper dans une commune réprobation la morale de Rousseau et celle du christianisme.

Il faut donc franchement reconnaître que Rousseau croit par moments — et autour de lui on croit presque toujours — qu'il est fondamentalement d'accord avec le christianisme.

Et cependant il ne l'est pas. Malgré toutes les apparences, Rousseau reste en fait un philosophe rationaliste, car le contenu de son sentiment moral, ou de sa conscience morale, c'est-à-dire sa loi morale — cette loi qui quant à la forme et au contenu répond à peu près point pour point à la loi de discipline morale des chrétiens — repose sur un fondement différent, de même elle a qu'un but différent.

Il ne s'agit pas du tout ici, en effet, d'une loi donnée par un Dieu qui défend certaines choses lesquelles sont mauvaises simplement parce qu'il les décrète telles, mais il s'agit d'un code de règles morales que l'expérience a forcé peu à peu les hommes intelligents à adopter en sorte de mener une existence aussi heureuse que possible. Et encore un coup, s'il y a coïncidence entre les données de cette sagesse de raison et la volonté du Dieu chrétien, tant mieux ou tant pis : cela n'a aucune importance pour la pensée de Rousseau ici.

Voici comment, en combinant la pensée du *Second Discours* et de la *Lettre sur les Spectacles* peut se résumer la pensée de Rousseau sur ce point si fondamental :

Les sociétés se sont constituées un peu au hasard des circonstances ; mais des règles de conduite se sont imposées peu à peu ; règles différentes parfois sur certains points particuliers, selon les pays, les climats, et autres conditions ; cependant en somme toujours les mêmes, car ayant toujours le même point de départ d'un accord à trouver entre bonheur individuel et bonheur de tous les autres. Ainsi ne pas voler son semblable, car cela amène la guerre, ne pas mentir car si l'on veut pouvoir agir il faut pouvoir se fier à la parole, s'organiser en famille (monogame, polygame) de sorte qu'ayant chaque rouage social en ordre, le tout ait plus de chance de fonctionner régulirement, et surtout que l'amour, le grand perturbateur, soit bien contrôlé dans ses effets.

Tout est à base rationnelle. Et en général un peu de réflexion suffit pour le voir. Même les violateurs en conviennent. Rousseau l'a fort bien dit dans son ouvrage, en reprenant la pensée de La Rochefoucault : « L'hypocrisie est un hommage que le vice rend à la vertu ». Un homme sait bien toujours qu'il a tout intérêt à ce que, les autres en tous cas, observent la loi morale, et par conséquent il la déclare bonne ; même s'il ne veut pas de la vertu pour lui, « parce qu'elle lui serait coûteuse, il l'aime toujours dans les autres parce qu'il espère en profiter » (193), parce qu'il sait bien qu'il est « l'autre » pour son voisin.

Et enfin la preuve indiscutable que même pour Rousseau

tout ce code est bien fondé sur la raison, c'est que quand on l'attaque, Rousseau le défend par des arguments rationnels. Un exemple excellent : « Les philosophes » ont essayé de faire de la conscience un inutile trouble-fête et de l'attaquer au nom de la raison ; or c'est justement au nom de la raison que Rousseau prend sa défense. Prenez la pudeur par exemple : « Préjugés populaires, nous crie-t-on, petites erreurs de l'enfance... pourquoi rougirions-nous des besoins que nous donna la nature ? Pourquoi l'homme aurait-il sur ce point d'autres lois que les animaux ? » — Réponse : « J'ai peur que ces grands scrutateurs des conseils de Dieu n'aient un peu légèrement pesé leur *raison*. Moi qui ne me pique pas de les connaître, j'en crois voir qui leur ont échappé... » (234). Et il explique très habilement, dans des observations qui sont encore très développés au Ve livre d'*Emile* que la pudeur est la « sauvegarde commune que la nature a donnée aux deux sexes dans un état de faiblesse et d'oubli d'eux-mêmes qui les livre à la merci du premier venu » (234) ; la pudeur est surtout forte chez les femmes car les conséquences sont surtout lourdes pour elles. Ces *raisons* sont excellentes.

Et que signifient dans la *Lettre à d'Alembert* des mots comme : « Une bonne conscience éteint le goût des plaisirs frivoles » (187), sinon que bonne conscience est bon entendement ? Terminons en rappelant un des morceaux les plus lucides qu'ait écrits Rousseau à cette époque, (dans sa *Préface à Narcisse* ; (1) il y montre qu'il avait au fond conçu les choses dès alors sans l'embarras de cet élément métaphysique de la conscience morale, et que « toute la morale est dans les coutumes » :

« Le moindre changement dans les coutumes, fût-il même avantageux à certains égards, tourne au préjudice des mœurs, car les coutumes sont la morale du peuple, et dès qu'il cesse de les respecter, il n'a plus de règle que les passions, ni de freins que les lois, qui peuvent quelquefois contenir les méchants mais jamais les rendre

(1) On le donne comme de 1752, car la pièce fut jouée en 1752, — ce n'est pas une preuve absolue.

bons. D'ailleurs quand la philosophie a une fois appris au peuple à mépriser ses coutumes, il trouve bientôt le secret d'éluder ses lois. Je dis donc qu'il en est des mœurs d'un peuple comme de l'honneur d'un homme : C'est un trésor qu'il faut conserver, mais qu'on ne recouvre plus une fois qu'on l'a perdu » (V. 108).

Mais alors, si c'est donc bien un code rationnel qui constitue le contenu du sentiment moral ou de la conscience morale de Rousseau, il est bien évident par là que Rousseau écarte du même coup la conscience morale comme un sentiment a-prioristique ou inné ; puisque, en effet, la raison humaine en rend compte parfaitement, il est inutile d'en chercher l'origine ailleurs — métaphysiquement ; *entia non sunt multiplicanda praeter necessitatem.*

Sans doute, sa conscience morale peut avoir toutes les *apparences* de l'innéité, d'être gravée au cœur de tout homme ; il *semble* à celui-ci n'avoir jamais *appris* les principes de conduite morale et cependant il les porte en lui. Mais c'est là une simple illusion. Il suffit que l'enfant ait vécu dans un milieu où ces principes étaient appliqués constamment et approuvés, pour qu'il les ait connus et probablement adoptés.

Si, maintenant, il résulte de tout ceci que Rousseau va en réalité contre son propre sentiment, en donnant la conscience morale comme innée, cette inconséquence, nous le répétons, n'a *en soi* pas d'importance ; c'est une *épi*-thète, si on nous permet cette expression, comme la conscience morale est un *épi*-phénomène pour les déterministes ; on peut l'ignorer. Elle est grave cependant, cette intrusion de l'élément métaphysique, en ce sens qu'elle contribue à amener dans l'esprit du lecteur cette confusion qui se perpétue depuis un siècle et demi. Car si tout l'esprit de la pensée de Rousseau depuis le *Second Discours* est évidemment en accord avec les maints passages où il fait marcher le sentiment moral ou la conscience morale la main dans la main avec la raison, il y en a d'autres tout aussi formels où on le voit s'ingénier à les opposer l'un à l'autre ; et en vérité si l'on compte les passages au lieu de les peser, la balance est en faveur des derniers —

ce qui amène à cette bien curieuse situation : Ce Rousseau qui croyait être d'accord avec le christianisme sur la loi morale, ne l'était pas ; mais il l'était en réalité avec la philosophie avec laquelle il croyait ne l'être pas.

Ce n'est pas assez cependant de constater cette anomalie ; Rousseau ne s'y serait pas laissé entraîner par simple accident ou négligence. Il doit y avoir une cause intéressante à ce souci extrême chez lui, nous dirions presque superstitieux, de voir sa cause confondue avec celle des « philosophes », — plus grand que de la voir confondue avec celle des théologiens. On est porté à penser que ce fanatisme anti-philosophique trahit, en même temps qu'une irritante impuissance à expliquer, une grande certitude (1).

Et tout aurait été clair en effet si Rousseau avait *souligné* une distinction qui est implicitement contenue dans tous ses passages se rapportant à cette question — et qui constitue la cause même de son litige avec les « philosophes » — à savoir la distinction entre *a*) le rationalisme moral de la philosophie tout court, et *b*) le rationalisme moral des « philosophes » ou Encyclopédistes du xviiie siècle. Tous invoquent la raison comme critère de la conduite humaine, Rousseau — et même quand il parle de conscience morale innée — aussi décidément que les Encyclopédistes. Mais par suite des circonstances dans lesquelles le rationalisme s'était élevé contre la métaphysique et la théologie au xviiie siècle, la plupart des « philosophes » avaient (par esprit de secte pour ainsi dire et *a priori*) combattu tout dogme moral prêché par l'Église ; pour eux, il avait suffi de prendre le contrepied de la morale chrétienne de contrainte et laisser parler la nature pour agir rationnellement ; l'argument est simpliste : La raison réprouve la contrainte des aspirations de l'homme au bonheur, *donc* elle

---

(1) Nous observons du reste en passant, que dès que Rousseau peut cesser de penser à sa polémique avec les « philosophes », il cesse aussi d'opposer la conscience morale et la raison ; seulement le fait est qu'il y pense presque constamment.

réprouve *toute* contrainte. Rousseau ne veut rien de cela qui lui paraît être à la fois d'une naïveté, d'un orgueil, et d'un danger immenses ; il s'efforce de suggérer — nous disons *il s'efforce* car il n'est qu'à moitié conscient de la chose — cette différence entre la raison telle qu'exercée par les « philosophes » du temps (selon laquelle l'homme n'aurait qu'à suivre une philosophie d'impulsions naturelles et primitives pour trouver le chemin du bonheur), et une raison mieux informée (pour laquelle la discipline morale est d'importance cardinale). Cette différence, elle est dans la nature des choses : Rousseau en la faisant est simplement plus philosophe que les « philosophes ». Il serait surprenant qu'un groupe de philosophes du XVIIIᵉ siècle, fussent-ils aussi intelligents et pondérés que possible, pussent trouver tout d'un coup mieux que la sagesse humaine de tant de siècles accumulés. Bref, Rousseau défend les droits de la raison collective de l'humanité, raison développée et confirmée — et à l'occasion corrigée — au cours des siècles, tandis que les Encyclopédistes (tels que les voit Rousseau) représentent les droits d'une raison contingente d'un groupe en rupture de ban avec la sagesse de tous les âges — et d'ailleurs sagesse dont la morale chrétienne dans ses préceptes au moins, se rapproche beaucoup plus.

Pour nous qui jugeons de loin le débat, nous voyons bien qu'en principe, Rousseau marche la main dans la main avec les « philosophes » ; car en fin de compte, la raison reste la raison. Cela est si vrai que maint « philosophe », du XVIIIᵉ siècle, et pas des moindres, quand ils se mettaient à réfléchir vraiment sur les questions de morale se rencontraient de façon frappante avec la morale de discipline de Rousseau — qui est celle des classiques, et qui est, en ce qui concerne la forme au moins, celle des chrétiens. Il y aurait un livre à faire sur *l'accord* du livre *De l'esprit* avec la philosophie morale de Rousseau. Voltaire même n'est pas si loin de Rousseau, et le frondeur du *Mondain* (qui est une boutade) ne doit pas nous faire oublier le « philosophe » du *Poème de la loi naturelle*.

Mais en attendant, il y avait conflit entre l'esprit *général* de cette « philosophie » du XVIIIᵉ siècle, et la philosophie ration-

nelle et universelle de Rousseau ; et celui-ci considérait comme important avant toute chose de se désolidariser d'avec cet esprit général — si important qu'il allait jusqu'à sacrifier selon la lettre le principe rationaliste à la pratique de discipline chrétienne et à la notion d'une *conscience morale* indépendante du rationalisme.

§ 2. Une seconde notion à élucider — ou à ré-examiner — pour éviter des malentendus et toucher le fond de la pensée de Rousseau, est ce qu'il entend par *vivre selon la nature* ; car il ne s'agit plus dans la *Lettre sur les Spectacles* de bonté naturelle primitive comme dans la première partie du *Second Discours* ; il est entendu que l'homme sort de l'état de nature pour atteindre au bonheur ; mais il s'agit de savoir si l'homme porte en lui *naturellement* la faculté de bonheur ; ou alors s'il doit acquérir d'abord cette faculté de bonheur (1).

En réalité, c'est le même problème que celui de la conscience morale sous une autre forme, ou sous un autre aspect ; et il se présente une fois encore à propos des rapports de Rousseau avec les « philosophes ». Mais, chose assez bizarre, tandis que, en ce qui concerne la conscience morale, Rousseau et les « philosophes » semblaient en parfait désaccord alors qu'ils étaient fondamentalement d'accord (sur la base rationnelle de la morale) ; au contraire, en ce qui concerne la question de la morale naturelle, il semblerait évident qu'il doit y avoir accord ; et cependant il y a justement là désaccord profond ; c'est-à-dire que les « philosophes » disent : *Oui*, l'homme peut tabler sur la nature ; et que Rousseau dit *Non*. Plus explicitement, les « philosophes » disent que l'homme qui vit bien (ou heureux) celui qui vit raisonnablement (et non selon les insolentes prétentions de la théologie dite révélée) vit selon

(1) « Naturellement » pris dans le sens d' « immédiatement », pas dans le sens de formation graduelle d'un être naturellement fruste par des moyens mis à sa disposition par la nature, — car l'homme ne peut agir en dehors de la nature. Comme le dit Shakespeare, *The art itself is nature* (l'art même est nature) ; ou comme le dit Havelock Ellis, dans sa *Danse of Life* (p. 313) : « L'art n'est guère davantage que la naturelle sage-femme de la nature ».

sa nature qui lui suggère de s'abandonner à ses dispositions
pour le plaisir. Rousseau, quoique lui aussi dise que l'homme
qui vit bien (ou heureux) est celui qui vit raisonnablement
ne dit plus du tout que l'homme qui vit raisonnablement vit
selon cette nature qui lui suggère de s'abandonner à ses dispositions pour le plaisir. S'abandonner à cette nature-là, c'est
selon Rousseau l'hérésie même, car elle ne conseille pas seulement le bonheur mais l'abandon aux appels de l'instinct et
des sens ; l'homme qui écoute ses passions est le plus sûrement égaré ; il est aveugle ; aucune mesure ne devrait être
épargnée quand il s'agit de l'arrêter. Et si la morale de la
nature prêchée par ces philosophes doit conduire l'humanité
à sa ruine, alors plutôt cent fois celle de leurs adversaires qui
disposent au moins de la conscience morale chrétienne pour
étouffer les passions funestes. Certes, la raison même ne désa-
vouera pas Rousseau ; voyez les Romains de l'Empire n'ayant
pas écouté Brutus et Caton et Fabricius ; voyez les Français
sous Louis XV qui se sont abandonnés à leurs sentiments
naturels de jouissance, de luxe, de sensualité... c'est l'abomi-
nation de la désolation ! Tout peuple qui fera comme eux aura
le même sort.

Tout cela est facile à saisir. Ce qu'il importe vraiment de
souligner c'est la cause qui a empêché qu'on s'entendît au
XVIIIe siècle — et qui fait qu'on continue à n'y voir pas clair.
Tout, encore une fois revient au mot « nature » ; car au nom de
quoi Rousseau combat-il ici les « philosophes » ? On le sait assez ;
il brandit le grand mot. Or, c'est-à-dire qu'il oppose donc la
voix de la nature à la voix de la nature, ou au moins *une* voix
de la nature à *une autre* voix de la nature. C'est qu'en effet
il y avait en réalité deux problèmes distincts relatifs à cette
question : faut-il ou non suivre la nature ? Le premier, c'est :
Faut-il suivre la nature quand elle nous dit qu'il est légitime
de chercher le bonheur ? A cette question Rousseau répond
avec enthousiasme, *oui*, de même que les « philosophes ». La
second c'est : Faut-il suivre la nature quand celle-ci nous dit
que pour le bonheur il faut céder à nos appétits et à nos pas-

sions. A cette question, tandis que les « philosophes » répon-
draient encore *oui*, Rousseau répondait *non*. Mais on a, avec
une surprenante légèreté et une non moins surprenante persistance, conclu que puisque Rousseau répondait *oui*, *il faut
écouter la nature*, à la première question comme les « philosophes », il répondait de même avec eux sur la seconde question, — alors qu'à celle-ci il répond *non*, quand même il
invoque le terme « nature ».

Maintenant, il est difficile de contester la légitimité d'une
terminologie commune dans aucun des deux cas : il est *naturel* de s'abandonner aux penchants de notre être ; mais il est
naturel aussi de résister aux penchants de notre être si ceux-
là nous rendent malheureux. De sorte que Rousseau et les
« philosophes » ont droit tous, avec leurs idées diamétralement opposées, au même mot *nature*. Et sans doute il serait
préférable de s'entendre ; un homme qui, comme Rousseau,
affectionne tant ces vocables, *nature* et *naturel* aurait dû être
plus attentif. Or, il faut reconnaître que Rousseau ne paraît
pas s'en soucier le moins du monde. Il suffit de lire par exemple
ses pages 233 et 234 où « nature » revient fréquemment, et
tantôt dans le sens d'appétits naturels, tantôt dans le sens
de morale de contrainte anti-naturelle. Tantôt Rousseau
parle de « cette philosophie d'un jour... qui veut étouffer le
cri (de « honte », et de « pudeur ») de la nature et la voix unanime du genre humain », — ici il faut donc *suivre* la voix de la
nature ; tantôt il discute l'objection des philosophes préten-
tieux que les penchants sexuels sont les mêmes chez les
hommes et les animaux, et que les passions des premiers sont
donc aussi légitimes que celles des seconds ; et il s'écrie : « Est-
ce à moi de rendre compte de ce qu'a fait la nature », — ici
il faut donc *ne pas suivre* la voix de la nature, mais obéir à
l'*anti-naturelle pudeur*. Enfin il faut même ajouter qu'en
somme, si l'on veut tenir compte de la terminologie la plus
usuelle — et il serait fort désirable d'en tenir compte — le
droit est plutôt du côté des « philosophes » de se proclamer les
philosophes *de la nature* que du côté de Rousseau ; car s'il y
a bien eu des penseurs qui ont proclamé que la voix de la

conscience morale était une voix naturelle au cœur de l'homme,
il y en a eu bien plus qui ont considéré comme naturels les
appétits des sens et de l'instinct ; et même les philosophes de
la conscience morale n'ont pas nié le caractère du naturel à ces
appétits physiques. (1) D'autre part, ayant concédé tout cela,
il est juste aussi de relever que les deux sens sont si différents,
si nettement opposés, et que celui des deux qu'il faut entendre
chaque fois dorénavant (c'est-à-dire depuis après le *Second
Discours* quand la pensée de Rousseau est bien plus avancée
dans son évolution) est si clairement indiqué par le contexte,
qu'en réalité on a un peu vergogne d'accuser Rousseau de
manque de clarté sur ce point ; réclamer la nécessité de réviser
cette terminologie revient presque à délivrer au lecteur un
brevet de sottise. Que répondre, cependant, à l'argument que
des critiques de renom persistent à se servir de ce terme de
« nature » pour accuser Rousseau de romantisme et d'anarchie ; que des Seillière, des Lasserre, des Babbit etc., n'ont
jamais eu vergogne, eux, de tirer parti de cette grossière
confusion pour déformer la pensée de Rousseau. Il n'y a que
deux explications, inintelligence ou déformation délibérée
de Rousseau : Il est souvent difficile de croire à la première (2).

(1) Diderot par exemple paraît bien plus *nature* que Rousseau dans le chapitre du *Supplément au Voyage de Bougainville* (qu'il n'osa du reste pas publier
et qui ne parut posthume qu'en 1795), intitulé « Dialogue sur l'inconvénient
d'attacher des idées morales à certaines actions qui n'en comportent point » ;
l'auteur s'appuie sur cette constatation : que le Tahitien est incapable de voir
un sens aux mots *fornication, inceste, adultère* ; et le prêtre du « Dialogue »
doit admettre qu'il est à bout d'argument : « Rien n'était mal de sa nature
(dans la société tahitienne avant l'arrivée des Européens, et par exemple) ;
la passion de l'amour réduite à un simple appétit physique n'y produisait
aucun de nos désordres » (Cité, Chinard, *Publ. Modern Lang. Assoc.*, March
1928, p. 294-5). Ajoutons du reste que les faits sont plus complexes que cela ;
l'inceste et l'adultère sont des crimes, voire plus grands que chez nous chez
certains primitifs. Voir Lévy-Bruhl, *l'Ame primitive*, Alcan, 1927, pp. 108,
121, 236, p. ex.).

(2) Exemple récent où on voit Rousseau rendu gratuitement responsable
de tous les méfaits des « philosophes » prêchant le retour à la nature : Bellessort, *La Pérouse* (Plon, 1927), page 115 : Après un acte de cruauté et de trahison

Il y a en outre des circonstances atténuantes pour Rousseau s'il a employé le mot « nature » là où il s'agit bien plutôt d'anti-nature.

Il y a d'abord une considération en quelque sorte historique, ou si on veut théologique. Rousseau affirmant souvent l'innéité de la conscience, l'épithète « naturelle » était alors légitime. Or il avait trouvé fort répandue la théorie paulinienne, augustinienne, janséniste et surtout protestante selon laquelle le but de l'existence est d'éprouver l'homme, et qui affirmait que Dieu avait mis en nous à la fois la voix naturelle des passions qui appellent au plaisir, et la voix de la conscience, *naturelle aussi car innée*, qui réclame le renoncement. Rousseau avait rejeté la doctrine du renoncement comme excellent en soi, cependant en tant qu'il comprend si bien la valeur du renoncement comme moyen de bonheur, il semble fort souvent disposé à adopter la doctrine chrétienne de la morale, innéité comprise.

Mais il y a surtout une autre considération qui explique et qui a légitimé peut-être les mots nature et naturel pour la morale anti-naturelle de Rousseau. Dans le *Second Discours* il a tout un long passage où il met en garde contre l'interprétation « historique » de son examen. Pour définir l'homme naturel, dit-il positivement, on ne peut procéder par l'histoire, car les historiens se contredisent sur ce premier homme ; et par exemple, « il est évident par la lecture des livres sacrés que le premier homme ayant reçu immédiatement de Dieu des lumières et des préceptes n'était point lui-même dans cet état ». Et c'est ici que Rousseau dit cette phrase fameuse et dont on a si traitreusement abusé : « Commençons donc par écarter tous les faits » (83-85), c'est-à-dire il faut les écarter, car nous ne savons jamais si nous aurons les véritables faits ;

horrible perpétré par les habitants de Tutuila, île de l'Océanie, La Pérouse écrivait : « Je suis mille fois plus en colère contre les philosophes qui préconisent les sauvages que contre les sauvages eux-mêmes ! » (p. 115). Et Bellessort d'ajouter : « Je ne dirai pas que s'il (M. de Langle) était mort, c'était la faute à Rousseau ; mais j'excuserais La Pérouse d'avoir pensé que les Jean-Jacques sont des malfaiteurs ». Il fallait dire « les Philosophes ».

on ne peut même pas dire avec certitude que l'homme *nature* dans le sens de « primitif » ait jamais existé ; ce qu'on peut seul étudier, ce que Rousseau étudiera, ce ne sera donc pas « l'état de nature » de l'homme, mais « la seule nature de l'homme ». L'importance de la distinction est énorme, mais elle ne ressortira qu'après le *Second Discours* où Rousseau flirte encore avec l'homme primitif. Ce sera donc dans « la nature de l'homme », non dans « l'homme à l'état de nature » qu'il trouve inscrite la loi morale de l'homme. Or, à ce titre, elle sera une loi « naturelle » encore. Etudier la « nature de l'homme », c'est étudier ce que serait l'homme social normalement développé. Rousseau dira explicitement dans *Émile* : « Il ne faut pas confondre ce qui est naturel à l'état sauvage, et ce qui est naturel à l'état civil ». C'est avec beaucoup de raison que Vial (*Doctrines d'éducation de Rousseau*, Delagrave, 1920, chap. II, p. 66) rappelle en note que Taine avait mis en rapport l'homme naturel de Rousseau et le type de l'homme classique (1), c'est-à-dire l'homme normal, chez qui existera l'équilibre des éléments constitutifs (appétits d'une part, raison ou conscience morale d'autre part). Règne normal, donc naturel. En d'autres termes, dans l'état social où l'homme trouvera le bonheur positif, l'anti-nature est devenu naturel. Et c'est bien ce qu'entend Rousseau dans cet autre passage d'*Emile* : « Voulant former *l'homme de la nature* (2), il ne s'agit pas pour cela d'en faire un sauvage ; mais enfermé dans le tourbillon social, il suffit qu'il ne s'y laisse pas entraîner, ni par les passions, ni par les opinions des hommes ; qu'il voie par ses yeux, qu'il sente par son cœur, qu'aucune autorité ne le gouverne hors celle de sa propre raison ».

Cette morale, dans son précepte paraît donc bien classique, ou chrétienne, bref anti-romantique, — encore qu'on puisse l'appeler *naturelle*.

---

(1) A propos de *La Nouvelle Héloïse* nous reviendrons sur ce rapprochement, et verrons combien Julie et Chimène loin d'être des « héroïnes » à opposer — romantique et classique —, sont sœurs au contraire.

(2) Qu'on remarque l'expression *former l'homme de la nature* — celui-ci n'existe donc pas en venant au monde.

Conclusion

On comprend maintenant comment on a pu interpréter la
Lettre sur les Spectacles comme appartenant à un groupe
d'écrits très austères, et pourquoi nous devons considérer
nous-mêmes cet écrit comme marquant un retour du pendule
dans le sens de ce que nous avons appelé le Rousseau romain,
par opposition au Rousseau romantique. C'est un retour à
l'idée de vertu discipline sans pourtant l'être à l'idée de vertu
renoncement et de sacrifice à Dieu ou État, du *Premier Discours.*

Rousseau ne renonçant pas à sa grande idée du *Second Discours* par laquelle il s'arrache au traditionalisme philosophique
ou théologique du *Premier Discours*, et par laquelle il rejoint
les « philosophes » qui disent que l'homme cherche légitime-
ment son bonheur terrestre, il a cependant deux motifs pour
insister très fortement — presque fanatiquement — sur l'élément de contrainte qui doit aller avec l'affirmation de la légitimité de la recherche de la jouissance.

1. Un motif d'ordre général : Précisément parce que
l'homme est faible seulement — dans l'amour par exemple —
et pas positivement méchant, il faut frapper *plus* fort. Si
vous dites à l'homme (comme Rousseau le faisait dans le
Premier Discours) qu'il est mauvais, il comprend tout de suite
qu'il doit agir contre ses dispositions spontanées ; mais si on
lui dit qu'il n'est pas mauvais, comme Rousseau le fait dans
le *Second Discours, et après,* (même en faisant la distinction
que *pas mauvais* ne signifie pas *bon*) il tire la conclusion que
quoi qu'il fasse il n'agira pas *mal* ; or justement en se reposant
sur cet oreiller de paresse il compromet son bonheur, il est
donc de bonne politique, il est donc urgent pour un écrivain
qui a tant soit peu de psychologie, d'appuyer avec d'autant
plus de force sur l'impératif disciplinaire ; et c'est parce qu'ils
ne lutte pas contre le franc mal du péché, mais contre la fai-

blesse, qui est en apparence moins mauvaise, mais en réalité
infiniment plus dangereuse, que Rousseau, sagement, s'est
montré plus sévère même dans la *Lettre sur les Spectacles*
que dans le *Premier Discours*.

2. Outre ce motif d'ordre psychologique et général, il en
est un autre pour Rousseau de faire jouer le romain, — et qui
est d'ordre contingent.

C'est que Rousseau dans le *Second Discours*, par sa
campagne en faveur du droit au bonheur contre la conception
théologique de la vertu renoncement, avait donné l'idée qu'il
était enrôlé sous le drapeau des « philosophes », et que maintenant il veut se reprendre. Il avait été avec eux, et il reste avec
eux du reste sur ce point, que la voix de la nature réclamant
du bonheur terrestre est légitime ; il demeurera encore d'accord avec eux en principe, qu'il faut demander à la philosophie et non à la métaphysique ou à la théologie, le moyen de
réaliser ce bonheur ; il ne se sépare d'eux que quand il s'agit
de formuler les préceptes de la philosophie dans la recherche
du bonheur, quand il oppose comme nous avons dit, à la philosophie du parti des « philosophes » (laquelle invite à suivre
la nature jusqu'au bout, non seulement quand elle dit de
rechercher le bonheur, mais encore quand elle dit qu'il faut
le chercher en s'abandonnant aux dispositions naturelles), la
philosophie tout court (qui dit qu'il faut lutter contre les
moyens de bonheur suggérés par la nature naturelle). *Mais là*,
il se sépare bien, et il *doit* parler très fort, car c'est justement
quand la question prend un intérêt *pratique*, que les deux
thèses vont en sens diamétralement opposé ; — et on comprend
que pour cette raison, la *Lettre sur les Spectacles* soit considérée
comme l'acte de séparation entre Rousseau et les Encyclopédistes ; ceux-ci le considèrent ainsi : et Rousseau de même.

C'est un point capital que cette distinction entre la philosophie tout court et la philosophie des « philosophes » ;
mais il y a toujours danger que le lecteur, tenant compte des
points de contacts (légitimité de la recherche naturelle du
bonheur, et critère philosophique et non métaphysique) oublie
le point de séparation. Rousseau a si peur de ce danger, et il

accuse dès lors le point de divergence si fortement, que c'est lui-même qui paraît oublier combien il y avait pourtant de rapports entre sa pensée et celle des « philosophes », et qu'il s'est fait passer pour leur ennemi ; car, voyant la morale chrétienne qui était, dans ses commandements sinon dans son inspiration, plus sage que celle des « philosophes », Rousseau se sentit peu de répulsion à adopter ce malheureux terme de *conscience morale*, bien plus se sentit poussé à se servir de la religion... Sur ce point l'auteur de la *Lettre sur les Spectacles* laisse clairement entrevoir déjà celui de la *Profession de foi du Vicaire Savoyard* où ce rapprochement sera consommé.

La position de Rousseau vis-à-vis des Encyclopédistes rappelle celle des Jansénistes vis-à-vis des Calvinistes : c'est parce que les point de contacts entre Jansénius et Calvin étaient si sérieux (péché originel et nécessité de la grâce) et les points de divergence étant si peu apparents que les Jansénistes furent si âpres dans leur polémique contre Genève : comme on ne voulait faire cause commune, on fit valoir furieusement des points secondaires qui n'étaient cependant que des applications pratiques de principes similaires.

De sorte qu'on peut dire que Rousseau a tort de se plaindre dans les *Confessions* (à propos de *la Nouvelle Héloïse* : VIII, 312) qu'en voulant s'efforcer de rapprocher les théologiens et les « philosophes », il n'avait réussi qu'à se mettre à dos les deux partis. Il a tort de se plaindre car il fallait qu'il s'expliquât plus clairement et plus franchement pour être bien compris. Aux Encyclopédistes, d'une part il devait dire : Vous êtes demeurés en chemin ; vous réclamiez les droits du bonheur terrestre ; je le veux aussi ; mais si vous aviez poussé vos réflexions, vous auriez donné toute son importance à ce fait que les hommes sont faibles et sots, et qu'il faut leur demander le renoncement à leurs inspirations primesautières et dangereuses pour pouvoir leur procurer le bonheur ; les enseignements de l'Eglise les amènent au bonheur, gardons-nous donc de combattre ceux-ci et de vouloir « écraser l'infâme » ; — et les Encyclopédistes n'auraient pas eu le droit de ne pas comprendre et de le repousser en disant : Tu veux aller avec l'Eglise, c'est *donc* que tu ne veux pas le bonheur dans le monde. D'autre part, à l'Eglise, il devait dire : Je vais avec vous ; la seule différence qu'il y ait entre nous est que je prêche votre morale et que je souscris partiellement à vos dogmes dans un autre but que vous ; mais ne me repoussez pas comme votre allié ; vous avez, au point de vue pratique des idées infiniment préférables à celles de vos adversaires ; et s'il fallait choisir, je me mettrais avec vous et contre eux, car ce qui importe avant tout à l'humanité, c'est d'arriver à réaliser le but du bonheur — peu importe du reste le principe invoqué publiquement ; en prêchant mes idées, je vous rends le service de rendre les hommes obéissants à vos préceptes. — Et l'Eglise n'aurait pas eu le droit de ne pas comprendre et de répondre : Tu veux un bonheur impie, c'est *donc* que tu veux ce que nous appelons mal.

Un mot encore. La position de Rousseau est excellente du reste, sa distinction entre la philosophie en soi et la philosophie des « philosophes » légitime, voire impérative ; mais elle ressort moins clairement de l'argumentation dialectique de Rousseau que de la présentation générale du sujet ; elle ressort particulièrement de ce fait qu'il a dans la *Lettre sur les Spectacles*, cessé absolument d'en appeler aux sauvages comme parangons d'excellence. Comme il avait abandonné dès le *Second Discours* les Romains, qui, voués à une vertu de renoncement, niaient les droits naturels au bonheur, pour les primitifs qui écoutaient la voix de la nature les appelant à jouir de la vie, il abandonne ici à leur tour ces sauvages représentant la course au bonheur spontané, animal et aveugle, pour les Suisses représentant l'aspiration à un bonheur social, un bonheur qui s'est arrêté devant les tentations d'une civilisation entraînant l'homme dans des maux bien pires que la simple privation de bonheur social des sauvages.

Nous n'avons pas voulu encombrer notre exposé de trop de polémique, et nous ajoutons ici quelques mots pour justifier notre

position vis-à-vis de récents commentateurs sur ces deux points :
de la conscience morale innée chez Rousseau ; et de la morale nature et anti-nature chez Rousseau.

I. La conscience morale innée.

Nous renvoyons à une page admirable de Hoeffding qui résume
de la façon la plus concise et avec autant de clarté que la chose
comporte, la pensée de Rousseau réduite en termes de sentiment.
Discuter cette page sera discuter les volumes innombrables où
Rousseau est représenté en sentimentaliste dans sa philosophie
morale (nous ne parlons pas ici de sa *religion* sentimentale).

« Rousseau, à cet égard [de la psychologie du sentiment], a exercé une influence décisive. Même s'il a pour devanciers Spinoza, Shaftesbury, Hutcheson
et Hume, on lui doit d'avoir reconnu au sentiment une part indépendante dans
la vie morale. Le sentiment est plus naturel que la raison. Il nous donne notre
propre valeur ; nous sommes petits par les lumières de notre raison, grands
par nos sentiments ! Le sentiment est, dans sa forme immédiate, c'est-à-dire
en tant que sentiment de la vie, indépendant du développement de la raison
et précisément ce sentiment immédiat joue un grand rôle pour Rousseau. Le
sentiment change plus lentement que les représentations et que les opinions,
même si, dans le cours du temps, il subit l'action de celles-ci. Un sentiment ne
peut être remplacé que par un autre sentiment : « On n'a de prise sur les passions que par les passions. » C'est un principe qui joue un grand rôle dans la
pédagogie de Rousseau. Enfin l'indépendance du sentiment vis-à-vis de la
raison se montre également en ceci que, dans certains moments, il peut s'élever
jusqu'à une extase dans laquelle il n'y a plus de représentation déterminée, où
le besoin et le pouvoir de penser n'existent plus, où tout notre être coule vers
l'infini. » (*Rousseau et sa philosophie*, Alcan, 1912, p. 118-119).

Ces mots réfléchissent bien la pensée de Rousseau : Le sentiment
moral (ou la loi morale qui est son contenu) est conféré, d'abord
tout constitué, à l'homme et comme une faculté distincte, — ce
sentiment peut être imaginé comme immédiat ou inné ; mais —
du moment que « les opinions et représentations » des hommes le
modifient après coup dans son contenu c'est qu'il est à base intellectuelle — il est ensuite convertible en termes de raison ; et puis la
raison, en retour, peut modifier le sentiment moral aperçu en bloc
dans une première perception.

Rien en cela qui ne soit d'accord avec notre interprétation intellec-
tualiste. Contestable cependant est l'affirmation que *semble* faire
Hoeffding, à savoir que la morale soit rationnelle et *en même temps*
immédiate. Nous avons expliqué comment le sentiment moral et la
loi morale peuvent *paraître* immédiats et innés sans l'être en effet ;
mais puisqu'on peut rendre compte de cette faculté morale tout aussi

SCHINZ. — Rousseau   16

bien par la raison seule, il est inutile de lui attribuer une origine métaphysique. Et même, on ne voit pas comment Hoeffding pourrait
prêter à Rousseau l'idée d'une modification après coup de la loi
morale par la raison, si cette loi morale soit être considérée comme
une donnée du sentiment *intégrale*. [*die Vorstellung.. (die) spaeter
auf das Gefuhl zuruckweisen kann*]. Supposé même d'ailleurs que
tout ceci valût, et que le sentiment donnât l'extase pour le bien
moral, il faudrait encore prouver que l'être humain ressent réellement cette extase pour le bien moral même sans avoir l'intelligence nécessaire pour saisir son sens en termes de raison ; on sait
par exemple, qu'on peut bien suggérer par hypnotisme à une personne de parler hébreu, mais on ne peut suggérer cela à une personne qui ne sait déjà l'hébreu ; de même ici : *nihil est in sentimento
quod non fuerit ante in intellectu* ; personne n'a prouvé que l'enthousiasme spontané pour le bien moral se rencontre ailleurs que dans
des intelligences qui au moins seraient capables de saisir son élément rationnel si celui-ci leur était présenté. Ce sont des Platon,
des Rousseau et des Kant qui font des hymnes à la « vertu » ; mais il
semble bien qu'on *apprend* aux enfants à aimer le bien, et peut-on se
représenter que les primitifs connaissent cet enthousiasme ? La seule
chose à concéder, ce serait que simplement l'homme intelligent a
psychologiquement le pouvoir de reconnaître ce qui est rationnel
sans que cette reconnaissance passe par l'intelligence consciente ;
et c'est tout ce que réclame la théorie morale de Rousseau indiquée
dans la *Lettre sur les Spectacles*. On se trouve ici devant la toute
grande question de l'inconscient, dont avec raison s'est tant préoccupé le XIXe siècle. Notre vie est pleine non seulement d'appréhen-
sions psychiques inconscientes quoique rationnelles, mais d'*actes*
présupposant indiscutablement du raisonnement : appliquer les
règles de l'orthographe sans raisonner chaque cas, faire de l'es-
crime, renvoyer une balle de tennis, etc... ou qu'on songe à ces
calculateurs phénomènes comme Inaudi, qui « mentalement »
c'est-à-dire inconsciemment peuvent résoudre des problèmes extrêmement complexes mais parfaitement analysables — résultats
d'une sorte de machine de calcul cérébral. On ne voit pas pourquoi
la raison ne pourrait pas travailler aussi bien d'une façon inconsciente dans le domaine des relations sociales ou de la morale que
dans celui des mathématiques. Si Rousseau, qui vivait à une
époque où l'inconscient n'était pas encore un élément psychologique formellement reconnu, n'a pas dit tout cela comme nous
pouvons le dire, qu'importe ; car cela est impliqué dans ses affirmations. Rappelons-nous ses remarques sur le sentiment de la pudeur réductible à la raison. Et l'extase morale — ou reconnaissance immédiate du bien — n'est pas la seule de son espèce. Quand

nous sommes frappés par la beauté d'un objet, est-ce à dire que le beau n'obéit pas à des lois esthétiques parce que nous ne connaissons pas toujours celles-ci par l'analyse ; enfin le cas de la musique, résultat de rapports infiniment complexes de nombres de vibrations, — rapports analysables à l'intelligence, — n'est contesté par personne.

II. La morale nature et anti-nature. Nous avons pris en considération seulement deux conceptions de nature morale dans l'œuvre de Rousseau, la nature des sens, et la nature morale ou rationnelle. On s'était aperçu depuis longtemps que chez lui cette notion de « nature » n'était pas claire ou conséquente, ou plutôt qu'il désignait sous ce nom plusieurs choses différentes, voire incohérentes. Depuis un quart de siècle on n'a pas mal discuté cela.

Par exemple, Masson écrira (*Religion de J.-J. Rousseau*, I, p. 260-261) :

« Disons tout suite que beaucoup reste à faire pour établir nettement les rapports de la nature telle que vue par les Encyclopédistes et telle qu'envisagée par Rousseau ; car — comme nous l'avons dit dès notre introduction, la nature était très communément invoquée quand vint Rousseau ; et, c'est la plus grande hérésie de croire que Rousseau a été un novateur en mettant en honneur la nature ».

Mornet dans ses divers travaux et Ducros entre autres ont posé des jalons importants pour ce travail particulier. Nous ne pouvons nous y arrêter ici.

De même nous passons rapidement sur la notion de nature mystique que certains commentateurs modernes de Rousseau et du romantisme ont essayé de remettre en honneur. Masson par exemple dans son grand ouvrage sur la religion de Rousseau, écrira :

« La nature qu'invoquent Diderot et d'Holbach nous le verrons ne sera pas celle de Rousseau [Cf. *Dialogues*, Ed. Hachette, p. 310] Quand Jean-Jacques s'écriera avec attendrissement : *O Nature ô ma mère, me voici sous ta seule garde* ! c'est à la Providence qu'il se confiera ; il traduira la prière de toutes les âmes sensibles qui depuis longtemps déjà cherchaient à surprendre dans l'univers la bonté de Dieu... » (vol. I, p. 260-1).

Et il montrera par exemple cette nature comme parente de celle dont avait parlé déjà Fénelon dans son *Education des filles* : « Il faut se contenter de suivre et d'aider la nature ». C'est là une interprétation particulière de Rousseau, et qui a été amenée par tout un système de commentaires, que nous avons analysé dans notre travail *La Pensée religieuse de Rousseau et ses récents interprètes* (Alcan, 1927).

Seillière, *Jean-Jacques Rousseau* (Garnier, 1921, p. 78-81), cherche bien loin l'origine des malentendus créés par le mot de na-

ture chez Rousseau. Sous le titre « De deux significations contradictoires de l'adjectif naturel.», et en en appelant savamment à Berkeley et à de Bonald, il souligne une distinction à faire du point de vue du temps. Il y a chez Rousseau une association de naturel avec sauvage ; mais aussi de naturel avec civilisé en ce sens que l'homme est devenu *naturellement bon* par éducation, civilisation, etc. Or, Rousseau aurait d'abord cru et affirmé la bonté naturelle originelle du primitif ; et puis voyant que c'était impossible, il aurait adopté la bonté acquise graduellement et *naturellement* ; mais ensuite, et uniquement « par mauvaise honte de se dédire » Rousseau aurait continué à affirmer la bonté originelle. On se demande pourquoi Seillière a écrit tant de livres pour réfuter un si triste sire sont les opinions sont faites par crainte de l'opinion publique, De la bien simple notion de *nature = passion*, et *anti-nature = vertu*, Seillière ne parle pas, — comme s'il se plaisait à demeurer dans le trouble, comme s'il avait peur de perdre une occasion d'accuser Rousseau.

Une autre discussion encore — et la plus intéressante — est, ici encore, celle de Hoeffding, qui dans son *Rousseau et sa philosophie*, Chap. IV. discute trois notions différentes de « nature » chez Rousseau. I. *La notion théologique* — la nature que Dieu a créée parfaite. 2. *La notion d'histoire naturelle* — la nature que l'on trouve chez l'homme primitif avec ses instincts et son manque de pensée culturelle. 3. *La notion psychologique* (de beaucoup la plus importante) — la nature telle qu'on la trouve chez l'homme en général, avec ses virtualités aussi bien que ses traits primitifs.

C'est fort juste, et d'ailleurs Hoeffding a raison de remarquer qu'il n'y a proprement guère de rapports entre la première et la deuxième : « Il est étonnant dit-il, que Rousseau n'ait pas vu qu'on ne saurait en appeler à la fois à la théologie et à la zoologie, car elles en appellent à un point de vue absolument différent ». Ce qui est étonnant, d'autre part, c'est que, lui, Hoeffding n'ait pas distingué psychologiquement entre nature passionnelle et nature morale ; certains éléments de la *distinction* sont impliqués, c'est vrai, dans ses deuxième et troisième sens, mais il ne semble pas apercevoir *l'opposition* dès qu'on discute la philosophie toute pratique de Rousseau. Et c'est là, dans la philosophie pratique, qu'est tout Rousseau ; la théologie n'est chez lui qu'une spéculation sans aucune valeur directe ; aussi bien n'en a-t-il fait usage que dans certains passages lyriques — dont nous aurons à nous occuper à propos de la Profession de foi du Vicaire savoyard. Du point de vue moral — qui est le sien — les deux seules notions de nature qui comptent sont celles que nous avons considérées : La passionnelle et la morale ou rationnelle, la seconde s'opposant, au nom de la raison, au règne de la première.

CHAPITRE IV

ROUSSEAU ET LES ANGLAIS

La nouvelle Héloïse

1. Mise au point du vocabulaire philosophique de la *Nouvelle Héloïse* : Raison des « philosophes » et raison en soi ; sentiment moral et sentiment naturel ; nature morale et nature romantique.
2. Histoire du roman. Attitudes successives de l'auteur vis-à-vis de son problème moral. Influences d'événements de la vie personnelle de Rousseau sur la composition.
3. Résumé de parties I à IV.
4. *La Nouvelle Héloïse avant le roman moral* : Première phase, Lettres d'amour ; Deuxième phase, le roman moderne, le « livre efféminé ».
5. *La Nouvelle Héloïse, roman sérieux* : Troisième phase, Morale romantique ; Quatrième phase, Morale de vertu-sagesse, — avec, en marge, l'idée du « ménage à trois » ; Cinquième phase, de l'insuffisance de la vertu-sagesse pour réaliser le vrai bonheur et de retour à des velléités romantiques.
6. La signification de l'anglomanie dans l'évolution de la pensée de Rousseau. *Deux Appendices.*
   Notes sur les modifications subies par le roman en cours de composition.
   Notes sur l'anglomanie de Rousseau.

§ **1**. Dès maintenant nous avons vu tous les éléments qui doivent entrer dans la discussion et qui tour à tour ont contribué à la formation de la pensée morale de Rousseau. Certains de ces éléments passeront de plus en plus au second plan, d'autres prendront plus de relief, d'autres encore auront des heures de faveur et des heures de défaveur. Mais il ne s'en ajoutera plus. Même la notion de la divinité comme ga-

rant et répondant de l'ordre moral (la « Providence ») est là par implication (1).

En outre, dès la *Lettre à d'Alembert* nous en savons assez pour affirmer une orientation assez nette. Après avoir abandonné la notion de *vertu de renoncement*, romaine ou calviniste, du *Premier Discours* (formulée elle-même en réaction contre les dispositions romantiques de l'auteur), et après avoir été fortement sollicité, dans son *Second Discours*, par une morale qui cherchait le bonheur dans l'abandon aux appels de la nature, *vertu d'innocence*, Rousseau avait passé maintenant à une morale de discipline rationnelle, une *vertu de sagesse*.

Il s'était, à vrai dire, présenté quelques difficultés à tirer les choses au clair, car il se trouvait que la vertu sagesse dans ses préceptes, se rapprochait plutôt de la vertu de renoncement, et paraissait plutôt en opposition avec la vertu romantique d'innocence. En réalité, du point de vue philosophique, ce rapprochement et cette opposition apparents n'avaient qu'une importance secondaire ; et Rousseau restait bien moins loin — selon l'esprit sinon la lettre — de la vertu romantique ; car il avait bien abandonné pour toujours l'idée de donner à la vertu d'autre but que celui du bonheur terrestre des hommes ; ce n'était que dans des moments d'oubli qu'il laissait couler de sa plume des mots qui semblaient ramener l'éloge de la vertu cultivée pour elle-même : seules la vertu romantique ou d'innocence, et la vertu de sagesse, toutes deux en vue du bonheur terrestre, demeuraient dans le rayon de son examen. Enfin dans ce dernier conflit, Rousseau s'est en fait prononcé déjà avec force pour une vertu de discipline.

D'autre part, si un examen attentif de l'œuvre dans son ensemble révèle que Rousseau s'en est toujours tenu dès lors à cette théorie de la discipline des passions et de la vertu sagesse, cependant cette même complexité des problèmes et

---

(1) Elle est du reste, dès cette époque, discutée ailleurs que dans des écrits publics ; dans la correspondace surtout, et par exemple dans la *Lettre à Voltaire*. d'août 1756 ; elle le sera plus tard abondamment dans la *Profession de foi du Vicaire savoyard* où nous la retrouverons).

ces mêmes confusions qui l'avaient empêché de formuler aussi clairement que nous croyons l'avoir fait ce qui constituait le fond de sa pensée dans la *Lettre à D'Alembert* (1), et cette même intrusion constante de la polémique dans les exposés, continueront à envelopper d'incertitude sa pensée dans ses grands écrits, et contribueront à la formation de ces « rousseauismes » sans fondement réel, dont nous avons parlé.

Rousseau, en effet est resté jusqu'au bout la première victime de son manque de mise au point et de ses polémiques. On ne pourra jamais dire, même après la *Lettre à D'Alembert*, que la vertu de sagesse ou de raison ait définitivement et nettement vaincu ; d'autre part, on pourra moins encore nier jamais que le fond de la pensée de Rousseau ne soit rationaliste foncièrement, et dès lors anti-romantique. Et c'est cette oscillation entre les deux tendances incompatibles, du romantisme (qui a sa source dans sa personnalité) et de la discipline (qui a sa source dans sa réflexion philosophique) qui continue à nous intéresser surtout. Elle est particulièrement très saisissable dans le moins systématique de ses grands écrits, le roman de *La Nouvelle Héloïse*.

Avant de l'étudier, formulons encore brièvement les différents éléments de confusion dont nous aurons à tenir compte.

Raison des philosophes et raison en soi.

Parce que Rousseau continue à se défier de la raison des « philosophes » de son siècle, — et de fait s'en défiera de plus en plus — il est sans cesse sur le *qui-vive* en ce qui concerne la raison tout court. Cette raison contingente, non absolue, a égaré les « philosophes », elle peut en égarer d'autres ; elle a

---

(1) Particulièrement faute de tenir compte de la distinction entre l'homme naturellement non-mauvais et l'homme naturellement bon, de la distinction entre une morale qui simplement reconnaît (contre le morale chrétienne traditionnelle) que la recherche du bonheur terrestre est naturelle et légitime, et une morale qui considère que la recherche naturelle du bonheur c'est-à-dire en cédant aux invites immédiates de la passion, est le moyen d'arriver à cette fin, et de la distinction entre une conscience morale innée de l'homme et une conscience morale expression de la sagesse accumulée au cours des âges.

égaré pour quelque temps Rousseau lui-même ; elle peut l'égarer encore. Or c'est contre la raison des « philosophes », en
réalité d'abord, mais par extension contre la philosophie tout
court aussi, que Rousseau invoque surtout le *sentiment* : sentiment est pour lui synonyme d'anti-raison, ou de a-raison.

Et cependant nous savons maintenant ce que Rousseau entend au fond par ce « sentiment », cette voix qu'il trouve en lui-
même pour lutter contre les appétits naturels, et qui n'est
réellement autre que la voix de la raison, — de la raison tout
court, supérieure, par opposition à la voix de la raison des
« philosophes » du XVIIIe siècle.

Sentiment moral et sentiment romantique.

Malheureusement nous savons que Rousseau appelle « sentiment » la voix aussi qui engage naturellement l'homme à
chercher le bonheur ; en d'autres termes, la voix qui est en
opposition avec la voix du sentiment moral. C'est-à-dire qu'il
y a donc deux sortes de *sentiments* chez Rousseau, — le
sentiment moral et le sentiment romantique, désignant des
choses contraires. On ne pourrait pas, en s'efforçant, trouver
mieux pour jeter de la confusion dans la pensée que cet emploi
du même terme dans deux acceptions opposées ; et on sait
d'ailleurs que Rousseau ne dit pas toujours *avec épithète* « sentiment moral », et qu'il ne dit jamais « sentiment romantique » (1).

Pourquoi Rousseau *a*) appelle-t-il ces deux notions « sentiment », et *b*) comment peut-il simultanément les approuver
toutes les deux puisqu'elles sont contraires ?

a) Il les appelle toutes deux « sentiment » car leurs données
à toutes deux lui semblent perçues immédiatement par
l'homme, et non acquises par l'intermédiaire des sens et surtout de la raison raisonnante. Il les considère comme innées ;
en réalité, l'une est innée réellement (sentiment romantique) ;

---

(1) « Romantique » et surtout « romantisme » étaient comme on le sait des
termes *très* rares encore du temps de Rousseau. Cf. A. François « Romantique »
Annales Rousseau, (1909 ; VI, 199-236).

l'autre l'est soi-disant (sentiment moral) — et nous avons vu qu'en fait, Rousseau infirme implicitement cette seconde innéité puisqu'il admet par ailleurs que les notions de morale sociale sont le résultat de l'expérience raisonnée de l'humanité, et n'ont ainsi pas besoin d'une explication métaphysique.

b) Et Rousseau peut approuver les deux « sentiments » quand bien même ils vont en sens contraire parce qu'il les trouve bons dans des sens différents. Le premier, — le sentiment romantique — il le trouve bon, car il ne veut pas que l'homme renonce à ses aspirations de bonheur pour une morale, à base religieuse ou politique. Le second — le sentiment moral — il le trouve bon, car il veut opposer aux « philosophes » en tant qu'ils recommandent la jouissance romantique, la discipline. C'est-à-dire qu'ici, par scrupule de laisser subsister quoi que ce soit qui puisse entraîner l'homme sur le chemin des misères humaines, il oppose le sentiment moral à son propre sentiment romantique : — céder à ce dernier n'est-ce pas déjà s'abandonner sur la pente glissante du malheur ? La sécurité consiste à ne jamais se livrer au romantisme, mais toujours de rester maître de soi. On peut se demander si cela ne va pas tuer la jouissance même et le bonheur ? C'est là un point délicat, et que Rousseau sentira, nous l'allons voir, surtout à propos des dernières parties de *la Nouvelle Héloïse*.

Nature morale et nature romantique

Nous ne revenons pas sur cette appellation, aussi regrettable que (et parallèle avec) celle de « sentiment moral » et « sentiment romantique ». Nous venons seulement d'expliquer que le terme moral est employé lui aussi dans deux sens absolument contraires, mais qu'une lecture attentive du contexte suffit à indiquer s'il s'agit de « nature romantique» ou de « nature morale ».

En résumé, en lisant Rousseau, et surtout en lisant *La Nouvelle Héloïse*, le lecteur se souviendra donc toujours de ceci, que selon le contexte :

Raison signifie { ou raison en soi,
{ ou son opposé, raison selon la « philosophie du
{ XVIIIᵉ siècle ».

Sentiment { ou sentiment romantique,
{ ou son contraire, sentiment moral.

Nature { ou nature romantique,
{ ou son contraire, nature morale.

D'autre part le lecteur se souviendra également que :

Raison (en soi), et *sentiment* (moral) ne sont pas opposés l'un à l'autre, mais se couvrent au contraire dans la philosophie entièrement pragmatique de Rousseau.

Enfin, en se rapportant aux commentateurs de Rousseau, il faudra ne pas oublier, en corollaire des distinctions et des rapprochements ci-dessus, que le « romantisme » de Rousseau signifie tantôt romantisme vraiment (lorsque ce romantisme se rattache à la nature et au sentiment romantiques), tantôt le contraire (lorsque ce terme se rattache à la nature et au sentiment moraux). Généralement, aujourd'hui, c'est dans le premier sens que le terme est le plus fréquemment employé ; quoique, du point de vue de Rousseau, il s'agirait plutôt du second (1).

§ 2. Maintenant arrivons aux oscillations curieuses qui se manifestent au cours du roman de *La Nouvelle Héloïse*, entre Rousseau romantique et Rousseau romain. Et, avant tout, entourons-nous des renseignements accessibles par ailleurs.

D'abord, les *Confessions*. Nous y apprenons que *La Nouvelle Héloïse* fut commencée tôt après l'arrivée de l'auteur à Montmorency, et dans un esprit tout semblable à celui qui présida à la rédaction du *Second Discours*, alors en cours de publication. Rousseau avait raconté au Livre VIII comment dans la forêt de Saint-Germain, en 1753, il avait « médité » le *Second Discours* en y cherchant « l'image des premiers temps » ; puis aussi comment il avait signifié à ses amis de

---

(1) Nous ne parlons pas ici de ce que Rousseau, *l'homme*, était peut-être, mais de ce que Rousseau, *le philosophe*, voulait.

Paris son intention de quitter la société et de vivre dans la
retraite. Il avait, sur ces entrefaites, entrepris son voyage
dans sa ville natale ; en route, il avait écrit la dédicace du
Second Discours aux magistrats de Genève ; et, de retour, il
avait trouvé la rustique demeure de l'Ermitage, offerte par la
générosité de Mme d'Epinay, à la lisière de la magnifique
Forêt de Montmorency. Il s'y était établi le 9 avril 1756.
Rendu à la solitude, tout ce qu'il y avait encore en lui de fiel
contre la société des hommes s'en était allé : « Quand je ne vis
plus les hommes, je cessai de les mépriser ; quand je ne vis
plus les méchants, je cessai de les haïr » (VIII, 299). Bref, il
avait retrouvé à Montmorency les belles heures de la Forêt
de Saint-Germain ; avec cette différence que des éléments
romantiques personnels venaient se mêler maintenant à ses
méditations, éléments qu'il avait écartés — en vertu même
du sujet à traiter — dans la *Lettre à D'Alembert* :

« Ces réflexions tristes, mais attendrissantes, me faisaient re-
plier sur moi-même avec un regret qui n'était pas sans douceur...
Je faisais ces méditations dans la plus belle saison de l'année,
au mois de juin, sous des bocages frais, au chant du rossignol,
au gazouillement des ruisseaux. Tout concourut à me replon-
ger dans cette mollesse trop séduisante pour laquelle j'étais
né, mais dont le ton dur et sévère où venait de me monter
une longue effervescence m'aurait dû délivrer pour toujours.
J'allai malheureusement me rappeler le dîner du château de
Toune (Cf. VIII 95-8), et ma rencontre avec ces deux charmantes
filles, dans la même saison et dans des lieux à peu près semblables
à ceux où j'étais dans ce moment. Ce souvenir que l'innocence qui
s'y joignait me rendait plus doux encore, m'en rappela d'autres de
la même espèce. Bientôt je vis rassemblés autour de moi tous les
objets qui m'avaient donné de l'émotion dans ma jeunesse, Mlle
Galley, Mlle de Graffenried, Mlle de Breil, Mme Bazile, Mme de Larnage, mes jolies écolières, et jusqu'à la piquante Zulietta ! que
mon cœur ne peut oublier. Je me vis entouré d'un sérail de
houris, de mes anciennes connaissances, pour qui le goût le plus
vif ne m'était pas un sentiment nouveau. Mon sang s'allume et pé-
tille, la tête me tourne malgré mes cheveux déjà grisonnants, et
voilà le grave citoyen de Genève, voilà l'austère Jean-Jacques, à
près de quarante-cinq ans redevenu tout à coup le berger extravagant ». (p. 305-6).

Et c'est ce printemps-là, et dans cet esprit qui est bien celui du *Second Discours*, qu'il avait commencé à écrire les pages d'où devait sortir le roman de Julie.

« Ces fictions (ou rêves relatifs à ses histoires d'enfance et de jeunesse) à force de revenir, prirent enfin plus de consistance, et se fixèrent dans mon cerveau sous une forme déterminée. Ce fut alors que la fantaisie me prit d'exprimer sur le papier quelques-unes des situations qu'elles m'offraient... Je jetai d'abord sur le papier quelques lettres éparses, sans suite et sans liaison... Les deux premières parties ont été écrites presque en entier de cette manière » (p. 309). Tout cela « sans prévoir qu'un jour je serais tenté d'en faire un ouvrage en règle ».

Et puis, un jour, l'idée s'était glissée dans son esprit qu'il pourrait peut-être en faire « une espèce de roman ». Ne pouvant faire cesser ces rêveries, même lorsque l'hiver l'empêcha de courir les bois, il s'était résigné :

« Quand la mauvaise saison commença de me renfermer au logis, je voulus reprendre mes occupations casanières ; il ne me fut pas possible. Je ne voyais partout que les deux charmantes amies, que leurs ami, leurs entours, le pays qu'elles habitaient, qu'objets créés ou embellis pour elles par mon imagination... Après beaucoup d'efforts inutiles pour écarter de moi toutes ces fictions, je fus enfin tout-à-fait séduit par elles et je ne m'occupai plus qu'à tâcher d'y mettre quelque ordre et quelque suite pour en faire une espèce de roman » (p. 311).

Tout cela est très plausible, et nous l'acceptons sans difficulté.

Depuis ici, cependant, la chose devient plus complexe ; mais justement Rousseau devient moins explicite. « Mon grand embarras, dit-il assez sommairement, était la honte de me démentir ainsi moi-même si nettement et si hautement ». Après avoir si violemment condamné les « livres efféminés qui respiraient l'amour et la mollesse », n'allait-il pas se ranger lui-même parmi les auteurs censurés ? Il en « rougit », mais s'avise d'un moyen : écrire un roman *moral* :

« Ce parti pris, je me jette à plein collier dans mes rêveries, et à force de les tourner et retourner dans ma tête, j'en forme enfin l'espèce de plan dont on a vu l'exécution » (p. 312).

Or, cette « espèce de plan » — qui succède comme on voit à l'idée d'une « espèce de roman » — comportait un nouveau compromis avec sa conscience, en ce sens qu'il laissait subsister à peu près telles quelles les « lettres brûlantes » : « Mes tableaux voluptueux auraient perdu toute leur grâce si le doux coloris de l'innocence y eût manqué » ; sa Julie devrait donc pécher, mais le péché de la jeunesse serait racheté par la vertu de la femme mariée. Du reste,

« Les êtres parfaits ne sont pas dans la nature, et leurs leçons ne sont pas assez près de nous. Mais qu'une jeune personne née avec un cœur aussi tendre qu'honnête, se laisse vaincre à l'amour étant fille, et retrouve étant femme des forces pour le vaincre à son tour et redevenir vertueuse, quiconque vous dira que ce tableau dans sa totalité est scandaleux et n'est pas utile, est un menteur et un hypocrite ; ne l'écoutez pas » (p. 312).

Il y aurait donc eu, selon Rousseau lui-même, après la phase des lettres amoureuses, deux phases : celle du roman dans le sens ordinaire du mot, roman mondain, et celle du roman moral. Il n'y a pas de raison ici encore pour douter de l'exactitude de ces affirmations. Elles restent cependant générales ; et si elles nous expliquent bien comment Rousseau a voulu se mettre en règle avec le public, ou avec des critiques (surtout les « philosophes » qui guettaient toujours les occasions de le trouver en faute ou en contradiction avec lui-même), elles ne disent pas assez sur ce qui est autrement intéressant pour nous, à savoir *comment* il se met en règle avec lui-même ; c'est-à-dire sur les altérations qu'il a dû faire subir à ses premières rédactions, pour réconcilier les points de vue divers qu'il signale lui-même dans son roman (lettres d'amour, roman mondain, et roman moralisateur), et puis sur des fluctuations de pensée *très évidentes* qui se sont produites même après que le roman mondain avait été absorbé par le roman moral. Qu'il y en eut encore, on pourrait avec assez

de certitude le deviner, même si le texte n'en révélait rien ;
d'abord en raison des oscillations de pensée chez Rousseau
en général ; et puis à cause des circonstances dans lesquelles
le roman fut composé.

En effet, la période de rédaction s'étend sur plus de trois
ans (il commence les « lettres brûlantes » dès le printemps
de 1756, et il envoie le manuscrit de la sixième et dernière
partie à l'imprimeur, le 18 janvier 1760). Et elle fut, — cette
période où l'auteur « tourne et retourne dans sa tête » l'œuvre
moralisatrice, — une des plus mouvementées de la vie de
Rousseau. Non seulement était-il interrompu par toutes sortes
de soucis domestiques (maladie, difficultés au sujet de, et
avec, la mère Levasseur qui faisait des dettes, et qui s'efforçait de détacher de lui Thérèse) ; non seulement s'occupe-t-il
de questions philosophiques variées (par exemple le problème de la Providence soulevé par le poème de Voltaire sur
Le Désastre de Lisbonne, et qu'il discute dans une longue et
fameuse lettre, 18 août 1756) ; mais il travaille déjà au
Contrat social, à l'*Emile,* et il écrit la *Lettre à D'Alembert* ; et
il vécut les mois douloureux des malentendus avec Mme
d'Epinay, lesquels ne sont à leur tour qu'un écho de ses disputes avec les Encyclopédistes ; et *surtout,* il éprouva sa
grande passion pour Mme d'Houdetot. Ces événements — et de
nombreuses lectures — ne lui fournirent pas seulement des
épisodes à ajouter à ceux suggérés par les souvenirs de jeunesse (Julie marquée de la petite vérole — comme Mme d'Houdetot ; le baiser de Julie à Saint-Preux devant le mari
de celle-ci — comme Mme d'Houdetot embrassant Rousseau
devant tous ses gens ; peut être le séjour de Wolmar et de
M. d'Etanges à l'armée — comme Saint-Lambert ; le voyage
de Saint-Preux autour du monde avec l'amiral Anson, etc.) ;
ou des digressions (le droit d'obliger un ami d'accepter des
services d'argent ; les réflexions sur les femmes de Paris ;
sur les Français, et les Anglais ; la lettre sur Genève ; les
mœurs des cultivateurs suisses, l'esprit philosophique, etc.)
mais ils lui révélèrent des aspects nouveaux, et lui suggé-
rèrent des idées nouvelles sur l'amour.

Donc les quelques phrases de Rousseau dans les *Confessions* sont loin de tout dire sur la rédaction de *La Nouvelle Héloïse*.

Nous pouvons ignorer deux « préfaces » écrites pour le roman en 1759-60. Disons seulement que Rousseau y suggérait déjà au lecteur l'interprétation qu'il désirait voir adoptée : l'histoire édifiante « d'une jeune fille offensant la vertu qu'elle aime, et ramenée au devoir par l'horreur d'un plus grand crime » (IV, p. 5), et « la chaste épouse, la femme sensée, la digne mère de famille [qui] font oublier la coupable amante » (p. 8).

On trouve d'autre part quelques données de valeur dans les fragments de correspondance publiés d'abord par M. Buffenoir, dans ses volumes sur Mme d'Houdetot (et incorporés, cela va sans dire, dans la Correspondance générale). Rousseau avait écrit dans les *Confessions* (VIII, p. 355) qu'au moment de se mettre à la *Lettre à D'Alembert*, le roman n'était qu'à moitié fait ; mais il écrit aussi à Mme d'Houdetot (1er oct. 1757) : « Dès que j'aurai fait ma copie des *Lettres de Julie*, je commencerai la vôtre ». On a pu conclure (M. Mornet, dans sa grande édition de *La Nouvelle Héloïse*, Hachette, vol. I, p. 82), que Rousseau avait fini le roman dès cette époque (1). Il paraît cependant probable qu'il ne s'agissait dans la lettre citée ci-dessus que des trois ou quatre premières parties — et cela semble bien confirmé par d'autre lettres à Mme d'Houdetot mises au jour en 1905 par M. Buffenoir. On y lit d'abord (28 janvier, 1758) : « Comme j'ai tout à fait changé d'idée et ne songe plus à la faire publier [la *Julie*]... » Et puis — nouveau changement d'idée chez Rousseau — 18 février 1758 : « Mon dessein est d'achever cet ouvrage et de l'achever pour vous seule ; car quand même les quatre parties verraient le jour, la cinquième que je vous destine ne le verra jamais ». On pourrait presque penser d'après cela, que la cinquième partie a été écrite deux fois, une fois pour Mme d'Houdetot, et une fois pour le public. L'auteur n'en dit rien dans les *Con-*

(1) (Cf. la discussion de ce point dans un article des *Publications of the Modern Language Association of America*, décembre 1926).

fessions, et il serait possible qu'il ait simplement *altéré* cette partie avant de l'imprimer, sans la recommencer. Mais certes la cinquième partie telle que nous la connaissons ne saurait être celle qu'il imagina pour Mme d'Houdetot, car on ne voit que la seule Lettre 5 qui fût d'un intérêt spécial pour elle (Lettre 2, ménage ; 3, éducation ; 6, religion, incrédulité de Wolmar ; 7, vendanges ; et puis les discussions des affaires de Lord Bomston, à Rome). Il y a du reste dans la rédaction finale, non pas une cinquième partie seulement, — qui devait « achever le roman » — mais aussi une sixième. Enfin, dans la lettre à Duclos, 19 nov. 1760, Rousseau déclare qu'il considère la quatrième partie comme « la meilleure de tout le recueil, et j'ai été tenté de supprimer les deux suivantes ». Il est difficile, on le voit, de suivre l'auteur dans tous ces tâtonnements, mais cela rend évident au moins que l'auteur a travaillé sur plus de deux plans différents, celui de « la jeune fille offensant la vertu », et celui de « la chaste épouse faisant oublier la coupable amante ».

Les lettres de Rousseau à son libraire Rey témoignent dans le même sens. Il semblerait ressortir de la lettre à Mme d'Houdetot, du 1er oct. 1757, que le roman était sinon terminé, du moins près de l'être, puisqu'il le recopiait déjà ; et voici qu'un ans après, le 1er sept. 1758, il écrivait seulement à l'imprimeur que le livre était fini ; et cela était confirmé dans une lettre du 24 oct. à Rey. Cependant, six mois se passent encore ; le 14 mars 1759, il va recopier le tout — qu'a-t-il fait tout ce temps ? — et deux mois et demi plus tard, le 25 mai, en parlant de sa copie, il dit une fois de plus : « J'ai changé beaucoup de choses ». Cela ne pouvait supposer seulement d'insignifiants changements de forme.

Enfin, un mot des manuscrits. Il y a à la Chambre des Députés, dit M. Mornet, trois manuscrits de *La Nouvelle Héloïse* (vol. cité, 158 ss) : Un premier brouillon, tout-à-fait fragmentaire, un deuxième brouillon pour les parties IV-VI, avec un certain nombre de lacunes, et la copie faite pour Mme de Luxembourg, complète. Nous n'avons pas réussi à obtenir l'autorisation de voir ces manuscrits ; mais M. M. Pellet,

dans la *Révolution Française*, de septembre 1906 (p. 199-202)
les décrit avec quelques détails. Il dit du premier : « C'est un
fouillis inextricable à première vue, probablement le premier
jet de la pensée de Rousseau ». [Il faut entendre probablement : le premier jet une fois que les lettres furent destinées à
devenir roman]. « 170 feuillets écrits serrés, à mi-pages, raturés
à outrance, les marges remplies de corrections ». C'est un
nouveau témoignage que Rousseau n'a pas seulement « tourné
et retourné » le roman dans sa tête avant de l'écrire, mais après
l'avoir couché sur le papier. Et le deuxième manuscrit nous
donne donc un brouillon spécial pour IV à VI (1). Cela, combiné avec ce que nous savons d'autre part, confirme nos suppo-
sitions : il y a eu une rédaction du roman s'arrêtant avec la
IVe Partie ; il y en a eu une comptant une Ve Partie (destinée
à Mme d'Houdetot) ; et une enfin où il y a eu IV, V et VI. Le
fait qu'il y a remaniement spécialement des parties IV et suivantes, prouve seulement que les trois premières pouvaient
demeurer les mêmes, avec des changements pas trop importants (2).

Ainsi les *Confessions*, la correspondance, les manuscrits
témoignent qu'il faut s'attendre à trouver dans le grand roman touffu de *Julie* (3), non seulement des hésitations et des
incohérences plus ou moins mal dissimulées, mais peut-être
bien toute une série d'attitudes changeantes sur la question
du mariage laquelle sert de sujet de démonstration des principes de morale ; attitudes qui ne sont pas fondues les unes
dans les autres, mais qui demeurent superposées les unes aux

---

(1) D'après M. Pellet, il peut sembler que les parties I à III manquent tout
simplement ; d'après M. Mornet, ce serait plutôt un manuscrit spécial pour ces
parties, et d'ailleurs un « brouillon ».

(2) Les comparaisons entre les manuscrits relatées par M. Mornet n'ont pour
but que d'établir un texte de la version imprimée, et n'ont pas autant d'intérêt pour nous. Nous en dirons autant pour les indications qu'il donne relativement aux quelques feuillets de brouillons qui se trouvent dans la collection
d'autographes de Victor Cousin, à la Bibliothèque de la Sorbonne, à la Bibliothèque de Genève, etc. (Cf. aussi *Annales Rousseau*, 1908, p. 269).

(3) Le premier titre du roman.

autres, soit parce qu'elles sont incompatibles simultanément,
soit dans certains cas aussi parce que Rousseau, plutôt que de
recourir au moyen rationnel d'une refonte générale avait
préféré — probablement par simple paresse — se livrer au
travail ingrat de réajuster au fur et à mesure les parties écrites
d'un ou plusieurs points de vue précédents. Il nous avertit
lui-même que les modifications des deux premières parties
furent légères ; ce sont celles contenant les plus brûlantes
lettres d'amour ; l'auteur ne voulut point les modifier comme
elles auraient vraiment dû l'être pour cadrer avec le tout
« puisque ces tableaux voluptueux auraient perdu toutes leurs
grâces si le coloris de l'innocence y eût manqué » (VIII, p. 312).
C'est dans les parties III et IV qu'il faut s'attendre à trouver
je plus de remaniements ; la Ve et la VIe étant écrites les dernières en auront beaucoup moins de nouveau ; et celles qu'on
y pourra soupçonner consisteront surtout à déplacer des
groupes de lettres (Ainsi, par suite de nombreuses pages rendues nécessaires dans la IVe partie pour préparer une nouvelle
et dernière conception du problème, cette IVe partie se trouvait enflée démesurément ; une partie des lettres qui y étaient
d'abord purent très facilement être transportées dans la Ve,
qui elle-même devint, en grande partie, la VIe.

§ 3. Maintenant arrivons enfin au roman lui-même. Pour
que nous puissions être bien clair, il faut que le lecteur souffre,
non à la vérité un résumé, mais une récapitulation rapide des
différentes péripéties de l'histoire. Et puis, pour simplifier
encore, nous détacherons d'abord les parties V et VI qui ont
été ajoutées après coup — comme nombre de textes déjà
cités suffiraient à l'établir.

Première partie. — Saint-Preux, apparemment orphelin,
donne des leçons à une voisine noble, Julie d'Étanges, et à sa
cousine Claire, à Vevey (Vevai), au bord du Lac Léman. Il
tombe amoureux de Julie, et il lui écrit pendant l'absence de
Claire qui est allée rendre les derniers devoirs à une vieille
gouvernante morte récemment. Après trois lettres, Julie
avoue qu'elle aime aussi ; elle a une mère bonne mais faible,

et un père sévère — absent en ce moment. Départ de Julie
pour la maison de campagne, au-dessus de Clarens, où Saint-
Preux est invité à lui rendre visite (1)... Et là, avec la conni-
vence de la cousine, Julie réserve dans un bosquet le premier
baiser à l'amoureux (Lettre 14) :

« Qu'as-tu fait, ah, qu'as-tu fait, ma Julie ! Tu voulais me récom-
penser et tu m'as perdu. Je suis ivre ou plutôt insensé. Mes sens
sont altérés, toutes mes facultés sont troublées par ce baiser mortel.
Tu voulais soulager mes maux ! Cruelle, tu les aigris. C'est du poison
que j'ai cueilli sur tes lèvres, il fermente, il embrase mon sang ;e
il me tue et ta pitié me fait mourir. — O souvenir immortel de cet
instant d'illusion, de délire et d'enchantement, jamais, jamais tu
ne t'effaceras de mon âme ;... tu feras le supplice et le bonheur de
ma vie » (p. 40-41). (2).

Quelque temps après tout le monde rentre à la ville (Vevey).
Mais Julie qui songe maintenant à la façon dont elle pourrait
s'unir à son amant par le mariage, propose l'éloignement pro-
visoire, Saint-Preux part pour le Valais d'où il envoie des
descriptions enchanteresses de la nature des Alpes, et surtout des mœurs des habitants de la vallée. Le père revient ;
on lui parle de Saint-Preux et des leçons qu'il a données aux
jeunes filles ; les difficultés commencent ; le père veut payer
le roturier (49), ce que Saint-Preux refusera (55). Il faut ajouter
ajouter que le père avait ramené avec lui Wolmar, « un étranger respectable, son ancien ami, qui lui a sauvé la vie à la
guerre » ; mais celui-ci ne reste pas (49).

L'hiver approche ; Julie rappelle Saint-Preux du Valais
où il fait froid ; mais il ne doit pas encore retourner à Vevey ;
il se fixe à Meillerie, village de la rive du lac en face de Vevey ;
des roches qui surplombent le village, il peut distinguer la
maison d'Étanges. L'éloignement excite la passion ; des lettres
enflammées sont échangées ; ils sont faits l'un pour l'autre :

(1) Clarens n'est qu'à une petite distance de Vevey, et Saint-Preux pouvait
s'y rendre à pied. S'il y allait aussi pour des leçons, n'est pas clair.

(2) Dans l'édition Hachette, les cinq premières parties sont au volume IV ;
nous indiquons seulement les pages.

« Non, connaissez-le enfin, ma Julie ; un arrêt éternel du ciel nous destina pour l'un l'autre ; c'est la première loi qu'il faut écouter, c'est le premier soin de la vie de s'unir à qui nous doit la rendre douce... L'enthousiasme de l'honnêteté t'ôte la raison [Julie n'a pu encore se résoudre à aller à l'encontre de la volonté de son père qui ne peut approuver le mariage], et la vertu n'est plus qu'un délire ». (p. 61).

Julie rongée de chagrin, et de soucis, et d'amour tombe malade ; une mauvaise fièvre menace sa vie, dans son délire elle nomme sans cesse Saint-Preux. Claire appelle celui-ci : « Venez sans différer... Ne perdez pas un moment si vous voulez revoir la plus tendre des amantes qui fût jamais » (p. 62).

Les événements se précipitent. Saint-Preux propose l'enlèvement ; et Julie apprend que son père a promis sa main à Wolmar. Elle se révolte.

« Enfin, mon père m'a donc vendue ! Il fait de sa fille une marchandise, une esclave ! Il s'acquitte à mes dépens ! Il paie sa vie de la mienne... Père barbare et dénaturé » (p. 62).

Et dans son désespoir, profitant d'une absence de Claire, elle se donne à Saint-Preux, expliquant après : « sans savoir ce que je faisais, je choisis ma propre infortune. J'oubliai tout et ne me souvins que de l'amour » (p. 64). Et Claire, qui représente à ce moment du roman le sang froid, trouve ces mots pour la réconforter :

« Garde-toi donc de tomber dans un abattement dangereux qui t'avilirait plus que ta faiblesse. Le véritable amour est-il fait pour dégrader l'âme ? » (p. 65).

Saint-Preux est d'accord :

« Qu'as-tu fait que les lois divines et humaines ne puissent et ne doivent autoriser ? Que manque-t-il au nœud qui nous joint qu'une déclaration publique ? Veuille être à moi, tu n'es plus coupable. O mon épouse ! O ma digne et chaste compagne ! O charme et bonheur de ma vie ! Non ce n'est point ce qu'a fait ton amour qui peut être un crime, mais ce que tu voudrais lui ôter : ce n'est qu'en acceptant un autre époux que tu peux offenser l'honneur » (p. 67).

Julie cependant semble répudier ses actions, elle parle un langage un peu inattendu, et à vrai dire suspect à cet endroit du roman (1) ; elle regrette la vertu :

« Crois-moi — écrit-elle à Saint-Preux — crois-en le cœur tendre de ta Julie, mon regret est bien moins d'avoir trop donné à l'amour que de l'avoir privé de son plus grand charme. Ce doux enchantement de vertu s'est évanoui comme un songe ; nos feux ont perdu cette ardeur divine qui les animait en les épurant ; nous avons recherché le plaisir, et le bonheur a fui loin de nous ». (p. 68).

Julie a donc un accès de vertu — appelons-le ainsi puisque Rousseau l'a fait — et souffre d'être sortie de la voie du devoir :

« Ma faute est irréparable, mes pleurs ne tariront point » (p. 68). [Et] : « Je ne sentis jamais mieux combien une conscience coupable arme contre nous de témoins qui n'y songent pas... Nous nous aimons trop pour pouvoir nous gêner ainsi » (p. 69).

Elle soupire de rentrer dans la routine sociale :

« Que ton mérite efface ma honte ; rends excusable, à force de vertu, la perte de celles que tu me coûtes... Hâte-toi donc avant que je sois forcé de reprendre les occupations ordinaires [après la maladie], de faire la démarche dont nous sommes convenus » (p. 68-9). [Il s'agit de la demande en mariage].

Cette sorte de crise n'occupe du reste que quelques pages. Puis, déjà, de nouveau elle s'écrie : « Ah ! si de mes fautes pouvait naître le moyen de les réparer ! Le doux espoir d'être un jour ...» (p. 70). Elle voudrait être mère pour forcer son père à accepter le mariage. Encore quelques pages et elle est redevenue tout à fait elle-même, et communique à Saint-Preux son projet dans une longue lettre commençant ainsi : « Baise cette lettre et saute de joie pour la nouvelle que je vais t'apporter... » (p. 74). Les parents s'en vont et les amoureux dans la maison de Claire, peuvent se voir librement.

---

(1) « Suspect » en ce sens qu'il suggère l'idée d'avoir été interpolé plus tard lorsque Rousseau introduisit un nouvel esprit.

Une certaine Fanchon, protégée de Julie, a des embarras d'argent ; pour l'aider, son fiancé veut s'engager comme soldat et le mariage est compromis. Julie envoie Saint-Preux pour arranger l'affaire, et empêcher que les exigences sociales compromettent ce mariage indiqué par la nature.

Peu après entre en scène, comme visite chez M. d'Étanges, Lord Bomston (p. 83-4), le gentilhomme qui représente toutes les vertus chevaleresque de l'Angleterre, par opposition à la légèreté et à la frivolité françaises. Saint-Preux se rappelle l'avoir vu à Sion, pendant son séjour au Valais. Tout de suite Bomston devient un acteur triomphant. Il est convié à un dîner chez les d'Étanges où il se rencontre avec Saint-Preux ; celui-ci remarque que Julie plaît à l'anglais (p. 86) ; et il est en effet question de mariage (p. 91) ; cependant Julie tranquillise son amant ; ni elle, ni son père ne songent à Bomston.

Julie avait proposé de célébrer le mariage de la Fanchon à la campagne pour se ménager un rendez-vous avec Saint-Preux. Le plan échoue, mais Julie est décidée à céder à son amour :

« Loin de rebuter mon courage, tant d'obstacles l'ont irrité ; je ne sais quelle nouvelle force m'anime, mais je me sens une hardiesse que je n'eus jamais ; et, si tu l'oses partager, ce soir, ce soir même peut acquitter mes promesses, et payer d'une seule fois toutes les dettes de l'amour. » (p. 97).

Et les lettres de Saint-Preux à ce sujet sont des plus passionnées (p. 98-101).

Intermède de la querelle entre Bomston et Saint-Preux chez Bomston, lequel se plaint que Julie fut bien froide pour lui, mais moins pour d'autres. Saint-Preux relève le gant. Duel proposé. Julie écrit à la fois à Saint-Preux pour combattre ce projet (qui du reste compromettrait tout) et à Bomston pour lui avouer son amour pour Saint-Preux (p. 109). Bomston alors fait des excuses « romaines » ou « anglaises » — des excuses à grand spectacle — à Saint-Preux (p. 110) ; mais non content de cela, il cherche à arranger l'union par le mariage des deux amants ; il demande à M. d'Étanges, la main

de Julie pour Saint-Preux (p. 113-115) ; il plaide pour les
roturiers qui ont noblesse de cœur et de manière ; il attaque
la noblesse, parle de celle d'Angleterre, « la plus éclairée, la
mieux instruite, la plus sage et la plus brave d'Europe » ; il
ajoute qu'il accepterait Saint-Preux pour son beau-frère à
lui et se déclare prêt à lui donner la moitié de sa propre fortune, etc. Mais tout ceci irrite M. d'Étanges, et le résultat est
que Saint-Preux doit partir (p. 117).

Grande scène entre le père et la fille. M. d'Étanges se laisse
aller à souffleter Julie ; en se reculant pour éviter les coups,
elle tombe, donne du visage contre un pied de table ; le sang
coule ; le père est rappelé à lui à cette vue... et tous sentent
dans la réconciliation la douceur des sentiments naturels :

« Douce et sainte innocence — écrit Julie — tu manquais seule
à mon cœur pour faire de cette scène de la nature le plus délicieux moment de ma vie... Pour moi, je lui ai dit [à son père], et je
le pense, que je serais trop heureuse d'être battue tous les jours au
même prix, et qu'il n'y a point de traitement si rude qu'une seule de
ses caresses n'efface au fond de mon cœur » (p. 119).

Cependant, en sortant le père défend à sa fille « de voir et
de parler de sa vie à Saint-Preux ». Et elle, Julie, termine :

« Ah, ma cousine, quels monstres d'enfer sont ces préjugés qui
dépravent les meilleurs cœurs et font taire à chaque instant la nature... Malgré tous les préjugés, tous les obstacles, tous les revers, le
ciel nous a faits l'un pour l'autre. Oui, oui, j'en suis sûre, il nous
destine à être unis ; il m'est impossible de perdre cette idée, il
m'est impossible de renoncer à l'espoir qui la suit » (p. 120).

Mais Julie même veut éloigner Saint-Preux. Claire et
M. d'Orbe (le fiancé de Claire) s'en chargent, avec l'assistance
de Lord Bomston qui offre sa chaise pour l'enlèvement de
l'amant. Grande scène émouvante du départ sans revoir
Julie (p. 125-8).

Deuxième partie. Lord Bomston emmène Saint-Preux à
Besançon où ils s'arrêtent quelques jours. Saint-Preux écrit
qu'il est temps encore, qu'il reviendra si Julie le rappelle

(p. 133). En même temps Bomston offre à Julie (et sans rien dire à Saint-Preux) un refuge dans ses terres d'York où l' « odieux préjugé n'a point d'accès », où elle échappera aisément aux « poursuites d'une famille irritée », et où, avec Saint-Preux ils pourraient vivre des produits de la terre (p. 135-6). Julie hésite entre l'amour pour Saint-Preux et l'amour filial ; elle demande à Claire de décider pour elle (p. 137). Claire penche pour le refus, mais jure qu'elle accompagnera Julie si celle-ci se décide à partir, abandonnant jusqu'à M. d'Orbe, son fiancé :

> « C'est à M. d'Orbe, s'il m'aime ,à s'en consoler. Pour moi, quoique j'estime son caractère, que je ne sois pas sans attachement pour sa personne, et que je regrette en lui un fort honnête homme, il ne m'est rien auprès de ma Julie. Dis-moi, mon enfant, l'âme a-t-elle un sexe » (p. 140).

Julie alors décline l'offre de Bomston (p. 141-3).

Dans un accès de délire, Saint-Preux s'imagine que Bomston a voulu l'éloigner de Julie pour épouser celle-ci lui-même. Bomston lui met sous les yeux la lettre où Julie refuse l'offre de la terre d'York. Saint-Preux tombe dans les bras de son bienfaiteur, « le cœur chargé d'admiration, de regret et de honte ». Les deux hommes vont du reste se séparer ; Bomston ira, pour ses affaires, en Italie, tandis que Saint-Preux l'attendra à Paris ; de Paris, ils se rendront plus tard ensemble en Angleterre, où Bomston s'occupera de procurer à Saint-Preux une position dans le monde. Bomston de plus, s'autorise, de l'ingratitude et des soupçons de son ami pour le forcer à accepter des moyens de subsistance à Paris :

> « Son âme sublime, écrit Saint Preux, est au-dessus de celle des hommes, et il n'est pas plus permis de résister à ses bienfaits qu'à ceux de la divinité » (p. 146, 149). [Et] : « apprends qu'il ose abuser du droit que lui donnent sur moi ses bienfaits pour les étendre même au delà de la bienséance. Je me vois, par une pension qu'il n'a pas tenu à lui de rendre irrévocable, en état de faire une figure fort-au-dessus de ma naissance ; et c'est peut-être ce que je serai forcé de faire à Londres pour suivre ses vues » (p. 157).

Julie est du reste d'accord avec Bomston. En vérité, c'est faire injure à un homme comme lui de le remercier (164).

Pendant que s'élaborent ces plans, continue l'aventure romanesque : Julie écrit qu'elle n'épousera pas Saint-Preux sans le consentement de son père, mais qu'elle n'épousera personne dans le consentement de Saint-Preux :

> « J'ai consulté, non mes devoirs, mon esprit égaré ne les connaît plus, mais mon cœur, dernière règle de qui n'en saurait plus suivre ; et voici le résultat de ses inspirations : Je ne t'épouserai jamais sans le consentement de mon père ; mais je n'en épouserai jamais un autre sans ton consentement ; je t'en donne ma parole » (p. 154).

Saint-Preux répond qu'il mourra « libre ou époux de Julie » (p. 155).

Saint-Preux maintenant seul à Paris, écrit de longues lettres (14, 17, 19 entre autres) à Julie sur la société, nouvelle pour lui, qu'il observe d'un œil pas trop complaisant. Comme diversion à ces très longues lettres (qui sont surtout une adaptation de Muralt aux théories sociales de Rousseau) les événements suivants nous rappellent encore que nous lisons un roman d'amour : Claire épouse M. d'Orbe (p. 163, 176). Deux « épouseurs » se présentent pour Julie, pas dangereux cependant (p. 179). Julie envoie son portrait à Saint-Preux (p. 181) qui écrit une lettre passionnée en la recevant (p. 192-3). Saint-Preux s'est laissé entraîner par surprise dans une maison publique où tout son péché consiste d'ailleurs à n'avoir pas *hautement* protesté en s'en allant ; il se confesse à Julie qui pardonne en sermonnant toujours (p. 204).

Les lettres de Saint-Preux à Julie sont découvertes par la mère (p. 212).

Troisième partie. Mᵐᵉ d'Étanges est malade, et Julie au désespoir d'avoir causé un grand chagrin à sa mère. Le « dangereux secret » des lettres d'amour est caché au père, mais Claire exige de Saint-Preux qu'il renonce à Julie pour cacher au moins « sous un voile éternel, cet odieux mystère » de leurs amours. Il n'y a du reste plus d'espoir ; car le père, cet « homme inflexible », dont la parole est « irrévocable » a promis Julie à Wolmar ; si Saint-Preux insiste encore à « corrompre une fille sage », « à déshonorer sans scrupule toute une famille pour satisfaire un moment de fureur », c'est alors de « l'obstination (p. 212-13). Et que Saint-Preux ne manque pas d'observer la *douceur de ces termes*, car Mᵐᵉ d'Étanges avait écrit elle-même, mais Claire pensant tout de même qu'il est « digne au moins qu'on n'emploie pas avec lui de pareils moyens », a « mis en pièce cette lettre accablante ». Saint-Preux écrit à Mᵐᵉ d'Étanges qu'il veut expier un « crime involontaire », et renoncer à Julie, laquelle lui a « trop appris comment il faut immoler le bonheur au devoir » (p. 215). Il renonce à voir celle qu'il aime, à lui écrire, et même, s'il faut, consent à ce qu'un autre épouse Julie. Mᵐᵉ d'Étanges meurt, et sa fille l'écrit au « barbare », « par qui je plonge le couteau dans le sein mater-nel », à celui qui doit sentir avec elle « l'horreur d'un parricide qui fut votre ouvrage » (p. 218). Saint-Preux écrit à Claire pour demander si son amour pour Julie est cause de la mort de Mᵐᵉ d'Étanges ; car, si c'est le cas « nous sommes deux monstres indignes de vivre » (p. 220). Claire répond que non, que les chagrins de Julie la trompent :

« Cette âme tendre croit toujours ne pas s'affliger assez, et c'est une sorte de plaisir pour elle d'ajouter au sentiment de ses peines tout ce qui peut les aigrir » (p. 222).

La vraie cause de la mort, c'est M. d'Étanges qui :

« Longtemps inconstant et volage, prodigua les flux de sa jeu-nesse à mille objets moins dignes de plaire que sa vertueuse com-pagne ; et quand l'âge le lui eut ramené, il conserva avec elle cette rudesse inflexible dont les maris infidèles ont accoutumé d'aggraver leurs torts » (p. 223).

Échange de billets entre le père de Julie et l'amant ; le pre-mier demandant au « suborneur » de rendre sa parole à Julie ; et le second envoyant au « père barbare et peu digne d'un nom si doux » un billet par lequel il « rend à Julie d'Étanges le droit de disposer d'elle-même et de donner sa main sans consul-ter son cœur » (226).

Julie de nouveau toute à son amour malheureux, fait une maladie ; est atteinte de la petite vérole ; dans son délire elle déclare qu'elle espère mourir, et quand elle est sauvée par les soins de Claire, elle exprime le souhait d'être défigurée par son mal en sorte que Wolmar ne veuille plus d'elle. « Son dégoût me garantira de sa tyrannie, et il me trouvera trop laide pour me rendre malheureuse » (227). Elle rêve que Saint-Preux est accouru de Paris, a pénétré dans la chambre et a embrassé sa main avec passion ; sa cousine lui avoue que ce n'est pas un rêve (229), et que son amant a été infecté de la maladie ; celui-ci s'est arrêté à Dijon où Lord Bomston l'a rejoint ; et après guérison, ils sont retournés ensemble à Paris (230). Ces détails impressionnent tant Julie qu'elle est prête à céder à tant d'amour, tandis que Saint-Preux écrit qu'il se révolte contre sa destinée injuste ; il ira en Angleterre où Bomston dit avoir besoin de lui, mais il projette de venir chaque année voir secrètement sa maîtresse (223).

Tout à coup, Claire écrit : « Votre amante n'est plus... Julie est mariée » (234). Et Julie fait suivre la nouvelle d'une très longue lettre où elle reprend, en la commentant, l'histoire de leur amour. Elle ajoute à ce que nous savons déjà, qu'entre temps Wolmar a perdu sa fortune, que M. d'Étanges s'est jeté aux pieds de sa fille pour lui demander de sacrifier une « passion honteuse » à l'honneur de son père ; car comment dirait-il à Wolmar :

« Monsieur, je vous ai promis ma fille tandis que vous étiez riche, mais à présent que vous n'avez plus rien, je me rétracte, et ma fille ne veut point de vous... Non, ma fille ,il est trop tard pour finir dans l'opprobre une vie sans tache, et soixante ans d'honneur ne s'abandonnent pas en un quart d'heure » (241-2).

Mais, surtout, Julie explique sa conversion à des idées opposées à celles qu'elle et Saint-Preux, et Lord Bomston avaient défendues auparavant :

« Il n'y a pas deux mois que je pensais encore ne m'être pas trompée. L'*aveugle amour* (1), me disais-je, avait raison ; nous étions faits l'un pour l'autre ; je serais à lui si l'ordre humain n'eût troublé les rapports de la nature ; et s'il était permis à quelqu'un d'être heureux, nous aurions dû l'être ensemble » (235).

Or elle s'était trompée, car : « La vertu est si nécessaire à nos cœurs, que quand on a une fois abandonné la véritable, on s'en fait une à sa mode, et l'on y tient plus fortement peut-être parce qu'elle est de notre choix » (239). Mais maintenant, après avoir cédé au cœur, du reste « si sincère » de Saint-Preux, elle a connu :

« Combien il est insensé de chercher dans l'*égarement de son cœur* un *repos* qu'on ne trouve que dans la *sagesse* » (240). « Prestige des passions, tu fascines ainsi la raison, tu trompes la sagesse et *changes la nature* avant qu'on s'en aperçoive » (244).

Julie souligne que c'est à l'église, où elle avait été entraînée pour la cérémonie du mariage malgré elle en somme, par le « père barbare » (lequel tout à coup est devenu un père « à entrailles », un « père attendri et fondant en larmes ») qu'elle se sentit convertie :

« Une puissance inconnue semble corriger tout à coup le *désordre de mes affections*, et les rétablir *selon la loi du devoir et de la nature* » (p. 245) ; [et] « je connus dès ce moment que j'étais réellement changée » (p. 246) ; « je déplorai le triste aveuglement qui me l'avait fait manquer si longtemps [mon devoir] » (p. 247) ; etc. etc...

« Comment s'est-il fait, cet heureux changement ? Je l'ignore. Ce que je sais, c'est que *je l'ai vivement désiré*. Dieu a fait le reste » (p. 252). Mais, « adorez l'Éternel, mon digne et sage ami ! ». Dans une lettre suivante, elle précise encore :

« Ce qui m'a longtemps abusée et peut-être vous abuse encore, c'est la pensée que l'amour est nécessaire pour former un heureux mariage » (p. 258).

---

(1) Nous soulignons certains termes auxquels il est bon que le lecteur fasse attention en vue de l'interprétation qui suit.

« Ce sentiment qui nous joint (M. de Wolmar et moi) n'est point l'*aveugle transport des cœurs passionnés*, mais l'immuable et constant attachement de deux personnes honnêtes et *raisonnables* » (p. 259). [Plus que cela :] « Je serais libre encore et maîtresse de me choisir un mari, je prends à témoin de ma sincérité, ce Dieu qui daigna m'éclairer et qui lit au fond de mon cœur, ce n'est pas vous que je choisirais, c'est M. de Wolmar » (p. 259).

Elle conservera à Saint-Preux son amitié, c'est-à-dire elle conservera de son « sentiment » pour lui, « ce qui peut s'accorder avec l'innocence... Oubliez tout le reste et *soyez l'amant de mon âme* » (p. 252).

Julie demande à son amant l'autorisation de révéler son passé à Wolmar ; Saint-Preux refuse (p. 253-4) ; — mais Julie finira par obtenir gain de cause, ou plutôt elle n'aura pas besoin de « révéler » à Wolmar quoi que ce soit, car celui-ci savait tout. Enfin Julie brise tout commerce direct de lettre avec Saint-Preux, mais ne voit pas d'objection à ce qu'il corresponde avec Claire (p. 260).

Intermède du suicide : entre temps Saint-Preux est à Londres, s'abandonnant à son désespoir. Bomston avait voulu l'envoyer à Rome pour ses affaires à lui, mais le voyant si peu homme, il renonce. Saint-Preux déclare qu'il va quitter la vie, car il en a le droit (p. 262 ss) ; Bomston répond à son ami qu'il est un lâche et qu'il doit vivre pour accomplir quelque chose et pour ne pas affliger ceux qui l'aiment (p. 269 ss). Il lui propose de faire le tour du monde « à titre d'ingénieur des troupes de débarquement » avec l'expédition de Lord Anson, lequel allait quitter Plymouth. Saint-Preux se résigne ; il vivra et ira : « Faites, Milord... » (p. 275). Au moment de s'embarquer, il apprend que Julie a un enfant :

« Adieu, charmantes cousines. Adieu beautés incomparables. Adieu pures et célestes âmes. Adieu tendres et inséparables amies, femmes uniques sur la terre... J'entends le signal et les cris des matelots ; je vois fraîchir le vent et déployer les voiles ; il faut monter à bord, il faut partir. Mer vaste, mer immense qui dois peut-être m'engloutir dans ton sein ; puissé-je retrouver sur tes flots le calme qui fuit mon cœur agité » (p. 276).

*
* *

La quatrième partie ,nous l'avons dit, a subi les altérations les plus importantes. Nous allons mettre en italiques — pour pouvoir nous y reporter dans les commentaires qui suivront — ce que nous considérons comme ajouté pour faire du roman simplement romanesque un roman moralisant.

Quatrième partie. Quatre ans se sont écoulés. Julie est devenue mère de deux garçons — l'un Marcelin, l'autre sans nom indiqué —, Claire d'une fille, Henriette. Claire étant devenue veuve, sa cousine lui demande de quitter Lausanne pour venir habiter Clarens ; Claire avait, sans le dire, projeté précisément cela, et même arrangé dans sa tête le mariage de sa fille avec l'aîné de Julie. La réunion aura lieu en automne. Le père de Julie va partir pour Berne d'où il ne reviendra pas avant d'avoir vu la fin d'un long procès.

Julie n'a toujours pas révélé à Wolmar son passé, et ce passé lui est toujours présent : « *Tu ne m'es pas seulement nécessaire,* écrit-elle à Claire, *quand je suis avec mes enfants ou mon mari, mais surtout quand je suis seule avec ta pauvre Julie ; et la solitude m'est dangereuse précisément parce qu'elle m'est douce et que souvent je la cherche sans y songer. Ce n'est pas, tu le sais, que mon cœur se ressente encore de ses anciennes blessures ; non, il est guéri, je le sens, j'en suis très sûre ; j'ose me croire vertueuse. Ce n'est point le présent que je crains, c'est le passé qui me tourmente* ». *Elle croit avoir un pressentiment que Saint-Preux est mort :* « *Il n'est plus, il n'est plus... Il manquait aux* tourments de ma conscience *d'avoir à me reprocher la mort d'un honnête homme. Ah, ma chère, quelle âme c'était que la sienne !... Comme il savait aimer !...* » (p. 279-80).

Saint-Preux revient. Il écrit à Claire qu'il ira en Italie avec Bomston, et puis demande à les voir : « Reviens-je plus libre et plus sage que je ne suis parti ? J'ose le croire et ne puis l'affirmer. La même image règne toujours dans mon cœur » (p. 288). Wolmar invite lui-même Saint-Preux dans sa maison : « L'innocence et la paix y règnent ; vous y trouverez l'amitié, l'hospitalité, l'estime, la confiance. Consultez votre cœur, et s'il n'y a rien là qui vous effraye, venez sans crainte » (p. 289). Claire ajoute : « Il [Wolmar] fait plus, il prétend vous guérir, et dit que ni Julie, ni lui, ni vous, ni moi ne pouvons être heureux sans cela » (p. 290).

Saint-Preux quitte l'Angleterre sans avoir vu Bomston qui est occupé de ses affaires, et qui ira plus tard en Italie. Lui se rend à Clarens. Émotion considérable en approchant de la maison de Julie, et confirmation de l'incertitude sur sa guérison : « Le cœur me battit fortement... mouvement d'effroi... terreur... tumulte universel... » (p. 292). Ce fut d'abord, quand ils furent dans les bras l'un de l'autre « un transport sacré », et « les tendres prémisses d'une amitié pure et sainte que nous emporterons dans le ciel ». Arrivent les enfants : « Que devins-je à cet aspect... O spectacle ! ô regrets ! Je me sentis déchiré de douleur et transporté de joie » ; c'était « la trop vive preuve qu'elle ne m'était plus rien » (p. 293). Toutefois il les embrasse de bon cœur, et « je commençais tout de bon à bien augurer de moi ». Puis les voici seuls un moment : « nouvel embarras, le plus pénible et le moins prévu de tous » (p. 294) : Mais voici Wolmar qui revient et lui serre la main en disant : « Embrassez votre sœur et amie ; traitez la toujours comme telle ». La confiance revient encore, jusqu'à ce que, « le soir, en me retirant, je passai devant la chambre des maîtres de la maison, je les y vis entrer ensemble : je gagnai tristement la mienne » (p. 295). En terminant sa lettre à Bomston, il dit : « Quelque doux qu'il me soit d'habiter cette maison, je l'ai résolu, je le jure, si je m'aperçois jamais que je m'y plais trop, j'en sortirai dans l'instant » (p. 296).

Quant à Julie, nous l'apprenons par sa lettre à Claire, elle est — malgré les apparences — plus craintive encore que Saint-Preux : « Ma chère, il faut tout dire : ces marques [de petite vérole, indice de l'amour éperdu de Saint-Preux] me font quelque peine à regarder, et je me surprends souvent à les regarder malgré moi même » (p. 297) ; elle s'impose de montrer toutes ses lettres à Wolmar — qui du reste refuse de les voir.

Claire répond : « je ne comptais que sur ta vertu, et je com-

mence à compter aussi sur ta raison ; je regarde à présent ta guérision sinon comme parfaite, au moins comme facile, et tu en as précisément assez fait pour te rendre inexcusable si tu n'achèves pas » (301).

Visite de Saint-Preux à Lausanne, chez Claire, qui n'ose le loger dans sa maison, cédant « en cette occasion, sans savoir pourquoi », aux « serviles bienséances » (ceci, en vue de ce que Rousseau dévelopera dans les Ve et VIe parties, l'amour de Claire pour Saint-Preux, p. 445 ss). Saint-Preux ramène à Clarens la fillette de Claire ; celle-ci suivra plus tard (p. 305).

Dans les lettres suivantes, — fort longues — Saint-Preux décrit « le spectacle agréable et touchant... d'une maison simple et bien réglée, où règnent l'ordre, la paix, l'innocence ; où l'on voit réuni sans apparat, sans éclat, tout ce qui répond à la véritable destination de l'homme ! » (p. 306) ; « où on ne voit rien qui n'associe l'agréable à l'utile » (p. 328), — bref, le bonheur de Julie. Notons en passant que dans ce roman de mœurs *suisses*, on retrouve à tout moment l'opposition des mœurs françaises et anglaises (par exemple p. 315, 320).

Lettre de l'Elysée. La lettre XI est fort importante ; c'est la fameuse lettre de l'Élysée où Saint-Preux apprend à connaître la Julie vertueuse. L'Élysée est une sorte de lieu consacré au recueillement et à la méditation ; tout y est disposé pour oublier les hommes ; c'est « le Jardin anglais » opposé au « jardin français » : « Vous ne voyez rien d'aligné, rien de nivelé ; jamais le cordeau n'entra dans ce lieu ; la nature ne plante rien au cordeau » (p. 334). Julie, Wolmar et Saint-Preux s'y promènent, parlent des délices de cette retraite, en compagnie des fleurs — et des oiseaux qui nichent librement :

« Madame, repris-je (Saint-Preux) assez tristement, vous êtes épouse et mère ; ce sont des plaisirs qu'il vous appartient de connaître. Aussitôt M. de Wolmar me prenant par la main me dit en la serrant : Vous avez des amis et ces amis ont des enfants ; comment l'affection paternelle vous serait-elle étrangère ». Je le regardai ; je regardai Julie : tous deux se regardèrent et me rendirent un re-

gard si touchant que, les embrassant l'un après l'autre, je leur dis
avec attendrissement : Ils me sont aussi chers qu'à vous. Je ne sais
par quel bizarre effet un mot peut ainsi changer une âme ; mais depuis ce moment M. de Wolmar me paraît un autre homme, et je
vois en lui moins le mari de celle que j'ai tant aimée que le père de
deux enfants pour lesquels je donnerais ma vie » (p. 333).

*Cependant autre-fois ce jardin anglais, après tout, un ouvrage
artificiel selon la nature, n'était pas là. Saint-Preux dit à ce
propos :* « Je n'ai qu'un reproche à votre Elysée, mais qui vous
paraîtra grave ; c'est d'être un amusement superflu. A quoi bon
vous faire une nouvelle promenade, ayant de l'autre côté de la
maison des bosquets si charmants et si négligés ?

*— Il est vrai, dit-elle, un peu embarrassée, mais j'aime mieux
ceci.*

*— Si vous aviez bien songé à votre question avant de la faire,
interrompit M. de Wolmar, elle serait plus qu'indiscrète. Jamais
ma femme depuis son mariage n'a mis les pieds dans les bosquets dont vous parlez. J'en sais la raison quoiqu'elle me l'ait
toujours tue. Vous qui ne l'ignorez pas, apprenez à respecter
les lieux où vous êtes ; ils sont plantés par les mains de la vertu »*
(p. 338).

*— Dans ces bosquets-là Julie avait donné à Saint-Preux le
baiser d'amour. Revenu le lendemain seul à l'Elysée, Saint-
Preux songe à cette dernière remarque :* « Le souvenir de ce seul
mot a changé sur le champ tout l'état de mon âme. J'ai cru voir
l'image de la vertu où je cherchais celle du plaisir : cette image
s'est confondue dans mon esprit avec les traits de Mme de Wolmar » *(p. 339). Et,* « j'ai trouvé qu'il y a dans la méditation des
pensées honnêtes une sorte de bien être que les méchants n'ont
jamais connu, c'est celui de se plaire avec soi-même » *(p. 340).*

*Qu'ici le lecteur soit particulièrement attentif ; car c'est ici
que les remaniements semblent avoir été profonds. La lettre XII
montre Julie et Saint-Preux mis à l'épreuve. Wolmar lui-même
entraîne les deux amants d'autrefois dans le bosquet du premier
baiser. C'est Julie qui écrit à Claire :* « Il nous a menés dans ce
même bosquet où commencèrent tous les malheurs de ma vie.

*En approchant de ce lieu fatal, je me suis senti un affreux batte-
ment de cœur, et j'aurais refusé d'entrer si la honte ne m'eût
retenue et si le souvenir d'un mot qui fut dit l'autre jour dans
l'Elysée [celui que nous avons rapporté] ne m'eût fait craindre
les interprétations. Je ne sais si le philosophe était plus tranquille, mais quelque temps après, ayant par hasard tourné les
yeux sur lui, je l'ai trouvé pâle, changé, et je ne puis te dire
quelle peine tout cela m'a fait »* (p. 342). *Wolmar s'assied entre
les deux, et raconte sa vie, esquisse son portrait d'homme de
raison* : « *J'ai naturellement l'âme tranquille et le cœur froid.
Je suis de ces hommes qu'on croit injurier en disant qu'ils ne
sentent rien, c'est-à-dire qu'ils n'ont point de passion qui les
détourne de suivre le vrai guide de l'homme (la raison). Peu
sensible au plaisir et à la douleur... mon seul principe actif est
le goût de l'ordre ; et le concours combiné du jeu de la fortune
et des actions des hommes me plaît exactement comme une belle
symétrie dans un tableau, ou comme une pièce bien construite
au théâtre »* (p. 342). *Cependant Julie l'a ému, et il l'a épousée,
sachant du reste toute son histoire* : « *J'osai croire à la vertu et
vous épousai* » (p. 345). *Et maintenant, il arrive à un plan qu'il a
formé* : « *Le seul tort que je vous trouve est de n'avoir pu reprendre
en vous la confiance que vous vous devez, et de vous estimer moins
que votre prix »* (p. 345). *Il veut la guérison, se fondant sur ce
qu'il n'y a* « *rien de bien qu'on n'obtienne des belles âmes avec
de la confiance et de la franchise »* (p. 346). *Et, première séance
de guérison* : « *En se levant, il nous embrassa et voulut que nous
nous embrassions aussi dans ce lieu... dans ce lieu même où
jadis... Claire, ô bonne Claire, combien tu m'as toujours aimée !
Je n'en fis aucune difficulté ; hélas, que j'aurais eu tort d'en
faire ! Ce baiser n'eut rien de celui qui m'avait rendu le bosquet
redoutable : je m'en félicitai* tristement (!?) *et je connus que
mon cœur était plus changé que jusque-là je n'avais osé le croire »*
(p. 346).

En s'en retournant Wolmar annonce la grande tentation :
il part, sous prétexte d'affaires, pour Étanges, y restera cinq
ou six jours, laissant Julie et Saint-Preux livrés à eux mêmes.

Julie alarmée, écrit tout de suite la chose à Claire : « Mon cœur est pur, ma conscience est tranquille... en un mot, je trouve que je n'ai pas même besoin du secours de la vertu pour être paisible en sa présence, et que quand l'horreur du crime n'existerait pas, les sentiments qu'elle a détruits auraient bien de la peine à renaître ». D'autre part : « je n'ignore pas que nulle considération ne peut être mise en balance avec un réel danger ; mais ce danger existe-t-il en effet ? Voilà précisément le doute que tu dois résoudre » (p. 348). Claire répond une longue lettre, et en appelle une fois encore simultanément à la vertu *et à la* raison *: « Ah, Julie, croirai-je qu'après tant de tourments et de peine, douze [?] ans de pleurs et six ans de gloire te laissent redouter une épreuve de huit jours ? En deux mots, sois sincère avec toi-même : si le péril existe, sauve ta personne et rougis de ton cœur ; s'il n'existe pas, c'est outrager ta raison, c'est flétrir ta vertu que de craindre un danger qui ne peut l'atteindre » (p. 351).*

Wolmar avant de partir, écrit à Claire qu'il pense faire de Saint-Preux le précepteur de ses enfants (p. 354), et explique que son plan doit révéler aux deux amoureux d'autrefois qu'ils sont guéris.

La lettre XIV apprend à Saint-Preux que Julie n'est pas heureuse ; son mari est incrédule, telle est la raison qu'elle en donne ; puis : « Mon cher ami, il n'y a point de vrai bonheur sur la terre. J'ai pour mari le plus honnête et le plus doux des hommes ...j'ai des enfants qui ne donnent et ne promettent que du plaisir à leur mère... (elle a Claire, elle a Saint-Preux lui-même)... Favorisée en toutes choses du ciel, de la fortune et des hommes, je vois tout concourir à mon bonheur. Un chagrin, un seul chagrin l'empoisonne. Je ne suis pas heureuse »...

Puis, Lettre XVI, ou plutôt billet de Julie : « Wolmar, il est vrai je crois mériter votre estime ; mais votre conduite n'en est pas plus convenable et vous jouissez durement de la vertu de votre femme » (p. 359).

Lettre de la Promenade sur le Lac. La promenade sur le lac, décrite Lettre XVII avait eu lieu. Le vent avait poussé Julie et Saint-Preux vers Meillerie ; ils avaient visité les lieux d'où il avait écrit les lettres les plus brûlantes à Julie au plus fort de leurs amours. Elle avait trouvé son chiffre et des vers amoureux gravés sur les arbres ; elle avait saisi la main de son compagnon (p. 363).

... « Puis, tout à coup, détournant la vue et me tirant par le bras : Allons-nous en, mon ami, me dit-elle d'une voix émue ; l'air de ce lieu n'est pas bon pour moi. Je partis en gémissant... » (p. 363).

Ils s'en retournent sur le lac, calmé et éclairé par la lune. Et, Saint-Preux songeait :

« C'en est fait... ces temps heureux ne sont plus ; ils ont disparu pour jamais. Hélas ! Ils ne reviendront plus ; et nous vivons, et nous sommes ensemble, et nos cœurs sont toujours unis !... Je me mis à verser des torrents de larmes... Quand je me trouvai bien remis, je revins auprès de Julie ; je repris sa main. Elle tenait son mouchoir ; je le sentis fort mouillé : Ah ! lui dis-je tout bas, je vois que nos cœurs n'ont jamais cessé de s'entendre ! Il est vrai, dit-elle d'une voix altérée ; mais que ce soit la dernière fois qu'ils auront parlé sur ce ton » (p. 365).

En terminant sa lettre, Saint-Preux dit à Bomston :

« J'espère qu'elles [ces émotions] seront la crise qui me rendra tout à fait à moi... Au reste, je vous dirai que cette aventure m'a plus convaincu que tous les arguments, de la liberté de l'homme et du mérite de la vertu... O Edouard... sans toi j'étais perdu peut-être. Cent fois dans ce jour périlleux, le souvenir de ta vertu m'a rendu la mienne » (p. 365).

Ajoutons les premiers mots de la Lettre 2, — de la Cinquième Partie — qui sert de transition :

« Oui, milord, je vous le confirme avec des transports de joie, la scène de Meillerie a été la crise de mes folies et de mes maux » (p. 368).

§ 4. Nous pouvons ici nous arrêter pour faire, d'après le résumé de ces quatre parties, et d'après ce que nous avons par ailleurs (correspondance, *Confessions*, et événements de sa vie), l'histoire de *la Nouvelle Héloïse*. Nous n'aurons pas toujours des preuves « documentaires » pour cette sorte de reconstitution psychologique du travail intérieur de Rousseau au cours de la rédaction ; nous en manquerons même pour quelques points surtout importants ; rappelons enfin que nous n'avons même pas vu les brouillons qui pourraient à l'occasion confirmer ou infirmer nos interprétations — ayant en vain essayé de forcer les portes de la Bibliothèque des Députés. Mais nous croyons que les arguments internes sur lesquels nous nous appuyons ne manquent pas de solidité (1).

La nouvelle héloïse avant le roman moral

Nous passons rapidement sur les deux premières phases de l'histoire, c'est-à-dire avant que Rousseau en soit arrivé au roman didactique.

Première phase : *Les lettres d'amour*. — Cette phase initiale est indiquée nettement par Rousseau lui-même ; et ces lettres, il ne les retouche guère, il l'a dit également ; et cela pour des raisons purement littéraires (en sorte de leur garder leur caractère spontané). C'est du romantisme, et du romantisme purement lyrique.

On peut cependant se poser la question : N'y-a-t-il pas dès ces premières lettres, à côté des sentiments idylliques, quelques

---

(1) Nous sommes d'ailleurs trop disposés de nos jours à nous laisser enchaîner — en refusant de considérer d'autres preuves que les externes, et nous nous méfions trop des évidences internes. Rappelons, par exemple, que M. Ritter avait déduit fort bien, par une simple lecture attentive des *Confessions* et de la correspondance de Rousseau, la falsification des *Mémoires d'Epinay* — Mme Macdonald n'a fait que confirmer par le document ce qui était prouvé déjà. Et nous avions nous-même pu conclure à la superposition de deux rédactions des premières pages de la *Profession de foi*, avant que P.-M. Massonn'ait mis la main sur les brouillons d'*Emile* qui ont démontré la chose par la vue en quelque sorte.

données ajoutées après coup, — celle par exemple de l'obstacle à l'amour de Julie et Saint-Preux ? Il n'y a pas lieu de le penser. Car l'introduction de cet élément après coup aurait entraîné une modification assez sérieuse dans les textes pour que cette spontanéité première à laquelle Rousseau tenait tant, fût sérieusement compromise. D'ailleurs, l'obstacle ne donne-t-il pas à l'amour en quelque sorte le sel littéraire ? N'est-ce pas lui qui permet de pousser jusqu'au paroxysme de l'émotion le thème lyrique ? L'amour béat, entraînerait l'ennui ou le sourire indulgent ; l'amour ingénu, légitime dans les conditions d'existence de Paul et Virginie, ne serait pas de saison ici. En outre, si Rousseau dit qu'il a conservé ces lettres à peu près intactes, il dit aussi qu'il a songé dès le début en les écrivant à Mlles Galley et de Graffenried ; or, par ailleurs nous savons bien que Rousseau avait pensé au mariage avec l'une d'elles. On sait enfin que Rousseau avait abandonné pour se mettre à *la Nouvelle Héloïse* un autre récit commencé *Le roman de Claire et de Marcelin* où la question de mésalliance paraît aux premières pages (1).

Deuxième phase : *Le roman mondain, frivole, le « livre efféminé »* (VIII, p. 311). — Comme il y aura encore trois conceptions du roman successivement superposées à celle-ci, ce seraient de véritables fouilles qu'il faudrait entreprendre sous le texte final pour la reconstituer à peu près. Nous ne nous proposons pas d'opérer ces fouilles ; aussi bien ce n'est pas nécessaire ; cette phase n'est guère plus intéressante pour notre examen philosophique que celle des lettres d'amour ; et ce serait un travail fastidieux pour le lecteur comme pour nous. Passons donc rapidement : Qui dit roman dans ces années-là, dit « roman anglais » ; et c'est bien une imitation de ce genre que Rousseau devait appeler « livre efféminé ». C'est avec Diderot, le coryphée de Richardson, qu'il s'était enthousiasmé pour les Anglais et surtout pour certains de

---

(1) Voir Strechkheisen-Moultou, *Œuvres et correspondance inédites de Rousseau*, 1861, « Le roman de Claire et de Marcelin », pp. 265-273. Voir aussi Lettre à Deleyre, 26 août 1756.

leurs romans. C'est chez Diderot qu'il avait fait la connaissance de Prévost, l'auteur de *Manon* et de *Cleveland* et dont
le nom revient sous sa plume à plusieurs reprises (« homme
très aimable et très simple, dont le cœur vivifiait les écrits
dignes de l'immortalité »). Rousseau proclama qu'on n'avait
« jamais fait encore, en quelque langue que ce soit, de roman
égal à Clarisse, ni même approchant » (I, p. 231). Ce jugement
exprimé, dans une note à la *Lettre à d'Alembert* et auquel il
fait du reste plus tard de sérieuses réserves, paraît trahir un
mouvement d'enthousiasme après une première lecture ;
Clarisse avait paru en français en 1751, d'après Texte, en
1753 d'après Dobson. En 1756-7, d'autre part, avait paru pour
la première fois en français le *Grandison* de Richardson qui
nous paraît avoir fourni un prototype de Lord Bomston plus
que n'importe quel grand seigneur anglais alors fameux dans
le roman européen. C'est peut-être bien la lecture de *Grandison*
et son intention de s'en servir pour Bomston qui a suggéré à
Rousseau de demander (ce même hiver 1756-7) à Deleyre, de
lui envoyer Muralt, *Lettres sur les Français et sur les Anglais...*
Dans sa lettre du 2 novembre, Deleyre écrit qu'il enverra le
volume après l'avoir lu. Rousseau lui-même l'aura lu dans
le courant de 1757. Comme on l'a démontré maintes fois avant
et depuis Texte, c'est une combinaison des effets de la lecture
de Prévost, Richardson et Muralt que nous avons dans le
tableau des Anglais et de l'Angleterre auquel Rousseau se
complait dans la *Nouvelle Héloïse* (1). L'opposition des « vertus
anglaises » à la frivolité des Français était très nettement indiquée et développée dans Muralt, et elle était trop selon les
sentiments de Rousseau à cette époque pour que celui-ci se
privât de faire usage d'un observateur de première main.

De sorte que nous nous représentons la conception du « roman efféminé » (nous disons *conception* car nous ne savons pas

---

(1) Parmi les discussions plus récentes sur les prototypes possibles de Bomston
(Cleveland, de Prevost, Morden, de la *Clarissa*, et Grandison, de Richardson,
par exemple) ,citons celle de Geo R. Havens. Voir le résumé du débat *Annales
Rousseau*, Vol. XIII, p. 247-8.

jusqu'à quel point il avait été réellement rédigé) telle qu'elle demeura enterrée sous les conceptions subséquentes, comme un roman ayant le programme et jusqu'à un certain point l'esprit anglicisant à la mode. D'abord des aventures d'amour, aventures assez théâtrales volontiers, au cours de voyages un peu par tout le monde et surtout en Italie où la froide nature anglaise trouvait son complément dans la chaude atmosphère des passions italiennes (—ces aventures étant un dernier écho des grandes aventures des romans précieux du XVIIᵉ siècle) ; ensuite sentimentalité à haute dose, — pas sentimentalité précieuse qui n'est qu'intellectuelle en quelque sorte, jeu d'esprit, mais sentimentalité passionnée, voluptueuse, un peu sauvage et primitive dans son tréfonds, violente — (Julie malade d'amour, espérant mourir ou être défigurée par la maladie pour être délivrée de l'amour du prétendant odieux, l'amant retournant en cachette auprès de la malade en délire, et espérant dans ses baisers s'inoculer à son tour la maladie, résolution de suicide, etc.) ; enfin ayant comme héros, ou au moins comme personnage de premier plan, le gentleman anglais ; — ce gentleman qui, d'un part, et jusque dans ses moindres actions, gestes et paroles, appartient au tout grand monde, qui d'autre part est au-dessus des conventions sociales, c'est-à-dire sait exactement quand il faut les observer, et quand il est légitime de s'en affranchir ; bref « homme de qualité », le « philosophe anglais » M. Cleveland et qui n'a pas honte d'être « fils naturel de Cromwell », — et qui s'appellera chez Rousseau Lord Bomston.

Le roman lui-même se façonne à peu près sur le roman de Clarissa Harlowe ; et Julie et Claire se décalquent de Mˡˡᵉ Galley et de Graffenried pour s'apparenter à Clarissa Harlowe et Nancy Howe ; le père sévère et inflexible se précise et prend les traits du père de Clarisse ; et la mère faible et tendre prend corps à son tour. Jamais Rousseau cependant, ne semble avoir songé à prendre dans son roman, ni un dégoûtant Roger Holmes, ni une franche canaille mondaine comme Lovelace (1).

(1) De même du reste dans les aventures du roman. Rousseau n'a pas cédé

Est-ce que le rival de Saint-Preux était déjà un sage Wolmar. ou n'était-ce pas plutôt le gentilhomme anglais, Bomston ? Impossible de le savoir. Le fragment en appendice de la Julie, « Les amours de Milors Bomsaton » et qui rappelle pas mal les aventures du Colonel Morden dans *Clarissa* et de Lord Grandison en Italie, était-il un écho ou un reste du roman effé miné » ; ou est-ce que d'emblée le gentleman anglais après avoir noblement cédé devant Saint-Preux, l'amoureux na ture, devait continuer ses aventures en Italie avec la marquise dont il tue le mari en duel mais qu'il refuse d'épouser à cause du sang qu'il y a maintenant entre lui et elle, puis avec la courtisane Laurette qui l'aime tant qu'elle va chercher re fuge dans un couvent pour fuir la tentation de déshonorer son Lord anglais par un mariage avec elle (1) — nous n'en savons pas davantage. Peu importe : du point de vue des idées de Rousseau, le roman depuis le moment où son auteur se décide à le traiter autrement que comme un jeu de son imagination romanesque et un simple objet de délassement au milieu de travaux plus austères, demeure seul intéressant.

Comme retouches faites par suite du passage de la première phase — des « Lettres d'amour » tout court — à la deuxième, du « roman efféminé », nous n'avons à retenir que l'intrigue ; celle-ci se précise sur le modèle de Clarissa Harlowe, et amène l'introduction du personnage de Lord Bomston avec le cor tège de l'anglomanie ; et peut-être l'insertion, à la fin d'une

---

au goût encore prévalant d'épisodes sensationnels ; la question d'argent joue un rôle passager et Rousseau insiste davantage sur la question de naissance ; pas d'enlèvement, pas de drogues soporifiques, pas de maison de prostituées pour Julie, pas de prison ; seulement un épisode de duel — évité du reste — et un enfant noyé avec un sauvetage émouvant... et encore est-ce pour amener une fin au roman.

(1) La sentimentalité de ce monde si aristocratique ont été poussés aux der nières limites par Rousseau ; ainsi la belle Laurette n'avait-elle pas été offerte à Bomston par la marquise elle-même quand celle-ci avait dû renoncer à être sa maîtresse, et offerte pour qu'il ait quelque chose comme compensation pour sa grande vertu : Laurette physiquement ressemblait comme une sœur à la marquise !

des lettres amoureuses (I, 22), des quelques lignes annonçant l'existence de Wolmar, le futur époux de Julie :

« Adieu, mon ami. Je ne puis m'entretenir plus longtemps avec vous. Vous savez de quelles précautions j'ai besoin pour écrire. Ce n'est pas tout ; mon père a amené un étranger respectable, son ancien ami, et qui lui a sauvé autrefois la vie à la guerre. Jugez si nous nous sommes efforcés de le bien recevoir. Il repart demain... On m'appelle : il faut finir. Adieu de rechef » (p. 49).

Un argument qui ferait peut être croire à la présence déjà dans le plan du roman efféminé et anglais, d'un autre rival à Saint-Preux que Bomston, serait que Rousseau se souvient positivement que la lettre de l'Élysée et celle du Lac avaient été écrites avant la phase du roman efféminé (VIII, p. 315) ; et on ne conçoit pas du tout la première au moins de ces lettres, avec Lord Bomston comme mari. Autrement, la petite cheville de la mention de Wolmar aurait été introduite au moment de la rédaction correspondant à une des phases du roman sérieux, soit la troisième, soit la quatrième.

Il y a d'autre part des restes du roman « anglais » qui sont en eux-mêmes bien inutiles aux versions postérieures, mais qui ont été adaptés au nouveau roman, — Rousseau, on le sait, n'en est pas à quelques digressions près. Il y a par exemple l'épisode du duel entre Saint-Preux et Bomston, un peu bien sensationnel quand on ne cherche pas le romanesque. Il y a aussi celui de Besançon, quand Saint-Preux soupçonne Bomston d'avoir voulu l'éloigner de Julie en sorte que lui, Bomston, puisse ensuite aller la courtiser ; le raccordement, du reste, est excellent ici.

LA NOUVELLE HÉLOÏSE, ROMAN SÉRIEUX

§ 5. A partir d'ici nous pouvons, croyons-nous, devenir beaucoup moins imprécis.

TROISIÈME PHASE DU ROMAN : *Morale romantique*. — Tout d'abord, quand Rousseau s'est proposé de faire un roman utile, c'est-à-dire non frivole et non « efféminé », il paraît s'être

senti impérieusement sollicité par la vieille vertu calviniste et
romaine du renoncement ; il s'abandonne sans méfiance ; et
nous assistons à un flirt prolongé — et de temps en temps
même renouvelé encore après — avec la muse du *Premier
Discours*. Il était très monté contre les « philosophes » qui
prêchaient sans vergogne la morale dangereuse du plaisir
sans restriction, et il affirme en proportion sa réaction en sens
contraire. Il y a une raison personnelle aussi : la passion pour
Mme d'Houdetot le tenait alors, et il s'exalte dans sa résolution de sacrifier son amour à celui de Saint-Lambert ; et il est
en train d'écrire les « lettres morales » à Sophie ; bref il se met
dans l'état d'esprit qui lui dictera bientôt sa philippique contre
la passion de l'amour dans la *Lettre à d'Alembert*. Dans ces
dispositions, fatalement en quelque sorte, la vertu de Julie
sera en vertu de renoncment : où serait sa « vertu » si elle pouvait trouver le bonheur dans le mariage avec Wolmar et dans
l'éloignement de Saint-Preux ? Sa supériorité consistera donc
à consommer ce « sacrifice héroïque auquel nous sommes tous
deux appelés », comme elle le dit à Saint-Preux.

Les deux lettres, de l'Élysée (IV, 11) et du Lac (IV, 17)
déjà écrites, se prêtaient tout à fait à cet esprit : plus le sacrifice était plus grand, plus les lettres étaient émouvantes pour
le lecteur.

Une sorte d'aveu de Rousseau lui-même qu'il a bien été
séduit de nouveau, au moins momentanément, par la vertu
de renoncement, c'est que douze ou treize ans après il mentionne la *Princesse de Clèves* à propos justement de la IVe partie où ces deux lettres sont essentielles : « Je mets sans crainte
la IVe partie à côté de la *Princesse de Clèves* » (*Confessions*,
IX, vol. IX, p. 2). Et qu'est-ce que cette Julie là sinon encore
la « romaine » Pauline de Corneille, cédant dans un esprit de
désintéressement complet à l'autorité paternelle, et épousant
celui qu'elle n'aime pas. Ajoutons que Rousseau nous a laissé
des fragments d'une *Lucrèce* (Vol. V, 177-180) ; il y a des raisons de penser que c'était lors de son voyage à Genève, en
1754, qu'il y avait travaillé, donc pas très longtemps avant
d'avoir rêvé d'une Julie (cf. VIII, p. 281), et il est bien pos-

sible que le souvenir en ait agi sur lui au moment où il tâton-
nait pour trouver une conception « vertueuse » de son roman ;
il fait une véritable orgie du mot « vertu » dans ces fragments.

Mais ce mouvement de retour ne pouvait durer, et ces flirts
avec l'idée du devoir austère étaient pareils à ceux que nous
avons relevés dans la *Lettre à d'Alembert*, lorsqu'au milieu
de ses éloges des montagnons neuchâtelois et des bourgeois
de Genève, il oublie qu'il est en train de prouver que ceux-ci
grâce à leur vie simple, sont *heureux*, et que dès lors le mot de
« vertu » qu'il emploie pour eux est susceptible d'interprétation calviniste ou romaine. En fait, Rousseau était trop loin
engagé dans la théorie du bonheur comme but de la vie pour
réellement y renoncer plus jamais sérieusement ; et, en vérité,
il mettra sa passion à chercher où est le *bonheur* de Julie et
non sa souffrance. En effet avant que ses héros aient écrit
de nombreuses lettres, l'auteur opère une nouvelle volte-face,
tournant le dos à l'esprit romain de renoncement et s'abandonnant à ces dispositions romantiques qui sont au cœur de
tout homme ; il semble oublier même momentanément que
ce sera pour une fois de plus rencontrer ces chaînes de la loi
morale qui, pour être les vrais garants du bonheur, sont cependant parfois désagréables. A vrai dire, jamais il n'aura été
plus éloquent que dans les lettres où il justifie Saint-Preux et
Julie dans leur résistance aux lois et coutumes de la société
pour s'abandonner à la voix de la passion : Si « naturelle » est
sa morale des droits de l'amour, si fortement présentée, que
la génération romantique n'a retenu que cela dans *la Nouvelle
Héloïse* (c'est elle qui a dicté à Lamartine son mot célèbre
« Grands Dieux ! Quel livre ! Comme c'est écrit. Je suis étonné
que le feu n'y prenne pas »), et que jusqu'aujourd'hui les
manuels de littérature enseignent que *la Nouvelle Héloïse* a proclamé les droits de l'amour dans le mariage par opposition au
mariage de raison... et un point, c'est tout (1). C'est là que

---

(1) Et les Seillière, les Babbitt exploitent cette interprétation traditionnelle,
si manifestement insuffisante, dans leurs attaques contre les manques de Rousseau romantique.

nous avons ces phrases passionnées (voir résumé ci-dessus) :
Saint-Preux à Julie qui hésite :

« Un arrêt éternel du ciel nous fit l'un pour l'autre ; c'est la première loi qu'il faut écouter... ta vertu n'est plus qu'un délire »
(p. 61).

Julie :

« Mon père m'a donc vendue (à Wolmar) ; il fait de sa fille une
marchandise, une esclave ! Il s'acquitte à mes dépens ; il paie sa
vie de la mienne » (p. 62).

Claire reprochant à Julie son abattement devant son père :

« Abattement dangereux qui t'avilirait plus que ta faiblesse. Le
véritable amour est-il fait pour dégrader l'âme ? » (p. 65).

Saint-Preux après la chute :

« Qu'as-tu fait que les lois divines et humaines ne puissent et ne
doivent autoriser... ô mon épouse, ô ma digne et chaste compagne !»
(p. 67).

C'est là que le père fait tout pour s'attirer notre réprobation : « Volage » qui tue sa femme de chagrin par ses infidélités et sa « rudesse inflexible » (p. 222-3) ; souffletant sa fille
qui résiste à la proposition d'épouser Wolmar (IX, p. 120) ;
écrivant une lettre d'une brutalité révoltante d'un « gentilhomme » à un homme « qui ne l'est pas », à Saint-Preux, le
« suborneur », le « premier venu ». C'est là enfin que nous allons
voir assumer un rôle de premier plan à l'anglais Bomston.
Le « Lord » ne sera plus un simple amoureux de Julie, grand
seigneur dans ses manières, éblouissant de correction, le point
de mire de tous les regards dès qu'il paraît ; il devient *philosophe*. Bomston sera le porte-parole de Rousseau, et celui qui
par ses actes autant que par son éloquence donnera sa sanction aux idées émancipatrices de Julie et de Saint-Preux ; il
va prêter à la « nature » la splendeur de son nom, de sa position sociale, de son argent. Du rôle de simple Lovelace qu'il

jouait probablement dans la conception du roman mondain — Lovelace assurément sans vices, mais aussi, à part la séduction de ses manières, sans « vertu » — il devient le rival généreux qui s'incline devant le sentiment naturel d'amour, et par conséquent acquiert comme un droit indiscutable à juger posément des choses de l'amour.

La transformation du personnage de l'Anglais — la retouche, comme nous avons dit — est tout à fait habile ; et peut-être ce mot *habile* n'est-il même pas le bon ; car quelques traits de plume suffisaient en quelque sorte. C'était en effet une partie déjà du caractère anglais que la tradition avait forgée si rapidement, que le « gentleman » d'Outre-Manche se distinguât par sa franchise à l'endroit des conventions sociales, et par son courage à laisser parler la raison plus haut que les coutumes ; c'était *au nom de la raison* qu'il invoquait des arguments romantiques, dits de la nature. Or, dans le cas particulier de Julie, tel que Rousseau le concevait dans son histoire en ce moment, la raison semblait en effet appuyer la nature « romantique », tandis que les considérations de fortune et de nom pouvaient être taxées « d'odieux préjugés », et donner lieu aux protestations passionnées des amants et de leur protecteur.

Celui qui a lu dans l'esprit dans lequel nous avons essayé de le faire, la *Lettre à d'Alembert*, et connaît la manière de voir de Rousseau réfléchi, sait bien ce qu'il y a de spécieux dans tout cela et comment Rousseau revenu à lui-même saura montrer que la révolte à fond de train contre la tradition sociale est à courte vue : Bomston manifeste justement cette raison insuffisamment réfléchie des « philosophes » contre lesquels Rousseau mettait en garde, et à laquelle il opposait la raison mieux informée : Ces deux arguments, de la fortune et du rang, qui pouvaient aller à l'encontre du bonheur dans ce cas particulier, pouvaient dans un autre cas au contraire empêcher une tragédie ; c'est précisément ce que démontrait le roman de Richardson (il est vrai qu'il l'eût démontré mieux si le père de Clarissa n'avait pas été présenté comme un odieux tyran) : tous les amoureux ne sont pas de touchants enthousiastes comme Saint-Preux, mais souvent des Lovelace. Maint roturier comme Saint-Preux n'aurait vu dans l'amour que son côté sensuel ; comme vice-versa s'il y avait des nobles canailles comme Lovelace, cela n'empêchait pas que la supériorité mentale, donc morale, de la classe noble ne fût peut-être normalement supérieure aussi.

D'ailleurs c'était réduire le problème de mariage à des proportions bien étroites de ne considérer que les obstacles de fortune et de rang ; et là sans doute Bomston pouvait réclamer toute notre sympathie pour son éloquence ; mais Rousseau laissait supposer qu'il n'y en avait pas d'autres ; et justement il devait s'en présenter.

C'est ici qu'il convient de placer deux mots sur la question de la sincérité de Rousseau. Le fait est certain qu'il a été amené à abandonner plus loin dans le roman cette attitude sur le rôle exclusif de l'amour dans le mariage ; mais cela ne saurait signifier qu'il n'a pas, à un moment donné, vraiment cru à la théorie égalitaire et « naturelle » de Bomston. Il serait fastidieux de prouver la chose à coup de citations ; du reste il a été obligé plus tard d'atténuer par endroits les paroles qu'il met dans les lettres de Bomston, d'introduire des réserves, etc ; bref, d'adapter celles-ci en quelque manière en sorte d'éviter des incohérences flagrantes. Mais telles qu'elles sont, il suffit de lire attentivement les scènes où Bomston intervient : l'impression qui se dégage est sans contestation possible celle de la sincérité : un auteur présente-t-il si fortement une cause qu'il compte réfuter ensuite ? Et notons que Julie sera même obligée d'avouer à Saint-Preux, quand elle lui raconte comment son père l'a convaincue d'épouser Wolmar : « Je ne manquais pas de bonnes raisons à opposer à ce discours » (p. 242). Ce qui revient à dire : Moi, Rousseau, je n'ai pas réussi à réfuter Rousseau. En effet, s'il avait eu d'emblée l'intention de blâmer Julie d'aimer Saint-Preux et de se révolter contre les arguments opposés à son bonheur par un père féru de préjugés, il devait employer d'autres arguments ; s'il ne l'a pas fait, c'est que quand il écrivait cela, il ne se souciait

pas de se réserver aucune porte de sortie. Et nous osons ris-
quer l'idée que c'est partiellement parce qu'il a trouvé sa position si irréfutable dans ces pages, qu'il n'a pas pu se résoudre à supprimer davantage des lettres bomstonniennes dans
le roman définitif. Il devait demeurer quelque chose de *vrai*
dans le plaidoyer de Saint-Preux, Julie, et Bomston, — et
donc on *devait* pouvoir le laisser.

QUATRIÈME PHASE DU ROMAN : *Morale de la vertu sagesse.* —
La ligne de démarcation entre les deux phases du roman tel
que Rousseau les veut distinguer — à savoir I, celle du roman
frivole et « efféminé », c'est-à-dire de Julie amante, et II, celle
du roman moral, c'est-à-dire celle de Julie, épouse modèle
qui fait oublier l'autre, — est très abrupte ; elle se trouve à la
Lettre 17 de la IIIᵉ partie, *De Claire à Saint-Preux* :

« Votre amante n'est plus... Julie est mariée et digne de rendre
heureux l'honnête homme qui vient d'unir son sort au sien... Après
tant d'imprudences, rendez grâce au ciel qui vous a sauvés tous
deux... (p. 234).

Nous avons voulu montrer qu'il y avait bien plus de variations que cela au cours de la rédaction, qu'il y avait eu d'abord
l'histoire inventée simplement comme prétexte des lettres
d'amour, et puis le roman anglicisant d'aventure, — cela
d'après les indications de Rousseau même dans les *Confessions* ; que donc ce qui, d'après Rousseau dans ses « Préfaces »
et dans sa correspondance serait son premier roman, est en
réalité sa troisième histoire ; — et celle-ci nous l'avons appelée
le roman romantique, c'est-à-dire où l'auteur avait cru *sincèrement* aux droits absolus de l'amour. Mais ce ne fut-là
encore qu'une première forme du roman didactique qui fut
bientôt suivie d'une autre où il prêchera la répression de
l'amour romantique : ce sera donc la quatrième phase du
roman complet et qui correspond à ce que Rousseau appelle
la phase du roman moral (il n'en accepte, lui, qu'une où il
aurait pris une attitude morale) par opposition au roman frivole. Après deux séries de retouches au manuscrit original

une troisième va donc devenir nécessaire ; on ne peut guère s'étonner de l'infinie confusion des brouillons.

La différence d'esprit de cette nouvelle conception par rapport à la précédente est aussi radicale que possible, mais notre lecteur est préparé à la saisir. Il s'agit tout simplement de renverser le sens des notions chères à Rousseau ; « sentiment » va cesser de signifier sentiment romantique pour signifier (comme dans la *Lettre à d'Alembert*, et un peu comme dans le *Second Discours*) le contraire ; et « sentiment (moral) » et « nature » vont cesser de se rapporter à la nature passionnelle de l'homme pour se rapporter à celle qui s'exprime par la conscience disciplinante.

Ce sera Claire, qui avait dit hier avec conviction : « le véritable amour est-il fait pour dégrader l'âme ? » (p. 65), qui dit aujourd'hui qu'il faut « cacher sous un voile éternel l'*odieux* mystère » (p. 212), et que Saint-Preux doit cesser de s'obstiner à vouloir « corrompre une fille sage ». Saint-Preux, de son côté, accepte d'expier « ce *crime* involontaire » (p. 215). Et tantôt, ce sera Julie qui fera part de la mort de sa mère au « barbare » Saint-Preux dont, du reste, elle est la « parricide » complice (218) pour devenir la Julie mariée, repentante et heureuse. *Repentante*, c'est le mot à employer surtout pour le roman tel que Rousseau veut le voir interprété, celui de l'épouse vertueuse qui rachète la faute de l'amour coupable ; — *heureuse*, c'est le mot à employer pour nous qui savons que Julie ne cherche que le bonheur, et que, si elle abandonne Saint-Preux, c'est que le bonheur (qu'elle appelle du reste « vertu ») n'est pas dans le mariage avec Saint-Preux ; et si le souvenir de l'amour coupable pour Saint-Preux demeure en Julie, le mot *repentante* ne peut être pris que sans le sens de regret pour une erreur de jugement ; il ne s'agit pas de remords d'un péché.

Voici dans cette conception du roman l'idée de Julie — qui est celle de Rousseau sûrement :

« Il n'y a pas deux mois que je pensais encore ne m'être pas trompée. L'aveugle amour, me disais-je, avait raison ; nous étions faits l'un pour l'autre, je serais à lui si l'ordre humain n'eût troublé les rapports de la nature » (p. 235) ; [mais] « j'entre dans une nouvelle carrière qui ne doit finir qu'avec la mort » (p. 235) ; [car je connais maintenant] « combien il est nécessaire de chercher dans l'égarement de son cœur un repos qu'on ne trouve que dans la sagesse » (p. 240). [Je veux] « corriger... le désordre de mes affections » (p. 245). « Ce qui m'a longtemps abusée et peut-être vous abuse encore, c'est la pensée que l'amour est nécessaire pour former un heureux mariage » (p. 259). [Ayant trouvé] « l'immuable attachement de deux personnes honnêtes et *raisonnables*, je prends Dieu à témoin que si c'était à refaire, ce n'est pas vous Saint-Preux, que je choisirais, c'est M. de Wolmar » (p. 259).

Les deux lettres 18 et 20 exposant la nouvelle attitude de Julie, surtout la première, sont remplies tour à tour de pathos et d'argutie, de motifs considérables et de prétextes. Il ne faut pas en conclure, comme la critique facile ou hostile, que Rousseau est un *sophiste* ; mais seulement, d'une part que Rousseau a eu parfois de la peine à affranchir sa pensée de considérations appartenant encore à une phase précédente de sa pensée ; et d'autre part que les retouches rendues nécessaires par ces rédactions antérieures, n'ont pas toujours effacé tous les vestiges de la pensée d'hier. En lisant avec quelque attention, il est facile de dégager ce que Rousseau veut dire maintenant, et ce qui forme encore dans l'état actuel du roman la pensée de beaucoup la plus abondamment représentée : à savoir, la pensée que la vie heureuse c'est la vie ordonnée, à l'abri des incertitudes et des vicissitudes du cœur. Ainsi nous voyons Julie jetant après son mariage un coup d'œil rétrospectif sur les événements des dernières années, et nous assurant que depuis quelque temps déjà s'était présentée à elle l'idée que la passion est mère de l'inquiétude. Quand Saint-Preux était à Paris, elle souffrait dans la crainte d'être oubliée de l'amant auquel elle pensait avec une tendresse passionnée ; celui-ci ne vivait-il pas dans la grande ville, voyant tant de femmes qui pouvaient solliciter son amour. Sans doute, les lettres de Saint-Preux la rassurent ; mais :

« Mon ami, je n'en fus pas plus heureuse ; pour un tourment de
moins, sans cesse il en renaissait mille autres, et je ne connus jamais mieux combien il est insencé de chercher dans l'égarement de
son cœur, un repos que je ne trouve que dans la sagesse » (p. 240)

Traduction : une passion comme la mienne embrouille la
vie tout entière ; jamais de repos ; et après tout, y a-t-il sans
repos, du bonheur ? Cette conviction s'accentue, s'impose à
elle impérativement à l'église ; et, après la cérémonie du mariage, quand elle réfléchit sur la transformation intérieure qui
s'est opérée en elle, elle la définit ainsi : « Le goût de la sagesse » qui « se réveillait en moi » (p. 246). Et quelques lignes
plus loin, ces mots : « un heureux instinct me porte au bien ;
quelque violente passion s'élève ; elle a sa racine dans le
même instinct ; que ferai-je pour le détruire ? [Réponse :]
De la considération de l'ordre, je tire la beauté de la vertu,
et la bonté de l'utilité commune » (p. 247). Donc, la passion
pour Saint-Preux, c'est le désordre, le mariage avec Wolmar
c'est l'ordre, l'ordre qui favorise « l'utilité commune », celle
de Julie aussi, bien entendu. Nous n'avons dans tout ceci
qu'un simple écho de la *Lettre sur les Spectacles*, ou plutôt
une longue démonstration.

Car Julie prouve tout cela point par point :

a) Le bonheur est avec Wolmar. — Julie va (lettre 20) parler
de Wolmar « d'une manière digne de lui, comme il convient
à son épouse et à une amie de la vérité » (p. 256). Savourons
ce portrait de l'homme qu'elle a choisi pour remplacer le
tendre et ardent Saint-Preux dans son cœur ; c'est plus que
du Grandison, plus que du Bomston, plus que du Muralt
même ; cela semble écrit par l'homme d'affaires anglais le
plus « matter of fact » possible, exposant froidement et parce
qu'il se sent absolument sûr de lui-même, la qualité supérieure de l'article qu'il offre à sa clientèle :

« M. de Wolmar a près de cinquante ans ; sa vie, unie, réglée, et
le calme des passions, lui ont conservé une constitution si saine et
un air si frais qu'il paraît en avoir à peine quarante ; et il n'a rien
d'un âge avancé que l'expérience et la sagesse. Sa physionomie est

noble et prévenante, son abord simple et ouvert ; ses manières sont
plus honnêtes qu'empressées ; il parle peu et d'un grand sens, mais
sans affecter ni précision, ni sentences. Il est le même pour tout le
monde, ne cherche et ne fuit personne, et n'a jamais d'autres pré-
férences que celles de la raison. -Malgré sa froideur naturelle, son
cœur, secondant les intentions de mon père, crut sentir que je lui
convenais et pour la première fois de sa vie il prit un attachement.
Ce goût modéré, mais durable, s'est si bien réglé sur les bienséances
et s'est maintenu dans une telle égalité, qu'il n'a pas eu besoin de
changer de ton en changeant d'état, et que, sans blesser la gravité
conjugale, il conserve avec moi depuis son mariage les mêmes manières qu'il avait auparavant. Je ne l'ai jamais vu ni gai, ni triste,
mais toujours content ; jamais il ne me parle de lui, rarement
de moi ; il ne me recherche pas, mais il n'est pas fâché que je le
cherche, et me quitte peu volontiers. Il ne rit point, il est sérieux
sans donner envie de l'être ; au contraire son abord serein semble
m'inviter à l'enjouement. Avec quelque soin que j'aie pu l'observer,
je n'ai su lui trouver de passion d'aucune espèce que celle qu'il a
pour moi ; encore cette passion est-elle si égale et si tempérée qu'on
dirait qu'il n'aime qu'autant qu'il veut aimer, et qu'il ne le veut
qu'autant que la raison le permet. Il est réellement ce que Milord
Édouard croit être [!]... Le plus grand goût de M. de Wolmar est
d'observer. Il aime à juger des caractères des hommes et des actions
qu'on voit faire. Il en juge avec une profonde sagesse et la plus parfaite impartialité. Si un ennemi lui faisait du mal, il en discute-
rait les motifs et les moyens aussi paisiblement que s'il s'agissait
d'une chose indifférente... » (p. 256-7) (1).

Et l'ex-romantique Julie prend encore la peine d'ajouter :
« J'oubliais de vous parler de nos revenus — écrit-elle à Saint-
Preux dont elle vient de briser le cœur — et de leur administration » (p. 257 ss). Le jeune ménage a une « fortune honnête,
mais modérée » ; pas de « luxe », mais « l'abondance » ; et elle
explique que l'ordre que Wolmar a dans sa maison est le
même qui « règne dans son cœur », et « semble imiter l'ordre
établi dans le gouvernement du monde ».

b) *Le bonheur ne saurait être avec Saint-Preux.* — Julie est
lancée, elle ne s'arrêtera plus ; sa logique est impitoyable.

---

(1) On trouvera le portrait de Wolmar tracé par lui-même, IV, Lettre 12 :
« J'ai naturellement l'âme tranquille, et le cœur froid... » Nous aurons à en re-
parler.

L'amour nécessaire dans le mariage ? « Mon ami, c'est une erreur » ; et qui plus est, l'amour est une illusion. Nous prenons la violence de ce sentiment pour un « signe de sa durée », mais « au contraire, c'est son ardeur même qui le consume » ; on doit « compter qu'on cessera de s'aimer tôt ou tard » ; alors « on se voit réciproquement tel qu'on est » ; on ne trouve plus « l'objet qu'on aima » ; « on se dépite contre celui qui reste », et il est à craindre que le « déclin » de l'amour ne s'arrête pas à l'indifférence, et aille jusqu'au « dégoût ». « Mon cher ami... Je ne vous ai jamais vu qu'amoureux », et quelquefois, après s'être trop aimés comme « amants » on se « hait comme époux » ; d'ailleurs il y a « des hommes vertueux qui ne laissent pas d'être des maris insupportables ». On peut aller plus loin encore : non seulement l'amour n'est pas nécessaire dans le mariage, mais il est positivement « importun » ; l'avantage d'une union avec un Wolmar c'est que « nulle illusions ne nous prévient l'un pour l'autre » ; il faut sans doute de l'affection, mais c'est assez : « S'il ne m'aimait point, nous vivrions mal ensemble ; (mais) s'il m'eût trop aimée, il m'eût été importun » (p. 259). Conclusion de tout cela : le pauvre Saint-Preux reçoit en guise de consolation, ce cri d'épicuréisme ineffable : « Mon bon et digne ami... oublions tout le reste, et soyez l'amant de mon âme » (p. 252) (1).

(1) Nous craindrions d'allonger la démonstration de la vérité de notre interprétation. Mais on verra que cette sagesse rationaliste se glisse partout. Par exemple : il s'était trouvé des philosophes pour déclarer que violer les lois du mariage au nom de la passion naturelle, n'était pas un mal, voire un bien. Rousseau déclare, lui, que c'est pire de pécher avec une femme mariée qu'avec une fille ; et il le prouve en *raisonnant* le cas : « Ne dirait-on pas qu'en s'attaquant directement au plus saint et au plus solennel des engagements ces dangereux raisonneurs ont résolu d'anéantir d'un seul coup toute la société humaine qui n'est fondée que sur la foi des conventions ? Mais, voyez, je vous prie, comme ils disculpent un adultère secret. C'est, disent-ils, qu'il n'en résulte aucun mal, pas même pour l'époux qui ignore : comme s'ils pouvaient être sûrs qu'il ignorera toujours... Quoi donc !... ce n'est pas un mal de se forcer soi-même de devenir fourbe et menteur ? ce n'est pas un mal de former des liens qui vous font désirer le mal et la mort d'autrui, la mort de celui-même qu'on doit le plus aimer et avec qui l'on a juré de vivre ? Ce n'est pas un mal

Suivent les longues lettres de la IVᵉ partie — aujourd'hui réparties entre la IVᵉ et la Vᵉ. Nous avons expliqué que lorsque Rousseau décida de continuer son roman au delà de la IVᵉ partie, ce fut pour y introduire de nouvelles et différentes considérations sur le thème du mariage et de l'amour, cela exigera une extension de la IVᵉ partie telle qu'il faudra pour garder les proportions déverser dans la Vᵉ partie quelques lettres qui avaient été destinées, et appartenaient par l'esprit à la IVᵉ. Il s'agit des trois premières de la Vᵉ partie actuelle ; la deuxième surtout est très étendue (1).

Ces lettres prouvent une seule et même chose : Julie qui a épousé « selon la sagesse » est heureuse, et avec elle tous ceux qui l'entourent. Dans son ménage, on voit réuni « tout ce qui

---

qu'un état dont mille autres crimes sont toujours le fruit ? Un bien qui produirait tant de maux serait par cela seul un mal lui-même » (p. 249). Et « comment prouvent-ils qu'il est indifférent à un père d'avoir des héritiers qui ne soient pas de son sang, d'être peut-être chargé de plus d'enfants qu'il n'en aurait eu et forcé de partager ses biens aux gages de son déshonneur... N'est-ce donc faire aucun mal à votre avis que d'anéantir ou troubler par un sang étranger cette union naturelle, et d'altérer dans son principe l'affection qui doit lier entre eux tous les membres d'une même famille ? Y a-t-il au monde un honnête homme qui n'eût horreur de changer un enfant en nourrice ? et le crime est-il moindre de le changer dans le sein de la mère ? » (p. 249-50).

Il est peut-être intéressant de relever ici que l'idée que l'homme qui pèche avec une femme mariée est plus coupable que celui qui pèche avec une fille se retrouve au début de la *Profession de Foi du Vicaire savoyard* ; et elle se retrouve encore dans l'histoire des amours de Lord Bomston. Rousseau en doit-il l'idée à Genève ? On lit — et G. Valette ne l'a pas relevé dans son *Rousseau Genevois* — dans Eugène Choisy, *La Théologie à Genève au temps de Calvin* (Eggiman, 1897, ch. VI) relativement à la discipline ecclésiastique du mariage, ceci : que le consentement du père n'est obligatoire qu'avant 20 ans pour les fils, avant 18 ans pour les filles ; et l'explication en est que « le législateur est tellement favorable au mariage — pour éviter la paillardise — qu'il fait fléchir l'autorité paternelle devant l'intérêt social et moral conformément à l'ordonnance de la parole de Dieu. La création de nouvelles familles, encouragée et facilitée autant que possible sera le remède au désordre des mœurs ».

(1) Au fond, il faudrait dire deux lettres et demie ; car Rousseau dit en note p. 389 que sa troisième lettre est formée de deux autrefois distinctes ; il a adroitement rattaché la longue lettre sur l'éducation à la brève scène de la « Matinée anglaise ».

répond à la véritable destination de l'homme » (p. 306) ; tout
y est orienté vers le bonheur, «spectacle agréable et touchant».
Rien n'est abandonné au hasard de la nature ; rien n'est laissé
à des impulsions romantiques. Ce sont des gens non riches,
mais opulents cependant ; car ne prenant pas de fermiers,
ils économisent les frais de fermage ; les fermiers n'ont pas
aussi grand soin en effet d'une terre louée que le propriétaire:
en outre, de cette façon, forcés de rester à la campagne les
maîtres ne dépenseront pas à la ville leur argent ; la vie cham-
pêtre détruit le goût des « fantaisies ruineuses » (p. 384).

Du même point de vue utilitaire sont traitées les questions
de choix de domestiques, de l'exploitation de la terre, du jar-
dinage, des vêtements, de l'usage du vin, et tant d'autres problèmes d'ordre pratique ; et à plus forte raison les grands problèmes d'éducation, de religion, de politique (1). Tout est
raison, tout est prudence, tout est calcul. Et Saint-Preux
lui-même doit être attiré dans le cercle de ce bonheur de la
vertu sagesse.

---

(1) Il n'est pas jusqu'aux jouissances sensuelles qui ne soient pesées et
exploitées avec une habileté surprenante par cette terrible Julie. Ainsi Julie a
trouvé — ce qui est fort juste, mais ce qui exige une sagacité fort peu « naturelle »
— que « tout ce qui tient aux sens et n'est pas nécessaire à la vie, change de
nature aussitôt qu'il tourne en habitude, qu'il cesse d'être un plaisir en devenant un besoin, que c'est à la fois une chaîne qu'on se donne et une jouissance
dont on se prive... » (p. 378). Et que fait-elle, cette âme que Rousseau appelle
« simple » et qui nous paraît au contraire extrêmement retorte ? elle développe
l'art « de donner du prix aux moindres choses ». La *nature* serait de jouir de
tout ce qu'on peut, et c'est ce que font les hommes, et ils épuisent ainsi la
coupe des jouissances ; or, il ne faut pas se laisser guider par la nature ; la nature
tend des pièges ; *l'art* consiste à « se refuser les choses vingt fois par jour pour
en jouir une ». « Par exemple, elle (Julie) aime beaucoup le café ; chez sa mère
elle en prenait tous les jours ; elle en a quitté l'habitude pour en augmenter le
goût ; elle s'est bornée à n'en prendre que quand elle a des hôtes... C'est une
petite sensualité qui la flatte plus, qui lui coûte moins, et par laquelle elle
aiguise et règle à la fois sa gourmandise » (p. 386). Elle a bien raison d'appeler
cela de la « volupté tempérante », ou ailleurs « le bonheur de la sagesse » qui
n'est pas celui des « vulgaires épicuriens » (p. 379). C'est l'histoire de l'abbé
dont parle Mme de Sévigné, lequel mangeait de la merluche dans ce monde
pour se rassasier de saumure dans l'autre.

On devine les modifications importantes qui vont s'imposer à Rousseau dans la rédaction du roman dès le moment où il eut admis ces nouvelles théories, les retouches aussi à faire dans les parties écrites déjà.

Parmi les *modifications*, nous voyons que Wolmar devient à son tour un personnage de premier plan ; il cesse d'être simplement le prétendant titré et riche qu'un père veut imposer à sa fille ; il est l'incarnation de la sagesse ; — et on lui ôte même sa fortune pour rendre plus évident que, quoique privé de biens de ce monde, cet homme est *le* mari parfait.

D'autre part, Bomston, le grand Lord anglais, qui souverainement s'était fait le champion de l'amour romantique, est une puissance déchue. De grand coryphée, il tombe au rang de comparse... Il est difficile de se passer de lui tout à fait ; mais c'est qu'il faut un correspondant qui à Saint-Preux puisse dire des choses que le lecteur doit connaître, et qui ne vont pas dans des lettres adressées aux grands rôles ; c'est qu'il faut un ami pour rendre possibles certaines péripéties ; c'est qu'il faut une entremise pour envoyer Saint-Preux faire son voyage de quatre ans autour du monde afin de tâcher d'apaiser son grand chagrin. Bomston est si bien tombé que l'on se moque aimablement de son cœur excellent associé à une intelligence naïve, et qu'on dit : Wolmar *est* ce que Bomston *croit* être.

C'est Julie ici qui devient porte-parole (dans les deux lettres 18 et 20 surtout, de la IIIᵉ partie) ; qui est chargée spécialement d'expliquer, à l'encontre du romantisme à courte vue de Bomston qu'il y a des choses plus fondamentales que la passion dans le mariage, et que cette passion est susceptible d'entraîner le désenchantement ; elle le fait avec une prolixité telle que Rousseau lui-même l'appelle « la prêcheuse ».

Parmi les *retouches* à faire dans les parties antérieures, et qui s'imposaient à Rousseau, il y avait d'abord celle du père « volage », « dur et inflexible » qui sera dorénavant « le tendre père » ; c'est ce père, en fin de compte, qui aura eu raison : quel triste champion de la vérité cependant, aux yeux du lecteur, que ce personnage de tout point haïssable ! Un

homme qui a tué sa femme de chagrin par ses infidélités, puis
par sa brutalité ; et qui ayant opposé l'argument de la pauvreté à propos d'un mariage qui lui déplaisait, pour invoquer
le même argument de la pauvreté du gendre en faveur d'un
mari qui lui agrée. N'ayant pas voulu récrire tout son roman,
Rousseau dut introduire le second (le père tendre) en gardant
le premier (le barbare) ; cette façon de procéder par simple
juxtaposition est aussi candide que maladroite, — et seul un
violent changement de front dans la conception du roman peut
expliquer qu'un écrivain de l'envergure de Rousseau acceptât
des compromis aussi grossiers avec l'art. Qu'est-ce par exemple
qui avait été indiqué comme cause de désaccord entre père et
fille : Julie voulait épouser Saint-Preux par sentiment opposé
à la raison. Mais maintenant — à côté même des arguments
tirés de la vertu dictée par la raison — Rousseau oppose au
sentiment d'amour pour Saint-Preux, le sentiment familial.
C'est dans la lettre 58 de la Ire Partie qui raconte l'épisode du
père souffletant sa fille (et qui, elle, porte les traces d'une
refonte) : après la brouille au nom des sentiments naturels,
vient la réconciliation au nom d'autres sentiments naturels.
Quand le père voit le sang couler, il est ému et une scène touchante suit : « Ici finit le triomphe de la colère et commence
celui de la nature » (1) (p. 118) ; — et le reste du jour fut témoin encore de scènes de sensibilité ; devant le feu, Julie
« couvre de baisers » et « inonde de ses larmes » ce père : « Je
sentis à celles qui lui coulaient des yeux qu'il était lui-même
soulagé d'une grande peine ; ma mère vint partager nos transports. Douce et paisible innocence, tu manquais seule à mon
cœur pour faire de cette scène de la nature le plus délicieux
moment de ma vie » (p. 119). Voilà le tour joué ; la *nature*
peut être du côté de Julie aimant Saint-Preux, et elle n'est
pas moins du côté de Julie aimant son père et sa mère. C'est
fort acceptable ; mais c'est-à-dire que Rousseau prépare ici
le lecteur à accepter plus tard l'idée que la *nature* est pour
Julie obéissant à son père aussi bien que pour elle lui déso-

(1) Et la *colère*, n'est pas de la nature non plus ?

béissant : la *nature* ne résout rien, et quand d'autres raisons seront données (les raisons de sagesse rationnelle que Julie exposera dans les lettres 18 et 20 de la IIIe partie après le mariage avec Wolmar) le lecteur se reportant à Julie encore l'amante de Saint-Preux trouvera de quoi écarter son objection : sentiment pour Saint-Preux, sentiment pour père — c'est toujours sentiment comme toujours nature. Disons, pour qui ne serait pas satisfait de voir ce père brutal, volage et inflexible, tout à coup adoré par sa fille, que Rousseau introduit plus loin une autre cheville rétroactive (IV, Lettre 12) ; il fait allusion à une sorte de conversion du vieux baron au moment où on agitait la question du mariage de Julie : Wolmar rapporte ainsi ses paroles (p. 344) : « Moi-même, après avoir vécu presqu'indépendant dans les liens du mariage, je sens que j'ai besoin de redevenir époux et père, et je vais me retirer dans le sein de ma famille ».

La même transition est ménagée au moyen de la mère. La voix de la nature avait parlé pour Saint-Preux seul ; mais pour faire mieux accepter le revirement de Julie, on va exploiter le sentiment pour une mère mourante (p. 212 ss.). Rousseau a beau jeu, devant ce spectacle, de montrer que la nature contre Saint-Preux est plus forte que la nature pour Saint-Preux. Quelle fille résisterait devant le lit de mort d'une mère demandant la renonciation à un amant au nom de l'amour filial ? C'est une situation mélodramatique exploitée trop souvent (*Atala*). On invoque la nature contre la nature et cela forcera à chercher ailleurs la raison déterminante — dans la sagesse philosophique.

Sera-t-on étonné ensuite de certaines juxtapositions curieuses, — des interpolations très certainement — dans les premières parties du roman, c'est-à-dire de phrases destinées à préparer le revirement en faveur du père ? C'est ainsi que (p. 62) à ces mots de Julie : « Mon père m'a donc vendue, il a fait de sa fille une vile marchandise... Père barbare et dénaturé », succèdent bientôt ces mots : « Quoi... c'est le meilleur des pères, il veut unir sa fille à son ami, voilà son crime ».

Et après ces mots (p. 64) : « J'oubliai tout et ne me souvins que de l'amour », écrits avec un accent de triomphe, on va lire : « C'est ainsi qu'un instant d'égarement m'a perdue à jamais ».

Tout lecteur attentif découvrira de ces solutions de continuité et de ces retouches. Rappelons-en une encore : Il est difficile de croire que Rousseau ait pu dans le même groupe des premières lettres, écrire d'une part ses plaidoyers chaleureux pour l'amour romantique de Saint-Preux et de Julie, et d'autre part parler comme il le fait du mariage le plus indifférent à l'amour qui puisse être et qui fut contracté entre Claire et M. d'Orbe ; un mariage qui « substitue aux feux de l'amour tout ce qui peut y suppléer dans le mariage » (p. 132), un mariage dont l'amie même de Julie peut dire :

« Un mari peut m'être utlie, mais il ne sera jamais pour moi qu'un mari ; et de ceux-là, libre encore et passable comme je suis, j'en puis trouver un par tout le monde » (p. 140).

C'est Claire encore qui lancera à Julie : « Dis-moi, mon enfant, l'âme a-t-elle un sexe » ? Aussi, nous voici bien préparés, quand Rousseau amènera la catastrophe pour Julie (c'est-à-dire quand elle doit renoncer à Saint-Preux) à voir Claire chargée par l'auteur de faire comprendre au lecteur qu'en vérité, il s'agit non d'une « catastrophe » mais plutôt d'un heureux concours de circonstances : « J'ose à peine vous dire les idées bizarres qui me viennent là-dessus, mais elles sont consolantes et cela m'enhardit » (p. 221). Voici ces réflexions : Premièrement, vous ne regretterez jamais rien, car la vertu plus que l'amour «dédommage de tout ce qu'on lui sacrifie»; et « on jouit en quelque sorte des privations qu'on s'impose par le sentiment même de ce qu'il en coûte et du motif qui nous y porte » ; donc par un « amour-propre exquis... vous vous direz, *je sais* aimer avec un plaisir plus durable et plus délicat que vous n'en goûterez à dire, *je possède ce que j'aime* » ; — c'est une variation sur la vertu stoïque ; nous connaissons. Mais ceci est mieux : Quand il serait même « naturel », et donc

quand même il aurait les droits profonds que confère tout ce
qui est naturel, l'amour passionné est passager — et voici la
« nature » bien arrangée :

« Le temps eût joint au dégoût d'une longue possession le progrès de l'âge et le déclin de la beauté ; il semble se fixer à votre faveur par la séparation ; vous serez toujours l'un pour l'autre à la
fleur des ans, vous vous verrez sans cesse tels que vous vous vîtes
en vous quittant ; et vos cœurs, unis jusqu'au tombeau, prolonge-
ront dans une illusion charmante votre jeunesse avec vos amours »
(p. 221).

Enfin, troisièmement, vous avez connu l'amour tout entier :

« L'amour n'a point de délices dont il ne vous ait comblés ». [Or,]
« mon ami, ce fut là le comble, et vos feux et votre bonheur ne
pouvaient plus que décliner... Consolez-vous donc de la perte d'un
bien qui vous eût toujours échappé, et vous eût de plus ravi celui
qui vous reste » (p. 222).

Il saute aux yeux que des paroles d'un objectivisme —
presque cynisme — tel, ne sont pas dans le ton des lettres
romantiques, et de la phase romantique. Elles sont ajoutées
après coup en vue des raccordements ultérieurs avec le roman
continué dans un esprit nouveau.

En marge du roman. Le ménage a trois

Cette confiance extraordinaire en la raison opposée à la
nature et qui en somme ignore l'amour romantique ou le
considère comme un *x* dans la vie, constitue le fondement de
ce que la critique est convenue d'appeler l'idée du ménage à
trois. Il ne faut pas nier probablement que l'idée en fut en
quelque sorte imposée à Rousseau par son malheureux amour
pour Mme d'Houdetot, l'amante en titre de Saint-Lambert
(Voir *Confessions*, et les livres de Brunel, d'Érich Schmidt,
Buffenoir, Mornet, etc.) et que le ton de langoureuse sentimentalité prêté par Rousseau à Saint-Preux, Julie, et Wolmar à

ce propos ait la même origine. Et il n'y a aucune raison pour douter que Rousseau ait été sincère quand il a déclaré croire, au moment où il écrivait ces pages de *La Nouvelle Héloïse*, que le trio pouvait vivre sur le pied de franche amitié, comme il avait été sincère dans l'étape de sa pensée où il réclamait les droits de la passion. Saint-Preux, revenu de son voyage autour du monde, est certain d'avoir en effet sous les yeux la réalisation des conditions du bonheur à trois :

« Que de plaisirs trop tard connus je goûte depuis trois semaines ! La douce chose que de couler ses jours dans le sein d'une tranquille amitié à l'abri de l'orage des passions impétueuses ! Milord, que c'est un spectacle agréable et touchant que celui d'une maison simple et bien réglée où règnent l'ordre, la paix, l'innocence ; où l'on voit réunis sans appareil, sans éclat, tout ce qui répond à la véritable destination de l'homme ! » (p. 306).

Le rêve va bien au delà de la réalité. Dans un passage de la lettre importante de l'Élysée, on voit, un jour, un nuage passer encore sur le front de l'ancien amant. En compagnie de Julie et de Wolmar, il disserte sur la beauté de la vie paisible, loin des hommes, en compagnie des fleurs et des oiseaux qui nichent librement :

« Madame, dit Saint-Preux, vous êtes épouse et mère ; ce sont des plaisirs qu'il vous appartient de connaître. Aussitôt M. de Wolmar me prenant par la main me dit en la serrant : *Vous avez des amis et ces amis ont des enfants ; comment l'affection paternelle vous serait-elle étrangère ?* Je le regardai ; je regardai Julie : tous deux se regardèrent et me rendirent un regard si touchant que, les embrassant l'un après l'autre, je leur dis avec attendrissement : *Ils me sont aussi chers qu'à vous.* Je ne sais par quel bizarre effet, un mot peut ainsi changer une âme ; mais depuis ce moment M. de Wolmar me paraît un autre homme, et je vois en lui moins le mari de celle que j'ai tant aimée que le père de deux enfants pour lesquels je donnerais ma vie » (p. 333).

Enfin, tout semble bien maintenant. L'ordre, un instant menacé une dernière fois par la scène des rochers de Meillerie lors de la promenade sur le lac, s'était rétabli ; c'était le

triomphe de la raison, la paix du ménage à trois. Rousseau peut introduire — inspiré comme on le sait par Muralt — la fameuse scène de « la Matinée à l'anglaise ». Des hôtes, écrit Saint-Preux, viennent de quitter Étanges.

« Et nous commençons entre nous trois une société d'autant plus charmante qu'il n'est rien resté dans le fond du cœur qu'on veuille se cacher l'un à l'autre... Nous avons passé une matinée à l'anglaise, réunis et dans le silence, goûtant à la fois le plaisir d'être ensemble et la douceur du recueillement... Deux heures se sont ainsi écoulées entre nous dans cette immobilité d'extase, plus douce mille fois que le froid repos des dieux d'Épicure » (p. 389-90).

Le roman devait s'arrêter là. La Matinée à l'Anglaise est une excellente chûte de rideau.

CINQUIÈME PHASE DU ROMAN : *Insuffisance de la vertu-sagesse pour réaliser le bonheur, et retour à des velléités romantiques.* — Le roman moralisant *devait* s'arrêter là. Toutefois le lecteur sera-t-il satisfait ; ou va-t-il se mettre à méditer encore ? Nommez « bonheur » si vous voulez, toute cette vertu conjugale, et domestique, et économique, mais est-ce là tout ? Est-ce surtout l'important ? Bref est-ce le bonheur vraiment, ou ne serait-ce que la condition du bonheur ? Et, si on n'a rien d'autre, est-ce la peine d'avoir cela ? — Rousseau a fini par ajouter deux parties nouvelles à son roman... C'est inquiétant : Est-ce encore une fois la voix du romantisme qui refuserait de se laisser subjuguer ?

Résumons les parties ajoutées, Ve et VIe.

Ve PARTIE : Claire devenue veuve, quitte Lausanne pour venir demeurer à Clarens. Son arrivée sera l'occasion de manifestations extraordinaires de joies sentimentales. Elle devient intendante de la maison ; Julie sera l'éducatrice des trois enfants (p. 419 ss.) (1). Le père de Julie revient au pays, et se

---

(1) Rousseau, qui écrivait en ce moment l'*Emile* concurremment avec *La Nouvelle Héloïse*, voulait que l'enfant fût d'abord élevé par la femme seule, et puis passât aux mains d'un homme ; c'est pour cette seconde phase de l'éducation que Wolmar arrêtera les services de Saint-Preux.

réconcilie avec Saint-Preux (p. 424). Quant à Milord, il vient
rejoindre Saint-Preux à Clarens pour l'emmener en Italie ;
cependant la saison est trop avancée pour passer les Alpes,
et le départ est remis au printemps (le but du séjour à Rome
était d'obtenir l'opinion de Saint-Preux sur la façon d'arranger les affaires d'amour de Bomston). Lorsque le voyage eut
lieu, les deux amis s'arrêtèrent pour leur première étape à
Villeneuve — comme lors de la fuite de Saint-Preux à Paris
quand il avait dû renoncer à Julie. Saint-Preux couche dans
la même chambre d'hôtel que six ans auparavant ; ses souvenirs l'envahissent ; tout son passé d'amour se dresse devant
lui ; il a par trois fois la vision de Julie couverte d'un suaire
(p. 423-4). Il est bouleversé (1) ; Bomston le traite d'enfant,
cependant retourne immédiatement avec lui à Clarens pour
s'assurer qu'aucun malheur n'est arrivé. Tout est bien ; ils
repartent sans avoir même laissé connaître leur retour. De
Milan, Saint-Preux écrit et fait part des alarmes que lui causa
sa vision. Claire est très frappée ; les autres apprécient différemment ; Julie ne dit rien. (A Milan, Saint-Preux apprend
que Wolmar l'a choisi comme précepteur de ses enfants).
Claire quitte Clarens pour aller préparer la noce de son frère
à Genève (p. 438) ; on apprend qu'elle aime Saint-Preux, et
Julie propose d'épouser (p. 445 ss.). VIᵉ PARTIE : Claire consent
à s'en remettre à Julie pour savoir si elle doit épouser Saint-
Preux. Saint-Preux en fait autant (vol. V, p. 35) ; et il retarde
son retour à Clarens, car s'il n'épouse pas, il vouera le reste
de sa vie à l'amitié, c'est-à-dire à Bomston, et il ira en Angleterre ; dans ce cas il ne veut pas passer par Clarens à cause de
la douleur qu'il aurait de se séparer de nouveau et pour toujours de Julie (Bomston ne lui a pas encore dit qu'il comptait
lui aussi aller demeurer à Clarens). Julie propose à Saint-
Preux, s'il n'épouse pas Claire et s'il ne veut pas vivre à Clarens
par crainte des souvenirs, de lui confier un de ses enfants.
Claire entre temps est revenue. Accident de Chillon (p. 47 ss.) :

---

(1) Il peut être bon de rappeler que la Promenade sur le lac et à Meillerie
avait alors eu lieu déjà.

Julie se jette dans le lac pour sauver son cadet Marcelin, et meurt d'une lente et douce agonie. M. d'Étanges qui était en séjour de l'autre côté du lac, en apprenant l'accident tombe et se casse la jambe ; il ne reverra pas sa fille. Une lettre posthume de Julie propose encore une fois le mariage de Saint-Preux et Claire, et apporte l'aveu qu'elle a aimé Saint-Preux jusqu'au bout. Saint-Preux fait une violente maladie en apprenant la mort de Julie (p. 76). Quant à Claire, elle écrit à Saint-Preux que celui qui a aimé Julie ne doit pas en épouser une autre ; elle sent du reste qu'elle va rejoindre Julie avant long-temps.

On entend que Wolmar va se convertir (p. 44, 50-1, 54, 59, 77) (1). Quant à Saint-Preux il va devenir le précepteur des enfants : « Il vous reste, écrit Wolmar, de grands devoirs à remplir » (p. 48).

Il faut distinguer deux motifs qui ont déterminé Rousseau à continuer son roman ; l'un purement contingent, l'autre plus fondamental, ou plutôt, plus directement en rapport avec le roman propre.

Le motif contingent est le désir de développer le rôle de la religion dans la vie. Le motif fondamental — si notre examen est exact — est que Rousseau a été repris de doute à l'endroit de sa Julie de la vertu-sagesse : le pendule, une fois de plus, aurait oscillé du pôle romain au pôle romantique.

C'est le premier de ces motifs que Rousseau a avoué, souligné même ; c'est le second — donc bien l'essentiel — qu'il semble vouloir exprimer avec réserve, avec tant de réserve qu'on ne l'a pas compris la plupart du temps.

---

(1) Pas assez au gré de quelques-uns. Mais Rousseau écrit à son ami Vernes le 24 juin 1761 : « Vous me reprochez de n'avoir pas fait changer de système à Wolmar sur la fin du roman ; mais, mon cher Vernes, vous n'avez pas lu cette fin, car sa conversion y est indiquée avec une clarté qui ne pouvait souffrir un plus grand développement sans vouloir faire une capucinade ». Comparez Sévère, de *Polyeucte*.

Commençons par écarter cet élément contingent, auquel Rousseau, si on en juge d'après la lettre, *paraît* tenir surtout.

On se souvient du passage des *Confessions* (IX) :

« Outre cet objet de mœurs et d'honnêteté conjugale qui tient radicalement à tout l'ordre social, je m'en fis un plus secret de concorde et de paix publique : objet plus grand, plus important peut-être en lui-même, et du moins pour le moment où l'on se trouvait. L'orage excité par l'*Encyclopédie*, loin de se calmer, était alors dans sa plus grande force. Les deux partis déchaînés l'un contre l'autre avec la dernière fureur, ressemblaient plutôt à des loups enragés, acharnés à s'entredéchirer, qu'à des chrétiens et des philosophes qui veulent réciproquement s'éclairer, se convaincre et se ramener dans la voie de la vérité... Je m'avisai d'un expédient, c'était d'adoucir leur haine réciproque et leurs préjugés, et de montrer à chaque parti la vérité et la vertu de l'autre... Ce projet, peu sensé, eut le succès qu'il devait avoir, il ne rapprocha point les partis, et ne les réunit que pour m'accabler » (VIII, p. 312).

Ces lignes sont écrites dix ans après le roman. Mais dès 1760, Rousseau désirait qu'on regardât ainsi les choses, et c'est à un ami en qui il avait grande confiance, Duclos, qu'il écrit le 19 novembre 1760 : « Je crois la IVe Partie la meilleure de tout le recueil, et j'ai été tenté de supprimer les deux suivantes : Mais peut-être compensent-elles l'agrément par l'utilité ; et c'est dans cette opinion que je les ai laissées. Si Wolmar pouvait ne pas déplaire aux dévôts, et que sa femme plût aux philosophes, j'aurais peut-être publié le livre le plus salutaire qu'on pût lire dans ce temps-ci ».

Or, comment dans le roman tel que nous le connaissons, cette discussion religieuse est-elle amenée ? Par le souci que témoigne un beau jour Julie pour le salut de l'âme de Wolmar. Si Wolmar ne croit pas, il ne sera pas sauvé, et elle veut le sauver (p. 412 ss,) :

« Quelle horreur pour une tendre épouse d'imaginer l'Être suprême vengeur de sa divinité méconnue, de songer que le bonheur de celui qui fait le sien doit finir avec sa vie, et de ne voir qu'un réprouvé dans le père de ses enfants ». [Et plus loin, elle veut :]

SCHINZ. — Rousseau   20

« rassembler autour de lui ces douceurs passagères auxquelles il borne sa félicité : Ah, dit-elle avec douleur, si l'infortuné fait son paradis en ce monde, rendons-le lui du moins aussi doux que possible » (p. 416-17).

Lorsqu'elle voit la mort approcher, elle affirme qu'elle veut mourir pour qu'il ait la foi (vol. V, p. 46) ; et jusque dans la grande lettre où elle raconte ses derniers moments elle exprime l'espoir que sa mort chrétienne servira à faire croire et à sauver Wolmar.

Mais, nous le demandons, n'y a-t-il pas quelque chose d'étrange à ce que Julie, qui depuis son mariage fait profession de sentiments religieux sincères et ne paraît pas avoir varié sur ce point, s'avise après six années de s'inquiéter du sort de Wolmar dans l'autre monde, — et quand d'ailleurs il n'y a aucune apparence que ni elle ni lui soit près de la tombe ? Et la chose devient tout à fait suspecte quand on réfléchit que la théologie de Julie rend parfaitement vaine cette crainte. Dieu, affirme-t-elle ne condamnera personne pour des questions de croyances dogmatiques ; c'est la conduite dans cette vie qui constitue un passe-droit pour la vie éternelle et bienheureuse ; elle est certaine que Wolmar, plus que n'importe qui mérite le paradis pour ses vertus :

« Le Dieu que je sers est un Dieu clément, un père : ce qui me touche est sa bonté ; elle efface à mes yeux tous les autres attributs ; elle est le seul que je conçois... Le Dieu vengeur est le Dieu des méchants » (p. 43).

Il est évident, à qui examine de près le texte publié de *La Nouvelle Héloïse*, que les nombreuses pages se rapportant à cette incrédulité de Wolmar sont le résultat d'un nouveau courant de pensée dans le roman ; il n'y avait rien dans les conceptions antérieures qui pouvait faire prévoir cela (1) ; et

(1) Tout au plus, cela pouvait-il se rattacher, à titre de hors d'œuvre aux élucubrations religieuses de Julie quand elle explique son renoncement à Saint-Preux pour Wolmar, et l'impression que fit la cérémonie religieuse du mariage.

il est évident pour nous que les deux uniques passages qui mentionnent ce problème avant la Ve partie ont été ajoutés après coup pour préparer le lecteur. Le plus important de ces passages se trouve à la fin de la IVe Partie (lettre 15) :

« Mon cher ami, écrit Julie à Saint-Preux, il n'y a point de vrai bonheur sur la terre... Favorisée en toutes choses du ciel, de la fortune et des hommes, je vois tout concourir à mon bonheur. Un chagrin secret, un seul chagrin l'empoisonne, et je ne suis pas heureuse » (p. 358).

Puis un autre est ajouté commodément sous forme de *note*, dès la IIIe Partie (lettre 20) :

« Apparemment elle (Julie) n'avait pas découvert encore le fatal secret qui la tourmenta si fort dans la suite, ou elle ne voulait pas alors le confier à son ami » (p. 258).

La gaucherie de la *note* est évidente : comme s'il était concevable que Julie ne sût pas depuis longtemps l'indifférence religieuse de Wolmar qui n'était pas un hypocrite ; alors on ajoute une seconde phrase, laquelle cependant montrerait qu'alors Julie aurait dû être depuis longtemps malheureuse.

En ce cas, qu'est-ce qui donc justifie ou explique cet épisode encombrant, et tout à coup introduit, de l'incrédulité de Wolmar ? Il est bien certain qu'il y a tout au cours de *La Nouvelle Héloïse* des quantités de disgressions sur tous les sujets imaginables ; mais il n'en est aucune qui comme celle-ci empiète tellement sur l'histoire qu'elle semble en modifier le cours entièrement.

Voici les causes que nous entrevoyons :

D'abord, Rousseau a vu l'occasion là de mêler un peu plus de Mme d'Houdetot à son roman. Il a avoué dans les *Confessions* qu'elle n'avait pas été sans influence sur la manière dont le roman avait été mené à fin (VIII, p. 314) ; elle l'avait replongé dans ses rêveries de « berger extravagant » ; puis le ménage à trois était une réminiscence évidente des projets caressés quelque temps pour un *modus vivendi* entre Saint-Lambert, Mme d'Houdetot, et Rousseau.

Et nous savons aussi que dans sa lettre du 18 février 1758, il faisait mention d'un désir d'ajouter une 5e Partie « pour elle seule » à *La nouvelle Héloïse* : cela pouvait viser les lettres du ménage à trois ; mais cela pouvait indiquer aussi autre chose : en effet, Rousseau rédigeait en ce moment ces fameuses *Lettres à Sophie* que M. Buffenoir a retrouvées et publiées (*La Comtesse d'Houdetot, sa famille, ses amis*, Paris 1905), et qui sont un vrai traité de morale et de religion. Nous pensons donc que nous avons dans les grands morceaux théologiques de la Ve Partie donnés en vue de la conversion de Wolmar, les échos de la tentative de conversion de Mme d'Houdetot, — ces lettres de *La Nouvelle Héloïse* écrites « pour elle seule » (1). Il est vrai que Rousseau avait dit que cette partie, si écrite, ne serait « jamais publiée », mais il a pu changer d'idée comme dans tant d'autres circonstances, et cela paraît confirmé par la lettre à Duclos citée plus haut (19 nov. 1760) où il dit qu'après avoir voulu supprimer les Parties V et VI, il les avait gardées pour « l'utilité », souhaitant que « Wolmar plût aux dévots et sa femme aux philosophes de ce temps-ci ».

Une autre explication — et qui ajoute à la précédente — de la présence de cette discussion philosophique interjetée après la IVe Partie, serait celle-ci : Rousseau ayant eu des doutes sur sa thèse que la sagesse était tout ce qui était nécessaire pour rendre le mariage heureux, tandis que l'amour serait un intrus plutôt qu'un élément normal du mariage, avait voulu être sincère jusqu'au bout ; mais, ne pouvant se dédire d'une façon trop patente — par souci artistique et par amour-propre — il avait senti qu'il serait opportun de couvrir sa reculade ; or, en jetant dans la marche des événements du roman proprement dit cet épisode de la conversion de Wolmar, il détournerait, ou en tous cas diviserait l'attention du lecteur ; puis, lorsqu'il reviendrait au thème proprement

---

(1) Masson a signalé des phrases prises textuellement de ces lettres jusque dans la *Profession de foi* (La religion de J. J. R. vol. II, p. 58-59, et index).

dit, — l'opposition aux quatre premières parties des deux
dernières —, le lecteur serait distrait et moins choqué.

Ceci nous amène à la troisième cause du hors d'œuvre :
Rousseau cherchait un moyen de faire avouer à Julie qu'elle
n'était pas heureuse. Or, celle-ci ne pouvait positivement
pas, après ces pages et ces pages, après ces arguments si défi-
nis démontrant qu'elle *devait* être heureuse, — elle ne pouvait
pas, sans paraître une étourdie consommée, avouer qu'elle
ne l'était pas pour des raisons simplement domestiques ou
même de cœur. Alors, Rousseau imagine cet expédient, le
plus plausible à sa disposition, de l'incrédulité de Wolmar.
Mais cela est et reste un expédient, et jusqu'au bout du roman
Rousseau sera mis en posture embarrassée, car il ne peut
lâcher son prétexte (Julie qui s'est déclarée non heureuse à
cause de l'incrédulité de Wolmar), et il veut arriver à faire
comprendre ce qui doit être compris (Julie non heureuse car
elle aime encore Saint-Preux).

On peut admirer la façon dont — après tout — Rousseau
s'est tiré de cet épineux compromis. On peut le blâmer d'y
avoir eu recours, au lieu de choisir entre deux alternatives
plus franches, *ou bien* de ne pas publier le roman qui n'exprimait plus sa vraie pensée, *ou bien* de publier le roman quand
même il ne représentait plus sa philosophie et à titre d'œuvre
purement littéraire (comme il avait publié en tous cas les
lettres des amants, de la 1re Partie) : — on doit reconnaître
que s'il voulait publier son roman en exprimant sa pensée de
la dernière heure, et sans le récrire tout entier à peu près, le
moyen employé était habile sinon acceptable.

Mais, venons maintenant sans ambages à ce que nous avons
appelé le motif fondamental qu'a Rousseau pour ajouter les
parties V et VI, donc au fait : En somme le problème de *La
Nouvelle Héloïse*, de la 1re à la VIe Partie, pouvait se résumer
— si on fait abstraction des quelques passages trahissant des
réminiscences et velléités de retour à la vertu romaine ou
puritaine de renoncement — dans cette question : De Saint-
Preux ou de Wolmar, lequel apportera le bonheur à Julie ?

Or, Rousseau, après s'être posé en champion décidé de Saint-Preux représentant les droits de l'amour romantique, s'était attaché à réfuter avec un grand luxe d'arguments, la thèse qui l'avait un moment séduit si fort, en faveur de la thèse opposée de contrôle du sentiment naturel par la raison. Eh bien, il s'agit pour nous, de montrer que les Parties Vᵉ et VIᵉ témoignent du fait que Rousseau a changé d'opinion une fois de plus : qu'il a récusé finalement *la* thèse du roman, c'est-à-dire celle qu'il a déclarée sienne jusque dans les *Confessions*, celle qu'il avait affirmée dans les deux « Préfaces », celle qui demeure de beaucoup la plus longuement, la plus minutieusement, la plus sérieusement élaborée, celle qu'un siècle et demi de tradition a affirmée, — celle qui décide en faveur de Wolmar.

Quelques citations, d'une parfaite clarté, suffiront (1) :

« Je ne vois partout, dit Julie dans la Lettre 6, que sujets de contentement, et je ne suis pas contente ; une langueur secrète s'insinue au fond de mon cœur ; je le sens vide et gonflé, comme vous (Saint-Preux) disiez autrefois du vôtre ; l'attachement que j'ai pour tout ce qui m'est cher ne suffit pas pour l'occuper, il lui reste une *force inutile* dont je ne sais que faire. Cette peine est bizarre, j'en conviens ; mais elle n'est pas moins réelle. Mon ami, je suis trop heureuse, le bonheur m'ennuie » (p. 41).

Et « ce dégoût du bien-être » a « je l'avoue... beaucoup ôté du prix que je donnais à la vie »... Je vis « inquiète, mon cœur ignore ce qui lui manque, il désire sans savoir quoi ». D'ailleurs, depuis quand dure cet état ? « Depuis mon mariage et depuis votre retour ». Quand elle avait écrit : « Je puis être faible devant tout le monde, mais je réponds de moi devant vous » (p. 37), qu'était-ce à dire sinon : je puis bien me vaincre avec vous, les grands combats sont plus faciles que les petits pour des caractères comme le mien ; *mais* à quoi bon cette victoire ? Il y en avait une autre qu'il eût valu la peine de gagner ; ce qui aurait pu être si nous avions tenu bon ne peut plus être aujourd'hui.

----

(1) Elles sont toutes du volume V, de l'édition Hachette.

« Vous n'ignorez pas combien vous m'êtes cher, mais vous aimez
à vous le faire redire ; et comme je n'aime guère moins à le répéter,
il vous est aisé d'obtenir ce que vous voulez sans que la plainte et
l'humeur s'emmêlent » (p. 36).

Et enfin :

« Faut-il aller jusqu'au bout et vous parler avec ma franchise
ordinaire ? Je vous avouerai sans détour que les six derniers mois
que nous avons passés ensemble ont été le temps le plus doux de
ma vie, et que j'ai goûté dans ce court espace tous les biens dont
ma sensibilité m'ait fourni l'idée » (p. 37).

Quel « vertueux » mensonge donc, que cette phrase : « Mon
cœur ignore ce qui lui manque, il désire sans savoir quoi ? »
(p. 41). *Sans savoir quoi*, — mais ailleurs elle avait confié à
Saint-Preux le secret de ses soucis : c'était l'incrédulité de
Wolmar !

Et maintenant Julie se meurt : Dans la nuit de crise, en
proie à la fièvre, deux noms errent sur ses lèvres, celui de
l'enfant qu'elle a sauvé, et celui de Saint-Preux (p. 59). Et
au dernier jour :

« Julie, ô ma Julie, — s'écrie Wolmar, qui raconte cette scène à
Saint-Preux — vous avez navré mon cœur !... Oui ! je vous ai pénétrée, vous vous réjouissez de mourir ; vous êtes bien aise de me
quitter. Rappelez-vous la conduite de votre époux depuis que nous
vivons ensemble : ai-je mérité de votre part un sentiment si cruel ?
A l'instant elle me prit les mains, et de ce ton qui savait aller chercher l'âme : Qui ? Moi ? Je veux vous quitter ? Est-ce ainsi que
vous lisez dans mon cœur ?... Cependant, repris-je, vous mourez
contente... Je l'ai vu... Je le vois... Arrêtez, dit-elle : il est vrai, je
meurs contente, mais c'est de mourir comme j'ai vécu, digne d'être
votre épouse. Ne m'en demandez pas davantage ; je ne vous dirai
rien de plus ; mais, continua-t-elle en tirant un papier de dessous
son chevet, voici où vous achèverez d'éclaircir ce mystère. Ce
papier était une lettre, et je vis qu'elle vous était adressée » (p. 59).

Ce mystère n'est point mystérieux. Mais qu'on ne s'attende
pas à voir Julie confier à Saint-Preux qu'elle compte sur sa

fin chrétienne pour convertir son époux au christianisme. De ces pages, nous ne retenons que ces mots :

« Nous songions à nous réunir : cette réunion n'était pas bonne. C'est un bienfait du ciel de l'avoir prévenue ; sans doute il prévient des malheurs. Je me suis longtemps fait illusion. Cette illusion me fut salutaire ; elle se détruit au moment que je n'en ai plus besoin. Vous m'avez crue guérie ; et j'ai cru l'être. Rendons grâce à Celui qui fit durer cette erreur autant qu'elle était utile : qui sait si, me voyant si près de l'abîme, la tête ne m'eût point tournée ? Oui, j'eus beau vouloir étouffer le premier sentiment qui m'a fait vivre, il s'est concentré dans mon cœur... Adieu, adieu, mon doux ami... Hélas ! J'achève de vivre comme j'ai commencé. J'en dis trop peut-être en ce moment où le cœur ne déguise plus rien... Eh ! pourquoi craindrais-je d'exprimer tout ce que je sens ? Ce n'est plus moi qui te parle : je suis déjà dans les bras de la mort. Quand tu verras cette lettre, les vers rongeront le visage de ton amante et son cœur où tu ne seras plus. Mais mon âme existerait-elle sans toi ? Sans toi, quelle félicité goûterais-je ? Non, je ne te quitte pas, je vais t'attendre. La vertu qui nous sépare sur la terre nous unira dans le séjour éternel : Je meurs dans cette douce attente : trop heureuse d'acheter au prix de ma vie le droit de t'aimer toujours sans crime et de te le dire encore une fois » (p. 76).

Il y a bien aussi quelques mots pour engager Saint-Preux à consommer la conversion : « Soyez chrétien pour l'engager à l'être. Le succès est peut-être plus près que vous ne pensez » (p. 76). Voici les choses remises dans leur juste proportion.

***

Un mot encore : Il est évident que Rousseau a amené l'accident et la mort de Julie pour mettre fin à une situation impossible. Si Rousseau avait eu foi en sa Julie, son roman non seulement pouvait, mais devait logiquement se terminer par un triomphe clair et net de Wolmar sur Saint-Preux. Et cette fin mélodramatique serait autrement, absolument déplacée chez un auteur qui voulait écrire un roman philosophique (*Confessions*, IX, vol. IX, p. 1), et qui justement reprochait à Richardson la manie des épisodes sensationnels (1).

Il y a plus ; Julie s'est suicidée, en ce sens au moins qu'elle a profité volontiers d'une occasion de trouver la mort tout en donnant aux autres (et peut-être un peu à elle-même) l'illusion d'accomplir un acte héroïque. Il y a à ce sujet dans la IVe Partie un passage assez curieux, et auquel on n'a pas en général prêté grande attention. Claire, après la mort de Julie, écrit ce billet à Saint-Preux :

« C'en est fait, homme imprudent, homme infortuné, malheureux visionnaire ! Jamais vous ne la reverrez... le voile... Julie n'est plus... » (p. 48).

Certains détails de son roman, Rousseau les travaillait avec minutie : s'il a délibérément introduit l'accident pour finir, il a *voulu* que Julie coure à la mort ; *mais* comme elle est en tout parfaite, il trouve à l'absoudre un peu en rendant Saint-Preux responsable en dernier ressort... Il vaut la peine d'examiner ce billet de près. Va pour « homme infortuné » ; va même pour « malheureux visionnaire » ; mais « homme imprudent », — il ne peut y avoir là qu'un seul sens : Avec vos fantômes et visions, n'avez-vous pas causé la mort de Julie ? Elle n'était pas heureuse, mais elle ne pensait pas à la mort pour se délivrer ; votre songe de Villeneuve où vous voyiez Julie morte, et dont vous nous avez fait part, lui a suggéré le moyen de sortir de son état de souffrance.

Rousseau aime à jouer avec le surnaturel *apparent*. Tout le *Devin du village* repose là-dessus ; et après *La Nouvelle Héloïse*, dans la « suite » qu'il voulait écrire pour *Emile*, il laissait penser à des matelots abordant dans une île perdue de l'océan (et qu'ils croient déserte) que la sainte Vierge intervient en leur faveur et leur apporte des provisions ; ils s'imaginent même entendre un chœur d'anges dans les grottes de l'île : en

(1) Voir aussi la *Préface* où Rousseau critique ceux qui veulent dans les romans « des hommes communs et des événements rares... Je crois que j'aimerais mieux le contraire » (vol. IV, p. 5).

réalité, c'est une femme qui vivait là et qui trompait (dans un
but très édifiant du reste) la foi naïve des naufragés ; qu'on
se reporte encore au livre VIII des *Confessions*, on y trouvera
la curieuse histoire de la magie de Venise (VIII, p. 172) ; et à
la troisième *Lettre de la Montagne* (III, p. 154, note). Ici c'est
Saint-Preux qui a eu un songe prophétique ; mais il n'y a eu
que les apparences du surnaturel, car le songe a opéré à la
façon d'une suggestion sur Julie ; en d'autres termes, le songe
n'a pas prédit l'action de Julie, mais l'action de Julie a réalisé
le songe.

Chose intéressante — quoique pas tout à fait étrange — il
n'y a que les deux femmes célèbres, disciples ardentes du
Rousseau romantique, qui aient vu tout à fait clair dans cette
fin de *La Nouvelle Héloïse* (du moins nous ne l'avons pas
trouvé ailleurs), Mme de Staël et George Sand. La première
fait allusion à ce désarroi de Rousseau, lorsqu'arrivé à la fin
de *La Nouvelle Héloïse* il s'était trouvé dans l'impossibilité
de finir selon son intention sur la note de la victoire de la
vertu sagesse ; voir les *Lettres sur les Ouvrages et le Caractère
de Rousseau* (1788), p. 44-46). Quant à George Sand c'est dans
ses *Lettres d'un voyageur*, d'abord, 1837, (I, 212) ; et puis
plus au long dans son roman *Jacques* qu'elle s'est occupé de
Julie et Saint-Preux. Benedetto a raison (*Revue d'Histoire
littéraire*, juillet 1911, p. 553-65) en pensant que *Jacques*
représente pour George Sand « la solution du problème » de
Julie et Saint-Preux : logiquement, en effet, c'est-à-dire si
Rousseau avait eu le courage de ne pas faire mourir Julie,
Wolmar (*Jacques*) se serait généreusement suicidé (en simulant
un accident) pour céder la place à Saint-Preux (à Octave pour
la possession de Fernande) : « Ne maudis pas ces deux amants
— écrit Jacques à Sylvie (une confidente à la manière de
Claire d'Orbe) qui vont profiter de ma mort. Ils ne sont pas
coupables ; ils s'aiment » (p. 349). — Mais, justement, Rousseau n'avait pas voulu de cela ; il voyait trop les conséquences
que tireraient beaucoup de lecteurs de ce romantisme justi-
fiant les appels de l'amour passion. Les femmes ne comptent
pas cela, et pour le bonheur individuel sont anarchistes tou-

jours : Mme de Stael et George Sand discutant *la Nouvelle
Héloïse*, c'est Marie de France écrivant *Eliduc*.

*

Est-il besoin de dire qu'un pareil changement dans les
dispositions de l'auteur devait amener de profondes retouches
une fois de plus et des chevilles évidentes au lecteur attentif.

Certaines de ces modifications ont été en quelque sorte
inconscientes, penserions-nous. Par exemple, pour bien ramener l'atmosphère « sentiment » (qui avait été non jamais sup-
primée, mais remisée au second plan avec la condamnation
de l'amour romantique de Saint-Preux et de Julie et avec
l'exaltation de la raison comme instrument de bonheur),
Rousseau pousse à nouveau cette note de façon presqu'alar-
mante. Et on peut voir en ceci non seulement l'affirmation
renouvelée des droits du sentiment, mais c'était en même
temps une manière de tonifier l'élément de la passion romantique, lequel baignant dans une atmosphère sentimentale
paraissait moins anormal. Donc, les scènes touchantes
abondent à Clarens : « Si quelquefois on y verse des larmes,
écrit Saint-Preux à Bomston, elles sont d'attendrissement et
de joie » (p. 368). Ici on s'attendrit sur la réconciliation du
baron d'Étanges avec Saint-Preux (424) ; là, on nous raconte
l'aventure de « ce vieux plaideur inflexible et entier », l'adversaire du père de Julie, et qui subjugué par les charmes de
Julie repart tout ému et honteux d'avoir fait un procès au
père d'une si tendre créature (419). Mais le chef-d'œuvre du
genre, c'est la scène épouvantable du retour de Claire (419-20)
où tous ceux qui ne tombaient pas évanouis d'émotion, cou-
raient affolés dans toutes les directions, et s'embrassaient
avec emportement ; Wolmar lui-même « se sentit ému » :

« Claire vole à son amie en s'écriant avec un emportement impossible à peindre : *Cousine, toujours, pour toujours, jusqu'à la
mort !* Henriette apercevant sa mère court au-devant d'elle en
criant aussi *Maman ! maman !* de toute sa force, et la rencontre

si rudement que la pauvre petite tomba du coup. Cette subite apparition, cette chute, la joie, le trouble saisirent Julie à tel point que, s'étant levée, en étendant les bras avec un cri très aigu, elle se laissa retomber et se trouva mal. Claire voulant relever sa fille, voit pâlir son amie ; elle hésite, elle ne sait à laquelle courir. Enfin me voyant relever Henriette, elle s'élance pour secourir Julie défaillante, et tombe sur elle dans le même état. Henriette les apercevant toutes deux sans mouvement se mit à pleurer, et pousser des cris qui firent accourir la Fanchon (une servante dévouée) : L'une court à sa mère, l'autre à sa maîtresse. Pour moi, saisi, transporté, hors de sens, j'errais à grands pas par la chambre sans savoir ce que je faisais avec des exclamations ininterrompues, et dans un mouvement convulsif dont je n'étais pas le maître. Wolmar lui-même, le froid Wolmar se sentit ému. O sentiment ! sentiment ! douce vie de l'âme »... (p. 419-420).

Jusqu'au soir cette « fête » continue.

D'autres modifications assurant un retour plausible du point de vue de la vertu-sagesse à celui de l'amour romantique, sont très conscientes et ont exigé pas mal de savoir-faire et de subtilité. Avant tout, il a fallu remanier avec un soin infini toute la IVe Partie : non seulement réarranger certains passages existant, mais en ajouter qui atténuaient la portée de certaines paroles qu'on ne pouvait supprimer du moment qu'on conservait à peu près telle quelle la rédaction précédente ; et aussi ajouter des passages destinés à positivement annoncer que Julie allait revenir à ses rêves d'amour de jeune fille.

Nous avons essayé de faire imprimer notre résumé de la IVe Partie en sorte de faire saisir au lecteur où il devait chercher les altérations, et surtout les additions : — ces passages sont en italiques. Nous croyons qu'en lisant ce résumé en omettant les passages en italiques, on retrouvera le roman de la vertu de sagesse tel qu'il était à peu près d'abord : Bonheur domestique, et les deux épisodes où le passé est rappelé à Julie (lettres de l'Élysée et du Lac) ; dans ce contexte, ces épisodes viennent confirmer la victoire de la Julie sage et Wolmarienne et la défaite finale de la Julie amante. En relisant ensuite le résumé avec les parties en italiques, on verra

paraître le roman sous sa dernière forme, et tel que développé
en détail dans les Parties V et VI.

Voici ce qu'on trouvera :

Les onze premières Lettres, telles quelles pour les deux conceptions (sauf les passages interjetés que nous avons indi-
qués par la même méthode — italiques) : Après six ans, Saint-
Preux revient de voyage ; déjà sont faits les plans que Claire
d'Orbe, devenue veuve, viendra habiter Clarens ; les enfants
des deux ménages seront élevés en commun ; bref le bonheur
domestique sera parfait ; Saint-Preux viendra lui aussi ;
Wolmar l'invite lui-même ; il arrive, il voit, il est vaincu... là
est le bonheur, car là est la sagesse.

La Lettre 11 est celle de « l'Élysée ». L'Élysée est, on se le
rappelle, ce jardin planté par Julie pour avoir, près de la
maison, un endroit où se promener qui ne soit pas le bosquet
où Saint-Preux avait obtenu le premier coupable baiser de
l'amour. A Saint-Preux qui allait glisser sur la pente du souvenir, Wolmar explique : « Apprenez à respecter les lieux où
vous êtes ; ils sont plantés par les mains de la vertu » (p. 338).
Et Saint-Preux écrira à Bomston : « Le souvenir de ce seul mot
a changé sur le champ tout l'état de mon âme. J'ai cru voir
l'image de la vertu où je cherchais celle du plaisir ; cette
image est confondue dans mon esprit avec celle de Mme de
Wolmar » (p. 339) ; et il voit là « la vivante preuve du triomphe
des vertus et de l'humanité sur le plus ardent amour. Ah ! quel
sentiment coupable eût pénétré jusqu'à elle à travers cette
inviolable escorte ? » (p. 340). Il n'y a rien à changer à cette
lettre, car par les mots elle s'adapte aux deux cas : c'est-à-dire
que dans le cas du roman vertueux, Julie et Saint-Preux
seraient guéris ou convertis, dans le roman tel que continué,
ils *paraîtraient* guéris ou convertis.

Mais viennent les Lettres 12 à 16 qui sont — selon notre interprétation — nouvelles, ou en tous cas profondément rema-
niées. La Lettre 16, très courte, est celle où Julie écrit à Wolmar : « Vous jouissez durement de la vertu de votre femme » ;
et la Lettre 17, de Saint-Preux à Bomston, est celle de la « Pro-

menade sur le lac », qui explique les mots de Julie et prépare la Ve Partie.

La Lettre 12 — assez longue — est celle où d'abord la nouvelle tournure du roman est nettement introduite et où nous apprenons que malgré ce qu'on venait de lire dans la Lettre 11, la guérison des amants était plus que douteuse. La fiction est celle-ci : Wolmar prétend faire la preuve de la guérison de Julie et Saint-Preux ; la scène est placée non plus dans le Jardin anglais, mais dans le bosquet même du premier baiser, et les deux anciens amants doivent s'embrasser devant le mari dans l'endroit du souvenir ; puis Wolmar annonce qu'il va partir pour quelque temps, laissant les anciens amoureux en présence. Julie est effrayée ; elle demande immédiatement conseil à Claire. Voici d'abord les mots de Julie se rapportant à la scène :

« Il (Wolmar) nous a menés dans ce même bosquet où commencèrent tous les malheurs de ma vie. En m'approchant de ce lieu fatal, je me suis senti un affreux battement de cœur, et j'aurais refusé d'entrer si la honte ne m'eût retenue, et si le souvenir d'un mot qui fut dit l'autre jour dans l'Élysée (nous l'avons rapporté) ne m'eût fait craindre les interprétations. Je ne sais si le philosophe était plus tranquille, mais quelque temps après, ayant par hasard tourné les yeux sur lui, je l'ai trouvé pâle, changé, et je ne puis te dire quelle peine cela m'a fait » (p. 342).

Plus bas, après le baiser :

« Ce baiser n'eût rien de celui qui m'avait rendu le bosquet redoutable : je m'en félicitai tristement [!] et je connus que mon cœur était plus changé que jusque-là je n'avais osé le croire » (p. 346).

Plus changé dans le sens de l'amour ou contre l'amour ? le mot « tristement » est révélateur ; et aussi l'appel à Claire : « Je n'ignore pas que nulle considération ne peut être mise en balance avec un danger réel ; mais ce danger existe-t-il en effet ? Voilà précisément le doute que tu dois résoudre » (p. 348). Voici pour Julie. Ce mot « tristement » est tout à fait

inconséquent dans le roman de la vertu-sagesse. Rien n'y avait préparé ; il faut donc ou bien que Rousseau soit un bien mauvais écrivain, ou bien qu'il y ait là une cheville ; — or personne encore n'a accusé Rousseau d'être un mauvais écrivain.

Venons à Wolmar. Dans cette Lettre 12, il se présente lui-même dans un discours où il s'affirme l'homme raisonnable ; mais Rousseau en fait cette fois un homme absolument de bois : « J'ai naturellement l'âme tranquille et le cœur froid. Je suis de ces hommes qu'on croit bien injurier en disant qu'ils ne sentent rien...(etc.) » (p. 342). Comment se défendre de l'idée que Rousseau ait voulu suggérer : il manque à cet homme une âme. Ce n'est pas tout : En présentant ce tableau de lui-même, Wolmar avoue qu'il a épousé Julie dans un moment où il n'était pas Wolmar, quand il fut saisi par une « ivresse d'amour », c'est-à-dire quand la raison avait cessé de parler :

« Comment réprimer la passion même la plus faible quand elle est sans contre-poids ? Voilà l'inconvénient des caractères froids et tranquilles. Tout va bien tant que leur froideur les garantit des tentations ; mais, s'il en survient une qui les atteigne, ils sont aussitôt vaincus qu'attaqués ; et la raison qui gouverne tandis qu'elle est seule, n'a jamais de force pour résister au moindre effort. Je n'ai été tenté qu'une fois et j'ai succombé » (p. 344).

Il oppose, c'est vrai la *passion de la vertu* aux autres *passions* ; mais comme la vertu consiste justement à réprimer les passions, c'est donc l'amour de la raison qu'il veut dire quand il dit « passion de vertu ». Bref, Rousseau veut — est forcé en somme de vouloir — que Wolmar lui-même discute s'il n'a pas « commis une faute » en épousant Julie (p. 344-5), et la façon dont celui-ci explique son mariage constitue un aveu de culpabilité. Sans doute Wolmar dit :

« Julie, je vous connaissais et n'en fis point [de faute] en vous épousant. Je sentis que de vous seule dépendait tout le bonheur dont je pouvais jouir, et que si quelqu'un était capable de vous rendre heureuse, c'était moi ».

Comme c'est commode ! Car enfin, si cela a pu faire le bonheur de Wolmar, celui de Julie, qu'en fait-on ? Aussi bien Rousseau est bien empêché de se tirer d'affaire, et le problème du mariage heureux de Julie doit être re-posé tout entier ; enfin, Wolmar est, bon gré mal gré, celui à qui échoit la part de le faire.

« J'ai fait, dira-t-il dans la Lettre 14, à Claire, une découverte que ni vous ni femme au monde, avec toute la subtilité qu'on prête à votre sexe, n'eussiez jamais faite (à savoir) que mes jeunes gens sont plus amoureux que jamais ; ce n'est pas sans doute merveille de vous l'apprendre [ce n'eût pas été vrai cependant dans le roman moralisant dont toute la conclusion eût été faussée par la suite des événements] ; de vous assurer au contraire qu'ils sont parfaitement guéris ; vous savez ce que peuvent la raison, la vertu ; ce n'est pas là non plus leur plus grand miracle. Mais que ces deux opposés soient vrais en même temps ; qu'ils brûlent plus ardemment que jamais l'un pour l'autre, et qu'il ne règne plus entre eux qu'un honnête attachement ; qu'ils soient toujours amants et ne soient plus qu'amis : c'est je pense, à quoi vous vous attendez moins, ce que vous aurez plus de peine à comprendre, et ce qui est pourtant l'exacte vérité » (p. 355).

Or, nous savons déjà — quelqu'effort que fasse Rousseau pour sauver les apparences et quoiqu'il affirme encore selon la lettre que tout est pour le mieux — que la suite des événements doit montrer la fragilité de tous ces discours. Wolmar même manque d'assurance au fond ; il y a « un voile de sagesse et d'honnêteté » qui protège Julie, c'est vrai, mais il y a pourtant « une chose qui me fait soupçonner qu'il lui reste encore quelque défiance à vaincre, qu'elle ne cesse de chercher en elle-même ce qu'elle ferait si elle était tout à fait guérie, et elle le fait avec tant d'exactitude que si elle était réellement guérie, elle ne le ferait pas si bien ». C'est clairement suggérer que le roman de la vertu-sagesse n'a pas définitivement résolu toutes choses.

Ces Lettres 13, 14 et 15 continuent la lettre 12, c'est-à-dire reprennent le problème qui paraissait résolu. La Lettre 13 est la réponse de Claire à Julie, et elle est assez caractéristique. Claire prend pour point de départ obligé (obligé pour ne pas

rompre la continuité avec le roman de la vertu-sagesse) la
conviction que Julie est guérie, et que c'est une trop scrupuleuse conscience seule qui la tourmente... Cependant après de
longues pages de pur bavardage sur l'innocence du tête à
tête, voici Claire conseillant parfaitement des mesures d'un
ordre très pratique pour conjurer ce danger qui soi-disant
n'existe pas :

« Impose toi la même réserve que si avec ta vertu tu pouvais
te défier encore de ton cœur et du sien ; évite les conversations
trop affectueuses, les tendres souvenirs du passé ; interromps ou
préviens les trop longs tête à tête ; entoure-toi sans cesse de tes
enfants ; reste peu seule avec lui dans la chambre, dans l'Élysée,
dans le bosquet... Tu aimes les promenades en bateau, tu t'en
prives pour ton mari, qui craint l'eau pour les enfants... Prends le
temps de cette absence pour te donner cet amusement... C'est le
moyen de te livrer aux doux épanchements de l'amitié, et de jouir
paisiblement d'un long tête à tête sous la protection des bateliers
qui voient sans entendre, et dont on ne peut s'éloigner avant de
penser à ce qu'on fait » (p. 352-53).

Qui peut en douter : la sérénité du mariage de Wolmar et
Julie est passée, et il ne fallait pas moins que les longues pages
serrées 341-359 pour endormir l'attention du lecteur converti
à la thèse de la vertu sagesse.

Alors vient la « Lettre du Lac » (13), la dernière de la IVᵉ
Partie actuelle. On se rappelle qu'elle faisait partie déjà de la
toute première ébauche, celle des lettres amoureuses ; elle
aura donc servi dans trois conceptions successives de l'histoire ; et elle s'encadre fort bien dans les trois cas sans nécessité d'altérations (nous ne disons pas que Rousseau n'en ait
pas vraiment fait quelques-unes). Dans le roman frivole
et « efféminé » c'est la lettre sentimentale relatant les émotions des deux amants, séparés et qui se retrouvent, — pur
sentimentalisme. Dans le réarrangement des lettres en vue
du roman moralisant, elle décrit une dernière épreuve des
deux amoureux, épreuve émouvante, mais d'où ils sont sortis
vainqueurs et heureux ; la lettre est suivie alors, (V, 1) de la
missive terriblement « anglaise » de Lord Bomston reprochant

à Saint-Preux d'avoir cédé même un peu, à la fascination du souvenir : « Sors de l'enfance, ami, réveille-toi ; ne livre pas ta vie entière au sommeil de la raison... Sois homme une fois avant la mort » (p. 365). Et Saint-Preux répond (V. 2) : « Oui, milord, je vous le confirme avec des transports de joie, la scène de Meillerie a été la crise de ma folie... Ce cœur faible est guéri autant qu'il peut l'être ».

Enfin dans le roman de la dernière phase, où Julie et Saint-Preux ne sont pas guéris, cette même lettre est alors, non, le dernier cri, mais le réveil de l'amour romantique, et qui introduit la catastrophe finale. Là encore, comme pour la Lettre II, il n'y avait pas nécessité de changer même un mot. Les petits remaniements apportés ailleurs (émotion de Julie quand elle voit les marques de petite vérole sur le visage de Saint-Preux, et quand elle le surprend regardant avec mélancolie les enfants) et l'interpolation des Lettres 12 à 16 suffisent pour que le lecteur lise autre chose dans le même texte. Quant aux mots émus de la fin, Saint-Preux s'y montre *passagèrement* rappelé au passé dans un cas, et *définitivement* dans le second. Et les lettres des parties V et VI développent cette dernière interprétation (1).

(1) Voici alors le réarrangement général des lettres du roman (sans compter les retouches au texte même) une fois qure Rousseau eut décidé d'ajouter les deux dernières parties :

Dans la IVe partie — du roman de Julie épouse satisfaite de Wolmar et qui rachète Julie amante de Saint-Preux — contenant les lettres du ménage modèle (1 à 10) plus les deux lettres de l'Élysée (11), et du Lac (17), deux changements interviennent :

1. Addition des portions qu'on voulait écrire pour Mme d'Houdetot seule et qui ont trait au « ménage à trois ».

2. Interpolation des chevilles pour préparer le changement d'idée sur le problème central (surtout les lettres aujourd'hui sous les numéros 12 et 16).

Cependant la IVe partie serait alors grossie démesurément, et on en enlève quelques lettres considérables relatives au ménage modèle de Julie pour les transporter dans la Ve partie (telles les 2, 3, 7 de Ve partie).

La *Ve Partie* sera alors disposée ainsi :

1. Lettre de ménage modèle transférées (telles les 2, 3, 7 actuelles).

2 Continuation du ménage à trois, et questions d'éducation des enfants qui sera confiée à Saint-Preux.

Doute-t-on toujours que Julie ait absolument changé d'opinion une fois encore, et que Rousseau (car Julie c'est Rousseau) ait incliné de nouveau vers le romantisme après avoir prôné la vertu opposée au romantisme ? — Ajoutons deux preuves additionnelles :

1° Julie est si persuadée maintenant que Saint-Preux fera un bon époux qu'elle le propose à Claire — à laquelle certes elle ne souhaiterait pas un mauvais parti. Lorsqu'en effet elle devine que la sémillante veuve éprouve pour Saint-Preux quelque chose de plus que de l'amitié (p. 420, 441 ss), on pourrait s'attendre à ce qu'elle , qui a dit si haut que l'amour est « importun » dans le mariage, et qu'elle avait épousé Wolmar parce qu'elle ne l'aimait pas d'amour, tandis qu'elle n'a pas épousé Saint-Preux parce qu'elle l'aimait d'amour, va tancer sa cousine. Point ! Non seulement elle ne soulève pas d'objections, mais elle réfute celles que Claire pourrait faire à un pareil mariage : Serait-ce une question d'inégalité sociale ? Mais non puisqu'un « homme élevé dans des sentiments d'honnêteté est l'égal de tout le monde » (p. 444) ; hésiterait-elle à « donner un successeur à l'époux défunt » ? Mais « tu aimes donc mieux te reprocher ton penchant que le justifier, et couver tes feux au fond de ton cœur que de les rendre légitimes ? » (p. 444). Non, tout cela n'est pas sérieux. La *vertu* ,puisqu'elle veut être vertueuse, c'est l'*amour*. L'amour est-il donc un crime :

« N'est-il pas le plus pur, ainsi que le plus doux penchant de la

3. Continuation des lettres rendant plausible le changement de front de Julie que le « bonheur avec Wolmar ennuie », et qui est toujours amoureuse de Saint-Preux (telles 9, 10, 11, 13).

4. Addition dans la Lettre 12 de ce qui est nécessaire à l'histoire des amours de Bomston pour amener le voyage de Saint-Preux en Italie pendant lequel se placera l'accident de Chillon, et pour amener la discussion sur le lieu de séjour de Saint-Preux (en Angleterre ou à Clarens).

5. Enfin quelques lettres sentimentales sur les joies de la famille et celles de l'amitié (telles 6, 14).

La *VI*e *Partie* contiendra les aveux de Julie que le bonheur n'existe pas sans romantisme... et la conclusion probable des efforts de Julie pour amener Wolmar à la religion.

nature ? N'est-il pas une fin bonne et louable ? Ne dédaigne-t-il
pas les âmes basses et rampantes ? N'anime-t-il pas les âmes
grandes et fortes ? N'ennoblit-il pas tous les sentiments ? Ne
double-t-il pas leur être ? Ne les élève-t-il pas au-dessus d'elles-
mêmes ? Ah ! si pour être honnête et sage, il faut être inaccessible à ses traits, dis, *que reste-t-il pour la vertu sur la terre* ? Le
rebut de la nature et les plus vils des mortels ! » (p. 444).

Il semble qu'on rêve vraiment !

Voilà pour Claire ; voici pour Saint-Preux, le second intéressé. Les conseils de Julie se résument en ceci : On ne joue
pas avec les appels de la nature. A la thèse des IIIe et IVe Parties, à savoir que le romantisme avec ses violences menace
l'équilibre de la vie, qu'il faut donc l'écarter pour le bonheur,
— elle oppose dans la IVe Partie celle-ci : Essayez de ne pas
satisfaire ces besoins romantiques, d'ignorer par exemple
l'amour, et alors il en résulte des désordres incessants ; et,
à tout considérer des désordres pires qu'en se soumettant à
ses exigences. Ainsi Julie qui avait dit *Casse-cou* à celui qui
cédait à la passion, dit aujourd'hui *Casse-cou* à celui qui
essaierait d'y résister. Lorsqu'enfin Saint-Preux écrit une
page d'une noble assurance en refusant d'oublier l'amour
de Julie pour celui de Claire, Julie lui répond d'un mot
admirable et féminin (VI, lettre 8) : « Mon cher philosophe,
ne cesserez-vous jamais d'être un enfant ? » (p. 36).

2º Dans les Parties V et VI on discute incidemment les
amours de Lord Bomston. Par une suite de circonstances
trop longues à rappeler, Bomston avait été mêlé à beaucoup
de romanesque en Italie avant de connaître Julie — et il n'en
a pas fini. Il avait aimé une marquise, dont il avait tué le mari
en duel, puis n'avait pas voulu épouser la marquise à cause
du sang qui était entre eux maintenant. La marquise qui voulait le bonheur de milord, a l'idée (bien XVIIIe siècle !) de
chercher un double physique d'elle-même qu'elle offre au
noble Lord ; c'est la courtisane Laurette. Celle-ci en compagnie du grand personnage sent naître en elle des sentiments
élevés qui lui font prendre en horreur sa vie passée. Bomston

finit par l'aimer, et la question est de savoir s'il l'épousera :
la raison dit *non*, et Claire, Saint-Preux, Bomston lui-même
trouvent *non* — à cause des exigences du rang de celui-ci dans
la société. Les conventions sociales, disait Claire, sont trop
contre une telle union, et Bomston lui-même ne saurait se
soustraire aux souffrances qui en résulteraient ; dans les circonstances particulières où ils se trouveraient, les amants
seraient plus malheureux qu'heureux (VIe Partie, Lettre 2) —
c'est ce dont Julie n'est plus sûre ; elle, a de chaudes paroles
pour appuyer ce mariage. Et au nom de quoi ? — du sentiment de l'amour qui sanctifie tout (p. 439-440). Elle hésite,
c'est vrai, mais déclare qu'elle a des raisons pour défendre
Laure, elle n'en a point pour la condamner (1).

Enfin, on nous a révélé il n'y a pas longtemps un fragment
de lettre de Rousseau qui doit mettre un terme à toute discussion sur ce point : « Vous la traitez d'infidèle (Julie) ; mais
à quoi je vous prie, est-elle infidèle ? A sa parole ? Elle n'a
rien promis qu'elle n'ait tenu. *A son amour ? On ne voit que
trop qu'il lui demeure tout entier.* A son devoir ? Vous élevez
là une grande question... » (cité par Mme Noelle Roger, *Revue*

_____

(1) Au moment où Rousseau rédigeait *l'Histoire des amours de Milord
Edouard Bomston*, publiée à Genève en 1781, mais écrite probablement à l'intention spéciale de Mme de Luxembourg (Voir Plan, *Rousseau jugé par les
Gazettes de son Temps*, 1912, p. 14-5, note) il était dans le même esprit que
quand il écrit les parties V et VI du grand roman ; et il doit se sentir plus libre
de laisser percer sa vraie pensée que dans le grand ouvrage qui doit affronter
la publicité. Or, ainsi considéré, ce petit récit supplémentaire ne serait-il pas
comme une satire contre les gens qui adorent la raison, s'en font les serviteurs
et se perdent dans d'interminables ratiocinations — comme il l'avait souvent
fait lui-même dans le gros du roman ? La vertu-sagesse en amour, c'est parfait ;
mais rend-elle heureux ? et du reste qui peut se vanter de savoir en quoi elle
consiste ? La raison du grand raisonneur anglais en particulier entraîne celui-ci
dans des situations de plus en plus embarrassées ; en s'en remettant à elle, il
manque commettre les plus grandes sottises : « Flottant sans cesse de l'une
(passion) à l'autre,... repoussé par cent raisons, rappelé par mille sentiments...
cédant tantôt au penchant et tantôt au devoir... toujours ardent, vif, passionné,
jamais faible ni coupable, et fort de son âme grande et belle quand il pensait
ne l'être que de sa raison... tous les jours méditant des folies et tous les jours
revenant à lui » (V, 85).

de Paris 15 sept. 1923, p. 245). Ce n'est bien certainement pas de l'amour pour Wolmar qu'il s'agit.

**

Et maintenant quelle sera notre conclusion à tout cela ? C'est que Rousseau a probablement ajouté cette fin (V et VI) *à contre-cœur* en quelque sorte. Ce n'est pas par préférence, ni moins encore par indifférence qu'il oscille ainsi toujours du romantisme à la raison calculatrice, et de la raison au romantisme ; et il nous semble que cette interpolation du problème de l'incrédulité de Wolmar contient un aveu ; qu'il y a là non seulement un moyen de se tirer d'affaire pour dissimuler un peu ses doutes sur la vertu-sagesse, au lecteur, mais pour se le dissimuler un peu à lui-même. En d'autres termes, il eût lui-même préféré pour l'humanité que sa théorie de la vertu-sagesse fût valable : tout serait alors bien plus simple ; mais sa probité d'observateur du cœur humain — et qui lui dit que tout de même Julie ne peut connaître le bonheur sans Saint-Preux — finit par l'emporter sur son scrupule littéraire : il avait compté terminer sur une Julie vertueuse *et* heureuse, elle finira vertueuse, mais *non heureuse*.

D'ailleurs Rousseau réduit au minimum les conséquences de sa rétractation, puisque, avant que Julie ne meure d'accident, les effets de son amour romantique persistant n'ont pas passé dans le monde des réalités (1).

§ 6. Il est un point sur lequel il faut revenir. Nous avons donné comme titre à ce chapitre « Rousseau et les Anglais ».

---

(1) Rousseau voulait, on le sait, reprendre ce problème à propos du roman de Sophie qu'il avait amorcé dans le Ve Livre d'*Emile*. Le mariage de Sophie et d'Émile était fondé sur le principe de la vertu-sagesse, contrôle très serré des mouvements de la nature. Or cette suite qu'il méditait, qu'il n'écrivit pas (en suite de ses errements en Suisse, en Angleterre et en France, qui le laissèrent épuisé), mais qu'il espérait voir écrite par Bernardin de Saint-Pierre, devait montrer Sophie mariée qui succombait au romantisme avant de se rendre à sa sagesse... des vieux jours.

C'est que l'on voit, dans *La Nouvelle Héloïse*, les Anglais suc-
céder dans l'admiration de Rousseau aux Suisses (de la *Lettre
à D'Alembert*), qui succédaient aux sauvages (du *Second Discours*), qui succédaient aux Romains (du *Premier Discours*)
Or, nous nous apercevons de plus en plus que ces admirations
successives, en même temps qu'elles trahissent une oscillation entre les dispositions romantiques de Rousseau, et sa
philosophie de discipline morale, comportent des nuances qui
indiquent peut-être une marche progressive vers une solution
ultime du conflit fondamental. C'est de ce point de vue que
nous intéresse particulièrement l'anglomanie de Rousseau.

Rousseau s'était aperçu dès le *Second Discours*, — en fait
dans le *Second Discours* même — que l'absence des misères de
la civilisation ne constituait pas encore du bonheur, et que
d'ailleurs le développement de l'intelligence et la civilisation qui en résulte, comportent seuls des jouissances autres
qu'animales et vraiment supérieures ; c'est lorsqu'il se fut
bien pénétré de cela, qu'abandonnant les sauvages, il s'était
tourné vers les bourgeois de la petite Genève et vers les
« montagnons neuchâtelois » ; ceux-ci lui semblaient mettre
à profit le développement intellectuel de l'homme, ses arts,
sa science, et cependant, vivant « dans l'obscurité », — on
pouvait presque dire en « sauvages » — ils ne connaissaient
pas les maux de la pernicieuse civilisation. Or, une fois engagé
dans ce genre d'argumentation, Rousseau ne pouvait s'en
tenir là. Les prémisses mêmes de son *Second Discours* (que
l'homme est susceptible de bonheur positif seulement après
avoir abandonné l'état de nature) lui imposait cette conséquence, que plus l'homme se développe, plus il sera susceptible
de jouissances profondes ; fût-il cent fois vrai qu'en fait il y
a plus de corruption, plus de mensonges, plus de mesquinerie
même qu'ailleurs, dans les classes les plus distantes de l'état
de nature, il y a cependant *là surtout* le terrain propre au développement du meilleur. Tout le monde d'ailleurs ne peut
vivre dans la petite Genève et dans les recoins des montagnes
neuchâteloises ; ces conditions de vie sont à tout prendre
exceptionnelles. Et en effet, Rousseau n'est pas sans avoir

conscience que la partie la plus intéressante de la société est
celle des classes supérieures, disons la plus civilisée (voir déjà
fin du *Premier Discours* et polémique suivant ce *discours*).

Voilà comment d'abord il est naturel que Rousseau — une
fois qu'il aura décidé d'écrire un roman philosophique —
choisira des personnages dans la classe normale ou supérieure de la société ; *normale*, car c'est elle qui, seule vivant
dans les conditions propres au bonheur, doit compter, — la
classe aisée et noble, celle qui a accès aux moyens de développer les instruments de bonheur. Bref tandis que la classe
du peuple intelligent, roturier, qui peut aspirer peut-être à
compter un jour, mais en tous cas ne compte guère au temps
de Rousseau, n'aura qu'un représentant, Saint-Preux, le
milieu propre où se déroulera le roman sera celui du baron
d'Etanges, de M. de Wolmar, de M. et Mme d'Orbe... Et c'est
ici que Rousseau va rencontrer les Anglais.

Rousseau, c'est bien évident, ne va pas tout à coup abandonner ses antipathies pour la société des grands, soit parce
qu'en effet cette société était souvent corrompue, soit parce
qu'elle n'offre le tableau que d'un bonheur apparemment
menteur. Mais il peut s'aviser maintenant d'une chose, à savoir que, dans cette classe qui l'intéresse, il n'a vu de ses
propres yeux que la société française, — et avec sa prompte
imagination romantique et romanesque, il est disposé à
croire que ces vices de la société qu'il connaît, ne sont pas des
vices en quelque sorte organiques. On n'a pas assez remarqué,
pensons-nous, les sentiments d'apparences contradictoires à
l'endroit de la haute société française elle-même ; en général
Rousseau malmène furieusement les Français, mais il les
aime ; ne dit-il pas que dans ces salons de Paris il trouve
malgré tout les seuls endroits encore où on soit intéressant.
Ainsi dans la Lettre 14 de la IIe Partie, Rousseau fait précéder ses attaques contre l'art du « mensonge », des « sophismes »,
contre les « préjugés », etc., par des mots comme : « Pourtant...
le Français est naturellement bon, ouvert, hospitalier, bienfaisant... » (IV, p. 158) ; ou « Au lieu de tous ces sentiments suspects de cette confiance trompeuse, veux-je chercher des

lumières et de l'instrucrion, c'en est ici l'aimable source »...
Quand il attaque le plus sévèrement leur « jargon de société »
il est obligé de convenir que : « un point de morale ne serait pas mieux discuté dans une société de philosophes que
dans celle d'une jolie femme de la société de Paris » (Lettre 17
v. p. 170). Et enfin Saint-Preux sait fort bien mettre en garde
Julie contre une interprétation hâtive de ses mots (II, Lettre
19) : « Je te le dis du fond de mon cœur : j'honore les Français
comme le seul peuple qui aime véritablement les hommes et
qui soit bienfaisant par caractère » (IV, p. 180) (1). Dès lors on
comprend que quand Rousseau va s'enthousiasmer maintenant pour les Anglais, son anglomanie ne sera en quelque manière qu'en fonction de sa francophobie. Il n'a pas vu les
Anglais de près ; il n'en connaît que ce qu'en racontent les
livres — et des livres qui eux-mêmes ne cherchent Outre-
Manche que des parangons de vertus sociales ; et par conséquent il peut en ignorer les défauts, lesquels quoique peut-
être différents de ceux de la noblesse française, constituent
probablement la rançon des qualités (2) : « Vous avez passé,
écrit Bomston à Saint-Preux, chez la seule nation d'hommes
(l'Anglaise) qui reste parmi les troupeaux divers dont la terre
est couverte » ; et là Saint-Preux a pu apprendre « à quels
signes on reconnaît cet organe sacré de la volonté d'un peuple,
et comment l'empire de la raison publique est le vrai fondement de la liberté » (IV, p. 366).

Puisque nous en sommes à ce sujet, il convient de rappeler
que la notion de ce qui est « anglais », et particulièrement dans
les romans, de ce qui constitue la supériorité du grand, noble
lord anglais, peut donner lieu à quelque confusion. Dans le

---

(1) C'est là que Rousseau dit aussi : « On sent combien Muralt les hait (les
Français) jusque dans les éloges qu'il leur donne ; et je suis trompé si même
dans ma critique on n'aperçoit le contraire » (IV, p. 180).

(2) C'est le cas du reste de tous les anglomanes, ses contemporains : ils
admirent des Anglais non en eux-mêmes, mais en tant qu'ils trouvent en eux
des qualités à proposer comme modèles aux Français, des fautes desquels ils
souffrent. Voltaire, même Montesquieu, Buffon, font exactement cela aussi.

vocabulaire du xviiie siècle chez Rousseau comme chez d'autres, *anglais* signifie tantôt adepte du romantisme senti- mental, tantôt adepte de la raison anti-romantique ; c'est-à- dire que nous retrouvons dans l'Anglais idéalisé, une fois de plus, les mêmes deux éléments sans cesse en conflit au xviiie siècle et chez Rousseau. En effet, ce gentleman anglais qui ose planer au-dessus des conventions sociales, nous l'admi- rons *tantôt* pour son courage à suivre ses impulsions naturelles en opposition aux règles de la morale courante c'est-à-dire pour son romantisme ; et *tantôt* parce qu'il sait opposer la raison à la voix de la passion ou de la nature, c'est-à-dire pour son caractère romain. Or, il est certain d'autre part que l'An- glais, champion de la raison (toujours la raison en soi, pas la raison des « philosophes » du xviiie siècle) peut parfois s'accor- der avec l'Anglais champion des sentiments romantiques pour répudier certains usages, traditions et règles de morale courante ; ainsi, le romantisme aussi bien que la raison répu- dient l'idée de considérer naissance et argent comme facteurs déterminants dans le mariage.

Et ceci explique certaines difficultés que nous avions cons- tatées en résumant le roman de Rousseau, à savoir : *D'abord* comment, tout en changeant sa position de défenseur de la nature en celle de défenseur de la raison anti-nature dans le mariage il avait pu cependant maintenir dans une position exaltée le même Bomston, — c'est que celui-ci défend au commencement du roman des idées en accord à la fois avec les principes du romantisme et avec ceux opposés de la raison (notamment donc, l'argument de l'argent et de la naissance comme sans valeur fondamentale dans la fondation de la fa- mille). Mais *ensuite* cela explique aussi pourquoi cependant Bomston a passé du rôle de porte-parole de Rousseau dans les phases du roman frivole et du roman romantique, à celui de comparse dans la phase du roman de la vertu-sagesse. D'autres éléments allaient entrer en ligne de compte, que l'argent et la naissance, et qui n'étaient plus communs au ro- mantisme et à la vertu sagesse, mais qui relevaient de celle-ci seule (tel surtout le fait que la passion amoureuse étant passa-

gère et la famille demeurant, la raison devait décompter la première). En outre, Lord Bomston s'étant compromis tout-à-fait d'abord dans sa défense de l'amour romantique de Julie, étant intervenu activement dans le conflit, et ayant même offert son aide de grand seigneur à un enlèvement, c'eût été décidément trop choquer le lecteur que de voir l'Anglais déployer le même zèle, et la même éloquence à condamner le mariage de Julie avec Saint-Preux, qu'il en avait déployé à le favoriser. Quand Rousseau s'est aperçu de la difficulté que lui créait cet Anglais à double personnalité, — qu'il aimait tout à tour, mais qu'il ne pouvait admirer en même temps c'était trop tard ; c'est-à-dire qu'il n'y avait qu'une alternative : récrire tout le roman, ou détrôner Bomston. Rousseau adopte le second moyen. Il donne donc à Julie elle-même, comme nous l'avons vu, le rôle de porte-parole pour défendre le mariage de raison et attaquer le mariage romantique. Elle n'avait pas été, à la manière de Bomston, présentée dans la première partie, comme arbitre des débats, mais comme partie ; seulement après le mariage d'ailleurs, avait-elle été à même de voir les deux aspects du problème ; Rousseau pouvait donc sans lui donner le rôle d'une sotte, la faire changer de sentiment ; tel changement était difficile à faire accepter chez le grand seigneur. C'était très habile de faire dire à Julie que Wolmar, le philosophe était véritablement ce que Bomston avait crû être.

Cela créa cette situation anormale — puisque quand Rousseau se montrait intéressé au peuple d'Outre-Manche, c'était bien l'Anglais homme de raison et non l'Anglais romantique qui était davantage dans son esprit — que Lord Bomston est à l'apogée de sa gloire dans la société de Clarens au moment où il représente plutôt *moins* les idées de Rousseau anglomane.

Maintenant ce que le lecteur peut retenir de tout ceci, le voici : L'examen des nuances successives de l'anglomanie de Rousseau reflète à sa manière exactement les conclusions de l'examen du roman ; à savoir que Rousseau a commencé par céder à son romantisme quand il a dessiné le Milord Edouard des premiers livres, le lord anglais qui réclame les

droits des sentiments de la nature ; qu'à la réflexion, il s'est ensuite rallié à l'admiration de l'Anglais essentiellement philosophe — quoique pas « philosophe » xviiiᵉ siècle ; — et quitte d'ailleurs à combattre à la fin de son histoire sa propre philosophie anglaise, qui admirable toujours, n'a pas peut-être le secret du bonheur.

DEUX APPENDICES AU CHAPITRE
SUR *LA NOUVELLE HELOÏSE*

APPENDICE I

Note sur les modifications subies par le roman au cours de la composition.

D'autres avaient vu avant nous le manque de cohérence, et l'avaient signalé. Déjà parmi les contemporains Duclos, l'ami de Rousseau écrivait à celui-ci : « Il me semble qu'il manque trois ou quatre lettres de liaison dans le premier volume... « (*Corr. gén.* V, p. 263). Puis Erich Schmidt, dans son *Richardson, Rousseau und Gœthe* (1875) signale des contradictions entre certains passages du texte et l'esprit du roman dans la Ire partie (p. 106) — ce sont des chevilles ou retouches que nous avons signalées et qui sont destinées à couvrir les inconséquences amenées par les conceptions successives de l'ouvrage. Nous n'insistons pas sur les quelques errements de chronologie signalés par Mornet (I, p. 316-17), et qui sont probablement de même origine. Ce n'est pas sans raison d'ailleurs que Rousseau insiste si volontiers sur le fait qu'il n'est que « l'éditeur » des lettres, donc pas responsable de incohérences, et il trouve commode d'expliquer des solutions de continuité par des lettres perdues. Ailleurs nous voyons Rousseau avoir recours à un autre procédé : après avoir mis dans la bouche de ses personnages des plaidoyers éloquents pour ou contre l'amour romantique, il s'arrange à neutraliser sa propre éloquence par des remarques ironiques introduites plus loin sous la plume de quelque autre correspondant ; il n'est aucun de ses personnages principaux qui y échappe ; pas plus Lord Bomston (III, 20, Vol. IV, p. 256 ; et surtout vol. V, p. 84-6, dans l'histoire des amours du lord Anglais) que Saint-Preux (VI, 8, Vol. V, p. 36) ; pas plus Wolmar (IV, 12, vol. IV, p. 344) que Julie (VI, 8, vol. V, p. 41) (1).

(1) « Quoi, Julie ! — met en note Rousseau lui-même — Aussi des contradictions ! Ah, je crains bien, charmante dévote, que vous ne soyez pas trop d'accord avec vous-même. Au reste j'avoue que cette lettre me paraît le chant du cygne » (Vol. V, p. 41, note). Et c'est à propos de ces mots de Julie : « Mon ami, je suis trop heureuse, le bonheur m'ennuie ».

Un joli exemple d'adaptation, ou réadaptation à l'histoire, c'est nous semble-t-il, celui qui est fourni par les fameuses lettres sur le suicide (III, 22 et 23), alors que Saint-Preux, perdant Julie, veut renoncer à la vie. L'idée de ces lettres semble bien appartenir au roman frivole ou efféminé, — et la rédaction de la première en tous cas, celle en faveur du suicide, Rousseau l'avait faite par jeu en imitation des grands romans anglais à la mode, où le suicide était considéré comme légitime et pratiqué communément. Dans le *M. Cleveland ou le philosophe anglais*, de Prévost (1732) on trouve résumé en quelques lignes toute l'argumentation de la Lettre 22 de Rousseau :

« Le souverain auteur de mon être... a marqué la durée de mes jours ; je viole ses ordres si j'en précipite la fin... [*Réponse*]. Mais s'il les a changées lui-même, ou du moins s'il les interprète autrement pour moi que pour le commun des hommes, dois-je moins de respect à ses dernières volontés que je n'en devais à ses premières ? En permettant que je sois tombé dans l'extrémité de l'infor-tune et de la douleur, il m'a excepté du nombre de ceux qu'il condamne à vivre longtemps, — l'excès même de mes peines est un témoignage clair et intelli-gible qu'il me permet de mourir » Vol. III, Livre V, p. 171-2. Cité : Woodbridge, « The Novels of the Abbé Prévost », *Publ. Modern. Lang. Assoc. of America*, June, 1911, p. 328).

Muralt avait souligné aussi dans ses *Lettres sur les Français et les Anglais*, cette manie du suicide Outre-Manche. Or, rien qu'à considérer la force des arguments en faveur (Lettre 22) et la fai-blesse de la réponse (Lettre 23), on est presque en droit de consi-dérer celle-ci comme une cheville ; mais, arrivé au roman moral, Rousseau aura pensé comme dans le cas des « lettres amoureuses », que le style était trop beau pour être perdu, et qu'il fallait conser-ver cette pro e — fût-ce au prix d'une mauvaise réfutation. Il y avait cependant une difficulté : Rousseau ne pouvait mettre la lettre du suicide sous la plume de son héros *anglais* — pour la simple raison que dans le roman sous la forme où nous l'avons, Bomston n'avait pas de raison de se suicider ; Rousseau *devait* donc la mettre sous la plume de Saint-Preux lequel est ici l'homme fatigué de la vie ; et contre toute tradition, il fallut que ce fût l'anglais qui réfutât Saint-Preux — avec de grands mots d'ailleurs, sinon avec de bons arguments. Même en cela du reste, il y avait avec les circonstances des accommodements ; il n'est pas certain en effet que l'acceptation du suicide soit, en soi, davantage con-forme à la philosophie « anglaise » que le rejet ; selon comme on le prend, le suicide peut être jugé comme révélant une énergie peu commune, ou une grande lâcheté ; or, si les anglomanes se plai-

saient à présenter le peuple français comme frivole, aimant le plaisir et fuyant l'effort stoïcien, et par contraste voyaient dans le suicide qui est anglais, un acte de stoïcisme, du point de vue d'une philosophie qui regarderait le monde comme un lieu d'épreuve et où l'endurance de l'homme est un critère de son excellence, le suicide serait à blâmer comme une lâcheté : et c'est de ce point de vue que Rousseau, sans être tout à fait infidèle à l'anglomanie en tant que synonyme de stoïcisme, aurait un peu le droit de faire de Bomston un adversaire du suicide. Bref, tout en admettant du reste parfaitement que Rousseau ait pu avoir d'emblée l'idée de réfuter le suicide quand il décida de faire des lettres sur le sujet, il nous paraît qu'il y a là bien des indices de remaniements.

Quant aux formes successives que le roman aurait revêtu dans la pensée de Rousseau et indiqué par tant d'indices, nous répétons qu'il ne faut pas essayer d'arriver à trop de précision ; elles demeurent en grande partie un objet de pure spéculation. Il ne paraît donc pas opportun de se livrer à de longues polémiques à ce sujet. Voici cependant les principaux ouvrages ayant abordé ce problème :

Erich Schmidt, *Richardson, Rousseau und Gœthe, Ein Beitrag zur Geschichte des Romans im XVIII Jahrhundert*, Jena 1875.

L. Brunel, *La Nouvelle Héloïse et Mme d'Houdetot*, Paris, 1888 ; 63 p. (Extrait des *Annales de l'Est*, oct. 1888).

Et surtout D. Mornet, *Jean-Jacques Rousseau, La Nouvelle Héloïse*, Coll. « Les grands écrivains de la France, vol. I, Hachette, 1925.

On trouvera aussi des données intéressantes dans les livres de M. Hippolyte Buffenoir, *La Comtesse d'Houdetot, une amie de J.-J. Rousseau*, Paris, 1901 ; et *La Comtesse d'Houdetot, sa famille et ses amis*, Paris 1905.

Erich Schmidt expose très consciencieusement, sans passion, clairement, ce qu'on peut appeler la théorie traditionnelle : Phase des lettres d'amour, *Das Erfühlte*. Puis, quand il s'agit du roman, imitation d'un de ces romans anglais à la mode, surtout Clarissa Harlowe, *Das Erlernte* (Julie et Claire se colorent de Clarissa et d'Anna Howe). Puis, note personnelle avec Mme d'Houdetot, *Das Erlebte* (surtout ménage à trois, et des détails, comme marques de petite vérole sur le visage, baiser de Mme d'Houdetot à Rousseau devant tous ses gens, etc.)... Et Schmidt s'arrête-là. Cette belle ordonnance, toute française du savant et brillant professeur allemand, souffre un peu de cet excès de systématisation dans un sujet très complexe.

L. Brunel insiste surtout sur l'élément personnel amené par

Mme d'Houdetot ; Julie, en somme finit par être tout à fait absorbée en Mme d'Houdetot (1). Mais Brunel, comme d'autres savants français (Maurras, Seillière, etc.) a une attitude si hostile à Rousseau que cela fausse tout-à-fait sa connaissance pourtant réelle des problèmes.

D. Mornet étudie bien plus à fond et impartialement les choses, mais pas — comme nous avons voulu le faire, — de ce point de vue du conflit, chez Rousseau, des attitudes romantiques et morales. Il ne se permet pas de sortir des données affirmées par le « document », par les textes (2). C'est-à-dire qu'il doit alors simplement contrôler les indications de Rousseau, à savoir d'une part la transformation du roman romanesque et sentimental en roman moralisateur, et d'autre part la transformation amenée par l'é'ément contingent de l'entrée, dans la vie de l'auteur, de Mme d'Houdetot.

Sur ces deux points la pensée de Mornet se ramène à ceci : Deux phases, mais la seconde comporte deux éléments : Première phase : roman d'amour qui est achevé fin 1756. Seconde phase, roman moralisant, lequel prend corps après l'entrée en scène de Mme d'Houdetot ; cette entrée décide (a) « et du mariage de Julie, (b) et de la vie à trois à Clarens » (p. 86). N'ayant pas consulté les manuscrits (nous avons expliqué que l'on nous en avait refusé l'accès) et d'ailleurs pas certain du tout qu'ils livreraient de grands secrets, nous devons nous en tenir aux arguments internes ; et nous nous bornons à deux brèves remarques.

1° D'après p. 90, il peut sembler que Mornet ait cru dans le roman d'amour (première phase), que « l'écolière » aurait « épousé son maître. » Soit, alors cependant, où est le roman sentimental et émouvant ? — Car ce sont les souffrances des amants qui nous arrachent des larmes, et dès que ces souffrances ne sont qu'épreuves passagères, dès que la note déchirante et passionnante manque, ce n'est plus *La Nouvelle Héloïse* ; l'idylle est à peu près absente, et Rousseau devrait avoir tellement changé le roman que ce serait un autre livre. Le mariage avec un autre que Saint-Preux nous semble donc en quelque sorte nécessaire, et cela donnait à Rousseau l'occasion de développer son thème moral, thème du reste déjà applaudi comme le dit Mornet lui-même (p. 63) : « On n'avait pas

(1) Un peu comme M. Montet identifie complètement Julie avec Mme de Warens (*Mme de Warens et le Pays de Vaud*, Lausanne, Bridel, 1889 ; XIII, 254 p.)

(2) Si nous ne nous sommes pas défendu l'examen philosophique, notre interprétation, cela va de soi, ne doit pas contredire les textes, elle peut cependant les dépasser.

attendu Julie pour justifier les femmes honnêtes »... Et cela, non seulement dans le roman, mais au théâtre. (*Le Préjugé à la mode* est de 1735). Et souvenons-nous aussi que Rousseau nous dit, dans les *Confessions*, se souvenir que les lettres de l'Elysée et du Lac — lesquelles présupposent le mariage de Julie avec un rival, sont toutes les deux écrites pour le premier roman. Mornet fait de cela un peu trop bon marché (p. 87) ; il prétend tout simplement que Rousseau s'est trompé ; c'est en tout cas se tromper sur un gros point.

2° Ceci nous amène à notre deuxième remarque : Mornet n'accorde pas assez selon nous aux travaux de réadaptation des Lettres déjà écrites une fois que l'esprit du roman eut changé. Pour préparer le revirement dans l'esprit du lecteur, pour emboiter tout cela, il fallait ménager les transitions, — matière délicate et complexe bien souvent ; et c'est ce que ces manuscrits si embrouillés semblent confirmer.

Faudrait-il considérer ici les vues de M. Seillière ? Depuis qu'il s'est laissé entraîner dans le grand mouvement rousseau-phobe, il y a un grand nombre d'années déjà, il a surpassé tous ses amis en violence et en fanatisme. Et pour lui comme pour eux le roman de Rousseau a fourni d'abondantes munitions. D'autre part, justement c'est en relisant le roman de *La Nouvelle Héloïse* que M. Seillière a fini par entrevoir lui-même que le Rousseau romanesque et anarchique qu'on chargeait si allègrement des péchés du monde, était en réalité un faux Rousseau. A-t-il cependant dès lors abandonné sa position ? Point. Et il serait sifficile de trouver un plus bel exemple d'un auteur luttant éperdûment pour ne pas devoir se rendre à l'évidence, un auteur voyant, mais se refusant à avouer qu'il voit. Qu'on lise son étude dans ses *Etapes du Mysticisme passionnel de Saint-Preux à Manfred* (Paris, Renaissance du Livre, 1919). Là donc, M. de Seillière, ayant relu sa *Nouvelle Héloïse* s'avise qu'elle est un plaidoyer *contre* le romantisme ; mais comment alors réconcilier cette découverte (un peu tardive) avec tant d'anathèmes anti-rousseauistes de toutes les années précédentes ? — Eh ! bien, c'est tout simple : *Rousseau a voulu donner le change à ses lecteurs*. Dans quelle intention ? N'allez pas le demander à M. Seillière ; aussi bien, que lui importe ! Mais sur les 57 pages de son chapitre, il en emploie 22 d'abord à essayer d'établir cette singulière thèse. Il voit certainement que sur six livres de *la Nouvelle Héloïse*, quatre environ — les derniers — récusent les droits du romantisme ; — eh ! bien, toute la concession faite à l'impartialité consiste à avouer que Rousseau est là « un peu plus rationnel » (et ces mots sous la plume d'un mangeur de Rousseau comme notre critique signifient déjà un monde) ; et encore, donc, tout cela est pour la galerie ; car rien ne saurait contrarier davantage M. Seillière que de voir comment de page en page, « Caton continue à morigéner ses contemporains » — cela n'annulle-t-il pas toutes ses critiques passées ? Mais un premier aveu en entraîne nécessairement d'autres ; et c'est dans la *Lettre sur les Spectacles* que M. Seillière découvre maintenant aussi un Rousseau anti-romantique : « Il n'est pour ainsi dire aucun de ses arguments contre le théâtre qui ne porte de façon directe contre le roman passionnel » (p. 9)... ; et malgré cela, M. Seillière continuant à jurer que Rousseau prêche les droits de la passion : C'est à faire rêver ! Et qu'on juge par cette phrase de la conviction avec laquelle peut écrire M. Seillière : « On n'a jamais mieux combattu le rousseausime en littérature que ne l'a fait ce jour-là Jean-Jacques. Aiguillonné par la satisfaction de prendre en faute un philosophe encyclopédiste » (p. 9)... : et cela continue ainsi : Rousseau est tout le temps rationnel, et c'est que tout le temps Rousseau ne songe qu'à « morigéner des adversaires » (p. 10). Quand M. Seillière n'exploite pas ces notes-là, alors c'est pour dire encore que Rousseau a prêché la morale, mais que lui-même dans sa personne était un passionnel. Belle découverte vraiment ! Comme si Rousseau avait prétendu en faire un secret ; aurait-il alors écrit les *Confessions* ? Mais c'est en grande partie justement parce qu'il savait si bien ce que veut dire « être un passionnel », que Rousseau combat tellement ces dispositions dans ses livres. Il n'y a « double jeu » (p. 11-12) chez Rousseau pour que celui qui veut absolument condamner Rousseau: Seillière voulant attaquer la philosophie de Rousseau, et ne pouvant le faire, se tourne contre l'homme Rousseau, lequel n'aurait écrit que pour mettre un « fard vertueux » sur sa vie, et un « fallacieux déguisement stoïco-chrétien » dans ses écrits (p. 17). On ne sait ce qu'il faut davantage déplorer alors, de l'*imbécillité de Rousseau* qui se donne tant de peine que d'écrire des volumes pour attirer l'attention sur ses tares. alors qu'il n'avait qu'à se taire et être ignoré et vivre en passionnel qu'il était, ou de l'*imbécillité du public* qui se laisse depuis un siècle et demi fasciner par un charlatan ou par un fou.

Il faut, ou bien simplement ignorer ces compromis de M. Seillière, ou alors lui reprocher sévèrement son manque de loyauté vis-à-vis de l'auteur qu'il attaque. Comment flétrir autrement que du terme de mauvaise foi des titres comme ceux-ci : *La béatification de Saint-Preux*, (p. 22), *La « vertu » de Saint-Preux après la chute de Julie* (p. 36), *La vertu de Saint-Preux après le mariage de Julie* (p. 39)... alors que M. Seillière nous a laissé voir si clairement qu'il comprenait que, selon la lettre au moins, Rousseau flétrissait la faiblesse romantique de l'amant de Julie ? D'autre part, ce que M. Seillière appelle — avec quel regret on le devine — « la clairvoyance psychologique et sociale de Mme de Wolmar » (laquelle représente bien, les idées de Rousseau), elle représente justement ce que M. Seillière propose comme remède contre « l'impérialisme mystique » de son Rousseau mannequin.

———————

APPENDICE II

Note sur l'anglomanie de Rousseau

Joseph Texte dans son ouvrage connu *Rousseau et les Origines du Cosmopolitisme littéraire* (Hachette, 1895) cherche à établir que cette sympathie pour les Anglais si manifeste dans *La Nouvelle Héloïse*, remontait très haut chez Jean-Jacques ; que celui-ci l'a conçue pour ainsi dire fatalement dès son enfance, à Genève. Se fondant sur ce fait que des rapports fréquents s'étaient établis entre les adeptes de Calvin et ceux de Knox, — rapports qui avaient eu pour résultat de faire de la Rome protestante une résidence aimée des Anglais sur le continent, — il arrivait à suggérer l'existence à Genève d'une sorte d'atmosphère anglaise qu'on respirait dans l'air ambiant. Cette idée est aujourd'hui généralement abandonnée. Évidemment Texte a pris l'effet pour la cause ; les Anglais venaient s'établir à Genève parce qu'ils y trouvaient établies des mœurs et une religion qu'ils aimaient chez eux, ils n'y apportaient rien de nouveau. Et vice-versâ, Rousseau aimera un jour les Anglais non parce qu'ils lui révéleront quelque chose, mais au contraire parce qu'il retrouvait chez eux des idées qui lui étaient depuis longtemps familières et au fond chères, et qui lui manquaient dans la société de Paris.

En tout cas, si Rousseau a subi une influence qui serait spécifiquement anglaise — anglaise et non genevoise — dans son enfance, il reste toujours à expliquer pourquoi ce n'est qu'à ce moment, c'est-à-dire aux années 1756 et 57, et lorsqu'il prépare la *Lettre à D'Alembert*, en 1758, qu'elle apparaît dans ses écrits, — après celles des Romains, des sauvages, et des Suisses. En effet, s'il est vrai qu'il raconte dans les *Confessions* qu'il avait lu aux Charmettes (car

il n'y a pas la moindre allusion aux choses anglaises à propos
de son enfance à Genève), ou, était-ce à Chambéry le *Spectateur*
d'Addison, et les *Lettres philosophiques* de Voltaire qui l'avaient
particulièrement intéressé ; et s'il est vrai qu'il raconte, encore dans
les *Confessions*, qu'en Savoie « la lecture des malheurs imaginaires
de M. Cleveland, faite avec fureur et souvent interrompue, m'a fait
faire je crois plus de mauvais sang que les miens » (VIII, p. 157) ; et
s'il est vrai en outre que plus tard, à Paris, il est en contact journalier avec des enthousiastes de l'Angleterre, Diderot en tête, —
pourtant quand il se met à écrire son *Premier Discours*, en 1749, qui
opposera-t-il aux faux civilisés ? Les Anglais ? Non, ce sont les
Romains. Puis, le voici qui change d'idées du *Premier* au *Second
Discours*, et remplace l'austère vertu romaine par l'innocence et la
sensibilité naïve. Or, c'est une des choses que particulièrement en
France autour de lui on célébrait dans les romans anglais à la mode;
c'est ce qui a ému Prévost, Diderot ; ce qui a donné naissance à la
« comédie larmoyante ». Enfin Rousseau doit avoir lu alors (étant
le compagnon journalier de Diderot) la *Clarissa Harlowe* de Richardson dont la traduction française paraît en 1751 (1). Ce serait
donc le moment, cette fois semble-t-il, que l'anglomanie se décla-
rât chez Rousseau. Cependant ce sont les sauvages qui ont les honneurs du *Second Discours*. Et dans la *Lettre sur les Spectacles*, ce ne
seront toujours pas encore les Anglais, ce seront les Suisses qui
serviront à Rousseau. On avouera que si Rousseau est si anglomane depuis son enfance, cette lenteur à s'en apercevoir est surprenante.

D'autre part, voici des *faits* qui sont dûment établis : au cours
de sa discussion avec d'Alembert, Rousseau arrive à formuler
vaguement cette conception de la vertu sagesse que nous avons
démêlée dans l'écrit de 1758 ; il ne l'avait pas nettement dégagée
lui-même car il était encore trop embarrassé dans la sensibilité du
sauvage. Mais c'est à ce moment — quand Rousseau songe à écrire
un roman, et cherche des personnages, que l'idée paraît s'être présentée à lui de se tourner du côté de l'Angleterre ; justement la
traduction du *Sir Grandison* venait de paraître et tournait une fois
de plus les regards de la France du côté d'Outre-Manche (hiver
de 1756-7). C'est alors que Rousseau songea à demander à son ami
Deleyre qui lui offrait constamment ses services (et entre autre
pour des livres) de lui envoyer les *Lettres sur les Anglais* du Suisse
Muralt. Ces lettres étaient beaucoup lues, comme le montre Texte
déjà, et encore mieux D. Mornet dans son article « Les enseigne-

---

(1) C'est la date de Texte. Mais Dobson, *Samuel Richardson*, dit 1753
(p. 103).

ments des bibliothèques privées de 1750-1780 » (*Revue d'Hist. Litt.* Juillet, 1910, p. 461) : dans cinq cents bibliothèques dont les catalogues ont été consultés on trouve, outre 449 exemplaires de romans anglais contre 369 français, 65 exemplaires de Muralt. Rousseau lut cet ouvrage au cours de l'hiver 1756-7 ; et c'est ainsi qu'il s'enflamma pour la nation du « bon sens », avec les résultats que nous avons exposés.

Telle, selon nous la véridique histoire de l'anglomanie (passagère) de Rousseau. Elle est moins impressionnante que celle de Texte. Après cela, que Rousseau, en vertu du fait que des écrivains ayant passé par une phase d'anglomanie il était en ce moment le plus discuté, soit devenu le plus puissant facteur dans la propagation de ce mouvement « cosmopolite », c'est encore une autre question, — mais pas de notre ressort.

CHAPITRE V

ENCORE ROUSSEAU ET LES ROMAINS
LE CONTRAT SOCIAL

A. — 1. Le *Contrat Social* n'est pas en marge de l'œuvre de Rousseau, comme cela a été souvent affirmé.

B. — 2. Diverses phases de composition du livre. *Première phase* : de méditation générale sans conclusion nette. *Deuxième phase* : de l'état contre l'individu (article « Economie politique » dans le volume V de l'*Encyclopédie*).

C. — 3. *Troisième phase* : Rousseau adoptait le même principe (rationaliste) de l'état contre l'individu ; mais cette première version du *Contrat Social* ne fut pas publiée.

    4. *Quatrième phase* : Dans le *Contrat social* imprimé Rousseau abandonne le point de vue rationaliste, et adopte celui de la tradition, comme le prouve le chapitre ajouté « De la Religion civile ».

    5. Cependant, chose curieuse, en réadoptant le principe traditionnel(Dieu qui ordonne la soumission à l'État) Rousseau n'abandonne pas le principe rationaliste d'un contrat social — qui était alors superflu.

    6. Cause de cet illogisme : Il voulait un principe rationaliste pour battre ses adversaires, les « philosophes », sur leur propre terrain de la raison ; et il veut essayer de modifier la notion du contrat social, c'est-à-dire d'un principe. de contrainte sociale faire un principe romantique d'affranchissement social. Vanité de cette tentative qui supposerait : (*a*) la négation du droit du plus fort, (*b*) l'existence d'un droit du faible. Rousseau ne réussit à établir ni l'une ni l'autre de ces propositions. Il n'en parle pas moins comme s'il avait réussi. Le pacte fondamental tel qu'il est défini dans le corps de l'ouvrage est absolument un contrat de contrainte. Les institutions de l'état basé sur ce contrat, trahissent à leur tour ce fait que l'individu doit abdiquer sa liberté.

    7. Rousseau essaie donc de présenter un système de contrainte sociale comme si c'était un système de liberté ; rien d'étonnant que la plus grande confusion règne parmi les commentateurs. C'est comme un cliché de photographie négatif où tout est exactement représenté, mais ce qui est réellement blanc apparaît noir, et *vice-versa*.

8. *Cinquième phase.* Ce que serait le *Contrat social* mis au point ; c'est-à-dire si Rousseau l'avait publié après avoir laissé sa pensée arriver à maturité. L'incertitude dans la conception de la « volonté générale » qu'il affirme tantôt infaillible (ce qui justifierait sa thèse d'un contrat social) tantôt faillible (ce qui lui enlève toute portée pratique) explique les solutions contradictoires données par les érudits à cette question : Rousseau est-il le père de la Révolution ? Il en est le père illégitime.

9. L'examen des institutions politiques romaines, admirables, aboutit cependant à cette conclusion : les meilleures institutions humaines sont vouées à l'échec final ; il faut une clef de voûte à tout édifice social : la religion civile.

10. Les Romains du *Premier Discours*, et les Romains du *Contrat social*.

Note sur la société athée de Bayle, et sur la « vertu civique » de Montesquieu, Rousseau et autres.

NOTE. — Nous nous aiderons pour expliquer la pensée politique de Rousseau de toutes les autres publications où, à côté du *Contrat social*, il a touché à ces matières, publications si admirablement éditées par Vaughan, Londres et New-York 1915. Rappelons que Rousseau a donné un rapide résumé du *Contrat social* dans l'*Emile* Livre V (II, 429-442). Nous renvoyons à l'excellente bibliographie de Beaulavon, édition du *Contrat Social* ; Paris, Rieder ; 2e éd. 1914, p. 105-113.

A

§ 1. La postérité a vu dans *la Nouvelle Héloïse* un livre romantique — qui suivit un livre austère, romain, puritain (*La Lettre sur les Spectacles*).

La postérité n'a pas eu tout à fait tort, car quand bien même Rousseau, lorsqu'il parle objectivement de son livre, souligne le caractère moral, *anti-nature* du roman (Julie amante, répudiée par Julie épouse vertueuse du vertueux Wolmar), cependant lui-même n'a pas voulu supprimer les parties passionnées, celles qui sont bien les plus prenantes, celles à propos desquelles Lamartine s'écriait : « Grands Dieux ! Quel livre ! Comme c'est écrit ! Je suis étonné que le feu n'y prenne pas » ; et par là même il a encouragé cette interprétation. Et puis, il indique plus qu'un doute à la fin du roman, sur la sagesse prêchée au cours de tant de pages avec tant de conviction ; car autant qu'il l'ose, sans paraître trop inconséquent, il finit par accorder une fois encore sa sympathie à Julie et Saint-Preux.

D'autre part, il reste que le grand effort de *la Nouvelle Héloïse* a bien été fait dans le sens d'une philosophie basée sur la discipline des passions : il y a chez l'auteur, de plus en plus, conscience de l'élément rationnel de la morale. Et même, on peut dire que, quand à la fin du roman, Rousseau comprend mieux de nouveau les aspirations romantiques du cœur, il parle encore en quelque sorte au nom de la raison — suggérant qu'il n'est pas possible, partant pas raisonnable, d'ignorer la nature comme a prétendu le faire Julie épouse.

Cette emprise de la raison sur le romantisme dans la pensée de Rousseau s'affirme dans le *Contrat Social* — lequel est en partie, sinon écrit, du moins arrangé pour la publication simultanément avec *la Nouvelle Héloïse*. Le *Contrat Social* est de beaucoup le plus nettement et le plus complètement rationaliste, et le plus anti-romantique des écrits de Rousseau. Tellement que, plus d'une fois, les commentateurs qui connaissaient le mieux leur Rousseau, l'ont considéré comme un écrit à part, un écrit en marge du reste de l'œuvre de l'écrivain, ou même en contradiction avec le reste. Pour Morley, par exemple, les théories du *Contrat* reviennent à « un abandon à peu près complet des principales thèses du *Second Discours*... C'est une enquête sur les principes de justice et l'organisation la plus appropriée de cette même société que les *Discours* avaient montrée basée sur l'injustice » (*Rousseau*, Vol. II, ch. III, p. 121) ; pour Chuquet : « Le *Contrat social* est en désaccord avec l'œuvre entière de Rousseau » (*Rousseau*, p. 147) ; pour Faguet (1) : « Les idées politiques de Rousseau me paraissent,

---

(1) Thèse reprise plus tard, et jusqu'en 1910-13, dans *Rousseau Penseur* : « Il est parfaitement certain que l'auteur de tous les ouvrages de Rousseau, et l'auteur du *Contrat social* sont deux hommes très différents. La question reste : comment l'un est devenu l'autre ? » (p. 305) ; Et il conclut : « que le *Contrat social* est un ouvrage de jeunesse de Rousseau, indépendant de ses autres œuvres... » (p. 333).

je le dis franchement, ne pas tenir à l'ensemble de ses idées » ;
« Oui, le *Contrat social* a l'air comme isolé dans l'œuvre de
Rousseau » (*Le* XVIIIe *siècle*, ch. VIII, p. 383, et al.) ; pour
D. Mornet : « Le *Contrat Social* est une œuvre à part » (*La
Pensée fr. au* XVIIIe *siècle*, p. 62). Il faut ajouter à ces noms,
ceux de Ducros (*J.-J. Rousseau, De Genève à l'Ermitage*, p. 283,
note) ; Beaudouin (*Vie et Œuvres de R.* Vol. I, p. 326-7) ;
E. Champion, dans ses diverses publications.

Nous ne pouvons pas, cela va de soi, souscrire à cette manière de voir après ce que nous avons dit du conflit permanent entre un Rousseau romantique et justement ce Rousseau
anti-romantique dont le *Contrat Social* est l'expression la plus
frappante. Comme esprit, le *Contrat Social* dans le domaine des
choses politiques, correspond par-dessus *la Nouvelle Héloïse*, à
la *Lettre à d'Alembert* dans le domaine de la morale générale, et
par delà le *Second Discours* romantique, au *Premier Discours*
romain. C'est si vrai que nous allons voir réapparaître comme
les parangons des vertus politiques, ces Romains que nous
avions vus adoptés au *Premier Discours*, et puis délaissés
pour les Sauvages, les Suisses, et les Anglais.

Il était opportun cependant de noter cette attitude de quelques grands maîtres ; elle prouve que le *Contrat Social* est une
œuvre particulière de Rousseau, et elle est particulière par la
façon dont y est poussée la note anti-romantique.

Ce n'est pas d'ailleurs que l'élément romantique soit absent.
Non seulement il est là indirectement, c'est-à-dire pour être
réfuté, mais il lève la tête dans quelques formules frappantes ;
entre autres dans la phrase qui est aujourd'hui tout au début
du premier chapitre du livre comme un coup de trompette
défiant : « L'homme est né libre, et partout il est dans les
fers ! » ; et il règne même positivement, cet esprit romantique,
dans quelques chapitres ; seulement c'est à titre d'intrus ;
dans certains cas très importants nous savons positivement
qu'il s'agit de morceaux intercalés dans les remaniements postérieurs, ou parfois dans des remaniements de remaniements.

Tout cela est assez complexe, aussi complexe presque que

l'histoire de la rédaction de *La Nouvelle Héloïse* ; c'est-à-dire que les problèmes traités restaient les mêmes (comme ç'avait été le cas dans la *Nouvelle Héloïse*), mais les solutions ont subi des fluctuations profondes et il faut ajouter que le *Contrat Social* dans sa dernière forme, — celle que Rousseau a livrée au public, — est une œuvre où sont assez hâtivement ajustés, comme dans un rapide et dernier effort désespéré, des morceaux appartenant à ces différentes et souvent incohérentes phases.

Nous n'irons pas jusqu'à dire avec Lamennais que la plus grande partie du *Contrat Social* n'est qu'un « informe assemblage d'incohérences et de contradictions », ni même avec Edme Champion que « Rousseau ne dément pas son système (comme on l'a dit parfois) ; il n'a pas de système » (*J.-J. Rousseau et la Révolution Française*, p. 70). Rousseau n'est *pas* sans système ; la difficulté vient au contraire de ce qu'il en a au moins deux — juxtaposés et non fondus. Rousseau était simplement très conscient de l'immense complexité du sujet ; et il l'a été jusqu'au bout comme le prouve la déclaration souvent citée à Dusaulx, et datant des derniers temps de sa vie : « Quant au *Contrat social*, ceux qui se vanteront de l'entendre tout entier sont plus habiles que moi. C'est un livre à refaire ; mais je n'en ai ni le temps, ni la force » (*De mes rapports avec Rousseau*, 1798, p. 102). Et déjà, à peine achevé le *Contrat*, dans le résumé qu'il en donne dans *Emile*, Rousseau écrivait : « Le droit politique est encore à naître, et il est à présumer qu'il ne naîtra jamais. » Et il ajoute même : « Le seul moderne en état de créer cette grande et inutile [*sic* dans l'édition Hachette] science eût été l'illustre Montesquieu ! Mais il eut garde de traiter le principe du droit politique » (II, 429-430) (1).

---

(1) Voir sur les réserves nombreuses de Rousseau en ce qui concerne son livre après qu'il l'eut publié, *Revue d'Histoire Litt.* : oct.-déc. 1912, Schinz, « Le Problème du Contrat social » p. 45-49.

B

§ 2. Essayons, comme pour *la Nouvelle Héloïse*, d'indiquer ces différentes phases de la pensée de Rousseau.

D'abord l'historique même de la composition du livre est instructive. Nous savons que l'idée d'un ouvrage sur les principes philosophiques des institutions politiques s'est présentée au moins deux fois, à des intervalles de plusieurs années, à l'esprit de Rousseau avant le moment où il a rassemblé et préparé pour l'impression l'écrit qui devint le *Contrat Social*.

PREMIÈRE PHASE. — *De méditation générale, sans conclusion nette*. — Rousseau nous raconte lui-même qu'il se mit à réfléchir sur ces problèmes à Venise, quand ses fonctions de secrétaire de l'ambassadeur (de septembre 1743, à août 1744) le confrontèrent avec le sujet (VIII, 288-9).

DEUXIÈME PHASE : *de l'article « Economie politique », imprimé au volume V de l'Encyclopédie*. — Revenu à Paris, et introduit dans le monde des « Philosophes », il continue sans doute à s'intéresser à ces questions ; mais pendant plusieurs années la musique l'accapare davantage. C'est en 1750 qu'on peut placer le moment du retour (1). Le *Premier Discours*, couronné, l'avait entraîné dans cette polémique qui le « préoccupait beaucoup » ; et déjà ces problèmes moraux avaient abouti à des problèmes politiques dans le *Second Discours* (fin 1753). Puis, l'Etat de Genève l'intéressa énormément, et c'est à son retour de cette ville (oct. 1754) qu'il écrivit son article « Économie politique » pour le V° volume de l'*Encyclopédie* ; (paru en novembre 1755). Il y dit en propres termes : « Pour exposer le système économique d'un bon gouvernement, j'ai souvent tourné les yeux sur celui de cette petite république » (III, 297) ; et les allusions qu'il fait à Genève indiquent assez qu'il s'agit d'observations de date récente, et non de souvenirs de son séjour dans la ville de Calvin avant l'âge de seize ans. Or, nous observons que Rousseau a

(1) Voir Lettre à Moultou, 18 janv. 1762. (*Corresp. gén.* VII, p. 63-4.)

eu alors (d'octobre 1754 au 6 avril, quand il part pour l'Ermitage), une période relativement oisive où il faut sans doute placer du travail préliminaire important pour le *Contrat Social*. Rousseau a certainement dû faire autre chose qu'écrire cet article pendant tous ces mois, et les rapports entre de gros morceaux de ce dernier et le livre imprimé autorisent l'affirmation que les deux écrits ont été faits concurremment, ou à des dates très rapprochées.

Il y a ici un petit fait à relever, à savoir le silence complet dans les *Confessions*, sur l'article « Économie politique ». Est-ce que Rousseau, qui parle en détail de ses autres écrits — ceux menés à chef et ceux qui sont demeurés à l'état de projets (VIII, 288) — a réellement oublié l'article « Économie politique », ou a-t-il *voulu* l'oublier et le faire oublier ? Nous penchons pour la seconde alternative, à savoir que Rousseau a intentionnellement omis la mention de l'article. Au moment où il écrivait les *Confessions*, il était l'auteur célèbre du *Contrat Social*, et le *Contrat Social* tel que publié est trop différent d'idée de l'article pour que Rousseau n'ait pas tenu à ce que celui-ci demeure ignoré. La notion de « contrat social » surtout, qui occupe l'avant-plan de la scène dans le livre publié, ne joue aucun rôle dans l'article, y est à peine mentionné ; et c'est dire que nous serons portés à croire que l'article « Économie politique » était rédigé dans le même esprit que ces *Institutions politiques* dont il paraît si désireux de faire disparaître les traces (VIII, 288-9 ; et III, 306, Préface au *Contrat*).

Quoiqu'il en soit de ces hypothèses, et que Rousseau ait voulu ou non oublier, pour nous qui suivons les vacillations de son esprit, nous ne saurions ignorer cette phase de sa pensée en matière politique. Elle va nous montrer un Rousseau qui, en matière de gouvernement, est nettement anti-romantique, ou anti-nature.

Voici en effet un résumé de l'article « Économie politique ».

Premier point : Il ne faut pas comparer l'organisation de la société à l'organisation de la famille ; et particulièrement l'autorité du père et l'autorité du souverain sont choses très différentes. Dans l'une, vous pouvez suivre la nature, c'est-à-dire vous pouvez être romantique, pour employer le terme familier ; dans l'autre vous allez directement à l'encontre des sentiments naturels. En effet, le père n'a qu'à écouter ses sentiments qui lui feront vouloir le bonheur des enfants : « Les devoirs du père lui sont dictés par des sentiments naturels, et d'un ton qui lui permet rarement de désobéir » (V. p. 238). Au contraire, si le souverain écoutait les sentiments naturels, ceux-ci le feraient se désolidariser d'avec le bonheur de ces individus qui ensemble constituent le souverain : « Loin que le chef (politique, ou souverain) ait un intérêt au bonheur des particuliers, il ne lui est pas rare de chercher le sien dans leur misère » (V. p. 239).

Il est fort intéressant de remarquer ici que Rousseau est en parfait désaccord avec le Diderot de l'article « Droit naturel ». C'est Diderot qui pense que l'organisation de l'état est fondée sur un droit « naturel » ; et c'est Rousseau qui dit que la nature est intéressée, et partant incompatible avec l'organisation sociale qui repose avant tout sur la contrainte des intérêts personnels pour la protection des intérêts de tous. Diderot fait le raisonnement à la mode et que la plupart des commentateurs prêtent à Rousseau : Nos institutions politiques et sociales sont injustes et mauvaises ; or elles sont artificielles ; donc ce qui est artificiel est mauvais [argumentation absurdement lâche ; *certain* artificiel est mauvais, mais pas nécessairement *tout* artificiel] ; puis, *vice-versâ*, ce qui n'est pas artificiel est naturel ; or, ce qui est naturel sera bon [autre énormité en logique] ; donc il faut un droit politique fondé sur la nature : — la mineure étant fausse, la conclusion le sera certainement. Rousseau, lui, est beaucoup moins superficiel ; il ne met pas la nature à toute sauce ; et ici il dit positivement que la nature porte le citoyen à ne pas sacrifier son intérêt, et porte le souverain (magistrat) à sacrifier l'intérêt des citoyens à son intérêt propre (1).

(1) Nous reviendrons sur cette question de l'opposition de la pensée de Rousseau et celle de Diderot, car Rousseau va lui-même attaquer directement les vues de Diderot.

Deuxième point : Ce n'est pas tout. On pourrait mieux, dit ensuite Rousseau, faire une autre comparaison ; celle du corps politique avec un corps organisé. Comme dans le corps physique, chaque organe est lésé par manque d'un organe qui monopolise le tout en sa faveur, ou qui néglige de faire sa part, ainsi dans le corps politique, le citoyen intéressé ou indifférent nuit à la marche de la société. Et de même qu'il faut donc une économie générale dans le corps physique pour que tout demeure à l'état normal, qu'il faut régler les rapports des parties au tout, ainsi il faudra une économie générale dans le corps politique qui règlera les rapports du citoyen à l'état.

Troisième point : Tout ceci n'est qu'une comparaison car, tandis que l'économie de l'organisme physique se fait par ajustement physique aussi et naturel, l'ajustement politique n'est pas un produit direct de la nature, mais une création de l'homme, et doit se faire par le moyen de la volonté intervenant dans le cours naturel des choses. C'est cette volonté qui est à la base de l'État et qu'il faut étudier (1).

Or, cet élément de la volonté générale qui est l'expression de la société civile ou État, va, elle aussi, contre la volonté particulière, c'est-à-dire elle va, elle aussi, à l'encontre de la nature de l'homme : pour revenir à notre vocabulaire, elle est anti-romantique. Et cette opposition à la nature, Rousseau la voit foncière : « L'intérêt personnel [romantique] se trouve toujours en raison inverse du devoir [vertu sociale ou civile], et augmente à mesure que l'association devient plus étroite et l'engagement moins sacré ; preuve invincible que la volonté la plus générale est aussi toujours la plus juste, et que

---

(1) Il faut donc bien prendre garde que la théorie de l'Etat de Rousseau n'a rien à faire avec la théorie de l'Etat = produit de la nature comme un champignon ou un cristal, une théorie déterministe qui a été proposée dans l'enthousiasme pour les sciences naturelles depuis Darwin, et qui se rattache à la théorie de Taine, que la vertu et le vice sont des produits naturels au même titre que le sucre et le vitriol. Rousseau ne se préoccupe pas (ici du moins) de cette question métaphysique ; il prend pour accordé que la volonté morale peut modifier le cours des événements physiques.

la voix du peuple est en effet la voix de Dieu » (V. I, 243) ; — la voix du peuple signifie la voix de tous, par opposition à la voix naturelle de chacun.

La volonté générale est considérée textuellement comme le « premier principe de l'économie politique et règle fondamentale du gouvernement » (V. I, 244), — la volonté générale, *et non un contrat social*. Rousseau ne remontera à un pacte social pour en faire le point de départ de toutes ses idées politiques, que plus tard ; et ici il ne le mentionne (comme un des clichés à la mode à cette époque (1)) qu'en passant et en rapport avec la propriété (V. I, 265) ; bien plus — et combien cela est intéressant ! — comme tel, c'est-à-dire comme point de départ de la propriété, le contrat social est ici considéré comme consacrant une injustice (cf. p. 265-8).

« Il faudra bien, finit par dire Rousseau, considérer la question des utilités que chacun retire de la confédération sociale, qui protège fortement les immenses possessions du riche, et laisse à peine un misérable jouir de la chaumière qu'il a construite de ses mains. Tous les avantages de la société ne sont-ils pas pour les puissants et les riches ? Tous les emplois lucratifs ne sont-ils pas remplis par eux seuls ? Toutes les grâces, toutes les exemptions ne leur sont-elles pas réservées ? Et l'autorité publique n'est-elle pas toute en leur faveur ? Qu'un homme de considération vole ses créanciers ou fasse d'autres friponneries, n'est-il pas toujours sûr de l'impunité ? » (267)...

« En un mot, toute assistance gratuite fuit au besoin le misérable, précisément parce qu'il n'a pas de quoi la payer ; msis je le tiens pour un homme perdu, s'il a le malheur d'avoir l'âme honnête, une fille aimable, et un puissant voisin » (268),

(1) La notion du contrat social a été en quelque sorte suggérée dans les temps modernes, par exemple, par La Boétie, *De la servitude volontaire* (1574) ; et elle avait pris un caractère défini dès le XVIe siècle chez Hooker (1594) ; puis, elle fut reprise au XVIIe siècle, d'abord chez Grotius (1625), puis chez Milton (1640) et surtout chez Hobbes, qui dans son *De Cive* (1642) partait de l'idée que l'homme étant méchant (*homo homini lupus*) il faut un contrat pour se garder en commun contre la méchanceté de chacun ; et chez Locke, qui dans ses *Two Treatises on Civil Governement* (1690) adoptait l'idée du contrat parce que les hommes sont bons et veulent s'associer pour développer leur bonté. Le *Tractatus Politicus* de Spinoza ne fut pas terminé.

Enfin :

« Résumons en quatre mots le pacte social des deux états : Vous avez besoin de moi, car je suis riche et vous êtes pauvres ; faisons donc un accord entre nous ; je permettrai que vous ayez l'honneur de me servir à condition que vous me donnerez le peu qui vous reste pour la peine que je prendrai de vous commander » (268).

C'est la grandiloquence du *Second Discours* : « Le premier qui, ayant enclos un terrain, s'avisa de dire : *Ceci est à moi*, et trouva des gens assez simples pour le croire fut le vrai fondateur de la société civile. Que de crimes... » etc.

Le véritable problème qui se présente à l'esprit du lecteur est celui-ci : Comment, au moment où les sociétés se sont constituées, les perdants ont-ils pu, le sachant et le voulant, accepter des conditions qui leur sont défavorables, et comment d'ailleurs aujourd'hui même peuvent-ils accepter de ne pas remettre tout en question ? Rousseau naturellement voit ce problème fort bien dans l'article « Économie politique », mais ne le résout pas. Il essaie de faire de « la Loi » le *Deus ex machinâ*, — dans un morceau très oratoire, mais tout à côté de la question :

« Par quel art inconcevable a-t-on pu trouver le moyen d'assujettir les hommes pour les rendre libres ? d'employer au service de l'Etat les biens, les bras et la vie même de tous ses membres, sans les contraindre et sans les consulter ? d'enchaîner leur volonté de leur propre aveu ? de faire valoir leur consentement contre leur refus, et de les forcer à se punir eux-mêmes quand ils font ce qu'ils n'ont pas voulu ? Comment se peut-il faire qu'ils obéissent et que personne ne commande, qu'ils servent et n'aient point de maître ; d'autant plus libres en effet que, sous une apparente sujétion, nul ne perd de sa liberté que ce qui peut nuire à celle d'un autre ? Ces prodiges sont l'ouvrage de la Loi. C'est à la Loi seule que les hommes doivent la justice et la liberté ; c'est cet organe salutaire de la volonté de tous qui rétablit l'égalité naturelle entre les hommes ; c'est cette voix céleste qui dicte à chaque citoyen les préceptes de la raison publique, et lui apprend à agir selon les maximes de son propre jugement, et à n'être pas en contradiction avec lui-même » (245).

Mais pourquoi l'homme obéit-il à la Loi, c'est-à-dire sacrifie t-il sa volonté particulière à la volonté générale ? Rousseau, en dernière analyse ne répond pas ; et l'article « Économie politique » finit par un aveu couvert d'impuissance. Pour s'en tirer, Rousseau déplace le problème et y substitue celui-ci : Comment les magistrats feront-ils observer la Loi ? — Qui est tout autre chose que : Pourquoi l'homme obéirait-il spontanément à la Loi quand celle-ci va contre ses intérêts, et quand il peut l'éluder impunément, c'est-à-dire justement quand le magistrat serait impuissant ?

Et d'ailleurs, comme les magistrats sont des hommes aussi, les choses deviennent pires — car non seulement ils ne voudront pas obéir à la loi quand elle va contre leurs intérêts, mais ils auront des pouvoirs qui leur permettront de tourner la loi en leur faveur à chaque coup. Comment les fera-t-on obéir à la loi, eux ? Ce sera à la fois bien plus important (parce que le bonheur de tous en dépend) et bien plus difficile (puisque, étant hommes, ils seront par les circonstances bien plus tentés que les autres). Rousseau donne sa langue au chat. Supposé dit-il, qu'on m'objecte que ceux qui gouvernent, et surtout ceux qui règlent les impôts, « les imposteurs, comme les appelle Bodin » fussent partiaux à leurs intérêts ?... Réponse : « Mais il faut rejeter de pareilles idées. Si dans chaque nation, ceux à qui le souverain confie le gouvernement des peuples en étaient les ennemis par état [par nature — et selon *Rousseau c'est justement ce qu'ils sont*], ce ne serait pas la peine de rechercher ce qu'ils doivent faire pour les rendre heureux ! » (273). Cela veut dire : le problème que j'avais à résoudre — un gouvernement qui soit le bonheur du peuple — est insoluble s'il ne se résout pas tout seul : tout dépend des gouverneurs, et s'ils sont par nature portés à être infidèles à leur mission de chefs d'État, c'est-à-dire s'ils sont par nature mauvais, comment les rendrions-nous bons ? C.-E. Vaughan a raison ; ceci est un morceau achevé d'ironie (*a finished piece of irony* », *Political Writings of Rousseau*, 1917, Vol. I, p. 273).

§ **3.** Troisième Phase : *La Première ébauche du Contrat Social.* — Rousseau ne pouvait s'en tenir là. Personne ne devait savoir mieux que lui qu'il avait mis le point final à l'article sur l' « Économie politique » par « un morceau achevé d'ironie »... Mais le volume V de l'*Encyclopédie* attendait ; il fallait s'en tirer, fût-ce en se moquant un peu.

Quand, trois ans plus tard, en vue de publier un ouvrage considérable, Rousseau reprend ses *Institutions politiques* (Hachette, VIII, 288) il espère encore faire usage de ses notes d'autrefois. C'est la notion de la Loi, expression de la volonté générale, qui lui paraît encore le point de départ de tout, le cœur de tous les problèmes politiques, et toujours pas la notion du *Contrat Social*.

Nous en avons une double preuve :

La première, dans les *Confessions*, où parlant du moment où il reprend ses notes manuscrites pour chercher à en tirer un ouvrage qui lui aide à vivre, Rousseau décrit ainsi l'état d'esprit dans lequel il conçut son travail : La grande question était celle de « la nature du gouvernement propre à former les peuples les plus vertueux, les plus éclairés, les plus sages ». Or, « j'avais cru que cette question tenait de bien près à cette autre, si même elle en était différente : *Quel est le gouvernement qui par sa nature se tient toujours le plus près de la loi* ? De là, qu'est-ce que la loi, et une chaîne de questions de toute importance. Je voyais que cela me ramenait à de grandes vérités utiles au bonheur du genre humain. » (VIII, 289).

L'autre preuve, c'est que même quand il a revu son manuscrit et s'est décidé à renoncer aux *Institutions politiques* dans l'ensemble, pour ne plus traiter que les Principes de droit politique (sous titre de *Contrat social*), et qu'il cherche ce principe dans un « contrat social », il ne supprime pas d'abord le passage sur la Loi comme la plus « sublime de toutes les institutions humaines » et celle qui a levé la difficulté qui semblait « insurmontable », la loi, le fondement de la société civile. On retrouve textuellement le passage cité plus haut, de l' « Économie politique » (p. 245) dans la première ébauche du *Contrat Social* :

« Ces difficultés, qui devaient paraître insurmontables, ont été

levées par la plus sublime de toutes les institutions humaines, ou
plutôt par une inspiration céleste qui apprit au peuple à imiter
ici-bas les décrets immuables de la divinité. Par quel art inconcevable a-t-on pu trouver le moyen d'assujettir les hommes... », etc.
(V. p. 475).

Cette répétition nous paraît un indice certain que le travail
sur les Institutions politiques doit avoir suivi de près en date
l' « Économie politique ». Rousseau n'aurait pas *écrit* ce passage après avoir donné au *pacte social* le rôle du principe de
la société civile ; on comprend seulement qu'il l'ait — par
inadvertence du reste bien compréhensible étant donné la
complexité de ces matières — *conservé*. De même qu'on comprend comment, quand il se relut bien des mois après, il se
soit avisé de l'incompatibilité de donner à deux notions la
première place (la Loi et le pacte) : le passage qui nous occupe,
en effet, dans le *Contrat Social* imprimé a été éliminé ; Rousseau ne fera plus que donner une importance très grande à la
Loi. (cf. Livre II, ch. VI et VII) (1).

Donc, dans cette troisième phase que nous résumons maintenant, le passage de la Loi, expression de la volonté générale,
c'est-à-dire *la lettre* reste, mais déjà l'*esprit* de Rousseau pas-
sera outre. La loi peut être encore « la plus sublime de toutes
les institutions humaines », déjà on sait qu'elle demeure
lettre morte aussi longtemps qu'on n'est pas certain qu'on
l'observe. L'*observation* à la loi, voilà le problème plus fondamental encore que l'*excellence* de la loi ; car, que la loi ordonne d'observer la loi, c'est un cercle ; ou selon la pittoresque
image des Anglais, c'est l'homme qui essaie de se soulever
par ses sous-pieds. Bref, quand Rousseau reprend ses notes des
Institutions politiques pour les publier, le premier problème

(1) « Les lois ne sont proprement que les conditions de l'association civile. Le
peuple soumis aux lois, en doit être l'auteur ; il n'appartient qu'à ceux qui
s'associent de régler les conditions de la société. Mais comment la règleront-ils ?...
Comment une multitude aveugle exécuterait-elle une entreprise aussi grande ?...
Il faudrait une intelligence supérieure... Il faudrait des dieux pour donner des
lois aux hommes » (VIII, 326-7).

qui se présente à lui, est celui-même qu'il avait commodément
éludé dans l' « Économie politique ». Rousseau probablement
avait cru être tout à fait d'accord avec Diderot quand il écrivait, lui, son article « Économie politique », et Diderot celui
de « Droit naturel » pour le même volume V de l'*Encyclopédie*.
Et ce dut être quand Rousseau lut, présentée systématiquement la pensée de Diderot sur le droit naturel, qu'il en comprit
les faiblesses, et qu'il comprit où était le vrai problème.

C'est tellement ce problème de l'observation de la loi qui
s'est poussé — et à bon droit — à l'avant des préoccupations
de Rousseau maintenant, qu'une grande partie, il faut dire la
partie la plus importante de ce long chapitre (plus tard sup-
primé) du début du premier *Contrat Social* est consacrée à
bien le mettre au centre des choses. Pour qu'il n'y ait pas
d'équivoque, Rousseau réfute directement cet article « Droit
naturel » où Diderot s'imaginait bénévolement que l'homme
est *naturellement* porté à observer la loi, — et on peut dire
que par là, Rousseau se réfute lui-même en tant qu'il avait au
moins tacitement accepté cette façon de voir. Comme dit
Vaughan, cette réfutation de Diderot est irréfutable. Il y a
là quelques pages d'une dialectique merveilleuse, et il faudra
des raisons bien fortes pour que Rousseau, comme nous le
verrons, les sacrifie.

Voici la marche des idées dans ce chapitre capital : chapitre II, « De la société générale du genre humain » (1).

Rousseau est un peu confus parfois, et nous résumons du
point de vue qui intéresse le problème central. L'homme a
passé de l'état de nature à l'état social pour deux raisons différentes, voire contraires :

a) A mesure que l'homme se développe, ses besoins dépassent
ses capacités de les satisfaire par ses seules forces, — et il a
besoin des autres ; « l'assistance des semblables lui devient
nécessaire » (447).

b) Mais en même temps, à mesure que chaque homme dé-

(1) Le Chap. I, en quelques lignes, dit le sujet de l'ouvrage : « étudier la nature du corps social ».

veloppe ses besoins, il se trouve en conflit avec les autres hommes, dont les besoins se développent aussi ; tous nous devenons « les ennemis de nos semblables » (447), — et l'homme a besoin des autres pour résister aux semblables.

Or, si nos besoins d'hommes sociaux à la fois nous rapprochent et nous divisent, en pratique c'est le problème de la division qui est le plus difficile à résoudre, qui est *le* problème social ; l'association *contre* le prochain est plus impérative que l'association *avec* le prochain. Il faut citer ce passage :

« La société générale, telle que nos besoins mutuels peuvent l'engendrer, n'offre donc point une assistance efficace à l'homme devenu misérable ; ou du moins elle ne donne de nouvelles forces qu'à celui qui en a déjà trop, tandis que le faible, perdu, étouffé, écrasé dans la multitude, ne trouve nul asile où se réfugier, nul support à sa faiblesse, et périt enfin victime de cette union trompeuse dont il attendait son bonheur ». (V. p. 448).

La société générale... n'offre donc point une assistance efficace à l'homme devenu misérable ! Mais en conséquence de la sortie de l'état de nature, où il était non pas heureux, mais non malheureux elle *doit* l'offrir. Et le problème c'est de remédier à cet état de choses.

Et c'est ici que Rousseau part contre la théorie de Diderot et des avocats de la bonté naturelle de l'homme laquelle était à la mode, et dont tellement à tort et d'une façon si persistante, on l'a rendu solidaire, — laquelle bonté ferait vouloir à l'homme l'intérêt de son semblable plutôt que son intérêt à lui. Le plaidoyer de Rousseau est parfait de logique, et il vise Diderot constamment :

« Il est faux que, dans l'état d'indépendance, la raison nous porte à concourir au bien commun par la vue de notre propre intérêt. Loin que l'intérêt particulier s'allie au bien général, ils s'excluent l'un l'autre dans l'ordre naturel des choses ; et les lois sociales sont un joug que chacun veut bien imposer aux autres mais non pas s'en charger lui-même. « Je sens que je porte l'épouvante et le trouble au milieu de l'espèce humaine » dit l'homme indépendant que le sage étouffe ; « mais il faut que je sois malheureux ou que je fasse le malheur des autres, et personne ne m'est plus

cher que moi. C'est vainement », pourra-t-il ajouter, « que je voudrais concilier mon intérêt avec celui d'autrui ; tout ce que vous
me dites des avantages de la loi sociale pourrait être bon si, tandis
que je l'observais scrupuleusement envers les autres, j'étais sûr
qu'ils l'observeraient envers moi. Mais quelle sûreté pouvez vous
me donner là-dessus ? et ma situation peut-elle être pire que de me
voir exposé à tous les maux que les plus forts voudront me faire
sans oser me dédommager sur les faibles ? Ou donnez-moi des
garants contre toute entreprise injuste, ou n'espérez pas que je m'en
abstienne à mon tour. Vous avez beau me dire qu'en renonçant
aux devoirs que m'impose la loi naturelle je me prive en même
temps de ses droits, et que mes violences autorisent toutes celles
dont on voudra user envers moi. J'y consens d'autant plus volontiers que je ne vois point comment ma modération pourrait m'en
garantir. Au surplus, ce sera mon affaire de mettre les forts dans
mes intérêts, en partageant avec eux les dépouilles des faibles ;
cela vaudra mieux que la justice pour mon avantage et pour ma
sûreté. » La preuve que c'est ainsi qu'eût raisonné l'homme
éclairé et indépendant est que c'est ainsi que raisonne toute société
souveraine qui ne rend compte de sa conduite qu'à elle-même.

Que répondre de solide à de pareils discours, si l'on ne veut
amener la religion à l'aide de la morale... » (V. p. 450-1).

Plus bas, on lit encore :

« Il ne s'agit pas de m'apprendre ce que c'est que justice ; il
s'agit de me montrer quel intérêt j'ai d'être juste » (452).

Ou :

« Ce que le raisonnement nous démontre à cet égard est parfaitement confirmé par les faits ; et pour peu qu'on remonte dans les
hautes antiquités, on voit aisément que les saines idées du droit
naturel et de la fraternité communes à tous les hommes se sont
répandues assez tard, et on fait des progrès si lents dans le monde
qu'il n'y a que le christianisme qui les ait suffisamment générali-
sées » (453) (1).

(1) « L'erreur de Hobbes, dit Rousseau, n'est donc pas d'avoir établi l'état
entre les hommes indépendants et devenus sociables ; mais d'avoir supposé
cet état naturel à l'espèce, et de l'avoir donné pour cause aux vices dont il est
l'effet » (453). La distinction est tout à fait légitime : Hobbes a placé l'opposition des intérêts humains à l'état de nature, — or là il n'y a pas occasion d'opposition ; l'opposition des intérêts, ou les conflits, ne deviennent normaux (et

Rousseau a donc vu le problème ; il l'a posé : L'individu cherche avant tout son bonheur, c'est légitime ; et la société, pour exister et donner à l'homme les avantages de l'existence sociale, doit contraindre la recherche libre de ce bonheur ; dès lors, si l'individu peut réaliser son bonheur personnel en violant la loi (cette loi qui, dicte une conduite au profit des autres et au désavantage de l'individu), — en violant cette loi sans être découvert, *est-il normal qu'il s'en abstienne* ? en s'en abstenant, n'est-il pas plutôt naïf, voire mauvais du point de vue du but final qui est sa jouissance personnelle ? Et, qu'il y ait de ces occasions de violer impunément la loi, personne n'en saurait douter ?

Il faut donc trouver le mobile qui fera que l'homme consente à obéir à la loi, même quand celle-ci est à son désavantage, et même quand il peut éviter de tomber sous le coup de la punition légale.

Alors Rousseau continue : On a proposé la volonté de Dieu ; et Rousseau la récuse, car on a toujours fait, et on fera toujonrs à la multitude « des dieux insensés comme elle » ; et, des institutions qu'on a tirées de la religion, « dérivent plus souvent le carnage et les meurtres que la concorde et la paix » (V. p. 451). Il faut s'adresser à la philosophie : « Rendons au philosophe l'examen d'une question que le théologien n'a jamais traitée qu'au préjudice du genre humain » (p. 452) (1). Sans doute, la philosophie s'y est essayée sans donner une solution satisfaisante jusqu'ici ; mais elle n'a pas épuisé ses possibilités ; elle peut, elle doit chercher dans un « art perfectionné » du gouvernement la solution : à savoir :

---

naturels) qu'à l'état social, et à cause de l'état social. Rousseau nie le *Homo homini lupus* avant l'état social ; il l'affirme absolument après, quand par le seul fait d'une organisation (pour le bien de tous), il y a limitations, donc oppositions d'appétits.

(1) Pour prévenir une objection, reconnaissons que Rousseau laisse ouverte ici la question du cas où on aurait une théologie bonne. Mais le fait est que Rousseau ne propose pas cette solution ; et qu'il l'écarte positivement dans la phrase : « Rendons au philosophe l'examen... »

choses de l'État ; comme telle, elle n'est pas en harmonie avec la religion civile. Voici les propres termes de l'auteur :

« Jésus vint établir sur la terre un royaume spirituel, ce qui, séparant le système théologique du système politique [l'union des deux avait fait la force des sociétés anciennes, et de Rome en particulier], fit que l'État cessa d'être un, et causa les divisions intestines qui n'ont jamais cessé d'agiter les peuples chrétiens... Le christianisme est une religion toute spirituelle, occupée uniquement des choses du ciel ; la patrie du chrétien n'est pas de ce monde. il fait son devoir, il est vrai, mais il le fait avec une profonde indifférence sur le bon ou le mauvais succès de ses soins. Pourvu qu'il n'ait rien à se reprocher, peu lui importe que tout aille bien ou mal ici-bas. Si l'État est florissant, à peine ose-t-il se réjouir de la félicité publique ; il craint de n'enorgueillir de la gloire de son pays : si l'État dépérit, il bénit la main de Dieu qui s'appesantit sur son peuple. » (p. 383-386).

Il ajoute encore que le chrétien ne résistera pas à un tyran, qui lui est une affliction bénie, envoyée par Dieu pour éprouver sa patience. De même, le chrétien ne prendra pas les armes pour verser le sang :

« Supposez votre république chrétienne vis-à-vis de Sparte ou de Rome : les pieux chrétiens seront battus, écrasés, détruits avant d'avoir eu le temps de se reconnaître, ou ne devront leur salut qu'au mépris que leur ennemi concevra pour eux. C'était un beau serment, à mon gré, que celui des soldats de Fabius ; ils ne jurèrent pas de vaincre ou de mourir, ils jurèrent de revenir vainqueurs, et tinrent leur serment. Jamais des chrétiens n'en eussent fait un pareil ; ils auraient cru tenter Dieu » (p. 387).

Bref, le christianisme dont parle Rousseau est celui de Tolstoï de nos jours, la religion de la non-résistance ; un pouvoir politique dépendant de tels citoyens est en bien mauvaise posture ; cette religion là, la politique de Rousseau ne peut l'accepter (1).

Rousseau n'en reconnaît pas moins que, *de toutes les religions*

_____

(1) Dans la première des *Lettres de la Montagne* (H. III, p. 129), Rousseau se plaindra, mais bien mal à propos, de ceux qui l'accusent de n'être pas chrétien.

ment une progression au cours de laquelle le Rousseau romain
au nom de la raison, l'emporte de plus en plus sur le Rousseau
romantique ou sentimental ; c'est-à-dire qu'en partant de
notions extrêmement générales, vagues et confuses d'abord,
il s'était acheminé vers un véritable système — système qu'il
n'a du reste jamais formulé de toutes pièces lui-même, car,
si tous les matériaux sont là, l'édifice est resté en voie de
construction du fait qu'il a renoncé à écrire avant d'être
arrivé à la complète clarification de ses idées ; et enfin si
nous avons réussi à montrer (6) que ces deux pôles de la
pensée de Rousseau l'ont mis en opposition directe avec les
deux grands courants de pensée de son temps, à savoir :
son affirmation *romantique* de la légitimité de désirer le bonheur sur la terre, d'une part, avec la tradition chrétienne
alors encore prévalante chez la grande majorité des hommes ;
et son affirmation de la nécessité d'une discipline *romaine*
de nos appétits, d'autre part, avec les révoltés qui prétendaient émanciper l'homme de toute contrainte et l'engager
à s'abandonner aux appels de la nature ; — si, disons-nous,
nous avons pu rendre acceptables ces divers points, nous
pouvons faire une très brève conclusion.

Laissant tomber les éléments de pensée que Rousseau a
abandonnés en cours de route (tels que la vertu de renoncement chrétien du *Premier Discours*), ou ceux qui sont proprement en marge de la pensée finale, mais qu'il n'a pas écartés
parce qu'il a cessé son activité philosophique avant d'avoir
réussi à mettre en forme systématique ses idées de la période
de maturité (telle la religion sentimentale et mystique de la
Profession de foi), et recueillant ici seulement ce qui appar-
tiendrait réellement au système tel que nous le voyons s'affirmer peu à peu, et avec une fermeté de plus en plus grande,
rappelons seulement une dernière fois les thèses qu'il importe
surtout de souligner.

Premièrement, ce grand point fondamental que chez Rousseau la vérité elle-même n'importe qu'indirectement, c'est-à-
dire seulement en tant que sa connaissance intéresse le bonheur

de l'homme — cette grande idée qu'il a probablement contribué plus que nul autre à faire triompher, et à faire triompher de manière profonde, pas violente ou sensationnelle comme tels de ses contemporains, Voltaire ou les Encyclopédistes — rend très importantes ces deux thèses : D'une part, que les jouissances de l'homme à l'état de nature ne sont pas des jouissances humaines au sens élevé que peut avoir ce mot ; elles ne sont qu'animales ; donc ce n'est pas d'elles qu'il doit s'agir ici ; ou en tous cas, disons qu'elles sont insuffisantes puisque aussi bien l'être humain peut en connaître de meilleures. D'autre part, que ces jouissances humaines, — que nous avons appelées romantiques, mais que Rousseau appelle encore « naturelles », par là créant un malentendu regrettable, — sont de celles où l'homme n'atteint qu'après être sorti de l'état de nature (amour psychologique ajouté au physique, affections familiales, arts, sciences, propriété, etc.).

Deuxièmement, ces jouissances qui sont supérieures et réelles, sont dangereuses : car, d'une part, passé un certain point, elles entraînent des maux (jalousies, guerres, privations, souffrances de toutes sortes, et d'autant plus cuisantes que les jouissances qui leur correspondent sont plus profondément connues) ; et, d'autre part, l'homme fatalement passe ce point, et donc fatalement arrive à la misère.

Il en résulte que Rousseau devrait donc apparemment les condamner. Il le fait ; pendant quelque temps, en effet, il se demande (*Second Discours*) si l'état de non-misère des premiers hommes n'est pas préférable à l'état de misère positive des civilisés.

Troisièmement, cependant, il ne les condamne pas tout à fait, ces jouissances de l'âge d'or. En fait, dès la fin du *Premier Discours*, il fait des réserves ; il revient à ces préoccupations tôt après dans la polémique relative au *Premier Discours* ; et dans le *Second Discours* même, qui est le plus confus de ses écrits on s'aperçoit que malgré tout ce qu'en ont dit les commentateurs, Rousseau a évité de demander à l'homme le renoncement aux jouissances romantiques de l'état social (Les « Notes » où ceci n'est plus toujours vrai, sont posté-

rieures). Et il s'est senti poussé irrésistiblement, par d'inces-
santes méditations — le génie n'est-il pas une longue patience — vers une solution qu'il a, sinon nettement formulée,
au moins nettement entrevue : S'il avait cru devoir condamner
pendant quelques temps la jouissance, ç'avait été non pour
elle-même, mais en vertu du danger qu'il y a pour le bonheur
de l'homme qui s'y adonne, et qui, dans l'état social, est fatalement entraîné au delà d'un point où cette jouissance s'abîme
en désillusion et misère. Or, le mot, « fatalement entraîné »
est-il juste ? Rousseau a fort bien montré qu'il l'était pour
le moment de l'âge d'or ; il l'a été au temps de l'écroulement
du monde antique ; il l'a été à l'époque de la Renaissance ;
Rousseau estimait qu'il l'était même au xviiie siècle ; *mais*
il ne le serait peut-être pas absolument ; il ne le serait peut-
être pas toujours. Supposé en effet que l'homme ait un jour
bien conscience des dangers, la fatalité ne pourrait-elle cesser ?
la raison ne pourrait-elle pas engager l'homme à ne céder à ses
penchants romantiques qu'aussi loin que le danger demeure
conjuré ? Bref, si on conçoit dans l'histoire de l'humanité un
état où l'homme échapperait aux misères de la civilisation
parce qu'il n'est *pas encore* menacé par ses dangers (l'âge
d'or), on en conçoit un autre où connaissant ces dangers,
l'homme n'en serait *plus* menacé. Ou si on veut, s'il y a l'état
où l'homme n'est *pas encore* victime de ses passions romantiques, il peut y avoir celui où il ne le serait *plus*.

Une fois ceci entrevu, Rousseau abandonne pour toujours
le remède d'un retour pour lequel il avait manifesté un penchant au cours du *Second Discours*.

Quatrièmement, il se jette alors dans les bras de la raison — malgré les apparences créées par des termes malheureux (*lumière intérieure, conscience morale*, etc.). Seulement
il suggère une distinction essentielle à faire entre la raison
absolue, et cette raison contingente encore, à l'état fruste,
telle qu'elle s'exerça sur les questions de morale, pendant de
longs siècles et jusqu'aux « philosophes » du xviiie siècle,
inclus ; la seconde ne voyait pas les dangers de l'abandon à
la voix de la nature, la première les comprend fort bien.

Cinquièmement, cette première distinction en entraîne une autre qu'il ne faut absolument jamais oublier, car là est la clef de toutes les polémiques soutenues par Rousseau parmi ses contemporains, et ce qui l'a conduit sur le vrai champ de bataille où il s'évertue, à savoir que, si la raison autorise l'homme à écouter (ou n'a pas de cause pour l'empêcher d'écouter) la nature qui lui dit de chercher à être heureux, la raison ne dit en aucune façon d'écouter les suggestions de cette même nature relatives aux *moyens* d'arriver au bonheur ; tout au contraire, elle lui dit de les rejeter.

Et Rousseau ne songera plus qu'à armer dès lors fortement l'homme contre ce romantisme conçu comme moyen, en sorte de réaliser le romantisme conçu comme but. Il va s'en expliquer d'abord dans la *Lettre sur les spectacles,* où pour la première fois, il réalise en plein le danger des jouissances mondaines et cela à l'occasion des plaisirs du théâtre ; puis dans *La Nouvelle Héloïse,* ou il étend son enquête à la vie en général ; il voudrait montrer en Julie raisonnable et sage, la réfutation du romantisme qui l'avait séduit lui-même ; il s'est même plu à conserver les tableaux de volupté du début du roman ,ceux qu'il avait tracés dans une de ses poussées romantiques, afin — se plaît-il à penser — de se réfuter lui-même. Mais il y a quelque chose de plus dans *La Nouvelle Héloïse* : c'est là que déjà se trouve indiqué que l'homme réduit à ses moyens, c'est-à-dire réduit à la raison seule, est cependant faible encore ; car tandis que Julie est délivrée par un coup de théâtre des menaces du romantisme renaissant (quand elle meurt, ou même se suicide avant la re-chute) Rousseau indique un moyen plus sûr que la raison ou tout moyen humain : *la religion* — c'est le testament philosophique de Julie mourante.

Sixièmement, le pragmatisme théologique, ajouté au rationaliste, est alors nettement accepté dans les deux ouvrages proprement philosophiques, le *Contrat Social* et l'*Emile* — nettement mais pas toujours clairement comme en témoignent les nombreux commentaires destinés à éclairer ceux-ci ; dans les deux, il part des aspirations de l'homme au bonheur sur la terre, pèse les dangers du *moi* qui s'abandonne à la nature, oppose au romantisme la raison humaine et les institutions des hommes nées de cette raison (institutions politiques d'une part, institutions d'éducation d'autre part, aussi loin que celles-ci pourront aller). Mais c'est pour aboutir dogmatiquement, dans les deux ouvrages, au recours à la religion comme garantie absolue — *religion civile* de l'homme d'état, *religion pragmatique* du vicaire savoyard.

*
* *

C'est le moment de revenir sur un point indiqué dans notre *Introduction* et qui peut être plus clairement entendu après notre long voyage à travers les écrits du philosophe de Genève.

Nous avions dit que la postérité se trouvait vraiment en face de deux Rousseau, celui de la tradition, le *Rousseau romantique*, et le Rousseau réel qui est au fond rationaliste dans sa morale, sa politique et sa théologie, le *Rousseau romain* ; et que le premier avait, aux yeux de cette postérité, presque complètement triomphé aux dépens du second.

Or ce triomphe ne doit pas nous étonner. *D'abord*, une philosophie romantique, c'est-à-dire autorisant l'homme à voir dans la vie son propre but, à viser au bonheur terrestre, était une révolution formidable contre la tradition chrétienne médiévale, et en profond accord avec les aspirations du temps. Et si Rousseau avait bien réellement repoussé ce qu'on peut appeler le romantisme intégral, c'est-à-dire celui qui proposait de réaliser le bonheur en cédant à la nature (qui est certainement le romantisme tel qu'on l'entend généralement), il avait cependant faite sienne cette idée romantique qui rejetait la morale du renoncement chrétien et qui autorisait la recherche du bonheur dans ce monde. Il n'était pas étonnant dès lors, que, ne faisant pas la distinction entre romantisme comme simple but et romantisme comme moyen, le lecteur n'ait pas évité la conclusion que Rousseau professant celui-là il devait professer aussi celui-ci ; et il était

naturel que se marquerait dans le public lecteur une préférence pour les pages où Rousseau soulignerait cette partie
de sa pensée ; et, en effet, le mouvement romantique tout
entier se réclama de cette partie de l'œuvre de Rousseau et
voulut ignorer l'autre. Il était naturel encore que la posérité
continuât à apprécier ces mêmes pages, à mesure que la
philosophie de la vie comme un moyen pour un autre but
(vertu de renoncement) allait perdre du terrain. Et *aussi*
reconnaissons une fois de plus que, quand bien même Rousseau combat dans ses écrits de maturité le prolongement de
la philosophie romantique, que voulaient les « libertins »
du XVIIᵉ siècle, et les « philosophes » du XVIIIᵉ siècle, c'est-à-
dire que tout en prêchant *le désir naturel du bonheur*, il
combattait ceux qui prêchaient encore *le bonheur par la
nature*, cependant il ne fit jamais assez nettement cette
distinction des deux phases romantiques en l'homme, —
pas même par devers lui — pour que ses lecteurs n'eussent
l'occasion de s'y tromper.

Toutefois ajoutons ceci : au point de vue de l'influence philosophique de Rousseau sur la postérité, il y a eu là peut être un
certain avantage ; car un gros problème comme celui des rapports des simples *aspirations romantiques* de l'homme avec les
conditions propres pour réaliser ces aspirations, gagne à n'être
pas présenté trop dogmatiquement, trop finalement ; quand on
se souvient de la complexité de toutes les questions concernant
les mobiles des actions humaines, présenter comme solution
une simple formule, qui, après tout, n'est pas difficile à saisir,
cela aurait presque l'air d'un escamotage. Et si l'on voulait
exprimer ceci sous une forme paradoxale un peu, Rousseau
ne serait-il pas ,en partie du moins, resté le plus vivant
des écrivains du passé, non pas *malgré* qu'il n'est pas
l'homme d'une philosophie systématiquement arrêtée par
lui (comme celle d'un Comte, ou d'un Taine, d'un Hegel ou
d'un Schopenhauer, d'un Mill ou d'un Spencer), mais au
contraire parce qu'il offre ce spectacle d'un homme, qui
hanté comme les autres par le problème des destinées
humaines, et sollicité par des solutions impératives mais

tirant en sens contraire, il n'a pas réussi comme les autres à s'arrêter à une formule définitive. Sa pensée demeure ainsi ouverte pour la postérité qui peut l'approfondir, la clarifier, la prolonger ; chaque étudiant de Rousseau peut avoir la sensation de devenir comme un collaborateur à l'œuvre entrevue, et à la solution également entrevue et rêvée.

Et un point encore. Le romantisme a une tendance à rester toujours romantique — dans ses moyens comme dans son but ; et l'homme reste toujours l'homme ; c'est-à-dire que reste toujours le danger signalé par Rousseau de l'être humain cédant pour son malheur aux appels de la nature ; qui pis est, le danger croît, avec la conscience en l'homme qu'on ne pourra plus lui contester son droit de tenter d'acquérir du bonheur et avec le développement des moyens offerts de toutes parts de satisfaire ses désirs de plaisir. Cela veut dire que vraiment le danger croit avec la victoire, et qu'à mesure qu'on s'éloigne de Rousseau, le penseur pragmatique doit veiller davantage aux égarements, doit apporter plus de freins ; il ne sera donc pas mauvais que de nos jours encore, et même toujours davantage, il y ait de ces hommes tout d'une pièce, ne distinguant pas le but romantique et les moyens romantiques, mais qui frappent *intégralement* le romantisme ; il faut en quelque sorte qu'il y ait encore de ces aveugles dans le domaine de la pensée, tels que nous en avons signalés en abondance dans notre Introduction ; et s'ils n'existaient pas, ces sombres prophètes maudissant le romantisme, — il faudrait les inventer. Ils sont nécessaires surtout dans les pays où les occasions de satisfaire les aspirations romantiques, en vertu des facilités de l'existence même, sont plus grandes — et en effet, en Amérique surtout et en Angleterre, il y a des Rousseauphobes aussi fanatiques que peut les désirer le Rousseau romain. Certes on ne saurait retourner tout de même aux doctrines sinistres de l'inquisition ; et telles que sont les choses, les foudres anti-romantiques et les foudres pragmatiques suffisent. Dans la vieille Europe, cependant, le moyen des Masson et des Giraud, que nous discutions au chapitre sur la « Profession de foi », sera peut-être plus habile et plus fructueux — ce moyen qui

SCHINZ — Rousseau   33

consiste à fondre le Rousseau romantique et le Rousseau romain en un Rousseau mystique, c'est-à-dire glissant la discipline chrétienne, classique et pragmatique sous le manteau de la religion de sentiment.

———

TABLE DES MATIÈRES

―――――――

AVANT-PROPOS XI

INTRODUCTION I

La modernité de Rousseau................................... I

I. La modernité prouvée : 1. Par les attaques jamais discontinuées contre lui (p. 1). 2. Par une formidable littérature rousseauiste (p. 10). 3. Le vrai Rousseau et le Rousseau de la tradition (p. 12). I

II. Les causes les plus souvent invoquées pour expliquer l'action de Rousseau sur ses contemporains et sur la postérité, et l'insuffisance de ces explications. 1. L'art de Rousseau (p. 16). 2. La personnalité de Rousseau (p. 17). 3. Rousseau novateur (p. 19). 16

III. Deux observations qui serviront de point de départ à une nouvelle interprétation. 1. Un facteur négligé : l'état des esprits en Europe au moment où parut Rousseau (p. 41). 2. Les commentateurs amenés à souligner de plus en plus un manque fondamental de cohésion philosophique chez Rousseau (p. 42). 41

PREMIÈRE PARTIE. — Le **Problème** 55

CHAPITRE I. — *L'avènement du romantisme au siècle de Rousseau* 55

1. Le problème, « comment concilier les aspirations romantiques de tout *moi* humain et les nécessités d'une discipline sociale », commence à se poser dès le moyen âge. Discipline ecclésiastique. 55

2. Première tentative d'affranchissement. Renaissance.......... 61

3. Suivie de réaction violente ; siècle de Louis XIV.............. 69

4. Le problème romantique se pose formidablement une seconde fois au XVIIIe siècle, et Rousseau va sentir ce problème et l'exprimer profondément.................................... 72

NOTE sur l'essence morale du Christianisme 81

CHAPITRE II. — *Rousseau devant son siècle. Le conflit chez l'homme Rousseau* 83

1. *Rousseau romantique et Rousseau romain.* De très bonne heure, deux dispositions en sens contraire se manifestent chez l'enfant :

l'une résultant des soins donnés à un être né très frêle et que l'on choie ; les souffrances intensifient la conscience du *moi* et la sensibilité, et constitueront une *nature romantique* ; l'autre sera le résultat de l'atmosphère calviniste de Genève et de lectures abondantes de Plutarque qui constituera ce qu'il a appelé lui-même une « âme romaine » 83

2. *Rousseau romantique.* A 11 ans, Rousseau est seul au monde. Tout concourt à affaiblir les aspirations romaines et accentuer au contraire le romantisme. La vie est sévère ; il s'étonne, puis se révolte, et quitte Genève. Son manque d'expérience et sa difficulté à comprendre les leçons de la vie en Italie, les bontés de Mme de Warens, son instruction décousue, sa gaucherie à Paris, ne font qu'exaspérer son *moi*. En même temps tout cela a accumulé en lui un profond dégoût de la vie de bohème et des mensonges sociaux, ce qui par contraste, le rejette aux idées « romaines ». La crise de Vincennes est à la porte.. 10

NOTE sur Rousseau et la Psychiâtrie................................ 129

SECONDE PARTIE. — **Le conflit chez Rousseau l'écrivain** 134

CHAPITRE I. — ROUSSEAU ET LES ROMAINS. *Discours sur les Sciences et les Arts*.. 134

Rousseau, désabusé de la vie « romantique », se reprend d'un grand enthousiasme pour la *vertu* 134

Le Premier Discours est un hymne à la vertu. Trois notions de vertu, *vertu romaine* de désintéressement ; *vertu d'innocence* ; *vertu de sagesse* ou philosophique. Rousseau exalte la vertu romaine, qu'il ne distingue pas de la vertu des chrétiens et qui vaut par le renoncement à toute prétention d'avantages personnels ou romantiques 138

Indices d'indécision cependant 149

NOTE *sur l'originalité du Paradoxe*................................ 155

CHAPITRE II. — ROUSSEAU ET LES SAUVAGES. *Discours sur l'Inégalité*.. 158

1. Rousseau conscient de la complexité des problèmes qu'il a soulevés. Incertitudes dans la conduite de sa vie et dans sa pensée philosophique 158

2. Il abandonne l'idéal de l'austérité et la vertu romaine, et pense trouver dans la vertu d'innocence des sauvages une solution au problème du bonheur. Il rejette la doctrine chrétienne de l'homme mauvais par nature.. 170

3. En réalité Rousseau n'a jamais prouvé que l'homme de la nature soit bon, mais seulement qu'il n'est pas mauvais ; mais il n'est malheureusement pas conscient de cette distinction. Trois sens du mot *bonté* dont Rousseau n'a que faire (*bonté chrétienne de*

discipline, bonté sentimentale de désintéressement sans sens aucun, *bonté eudaimoniste* qui n'est pas à proprement parler de la bonté, étant naïvement intéressée) 174

4. Encore moins qu'il n'a prouvé que l'homme est naturellement bon, Rousseau n'a prouvé que l'homme est naturellement heureux ; celui-ci est seulement non malheureux à l'état sauvage. D'où résulte que Rousseau est justifié en récusant l'accusation qu'il prêche le retour à l'état de nature 179

5. Tout ceci conduit à une nouvelle conception de « bonté » et de « vertu » 196

CHAPITRE III. — ROUSSEAU ET LES SUISSES. *Lettre sur les Spectacles* 197

A. 1. Ton austère de « vertu romaine ». Et cependant pas en accord avec la vertu du *Premier Discours,* ni en désaccord avec le romantisme du *Second* 198

2. Différence fondamentale des opinions de Rousseau et de Bossuet sur le théâtre, malgré des apparences d'accord jusque dans les termes employés pour censurer les spectacles 202

3. Différence des idées de Rousseau d'avec celles de D'Alembert et des « philosophes » ; ceux-ci adoptent sans autre que l'homme interprètera intelligemment les héros de théâtre ; Rousseau prend en considération la majorité du public qui interprètera de façon funeste à son « utilité » c'est-à-dire à son bonheur 204

4. Même à supposer que le peuple comprenne les spectacles qu'on lui offre, le théâtre tel qu'il existe est funeste à l'homme — qui y cherche *naturellement* le fruit défendu 212

5. Rousseau esquisse d'autres plaisirs que le théâtre, qui, ceux-ci seront légitimes par le fait qu'ils portent en eux le bonheur plus vrai et plus durable 217

B. 1. Notions à élucider pour bien comprendre la philosophie morale de Rousseau 224

La conscience morale ou *sentiment moral inné* ; cette notion paraît l'éloigner des « philosophes » et le rapprocher du christianisme traditionnel ; la vérité est juste l'opposé ; mais Rousseau a contribué lui-même à créer la confusion sur ce point, car, il a *appelé* ces notions « innées », et il a *démontré* qu'elles ne l'étaient pas. Sa conscience morale est d'essence rationaliste 224

2. *Vivre selon la nature* signifie maintenant chez Rousseau non plus : selon la nature primitive, mais — dans l'état social — vivre selon la nature de l'homme, laquelle comporte la raison, c'est-à-dire contrôle la passion romantique ; et il s'agit ici de *la* raison (dans le sens absolu du terme) qui est opposée chez Rousseau à la raison telle que développée par un groupe de philosophes du XVIIIᵉ siècle

et qui *prétendaient* à faux avoir la raison parfaite. Donc, sur ce terrain de la raison, le propre terrain choisi par eux, Rousseau se sépare des « philosophes » 231

Conclusion.. 227

Notes *sur deux points contestés*............................ 240

Chapitre IV. — Rousseau et les Anglais. *La Nouvelle Héloïse* 245

 1. Mise au point du vocabulaire philosophique de la *Nouvelle Héloïse*. Raison des « philosophes » et raison en soi ; sentiment moral et sentiment naturel ; nature morale et nature romantique. 245

 2. Histoire du roman. Attitudes successives de l'auteur vis-à-vis de son problème moral. Influences d'événements de la vie personnelle de Rousseau sur la composition 250

 3. Résumé de Parties I à IV............................ 258

 4. *La Nouvelle Héloïse avant le roman moral* : Première phase, Lettres d'amour ; Deuxième phase, le roman moderne, le « livre efféminé » 276

 5. *La Nouvelle Héloïse, roman sérieux* : Troisième phase, Morale romantique ; Quatrième phase, Morale de vertu-sagesse, avec, en marge, l'idée du « ménage à trois » ; Cinquième phase, De l'insuffisance de la vertu-sagesse pour réaliser le vrai bonheur et de retour à des velléités romantiques........................ 282

 6. La signification de l'anglomanie dans l'évolution de la pensée de Rousseau.. 333

 Deux Appendices.

 Notes sur les modifications subies par le roman en cours de composition 333

Note sur « l'anglomanie » de Rousseau........................ 339

Chapitre V. — Encore Rousseau et les Romains. *Le Contrat social.* 342

 A. 1. Le *Contrat Social* n'est pas en marge de l'œuvre de Rousseau, comme cela a été souvent affirmé........................ 343

 B. 2. Diverses phases de composition du livre. *Première phase* : de méditation générale sans conclusion nette. *Deuxième phase* : de l'état contre l'individu (article « Economie politique » dans le volume V de l'*Encyclopédie*) 347

 C. 3. *Troisième phase* : Rousseau adoptait le même principe (rationaliste) de l'état contre l'individu ; mais cette version ne fut pas publiée.. 353

 4. *Quatrième phase* : Dans le Contrat social imprimé, Rousseau abandonne le point de vue rationaliste, et adopte celui de la tradition, comme le prouve le chapitre ajouté « De la Religion civile ».. 364

5. Cependant, chose curieuse, en réadoptant le principe traditionnel
(Dieu qui ordonne la soumission à l'Etat) Rousseau n'abandonne
pas le principe rationaliste d'un contrat social qui était alors
superflu 376

6. Cause de cet illogisme : Il voulait un principe rationaliste pour
battre ses adversaires, les « philosophes » sur leur propre terrain de
la raison ; et il veut essayer de modifier la notion du contrat social,
c'est-à-dire d'un principe de contrainte sociale faire un principe
romantique d'affranchissement social. Vanité de cette tentative
qui supposerait : (a) la négation du droit du plus fort, (b) l'existence d'un droit du faible. Rousseau ne réussit à établir ni l'une,
ni l'autre de ces propositions. Il n'en parle pas moins comme s'il
avait réussi. Le pacte fondamental tel qu'il est défini dans le corps
de l'ouvrage est absolument un contrat de contrainte. Les institutions de l'état basé sur ce contrat trahissent, à leur tour, ce fait
que l'individu doit abdiquer sa liberté....................... 381

7. Rousseau essaie donc de présenter un système de contrainte
social comme si c'était un système de liberté ; rien d'étonnant que
la plus grande confusion règne parmi les commentateurs. C'est
comme un cliché de photographie négatif où tout est exactement
représenté, mais ce qui est réellement blanc apparaît noir et
vice-versa 390

8. Cinquième phase. Ce que serait le Contrat social mis au point ;
c'est-à-dire si Rousseau l'avait publié après avoir laissé sa pensée
arriver à maturité. L'incertitude dans la conception de la « volonté générale », qu'il affirme tantôt infaillilble (ce qui justifierait
sa thèse d'un contrat social) tantôt faillible (ce qui lui enlève
toute portée pratique) explique les solutions contradictoires
données par les érudits à cette question : Rousseau est-il le père
de la Révolution ? Il en est le père illégitime 399

9. L'examen des institutions politiques romaines, admirables,
aboutit cependant à cette conclusion : les meilleures institutions
sont vouées à l'échec final ; il faut une clef de voûte à tout
édifice social : la religion civile............................ 412

10. Les Romains du Premier Discours, et les Romains du Contrat
social. 417

NOTES sur la société athée de Bayle, et sur la « vertu civique » de
Montesquieu, Rousseau et autres............................. 418

CHAPITRE VI. — ROUSSEAU ROMANTIQUE ET ROUSSEAU ROMAIN. Émile   421

A. Les quatre Premiers Livres 421

1. Émile, dernier grand effort de Rousseau pour systématiser sa
pensée. Il s'avère philosophe pragmatique. Malgré des termes

souvent trompeurs, le but demeure romantique ; la philosophie doit procurer le bonheur à l'homme. Son éducation doit viser à ce but. *Premier âge. Deuxième âge* de l'enfant.................... 422

2. *Troisième âge.* La notion de l'« utile » introduite, mais sans changer vraiment le point de vue romantique et pragmatique .. 435

3. *Quatrième âge.* Rousseau voit le moment venu de transformer les dispositions de l'enfant ; nouvelle tentative d'introduire la notion d'une morale désintéressée, — et qui n'aboutit pas. Alors, il ne reste à Rousseau que le recours à la sanction religieuse...... 441

B. **« Profession de foi du Vicaire savoyard »**, qui correspond exactement au chapitre de la « Religion » civile dans le *Contrat social* : La conscience morale sans sanction religieuse n'aboutit pas plus que la vertu politique sans sanction religieuse............ 451

1. Introduction abrupte de la religion dans la vie d'Emile. Rapport avec les quatre premiers livres d'*Émile* est encore le pragmatisme. Rousseau doit trouver un Dieu favorisant le romantisme, c'est-à-dire qui veille au bonheur de l'homme. Cependant, nous savons que le bonheur est atteint par le contrôle des passions humaines ; le Dieu de Rousseau voudra donc cette contrainte des passions. 452

2. Tous les articles de foi seront adoptés ou rejetés selon qu'ils composent ou ne composent pas une religion forçant l'homme à vouloir choisir les voies du bonheur. Rousseau ne formule pas son principe directeur ; il prétend invoquer la *raison* et la *lumière intérieure,* la première si elle suffit à donner les dogmes voulus, la seconde quand la raison ne fournit pas ce qui est nécessaire ; en réalité le critère final est toujours pragmatique............ 457

3. Examen détaillé des dogmes. La *bonté divine* est le plus important de tous, sans excepter l'existence même de Dieu ; mais n'étant pas fondé en raison, Rousseau ne le donne que comme corollaire de puissance et intelligence divines. Conflit entre les deux croyances en la bonté naturelle de l'homme et en la bonté divine amène les dogmes de la liberté morale, de l'immatérialité de l'âme, etc.. 463

Conscience morale.................................... 475

4. La Religion du Vicaire et les autres religions............... 483

5. La religion sentimentale ou mystique de Rousseau n'a au fond pas de rapport direct avec sa religion pragmatique ou rationaliste, ni avec sa philosophie en général. L'idée de faire de cette religion sentimentale de Rousseau sa religion même, et même à l'exclusion d'une religion amenée par l'exercice de la raison, comme cela s'est fait depuis Chateaubriand et Mme de Stael jusqu'à MM. Masson et Giraud, c'est trahir la pensée philosophique de Rousseau 485

6. Comment Rousseau s'est laissé aller à introduire à côté de la

religion pragmatique, cette religion sentimentale — hors-d'œuvre au fond — dans la Profession de foi.................. 492

C. Émile après l'imitation religieuse, et le Vᵉ Livre 498

1. Le mariage................. 498

2. Sophie.. 499

CONCLUSION... 506